HARCOURT SCHOOL PUBLISHERS

STORY town

Oh, the do   pen!

Harcourt School Publishers

StoryTown is the new PreK–6 reading/language arts program from **Harcourt School Publishers.** With surprises around every corner and adventure just down the street, you'll find *StoryTown* is a great place to read.

Welcome to *StoryTown!*

StoryTown is filled with a variety of literature—nonfiction that supports reading include news articles, biographies, research, and more. Fiction stories include wonderful narratives, poems, plays, and fantasy. *StoryTown* also:

- offers materials tailored to each students' reading level.
- provides teachers with materials that deliver differentiated instruction.
- helps teachers plan effectively, and manage their entire classroom.

Harcourt School Publishers

StoryTown—a great place to read!

Beginning readers feel right at home with

StoryTown's Kindergarten program.

5 Teacher Editions

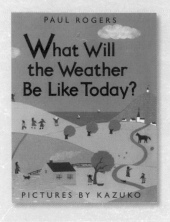

20 Big Books

20 Little Books

45 Pre-decodable and Decodable Books

30 On-Level Readers

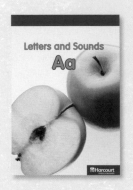

30 Below-Level Readers

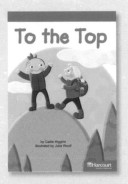

30 Advanced Readers

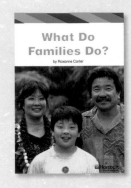

30 ELL Readers

Library Books Collection (20 titles)

15 Trade Books in Challenge Resource Kits

Read-Aloud Anthology

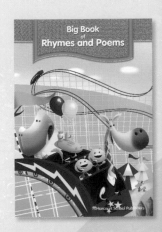

Big Book of Rhymes and Poems

The *StoryTown* **Kindergarten program** also includes:

- Professional Development Book
- Teacher Resource Book
- Big Book Audiotext CDs
- Leveled Readers Teacher Guides
- Leveled Readers Benchmark Assessment
- Photo Cards
- Sound/Spelling Cards
- Phonics Practice Book and Teacher Edition
- Practice Book Collection (10 titles)
- Word Builder and Word Builder Cards
- High-Frequency Word Cards
- Alphabet Cards

- Music CD
- Sounds of Letters CD
- Letter/Sound Rhymes Chart
- Tactile Letter Cards
- Write-on/Wipe-off Board
- Story Retelling Cards
- Instructional Routine Cards
- Kindergarten Assessments
- Magnetic Letters

Great instruction for *StoryTown's* smallest residents, too!

The *StoryTown* **Pre-Kindergarten Program** includes:

- Teacher Edition
- Teacher Resource Book
- Picture/Picture Word Cards
- Magnetic Letters
- Big Alphabet Cards
- Center Activity Cards
- Alphabet Masters
- School Friends Puppets

- Stories and More
- Nursery Rhymes Anthology
- Big Book of Rhymes and Songs
- Big Book Collection
- Lap Book Collection
- Music CD
- Oral Language Development Cards

StoryTown offers students a collection of tools for reading.

StoryTown *Student Editions*
Grades 1–6

StoryTown's motivating *Student Editions* include the perfect mix of nonfiction and narrative selections. Students develop robust vocabularies in *StoryTown* based on carefully selected words for instruction. Student-friendly explanations and meaningful learning activities get students involved in thinking about, using, and noticing new words in school and all around town.

The **StoryTown Library Books Collection** (Grades 1–6) includes twelve trade books per grade to engage students through easy, average, and challenging books.

Grade 6 shown

Students can visit **StoryTown** whenever they want with the **StoryTown Student eBook** (Grades 1–6). The **Student eBook** provides an interactive way for students to engage with text. A state-of-the-art interface presents **StoryTown** literature, instructional audio, interactive story maps, and activities.

StoryTown delivers differentiated instruction.

Leveled Readers (Grades K–6) with individual Teacher Guides for each title

StoryTown residents can find 120 different titles at each grade level for On-Level, Below-Level, Advanced, and ELL Readers. Each reader aligns to weekly skills, reinforcing high frequency words, vocabulary, phonics, and comprehension.

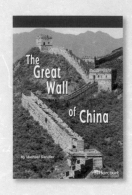

30 On-Level Readers   30 Below-Level Readers   30 Advanced Readers   30 ELL Readers

The *StoryTown Leveled Reader System* (Grades K–6) includes a single copy of 120 leveled readers and individual 8-page guided reading lessons for each title. In addition, the system includes 4 spiral charts with activities for each title organized around the On-Level, Below-Level, Advanced, and English Language Learner Collections. Benchmark Assessments are available for each grade.

The *Harcourt Leveled Readers Online* database provides access to 840 new *StoryTown* leveled readers that can be assigned to students in school, at home, anywhere!

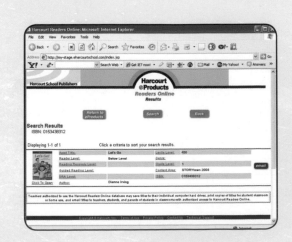

In **StoryTown,** leveled practice reinforces what students are learning.

- **StoryTown Practice Books** provide on-level activities to strengthen reading and language skills.
- **StoryTown's Extra Support Copying Masters** provide reproducible pages that parallel **Practice Book** activities—accommodating the below-level readers.
- The **Challenge Copying Masters,** for above-level readers, provide leveled practice for the advanced student, mirroring the skills found in the **Practice Book.**

Teacher Resource Books include useful instructional materials such as blackline versions of Readers' Theater selections and copying masters for patterns, manipulatives, and graphic organizers.

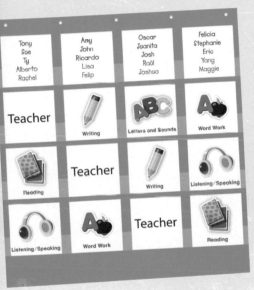

Literacy Center Kit (Grades K–6) strengthens skills taught each week in the critical areas of reading. Kit components include:

- Literacy Center Activity Cards on table top easels
- Literacy Center Pocket Chart
- Literacy Center Pocket Chart Icon Cards

StoryTown supports all levels of readers

StoryTown includes scaffolded materials to help every student.

The **Strategic Intervention Resource Kit** (Grades K–6) is designed for students who need extra support. Teachers can preteach and reteach the same comprehension and vocabulary skills that are taught each week in the core program. The kit includes a **Strategic Intervention Interactive Reader, Teacher Guide, Teacher Resource Book, Practice Book and Teacher's Guide,** and **Audiotext CD.** Each grade-level kit includes additional components, such as the **Sounds of Letters CD, Alphabet Masters, Builder Cards, Phoneme Phone**…and more!

The **Challenge Resource Kit** (Grades K–6) stimulates students with motivating trade books that serve as the springboard for author studies, genre studies, and critical thinking. Each grade-level kit includes a **Teacher Guide, Challenge Student Activities,** and **Challenge Book Packs.**

The **ELL Extra Support Kit** (Grades K–6) provides additional support to ELL students and helps teachers preteach and reteach the core skills, strategies, and vocabulary. A **Teacher Guide, Student Handbook,** and **Copying Masters** are included.

PLUS **StoryTown** has an **Intensive Intervention Program** for students who are reading below grade level. The **Primary** Program (Grades K–3) includes **Teacher Guides, Student Practice Books,** and additional components, such as the **Magnetic Letters, Reading Rods®,** and **Photo Cards**. The **Intermediate** Program (Grades 4–6) includes **Teacher Guides** and **Practice Masters,** each focusing on the essential elements of reading—phonemic awareness, phonics, vocabulary, fluency, and text comprehension.

StoryTown isn't only for students.

StoryTown teacher materials provide teachers with the opportunity to focus their attention on what is important—their students!

StoryTown Teacher Editions
Grades 1–6

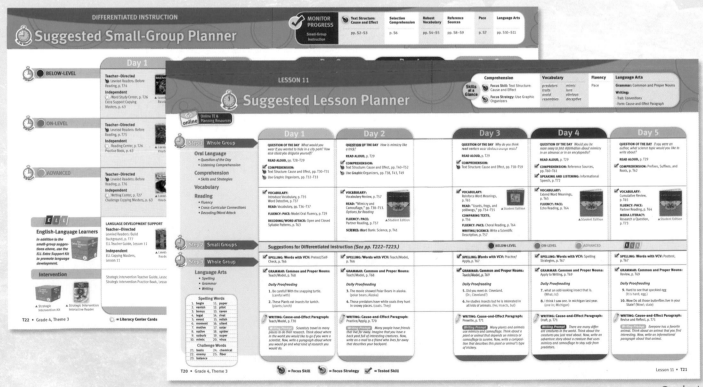

Grade 4

Teachers will benefit from *StoryTown's* well-organized instructional planners. Planners help organize daily lessons and differentiate instruction.

StoryTown is connected!

State-of-the-art technology makes the experience effortless by packing all the tools and resources in the right places.

The **StoryTown Online Teacher Edition and Planning Resources** is the perfect solution for the busy teacher. It can be accessed from anywhere there is an Internet connection. It organizes the instructional path and provides support resources including **Spelling, Phonics, and Grammar Practice Books**, plus **Leveled Readers**.

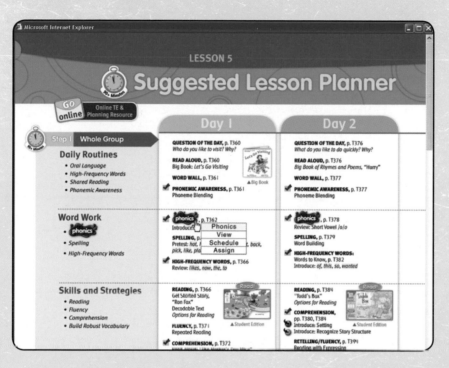

 Professional Development videos are part of the **Online TE and Planning Resources,** and are available online through podcasting, making them accessible and a great way to learn on the go!

 Teachers who do not have Internet access can use the **StoryTown One-Stop Planner CD-ROM**. Included on the CD-ROM are:
- **Teacher Edition** pages with a calendar planner
- Point-of-use instructional support resources that will print, view, and schedule instruction
- Differentiated instruction using **Leveled Readers**

StoryTown makes classroom planning easier and faster for teachers!

StoryTown offers additional resources for success.

The **Writer's Companion Student Edition** (Grades 1–6) and **Teacher Edition** (Grades K–6) deepen students' understanding of the elements and traits of effective writing. These components explicitly demonstrate how students can incorporate those elements and traits into their own writing.

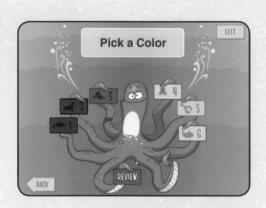

In the **Splash into Phonics** (Grades K–3) CD-ROM, games and activities are submerged in scenic ocean destinations and provide the background for reinforcing phonics.

In the **Comprehension Expedition** (Grades 3–6) CD-ROM, Special Agent Bird takes readers on exciting expeditions through swamps, forests, mountains, and beyond. Their journey provides practice and reinforcement of comprehension skills taught and tested in **StoryTown.**

StoryTown equips teachers with a variety of tools to evaluate students, maximizing their learning potential. **Assessment options include:**

Monitor Progress (Grades K–6)

Daily Monitor Progress notes, which inform instruction, are provided in the **Teacher Edition.**

Weekly Lesson Tests Copying Masters and Teacher Editions (Grades 1–6) monitor

student comprehension of the literature selections and the skills taught. Test sections include:

- Selection Comprehension, including open-ended questions
- Focus Skill
- Robust Vocabulary
- Grammar

- Research Skill or Vocabulary Skill
- High-Frequency Words (Grades 1 & 2)
- Decoding/Phonics (Grades 1–3)
- Fluency ("Fresh Reads")

Additional Assessment Options (Grades 1–6):

- Theme Tests and Teacher Edition
- Benchmark Assessments and Teacher Edition
- Diagnostic Assessments
- Online Assessment

Additional Resources Available (Grades 1–6):

- Grammar Practice Book and Teacher Edition (TE)
- Spelling Practice Book and TE
- Phonics Practice Book and TE
- Test Prep System
- Questioning the Author Comprehension Guide
- Story Retelling Cards (Grades K–2)

- Reading Transparencies
- Language Arts Transparencies
- Fluency Builders
- Instructional Routine Cards
- Read-Aloud Anthology (Grades K–3)
- Sound/Spelling Cards (Grades 1, 2)
- Photo Cards (Grade 1)
- Audiotext CDs

LESS
11

LESS
12

LESS
13

LESS
14

LESS
15

Grade 2 • Theme 3

At a Glance

HARCOURT SCHOOL PUBLISHERS

STORYtown

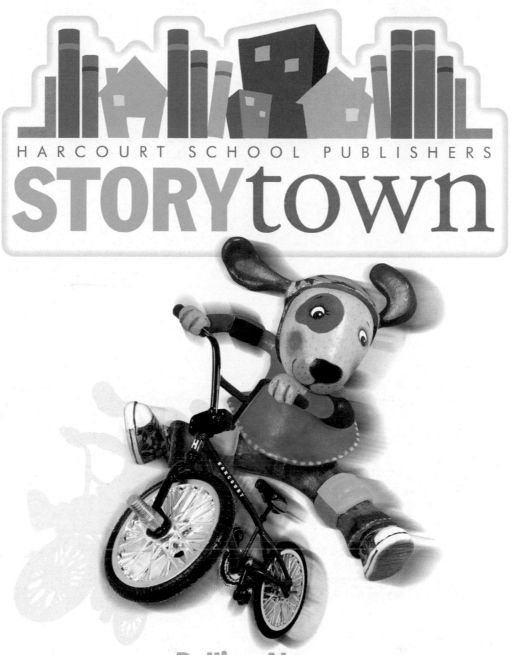

Rolling Along

TEACHER EDITION

Senior Authors
Isabel L. Beck • Roger C. Farr • Dorothy S. Strickland

Authors
Alma Flor Ada • Roxanne F. Hudson • Margaret G. McKeown
Robin C. Scarcella • Julie A. Washington

Consultants
F. Isabel Campoy • Tyrone C. Howard • David A. Monti

Harcourt
SCHOOL PUBLISHERS

www.harcourtschool.com

ISBN 10 0-15-353675-6
ISBN 13 978-0-15-353675-5

1 2 3 4 5 6 7 8 9 10   030   17 16 15 14 13 12 11 10 09 08 07

Program Authors

SENIOR AUTHORS

Isabel L. Beck
Professor of Education and Senior
Scientist at the Learning Research
and Development Center,
University of Pittsburgh

RESEARCH CONTRIBUTIONS:
Reading Comprehension, Vocabulary,
Beginning Reading, Phonics

Roger C. Farr
Chancellor's Professor Emeritus
of Education and Former Director
for the Center for Innovation in
Assessment,
Indiana University, Bloomington

RESEARCH CONTRIBUTIONS:
Instructional Assessment, Reading
Strategies, Reading in the Content Areas

Dorothy S. Strickland
Samuel DeWitt Proctor Professor
of Education and The State of New
Jersey Professor of Reading,
*Rutgers University, The State
University of New Jersey*

RESEARCH CONTRIBUTIONS:
Early Literacy, Elementary Reading/
Language Arts, Writing, Intervention

AUTHORS

Alma Flor Ada
Professor Emerita,
University of San Francisco

RESEARCH CONTRIBUTIONS:
Literacy, Biliteracy, Multicultural
Children's Literature, Home-School
Interaction, First and Second
Language Acquisition

Roxanne F. Hudson
Assistant Professor, Area of
Special Education
University of Washington

RESEARCH CONTRIBUTIONS:
Reading Fluency, Learning
Disabilities, Interventions

Margaret G. McKeown
Senior Scientist at the Learning
Research and Development Center,
University of Pittsburgh

RESEARCH CONTRIBUTIONS:
Vocabulary, Reading Comprehension

Robin C. Scarcella
Professor, Director of Academic
English and ESL,
University of California, Irvine

RESEARCH CONTRIBUTIONS:
English as a Second Language

Julie A. Washington
Professor, College of Letters and
Sciences,
University of Wisconsin

RESEARCH CONTRIBUTIONS:
Understanding of Cultural Dialect
with an emphasis on Language
Assessment, Specific Language
Impairment and Academic
Performance; Early Childhood
Language and Early Literacy of
African American Children

CONSULTANTS

F. Isabel Campoy
President, Transformative
Educational Services

RESEARCH CONTRIBUTIONS:
English as a Second Language,
Applied Linguistics, Writing in the
Curriculum, Family Involvement

David A. Monti
Professor Emeritus Department of
Reading and Language Arts,
Central Connecticut State University

RESEARCH CONTRIBUTIONS:
Reading Comprehension, Alternative
Assessments, Flexible Grouping

Tyrone C. Howard
Associate Professor Urban
Schooling,
*University of California,
Los Angeles*

RESEARCH CONTRIBUTIONS:
Multicultural Education, The Social
and Political Context of Schools,
Urban Education

Theme: Changing Times

Lesson 11

ART   LANGUAGE ARTS

Theme Writing | **Reading-Writing Connection**

Student Writing Model: Friendly Letter

Lesson 12

SOCIAL STUDIES

Reference Materials

Additional Resources

Data-Driven Instruction

1 ASSESS

Use assessments to track student progress.

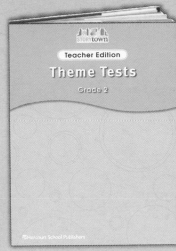

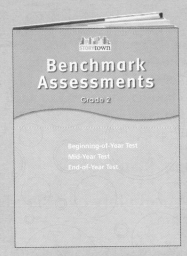

▲ Weekly Lesson Tests (grades 1–6)

▲ Theme Tests

▲ Benchmark Assessments
- Beginning-of-Year
- Mid-Year
- End-of-Year

 StoryTown Online Assessment

2 TEACH

Provide instruction in key areas of reading.

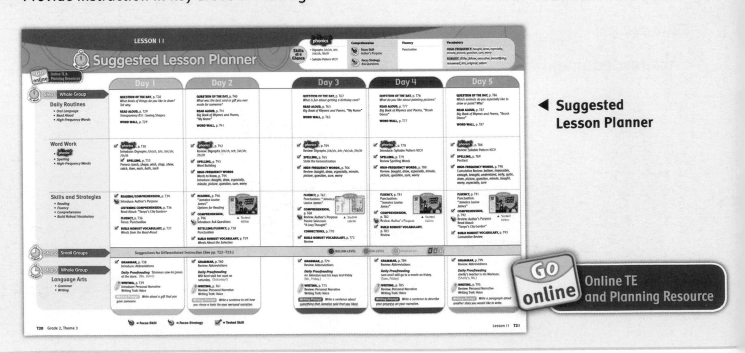

◀ Suggested Lesson Planner

DIFFERENTIATE INSTRUCTION

Use daily Monitor Progress notes to inform instruction.

MONITOR PROGRESS

Partner Reading

IF students need more support in fluency-building and in using appropriate pace,	THEN have them echo-read with you, paying close attention to punctuation marks to direct their pace.

Small-Group Instruction, p. S105:

● **BELOW-LEVEL: Reteach**
● **ON-LEVEL: Reinforce**
● **ADVANCED: Extend**

▲ Suggested Small-Group Planner

ASSESS, REMEDIATE, AND EXTEND

Use assessment results to remediate instruction.

INTENSIVE INTERVENTION PROGRAM

▲ Strategic Intervention Resource Kit

▲ Challenge Resource Kit

- Phonics
- Comprehension
- Vocabulary
- Fluency

Overview of a Theme

CORE LESSONS

- **Explicit, Systematic Instruction**

- **Spiraled Review of Key Skills**

- **Abundant Practice and Application**

- **Point-of-Use Progress Monitoring**

- **Support for *Leveled Readers***

- **Digital Support for Teachers and Students**

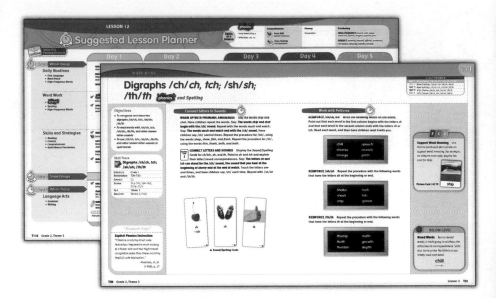

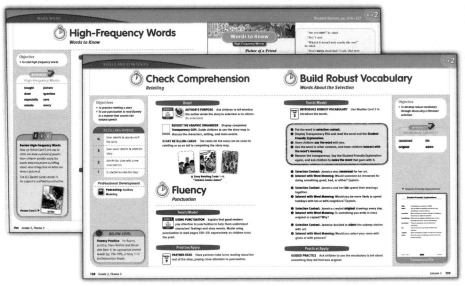

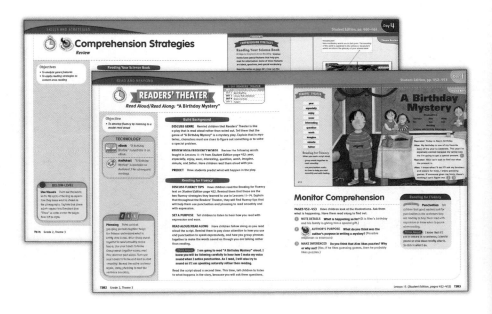

READING-WRITING CONNECTION

- **Reading-Writing Connection in *Student Edition***

- **Instruction in *Teacher Edition***

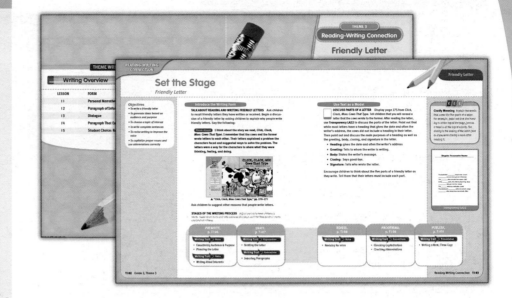

- **Focus on the Six Traits of Good Writing**
  - Organization
  - Ideas
  - Sentence Fluency
  - Word Choice
  - Voice
  - Conventions

- **Develop a Variety of Writing Strategies**

- **Develop <u>One</u> Major Form Through the Writing Process:**
  - Personal Narrative
  - Respond to a Story
  - Friendly Letter
  - Story
  - Description
  - Research Report

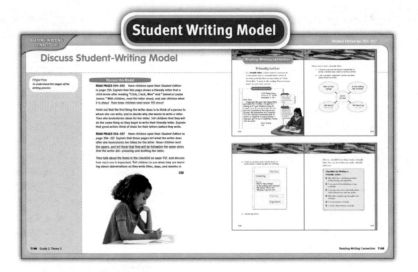

Overview of a Lesson

- **Lesson Resources**

- **Suggested Lesson Planner**

- **Suggested Small-Group Planner**

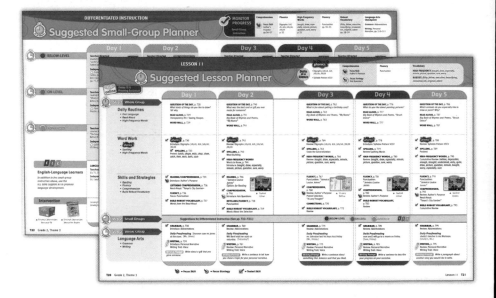

- *Leveled Readers* and **Leveled Practice**

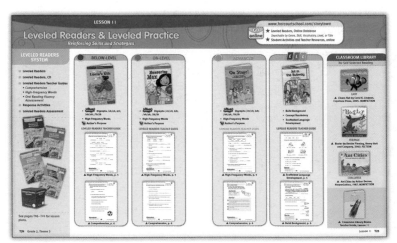

- Oral Language
- Read Aloud
- Word Wall

- Connect Letter and Sound
- Word Building
- Work with Patterns
- Spelling Pretest and Posttest
- Introduce and Review Structural Elements

- New Words for Each Lesson
- Instructional Routines
- Apply in the *Student Edition*
- Spiraled Review

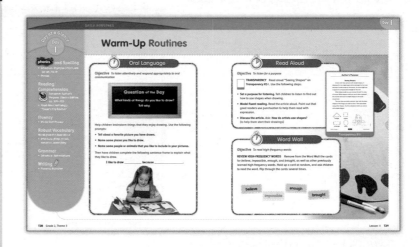

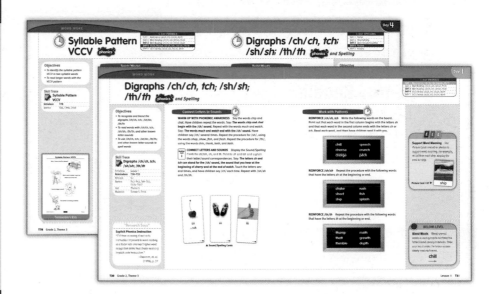

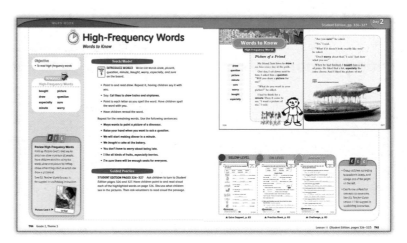

Overview of a Lesson (continued)

READING

- Main Selections
- Paired Selections

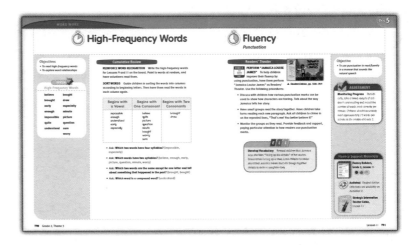

FLUENCY

- Explicit Instruction in Rate, Accuracy, and Prosody
- Repeated Readings
- Readers' Theater

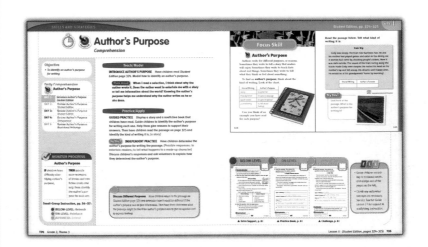

COMPREHENSION

- Focus Skills
- Focus Strategies
- Listening Comprehension

ROBUST VOCABULARY

- **Robust Vocabulary**
  - Tier Two Words

- **Instructional Routines**

- **Student-Friendly Explanations**

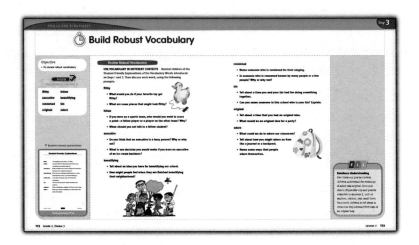

LANGUAGE ARTS

- **Grammar**

- **Writing**

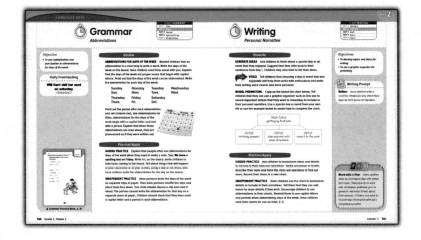

LEVELED READERS

- **Reinforce Skills and Strategies**

- **Review High-Frequency Words**

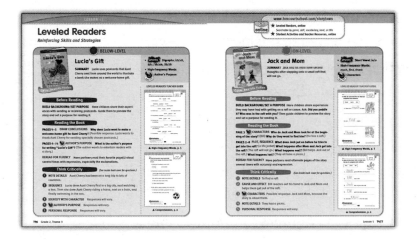

Introducing the Book

EXAMINE *THE STUDENT EDITION* Have children turn to each of the following features in the *Student Edition*. Briefly discuss how each part helps readers use the book and understand the stories.

- **Contents** Shows titles, authors, and page numbers.

- **Comprehension Strategies** Describes tools readers can use to read well.

- **Theme Overview** Lists literature, skills, and strategies in that theme.

- **Lesson Overview** Lists literature, focus skill, and focus strategy in that lesson.

- **Focus/Phonics Skill** Provides instruction in skills related to the literature.

- **Words to Know/Vocabulary** Introduces new high-frequency words or robust vocabulary words from the selection.

- **Genre Study** Describes the characteristic of the selection's genre.

- **Focus Strategy** Tells how to use strategies during reading.

- **Paired Selection** Presents poetry and other selections connected to the main selection.

- **Connections** Provides questions and activities related to both selections.

- **Reading-Writing Connection** Connects the literature to a good model of student writing.

- **Glossary** Provides student-friendly explanations for robust vocabulary words from each selection.

- **Index of Titles and Authors** Show titles and authors in alphabetical order.

Introduce Strategies

USING *STUDENT EDITION* PAGES 10–13 Have children open their *Student Editions* to page 10, and explain to them that these pages will help them think about ways to better understand what they read. Tell them that these ways are called "strategies," and that they can use strategies before they read, while they read, and after they read.

BEFORE YOU READ Tell children that before they read, they can think about what they already know about a topic to help them understand. They can also set a purpose for reading.

> **Think Aloud** If I was going to read a book about dogs, I could think about what I already know about dogs. I could also think about why I'm reading. These would help me understand the book better.

WHILE YOU READ Model strategies children can use while they read as follows:

> **Think Aloud** Asking questions about what I'm reading helps me know if I'm understanding it. If I'm not understanding, I can go back and reread parts of the book. When I answer questions about a book, I can be sure that I understood it.

AFTER YOU READ Explain how retelling and making connections can help children understand what they read. Say:

> **Think Aloud** After I read something, I tell myself what I just read. This helps me remember and understand. I also think about other things I have read, heard, or learned. Sometimes I can make connections between two different books.

Comprehension Strategies

Before You Read

Think about what you already know.
Look over the words and pictures before you read.

Set a purpose.
Decide why you are reading.

I want to enjoy reading a story.

While You Read

Use story structure.
Think about a story's characters, setting, and plot.

Use graphic organizers.
Use a story map, web, or chart to help you read.

Monitor your reading.
Use fix-up strategies such as reading ahead or rereading.

Ask questions.
Ask yourself and others questions about what you read.

Answer questions.
Answer your teacher's questions to help you understand what you read.

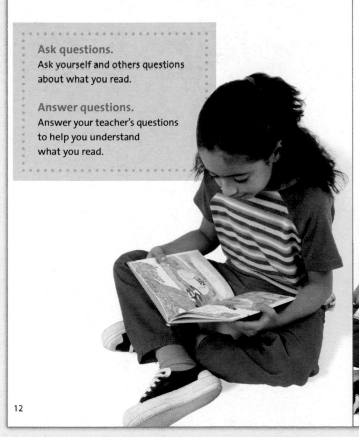

After You Read

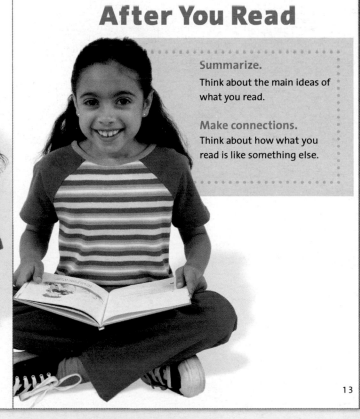

Summarize.
Think about the main ideas of what you read.

Make connections.
Think about how what you read is like something else.

Changing Times

Theme Resources

STUDENT EDITION LITERATURE

Lesson 11

PAIRED SELECTIONS

"Jamaica Louise James," pp. 328–349
REALISTIC FICTION

"A Lazy Thought,"
pp. 350–351
POETRY

Lesson 14

PAIRED SELECTIONS

"Rain Forest Babies," pp. 428–445
NONFICTION

"Baby Tapir Is Born!" pp. 446–447
WEBSITE

Lesson 12

PAIRED SELECTIONS

"At Play: Long Ago and Today," pp. 364–381
NONFICTION

"A History of Games and Toys in the United States,"
pp. 382–383
NONFICTION

Lesson 15 Theme Review

READERS' THEATER

"A Birthday Mystery,"
pp. 452–459
FICTION

Lesson 13

PAIRED SELECTIONS

"Big Bushy Mustache,"
pp. 392–417
REALISTIC FICTION

"Changing,"
pp. 418–419
POETRY

COMPREHENSION STRATEGIES

"The Life Cycle of a Frog,"
pp. 460–463
SCIENCE TEXTBOOK

 Literature selections are available on Audiotext 2.

THEME 3 CLASSROOM LIBRARY

For Self-Selected Reading

▲ **Buster**
by Denise Fleming

Buster the dog thinks his perfect life is spoiled when Betty the cat comes to live with him, until he learns not to be afraid of cats.

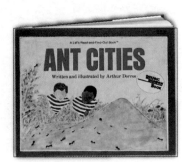

▲ **Ant Cities**
by Arthur Dorros

Explains how ants live and work together to build and maintain their cities.

▲ **Classroom Library Books Teacher Guide**

ADDITIONAL RESOURCES

▲ **Writer's Companion**

▲ **Grammar Practice Book**

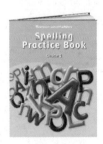

▲ **Spelling Practice Book**

▲ **Literacy Center Kit**

▲ **Reading Transparencies**

▲ **Language Arts Transparencies**

▲ **Fluency Builders**

▲ **Picture Card Collection**

PROFESSIONAL DEVELOPMENT

- **Professional Development Booklet**
- GO online **Online Professional Development**
- 🖥 **Videos for Podcasting**

Leveled Resources

 BELOW-LEVEL

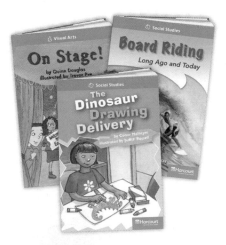

-  **Phonics**
- ☑ **High-Frequency Words**
- 🌀 **Focus Skills**

 ON-LEVEL

- **Phonics**
- ☑ **High-Frequency Words**
- 🌀 **Focus Skills**

ADVANCED

- **Phonics**
- ☑ **High-Frequency Words**
- 🌀 **Focus Skills**

E L L

- **Build Background**
- **Concept Vocabulary**
- **Scaffolded Language Development**

Leveled Reader System

- **Leveled Readers**
- **Leveled Readers CD**
- **Leveled Reader Teacher Guides**
  - High-Frequency Words
  - Comprehension
  - Oral Reading Fluency
- **Response Activities Flip Charts**
- **Leveled Readers Assessment**

TECHNOLOGY

 www.harcourtschool.com/storytown

✔ **Leveled Readers, *online***
  Searchable by Genre, Skill, Vocabulary, Level or Title

✔ **Student Activities and Teacher Resources, *online***

Teaching suggestions for the Leveled Readers can be found on pp. T96–T99, T190–T193, T276–T279, T358–T361, T430–T433

Strategic Intervention Resource Kit,
Lessons 11–15

Interaction Intervention Reader: *Title TK*

- "A Garden for Marta"
- "How We Play"
- "The Lost Watch"
- "Cats"
- "The Picnic"

Also available:

- Strategic Intervention Teacher Guide
- Game Boards
- Strategic Intervention Practice Book
- Skill Cards

- *Interactive Intervention Reader eBook*

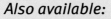 ELL Extra Support Kit,
Lessons 11–15

- ELL Teacher Guide
- ELL Readers
- ELL Practice Book

Challenge Resource Kit,
Theme 3

- Challenge Book Pack
- Challenge Cards
- Teacher Guide

Leveled Practice

 BELOW-LEVEL
Extra Support Copying Masters

 ON-LEVEL
Practice Book

 ADVANCED
Challenge Copying Masters

English Language Learners Copying Masters

INTENSIVE INTERVENTION PROGRAM

GRADES K–3 Set of Intervention material providing targeted instruction in:

- Phonics
- Comprehension
- Vocabulary
- Fluency

Digital Classroom
to go along with your Print Program

 online www.harcourtschool.com/storytown

FOR THE TEACHER

Prepare

GO online Professional Development In the Online TE

PROFESSIONAL DEVELOPMENT

▮ Videos for Podcasting

Plan & Organize

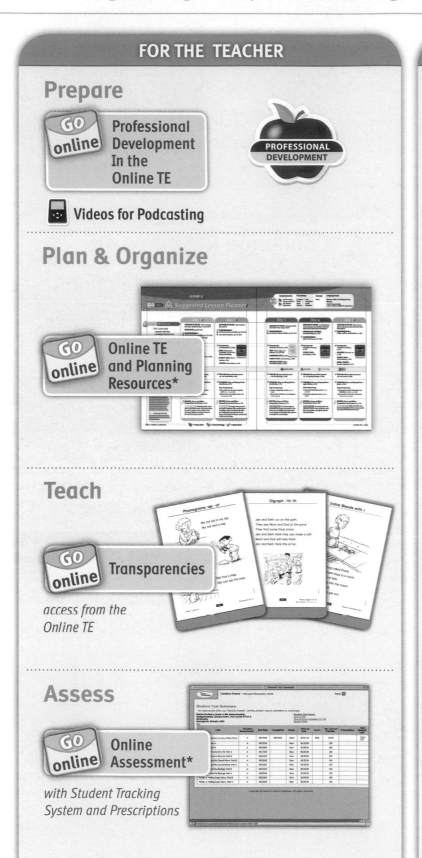

GO online Online TE and Planning Resources*

Teach

GO online Transparencies

access from the Online TE

Assess

GO online Online Assessment*

with Student Tracking System and Prescriptions

FOR THE STUDENT

Read

GO online Student eBook*

GO online Strategic Intervention Interactive Reader

GO online Leveled Readers

● **BELOW-LEVEL**
● **ON-LEVEL**
● **ADVANCED**
ELL

Practice & Apply

◉ Splash into Phonics CD-ROM

 Also available on CD-ROM

Monitor Progress

Plan Ahead

to inform instruction for Theme 3

MONITOR PROGRESS

Looking Back to Theme 2

IF performance was	THEN, in addition to core instruction, use these resources:
● **BELOW-LEVEL: Reteach**	• Below-Level Leveled Readers • Leveled Reader System • Extra Support Copying Masters • Strategic Intervention Resource Kit • Intensive Intervention Program
● **ON-LEVEL Reinforce**	• On-Level Leveled Readers • Leveled Reader System • Practice Book
○ **ADVANCED: Extend**	• Advanced Leveled Readers • Leveled Reader System • Challenge Copying Masters • Challenge Resource Kit

 ## ONLINE ASSESSMENT

✔ Prescriptions for Reteaching

✔ Weekly Lesson Tests

✔ End-of-Book Tests

✔ Student Profile System to track student growth

 www.harcourtschool.com/storytown

THEME 3 TESTED SKILLS

Tested

Domain	Skills
PHONICS/SPELLING	• Digraphs /ch/*ch*, *tch*; /sh/*sh*; /th/*th* • Long Vowel $\bar{e}$ • Consonants /s/*c*; /j/*g*, *dge* • *r*-Controlled Vowel /ûr/*ir*, *ur*, *er*, *ear*
HIGH FREQUENCY WORDS	• Words from Lessons 11-14
COMPREHENSION	• Comprehension of Grade-level Text 🔎 Author's Purpose 🔎 Fiction and Nonfiction
VOCABULARY	• Robust Vocabulary
FLUENCY	• Oral Reading Fluency 📟 Podcasting: Assessing Fluency
GRAMMAR	• Abbreviations • Singular Possessive Nouns • Plural Possessive Nouns • Pronouns
WRITING	• Friendly Letter
WRITING TRAITS	• Voice • Conventions

Theme at a Glance

	LESSON 11  pp. 328–349	LESSON 12  pp. 364–381	LESSON 13  pp. 392–417
Phonics/ Spelling	**DIGRAPHS** /ch/*ch, tch*; /sh/*sh*; /th/*th*	**LONG VOWEL** /ē/*ey, y*	**CONSONANTS** /s/*c*; /j/*g, dge*
Comprehension	✓ Author's Purpose Ask Questions	✓ Author's Purpose Ask Questions	✓ Fiction and Nonfiction Monitor Comprehension: Reread
Reading	**PAIRED SELECTIONS** "Jamaica Louise James" REALISTIC FICTION "A Lazy Thought" POETRY	**PAIRED SELECTIONS** "At Play: Long Ago and Today" NONFICTION "A History of Games and Toys in the United States" NONFICTION	**PAIRED SELECTIONS** "Big Bushy Mustache" REALISTIC FICTION "Changing" POETRY
High-Frequency Words	✓ **HIGH-FREQUENCY WORDS** *draw, picture, question , minute, bought, worry, especially, sure*	✓ **HIGH-FREQUENCY WORDS** *imagine, favorite, year , enjoy, cook, board, popular, expensive*	✓ **HIGH-FREQUENCY WORDS** *wear, tough, woman, young, shoes, wash, above*
Robust Vocabulary	**ROBUST VOCABULARY** *filthy, twinkle, executive, beautifying, renowned, kin, original, adorn*	**ROBUST VOCABULARY** *recently, housed, official, nominate, recreation, leisurely, ramble, archaic*	**ROBUST VOCABULARY** *wilting, flitted, gobble, trance, route, semblance, distraught, improvise*

Theme Writing ▌ **Reading-Writing Connection** ▶ Letter pp. T100–T111

Grammar	✓ **GRAMMAR:** Abbreviations	✓ **GRAMMAR:** Singular Possessive Nouns	✓ **GRAMMAR:** Plural Possessive Nouns
Writing	**WRITING FORM:** Personal Narrative **WRITING TRAIT:** Voice	**WRITING FORM:** Paragraph That Gives Information **WRITING TRAIT:** Voice	**WRITING FORM:** Story: Dialogue **WRITING TRAIT:** Conventions

THEME 3

Theme Project

 = Focus Skill   = Focus Strategy   ✓ = Tested Skill

LESSON 14

pp. 428–445

r-CONTROLLED VOWEL /ûr/*ir*, *ur*, *ear*

 Fiction and Nonfiction

Monitor Comprehension: Reread

PAIRED SELECTIONS
"Rain Forest Babies" NONFICTION
"Baby Tapir is Born!" WEBSITE

 HIGH-FREQUENCY WORDS
interesting, thumb, touch, care, sweat, father

ROBUST VOCABULARY
dappled, entranced, trooped, circling, adorable, assortment, habitat, immense

---

LESSON 15

pp. 452–459

READERS' THEATER

"A Birthday Mystery"

- **Build Fluency**

- **Review and Build Vocabulary**

COMPREHENSION STRATEGIES

"The Life Cycle of a Frog"

REVIEW FOCUS STRATEGIES

- Ask Questions

- Monitor Comprehension: Reread

Writing Traits Voice, Conventions

 GRAMMAR: Pronouns

 WRITING FORM: Paragraph That Explains

 WRITING TRAIT: Conventions

ADDITIONAL REVIEW

Focus Skills

- Author's Purpose

- Fiction and Nonfiction

- and Spelling

- Grammar

 **Writing:** Revise and Publish

Planning for Reading Success

Tested Skill	Teach/Model	Monitor Progress	Additional Support
PHONICS/SPELLING • Digraphs /ch/*ch*, *tch*; /sh/*sh*; /th/*th* • Long Vowel /ē /*ey*, *y* • Consonants /s/*c*; /j/*g*, *dge* • r-Controlled Vowel /ûr/*ir*, *ur*, *ear*	Lesson 11, pp. T00–T00 Lesson 12, pp. T00–T00 Lesson 13, pp. T00–T00 Lesson 14, pp. T00–T00	Lesson 11, p. T42 Lesson 12, p. T138 Lesson 13, p. T220 Lesson 14, p. T306	Small-Group Instruction, p. S000 Small-Group Instruction, p. S000 Small-Group Instruction, p. S000 Small-Group Instruction, p. S000
HIGH-FREQUENCY WORDS	Lesson 11–14, pp. 000–000, pp. 000–000, pp. 000–000, pp. 000–000, pp. 000–000	Lesson 11–14, pp. T66, T160, T246, T328, T405	Small-Group Instruction, p. S000; S000; S000; S000; S000;
ROBUST VOCABULARY	Lessons 11–15, pp. T00, 000, 000, 000, 000 Lessons 11–15, Extend Word Meanings, pp. T00, 000, 000, 000, 000	Lessons 11–15, pp. T93, T187, T273, T355	Small-Group Instruction, p. S000; S000; S000; S000; S000;
COMPREHENSION 🌀 Author's Purpose 🌀 Fiction and Nonfiction	Lesson 11, pp. T00–T00 Lesson 13, pp. T00–T00	Lessons 11–12, pp. T34, T130 Lessons 13–14, pp. T212, T298	Small-Group Instruction, p. S000 Small-Group Instruction, p. S000
DIBELS **FLUENCY** • Punctuation • Phrasing	Lesson 11, pp. T00, T000 Lesson 13, pp. T00, T000	Lesson 11–12, pp. T81, T175 Lesson 13–14, pp. T261, T343	Small-Group Instruction p. S000 Small-Group Instruction p. S000
WRITING • Trait Voice • Trait Conventions **FORM: FRIENDLY LETTER**	Lesson 11, pp. T000 Lesson 13, pp. T00–T00 Reading-Writing Connection, pp. T100–T111	Scoring Rubric, p. T95, T189 Scoring Rubric, p. T275, T429 Scoring Rubric, p. 000	Lesson 11, p. 000 Lesson 13, p. 000 p. 000
GRAMMAR	Lessons 11–14, pp. T00–T00, T00–T00, T00–T00, T00–T00	Lessons 11–14, pp. T00–T00, T00–T00, T00–T00, T00–T00	Lesson 11–14 Reteach Activities, pp. S000–S000, S000–S000, S000–S000, S000–S000

🌀 = Focus Skill

Review	Assess
Lesson 11, p. T00 Lesson 12, p. T00 Lesson 13, p. T00 Lesson 14, p. T00	Weekly Lesson Tests 11–15 Theme 3 Benchmark Test
Lesson 11–14, pp. 000–000, pp. 000–000, pp. 000–000, pp. 000– 000, pp. 000–000	Mini-Benchmark Tests 00, 00 Theme 3 Benchmark Test
Lessons 11–015, Cumulative Review, pp. 000–000, 000–000, 000	Weekly Lesson Tests 11–16 Theme 3 Benchmark Test
Lesson 11, p. T00 Lesson 13, p. T000	Weekly Lesson Tests 00, 00 Theme 3 Benchmark Test
Lesson 11, pp. T00 Lesson 13, pp. T00	Oral Reading Fluency Tests
Lesson 11, pp. T000 Lesson 13, pp. T00–T00	Weekly Lesson Tests 00, 00 Theme 3 Benchmark Test
Lesson 11, p. 000 Lesson 12, p. 000 Lesson 13, p. 000 Lesson 14, p. 000	Weekly Lesson Tests Theme 3 Benchmark Test

INTEGRATED TEST PREP

In the *Teacher Edition*

- Test Rubric, p.R000

- Test Short Response, pp. T57, T151, T236, T319

- Writing on Demand, pp. T110–T111

TEST PREP SYSTEM

- Teach/Model Transparencies

- Practice Workbook: Reading and Writing

TEST PREP MINUTES

For early finishers, beginning of class, or anytime:

- **ABBREVIATIONS Write a few sentences using some of the abbreviations you know.** (I went to see Dr. Miller on Wed. in Orlando, FL.)

- **WRITING/FICTION AND NONFICTION Write a few nonfiction sentences about something exciting thing that has happened in your life. Then write a few fiction sentences about something that has happened in your life.** (Nonfiction: My cousins came to visit me for a week. We spent a lot of time together and had fun. Fiction: I won a trip to a theme park for my whole school. We got to go on an airplane and stay in a fancy hotel.)

- **ROBUST VOCABULARY Draw a picture of how you would beautify your school or your house. Write a sentence about what beautifying your school or house would be like.** (Beautifying my house would be easy because I would add all of the things I like.)

- **WRITING Think about a time when you learned a lesson. Write a few sentences about it.**

Theme Project
Then-and-Now Display

Objectives
- *To gather information by interviewing*
- *To organize and present information in a tabletop display*

Materials
- posterboard
- pencils, markers, crayons
- scissors, glue, masking tape
- sides from cardboard cartons (or other backing for support)

See **Project Ideas from The Bag Ladies**

Getting Started

Point out a computer, and ask children if they think classrooms of fifty years ago had the same technology. Explain that children of fifty years ago learned in school and played with friends, just as children do today, but many changes have taken place from then to now. Tell children that they will make a tabletop display that shows some of these changes.

Along the Way

1 Brainstorm   Write the words *School*, *Play*, and *Home* on the board. Have children brainstorm questions about life fifty years ago in each of these categories. List the questions on the board.

2 Research   Tell children that they will answer their questions by interviewing adults who were schoolchildren fifty years ago. Talk about likely interviewees in children's families and in the school and local communities. Model how to ask an interview question, listen carefully, and take notes on the answers. Give children time to practice before they conduct the actual interviews. Then invite interviewees to speak to the class about their life fifty years ago.

3 Plan   Organize children into groups. Guide each group in deciding what to show in a "Then" and "Now" tabletop display. Explain how to organize information and present it clearly. Children will combine pictures (drawings, copies of photos, images downloaded from approved websites), objects if available, and sentences pointing out differences between then and now.

4 COMPLETE THE DISPLAY   Have each group lay out their pictures and sentences on a "Then" and "Now" poster before using glue. Remind them that their sentences must be neatly written and easy to read. The two posters are then taped together and propped up for the tabletop display.

LISTENING AND SPEAKING

Children can develop listening and speaking skills as they conduct their interviews and as they work in small groups to divide and complete a project. Emphasize the rules of effective listening and speaking:

- **Show interest while listening to a speaker.**
- **Pu the speaker's answers in your own words to show understanding. Ask follow-up questions if you don't understand an answer.**
- **Wait for a speaker to finish before making comments.**
- **Participate in group discussions by sharing comments.**

SUGGESTIONS FOR INQUIRY

The theme project can be a springboard for inquiry into a variety of topics and ideas. Help children formulate questions about changes over time, such as:

- **What are stories children read or movies they watched 50 years ago?**
- **How can we find out what our city or town looked like 50 or 100 years ago?**

Guide children in locating answers to some of their questions. Invite them to present their findings to the class.

Modify Research Children may use their home language to interview an older adult who speaks the language. Children may then use pictures to show what they learned about life in the past. Prompt them to describe the pictures in English.

BELOW-LEVEL

Support Concepts Illustrated works about historical decades are available in many public libraries. Use the photographs in such books or from online sources to show children clothing, cars, fads, entertainment, and other features of everyday life from fifty years ago. Ask children to point out how the features are like and unlike those of today.

School-Home Connection

Children may interview family members. If possible, interviewees may also provide objects for children to display and photos to scan or photocopy.

Build Theme Connections
Changing Times

Relate To Personal Experience

Discuss Change From Past To Future   Have children recall experiences from last summer or from first grade, and briefly tell about them. Then ask whether children remember experiences from when they were five years old. Ask children if they remember what they did as babies. Talk about the sequence from baby to toddler to preschooler to schoolchild to adult. Then read aloud the poem. Explain that it expresses the viewpoint of a young boy looking into his future.

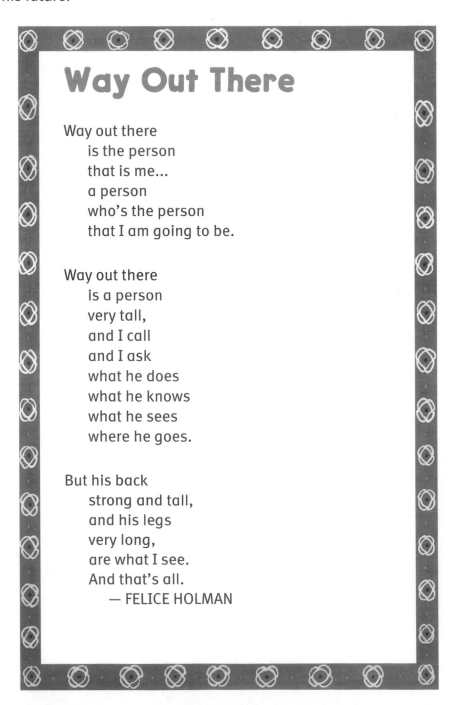

Way Out There

Way out there
   is the person
   that is me...
   a person
   who's the person
   that I am going to be.

Way out there
   is a person
   very tall,
   and I call
   and I ask
   what he does
   what he knows
   what he sees
   where he goes.

But his back
   strong and tall,
   and his legs
   very long,
   are what I see.
   And that's all.
      — FELICE HOLMAN

Winter on the Grand Canal, Hou Bao Ming

Talk About the Theme

DISCUSS THE THEME TITLE   Have children read the theme title, "Changing Times," and offer several ideas about its possible meanings. Tell children that the artwork shows a winter scene and is one of four pictures that the artist made of the same scene. The other pictures show spring, summer, and fall. Ask children what the seasons of the year might have to do with the theme of change.

PREVIEW THE THEME   Have children page through the selections in this theme. Tell them to read the selection titles and look at the illustrations. Ask for ideas about the kinds of changes that might be shown in this theme—in fictional characters and in real-life people and animals.

Talk About Fine Art

DISCUSS THE ARTWORK   Have children look closely at *Winter on the Grand Canal* by Hou Bao Ming. Ask questions to get children thinking about details and techniques; **Why do you think the artist chose blues and purples for this scene? What colors might the artist have used to show this scene in summer or spring? What kinds of activities are the people doing on this canal? Do you think the artist imagined this scene or showed it exactly as it is?** Encourage children to ask their own questions about the artwork. Encourage more than one answer.

Lesson 11

✔ Phonics
Digraphs /ch/*ch, tch*; /sh/*sh*; /th/*th*
Syllable Pattern VCCV

✔ Spelling
lunch, shape, wish, chop, show, catch, then, each, bath, such

✔ High-Frequency Words
bought, draw, especially, minute, picture, question, sure, worry

Reading
"Jamaica Louise James" by Amy Hest
REALISTIC FICTION

"A Lazy Thought" by Eve Merriam POETRY

✔ Fluency
Punctuation

✔ Comprehension
🌀 Author's Purpose
🌀 Ask Questions

✔ Robust Vocabulary
filthy, fellow, executive, beautifying, renowned, kin, original, adorn

✔ Grammar
Abbreviations

Writing
Form: Personal Narrative
Trait: Voice

✔ Weekly Lesson Test

🌀 = Focus Skill 🌀 = Focus Strategy ✔ = Tested Skill

One stop
for all
your **Digital** *needs*

Digital
CLASSROOM

 www.harcourtschool.com/storytown
To go along with your print program

FOR THE TEACHER

Prepare Professional Development

 Videos for Podcasting

Plan & Organize Online TE & Planning Resources*

Teach Transparencies

for electronic projection

Assess Online Assessment*

with Student Tracking System and Prescriptions

FOR THE STUDENT

Read  Student eBook*

 Strategic Intervention Interactive Reader

 Decodable Books

 Leveled Readers

Practice & Apply Splash into Phonics CD-ROM

 Comprehension Expedition CD-ROM

 Also available on CD-ROM

Literature Resources

STUDENT
EDITION

GO online
eBook
STUDENT EDITION

Genre: Realistic Fiction

Genre: Poetry

 ◄ **Audiotext** *Student Edition selections are available on Audiotext 2.*

Accelerated Reader ◄ *Practice Quizzes for the Selection*

THEME CONNECTION: CHANGING TIMES
Comparing Realistic Fiction and Poetry

 ART   **Jamaica Louise James, pp. 328–349**

SUMMARY   As a surprise for her grandmother's birthday, Jamaica Louise James hangs her painted artwork in the drab subway station where her grandmother works.

 LANGUAGE ARTS   **A Lazy Thought, pp. 350–351**

SUMMARY   In this poem, a child reflects on the busy, hectic life of adults.

Paired Selections

Support for Differentiated Instruction

Go online **LEVELED READERS**

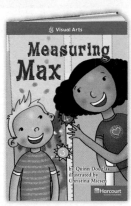

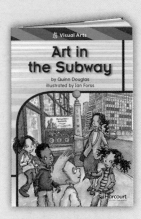

● **BELOW-LEVEL**　　● **ON-LEVEL**　　● **ADVANCED**

E L L

LEVELED PRACTICE

◀ **Strategic Intervention Resource Kit, Lesson 11**

◀ **Strategic Intervention Interactive Reader, Lesson 11**

Strategic Intervention Interactive Reader Online

◀ **ELL Extra Support Kit, Lesson 11**

◀ **Challenge Resource Kit, Lesson 11**

● **BELOW-LEVEL**

Extra Support Copying Masters, pp. 79, 81–84

● **ON-LEVEL**

Practice Book, pp. 79–85

● **ADVANCED**

Challenge Copying Masters, pp. 79, 81–84

E L L

ELL Copying Masters, Lesson 11

ADDITIONAL RESOURCES

- Decodable Book 9
- Spelling Practice Book, pp. 35–37
- Grammar Practice Book, pp. 37–40
- Reading Transparencies R51–R56
- Language Arts Transparencies LA21–LA22
- Test Prep System
◀ Literacy Center Kit, Cards 51–55
- Sound/Spelling Cards
◀ Fluency Builders
◀ Picture Card Collection
- Read-Aloud Anthology, pp. 42–45

✓ ASSESSMENT

✔ **Monitor Progress**

✔ **Weekly Lesson Tests, Lesson 11**

- Comprehension
- Robust Vocabulary
- Phonics and Spelling
- High-Frequency Words
- Focus Skill
- Grammar

 www.harcourtschool.com/ storytown
Online Assessment
Also available on CD-ROM—Exam View

Suggested Lesson Planner

Go online Online TE & Planning Resources

	Day 1	Day 2
Step 1 Whole Group		

Daily Routines
- Oral Language
- Read Aloud
- High-Frequency Words

Day 1

QUESTION OF THE DAY, p. T28
What kinds of things do you like to draw? Tell why.

READ ALOUD, p. T29
Transparency R51: Seeing Shapes

WORD WALL, p. T29

Day 2

QUESTION OF THE DAY, p. T40
What was the best card or gift you ever made for someone?

READ ALOUD, p. T41
Big Book of Rhymes and Poems, "My Name"

WORD WALL, p. T41

Word Work
- **phonics**
- Spelling
- High-Frequency Words

Day 1

 phonics, p. T30
Introduce: Digraphs /ch/*ch, tch*; /sh/*sh*; /th/*th*

 **SPELLING,** p. T33
Pretest: *lunch, shape, wish, chop, show, catch, then, each, bath, such*

Day 2

 phonics, p. T42
Review: Digraphs /ch/*ch, tch*; /sh/*sh*; /th/*th*

SPELLING, p. T43
Word Building

HIGH-FREQUENCY WORDS
Words to Know, p. T44
Introduce: *bought, draw, especially, minute, picture, question, sure, worry*

Skills and Strategies
- Reading
- Fluency
- Comprehension
- Build Robust Vocabulary

Day 1

READING/COMPREHENSION, p. T34
Introduce: Author's Purpose

LISTENING COMPREHENSION, p. T36
Read-Aloud: "Tanya's City Garden"

FLUENCY, p. T36
Focus: Punctuation

BUILD ROBUST VOCABULARY, p. T37
Words from the Read-Aloud

Day 2

READING, p. T46
"Jamaica Louise James"
Options for Reading

COMPREHENSION, p. T46
 Introduce: Ask Questions

▲ Student Edition

RETELLING/FLUENCY, p. T58
Punctuation

BUILD ROBUST VOCABULARY, p. T59
Words About the Selection

Step 2 Small Groups	Suggestions for Differentiated Instruction (See pp. T22–T23.)	

Step 3 Whole Group

Language Arts
- Grammar
- Writing

Day 1

GRAMMAR, p. T38
Introduce: Abbreviations

Daily Proofreading Shannon saw ms jones at the store. (Ms. Jones)

 WRITING, p. T39
Introduce: Personal Narrative
Writing Trait: Voice

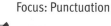 **Writing Prompt** *Write about a gift that you gave someone.*

Day 2

GRAMMAR, p. T60
Review: Abbreviations

Daily Proofreading
Will Kerri visit her aunt on saturday. (Saturday?)

 WRITING, p. T61
Review: Personal Narrative
Writing Trait: Voice

 Writing Prompt *Write a sentence to tell how you chose a topic for your personal narrative.*

 = Focus Skill   = Focus Strategy    = Tested Skill

Skills at a Glance

phonics

- Digraphs /ch/*ch*, *tch*; /sh/*sh*; /th/*th*
- Syllable Pattern VCCV

Comprehension

 Focus Skill
Author's Purpose

 Focus Strategy
Ask Questions

Fluency

Punctuation

Vocabulary

HIGH-FREQUENCY: *bought, draw, especially, minute, picture, question, sure, worry*

ROBUST: *filthy, fellow, executive, beautifying, renowned, kin, original, adorn*

Day 3

QUESTION OF THE DAY, p. T62
What is fun about getting a birthday card?

READ ALOUD, p. T63
Big Book of Rhymes and Poems, "My Name"

WORD WALL, p. T63

, p. T64
Review: Digraphs /ch/*ch*, *tch*; /sh/*sh*; /th/*th*

SPELLING, p. T65
State the Generalization

HIGH-FREQUENCY WORDS, p. T66
Review: *bought, draw, especially, minute, picture, question, sure, worry*

FLUENCY, p. T67
Punctuation: "Jamaica Louise James"

COMPREHENSION, p. T68
 Review: Author's Purpose
Paired Selection:
"A Lazy Thought"

▲ Student Edition

CONNECTIONS, p. T70

BUILD ROBUST VOCABULARY, p. T72
Review

Day 4

QUESTION OF THE DAY, p. T76
What do you like about painting pictures?

READ ALOUD, p. T77
Big Book of Rhymes and Poems, "Brush Dance"

WORD WALL, p. T77

, p. T78
Introduce: Syllable Pattern VCCV

SPELLING, p. T79
Review Spelling Words

HIGH-FREQUENCY WORDS, p. T80
Review: *bought, draw, especially, minute, picture, question, sure, worry*

FLUENCY, p. T81
Punctuation: "Jamaica Louise James"

COMPREHENSION, p. T82
 Review: Author's Purpose

▲ Student Edition

BUILD ROBUST VOCABULARY, p. T83
Review

Day 5

QUESTION OF THE DAY, p. T86
Which animals do you especially like to draw or paint? Why?

READ ALOUD, p. T87
Big Book of Rhymes and Poems, "Brush Dance"

WORD WALL, p. T87

, p. T88
Review: Syllable Pattern VCCV

SPELLING, p. T89
Posttest

HIGH-FREQUENCY WORDS, p. T90
Cumulative Review: *believe, impossible, enough, brought, understand, early, quite, draw, picture, question, minute, bought, worry, especially, sure*

FLUENCY, p. T91
Punctuation: "Jamaica Louise James"

COMPREHENSION, p. T92
 Review: Author's Purpose
Read-Aloud:
"Tanya's City Garden"

▲ Student Edition

BUILD ROBUST VOCABULARY, p. T93
Cumulative Review

● **BELOW-LEVEL** ● **ON-LEVEL** ● **ADVANCED** **E L L**

GRAMMAR, p. T74
Review: Abbreviations

Daily Proofreading
mr Johnston lost his keys last friday
(Mr., Friday.)

 WRITING, p. T75
Review: Personal Narrative
Writing Trait: Voice

Writing Prompt *Write a sentence about something that Jamaica said that you liked.*

GRAMMAR, p. T84
Review: Abbreviations

Daily Proofreading
sam and I will go to a movie on friday.
(Sam, Friday)

WRITING, p. T85
Review: Personal Narrative
Writing Trait: Voice

Writing Prompt *Write a sentence to describe your progress on your narrative.*

GRAMMAR, p. T94
Review: Abbreviations

Daily Proofreading
shelly's teacher is ms Markson.
(Shelly's, Ms.)

WRITING, p. T95
Review: Personal Narrative
Writing Trait: Voice

Writing Prompt *Write a paragraph about another story you would like to write.*

Suggested Small-Group Planner

45–60 Minutes

	Day 1	**Day 2**

 BELOW-LEVEL
15–20 Minutes

Day 1

Teacher-Directed
Leveled Reader:
"Lucia's Gift," p. T96
Before Reading

Independent
⭐ Listening/Speaking
Center, p. T26
Extra Support Copying Masters,
pp. 79, 81

▲ Leveled Reader

Day 2

Teacher-Directed
Student Edition:
"Jamaica Louise James,"
p. T46

Independent
⭐ Reading Center, p. T26
Extra Support Copying Masters,
pp. 82–83

▲ Student Edition

 ON-LEVEL
15–20 Minutes

Day 1

Teacher-Directed
Leveled Reader:
"Measuring Max," p. T97
Before Reading

Independent
⭐ Reading Center, p. T26
Practice Book, pp. 79, 81

▲ Leveled Reader

Day 2

Teacher-Directed
Student Edition:
"Jamaica Louise James,"
p. T46

Independent
⭐ Letters and Sounds
Center, p. T27
Practice Book, pp. 82–83

▲ Student Edition

 ADVANCED
15–20 Minutes

Day 1

Teacher-Directed
Leveled Reader:
"On Stage!," p. T98
Before Reading

Independent
⭐ Letters and Sounds Center, p. T27
Challenge Copying Masters, pp. 79, 81

▲ Leveled Reader

Day 2

Teacher-Directed
Leveled Reader:
"On Stage!," p. T98
Read the Book

Independent
⭐ Word Work Center, p. T27
Challenge Copying Masters,
pp. 82–83

▲ Leveled Reader

ELL

English-Language Learners

In addition to the small-group instruction above, use the ELL Extra Support Kit to promote language development.

LANGUAGE DEVELOPMENT SUPPORT
Teacher-Directed
ELL TG, Day 1
Independent
ELL Copying Masters, Lesson 11

▲ ELL Student Handbook

LANGUAGE DEVELOPMENT SUPPORT
Teacher-Directed
ELL TG, Day 2
Independent
ELL Copying Masters, Lesson 11

▲ ELL Student Handbook

Intervention

▲ Strategic Intervention Resource Kit

▲ Strategic Intervention Interactive Reader

Strategic Intervention TG, Day 1
Strategic Intervention Practice Book, Lesson 11

Strategic Intervention TG, Day 2
Strategic Intervention Interactive Reader, Lesson 11

▲ Strategic Intervention Interactive Reader

MONITOR PROGRESS

Small-Group Instruction

Comprehension	Phonics	High-Frequency Words	Fluency	Robust Vocabulary	Language Arts Checkpoint
Focus Skill Author's Purpose pp. S6–S7	Digraphs /ch/ *ch, tch*; /sh/*sh*; /th/*th* p. S2	*bought, draw, especially, minute, picture, question, sure, worry* p. S3	Punctuation pp. S4–S5	*filthy, fellow, executive, beautifying, renowned, kin, original, adorn* pp. S8–S9	**Grammar:** Abbreviations **Writing:** Personal Narrative, pp. S10–S11

Day 3

Teacher-Directed
Leveled Reader:
"Lucia's Gift," p. T96
Read the Book

Independent
 Word Work Center, p. T27

 ▲ Leveled Reader

Teacher-Directed
Leveled Reader:
"Measuring Max," p. T97
Read the Book

Independent
 Writing Center, p. T27

▲ Leveled Reader

Teacher-Directed
Leveled Reader:
"On Stage!," p. T98
Think Critically

Independent
 Listening/Speaking Center, p. T26

▲ Leveled Reader

LANGUAGE DEVELOPMENT SUPPORT

Teacher-Directed
Leveled Reader: "Art in the Subway," p. T99
Before Reading; Read the Book
ELL TG, Day 3

Independent
ELL Copying Masters, Lesson 11

 ▲ Leveled Reader

Strategic Intervention TG, Day 3
Strategic Intervention Interactive Reader, Lesson 11
Strategic Intervention Practice Book, Lesson 11

▲ Strategic Intervention Interactive Reader

Day 4

Teacher-Directed
Leveled Reader:
"Lucia's Gift," p. T96
Reread for Fluency

Independent
 Letters and Sounds Center, p. T27

▲ Leveled Reader

Teacher-Directed
Leveled Reader:
"Measuring Max," p. T97
Reread for Fluency

Independent
 Word Work Center, p. T27

▲ Leveled Reader

Teacher-Directed
Leveled Reader:
"On Stage!," p. T98
Reread for Fluency

Independent
 Writing Center, p. T27
Self-Selected Reading: Classroom Library Collection

▲ Leveled Reader

LANGUAGE DEVELOPMENT SUPPORT

Teacher-Directed
Leveled Reader: "Art in the Subway," p. T99
Reread for Fluency
ELL TG, Day 4

Independent
ELL Copying Masters, Lesson 11

 ▲ Leveled Reader

Strategic Intervention TG, Day 4
Strategic Intervention Interactive Reader, Lesson 11

▲ Strategic Intervention Interactive Reader

Day 5

Teacher-Directed
Leveled Reader:
"Lucia's Gift," p. T96
Think Critically

Independent
 Writing Center, p. T27
Leveled Reader: Reread for Fluency
Extra Support Copying Masters, p. 84

▲ Leveled Reader

Teacher-Directed
Leveled Reader:
"Measuring Max," p. T97
Think Critically

Independent
 Listening/Speaking Center, p. T26
Leveled Reader: Reread for Fluency
Practice Book, p. 84

▲ Leveled Reader

Teacher-Directed
Leveled Reader:
"On Stage!," p. T98
Reread for Fluency

Independent
 Reading Center, p. T26
Leveled Reader: Reread for Fluency
Self-Selected Reading: Classroom Library Collection
Challenge Copying Masters, p. 84

▲ Leveled Reader

LANGUAGE DEVELOPMENT SUPPORT

Teacher-Directed
Leveled Reader: "Art in the Subway," p. T99
Think Critically
ELL TG, Day 5

Independent
Leveled Reader: Reread for Fluency
ELL Copying Masters, Lesson 11

 ▲ Leveled Reader

Strategic Intervention TG, Day 5
Strategic Intervention Interactive Reader, Lesson 11

 ▲ Strategic Intervention Interactive Reader

Leveled Readers & Leveled Practice
Reinforcing Skills and Strategies

LEVELED READERS SYSTEM

- **Leveled Readers**
- **Leveled Readers, CD**
- **Leveled Readers Teacher Guides**
  - *Comprehension*
  - *High-Frequency Words*
  - *Oral Reading Fluency Assessement*
- **Response Activities**
- **Leveled Readers Assessment**

See pages T96–T99 for lesson plans.

BELOW-LEVEL

- **phonics** Digraphs /ch/*ch, tch*; /sh/*sh*; /th/*th*
- **High-Frequency Words**
- **Author's Purpose**

LEVELED READERS TEACHER GUIDE

▲ High-Frequency Words, p. 5

▲ Comprehension, p. 6

ON-LEVEL

- **phonics** Digraphs /ch/*ch, tch*; /sh/*sh*; /th/*th*
- **High-Frequency Words**
- **Author's Purpose**

LEVELED READERS TEACHER GUIDE

▲ High-Frequency Words, p. 5

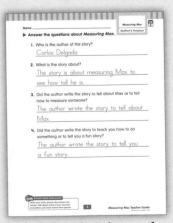

▲ Comprehension, p. 6

www.harcourtschool.com/storytown

Go online

★ **Leveled Readers, Online Database**
Searchable by Genre, Skill, Vocabulary, Level, or Title
★ **Student Activities and Teacher Resources, online**

ADVANCED

On Stage!
by Quinn Douglas
illustrated by Trevor Pye

- 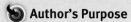 **phonics** Digraphs /ch/*ch, tch*;
/sh/*sh*; /th/*th*
- **High-Frequency Words**
- **Author's Purpose**

LEVELED READERS TEACHER GUIDE

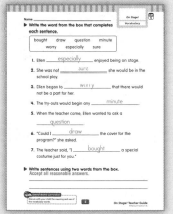

▲ High-Frequency Words, p. 5

▲ Comprehension, p. 6

ELL

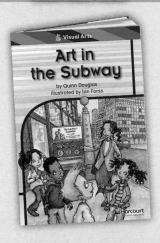

Art in
the Subway
by Quinn Douglas
illustrated by Ian Forss

- **Build Background**
- **Concept Vocabulary**
- **Scaffolded Language Development**

LEVELED READERS TEACHER GUIDE

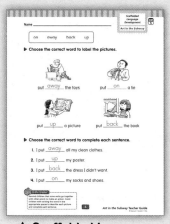

▲ Scaffolded Language
Development, p. 5

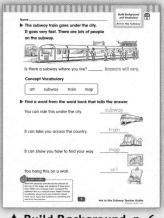

▲ Build Background, p. 6

CLASSROOM LIBRARY

for Self-Selected Reading

EASY

▲ *Clown Fish* by Carol K. Lindeen,
Capstone Press, 2005. NONFICTION

AVERAGE

▲ *Buster* by Denise Fleming, Henry Holt
and Company, 2003. FICTION

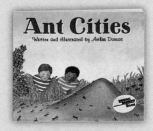

CHALLENGE

▲ *Ant Cities* by Arthur Dorros,
HarperCollins, 1987. NONFICTION

▲ Classroom Library Books
Teacher Guide, Lesson 11

Literacy Centers

15 Min. each

Management Support

While you provide direct instruction to individuals or small groups, other children can work on literacy center activities.

▲ **Literacy Center Pocket Chart**

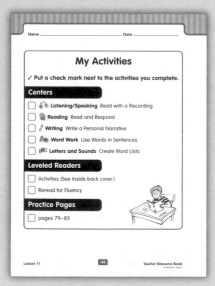

My Activities

✓ Put a check mark next to the activities you complete.

Centers

- ☐ Listening/Speaking Read with a Recording
- ☐ Reading Read and Respond
- ☐ Writing Write a Personal Narrative
- ☐ Word Work Use Words in Sentences
- ☐ Letters and Sounds Create Word Lists

Leveled Readers

- ☐ Activities (See inside back cover.)
- ☐ Reread for Fluency

Practice Pages

- ☐ pages 79–85

Lesson 11   44   Teacher Resource Book

▲ **Teacher Resource Book, p. 44**

Homework for the Week

TEACHER RESOURCE BOOK, PAGE 44

The Homework Copying Master provides activities to complete for each day of the week.

LISTENING/SPEAKING

Read with a Recording

Objective
To develop fluency by reading and recording a familiar story

LISTENING/SPEAKING   Card 51

Read with a Recording

MATERIALS
- CD/cassette player
- Audiotext
- Student Edition
- Reading Log or paper
- pencil

With a partner, listen to "Jamaica Louise James" on the *Audiotext.*

❶ Follow along in your book while you listen.

❷ Listen to it again, and read aloud with the recording.

❸ Use your Reading Log to record what you read.

Grade 2 Lesson 11

⭐ **Literacy Center Kit • Card 51**

READING

Read and Respond

Objective
To develop comprehension by rereading familiar stories and responding to them

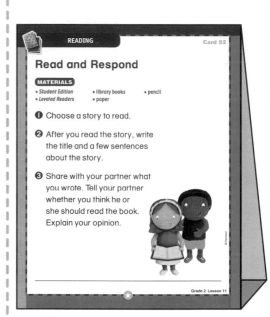

READING   Card 52

Read and Respond

MATERIALS
- Student Edition
- Leveled Readers
- library books
- paper
- pencil

❶ Choose a story to read.

❷ After you read the story, write the title and a few sentences about the story.

❸ Share with your partner what you wrote. Tell your partner whether you think he or she should read the book. Explain your opinion.

Grade 2 Lesson 11

⭐ **Literacy Center Kit • Card 52**

WRITING

Write a Personal Narrative

Objective
To practice writing a personal narrative

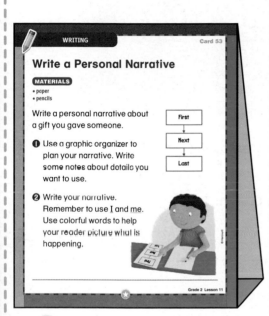

My Mom loves shells, so for her birthday one year I gave her

★ **Literacy Center Kit • Card 53**

 WORD WORK

Use Words in Sentences

Objective
To practice using and writing high-frequency words

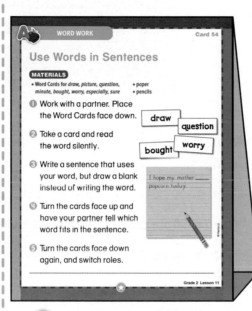

draw
picture
question
minute
bought
worry
especially
sure

★ **Literacy Center Kit • Card 54**

ABC **LETTERS AND SOUNDS**

Create Word Lists

Objective
To use common spelling patterns to write words

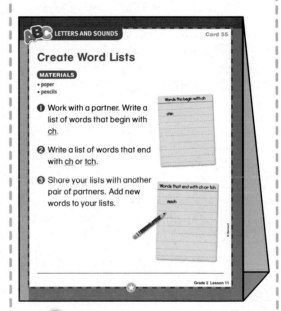

Words that begin with ch	Words that end with ch or tch
chat chip	catch beach

★ **Literacy Center Kit • Card 55**

Day at a Glance

Day 1

 phonics and Spelling

- Introduce: Digraphs /ch/*ch, tch*; /sh/*sh*; /th/*th*
- Pretest

Reading/ Comprehension

 Introduce: Author's Purpose, *Student Edition*, pp. 324–325

- *Read-Aloud Anthology*: "Tanya's City Garden"

Fluency

- Model Oral Fluency

Robust Vocabulary

Words from the Read-Aloud
- Introduce: *filthy, fellow, executive, beautifying*

Grammar

- Introduce: Abbreviations

Writing ✏

- Personal Narrative

Warm-Up Routines

 Oral Language

Objective *To listen attentively and respond appropriately to oral communication*

Question of the Day

What kinds of things do you like to draw?
Tell why.

Help children brainstorm things that they enjoy drawing. Use the following prompts:

- **Tell about a favorite picture you have drawn.**
- **Name some places you like to draw.**
- **Name some people or animals that you like to include in your pictures.**

Then have children complete the following sentence frame to explain what they like to draw.

I like to draw _____ because _____.

Read Aloud

Objective *To listen for a purpose*

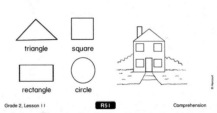

TRANSPARENCY Read aloud "Seeing Shapes" on **Transparency R51**. Use the following steps:

- **Set a purpose for listening.** Tell children to listen to find out how to use shapes when drawing.

- **Model fluent reading.** Read the article aloud. Point out that good readers use punctuation to help them read with expression.

- **Discuss the article.** Ask: **How do artists use shapes?** (to help them start their drawings)

Author's Purpose

Seeing Shapes

Artists start their pictures with simple shapes. A drawing of a tree might begin with a rectangle for the trunk and lots of small circles for the leaves. An artist might use a square for a house and a triangle for the roof.

What shape could you use to draw the sun? A circle, of course! What shapes could you use to draw a person? Be an artist and look for simple shapes in the world around you.

The next time you draw a picture, start with the basic shapes of the things you want to show. Then add details using other shapes. You'll be amazed at what you can do with simple shapes!

triangle　　square

rectangle　　circle

Grade 2, Lesson 11　　R51　　Comprehension

Transparency R51

Word Wall

Objective *To read high-frequency words*

REVIEW HIGH-FREQUENCY WORDS Remove from the Word Wall the cards for *believe*, *impossible*, *enough*, and *brought*, as well as other previously learned high-frequency words. Hold up a card at random, and ask children to read the word. Flip through the cards several times.

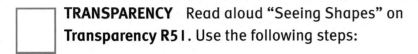

believe

impossible

enough

brought

Digraphs /ch/ *ch, tch;* /sh/ *sh;* /th/ *th* **phonics** *and Spelling*

Objectives

- *To recognize and blend the digraphs /ch/ch, tch; /sh/sh; /th/th*
- *To read words with /ch/ch, tch; /sh/sh; /th/th; and other known letter-sounds*
- *To use /ch/ch, tch; /sh/sh; /th/th; and other known letter-sounds to spell words*

Skill Trace

 Tested **Digraphs /ch/ *ch, tch;* /sh/*sh;* /th/*th***

Introduce	Grade 1
Reintroduce	**T30–T33**
Reteach	S2
Review	T42–T43, T64–T65, T376–T377
Test	Theme 3
Maintain	Theme 5, T166

"Research Says"

Explicit Phonics Instruction

"Children receiving direct code instruction improved in word reading at a faster rate and had higher word recognition skills than those receiving implicit code instruction."

–Foorman, et. al.
(1998), p. 37

Connect Letters to Sounds

WARM UP WITH PHONEMIC AWARENESS   Say the words *chip* and *chat*. Have children repeat the words. Say: **The words *chip* and *chat* begin with the /ch/ sound.** Repeat with the words *much* and *watch*. Say: **The words *much* and *watch* end with the /ch/ sound.** Have children say /ch/ several times. Repeat the procedure for /sh/, using the words *shop*, *show*, *fish*, and *fresh*. Repeat the procedure for /th/, using the words *thin*, *thank*, *both*, and *bath*.

Routine Card I   **CONNECT LETTERS AND SOUNDS**   Display the *Sound/Spelling Cards* for *ch/tch*, *sh*, and *th*. Point to *ch* and *tch* and explain their letter/sound correspondences. Say: **The letters *ch* and *tch* can stand for the /ch/ sound, the sound that you hear at the beginning of *cherry* and at the end of *watch*.** Touch the letters several times, and have children say /ch/ each time. Repeat with /sh/*sh* and /th/*th*.

ch
▪tch

sh

th

▲ **Sound/Spelling Cards**

5-DAY PHONICS

DAY 1	Reintroduce /ch/*ch, tch*; /sh/*sh*; /th/*th*
DAY 2	Word Building: /ch/*ch, tch*; /sh/*sh*; /th/*th*
DAY 3	Word Building: /ch/*ch, tch*; /sh/*sh*; /th/*th*
DAY 4	VCCV; Review /ch/*ch, tch*; /sh/*sh*; /th/*th*
DAY 5	VCCV; Review /ch/*ch, tch*; /sh/*sh*; /th/*th*

Work with Patterns

REINFORCE /ch/*ch, tch* Write the following words on the board. Point out that each word in the first column begins with the letters *ch* and that each word in the second column ends with the letters *ch* or *tch*. Read each word, and then have children read it with you.

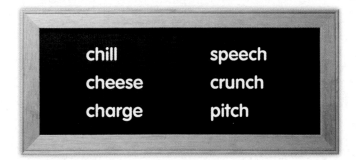

chill	speech
cheese	crunch
charge	pitch

REINFORCE /sh/*sh* Repeat the procedure with the following words that have the letters *sh* at the beginning or end.

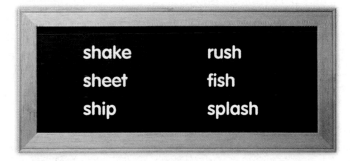

shake	rush
sheet	fish
ship	splash

REINFORCE /th/*th* Repeat the procedure with the following words that have the letters *th* at the beginning or end.

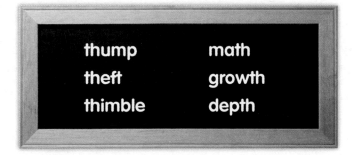

thump	math
theft	growth
thimble	depth

E L L

Support Word Meaning Use *Picture Cards* and other photos to support word meaning. For example, as children read *ship*, display the card for *ship*.

Picture Card 107 ▶ **ship**

BELOW-LEVEL

Blend Words Blend several words in each group to reinforce the letter/sound correspondences. Slide your hand under the letters as you slowly read each word.

chill

➡

Digraphs /ch/ *ch, tch;* /sh/ *sh;* /th/ *th* phonics *and Spelling*

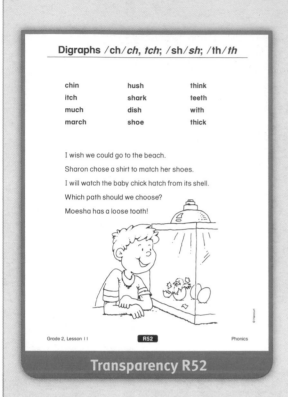

Digraphs /ch/*ch, tch;* /sh/*sh;* /th/*th*

chin	hush	think
itch	shark	teeth
much	dish	with
march	shoe	thick

I wish we could go to the beach.

Sharon chose a shirt to match her shoes.

I will watch the baby chick hatch from its shell.

Which path should we choose?

Moesha has a loose tooth!

Grade 2, Lesson 11   R52   Phonics

Transparency R52

Reading Words

GUIDED PRACTICE Display **Transparency R52** or write the words and sentences on the board. Point to the word *chin*. Read the word, and then have children read it with you.

INDEPENDENT PRACTICE Point to the remaining words in the top portion and have children read them. Then have children read aloud the sentences and identify words with *ch, tch, sh,* or *th*.

Decodable Books

Additional Decoding Practice

- **Phonics**
  Digraphs /ch/*ch, tch;* /sh/*sh;* /th/*th*
- **Decodable Words**
- **High-Frequency Words**
  See lists in *Decodable Book 9.*

  See also *Decodable Books,*
  online (Take-Home Version).

▲ Decodable Book 9: "The Bad Itch," "Flash Gets a Shave," and "Beth, Seth, and the Pie Contest"

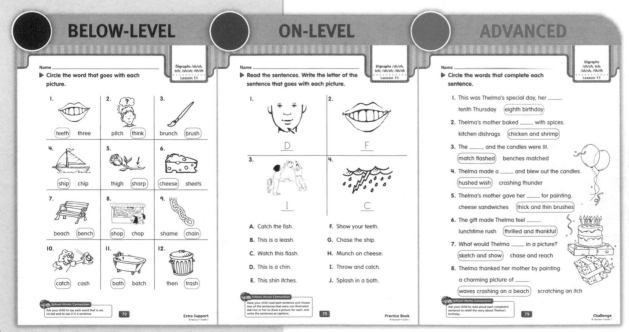

BELOW-LEVEL

▲ **Extra Support, p. 79**

ON-LEVEL

▲ **Practice Book, p. 79**

ADVANCED

▲ **Challenge, p. 79**

ELL

- Group children according to academic levels, and assign one of the pages on the left.

- Clarify any unfamiliar concepts as necessary. See *ELL Teacher Guide* Lesson 11 for support in scaffolding instruction.

5-DAY SPELLING

DAY 1 Pretest
DAY 2 Word Building
DAY 3 State the Generalization
DAY 4 Review
DAY 5 Posttest

Introduce Spelling Words

PRETEST Say the first word and read the dictation sentence. Repeat the word as children write it. Write the word on the board and have children check their spelling. Tell them to circle the word if they spelled it correctly or write it correctly if they did not. Repeat for words 2–10.

Words with /ch/ch, tch; /sh/sh; or /th/th

1. lunch — I would like to have soup for **lunch**.
2. shape — Sean made a kite in the **shape** of a rainbow.
3. wish — I **wish** I could fly like a bird.
4. chop — Trina will **chop** wood for the campfire.
5. show — Would you **show** me your paintings?
6. catch — Get ready to **catch** the ball!
7. then — When Tyrell is done, **then** it will be your turn.
8. each — Mom said we could have two slices **each**.
9. bath — The baby likes to splash in the **bath**.
10. such — I had **such** a great time at the game!

ADVANCED

Challenge Words Use the challenge words in these dictation sentences.

11. shadow — We sat in the **shadow** of a big umbrella at the beach.
12. bathtub — Our plastic raft was about as big as a **bathtub**.
13. starfish — My sister wanted to look for **starfish** at the shore.
14. matchbox — I kept the tiny shells I found in a **matchbox**.
15. sandwich — I bought an ice cream **sandwich** for a snack.

Spelling Words

1. lunch*   6. catch*
2. shape   7. then
3. wish   8. each*
4. chop   9. bath
5. show*   10. such*

Challenge Words

11. shadow   14. matchbox
12. bathtub   15. sandwich
13. starfish

* Words from "Jamaica Louise James"

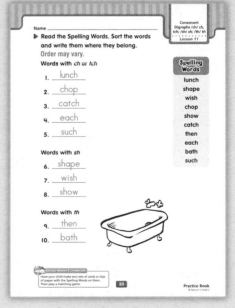

▲ Practice Book, p. 80

Author's Purpose

Comprehension

Objective

- *To identify an author's purpose for writing*

Daily Comprehension

 Author's Purpose

DAY 1:	Introduce Author's Purpose *Student Edition*
DAY 2:	Review Author's Purpose *Student Edition*
DAY 3:	Review Author's Purpose *Student Edition*
DAY 4:	Review Author's Purpose *Transparency*
DAY 5:	Review Author's Purpose *Read-Aloud Anthology*

✓ MONITOR PROGRESS

Author's Purpose

IF children have difficulty identifying author's purpose,	**THEN** provide more examples of stories and nonfiction books and help them identify the author's purpose for each one.

Small-Group Instruction, pp. S6–S7:

- ● **BELOW-LEVEL:** Reteach
- ● **ON-LEVEL:** Reinforce
- ● **ADVANCED:** Extend

Teach/Model

INTRODUCE AUTHOR'S PURPOSE Have children read *Student Edition* page 324. Model how to identify an author's purpose.

Think Aloud When I read a selection, I think about why the author wrote it. Does the author want to entertain me with a story or tell me information about the world? Knowing the author's purpose helps me understand why the author writes as he or she does.

Practice/Apply

GUIDED PRACTICE Display a story and a nonfiction book that children have read. Guide children to identify the author's purpose for writing each one. Help them give reasons to support their answers. Then have children read the passage on page 325 and identify the kind of writing it is. (a story)

Try This! **INDEPENDENT PRACTICE** Have children determine the author's purpose for writing the passage. (Possible responses: to entertain readers; to tell what happens to a made-up character) Discuss children's responses and ask volunteers to explain how they determined the author's purpose.

ADVANCED

Discuss Different Purposes Have children return to the passage on *Student Edition* page 325 and determine how it would be different if the author's purpose was to give information. Then have them determine what the passage might be like if the author's purpose was to give an opinion and to express feelings.

Focus Skill

 Author's Purpose

Authors write for different purposes, or reasons. Sometimes they write to tell a story that readers will enjoy. Sometimes they write to teach facts about real things. Sometimes they write to tell what they think or feel about something.

To find an **author's purpose**, think about the kind of writing. Look at the chart.

Kind of Writing	Author's Purpose
story	to entertain
friendly letter	to send a message
book review	to give an opinion
journal entry	to tell about feelings

Can you think of an example you have read for each purpose?

324

Read the passage below. Tell what kind of writing it is.

Train Trip

Cody was sleepy. The train ride had been fun. He and his mother had played games and eaten in the dining car. A woman had come by, checking people's tickets. Now it was dark outside. The sound of the train racing along the tracks made Cody even sleepier. He rested his head on his mother's lap and fell asleep. His dreams were happy ones. He would be at his grandparents' home by morning!

Kind of Writing	Author's Purpose

Try This!

Look back at the passage. What is the author's purpose for writing it?

GO online www.harcourtschool.com/storytown

325

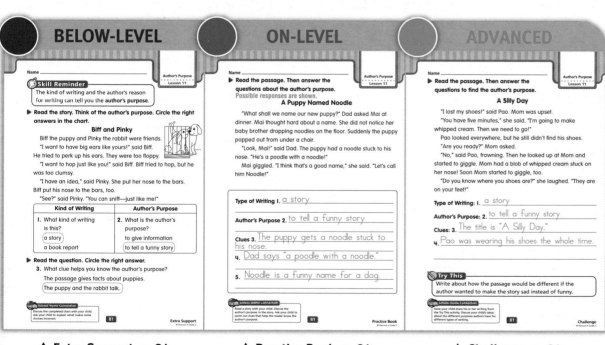

BELOW-LEVEL

Name _____

Skill Reminder
The kind of writing and the author's reason for writing can tell you the author's purpose.

▶ Read the story. Think of the author's purpose. Circle the right answers in the chart.

Biff and Pinky

Biff the puppy and Pinky the rabbit were friends.
"I want to have big ears like yours!" said Biff. He tried to perk up his ears. They were too floppy.
"I want to hop just like you!" said Biff. Biff tried to hop, but he was too clumsy.
"I have an idea," said Pinky. She put her nose to the bars. Biff put his nose to the bars, too.
"See?" said Pinky. "You can sniff—just like me!"

Kind of Writing	Author's Purpose
1. What kind of writing is this? (a story) a book report	2. What is the author's purpose? to give information (to tell a funny story)

▶ Read the question. Circle the right answer.
3. What clue helps you know the author's purpose?
The passage gives facts about puppies.
(The puppy and the rabbit talk.)

▲ **Extra Support, p. 81**

ON-LEVEL

Name _____

▶ Read the passage. Then answer the questions about the author's purpose.
Possible responses are shown.

A Puppy Named Noodle

"What shall we name our new puppy?" Dad asked Mai at dinner. Mai thought hard about a name. She did not notice her baby brother dropping noodles on the floor. Suddenly the puppy popped out from under a chair.
"Look, Mai!" said Dad. The puppy had a noodle stuck to his nose. "He's a poodle with a noodle!"
Mai giggled. "I think that's a good name," she said. "Let's call him Noodle!"

Type of Writing 1. a story

Author's Purpose 2. to tell a funny story

Clues 3. The puppy gets a noodle stuck to his nose.

4. Dad says "a poodle with a noodle."

5. Noodle is a funny name for a dog.

▲ **Practice Book, p. 81**

ADVANCED

Name _____

▶ Read the passage. Then answer the questions to find the author's purpose.

A Silly Day

"I lost my shoes!" said Pao. Mom was upset.
"You have five minutes," she said. "I'm going to make whipped cream. Then we need to go!"
Pao looked everywhere, but he still didn't find his shoes.
"Are you ready?" Mom asked.
"No," said Pao, frowning. Then he looked up at Mom and started to giggle. Mom had a blob of whipped cream stuck on her nose! Soon Mom started to giggle, too.
"Do you know where you shoes are?" she laughed. "They are on your feet!"

Type of Writing: 1. a story

Author's Purpose: 2. to tell a funny story

Clues: 3. The title is "A Silly Day."

4. Pao was wearing his shoes the whole time.

Try This
Write about how the passage would be different if the author wanted to make the story sad instead of funny.

▲ **Challenge, p. 81**

ELL

• Group children according to academic levels, and assign one of the pages on the left.

• Clarify any unfamiliar concepts as necessary. See *ELL Teacher Guide* Lesson 11 for support in scaffolding instruction.

Listening Comprehension
Read Aloud

Objectives

- *To set a purpose for listening*
- *To identify an author's purpose for writing*

Build Fluency

Focus: Punctuation Tell children that good readers pay attention to punctuation marks to help them make sense of what they read.

E L L

Connect to Prior Knowledge

As you read "Tanya's City Garden," help children visualize the action by using drawings and photographs to show the meanings of words such as *geranium*, *bench*, *camera crew*, and *ribbon*.

Before Reading

CONNECT TO PRIOR KNOWLEDGE Tell children that they will listen to a story about a girl who helps make her neighborhood a nicer place to live. Ask children to share ideas about making neighborhoods nicer.

▲ Read-Aloud Anthology, "Tanya's City Garden," p. 42

Routine Card 2 **GENRE STUDY: REALISTIC FICTION** Tell children that the story, "Tanya's City Garden," is realistic fiction. Remind them of the characteristics of this genre:

Think Aloud In realistic fiction, the characters, setting, and plot are like people, places, and events in real life.

After Reading

RESPOND Work with children to create a chart that shows the sequence of important events in the story. Record the events on the board.

> ## Beginning
> Tanya sees that the alley is dirty and ugly to look at.

> ## Middle
> She sweeps the alley and decorates it with a flower. Her neighbors see the garden and add things to improve it.

> ## End
> The mayor gives Tanya an award.

 REVIEW AUTHOR'S PURPOSE Have children identify the author's purpose in writing "Tanya's City Garden."

Build Robust Vocabulary

Words from the Read-Aloud

Teach/Model

Routine Card 3

INTRODUCE ROBUST VOCABULARY Use *Routine Card 3* to introduce the words.

❶ Put the word in **selection context**.
❷ Display Transparency R56 and read the word and the **Student-Friendly Explanation**.
❸ Have children **say the word** with you.
❹ Use the word in other contexts, and have children **interact with the word's meaning**.
❺ Remove the transparency. Say the Student-Friendly Explanation again, and ask children to **name the word** that goes with it.

❶ **Selection Context:** The alley was **filthy** and needed cleaning.
❹ **Interact with Word Meaning:** Would you get filthy after playing in the sprinkler or digging a hole in the ground? Why?

❶ **Selection Context:** Tanya's neighbors are **fellow** city gardeners.
❹ **Interact with Word Meaning:** Who are you more likely to see at school every day—the principal or a fellow student?

❶ **Selection Context:** Miriam Grand was an **executive** at the TV station.
❹ **Interact with Word Meaning:** Would you be more likely to find an executive in an office or at a park?

❶ **Selection Context:** The mayor thanked Tanya for **beautifying** the city.
❹ **Interact with Word Meaning:** Which might need beautifying, a new car or an old house? Why?

Practice/Apply

GUIDED PRACTICE Ask children to use the vocabulary to tell about a place that is *filthy* and how people might *beautify* it.

Objective

• *To develop robust vocabulary through discussing a literature selection*

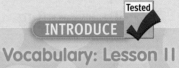

INTRODUCE **Tested** ✓

Vocabulary: Lesson 11

filthy	fellow
executive	beautifying

▼ **Student-Friendly Explanations**

Student-Friendly Explanations

filthy	If something is very dirty, it is filthy.
fellow	You use fellow to describe a person who has something in common with you.
executive	When someone is a boss in charge of a business, that person is called an executive.
beautifying	When you are making something nicer or more beautiful than it was, you are beautifying it.
renowned	If you are renowned, you are famous for something.
kin	Your kin are all of your family members and relatives.
original	When something is original, it is the first of its kind.
adorn	When you adorn something, you decorate it and make it beautiful.

Grade 2, Theme 3   R56   Vocabulary

Transparency R56

Grammar
Abbreviations

5-DAY GRAMMAR	
DAY 1	Titles
DAY 2	Days
DAY 3	Months
DAY 4	Apply to Writing
DAY 5	Weekly Review

Objective

- *To use correct capitalization and punctuation in abbreviations for titles*

Daily Proofreading

Shannon saw ms jones at the store.

(Ms. Jones)

TECHNOLOGY

 www.harcourtschool.com/ storytown
Grammar Glossary

Abbreviations

Titles of People	
Mr.	Mr. Hector Gonzalez
Mrs.	Mrs. Lucy Robertson
Ms.	Ms. Alicia Flores
Dr.	Dr. Edward Horn
	Dr. Eva Lewis

1. Does ms harris work at the bank?
2. I will see dr rodriguez next week.
3. Gloria gave her homework to mr spellman.
4. I live next door to mrs johnson.

Grade 2, Lesson 11   **LA21**   Grammar

Transparency LA21

Teach/Model

INTRODUCE ABBREVIATIONS AND TITLES Remind children that names of people are proper nouns and begin with a capital letter. Write these names from "Tanya's City Garden" on the board:

Ms. Jones   Ms. Metoyer   Mrs. Primrose

Read the names aloud and have children repeat them with you. Tell children that *Ms.* and *Mrs.* are titles that are abbreviations. Explain that an abbreviation is a short way to write a word. Point out the capital letter and period in each abbreviation.

Next, write these names on the board:

Mr. Marshall   **Dr. Lopez**

Read each name aloud and have children repeat it. Point out the titles. Explain that *Mr.* and *Dr.* are also titles that are abbreviations. Tell children that *Dr.* can refer to a man or a woman. Be sure children notice the capital letter and period in each abbreviation.

Guided Practice

READ ABBREVIATIONS Display **Transparency LA21**. Read aloud the list of abbreviated titles and names, and have children repeat after you. For sentences 1–4, invite volunteers to identify the abbreviated titles. Work together to add capital letters and periods.

Practice/Apply

WRITE ABBREVIATIONS Have children write sentences about people they know, using the abbreviated titles *Mr.*, *Mrs.*, *Ms.*, and *Dr.* Have them share their sentences with a partner. Partners should check that they have used a capital letter and a period for each title.

5-DAY WRITING	
DAY 1	Introduce
DAY 2	Prewrite
DAY 3	Draft
DAY 4	Revise
DAY 5	Revise

Writing
Personal Narrative

Teach/Model

INTRODUCE PERSONAL NARRATIVE Display **Transparency LA22,** and explain that this piece was written by a child to tell about something that happened to her. Read aloud "Our Little Gardens." Then together, develop a list of characteristics for a personal narrative. Keep it on display for children to refer to.

Personal Narrative

- A personal narrative tells a true story about something that happened in your life.
- Use the words *I, me, we,* and *us.*
- Tell about your thoughts and feelings.
- Use capital letters and periods in abbreviated titles such as *Mr.* and *Dr.*

WRITING TRAIT **VOICE** Point out examples from "Our Little Gardens" that show how the author shares her enthusiasm, such as "This part was a lot of fun!" Explain that writing with energy and enthusiasm draws the reader into a story.

Guided Practice

DRAFT AN OPENING SENTENCE Model writing an opening sentence for a personal narrative, such as "I went to the circus with my family and Ms. Lewis last weekend." Discuss how the sentence uses the words *I* and *my* and how it presents the narrative's main idea. Point out the capitalized abbreviation.

Practice/Apply

WRITE AN OPENING SENTENCE Have children write a sentence that tells something they did recently. They may want to save their sentences for use on Days 2–5.

Objectives

- *To read and respond to a personal narrative as a model for writing*
- *To develop an understanding of a personal narrative*
- *To write an opening sentence for a personal narrative*

Writing Prompt

Describe Have children write a sentence to tell about a gift they gave to someone.

Student Model: Personal Narrative

Our Little Gardens

My brother and I had a great idea for a birthday present for our mother. First, we each painted a clay flowerpot. This part was a lot of fun! I put rainbows and clouds on mine. My brother painted his blue with yellow stars. Next, we filled the pots with dirt and planted flower seeds. We had to water the seeds every day. Soon, lots of little green plants were shooting up! Our mother loved her presents. Do you know what I like best? We all get to enjoy our little gardens!

Grade 2, Lesson 11 — LA22 — Writing

Transparency LA22

Day at a Glance

Day 2

 phonics and Spelling

- Review: Digraphs /ch/*ch*, *tch*; /sh/*sh*; /th/*th*
- Build Words

High-Frequency Words

- Introduce: *draw, picture, question, minute, bought, worry, especially, sure*

Comprehension

 Ask Questions

Author's Purpose

Reading

- "Jamaica Louise James," *Student Edition*, pp. 328–349

Read!

Fluency

- Punctuation

Robust Vocabulary

Words About the Selection

- Introduce: *renowned, kin, original, adorn*

Grammar

- Review: Abbreviations

Writing

- Personal Narrative

Warm-Up Routines

Oral Language

Objective *To listen attentively and respond appropriately to oral communication*

Question of the Day

What was the best card or gift you ever made for someone?

Help children think about cards or gifts they have made for someone, rather than buying a card or gift at a store. Use the following prompts:

- **Who was your card or gift for?**
- **Tell about how you made it.**
- **When you gave the person your card or gift, what did he or she do?**

Then have children complete the following sentence to tell more about making presents:

Making a present for someone can be fun because _____.

Read Aloud

Objective *To listen for a purpose*

BIG BOOK OF RHYMES AND POEMS
Display the poem "My Name" on page 21 and
read the title aloud. Ask children to listen for
what happens each time the speaker writes
his name. Then track the print as you read
the poem aloud. Ask volunteers to use their
own words to tell where the speaker wrote his
name and what happened to it each time.

▲ **Big Book of Rhymes
and Poems, p. 21**

Word Wall

Objective *To read high-frequency words*

REVIEW HIGH-FREQUENCY WORDS Review the words *enough, brought,
understand, early,* and *quite,* as well as other previously learned high-
frequency words on the Word Wall. Point to each word, and have children
read it, spell it, and then read it again. Then point to words at random and
have children read them.

Digraphs /ch/ *ch, tch;* /sh/ *sh;* /th/ *th* phonics *and Spelling*

Objectives

- *To blend sounds into words*
- *To spell words that include the digraphs /ch/ch, tch; /sh/sh; and /th/th*

Skill Trace

 Tested ✓ Digraphs /ch/ *ch, tch;* **/sh/** *sh;* **/th/** *th*

Introduce	Grade 1
Reintroduce	T30–T33
Reteach	S2
Review	**T42–T43, T64–T65, T376–T377**
Test	Theme 3
Maintain	Theme 5, T166

Spelling Words

1. **lunch***	6. **catch***
2. **shape**	7. **then**
3. **wish**	8. **each***
4. **chop**	9. **bath**
5. **show***	10. **such***

Challenge Words

11. **shadow**	14. **matchbox**
12. **bathtub**	15. **sandwich**
13. **starfish**	

* Words from "Jamaica Louise James"

Word Building

READ A SPELLING WORD Write the word *such* on the board. Ask children to identify the letters that stand for the /ch/ sound. Then read the word, and have children do the same.

BUILD SPELLING WORDS Ask children which letters you should change to make *such* become *lunch*. (Change *s* to *l*, and add *n* before *ch*.) Write the word *lunch* on the board, and have children read it. Continue building the spelling words in this manner. Say:

- **Which letters do I have to change to make the word *each*?** (Change *lun* to *ea.*)

- **Which letters do I have to change to make the word *catch*?** (Change *e* to *c*, and change *ch* to *tch.*)

- **Which letters do I have to change to make the word *chop*?** (Erase *cat*, and add *op* after *ch.*)

- **Which letters do I have to change to make the word *show*?** (Change *ch* to *sh*, and change *p* to *w.*)

such
lunch
each
catch
chop
show

Continue building the remaining spelling words in this manner.

BELOW-LEVEL	ADVANCED
Digraph Chant Focus on one digraph at a time and have children practice building the spelling words by chanting and spelling. For example: "ch, ch, ch, ch, lunch, l-u-n-c-h."	**Questions and Answers** Have children work with a partner. One child should write a question using one of the spelling words. The partner should write an answer using another of the spelling words. Children should continue until they have used each word.

Day 2

5-DAY PHONICS/SPELLING	
DAY 1	Pretest
DAY 2	Word Building
DAY 3	State the Generalization
DAY 4	Review
DAY 5	Posttest

Read Words in Context

APPLY PHONICS Write the following sentences on the board or on chart paper. Have children read each sentence silently. Then track the print as children read the sentence aloud.

Will you <u>show</u> me where to put my <u>lunch</u>?

Dad needs to <u>chop</u> more fruit for <u>each</u> salad.

I can mold clay into the <u>shape</u> of a horse.

I <u>wish</u> I could <u>catch</u> <u>such</u> a huge moth!

After I take a <u>bath</u>, <u>then</u> I brush my teeth.

WRITE Dictate several spelling words. Have children write the words in their notebook or on a dry-erase board.

 phonics Resources

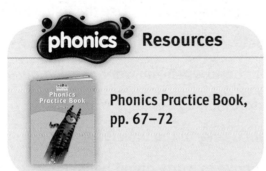

Phonics Practice Book, pp. 67–72

MONITOR PROGRESS

Digraphs /ch/*ch*, *tch*; /sh/*sh*; /th/*th*

IF children have difficulty building and reading words with the digraphs /ch/*ch*, *tch*, /sh/*sh*, and /th/*th*,	**THEN** help them blend and read the words *chip*, *chap*, *rush*, *hush*, *path*, and *math*.

Small-Group Instruction, p. S2:

● **BELOW-LEVEL:** Reteach

● **ON-LEVEL:** Reinforce

○ **ADVANCED:** Extend

BELOW-LEVEL   ON-LEVEL   ADVANCED

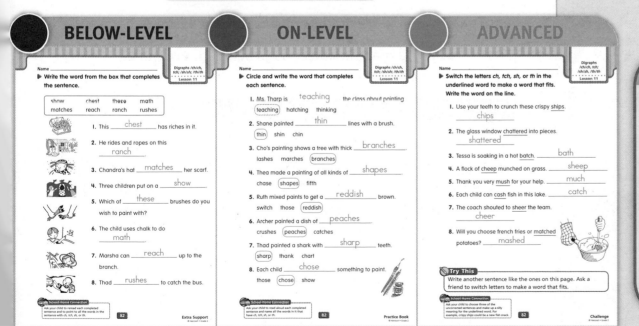

▲ Extra Support, p. 82   ▲ Practice Book, p. 82   ▲ Challenge, p. 82

ELL

• Group children according to academic levels, and assign one of the pages on the left.

• Clarify any unfamiliar concepts as necessary. See *ELL Teacher Guide* Lesson 11 for support in scaffolding instruction.

High-Frequency Words
Words to Know

Objective

- *To read high-frequency words*

INTRODUCE ✓ Tested

High-Frequency Words

bought	picture
draw	question
especially	sure
minute	worry

Review High-Frequency Words

Hold up *Picture Card* 5 and say *An artist can draw a picture of people.* Have children practice using the words *draw* and *picture* by telling about other things that an artist can draw a picture of.

See *ELL Teacher Guide* Lesson 11 for support in scaffolding instruction.

Picture Card 5 ▶ artist

Teach/Model

Routine Card 5

INTRODUCE WORDS Write the words *draw*, *picture*, *question*, *minute*, *bought*, *worry*, *especially*, and *sure* on the board.

- Point to and read *draw*. Repeat it, having children say it with you.
- Say: **Cal likes to *draw* trains and airplanes.**
- Point to each letter as you spell the word. Have children spell the word with you.
- Have children reread the word.

Repeat for the remaining words. Use the following sentences:

- **Maya wants to paint a *picture* of a dinosaur.**
- **Raise your hand when you want to ask a *question*.**
- **We will start making dinner in a *minute*.**
- **We *bought* a cake at the bakery.**
- **You don't have to *worry* about being late.**
- **I like all kinds of fruits, *especially* berries.**
- **I'm *sure* there will be enough seats for everyone.**

Guided Practice

STUDENT EDITION PAGES 326–327 Ask children to turn to *Student Edition* pages 326 and 327. Have children point to and read aloud each of the highlighted words on page 326. Discuss what children see in the pictures. Then ask volunteers to read aloud the passage.

Words to Know

High-Frequency Words

draw

question

picture

minute

sure

worry

bought

especially

Picture of a Friend

My friend Sam loves to **draw**. I see him every day at the park.

One day, I sat down next to him. I asked him a **question**. "Will you draw a **picture** for me?"

"What do you want in your picture?" he asked.

I had to think for a **minute**. Then it came to me. "I want a picture of me," I said.

"Are you **sure**?" he asked.

"Yes," I said.

"What if it doesn't look exactly like you?" he asked.

"Don't **worry** about that," I said. "Just draw what you see."

When he had finished, I **bought** him a slice of pizza. He liked that a lot, **especially** the extra cheese. And I liked his picture of me!

www.harcourtschool.com/storytown

326

327

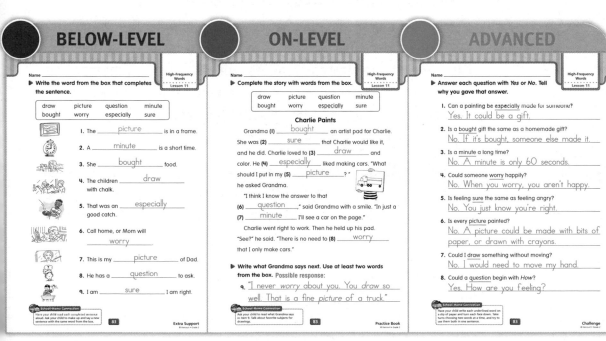

BELOW-LEVEL

▶ Write the word from the box that completes the sentence.

| draw | picture | question | minute |
| bought | worry | especially | sure |

1. The ___picture___ is in a frame.

2. A ___minute___ is a short time.

3. She ___bought___ food.

4. The children ___draw___ with chalk.

5. That was an ___especially___ good catch.

6. Call home, or Mom will ___worry___

7. This is my ___picture___ of Dad.

8. He has a ___question___ to ask.

9. I am ___sure___ I am right.

▲ Extra Support, p. 83

ON-LEVEL

▶ Complete the story with words from the box.

| draw | picture | question | minute |
| bought | worry | especially | sure |

Charlie Paints

Grandma (1) ___bought___ an artist pad for Charlie. She was (2) ___sure___ that Charlie would like it, and he did. Charlie loved to (3) ___draw___ and color. He (4) ___especially___ liked making cars. "What should I put in my (5) ___picture___ ?" he asked Grandma.

"I think I know the answer to that (6) ___question___ ," said Grandma with a smile. "In just a (7) ___minute___ I'll see a car on the page."

Charlie went right to work. Then he held up his pad. "See?" he said. "There is no need to (8) ___worry___ that I only make cars."

▶ Write what Grandma says next. Use at least two words from the box. Possible response:

9. "I never *worry* about you. You *draw* so well. That is a fine *picture* of a truck."

▲ Practice Book, p. 83

ADVANCED

▶ Answer each question with *Yes* or *No*. Tell why you gave that answer.

1. Can a painting be especially made for someone? Yes. It could be a gift.

2. Is a bought gift the same as a homemade gift? No. If it's bought, someone else made it.

3. Is a minute a long time? No. A minute is only 60 seconds.

4. Could someone worry happily? No. When you worry, you aren't happy.

5. Is feeling sure the same as feeling angry? No. You just know you're right.

6. Is every picture painted? No. A picture could be made with bits of paper, or drawn with crayons.

7. Could I draw something without moving? No. I would need to move my hand.

8. Could a question begin with How? Yes. How are you feeling?

▲ Challenge, p. 83

E L L

• Group children according to academic levels, and assign one of the pages on the left.

• Clarify any unfamiliar concepts as necessary. See *ELL Teacher Guide* Lesson 11 for support in scaffolding instruction.

Reading

Student Edition: "Jamaica Louise James"

Objectives

- *To understand characteristics of realistic fiction*
- *To ask questions as a strategy for comprehension*
- *To apply word knowledge to the reading of a text*

Options for Reading

BELOW-LEVEL

Preview Have children preview the story by looking at the illustrations. Guide them to predict who the characters are. Read each page to children, and have them read it after you.

ON-LEVEL

Monitor Comprehension Have children read the story aloud, page by page. Ask the Monitor Comprehension questions as you go. Then lead them in retelling the story and describing their favorite part.

ADVANCED

Independent Reading Have children read each page silently, looking up each time they finish a page. Ask the Monitor Comprehension questions as you go. Then lead them in a discussion about the change Jamaica made to the station.

Genre Study

DISCUSS REALISTIC FICTION: PAGE 328 Ask children to read the genre information on *Student Edition* page 328. Remind them that realistic fiction stories have characters, a setting, and a plot that are like people, places, and events in real life. Then use **Transparency GO4** or copy the graphic organizer from page 328 on the board. Tell children that they will work together to fill in the story map as they read "Jamaica Louise James."

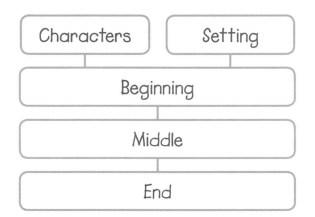

Comprehension Strategies

ASK QUESTIONS: PAGE 328 Remind children that good readers use strategies to make sense of what they read. Explain that one strategy readers can use is asking themselves questions as they read. Have children read the Comprehension Strategy information on page 328. Give examples of questions that children might ask themselves.

Think Aloud When I read a fiction story such as "Jamaica Louise James," I ask myself questions such as "Who are the main characters?" "How is the setting important?" "Why is this character acting in this way?"

Explain that readers may find that they have to reread or read ahead for the answers to their questions.

Realistic Fiction

Genre Study

Realistic fiction is a story with events that might happen in real life. Look for

- a beginning, a middle, and an end.

- a realistic setting.

Characters	Setting
Beginning	
Middle	
End	

Comprehension Strategy

Ask questions about the story's important ideas.

328

JAMAICA LOUISE JAMES

by
AMY HEST

illustrated by
Sheila White Samton

329

Build Background

DISCUSS HAVING BIG IDEAS   Tell children that they are going to read a story about a young girl who has a big idea and then sets out to make it happen. Ask volunteers to tell about a time they had a big idea and to describe how they brought it to life.

Routine Card 6

SET A PURPOSE AND PREDICT   Tell children that this is a story they will read to enjoy.

- Have children read the title.

- Identify Jamaica Louise James. Ask children where they think she might live and what she might enjoy doing.

- List their predictions on the board.

- Have children read the story to learn about Jamaica's big idea and what she does to make it happen.

TECHNOLOGY

 GO online **eBook**   "Jamaica Louise James" is available in an eBook.

 Audiotext   "Jamaica Louise James" is available on *Audiotext 2* for subsequent readings.

I was the <u>one</u> with the COOL idea...

It happened last winter and the mayor put my name on a golden plaque. It's down in the subway station at 86th and Main. You can see it if you go there.

That's me. You better believe it! Want to hear my big idea?

I'll tell but you've got to listen to the whole story, not just a part of it. Mama says my stories go on . . . and on . . . Whenever I'm just at the beginning of one, she tells me, "Get to the point, Jamaica!" or "Snap to it, baby!" But I like lacing up the details, this way and that. ② ③

Monitor Comprehension

PAGES 330–331   Say: **Jamaica says she had a "cool idea." Read to find out more about it.**

① **NOTE DETAILS**   **What have you learned about Jamaica's "cool idea" so far?** (Possible responses: It happened last winter. It has something to do with a subway station.)

② **CHARACTERS' TRAITS**   **What are some words you could use to describe Jamaica?** (Possible responses: creative, interesting, proud, funny)

③ **AUTHOR'S PURPOSE**   **Why do you think the author has Jamaica tell her own story? How does it help you learn about Jamaica?** (Possible response: The reader hears Jamaica's own voice. This helps her seem real and lets the reader understand her personality better.)

Apply
Comprehension Strategies

Ask Questions   Demonstrate how to ask questions to comprehend the story to this point.

Think Aloud   Asking questions about a story helps me think about what I read. I can ask myself, "What does Jamaica do to get her name on a plaque at a subway station?" That seems like an important idea in the story, so I'll try to answer the question as I read on.

This story begins with me. I have a big artist pad with one hundred big pages and five colored pencils with perfect skinny points. Sometimes I set myself up on the top step of our building, where everyone can see me. Everything I see is something I want to draw. **1**

At night, Mama and Grammy and I cuddle on the couch while the city quiets down. I show them every picture every night. Sometimes I tell a story as I go. Sometimes they ask a question like, Why does the man's coat have triangle pockets? Other times we don't say a word. **3**

2

332

333

Monitor Comprehension

PAGES 332–333   Say: **I see that Jamaica is drawing on a sketchpad. Read to find out about what she likes to draw.**

1 **NOTE DETAILS**   **What does Jamaica like to draw?** (She likes to draw everything she sees while sitting on the top step of her building.)

2 **MAKE INFERENCES**   **How can you tell that Jamaica lives in a city?** (Possible responses: Her drawing shows a busy city street. The plaque with her name on it is at a subway station; many subway stations are in cities.)

3 **DRAW CONCLUSIONS**   **How can you tell that Jamaica's family enjoys her drawings?** (Possible response: They look at Jamaica's drawings every night, listen to her talk about them, and ask questions about her work.)

E L L

Use Illustrations   Point out that Jamaica's drawings help readers see what Jamaica's world looks like to her. They also tell about the things she likes to draw. Point out items in Jamaica's drawings and ask children to name them, providing help as needed.

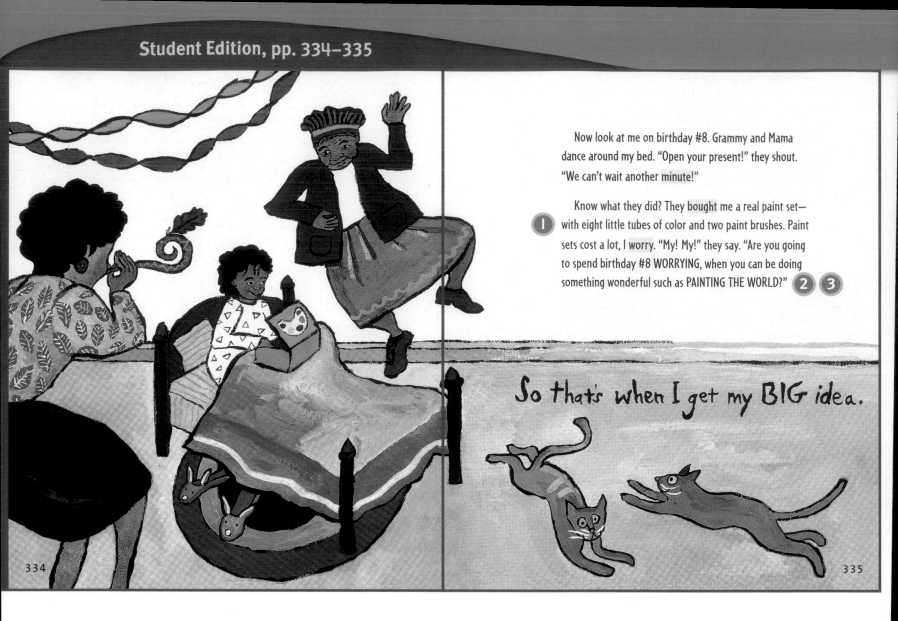

Now look at me on birthday #8. Grammy and Mama dance around my bed. "Open your present!" they shout. "We can't wait another minute!"

Know what they did? They bought me a real paint set—with eight little tubes of color and two paint brushes. Paint sets cost a lot, I worry. "My! My!" they say. "Are you going to spend birthday #8 WORRYING, when you can be doing something wonderful such as PAINTING THE WORLD?" ② ③

So that's when I get my BIG idea.

334

335

Monitor Comprehension

PAGES 334–335 Have children describe what they see and predict what might be happening. Say: **Read to find out what's happening.**

① **SUMMARIZE** **What is happening on these pages?** (It's Jamaica's eighth birthday. Grammy and Mama give her a paint set.)

② **DRAW CONCLUSIONS** **Why do you think Jamaica worries that the paint set might cost a lot?** (Possible response: She may think that her family doesn't have a lot of money to spare.)

③ **CHARACTERS' MOTIVATIONS** **Why do you think Jamaica's family chooses this present for her?** (Possible response: They think Jamaica is a good artist, and they want to encourage her.)

Use Multiple Strategies

Use Graphic Organizers Demonstrate how to use the story map to comprehend the story to this point.

Think Aloud After reading, I know the characters, the setting, and the beginning of the plot.

Characters Jamaica, Mama, Grammy	Setting the city

Beginning Jamaica gets a real paint set for her birthday.

Middle

End

I'm scared in the night. Not Grammy. At 86th and Main she goes down . . . and down . . . into the subway station.

All day long people line up at Grammy's token booth. They give her a dollar or four quarters, and she slides a token into their hand. Then they rush off to catch the train. ① ②

Now, this part of the story tells about my grammy, who leaves for work when it is still dark. Sometimes I wake up halfway when she slides out of bed. In winter she gets all layered, starting with the long-underwear layer.

She and Mama whisper in the kitchen. They drink that strong black coffee. Grammy scoops up her brown lunch bag and goes outside.

Subway

336

337

Monitor Comprehension

PAGES 336–337   Have children describe what they see. Say: **Read to find out where Grammy is going.**

① **MAIN IDEA   Where is Grammy going?** (into the subway station) **What does she do there?** (She works in a token booth. She sells people tokens so they can ride the subway.)

② **Focus Skill**   **AUTHOR'S PURPOSE   Why do you think the author describes Grammy and her job?** (Possible response: The author wants to show that Grammy's job isn't easy. She has to get up very early in all kinds of weather. She works a long day.)

Now, I like subways because the seats are hot pink and because they go very fast. But I don't like subway stations. Especially the one at 86th and Main. There are too many steep steps (fifty-six) and too many grownups who all look mad. The walls are old tile walls without any color.

Monitor Comprehension

PAGES 338–339 Say: **I see that the subway station is busy, and that people are in a hurry. Read to find out what Jamaica thinks about that.**

1 NOTE DETAILS **What does Jamaica like about the subway?** (She likes that subway trains have hot pink seats, and that the train moves fast.) **What things doesn't she like about subway stations?** (She doesn't like the station's steep steps, the grown-ups who look mad, and the old tile walls.)

2 CHARACTERS' EMOTIONS **Can you find Grammy and Jamaica in the illustration? How do you think they are feeling?** (Possible response: Grammy is at the token booth and Jamaica is on the train. They both look sad and unhappy.)

SUPPORTING STANDARDS

Subways Explain that subways are trains that run underground in many cities. The first subway station in the United States opened in 1898 in Boston, Massachusetts. Back then, riders paid a nickel to ride the subway. Today, it costs more than a dollar to ride Boston's subway. The construction of subways and other forms of mass transportation helped many cities grow during the twentieth century.

When Grammy comes home, she sews and talks about the people she sees, like Green-Hat Lady or Gentleman ① ② with the Red Bow Tie. Mama reads and hums. But I paint, blending all those colors until they look just right. Every day I add a picture to my collection and every day I think about my cool idea. ③

340

341

Monitor Comprehension

PAGES 340–341 Ask children to describe what is happening in the illustration. Say: **Read to find out what Grammy is talking about.**

① **NOTE DETAILS** What does Grammy talk about as she sews? (the people she saw while at work)

② **GENERALIZE** Why do you think Grammy likes to tell about her day at the subway station? (Possible response: She probably likes to tell about people she saw as a way for her to relax after a workday.)

③ **THEME** How can you tell that Grammy's stories have an influence on Jamaica? (Jamaica paints pictures of people Grammy tells about. Grammy tells about a woman with a green hat, and Jamaica is painting a picture of a woman like her.)

Descriptive Names Point out the descriptive names Grammy uses to tell about people, like "Green-Hat Lady" and "Gentleman with the Red Bow Tie." Elicit that Grammy may use these names because she doesn't know the actual names of the people she's describing. Explain that her descriptions also help the reader "see" these people. Have children think of fun, descriptive names for the characters and animals on pages 340–341, such as "Sleepy Orange Cat" and "Newspaper Lady."

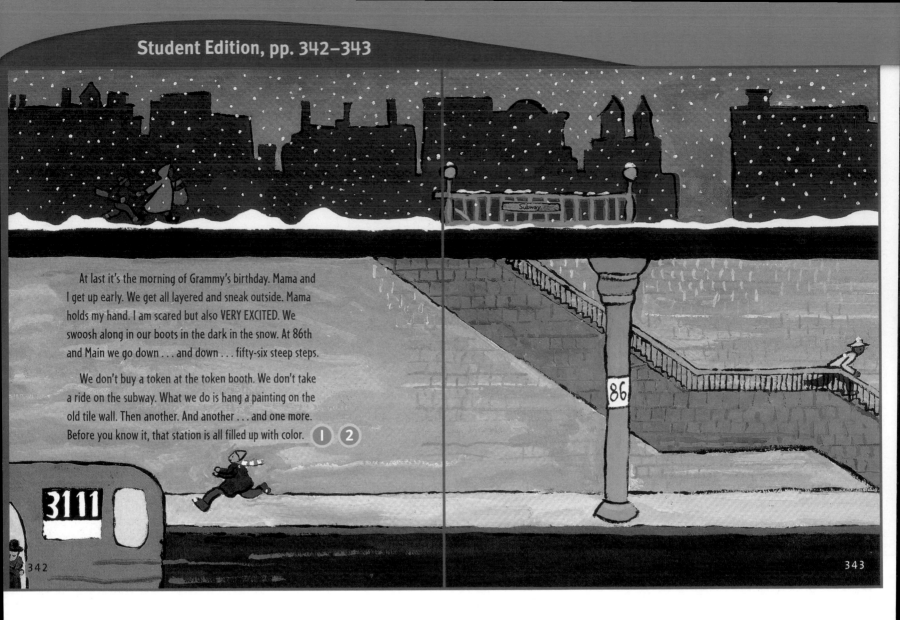

At last it's the morning of Grammy's birthday. Mama and I get up early. We get all layered and sneak outside. Mama holds my hand. I am scared but also VERY EXCITED. We swoosh along in our boots in the dark in the snow. At 86th and Main we go down . . . and down . . . fifty-six steep steps.

We don't buy a token at the token booth. We don't take a ride on the subway. What we do is hang a painting on the old tile wall. Then another. And another . . . and one more. Before you know it, that station is all filled up with color. **①** **②**

342

343

Monitor Comprehension

PAGES 342–343 Say: **Jamaica and her mother look as if they are going to the subway station. Read to find out what they are doing and whether it has to do with Jamaica's big idea.**

① **SUMMARIZE** **What are Jamaica and her mother doing?** (They are decorating the walls of the subway station with Jamaica's paintings. It has something to do with Grammy's birthday.)

② **AUTHOR'S PURPOSE** **Why do you think the author includes so many details on this page?** (The author wants to give a clear description of how Jamaica feels and thinks as she carries out her big idea.)

Apply
Comprehension Strategies

Ask Questions Model how to ask questions as you read.

Think Aloud I can ask myself questions about what is happening in the story, such as, "Why does Jamaica hang pictures in the subway station? What does this have to do with Grammy's birthday?" I'll look for answers to these questions as I read on.

Monitor Comprehension

PAGES 344–345   Say: **I see that Grammy has arrived at the subway station. Read to find out what she thinks about the pictures.**

① **CHARACTERS' EMOTIONS**   How does Grammy feel about Jamaica's surprise gift? How can you tell? (She feels pleased and happy; she wants to hug Jamaica because she likes it so much.)

② **EXPRESS PERSONAL OPINIONS**   What do you think of Jamaica's surprise for her grandmother? (Possible response: I think it is a good surprise because it shows how much Jamaica thinks about Grammy. It also helps make the subway station a nicer place for Grammy to work.)

ANALYZE AUTHOR'S PURPOSE

Author's Purpose   Remind children that authors have a purpose, or reason, for writing. After children have finished reading the story, ask:

Why did the author write "Jamaica Louise James"?

- to tell facts about subway stations
- to inform readers about a real artist
- **to entertain readers with a story about a girl and her family**

Lesson 11 (*Student Edition*, pages 344–345)   **T55**

So now you know the whole story. Everyone sure is in love with my subway station! You'd be surprised. People are talking to each other—some even smile. "That looks like me!" says a lady in a green hat to a gentleman with a red bow tie. Then Grammy tells everyone about Jamaica Louise James, age 8.

THAT'S ME. YOU BETTER BELIEVE IT!

Monitor Comprehension

PAGES 346–347 Ask children to describe what they see. Say: **Read to find out how people in the subway station react to Jamaica's paintings.**

1 **CAUSE/EFFECT** **How do people react to Jamaica's paintings?** (They talk to each other about the paintings. They smile.)

2 **DRAW CONCLUSIONS** **How is Jamaica's birthday surprise for Grammy also a gift to people who use the subway?** (Possible response: Her paintings make the subway a nicer place, and they encourage people to talk to each other.)

3 **AUTHOR'S PURPOSE** **What phrases from earlier in the story does the author repeat on these pages? Why do you think the author does this?** (The author repeats *Jamaica Louise James, age 8* and *That's me. You better believe it!* These phrases remind readers of how the story began and of Jamaica's personality.)

BELOW-LEVEL

Make Connections Guide children to notice that the illustrator includes characters that were mentioned earlier in the story. Point out the woman in a green hat. Ask: **Where did you hear about this woman before? Did Jamaica mention a gentleman with a red bow tie earlier in the story?** Help children connect the earlier descriptions of these characters with the scene shown on pages 346–347.

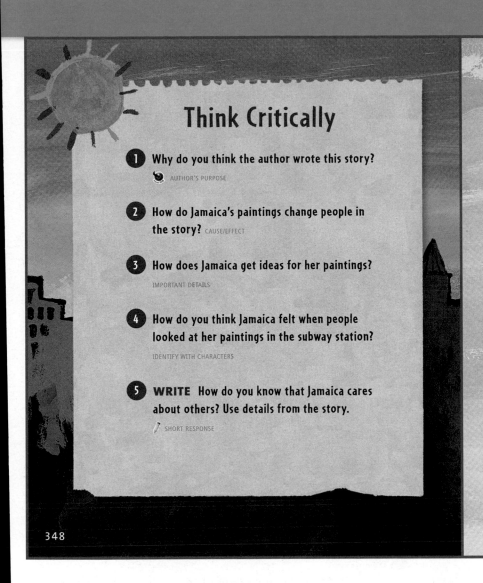

Think Critically

1. Why do you think the author wrote this story?
   AUTHOR'S PURPOSE

2. How do Jamaica's paintings change people in the story? CAUSE/EFFECT

3. How does Jamaica get ideas for her paintings?
   IMPORTANT DETAILS

4. How do you think Jamaica felt when people looked at her paintings in the subway station?
   IDENTIFY WITH CHARACTERS

5. **WRITE** How do you know that Jamaica cares about others? Use details from the story.
   SHORT RESPONSE

348

Meet the Author and Illustrator

Amy Hest

Many of Amy Hest's books are about families. As a child, she spent lots of time with her grandparents. One of her favorite things to do was to get up early to be alone with her grandfather.

Sheila White Samton

Sheila White Samton lives in New York City. She learned to use the subway system when she was about the same age as Jamaica Louise James.

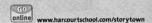 www.harcourtschool.com/storytown

349

Think Critically

Respond to the Literature

1. Possible response: to entertain her readers   **AUTHOR'S PURPOSE**

2. Possible response: Jamaica's paintings make people happier.   **CAUSE/EFFECT**

3. She gets ideas from people and things that she sees and from listening to Grammy talk about her day.   **IMPORTANT DETAILS**

4. Possible response: proud and happy   **IDENTIFY WITH CHARACTERS**

5. **WRITE** Possible response: I know that she cares about others because she wants to hang her art in the subway station to make Grammy and the other grownups happy.   **SHORT RESPONSE**

Meet the Author and the Illustrator

PAGE 349 Read page 349 aloud. Tell children that Amy Hest and Sheila White Samton did not know each other before working on "Jamaica Louise James," but while working on it, they found out that they lived less than half a block away from each other! Guide children to make connections between this and the story's theme.

Check Comprehension
Retelling

Objectives

- *To practice retelling a story*
- *To use punctuation to read fluently in a manner that sounds like natural speech*

RETELLING RUBRIC

4	Uses details to clearly retell the story
3	Uses some details to retell the story
2	Retells the story with some inaccuracies
1	Is unable to retell the story

Professional Development

 Podcasting: Auditory Modeling

BELOW-LEVEL

Fluency Practice   For fluency practice, have children read *Decodable Book 9*, the appropriate *Leveled Reader* (pp. T96–T99), or Story 11 in the *Strategic Intervention Interactive Reader*.

Retell

  AUTHOR'S PURPOSE   Ask children to tell whether the author wrote the story to entertain or to inform. (to entertain)

 REVISIT THE GRAPHIC ORGANIZER   Display completed **Transparency GO4**. Guide children to use the story map to discuss the characters, setting, and main events.

STORY RETELLING CARDS   The cards for the story can be used for retelling or as an aid to completing the story map.

▲ Story Retelling Cards 1–6, "Jamaica Louise James"

 # Fluency
Punctuation

Teach/Model

 **USING PUNCTUATION**   Explain that good readers pay attention to punctuation to help them understand characters' feelings and story events. Model using punctuation to read pages 330–331 expressively as children track the print.

Practice/Apply

 PARTNER-READ   Have partners take turns reading aloud the rest of the story, paying close attention to punctuation.

Build Robust Vocabulary

Words About the Selection

Teach/Model

Routine Card 3 **INTRODUCE ROBUST VOCABULARY** Use *Routine Card 3* to introduce the words.

❶ Put the word in **selection context**.

❷ Display Transparency R56 and read the word and the **Student-Friendly Explanation**.

❸ Have children **say the word** with you.

❹ Use the word in other contexts, and have children **interact with the word's meaning**.

❺ Remove the transparency. Say the Student-Friendly Explanation again, and ask children to **name the word** that goes with it.

❶ **Selection Context:** Jamaica was **renowned** for her art.

❹ **Interact with Word Meaning:** Would someone be renowned for doing something good, bad, or either? Explain.

❶ **Selection Context:** Jamaica and her **kin** spend their evenings together.

❹ **Interact with Word Meaning:** Would you be more likely to spend holidays with kin or with neighbors? Explain.

❶ **Selection Context:** Jamaica created **original** drawings every day.

❹ **Interact with Word Meaning:** Is something you write in class original or copied? Why?

❶ **Selection Context:** Jamaica decided to **adorn** the subway station with art.

❹ **Interact with Word Meaning:** Would you adorn your room with grass or with pictures?

Practice/Apply

GUIDED PRACTICE Ask children to use the vocabulary to tell about something they did that was *original*.

Objective

• To develop robust vocabulary through discussing a literature selection

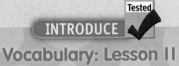

Tested
INTRODUCE ✓
Vocabulary: Lesson 11

renowned	**kin**
original	**adorn**

▼ **Student-Friendly Explanations**

Student-Friendly Explanations

filthy	If something is very dirty, it is filthy.
fellow	You use fellow to describe a person who has something in common with you.
executive	When someone is a boss in charge of a business, that person is called an executive.
beautifying	When you are making something nicer or more beautiful than it was, you are beautifying it.
renowned	If you are renowned, you are famous for something.
kin	Your kin are all of your family members and relatives.
original	When something is original, it is the first of its kind.
adorn	When you adorn something, you decorate it and make it beautiful.

Grade 2, Theme 3   R56   Vocabulary

Transparency R56

Grammar
Abbreviations

5-DAY GRAMMAR

DAY 1	Titles
DAY 2	Days
DAY 3	Months
DAY 4	Apply to Writing
DAY 5	Weekly Review

Objective

• *To use capitalization and punctuation in abbreviations for days of the week*

Daily Proofreading

Will Kerri visit her aunt on saturday.
(Saturday?)

▶ Read each word. Write *yes*, if it is an abbreviation. Write *no*, if it is not an abbreviation.

Abbreviations
Lesson 11

1. Jamaica ___no___
2. Sat. ___yes___
3. Mrs. ___yes___
4. Mon. ___yes___
5. Thursday ___no___
6. Dr. ___yes___
7. Tues. ___yes___
8. Friday ___no___

37
Grammar Practice Book

▲ **Grammar Practice Book, p. 37**

Review

ABBREVIATIONS FOR DAYS OF THE WEEK Remind children that an abbreviation is a short way to write a word. Write the days of the week on the board. Have children read them aloud with you. Explain that the days of the week are proper nouns that begin with capital letters. Point out that the days of the week can be abbreviated. Write the abbreviation for each day of the week:

Sunday	**Monday**	**Tuesday**	**Wednesday**
Sun.	**Mon.**	**Tues.**	**Wed.**
Thursday	**Friday**	**Saturday**	
Thurs.	**Fri.**	**Sat.**	

Point out the period after each abbreviation and tell children that, like abbreviations for titles, abbreviations for the days of the week begin with a capital letter and end with a period. Explain that when these abbreviations are read aloud, they are pronounced as if they were written out.

Practice/Apply

GUIDED PRACTICE Explain that people often use abbreviations for days of the week when they need to make a note. Say: **We have a spelling test on Friday.** Write *Fri.* on the board. Invite children to take turns coming to the board. Tell about things that will happen in your classroom or at your school, using a day of the week, and have children write the abbreviation for the day on the board.

INDEPENDENT PRACTICE Have partners write the days of the week on separate slips of paper. Then have partners shuffle the slips and place them face down. One child should choose a slip and read it aloud. The partner should write the abbreviation for that day on a separate piece of paper. Children should check that they have used a capital letter and a period in each abbreviation.

5-DAY WRITING	
DAY 1	Introduce
DAY 2	Prewrite
DAY 3	Draft
DAY 4	Revise
DAY 5	Revise

Writing
Personal Narrative

Prewrite

GENERATE IDEAS   Ask children to think about a special day or an event that they enjoyed. Suggest that they refer back to their sentences from Day 1. Children may also wish to list their ideas.

 VOICE   Tell children that choosing a day or event that was enjoyable will help them write with enthusiasm and make their writing voice clearer and more personal.

MODEL PREWRITING   Copy on the board the chart below. Tell children that they can use a graphic organizer such as this one to record important details that they want to remember to include in their personal narrative. Use a special day or event from your own life or use the example below to model how to complete the chart.

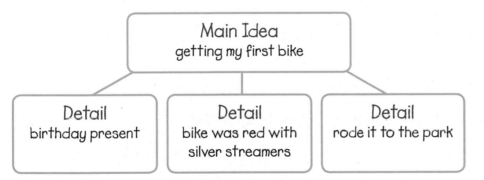

Main Idea
getting my first bike

Detail
birthday present

Detail
bike was red with silver streamers

Detail
rode it to the park

Practice/Apply

GUIDED PRACTICE   Ask children to brainstorm ideas and details to include in their personal narratives. Invite volunteers to briefly describe their topic and have the class ask questions to find out more. Record their ideas in a new chart.

INDEPENDENT PRACTICE   Have children use the chart to brainstorm details to include in their narratives. Tell them that they can add boxes for more details if they wish. Encourage children to use abbreviations in their charts. Remind them to use capital letters and periods when abbreviating days of the week. Have children save their charts for use on Days 3–5.

Objectives

- *To develop topics and ideas for writing*
- *To use a graphic organizer for prewriting*

Writing Prompt

Reflect   Have children write a sentence about how they chose their topic for their personal narrative.

Work with a Peer   Have children draw an illustration that tells about their topic. Then have them work with an English-proficient peer to generate and write details about their pictures. Children may wish to include their illustration with their completed narrative.

Day at a Glance

Day 3

 phonics and Spelling

- Review: Digraphs /ch/*ch*, *tch*; /sh/*sh*; /th/*th*
- State the Generalization

High-Frequency Words

- Review: *draw*, *picture*, *question*, *minute*, *bought*, *worry*, *especially*, *sure*

Fluency

- Punctuation
- "Jamaica Louise James," *Student Edition*, pp. 328–349

Comprehension

Review: Author's Purpose

- "A Lazy Thought," *Student Edition*, pp. 350–351 **Read!**

Robust Vocabulary

- Review: *filthy, fellow, executive, beautifying, renowned, kin, original, adorn*

Grammar

- Review: Abbreviations

Writing

- Personal Narrative

 Oral Language

Warm-Up Routines

Objective *To listen attentively and respond appropriately to oral communication*

Question of the Day

What is fun about getting a birthday card?

Guide children to think about cards they have received that were especially memorable and fun. Use the following prompts:

- **Do you like to receive pretty cards or funny cards? Why?**
- **What do you like best about birthday cards?**

Have children complete the following sentence frame to discuss their ideas:

Birthday cards are fun to receive because _____.

Read Aloud

Objective *To identify repetition in poetry*

BIG BOOK OF RHYMES AND POEMS
Display "My Name" on page 21 and have children tell what they remember about it. Ask children to listen for repeated lines and words as you read the poem aloud. Guide them to identify *I wrote my name* and *washed it away* as repeated phrases. Then read the poem again, having children chime in on *I wrote my name* and *washed it away*.

▲ **Big Book of Rhymes and Poems, p. 21**

Word Wall

Objective *To read high-frequency words*

REVIEW HIGH-FREQUENCY WORDS   Assign each child a partner. Point to and read one of the high-frequency words below. Have children repeat it with you. Then have one child spell the word to his or her partner, and have the partner spell it back. Repeat the process until each word has been spelled several times.

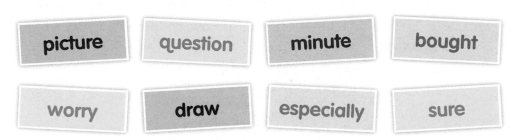

picture	question	minute	bought
worry	draw	especially	sure

Digraphs /ch/ *ch, tch;* /sh/*sh;* /th/*th* *phonics and Spelling*

5-DAY PHONICS

DAY 1	Reintroduce /ch/*ch, tch;* /sh/*sh;* /th/*th*
DAY 2	Word Building: /ch/*ch, tch;* /sh/*sh;* /th/*th*
DAY 3	Word Building: /ch/*ch, tch;* /sh/*sh;* /th/*th*
DAY 4	VCCV; Review /ch/*ch, tch;* /sh/*sh;* /th/*th*
DAY 5	VCCV; Review /ch/*ch, tch;* /sh/*sh;* /th/*th*

Objectives

- *To read phonetically regular words*
- *To read and write common word families*
- *To recognize spelling patterns*

Skill Trace

 Tested **Digraphs /ch/*ch, tch;* /sh/*sh;* /th/*th***

Introduce	Grade 1
Reintroduce	T30–T33
Reteach	S2
Review	**T42–T43, T64–T65, T376–T377**
Test	Theme 3
Maintain	Theme 5, T166

Digraphs /ch/*ch, tch;* /sh/*sh;* /th/*th*

Ruth has a cheese sandwich and a fresh peach for lunch.
Brendan chose mashed potatoes.
Sheena wanted french fries.
My brother made a batch of chocolate chip cookies.
I wish I could munch on an apple right now!

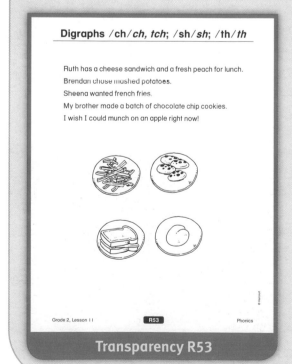

Grade 2, Lesson 11   **R53**   Phonics

Transparency R53

Work with Patterns

INTRODUCE PHONOGRAMS Write the following phonograms at the top of six columns.

> -ash   -ish   -ath   -atch   -each   -unch

Tell children that these are the endings of some words. Slide your hand under the letters as you read each phonogram. Repeat, and have children read the phonograms with you.

BUILD AND READ WORDS Write the words *dash* and *dish* under the phonograms *-ash* and *-ish*. Guide children to read each word: /d/-*ash, dash;* /d/-*ish, dish.* Repeat the process, using the letter *m* to build *math* and *match* and the letter *b* to build *beach* and *bunch.*

Then have children name other words that end with *-ash, ish, -ath, -atch, -each,* or *-unch.* Have them tell which letter or letters to add to build each word, and write the word in the appropriate column. Have children read each column of words. Then point to words at random and have children read them.

Read Words in Context

READ SENTENCES Display **Transparency R53** or write the sentences on the board. Have children choral-read the sentences as you track the print. Then have volunteers read each sentence aloud and underline words with the digraph *ch, tch, sh,* or *th.* Invite volunteers to add the words *peach, lunch, mash(ed), batch, wish,* and *munch* to the appropriate columns.

5-DAY SPELLING

DAY 1	Pretest
DAY 2	Word Building
DAY 3	State the Generalization
DAY 4	Review
DAY 5	Posttest

Review Spelling Words

STATE THE GENERALIZATION FOR /ch/ch, tch; /sh/sh; /th/th   List spelling words 1–10 on chart paper or on the board. Circle the words *lunch* and *chop*, and have children read them aloud. Ask: **What is the same in each word?** (The letters *ch* stand for the /ch/ sound.) Ask volunteers to name the other spelling words with /ch/ch. (each, such) Circle each one. Then circle the word *catch*, and remind children that the letters *tch* can also stand for the /ch/ sound.

Repeat the procedure for /sh/sh and /th/th, using different color pens to circle each group of words.

WRITE   Have children write the spelling words in their notebooks. Remind them to use their best handwriting.

Handwriting

STRAIGHT AND CURVED LINES IN LETTERS   Remind children that some letters, like *h* and *p*, are written using straight and curved lines.

Decodable Books

Additional Decoding Practice

- **Phonics**
  Digraphs /ch/ch, tch; /sh/sh; /th/th
- **Decodable Words**
- **High-Frequency Words**
  See lists in *Decodable Book 9.*

  See also Decodable Books, online (Take-Home Version).

▲ Decodable Book 9: "Hatch!" "Shark Cove," "These Are the Ways We Travel"

Spelling Words

1.	lunch*	6.	catch*
2.	shape	7.	then
3.	wish	8.	each*
4.	chop	9.	bath
5.	show*	10.	such*

Challenge Words

11.	shadow	14.	matchbox
12.	bathtub	15.	sandwich
13.	starfish		

* Words from "Jamaica Louise James"

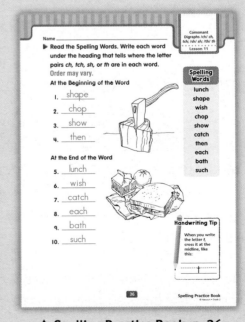

▲ Spelling Practice Book, p. 36

High-Frequency Words

Objective

- *To read high-frequency words*

 **REVIEW** Tested

High-Frequency Words

bought	picture
draw	question
especially	sure
minute	worry

Review

DISPLAY THE WORDS Write the words *draw, picture, question, minute, bought, worry, especially,* and *sure* on the board. Point to each word and ask a volunteer to read it.

Practice/Apply

GUIDED PRACTICE Give each child a set of word cards (*Teacher Resource Book,* p. 76) and have children spread the cards out in front of them. Randomly call out each of the words, and have children hold up the matching card. Point to the word on the board. Repeat until children respond quickly and accurately.

INDEPENDENT PRACTICE Have children work with a partner. One child should read a word from his or her set of cards. The partner should hold up his or her matching card, and use the word in a sentence. Have children repeat the process for all the words. Then have them switch roles and repeat.

 **ELL**

Model Usage Explain that *bought* is the past tense of *buy.* Say: **I went to the store yesterday to buy apples. I bought apples yesterday.** Then say other sentences about things you need to buy and have children place the action in the past, using *bought.*

 MONITOR PROGRESS

High-Frequency Words

IF children have difficulty reading the high-frequency words,	**THEN** display two sets of word cards, and have them read and match the words.

Small-Group Instruction, p. S3:

- **BELOW-LEVEL:** Reteach
- **ON-LEVEL:** Reinforce
- **ADVANCED:** Extend

Fluency
Punctuation

Review

DIBELS
Oral Reading Fluency
ORF

MODEL USING PUNCTUATION Remind children that good readers pay attention to punctuation marks to help them understand characters' feelings and story events. Tell children to

▲ Student Edition, pp. 328–349

- pause when they come to commas, periods, and ellipses.

- think about how a character would sound when they come to quotation marks.

- use their voice to show how a character feels when they come to exclamation points and question marks.

Think Aloud I'm going to read aloud part of "Jamaica Louise James." I'll pay attention to punctuation to help me show what is happening or how a character is feeling.

Practice/Apply

Routine Card 9

GUIDED PRACTICE Read pages 342–345 aloud. Then have children practice reading the same pages several times with a partner. Listen for pauses and changes in tone in response to punctuation, and discuss them with children. Point out when children react to punctuation effectively.

INDEPENDENT PRACTICE
Have partners take turns reading "Jamaica Louise James" aloud, a page at a time. Before they begin reading each page, have partners identify and discuss the punctuation.

Objective

- *To use punctuation to read fluently in a manner that sounds like natural speech*

BELOW-LEVEL

Fluency Practice Have children reread *Decodable Book 9*, Story 11 in the *Strategic Intervention Interactive Reader*, or the appropriate *Leveled Reader* (pp. T96–T99). Have them practice reading the text several times.

Additional Related Reading

- *Artist* by Heather Miller. Heinemann, 2003. **EASY**

- *The Art Box* by Gail Gibbons. Holiday House, 1998. **AVERAGE**

- *Micawber* by John Lithgow. Simon & Schuster, 2002. **CHALLENGE**

Author's Purpose
Comprehension

Objective

• *To identify an author's purpose for writing*

Skill Trace

 Author's Purpose

Introduce	T34–T35
Reteach	S6–S7
Review	**T68, T82, T92, T130–T131, T162, T176, T186, T379, T394**
Test	Theme 3
Maintain	Theme 5, T278

Review

REVIEW AUTHOR'S PURPOSE Remind children that authors have a purpose, or reason, for writing. Guide them to identify some purposes. (Possible responses: to entertain readers; to give information; to give an opinion) Tell children that identifying an author's purpose can help them make sense of what they read.

Practice/Apply

GUIDED PRACTICE Have children turn to "Arthur's Reading Race" on *Student Edition* page 22. Flip through the selection together, and ask volunteers to recall what the story is about. Elicit from children that the characters and events are made-up. Ask: **What is the author's purpose for writing this selection?** (to entertain readers with a made-up story)

INDEPENDENT PRACTICE Have children turn to other selections in the *Student Edition* that they have read. Ask them to identify the author's purpose for writing each one.

★ Language Arts

A Lazy Thought

by Eve Merriam
illustrated by Simon James

There go the grownups
To the office,
To the store.
Subway rush,
Traffic crush;
Hurry, scurry,
Worry, flurry.

No wonder
Grownups
Don't grow up
Any more.

It takes a lot
Of slow
To grow.

350

351

Reading

Student Edition: Paired Selection

Read and Respond

USE PRIOR KNOWLEDGE/SET A PURPOSE Guide children to use prior knowledge and set a purpose for reading. Then have children read the poem.

MONITOR COMPREHENSION Ask:

- **GENRE** **What are some rhyming words in the poem?** (*rush, crush; hurry, scurry, worry, flurry; slow, grow*)

- **PERSONAL RESPONSE** **How can you tell that the speaker of this poem is a child?** (He or she is telling about grown-ups.) **Do you agree with the speaker's ideas? Tell why.** (Possible response: I think the speaker is right; many grownups are often in a hurry.)

SCIENCE

SUPPORTING STANDARDS

Life Sciences Tell children that humans become "grownups," or reach physical maturity, roughly around age 25. Explain that *maturity* is the stage when the human body has reached its full growth. Go on to explain that while humans grow in stages, every person is different, and every person grows at a different rate.

 Connections

Objectives

- *To compare texts*
- *To connect texts to personal experiences*

Comparing Texts

1 Possible response: Yes; Jamaica sees many grownups in the subway station who look mad and who are rushing to get on the subway. She would agree that children shouldn't rush around like that. **TEXT TO TEXT**

2 Possible responses: I would make a nice dinner; I would give something I made. **TEXT TO SELF**

3 Possible responses: People can pick up and throw away litter they see. They can be friendlier to others. **TEXT TO WORLD**

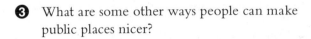

Connections

Comparing Texts

❶ Do you think Jamaica Louise would agree with the poem "A Lazy Thought"? Why or why not?

❷ Jamaica Louise gives a special birthday present. What special gifts would you like to give?

❸ What are some other ways people can make public places nicer?

Phonics

Make Sentences

Write the letters *ch*, *tch*, *sh*, and *th* at the top of a chart. With a partner, write as many words with those letters as you can. Then take turns choosing a word. Read the word aloud, and use it in a sentence.

ch	tch	sh	th
chain	patch	shut	thumb

352

Fluency Practice

Read with a Partner

With a partner, take turns reading the story aloud. Listen carefully to each other. Remember to add a little more stress to the most important words in each sentence.

Writing

Write a Story Paragraph

What else could Jamaica do with her artwork? Fill in a story map with another "cool idea" for Jamaica. Write a paragraph about Jamaica and her next cool idea.

Characters Setting

↓

Beginning

↓

Middle

↓

End

My Writing Checklist

Writing Trait ▶ Voice

✓ I use a story map to plan my writing.

✓ I use strong, interesting words to show that I care about this story.

353

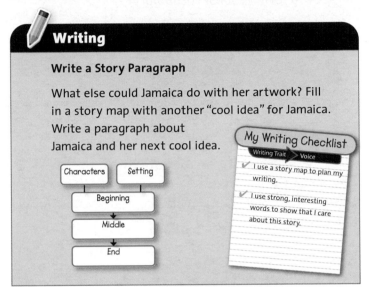

⏱ **PHONICS**

Make Sentences Suggest that children think of rhyming words to help them add words to their charts. Once children have used each of their words in a sentence, challenge them to go back and use two words from their chart in one sentence.

I like to *munch* apples at lunch.

⏱ **FLUENCY**

Read with a Partner Before they begin reading, have partners decide how they will take turns reading the story aloud. Model how to add stress to important words in a sentence. Read the sentence on *Student Edition* page 330, emphasizing the words *cool* and *idea*.

⏱ **WRITING**

Write a Story Paragraph Help children brainstorm things that Jamaica can do with her paintings, such as make a scrapbook. Copy and distribute story maps (*Teacher Resource Book*, p. 97).

📁 **Portfolio Opportunity** Children may choose to place their paragraphs in their portfolios.

Scrapbook

Build Robust Vocabulary

Objective

• *To review robust vocabulary*

REVIEW ✓

Vocabulary: Lesson II

filthy	**fellow**
executive	**beautifying**
renowned	**kin**
original	**adorn**

▼ **Student-Friendly Explanations**

Student-Friendly Explanations

filthy	If something is very dirty, it is filthy.
fellow	You use fellow to describe a person who has something in common with you.
executive	When someone is a boss in charge of a business, that person is called an executive.
beautifying	When you are making something nicer or more beautiful than it was, you are beautifying it.
renowned	If you are renowned, you are famous for something.
kin	Your kin are all of your family members and relatives.
original	When something is original, it is the first of its kind.
adorn	When you adorn something, you decorate it and make it beautiful.

Grade 2, Theme 3   R56   Vocabulary

Transparency R56

Review Robust Vocabulary

USE VOCABULARY IN DIFFERENT CONTEXTS   Remind children of the Student-Friendly Explanations of the Vocabulary Words introduced on Days I and 2. Then discuss each word, using the following prompts:

filthy

- **What would you do if your favorite toy got filthy?**

- **What are some places that might look filthy?**

fellow

- **If you were on a sports team, who would you want to score a point—a fellow player or a player on the other team? Why?**

- **When should you not talk to a fellow student?**

executive

- **Do you think that an executive is a busy person? Why or why not?**

- **What is one decision you would make if you were an executive of an ice cream business?**

beautifying

- **Tell about an idea you have for beautifying our school.**

- **How might people feel when they are finished beautifying their neighborhood?**

renowned

- Name someone who is renowned for their singing.

- Is someone who is renowned known by many people or a few people? Explain.

kin

- Tell about a time you and your kin had fun doing something together.

- Can you name someone in this school who is your kin? Explain.

original

- Tell about a time that you had an original idea.

- What would be an original idea for a party?

adorn

- What could we do to adorn our classroom?

- Tell about how you might adorn an item like a journal or a backpack.

- Name some ways that people adorn themselves.

Reinforce Understanding

Give hands-on practice to help children understand the meanings of *adorn* and *original*. Give each child a disposable cup and provide materials to decorate it, such as markers, stickers, and small items. Then invite children to tell about or show how they adorned their cups in an original way.

Grammar
Abbreviations

5-DAY GRAMMAR	
DAY 1	Titles
DAY 2	Days
DAY 3	**Months**
DAY 4	Apply to Writing
DAY 5	Weekly Review

Objective

- *To use capitalization and punctuation in abbreviations for months of the year*

Daily Proofreading

mr Johnston lost his keys last friday

(Mr., Friday.)

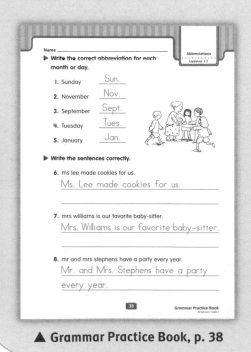

▲ **Grammar Practice Book, p. 38**

Review

ABBREVIATIONS FOR MONTHS   Tell children that months of the year have abbreviations. Write the months and their abbreviations on the board.

January	Jan.
February	Feb.
March	Mar.

Explain that abbreviations for months begin with a capital letter and end with a period, and that when they are read aloud, they are pronounced as if they were written out. Point out that there is no abbreviation for the month of May because the word is already short.

Practice/Apply

GUIDED PRACTICE   Explain that people often use abbreviations for months when they need to make a note. Write the following dates on the board. Model how to write the abbreviation for the first date. Then have volunteers write the remaining dates on the board.

September 29
January 13
February 6
March 10

INDEPENDENT PRACTICE   Have children work with a partner. Have each child write two dates without abbreviations and two other dates that do use abbreviations. Have partners switch papers and rewrite each date so that abbreviations are spelled out and full words are abbreviated.

5-DAY WRITING	
DAY 1	Introduce
DAY 2	Prewrite
DAY 3	**Draft**
DAY 4	Revise
DAY 5	Revise

Writing
Personal Narrative

Draft a Personal Narrative

REVIEW WITH A LITERATURE MODEL   Tell children that the story "Jamaica Louise James" is written like a personal narrative. Point out the following:

- Jamaica tells about something that happened in her life.
- She uses *I, me,* and *we* to tell her story.
- She tells about her excitement on this special day.
- Her personal voice is clear to the reader.
- Her story includes colorful words and details.

Have children turn to pages 342–345 in their *Student Edition,* and invite them to point out how Jamaica includes colorful details to tell her story.

DRAFT A PERSONAL NARRATIVE   Have children use their ideas, their graphic organizers, and what they now know to write a draft of their personal narrative.

 VOICE   As children write their drafts, remind them to use words that express energy and enthusiasm, and to include how they felt at the time.

CONFER WITH CHILDREN   Meet with children, helping them as they write their personal narratives. Offer encouragement for what they are doing well and make constructive suggestions for improving an aspect of the writing, as needed. Remind them to use capital letters and periods in abbreviated titles such as *Mrs.*

Objectives

- *To write a draft of a personal narrative*
- *To include effective word choice in writing*

 ## Writing Prompt

Write a Sentence   Have children write a sentence to tell what they liked about something that Jamaica said.

▲ **Writer's Companion, Lesson 11**

BELOW-LEVEL

Compose Draft As a List   If children seem daunted by writing a story, encourage them to write the draft as a list. Explain that later they can put the entries together to compose the narrative as a paragraph.

Day at a Glance

Day 4

phonics and Spelling
- Introduce: Syllable Pattern VCCV
- Review: Digraphs /ch/*ch, tch*; /sh/*sh*; /th/*th*

High-Frequency Words
- Review: *draw, picture, question, minute, bought, worry, especially, sure*

Fluency
- Punctuation
- "Jamaica Louise James," *Student Edition*, pp. 328–349

Read!

Comprehension

Review: Author's Purpose

Robust Vocabulary
- Review: *filthy, fellow, executive, beautifying, renowned, kin, original, adorn*

Grammar
- Review: Abbreviations

Writing ✏️
- Personal Narrative

Warm-Up Routines

 ## Oral Language

Objective *To listen attentively and respond appropriately to oral communication*

Question of the Day

What do you like about painting pictures?

Guide children to discuss the materials and the process involved in painting. Use the following prompts:

- **What makes painting different from drawing with crayons or pencils?**

- **Why do we often wear special clothes when painting pictures?**

- **Tell about some ways you like to use a brush when you paint a picture.**

Read Aloud

Objective *To listen for enjoyment*

BIG BOOK OF RHYMES AND POEMS
Display "Brush Dance" on page 22 and read the title aloud. Tell children to listen for enjoyment. Then read the poem aloud. After reading, discuss words the poet uses about painting, such as *smear*, *squiggle*, and *dab*. Use gestures to help illustrate the words' meanings. Then read the poem again, and invite children to use gestures to illustrate how a painter uses a brush.

▲ **Big Book of Rhymes and Poems, p. 22**

Word Wall

Objective *To read high-frequency words*

REVIEW HIGH-FREQUENCY WORDS
Arrange the words *draw*, *picture*, *question*, *minute*, *bought*, *worry*, *especially*, and *sure* in two columns. Divide the class into two groups. Have children in the first group choral-read the first column of words, snapping their fingers to keep time. Have the second group do the same with the second column of words. Then have the groups switch columns and repeat.

draw	bought
picture	worry
question	especially
minute	sure

Syllable Pattern VCCV phonics

5-DAY PHONICS	
DAY 1	Reintroduce /ch/*ch*, *tch*; /sh/*sh*; /th/*th*
DAY 2	Word Building· /ch/*ch*, *tch*; /sh/*sh*; /th/*th*
DAY 3	Word Building: /ch/*ch*, *tch*; /sh/*sh*; /th/*th*
DAY 4	**VCCV; Review /ch/*ch*, *tch*; /sh/*sh*; /th/*th***
DAY 5	VCCV; Review /ch/*ch*, *tch*; /sh/*sh*; /th/*th*

Objectives

• To identify the syllable pattern VCCV in two-syllable words
• To read longer words with the VCCV pattern

Skill Trace

 Tested **Syllable Pattern VCCV**

Introduce	T78
Review	T88, T340, T350

Syllable Pattern VCCV

May I have a muffin, please?

Mom used a ladder to get our kitten out of the tree.

I need a bigger pencil!

The batter is wearing a helmet.

Grade 2, Lesson 11   R54   Phonics

Transparency R54

Teach/Model

Routine Card 11

INTRODUCE VCCV Write *pencil* on the board. Ask: **How many vowels do you see? How many consonants come between the vowels?** Label the vowels with *V* and the middle consonants with *C*.

Say: **When a word has the VCCV pattern, divide the word between the consonants.** Draw a line between *n* and *c* in *pencil*. Have children blend the syllables together to read *pencil*.

• Cover the second syllable and have children read /pen/.

• Cover the first syllable and have children read /sil/.

• Then have children read the word, *pencil*.

Distribute Syllabication Card 8 (*Teacher Resource Book*, p. 91) and read it aloud. Write the examples (*number, picnic, muffin,* and *basket*) on the board. Have children label the VCCV pattern in each word and read it aloud.

Guided Practice

NONSENSE WORDS Write *melkip, subbin,* and *sheptin* on the board. Note that the words are made-up. Have children identify the VCCV pattern and blend the syllables to read each word.

Practice/Apply

INDEPENDENT PRACTICE Display **Transparency R54** or write the sentences on the board or on chart paper. Have children read the sentences aloud.

Digraphs /ch/ch, tch; /sh/sh; /th/th phonics and Spelling

5-DAY SPELLING
DAY 1	Pretest
DAY 2	Word Building
DAY 3	State the Generalization
DAY 4	**Review**
DAY 5	Posttest

Build Words

REVIEW THE WORDS   Have children open their notebooks to the spelling words that they wrote on Day 3. Have them read the words several times and then close their notebooks.

MAP LETTERS TO SOUNDS   Have children follow your directions to change one letter in each of the following words to make a spelling word. Have them write the spelling word on a sheet of paper. Then have a volunteer change the spelling of the word on the board so that children can self-check their spelling.

- Write *fish* on the board. Ask: **Which spelling word can you make by changing the first letter?** (wish)

- Write *chip* on the board. Ask: **Which spelling word can you make by changing the third letter?** (chop)

- Write *shave* on the board. Ask: **Which spelling word can you make by changing the fourth letter?** (shape)

fish
wish

chip
chop

shave
shape

Follow a similar procedure with the following words: *bunch (lunch), match (catch), eats (each), than (then), much (such), shot (show), both (bath)*.

CHALLENGE WORDS   Write the first two letters of each challenge word on the board. Tell children to write each word in its entirety.

BELOW-LEVEL

Identify Missing Digraphs Write *ch, tch, sh,* and *th* on the board. Then write the spelling words with a blank where the digraph should be. Guide children to add the appropriate digraph to complete each spelling word.

Objective

- *To use /ch/ch, tch; /sh/sh; /th/th; and other known letter-sounds to spell and write words*

Spelling Words

1.	**lunch***	6.	**catch***
2.	**shape**	7.	**then**
3.	**wish**	8.	**each***
4.	**chop**	9.	**bath**
5.	**show***	10.	**such***

Challenge Words

11.	**shadow**	14. **matchbox**
12.	**bathtub**	15. **sandwich**
13.	**starfish**	

* Words from "Jamaica Louise James"

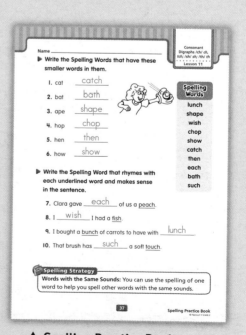

▲ Spelling Practice Book, p. 37

High-Frequency Words

Objective

- *To read high-frequency words*

High-Frequency Words

bought	picture
draw	question
especially	sure
minute	worry

Review

 READ WORDS   Display **Transparency R55**. Have children read the words at the top in order. Then point to the words at random and have children read them.

Practice/Apply

GUIDED PRACTICE   Talk about the illustration. Then track the print as children choral-read the sentences.

Then ask volunteers to create their own sentences using the high-frequency words. Write each sentence on the board, and read it with children.

INDEPENDENT PRACTICE   Have children write three sentences, using at least one high-frequency word in each. Ask children to read their sentences to a partner.

High-Frequency Words

bought	draw	especially	minute
picture	question	sure	worry

I am going to start a special art project in a <u>minute</u>.
I plan to paint a <u>picture</u> for Aunt Sadie on her birthday.
I'm <u>sure</u> she will like a painting of her flower garden.
I <u>bought</u> a new paint set with lots of bright colors.
First I will use a pencil to <u>draw</u> the flowers.
I know I will <u>worry</u> a little about making every flower look perfect.
I will ask Aunt Sadie this <u>question</u> — "How can you see your garden all year long?"
I think she will like my present, <u>especially</u> in the winter!

Grade 2, Lesson 11   R55   High-Frequency Words

Transparency R55

Fluency
Punctuation

Review

DIBELS
Oral
Reading
Fluency
ORF

MODEL USING PUNCTUATION
Read aloud page 347 of
"Jamaica Louise James."
Point out the exclamation point at
the end of the second sentence.

▲ **Student Edition, pp. 328–349**

Think Aloud The exclamation point at the end of this sentence
shows how excited Jamaica feels when she sees that people are
enjoying her art in the subway station. The exclamation point tells
me to show her excitement as I read the sentence.

Practice /Apply

Routine Card 8

GUIDED PRACTICE Have children echo-read page 347
with you, matching your expression and pauses as you
use punctuation marks.

INDEPENDENT PRACTICE Have children read along as they listen
to "Jamaica Louise James" on *Audiotext 2*. Stop the recording
periodically to note how the reader uses punctuation marks. Have
children practice reading aloud at these points.

BELOW-LEVEL

Choral-Read Have children turn to pages 330–331.
Have them identify various punctuation marks, and
discuss how to use them in reading. Then have children
practice choral-reading the pages so that they are all using expression appropriate to the punctuation marks.

Objective

• *To use punctuation to read fluently
in a manner that sounds like
natural speech*

 **MONITOR PROGRESS**

Fluency

IF children have difficulty using punctuation to read fluently,	**THEN** read aloud sentences from the story with different forms of punctuation and have children repeat.

Small-Group Instruction, p. S4–S5:

● **BELOW-LEVEL:** Reteach
● **ON-LEVEL:** Reinforce
● **ADVANCED:** Extend

Author's Purpose
Comprehension

Objective

- *To identify an author's purpose for writing*

Skill Trace

 Author's Purpose

Tested	
Introduce	T34–T35
Reteach	S6–S7
Review	**T68, T82, T92, T130–T131, T162, T176, T186, T379, T394**
Test	Theme 3
Maintain	Theme 5, T278

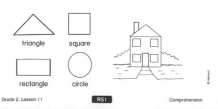

Author's Purpose

Seeing Shapes

Artists start their pictures with simple shapes. A drawing of a tree might begin with a rectangle for the trunk and lots of small circles for the leaves. An artist might use a square for a house and a triangle for the roof.

What shape could you use to draw the sun? A circle, of course! What shapes could you use to draw a person? Be an artist and look for simple shapes in the world around you.

The next time you draw a picture, start with the basic shapes of the things you want to show. Then add details using other shapes. You'll be amazed at what you can do with simple shapes!

triangle   square

rectangle   circle

Grade 2, Lesson 11   R51   Comprehension

Transparency R51

Review

EXPLAIN AUTHOR'S PURPOSE   Remind children that authors have a purpose for writing. Ask: **What is an author's purpose for writing a fiction story?** (for the reader's enjoyment, to entertain) **What are some other kinds of writing? What might be the author's purpose for these kinds of writing?** (Possible responses: nonfiction, to inform; reviews, to give an opinion; journals, to express feelings.)

Practice/Apply

GUIDED PRACTICE   Display **Transparency R51**. Reread the passage aloud to children. Guide children to identify the author's purpose. Ask:

- **Do you think "Seeing Shapes" is fiction or nonfiction? How can you tell?** (nonfiction; the passage gives information)

- **Why do you think the author wrote this passage?** (to tell about how artists use shapes in their work, and how shapes are everywhere)

- **Which of these tells the author's purpose—to entertain, to inform, to give an opinion, or to express feelings?** (to inform)

INDEPENDENT PRACTICE   Ask children to identify the author's purpose for writing "A Lazy Thought" and to tell how they know. (Possible response: to entertain; it is a poem that is enjoyable to read.)

Build Robust Vocabulary

Review Robust Vocabulary

USE VOCABULARY IN DIFFERENT CONTEXTS Remind children of the Student-Friendly Explanations of the Vocabulary Words. Then discuss the words, using the following activities:

filthy, beautifying Tell children that you will describe some items or places. After each description, children should respond, "That sounds nice!" or "That sounds filthy! It needs beautifying!" Then have children tell how they might beautify each filthy thing or place.

> **a teddy bear that has been dragged through the mud**
>
> **a birthday gift wrapped with paper and ribbons**
>
> **a grassy field littered with trash**

executive Have children listen as you make some statements. If the statement sounds like something an executive might say, children should respond, "That sounds like an executive!" If not, they should say nothing.

> **"I'll make a decision on that by the end of the day."**
>
> **"Could I stay home tomorrow?"**
>
> **"My plan will increase our business and please our customers."**
>
> **"Please schedule a meeting on that for this afternoon."**

adorn, original Tell children that you will name some things. Have children take turns telling how they might adorn each thing in an original way.

> a birthday cake
>
> a sweatshirt
>
> a pair of gym shoes
>
> a bicycle

Objective

• *To review robust vocabulary*

REVIEW ✔ **Tested**

Vocabulary: Lesson 11

filthy	fellow
executive	beautifying
renowned	kin
original	adorn

▼ **Student-Friendly Explanations**

Student-Friendly Explanations

filthy	If something is very dirty, it is filthy.
fellow	You use fellow to describe a person who has something in common with you.
executive	When someone is a boss in charge of a business, that person is called an executive.
beautifying	When you are making something nicer or more beautiful than it was, you are beautifying it.
renowned	If you are renowned, you are famous for something.
kin	Your kin are all of your family members and relatives.
original	When something is original, it is the first of its kind.
adorn	When you adorn something, you decorate it and make it beautiful.

Grade 2, Theme 3   R56   Vocabulary

Transparency R56

Grammar
Abbreviations

5-DAY GRAMMAR	
DAY 1	Titles
DAY 2	Days
DAY 3	Months
DAY 4	**Apply to Writing**
DAY 5	Weekly Review

Objective

- *To use abbreviations for titles, days, and months in writing*

Daily Proofreading

sam and I will go to a movie on friday.

(Sam, Friday)

Review

DISCUSS ABBREVIATIONS Review what children have learned about abbreviations, using the following points:

- An abbreviation is a short way to write a word.

- Most abbreviations end with a period.

- Abbreviations for proper nouns begin with capital letters.

- Abbreviations are pronounced as if they were written out.

Write the following names and dates on the board.

Mrs. Jackson	**Mon.**	**Apr. 19**
Dr. Hodges	**Thurs.**	**Dec. 8**

Have children point out and read aloud each abbreviation.

Practice/Apply

GUIDED PRACTICE Read aloud the following names and dates, one at a time, and have children write the abbreviations for each: *Ms. Brown, January 5, Tuesday, November 18, Mrs. White, Dr. Black, Friday, August 9, Wednesday.* For each item, write the correct response on the board and read it aloud.

INDEPENDENT PRACTICE Provide a current calendar so that children can find their birthday days and dates. Have children write on a sheet of construction paper the complete day and date, as well as the abbreviated day and date. Have children include their names, using their appropriate titles, and decorate their papers. Use the papers to create a classroom birthday bulletin board.

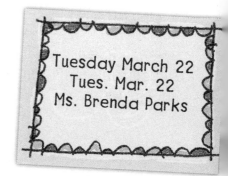

Tuesday March 22
Tues. Mar. 22
Ms. Brenda Parks

Grammar Practice Book, p. 39

Name _____

▶ Circle the correct abbreviation for each word.

Abbreviations
Lesson 11

1. March   Mr.   Mon.   (Mar.)

2. Wednesday   Wdsy.   (Wed.)   Wedn.

3. February   Fri.   Fbry.   (Feb.)

4. December   (Dec.)   Thurs.   Dmbr.

▶ Read each item below. Rewrite each item, using abbreviations correctly.

5. jan 16   Jan. 16

6. mr anthony martin   Mr. Anthony Martin

7. mon, dec 29   Mon., Dec. 29

8. dr joy hardin   Dr. Joy Hardin

39   Grammar Practice Book

▲ Grammar Practice Book, p. 39

Writing
Personal Narrative

5-DAY WRITING

DAY 1	Introduce
DAY 2	Prewrite
DAY 3	Draft
DAY 4	**Revise**
DAY 5	Revise

Write and Revise

WRITE Have children continue writing their personal narratives. Remind them to include colorful words and details that help the reader "see" the story.

WRITING TRAIT **VOICE** Remind children to use words that describe how they felt and that express their enthusiasm. Say: **A sentence like "We will go tomorrow" gives some information, but saying "I could hardly wait till tomorrow to go!" is more energetic and tells about the author's excitement.**

REVISE Have children read their personal narrative to a partner. They can use the list of criteria for a personal narrative to check and improve their writing.

Personal Narrative

- A personal narrative tells a true story about something that happened in your life.
- Use the words *I, me, we,* and *us.*
- Tell about your thoughts and feelings.
- Use capital letters and periods in abbreviated titles such as *Mr.* and *Dr.*

Tell children to make notes on their drafts of the changes they will make. Encourage them to use Editor's Marks. Remind children to check that they have abbreviated any titles correctly. Then have children begin revising their drafts. Tell them that they will make more revisions on Day 5.

Editor's Marks

∧	Add
⤴	Take out
⌐	Change
⊙	Add a period
≡	Capitalize
⌒	Check Spelling

Objectives

- *To revise a draft of a personal narrative*
- *To edit a draft for appropriate grammar, spelling, and punctuation*

Writing Prompt

Describe Have children write a sentence describing the progress they have made on their narratives.

Confer with Children Encourage children to share their revisions with you. Invite children to tell what they would like to change, and provide support. Work with them to identify colorful synonyms for some of the words used in their drafts.

Day at a Glance

Day 5

 phonics and Spelling
- Review: Syllable Pattern VCCV
- Posttest: Digraphs /ch/*ch*, *tch*; /sh/*sh*; /th/*th*

High-Frequency Words
- Cumulative Review

Fluency
- Punctuation
- "Jamaica Louise James," *Student Edition*, pp. 328–349

 **Read!**

Comprehension
- Review: Author's Purpose
- *Read-Aloud Anthology:* "Tanya's City Garden"

Robust Vocabulary
- Cumulative Review

Grammar
- Review: Abbreviations

Writing
- Personal Narrative

Warm-Up Routines

 ### Oral Language

Objective *To listen attentively and respond appropriately to oral communication*

Question of the Day

Which animals do you especially like to draw or paint? Why?

Use the following prompts to help children think about animals they like to draw or paint.

- **Do you like animals with stripes or animals with spots? Which ones?**
- **Which animals do you think are an interesting color?**
- **Which animals do you think have an interesting shape?**

Have children complete one of the following sentence frames to explain their preference:

I like to draw pictures of _____ because _____.

I like to paint pictures of _____ because _____.

Read Aloud

Objective *To identify rhymes and alliteration in poetry*

BIG BOOK OF RHYMES AND POEMS
Display "Brush Dance" on page 22, and read the poem aloud. Ask children to identify the rhyming words. (dot/blot, smear/here, splat/cat) Tell children that the poet also uses repeated sounds at the beginnings of words. Tell children to listen for these sounds as together you read the poem again. Guide children to identify the alliterative /sm/, /d/, and /spl/ sounds.

▲ **Big Book of Rhymes and Poems, p. 22**

Word Wall

Objective *To read high-frequency words*

REVIEW HIGH-FREQUENCY WORDS   Review the words *draw, picture, question, minute, bought, worry, especially,* and *sure*. Point to a card at random, and ask children to read the word. Have children read the words several times.

draw	picture	question	minute
bought	especially	worry	sure

 # Syllable Pattern VCCV *phonics*

5-DAY SPELLING	
DAY 1	Reintroduce /ch/*ch, tch*; /sh/*sh*; /th/*th*
DAY 2	Word Building: /ch/*ch, tch*; /sh/*sh*; /th/*th*
DAY 3	Word Building: /ch/*ch, tch*; /sh/*sh*; /th/*th*
DAY 4	VCCV; Review /ch/*ch, tch*; /sh/*sh*; /th/*th*
DAY 5	VCCV; Review /ch/*ch, tch*; /sh/*sh*; /th/*th*

Objectives

- To identify the VCCV pattern in two-syllable words
- To read two-syllable words with the VCCV pattern

Skill Trace

 Tested **Syllable Pattern VCCV**

Introduce	T78
Review	T88, T340, T350

Review

READ VCCV WORDS   Write the words *matter* and *helmet* on the board. Guide children to label the VCCV pattern in each word and read it aloud.

Practice/Apply

GUIDED PRACTICE   Write the following words on the board: *traffic, bottom, frozen, invent, napkin,* and *music.* Then make a chart as shown. Guide children to sort the words and add them to the chart.

VCCV Words	Not VCCV Words
traffic	frozen
bottom	music
invent	
napkin	

INDEPENDENT PRACTICE   Have children read aloud the words in the chart.

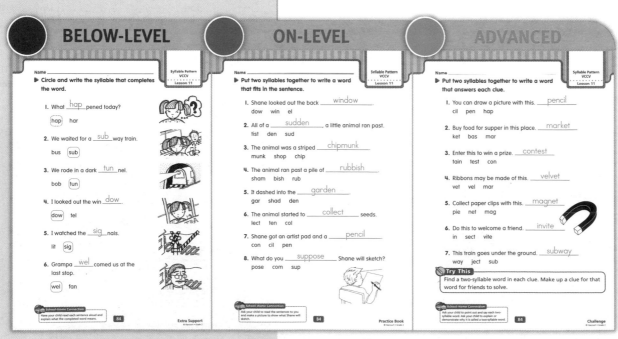

▲ **Extra Support, p. 84**   ▲ **Practice Book, p. 84**   ▲ **Challenge, p. 84**

 **ELL**

- Group children according to academic levels, and assign one of the pages on the left.

- Clarify any unfamiliar concepts as necessary. See *ELL Teacher Guide* Lesson 11 for support in scaffolding instruction.

Digraphs /ch/*ch, tch;* /sh/*sh;* /th/*th* phonics *and Spelling*

5-DAY SPELLING
DAY 1 Pretest
DAY 2 Word Building
DAY 3 State the Generalization
DAY 4 Review
DAY 5 Posttest

Assess

POSTTEST   Assess children's progress. Use the dictation sentences from Day 1.

Words with Digraphs /ch/*ch, tch,* /sh/*sh,* /th/*th*

1.	lunch	I would like to have soup for **lunch**.
2.	shape	Sean made a kite in the **shape** of a rainbow.
3.	wish	I **wish** I could fly like a bird.
4.	chop	Trina will **chop** wood for the campfire.
5.	show	Would you **show** me your paintings?
6.	catch	Get ready to **catch** the ball!
7.	then	When Tyrell is done, **then** it will be your turn.
8.	each	Mom said we could have two slices **each**.
9.	bath	The baby likes to splash in the **bath**.
10.	such	I had **such** a great time at the game!

ADVANCED

Challenge Words   Use the challenge words in these dictation sentences.

11.	shadow	We sat in the **shadow** of a big umbrella at the beach.
12.	bathtub	Our plastic raft was about as big as a **bathtub**.
13.	starfish	My sister wanted to look for **starfish** at the shore.
14.	matchbox	I kept the tiny shells I found in a **matchbox**.
15.	sandwich	I bought an ice cream **sandwich** for a snack.

WRITING APPLICATION
   Have children use at least two spelling words to write a funny sentence. Encourage children to illustrate their sentence.

I will catch a whale for lunch!

Objective

• *To use /ch/ch, tch; /sh/sh; /th/th; and other known letter-sounds to spell and write words*

Spelling Words

1.	lunch*	6.	catch*
2.	shape	7.	then
3.	wish	8.	each*
4.	chop	9.	bath
5.	show*	10.	such*

Challenge Words

11.	shadow	14.	matchbox
12.	bathtub	15.	sandwich
13.	starfish		

* Words from "Jamaica Louise James"

High-Frequency Words

Objectives

- *To read high-frequency words*
- *To explore word relationships*

High-Frequency Words

believe	bought
brought	draw
early	especially
enough	minute
impossible	picture
quite	question
understand	sure
	worry

Cumulative Review

REINFORCE WORD RECOGNITION   Write the high-frequency words for Lessons 9 and 11 on the board. Point to words at random, and have volunteers read them.

SORT WORDS   Guide children in sorting the words into columns according to beginning letters. Then have them read the words in each column again.

Begins with a Vowel	Begins with One Consonant	Begins with Two Consonants
impossible enough understand early especially	believe quite picture question minute bought worry sure	brought draw

- Ask: **Which two words have four syllables?** (impossible, especially)

- Ask: **Which words have two syllables?** (believe, enough, early, picture, question, minute, worry)

- Ask: **Which two words are the same except for one letter and tell about something that happened in the past?** (brought, bought)

- Ask: **Which word is a compound word?** (understand)

Fluency
Punctuation

Readers' Theater

DIBELS
Oral Reading Fluency
ORF

PERFORM "JAMAICA LOUISE JAMES" To help children improve their fluency by using punctuation, have them perform "Jamaica Louise James" as Readers' Theater. Use the following procedures:

▲ *Student Edition*, pp. 328–349

- Discuss with children how various punctuation marks can be used to show how characters are feeling. Talk about the way Jamaica tells her story.

- Have small groups read the story together. Have children take turns reading each new paragraph. Ask all children to chime in on the repeated lines, "That's me! You better believe it!"

- Monitor the groups as they read. Provide feedback and support, paying particular attention to how readers use punctuation marks.

Develop Vocabulary Remind children that Jamaica says she likes "lacing up the details" of her stories. Demonstrate lacing up a shoe. Lead children to understand that Jamaica means that she brings together details to make a complete story.

Objective

- *To use punctuation to read fluently in a manner that sounds like natural speech*

 ASSESSMENT

Monitoring Progress Periodically, take a timed sample of children's oral reading and record the number of words read correctly per minute. Children should accurately read approximately 72 words per minute in the middle of Grade 2.

Fluency Support Materials

 Fluency Builders, Grade 2, Lesson 11

 Audiotext *Student Edition* selections are available on *Audiotext 2.*

 Strategic Intervention Teacher Guide, Lesson 11

Author's Purpose
Comprehension

Objective

- *To identify an author's purpose for writing*

Skill Trace

 Tested **Author's Purpose**

Introduce	T34–T35
Reteach	S6–S7
Review	T68, T82, T92, T130–T131, T162, T176, T186, T379, T394
Test	Theme 3
Maintain	Theme 5, T278

E L L

Discuss Dialogue   If children have difficulty identifying the author's purpose, review "Tanya's City Garden" with them. Point out the dialogue and explain that many selections that are written to entertain are fiction stories that include conversations between made-up characters.

▲ **Read-Aloud Anthology, "Tanya's City Garden,"** p. 42

Review

REVIEW THE SKILL   Remind children that good readers identify the author's purpose in writing to help them better understand what they read. Remind them that an author's purpose may be to entertain or to inform.

SET A PURPOSE FOR LISTENING   Guide children to set a purpose for listening that includes

- listening to find out whether the selection is fiction or nonfiction.

- listening to find out why the author wrote the selection.

Practice/Apply

GUIDED PRACTICE   As you read aloud "Tanya's City Garden," use a chart like the one below to identify and discuss the author's purpose.

Kind of Writing	Author's Purpose
story	to entertain by telling about how a young girl makes an alley a nicer place

INDEPENDENT PRACTICE   Have children use the chart to review author's purpose. Ask children to imagine that the story had been in the form of a news report or article and tell what the author's purpose would be. (to inform) Invite volunteers to suggest an opening sentence for a newspaper article about Tanya's work.

Build Robust Vocabulary

Cumulative Review

REINFORCE MEANINGS   Ask children to respond to the following:

- **Tell about one of your kin who is renowned for something.**

- **What kind of request might an executive make?**

- **What kind of compromise might you make with a fellow student?**

MAKE WORD WEBS   Using **Transparency GO9,** work with children to complete word webs for *kin* and *improve*. Write *kin* in the center of the web and invite children to name people who are their kin. Record their responses in the web.

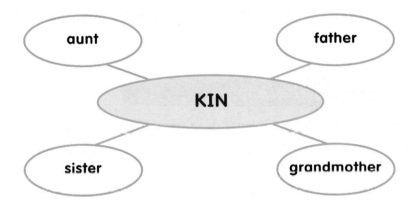

Then have children create their own web for *improve*. Have them fill in the web with things they could improve.

Objective

- *To review robust vocabulary*

REVIEW
Vocabulary

Lesson 9	Lesson 11
brisk	filthy
strutted	fellow
gobbled	executive
paced	beautifying
request	renowned
negotiate	kin
compromise	original
improve	adorn

✓ MONITOR PROGRESS

Build Robust Vocabulary

IF children do not demonstrate understanding of the words and have difficulty using them,	**THEN** model using each word in several sentences, and have children repeat each sentence.

Small-Group Instruction, p. S8–S9:

● **BELOW-LEVEL:** Reteach
● **ON-LEVEL:** Reinforce
● **ADVANCED:** Extend

Lesson 11   **T93**

Grammar
Abbreviations

5-DAY GRAMMAR	
DAY 1	Titles
DAY 2	Days
DAY 3	Months
DAY 4	Apply to Writing
DAY 5	Weekly Review

Objectives

- *To use abbreviations for titles, days, and months in writing*
- *To pronounce abbreviations as if they were written out*

Daily Proofreading

shelly's teacher is ms Markson.

(Shelly's, Ms.)

 Language Arts Checkpoint

If children have difficulty with the concepts, see pages S10–S11 to reteach.

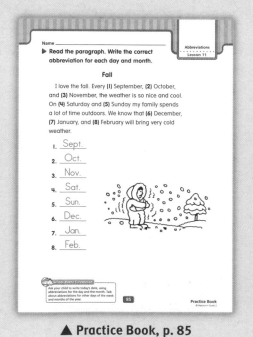

▲ **Practice Book, p. 85**

Review

REVIEW ABBREVIATIONS   Use the following questions to review what children have learned about abbreviations. Have volunteers write answers on the board as they are provided. Ask:

- **What abbreviations are used for titles? How are they spelled?** (Mr., Mrs., Ms., Dr.)

- **What are the abbreviations we use for the days of the week? How are they spelled?** (Sun., Mon., Tues., Wed., Thurs., Fri., Sat.)

- **What abbreviations are used for the months of the year? How are they spelled?** (Jan., Feb., Mar., Apr., Jun., Jul., Aug., Sept., Oct., Nov., Dec.)

Practice/Apply

GUIDED PRACTICE   Tell children that they will correct some abbreviations. One at a time, write the following examples on the board: *Mz Cooper, Sep. 8, thrus., Weds, Doct. Green, fri, Jul 12, Mrs Reed*. Have children write the corrected abbreviations on a sheet of paper. After each example, have a volunteer write the correct abbreviation on the board and read it aloud.

INDEPENDENT PRACTICE   Have pairs of children take turns saying a person's name (including a title), a day of the week, and a month of the year. Have the partner write the abbreviation for each example and then read it aloud. Then have children switch roles and repeat the process.

Writing
Personal Narrative

5-DAY WRITING	
DAY 1	Introduce
DAY 2	Prewrite
DAY 3	Draft
DAY 4	Revise
DAY 5	Revise

Revise

REVISE NARRATIVES Explain that good writers look back after a day or so to see if their writing is clear and to add any new ideas they have thought of. Tell children to reread their narratives and ask themselves these questions:

- Have I included details that help the reader "see" the story?

- Have I described how I felt about what happened?

- Does my story sound as though I am speaking to someone?

 VOICE Ask children to identify words in their personal narratives that express enthusiasm. Encourage them to read aloud their writing to see if it sounds like the way they talk.

Ask children to revise their personal narratives to clarify ideas and add any new information they want to include.

Objective

- *To revise a personal narrative*

Writing Prompt

Write a Paragraph Have children write a paragraph about another story they would like to write.

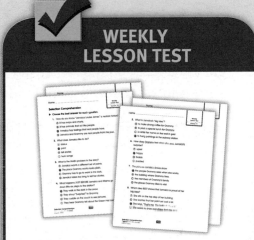

WEEKLY LESSON TEST

▲ **Weekly Lesson Tests, pp. 111–122**

- Selection Comprehension with Short Response
- Phonics and Spelling
- High-Frequency Words
- Focus Skill
- Robust Vocabulary
- Grammar
- Fluency Passage

 For prescriptions, see pp. A2–A6. Also available electronically on StoryTown Online Assessment and ExamView.

 Podcasting: Assessing Fluency

NOTE: A 4-point rubric appears on page R8.

SCORING RUBRIC						
	6	**5**	**4**	**3**	**2**	**1**
FOCUS	Completely focused, purposeful.	Focused on topic and purpose.	Generally focused on topic and purpose.	Somewhat focused on topic and purpose.	Related to topic but does not maintain focus.	Lacks focus and purpose.
ORGANIZATION	Ideas progress logically; paper conveys sense of completeness.	Organization mostly clear; paper gives sense of completeness.	Organization mostly clear, but some lapses occur; may seem unfinished.	Some sense of organization; seems unfinished.	Little sense of organization.	Little or no sense of organization.
SUPPORT	Strong, specific details; clear, exact language; freshness of expression.	Strong, specific details; clear, exact language.	Adequate support and word choice.	Limited supporting details; limited word choice.	Few supporting details; limited word choice.	Little development; limited or unclear word choice.
CONVENTIONS	Varied sentences; few, if any, errors.	Varied sentences; few errors.	Some sentence variety; few errors.	Simple sentence structures; some errors.	Simple sentence structures; many errors.	Unclear sentence structures; many errors.

REPRODUCIBLE RUBRICS for specific writing purposes and presentations are available on pages R2–R8.

Leveled Readers
Reinforcing Skills and Strategies

Genre: Realistic Fiction

BELOW-LEVEL

Lucia's Gift

SUMMARY Lucia uses postcards that Aunt Cherry sent from around the world to illustrate a book she makes as a welcome-home gift.

- **phonics** Digraphs /ch/*ch*, *tch*; /sh/*sh*; /th/*th*
- **High-Frequency Words**
- **Author's Purpose**

Focus Skill

Before Reading

BUILD BACKGROUND/SET PURPOSE Have children share their experiences with sending or receiving postcards. Guide them to preview the story and set a purpose for reading it.

Reading the Book

PAGES 4–5 DRAW CONCLUSIONS Why does Lucia want to make a welcome-home gift for Aunt Cherry? (Possible response: Lucia wants to thank Aunt Cherry for sending specially chosen postcards.)

PAGES 6–14 AUTHOR'S PURPOSE What is the author's purpose for writing "Lucia's Gift"? (The author wants to entertain readers with a story.)

REREAD FOR FLUENCY Have partners read their favorite page(s) aloud several times with expression, especially the exclamations.

Think Critically   *(See inside back cover for questions.)*

1 NOTE DETAILS Aunt Cherry had been on a long trip to lots of countries.

2 SEQUENCE Lucia drew Aunt Cherry first in a big city, next watching a lion. Then she drew Aunt Cherry riding a horse, next on a train, and finally swimming in the sea.

3 IDENTIFY WITH CHARACTER Responses will vary.

4 AUTHOR'S PURPOSE Responses will vary.

5 PERSONAL RESPONSE Responses will vary.

LEVELED READERS TEACHER GUIDE

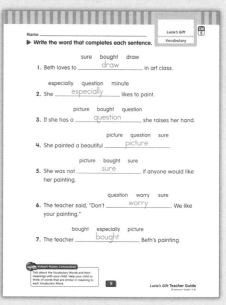

▲ **High-Frequency Words, p. 5**

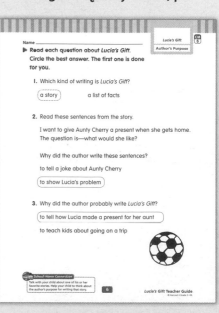

▲ **Comprehension, p. 6**

www.harcourtschool.com/storytown

Go online

★ **Leveled Readers Online Database**
Searchable by Genre, Skill, Vocabulary, Level, or Title
★ **Student Activities and Teacher Resources, online**

Genre: Realistic Fiction

ON-LEVEL

Measuring Max

SUMMARY As a birthday gift, Carla makes her younger friend Max a measuring chart to record how tall he is at age three. At his fourth birthday party, everyone checks to see how much he has grown.

- **phonics** Digraphs /ch/*ch*, *tch*; /sh/*sh*; /th/*th*
- **High-Frequency Words**
- **Author's Purpose**

Focus Skill

Before Reading

BUILD BACKGROUND/SET PURPOSE Ask children to recall their previous birthdays. Discuss ways in which they have changed or grown since then. Guide them to preview the story and set a purpose for reading it.

Reading the Book

PAGES 6–7 AUTHOR'S PURPOSE What is the author's purpose for writing "Measuring Max?" (The author wants to entertain readers with a story.)

PAGES 12–13 DRAW CONCLUSIONS How has Max changed since his third birthday? How is he the same? (Possible response: Max is taller. He still likes lions, and he is still friends with Carla.)

REREAD FOR FLUENCY Have groups of three children read the story as Readers' Theater. One child should read Carla's part, another should read her mother's part, and the third child should be the narrator. Remind children to be aware of punctuation.

Think Critically *(See inside back cover for questions.)*

1 NOTE DETAILS Carla got the idea from a store.

2 SEQUENCE First she drew zoo animals on the chart, next she painted them, and finally she pasted a measuring tape on the chart.

3 IDENTIFY WITH CHARACTER Responses will vary.

4 AUTHOR'S PURPOSE Responses will vary.

5 PERSONAL RESPONSE Responses will vary.

LEVELED READERS TEACHER GUIDE

▲ High-Frequency Words, p. 5

▲ Comprehension, p. 6

Leveled Readers

Reinforcing Skills and Strategies

ADVANCED

Genre: Realistic Fiction

On Stage!

SUMMARY Dion is shy about appearing in his class play, but thanks to his skill as an artist, he is still able to play an important role.

- **phonics** Digraphs /ch/*ch*, *tch*; /sh/*sh*; /th/*th*
- **High-Frequency Words**
- **Author's Purpose** *Focus Skill*

Before Reading

BUILD BACKGROUND/SET PURPOSE Ask children to recall plays or concerts in which they have been involved. Lead them to discuss key off-stage tasks. Guide them to preview the story and set a purpose for reading it.

Reading the Book

PAGES 4–5 DRAW CONCLUSIONS Why is Dion nervous about being in a class play? (Possible response: He may be shy about appearing on stage. He may be worried about forgetting lines or looking silly.)

PAGES 12–14 AUTHOR'S PURPOSE What is the author's purpose for writing "On Stage!?" (The author wants to entertain readers with a story.)

REREAD FOR FLUENCY Have partners take turns reading the story a page at a time. Suggest that they alternate by paragraphs or pages. Remind children to be aware of punctuation.

Think Critically *(See inside back cover for questions.)*

1. **PROBLEM/SOLUTION** Mom suggested that Dion paint the scenery.

2. **COMPARE/CONTRAST** Before he spoke to Mom he was worried; after he spoke to Mom he was happy and excited.

3. **NOTE DETAILS** The audience clapped loudly when Ms. Lopez pointed to the scenery.

4. **AUTHOR'S PURPOSE** Responses will vary.

5. **PERSONAL RESPONSE** Responses will vary.

LEVELED READERS TEACHER GUIDE

▲ High-Frequency Words, p. 5

▲ Comprehension, p. 6

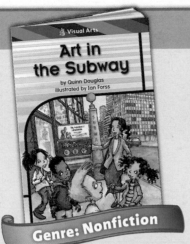

E L L

Art in the Subway

SUMMARY Through a class field trip, this nonfiction selection shows and explains the New York City subway system. The trip ends at the Brooklyn Bridge stop, where the class views a special artwork.

Genre: Nonfiction

- • **Build Background**
- • **Concept Vocabulary**
- • **Scaffolded Language Development**

Before Reading

BUILD BACKGROUND/SET PURPOSE Ask children to share experiences with the types of public transportation they have taken or know about. Be sure to include trains or subways in the discussion. Guide children to preview the story and set a purpose for reading it.

Reading the Book

PAGES 4–5 DRAW CONCLUSIONS Why do you think there is artwork in the subway stations? (to make the stations look nicer or brighter)

PAGES 12–14 AUTHOR'S PURPOSE Why do you think the author wrote "Art in the Subway"? (to give information about subways; to show artwork that appears in the New York subway system)

REREAD FOR FLUENCY Have partners take turns reading the story a page at a time. Suggest that they alternate by paragraphs or pages. Remind children to be aware of punctuation.

Scaffolded Language Development

(See inside back cover for teacher-led activity.)

Provide additional examples and explanation as needed.

LEVELED READERS TEACHER GUIDE

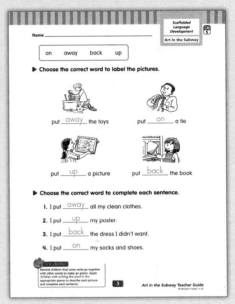

▲ Scaffolded Language Development, p. 5

▲ Build Background and Vocabulary, p. 6

Writing Overview  Friendly Letter

LESSON	FORM	TRAIT
11	Personal Narrative	Voice
12	Paragraph of Information	Voice
13	Dialogue	Conventions
14	Paragraph That Explains	Conventions
15	Student Choice: Revise and Publish	Voice and Conventions

Reading-Writing Connection

Friendly Letter

Focus on

Voice and Conventions

Children will

- Use a literature model to generate ideas

- Select a topic

- Plan and draft a friendly letter

- Revise the letter for voice by adding interesting words and phrases

- Proofread the letter, checking for correct capitalization, punctuation, and other conventions

- Publish a final version of the friendly letter

Set the Stage

Friendly Letter

Objectives

- *To write a friendly letter*
- *To generate ideas based on audience and purpose*
- *To choose a topic of interest*
- *To write complete sentences*
- *To revise writing to improve the voice*
- *To capitalize proper nouns and use abbreviations correctly*

Introduce the Writing Form

TALK ABOUT READING AND WRITING FRIENDLY LETTERS Ask children to recall friendly letters they have written or received. Begin a discussion of a friendly letter by asking children to explain why people write friendly letters. Then say the following:

> **Think Aloud** I think about the story we read, *Click, Clack, Moo: Cows That Type.* I remember that the cows and the farmer wrote letters to each other. Their letters explained a problem the characters faced and suggested ways to solve the problem. The letters were a way for the characters to share what they were thinking, feeling, and doing.

▲ Student Edition, pp. 270–271

Ask children to suggest other reasons that people write letters.

STAGES OF THE WRITING PROCESS Adjust pacing to meet children's needs. Guide them back and forth between the steps until the final product meets established criteria.

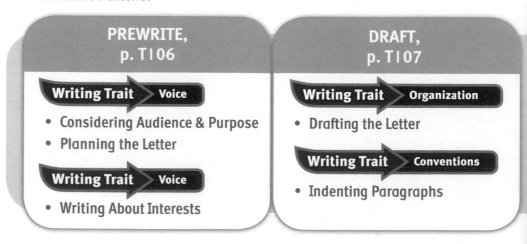

PREWRITE, p. T106	DRAFT, p. T107
Writing Trait > Voice	**Writing Trait > Organization**
• Considering Audience & Purpose	• Drafting the Letter
• Planning the Letter	**Writing Trait > Conventions**
Writing Trait > Voice	• Indenting Paragraphs
• Writing About Interests	

Use Text as a Model

DISCUSS PARTS OF A LETTER   Display *Student Edition* page 275, or have children open their books and turn to this page. Tell children that you will reread a letter that the cows wrote to the farmer. After reading the letter, use **Transparency LA23** to discuss the parts of the letter. Point out that while most letters have a heading that gives the date and often the writer's address, the cows did not include a heading in their letter. Then point out and discuss the main purposes of a heading as well as the greeting, body, closing, and signature in the letter.

- **Heading:** Gives the date and often the writer's address.
- **Greeting:** Tells to whom the writer is writing.
- **Body:** States the writer's message.
- **Closing:** Says good-bye.
- **Signature:** Tells who wrote the letter.

Encourage children to think about the five parts of a friendly letter as they write. Tell them that their letters must include each part.

Clarify Meaning Explain the words that name the five parts of a letter. For example, point out that the *heading* is at the top of the page, just as a head is at the top of a body. The *closing* is the ending of the letter, just as if you were closing a book after reading it.

Singular Possessive Nouns

The basketball _____ hoop is new. (court)

_____ soccer shoes got wet. (Vanessa)

The _____ plan is to play four-square. (girl)

At the _____ party, the children played tag. (boy)

_____ bike got a flat tire. (Liang)

The _____ slide has a tall ladder. (park)

The skateboard _____ sides are curved. (ramp)

_____ roller-skates have new wheels. (Min)

Transparency LA23

REVISE, p. T108

Writing Trait ▷ Voice

- Revising for voice

PROOFREAD, p. T108

Writing Trait ▷ Conventions

- Checking Capitalization
- Checking Abbreviations

PUBLISH, p. T109

Writing Trait ▷ Presentation

- Writing a Neat, Clean Copy

Discuss Student-Writing Model

Objective
To understand the stages of the writing process

Discuss the Model

READ PAGES 354–355   Have children open their *Student Edition* to page 354. Explain that this page shows a friendly letter that a child wrote after reading "Click, Clack, Moo" and "Jamaica Louise James." With children, read the letter aloud, and ask them what it is about. Then have children read page 355 aloud.

Point out that the first thing the writer does is to think of a person to whom she can write, and to decide why she wants to write a letter. Then she brainstorms ideas for her letter. Explain that good writers think of ideas for their letters before they write.

READ PAGES 356–357   Have children turn to pages 356–357. Explain that these pages tell what the writer does after she brainstorms ideas for her letter. Have children read the pages. Tell them that they will follow the same steps as they write a friendly letter.

Discuss how each item in the checklist is important. Tell children to use what they are learning about abbreviations as they write titles, days, and months in their letters. Explain that they will also be learning about pronouns, such as *I* and *me*, in this theme. Encourage children to keep the checklist in mind as they write and revise.

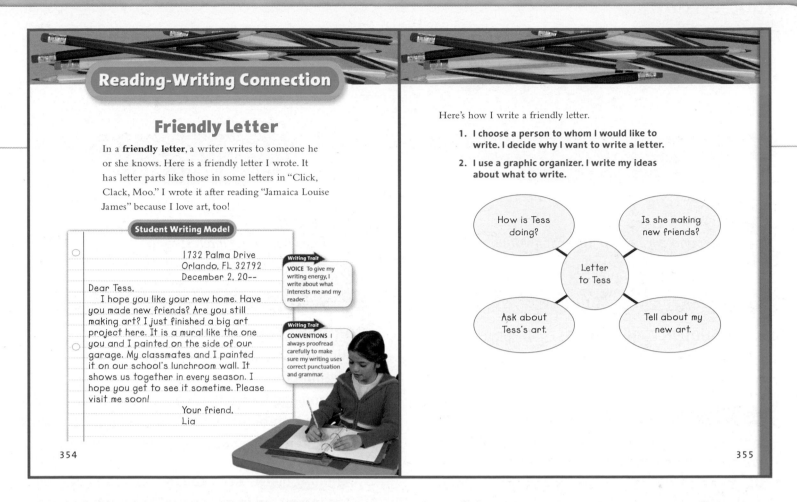

Reading-Writing Connection

Friendly Letter

In a **friendly letter**, a writer writes to someone he or she knows. Here is a friendly letter I wrote. It has letter parts like those in some letters in "Click, Clack, Moo." I wrote it after reading "Jamaica Louise James" because I love art, too!

Student Writing Model

1732 Palma Drive
Orlando, FL 32792
December 2, 20--

Dear Tess,

I hope you like your new home. Have you made new friends? Are you still making art? I just finished a big art project here. It is a mural like the one you and I painted on the side of our garage. My classmates and I painted it on our school's lunchroom wall. It shows us together in every season. I hope you get to see it sometime. Please visit me soon!

Your friend,
Lia

Writing Trait
VOICE To give my writing energy, I write about what interests me and my reader.

Writing Trait
CONVENTIONS I always proofread carefully to make sure my writing uses correct punctuation and grammar.

354

Here's how I write a friendly letter.

1. I choose a person to whom I would like to write. I decide why I want to write a letter.

2. I use a graphic organizer. I write my ideas about what to write.

- How is Tess doing?
- Is she making new friends?
- Letter to Tess
- Ask about Tess's art.
- Tell about my new art.

355

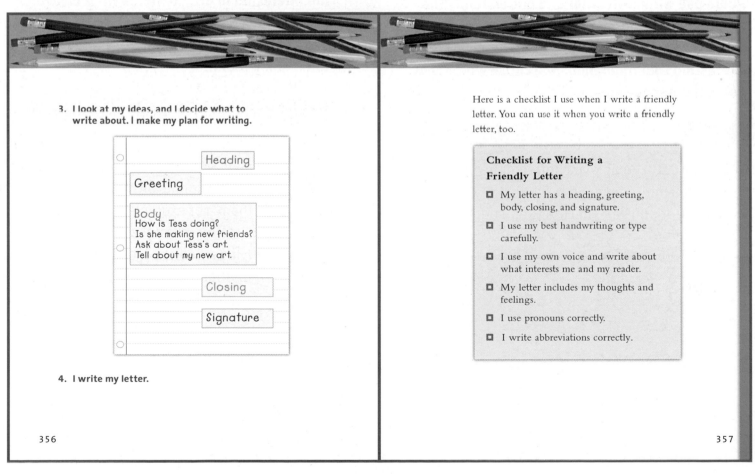

3. I look at my ideas, and I decide what to write about. I make my plan for writing.

Heading

Greeting

Body
How is Tess doing?
Is she making new friends?
Ask about Tess's art.
Tell about my new art.

Closing

Signature

4. I write my letter.

356

Here is a checklist I use when I write a friendly letter. You can use it when you write a friendly letter, too.

Checklist for Writing a Friendly Letter

- ☐ My letter has a heading, greeting, body, closing, and signature.
- ☐ I use my best handwriting or type carefully.
- ☐ I use my own voice and write about what interests me and my reader.
- ☐ My letter includes my thoughts and feelings.
- ☐ I use pronouns correctly.
- ☐ I write abbreviations correctly.

357

Prewrite

CONSIDERING AUDIENCE AND PURPOSSE

Writing Trait > Ideas

Objective
To consider audience and purpose for writing

Teach/Model

DISCUSS AUDIENCE AND PURPOSE   Display and read aloud what Jamaica Louise James says on *Student Edition* pages, 330–331. Say:

Think Aloud   **I can tell by the words the author uses, such as *cool idea*, that she thought carefully about who would read her writing—her audience. She made sure that she used words that children would use with each other and understand. She also thought about her reason, or purpose, for writing: to tell children a story about something interesting that happened. She chose words that would get her message across.**

Apply to Writing

GUIDED PRACTICE   Make a chart like the one below. Discuss with children people to whom they might like to write a letter and why. Record their suggestions on the board.

Audience	Purpose
friend	to tell about a new puppy
grandfather	to say thank you for a gift
cousin	to plan a vacation trip

PLANNING THE LETTER

Writing Trait > Voice

Objective
To write about what interests you

Teach/Model

INTRODUCE THE CONCEPT   Tell children that when writing friendly letters, they should also choose something that interests them to write about. Explain that choosing topics they care about will help their voice come through as they write their letters. Have children reread on page 354 the letter that Lia wrote.

Think Aloud   **I can see that Lia and her friend are interested in art, so that is what Lia wrote about. If I were writing a letter to a friend, I might write about a hobby I have that I think might also interest my friend.**

Apply to Writing

GUIDED PRACTICE   Have children review Lia's choice of writing ideas on page 355. Guide them to make and fill in their own graphic organizer with ideas that most interest them. For example, suggest that topics for a friendly letter might include school projects or favorite activities. Tell children to choose topics they are excited about so that their voice will come through clearly in their writing.

Draft

DRAFTING THE LETTER
Writing Trait ▸ Organization

Objective
To draft a friendly letter

Teach/Model

WRITING WITH A PLAN   Remind children that a friendly letter has five parts: heading, greeting, body, closing, and signature. Briefly review the content and purpose of each of the parts using **Transparency LA23**. Tell children that when they draft a letter, they can revise it later, but that making a plan and following it will help them write a better first draft. Have children review how Lia used a plan for writing on page 356. Remind them to think about their audience and purpose as they write their drafts.

Apply to Writing

GUIDED PRACTICE   Display **Transparency LA23** to guide children in correctly formatting their letter as they begin drafting. As they write, remind them to think about topics they chose for their letters.

Singular Possessive Nouns

The basketball _____ hoop is new. (court)

_____ soccer shoes got wet. (Vanessa)

The _____ plan is to play four-square. (girl)

At the _____ party, the children played tag. (boy)

_____ bike got a flat tire. (Liang)

The _____ slide has a tall ladder. (park)

The skateboard _____ sides are curved. (ramp)

_____ roller-skates have new wheels. (Min)

Transparency LA23

INDENTING PARAGRAPHS
Writing Trait ▸ Conventions

Objective
To write and indent paragraphs

Review

REVIEW PARAGRAPHS   Review the following points with children.

- Sentences always begin with a capital letter and end with an end mark: a period, a question mark, or an exclamation mark.
- A paragraph is about one topic and is indented.
- A paragraph is made up of a main idea and details.

Write the following sentences on the board, and have children identify the indent, initial capital letters, and the end marks.

> My first soccer game was last Saturday. I scored the first goal! My big brother really cheered for me.

Apply to Writing

GUIDED PRACTICE   Point out to children that as they write, thinking about sentence and paragraph rules can help them write better first drafts. Confer with children as they continue drafting. Remind them that they can always correct any incomplete sentences later when they revise.

E L L

Support the Writing   Help children focus their thoughts as they begin to write. Have them orally complete sentence starters such as "I am writing to ___. My letter is about ___."

Revise/Proofread

REVISING FOR VOICE

Writing Trait ▶ Voice

> **Objective**
> *To revise writing to improve the voice*

Teach/Model

GIVING WRITING ENGERGY Have children turn to *Student Edition* pages 330–331 and read aloud the text. Point out that the author used underlining, big letters, and pictures to give importance to the words. Mention that the author gave energy to the writing by including the sentence *You better believe it!* Explain that these things help readers "hear" the author's voice in the story. They help show the writer's thoughts and feelings.

Then have children think about their own letters and whether their voice shows through. If not, suggest that they change or add words to put energy into their writing. Write the following sentences and revisions on the board to review how to use editing marks to revise.

What a great party!   chocolate   the best
~~The party was fun.~~ We ate cake. We ate ice cream
                      ^   ^   ^
I ever had !
          ^

Apply to Writing

GUIDED PRACTICE Confer with children as they make revisions to improve their letters for voice. Encourage them to use the checklist on page 357 to help them revise.

CHECKING CAPITALIZATION & ABBREVIATIONS

Writing Trait ▶ Conventions

> **Objective**
> *To capitalize proper nouns and abbreviations*

Review

REVIEWING CAPITALIZATION Remind children that they have learned about nouns that name specific people and places as well as about titles, months, and the days of the week and how to abbreviate them. Guide them to recall that these kinds of nouns begin with a capital letter.

Tell children that good writers proofread their writing to be sure that each proper noun begins with a capital letter. Demonstrate for children how to mark capital letters correctly.

Dear Mr. paul

Apply to Writing

GUIDED PRACTICE Have children review their letters to make sure they used capital letters for proper nouns and abbreviations. Tell them to proofread their drafts for any other errors, mark corrections, and share their corrections with partners. Circulate as children proofread and offer guidance as needed.

Evaluate/Publish

WRITING A NEAT, CLEAN COPY

Writing Trait ▸ Presentation

Objective
To publish a friendly letter

Write the Letter

MAKING A CLEAN COPY Have children make clean copies of their revised letters. Encourage them to use their best handwriting. Then have them read their letter to a partner.

> January 3, 20--
>
> Dear Sue,
>   Our class went on a field trip. We saw big sharks in a tank. They looked really scary! Wait until you see the pictures I took.
>
>   Your friend,
>   Wendy

 TECHNOLOGY

Use a Computer Encourage children to publish their letters using a computer. Help them experiment with different print sizes and styles.

PORTFOLIO OPPORTUNITY
    Place children's letters in their portfolios as a record of their developing writing skills.

 ASSESSMENT

SELF-ASSESSMENT CHECKLIST Talk about the checklist children used to write their friendly letters. Then have them self-assess their writing in small groups and discuss with each other how they met each of the points. Discuss how each of these points supports the traits of writing and appears in rubrics.

- ☐ Includes the five parts of a friendly letter: heading, greeting, body, closing, signature.
- ☐ Uses neat handwriting or careful typing.
- ☐ Uses own voice to write about a topic of interest.
- ☐ Includes writer's thoughts and feelings.
- ☐ Writes complete sentences.
- ☐ Uses capital letters for proper nouns and abbreviations.

RUBRIC for Presentations — Scoring

	Score of 4	Score of 3	Score of 2	Score of 1
CONVENTIONS	The writer uses standard writing conventions well, with few or no errors.	The writer uses most standard writing conventions well, but makes some errors.	The writer uses some writing conventions well, but makes distracting errors.	The writer makes continuous errors with most writing conventions, making text difficult to read.
SENTENCE FLUENCY	The writing flows smoothly. The writer uses a good variety of sentences.	The writing flows generally well. The writer uses some variety in sentences.	The writing flows somewhat. The writer does not use much variety in their sentences.	The writing does not flow. The writer uses little or no variety in sentences, and some sentences are unclear.
WORD CHOICE	The writing uses vivid verbs, specific nouns, and colorful adjectives well. The writing is very detailed.	The writing may use some vivid verbs, specific nouns, and colorful adjectives. The writing is detailed.	The writing may use few interesting words. The writing is only somewhat detailed.	The writing lacks interesting word choice. The writing also lacks detail.
VOICE	The writer consistently uses creative ideas and expressions.	The writer's ideas and expressions are generally creative.	The writer's ideas and expressions are somewhat creative.	The writer lacks creativity in ideas and expressions.
ORGANIZATION	The ideas are well organized and in a logical order.	The ideas are generally well organized and in a logical order.	The ideas are somewhat organized.	The ideas are not well organized and there is no logical order.
IDEAS	The paper is clear and focused. It is engaging and includes enriching details.	The paper is generally clear and includes good supporting details, with minor focusing problems.	The paper is somewhat clear but the writer does not effectively use supporting details.	The paper has no clear central theme. The details are either missing or sketchy.

Writing on Demand

PREPARATION

Objectives
- *To write in response to a narrative prompt*
- *To organize ideas using graphic organizers*
- *To revise and proofread for grammar, punctuation, capitalization, and spelling*

Prepare to Write

DISCUSS TIMED WRITING   Tell children that in this theme, they have written or are writing a friendly letter in which they tell about an experience. Tell them that in a timed writing, they may be asked to write about an experience in 30 or 45 minutes. Explain that they will be given a narrative prompt, which will ask them to tell about an experience that they have had. Tell children that they will practice writing to this type of prompt.

ANALYZE THE PROMPT   Display **Transparency LA24**. Have children read the prompt. Explain that the topic of the prompt is a favorite playground experience.

The prompt limits the topic to a *playground experience*. Explain that an experience outside of the playground would not belong in children's writing. Point out that the prompt asks children to *think and write* about a favorite playground experience.

DISCUSS ORGANIZATION   Tell children that to do well on a timed writing such as this one, they should remember what they already learned about narrative writing.

- Tell what happened in time order.
- Use facts and details to support the main idea.
- Use your own voice to bring details to life.

DISCUSS STAYING FOCUSED   Remind children that they have 30 minutes to write, so it is important to plan their time and stay on task. Briefly review the steps of the writing process. Remind children to use prewriting graphic organizers to help keep their writing focused. Recommend that they plan to use their time as follows:

Planning Your Time	
Prewrite	5 minutes
Draft	20 minutes
Revise and Proofread	5 minutes

Explain that some children will need more or less time for each step and that you will let them know how much time is left while they are writing.

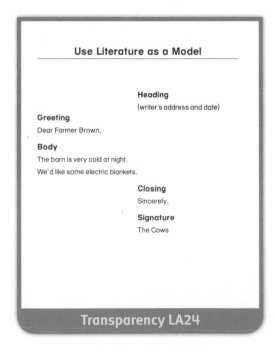

Use Literature as a Model

Heading
(writer's address and date)

Greeting
Dear Farmer Brown,

Body
The barn is very cold at night.
We'd like some electric blankets.

Closing
Sincerely,

Signature
The Cows

Transparency LA24

NARRATIVE WRITING

Write the Narrative

RESPOND TO A PROMPT Write the following prompt on the board and have children begin prewriting. Remind them when 5 minutes have passed that it is time to begin drafting. Let children know to revise and proofread when 5 minutes remain in the writing time. After 30 minutes, ask children to stop writing.

> Everyone has visited a special place.
>
> Think about a special place you have visited that you liked.
>
> Now write a story about what happened during your visit to that special place.

TIMED-WRITING STRATEGY When time runs out, ask If any children are not done. Have those children continue writing for up to 10 minutes longer, using another color of pencil. Then have them look at how much they wrote before changing pencil color, as a way to see how much was written within the time limit.

DISCUSS TIMED WRITING Ask children to discuss their experiences during the timed writing assignment. Ask questions such as the following:

- Were you able to finish on time? Why or why not?
- Does your writing follow the prompt? How?
- How did your prewriting help you write your draft?
- What changes did you make to revise?
- Did you proofread and correct errors?
- What could you do better on the next timed writing?

EVALUATE Display the rubric on page R7 and discuss what is necessary for receiving a score of 6. Provide copies of the rubric for children, and have them work independently or in pairs to evaluate their papers.

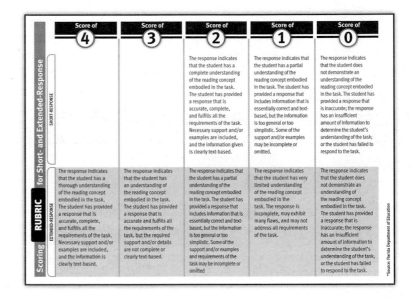

PORTFOLIO OPPORTUNITY Children may keep their writing in portfolios and compare them with earlier narrative writing to assess their own progress.

Lesson 12

WEEK AT A GLANCE

✔ Phonics
Long Vowel /ē/ey, y
Inflections -ed, -es (y to i)

✔ Spelling
very, messy, lady, happy, key, baby, money, funny, candy, sunny

✔ High-Frequency Words
board, cook, enjoy, expensive, favorite, imagine, popular, year

Reading
"At Play: Long Ago and Today" by Lynnette R. Brent NONFICTION

"A History of Games and Toys in the United States" NONFICTION

✔ Fluency
Punctuation

✔ Comprehension
 Author's Purpose
 Ask Questions

✔ Robust Vocabulary
recently, housed, official, nominate, recreation, leisurely, ramble, archaic

✔ Grammar
Singular Possessive Nouns

Writing
Form: Paragraph That Gives Information
Trait: Voice

✔ Weekly Lesson Test

 = Focus Skill   = Focus Strategy   ✔ = Tested Skill

One stop *for all* your **Digital** *needs*

Digital
CLASSROOM

 www.harcourtschool.com/storytown
To go along with your print program

FOR THE TEACHER

Prepare Professional Development

 Videos for Podcasting

Plan & Organize Online TE & Planning Resources*

Teach Transparencies

for electronic projection

Assess Online Assessment*

with Student Tracking System and Prescriptions

FOR THE STUDENT

Read  Student eBook*

 Strategic Intervention Interactive Reader

 Decodable Books

 Leveled Readers

Practice & Apply Splash into Phonics CD-ROM

 Comprehension Expedition CD-ROM

 Also available on CD-ROM

Literature Resources

STUDENT EDITION

GO online eBook **STUDENT EDITION**

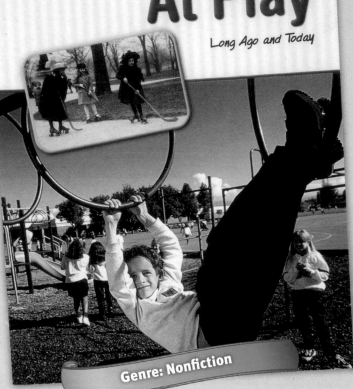

Times Change

At Play
Long Ago and Today

Genre: Nonfiction

A History of **Games and Toys** in the United States

Genre: Nonfiction

 ◀ **Audiotext** *Student Edition selections are available on Audiotext 2.*

 **Accelerated Reader** ◀ *Practice Quizzes for the Selection*

THEME CONNECTION: CHANGING TIMES
Comparing Nonfiction and a Time Line

 SOCIAL STUDIES **At Play: Long Ago and Today, pp. 364–381**

Paired Selections

SUMMARY This nonfiction selection compares how children and families in America enjoyed their leisure time long ago and today.

 SOCIAL STUDIES **A History of Games and Toys in the United States, pp. 382–383**

SUMMARY This timeline shows a history of games and toys in the United States.

Support for Differentiated Instruction

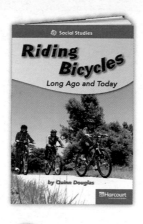

● **BELOW-LEVEL** ● **ON-LEVEL** ● **ADVANCED** **E L L**

LEVELED PRACTICE

◀ **Strategic Intervention Resource Kit,**
Lesson 12

◀ **Strategic Intervention Interactive**
Reader, Lesson 12
Strategic Intervention Interactive Reader
Online

◀ **ELL Extra Support Kit, Lesson 12**

◀ **Challenge Resource Kit, Lesson 12**

● **BELOW-LEVEL**
Extra Support Copying Masters,
pp. 86, 88–91

● **ON-LEVEL**
Practice Book, pp. 86–92

● **ADVANCED**
Challenge Copying Masters,
pp. 86, 88–91

E L L

ELL Copying Masters Lesson 12

ADDITIONAL RESOURCES

park baby

Read with a Recording

- Decodable Book 10
- Spelling Practice Book, pp. 38–40
- Grammar Practice Book, pp. 41–44
- Reading Transparencies R57–R62
- Language Arts Transparencies LA24–LA25
- Test Prep System
◀ Literacy Center Kit, Cards 56–60
- Sound/Spelling Card
◀ **Fluency Builders**
◀ **Picture Card Collection**
- Read-Aloud Anthology, pp. 46–47

✓ ASSESSMENT

✔ **Monitor Progress**

✔ **Weekly Lesson Tests, Lesson 12**
- Comprehension
- Phonics and Spelling
- Focus Skill
- Robust Vocabulary
- High-Frequency Words
- Grammar

 www.harcourtschool.com/
storytown
Online Assessment
Also available on CD-ROM—Exam View

Suggested Lesson Planner

90+ Minutes

 GO online Online TE & Planning Resources

	Day 1	**Day 2**
Step 1 Whole Group 90+ Minutes		
Daily Routines • Oral Language • Read Aloud • High-Frequency Words	**QUESTION OF THE DAY,** p. T124 *How do you play with your friends?* **READ ALOUD,** p. T125 *Transparency R57:* Native American Toys and Games **WORD WALL,** p. T125	**QUESTION OF THE DAY,** p. T136 *How would you play a game with the sun, the Earth, or the sky?* **READ ALOUD,** p. T137 *Big Book of Rhymes and Poems,* "Play" **WORD WALL,** p. T137
Word Work • phonics • Spelling • High-Frequency Words	✔ phonics, p. T126 Introduce: Long Vowel /ē/*ey, y* ✔ **SPELLING,** p. T129 Pretest: *very, messy, lady, happy, key, baby, money, funny, candy, sunny*	✔ phonics, p. T138 Review: Long Vowel /ē/*ey, y* ✔ **SPELLING,** p. T139 Word Building ✔ **HIGH-FREQUENCY WORDS** Words to Know, p. T140 Introduce: *board, cook, enjoy, expensive, favorite, imagine, popular, year*
Skills and Strategies • Reading • Fluency • Comprehension • Build Robust Vocabulary	✔ **READING/COMPREHENSION,** p. T130 Introduce: Author's Purpose **LISTENING COMPREHENSION,** p. T132 Read-Aloud: "Cardboard Box Joins Toy Hall of Fame" **FLUENCY,** p. T132 Focus: Punctuation ✔ **BUILD ROBUST VOCABULARY,** p. T133 *Words from the Read-Aloud*	✔ **READING,** p. T142 "At Play: Long Ago and Today" *Options for Reading* ✔ **COMPREHENSION,** p. T142  Introduce: Ask Questions ▲ Student Edition **RETELLING/FLUENCY,** p. T152 Punctuation ✔ **BUILD ROBUST VOCABULARY,** p. T153 *Words About the Selection*
Step 2 Small Groups 45 Minutes	**Suggestions for Differentiated Instruction (See pp. T118–T119.)**	
Step 3 Whole Group 15-20 Minutes **Language Arts** • Grammar • Writing	✔ **GRAMMAR,** p. T134 Introduce: Singular Possessive Nouns ***Daily Proofreading*** Mr Lynch threw the ball to home plate (Mr., plate.) ✏ **WRITING,** p. T135 Introduce: Paragraph That Gives Information Writing Trait: Voice **Writing Prompt** *Draw and write about a game that you played recently.*	✔ **GRAMMAR,** p. T154 Introduce: Singular Possessive Nouns ***Daily Proofreading*** vicky soccer ball is white and black (Vicky's, black.) ✏ **WRITING,** p. T155 Review: Paragraph That Gives Information Writing Trait: Voice **Writing Prompt** *Write your reflections about a popular game.*

 = Focus Skill   = Focus Strategy    = Tested Skill

- Long Vowel /ē/ey, y
- Inflections -ed, -es

Comprehension

 Focus Skill
Author's Purpose

 Focus Strategy
Ask Questions

Fluency
Punctuation

Vocabulary

HIGH-FREQUENCY: *board, cook, enjoy, expensive, favorite, imagine, popular, year*

ROBUST: *recently, housed, official, nominate, recreation, leisurely, ramble, archaic*

Day 3

QUESTION OF THE DAY, p. T156
What would you like about being a kite?

READ ALOUD, p. T157
Big Book of Rhymes and Poems, "Play"

WORD WALL, p. T157

 phonics, p. T158
Review: Long Vowel /ē/ey, y

✔ **SPELLING,** p. T159
State the Generalization

✔ **HIGH-FREQUENCY WORDS,** p. T160
Review: *board, cook, enjoy, expensive, favorite, imagine, popular, year*

FLUENCY, p. T161
Punctuation:
"At Play: Long Ago and Today"

 COMPREHENSION, p. T162
Review: Author's Purpose
Paired Selection: "A History of Games and Toys in the United States"

CONNECTIONS, p. T164

✔ **BUILD ROBUST VOCABULARY,** p. T166
Review

▲ **Student Edition**

Day 4

QUESTION OF THE DAY, p. T170
Do you like to play alone or with friends?

READ ALOUD, p. T171
Big Book of Rhymes and Poems, "Sharing the Swing"

WORD WALL, p. T171

 **phonics**, p. T172
Introduce: Inflections -ed, -es

✔ **SPELLING,** p. T175
Review Spelling Words

✔ **HIGH-FREQUENCY WORDS,** p. T176
Review: *board, cook, enjoy, expensive, favorite, imagine, popular, year*

FLUENCY, p. T175
Punctuation:
"At Play: Long Ago and Today"

 COMPREHENSION, p. T176
Review: Author's Purpose

✔ **BUILD ROBUST VOCABULARY,** p. T177
Review

▲ **Student Edition**

Day 5

QUESTION OF THE DAY, p. T180
What are some ways to have fun with friends and family members?

READ ALOUD, p. T181
Big Book of Rhymes and Poems, "Sharing the Swing"

WORD WALL, p. T181

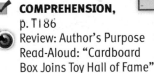 **phonics**, p. T182
Introduce: Inflections -ed, -es

✔ **SPELLING,** p. T183
Posttest

✔ **HIGH-FREQUENCY WORDS,** p. T184
Cumulative Review: *draw, picture, question, minute, bought, worry, especially, sure, imagine, favorite, year, enjoy, cook, board, popular, expensive*

FLUENCY, p. T185
Punctuation:
"At Play: Long Ago and Today"

 COMPREHENSION, p. T186
Review: Author's Purpose
Read-Aloud: "Cardboard Box Joins Toy Hall of Fame"

✔ **BUILD ROBUST VOCABULARY,** p. T187
Cumulative Review

▲ **Student Edition**

 BELOW-LEVEL  **ON-LEVEL** **ADVANCED** **E L L**

✔ **GRAMMAR,** p. T167
Review: Singular Possessive Nouns

Daily Proofreading
Leticias favorite game tag is.
(Leticia's, is tag.)

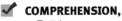 **WRITING,** p. T168
Review: Paragraph That Gives Information
Writing Trait: Voice

Writing Prompt *Write whether you think the author had fun writing "At Play: Long Ago and Today."*

✔ **GRAMMAR,** p. T178
Review: Singular Possessive Nouns

Daily Proofreading
ted ran laps at the schools track.
(Ted, school's)

WRITING, p. T179
Review: Paragraph That Gives Information
Writing Trait: Voice

Writing Prompt *Write what you like about your partner's paragraph.*

✔ **GRAMMAR,** p. T188
Review: Singular Possessive Nouns

Daily Proofreading
We picked the bushs berryes.
(bush's, berries)

WRITING, p. T189
Review: Paragraph That Gives Information
Writing Trait: Voice

Writing Prompt *Write about a game that you learned about from a classmate's paragraph.*

Suggested Small-Group Planner

45-60 Minutes

	Day 1	**Day 2**

  BELOW-LEVEL 15-20 Minutes

Day 1

Teacher-Directed
Leveled Reader:
"Having Fun: Long Ago and Today," p. T190
Before Reading

Independent
⭐ Listening/Speaking Center, p. T122
Extra Support Copying Masters, pp. 79, 81

▲ Leveled Reader

Day 2

Teacher-Directed
Student Edition:
"At Play: Long Ago and Today," p. T142

Independent
⭐ Reading Center, p. T122
Extra Support Copying Masters, pp. 89–90

▲ Student Edition

  ON-LEVEL 15-20 Minutes

Teacher-Directed
Leveled Reader:
"Riding Bicycles: Long Ago and Today," p. T191
Before Reading

Independent
⭐ Reading Center, p. T122
Practice Book, pp. 79, 81

▲ Leveled Reader

Teacher-Directed
Student Edition:
"At Play: Long Ago and Today," p. T142

Independent
⭐ Letters and Sounds Center, p. T123
Practice Book, pp. 89–90

▲ Student Edition

ADVANCED 15-20 Minutes

Teacher-Directed
Leveled Reader:
"Board Riding: Long Ago and Today," p. T192
Before Reading

Independent
⭐ Letters and Sounds Center, p. T123
Challenge Copying Masters, pp. 79, 81

▲ Leveled Reader

Teacher-Directed
Leveled Reader: "Board Riding: Long Ago and Today," p. T192
Read the Book

Independent
⭐ Word Work Center, p. T123
Challenge Copying Masters, pp. 89–90

▲ Leveled Reader

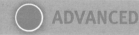

English-Language Learners

In addition to the small-group instruction above, use the ELL Extra Support Kit to promote language development.

LANGUAGE DEVELOPMENT SUPPORT
Teacher-Directed
ELL TG, Day 1
Independent
ELL Copying Masters, Lesson 12

▲ ELL Student Handbook

LANGUAGE DEVELOPMENT SUPPORT
Teacher-Directed
ELL TG, Day 2
Independent
ELL Copying Masters, Lesson 12

▲ ELL Student Handbook

Intervention

▲ Strategic Intervention Resource Kit   ▲ Strategic Intervention Interactive Reader

Strategic Intervention TG, Day 1
Strategic Intervention Practice Book, Lesson 12

Strategic Intervention TG, Day 2
Strategic Intervention Interactive Reader, Lesson 12

▲ Strategic Intervention Interactive Reader

MONITOR PROGRESS

Small-Group Instruction

Comprehension	Phonics	High-Frequency Words	Fluency	Robust Vocabulary	Language Arts Checkpoint
Focus Skill Author's Purpose pp. S16–S17	Long Vowel /ē/ey, y p. S12	*board, cook, enjoy, expensive, favorite, imagine, popular, year,* p. S13	Punctuation pp. S14–S15	*recently, housed, official, nominate, recreation, leisurely, ramble, archaic,* pp. S18–S19	**Grammar:** Singular Possessive Nouns **Writing:** Paragraph That Gives Information, pp. S20–S21

Day 3

Teacher-Directed
Leveled Reader:
"Having Fun: Long Ago and Today,"
p. T190
Read the Book

Independent
⭐ Word Work Center, p. T123

▲ Leveled Reader

Teacher-Directed
Leveled Reader:
"Riding Bicycles: Long Ago and Today," p. T191
Read the Book

Independent
⭐ Writing Center, p. T123

▲ Leveled Reader

Teacher-Directed
Leveled Reader:
"Board Riding: Long Ago and Today,"
p. T192
Think Critically

Independent
⭐ Listening/Speaking Center, p. T122

▲ Leveled Reader

LANGUAGE DEVELOPMENT SUPPORT

Teacher-Directed
Leveled Reader: "Toys: Long Ago and Today," p. T193
Before Reading; Read the Book
ELL TG, Day 3

Independent
ELL Copying Masters, Lesson 12

▲ Leveled Reader

Strategic Intervention TG, Day 3
Strategic Intervention Interactive Reader, Lesson 12
Intervention Practice Book, Lesson 12

▲ Strategic Intervention Interactive Reader

Day 4

Teacher-Directed
Leveled Reader:
"Having Fun: Long Ago and Today,"
p. T190
Reread for Fluency

Independent
⭐ Letters and Sounds Center, p. T123

▲ Leveled Reader

Teacher-Directed
Leveled Reader:
"Riding Bicycles: Long Ago and Today," p. T191
Reread for Fluency

Independent
⭐ Word Work Center, p. T123

▲ Leveled Reader

Teacher-Directed
Leveled Reader:
"Board Riding: Long Ago and Today,"
p. T192
Reread for Fluency

Independent
⭐ Writing Center, p. T123
Self-Selected Reading: Classroom Library Collection

▲ Leveled Reader

LANGUAGE DEVELOPMENT SUPPORT

Teacher-Directed
Leveled Reader: "Toys: Long Ago and Today," p. T193
Reread for Fluency
ELL TG, Day 4

Independent
ELL Copying Masters, Lesson 12

▲ Leveled Reader

Strategic Intervention TG, Day 4
Strategic Intervention Interactive Reader, Lesson 12

▲ Strategic Intervention Interactive Reader

Day 5

Teacher-Directed
Leveled Reader:
"Having Fun: Long Ago and Today,"
p. T190
Think Critically

Independent
⭐ Writing Center, p. T123
Leveled Reader: Reread for Fluency
Extra Support Copying Masters, p. 91

▲ Leveled Reader

Teacher-Directed
Leveled Reader:
"Riding Bicycles: Long Ago and Today," p. T191
Think Critically

Independent
⭐ Listening/Speaking Center, p. T122
Leveled Reader: Reread for Fluency
Practice Book, p. 91

▲ Leveled Reader

Teacher-Directed
Leveled Reader:
"Board Riding: Long Ago and Today,"
p. T192
Reread for Fluency

Independent
⭐ Reading Center, p. T122
Leveled Reader: Reread for Fluency
Self-Selected Reading: Classroom Library Collection
Challenge Copying Masters, p. 91

▲ Leveled Reader

LANGUAGE DEVELOPMENT SUPPORT

Teacher-Directed
Leveled Reader: "Toys: Long Ago and Today," p. T193
Think Critically
ELL TG, Day 5

Independent
Leveled Reader: Reread for Fluency
ELL Copying Masters, Lesson 12

▲ Leveled Reader

Strategic Intervention TG, Day 5
Strategic Intervention Interactive Reader, Lesson 12

▲ Strategic Intervention Interactive Reader

Leveled Readers & Leveled Practice
Reinforcing Skills and Strategies

LEVELED READERS SYSTEM

- Leveled Readers
- Leveled Readers, CD
- Leveled Readers Teacher Guides
  - *Comprehension*
  - *High-Frequency Words*
  - *Oral Reading Fluency Assessement*
- Response Activities
- Leveled Readers Assessment

See pages T192–T195 for lesson plans.

BELOW-LEVEL

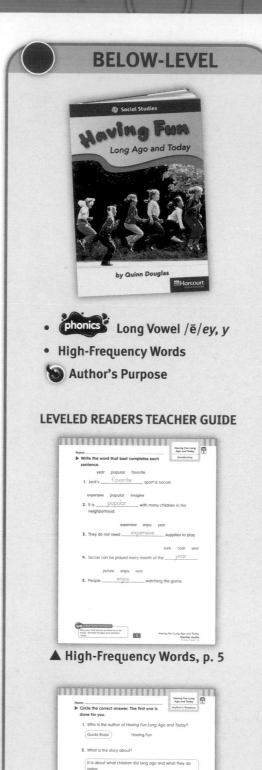

- **phonics** Long Vowel /ē/*ey, y*
- High-Frequency Words
- Author's Purpose

LEVELED READERS TEACHER GUIDE

▲ High-Frequency Words, p. 5

▲ Comprehension, p. 6

ON-LEVEL

- **phonics** Long Vowel /ē/*ey, y*
- High-Frequency Words
- Author's Purpose

LEVELED READERS TEACHER GUIDE

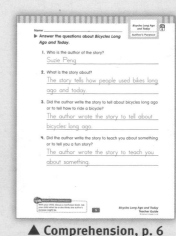

▲ High-Frequency Words, p. 5

▲ Comprehension, p. 6

www.harcourtschool.com/storytown

Go online

★ **Leveled Readers, Online Database**
Searchable by Genre, Skill, Vocabulary, Level, or Title
★ **Student Activities and Teacher Resources, online**

ADVANCED

Social Studies
Board Riding
Long Ago and Today
by Quinn Douglas

-  **phonics** Long Vowel /ē/*ey, y*
- **High-Frequency Words**
- **Author's Purpose**

LEVELED READERS TEACHER GUIDE

▲ High-Frequency Words, p. 5

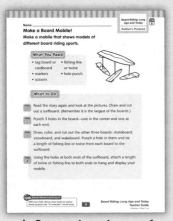

▲ Comprehension, p. 6

E L L

Social Studies
Toys
Long Ago and Today
by Dot Meharry
Illustrated by Naomi Lewis

- **Build Background**
- **Concept Vocabulary**
- **Scaffolded Language Development**

LEVELED READERS TEACHER GUIDE

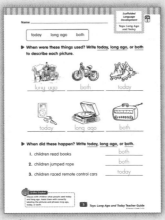

▲ Scaffolded Language Development, p. 5

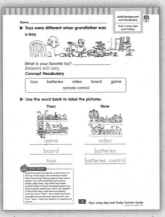

▲ Build Background, p. 6

CLASSROOM LIBRARY
for Self-Selected Reading

EASY
▲ *Clown Fish* by Carol K. Lindeen, Capstone Press, 2005. NONFICTION

AVERAGE
▲ *Buster* by Denise Fleming, Henry Holt and Company, 2003. FICTION

CHALLENGE
▲ *Ant Cities* by Arthur Dorros, HarperCollins, 1987. NONFICTION

▲ Classroom Library Books Teacher Guide, Lesson 12

Literacy Centers

15 Min. each

Management Support

While you provide direct instruction to individuals or small groups, other children can work on literacy center activities.

▲ **Literacy Center Pocket Chart**

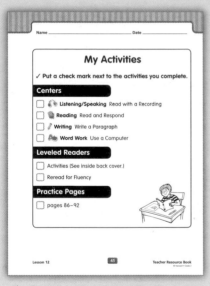

My Activities

✓ Put a check mark next to the activities you complete.

Centers
- ☐ 🎧 Listening/Speaking Read with a Recording
- ☐ 📖 Reading Read and Respond
- ☐ ✏️ Writing Write a Paragraph
- ☐ 🔤 Word Work Use a Computer

Leveled Readers
- ☐ Activities (See inside back cover.)
- ☐ Reread for Fluency

Practice Pages
- ☐ pages 86–92

Lesson 12   45   Teacher Resource Book

▲ **Teacher Resource Book, p. 45**

Homework for the Week

TEACHER RESOURCE BOOK, PAGE 45
The *Homework Copying Master* provides activities to complete for each day of the week.

Read with a Recording

Objective
To develop fluency by listening to familiar selections and reading them aloud

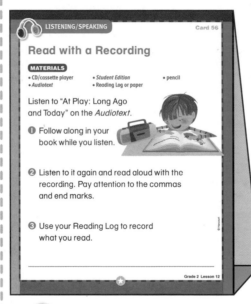

LISTENING/SPEAKING — Card 56

Read with a Recording

MATERIALS
- CD/cassette player
- Audiotext
- Student Edition
- Reading Log or paper
- pencil

Listen to "At Play: Long Ago and Today" on the *Audiotext*.

❶ Follow along in your book while you listen.

❷ Listen to it again and read aloud with the recording. Pay attention to the commas and end marks.

❸ Use your Reading Log to record what you read.

Grade 2 Lesson 12

⭐ **Literacy Center Kit • Card 56**

READING

Read and Respond

Objective
To develop comprehension by reading nonfiction selections and responding to them

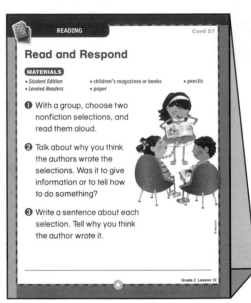

READING — Card 57

Read and Respond

MATERIALS
- Student Edition
- Leveled Readers
- children's magazines or books
- paper
- pencils

❶ With a group, choose two nonfiction selections, and read them aloud.

❷ Talk about why you think the authors wrote the selections. Was it to give information or to tell how to do something?

❸ Write a sentence about each selection. Tell why you think the author wrote it.

Grade 2 Lesson 12

⭐ **Literacy Center Kit • Card 57**

WRITING

Write a Paragraph

Objective
To practice writing a paragraph that gives information

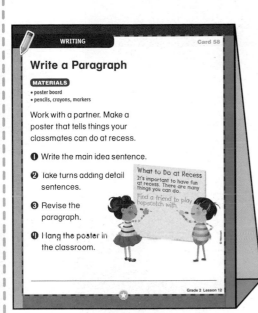

Literacy Center Kit • Card 58

WRITING
Card 58

Write a Paragraph

MATERIALS
• poster board
• pencils, crayons, markers

Work with a partner. Make a poster that tells things your classmates can do at recess.

❶ Write the main idea sentence.

❷ Take turns adding detail sentences.

❸ Revise the paragraph.

❹ Hang the poster in the classroom.

Grade 2 Lesson 12

WORD WORK

Use a Computer

Objective
To practice spelling and writing high-frequency words

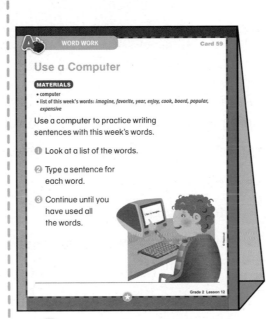

Literacy Center Kit • Card 59

WORD WORK
Card 59

Use a Computer

MATERIALS
• computer
• list of this week's words: *imagine, favorite, year, enjoy, cook, board, popular, expensive*

Use a computer to practice writing sentences with this week's words.

❶ Look at a list of the words.

❷ Type a sentence for each word.

❸ Continue until you have used all the words.

Grade 2 Lesson 12

LETTERS AND SOUNDS

Complete Words

Objective
To use common spelling patterns to read and write words

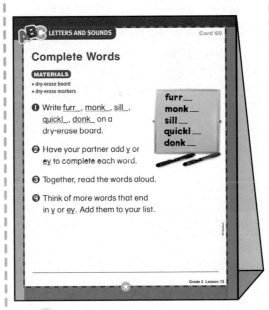

Literacy Center Kit • Card 60

LETTERS AND SOUNDS
Card 60

Complete Words

MATERIALS
• dry-erase board
• dry-erase markers

❶ Write furr__, monk__, sill__, quickl__, donk__ on a dry-erase board.

furr__
monk__
sill__
quickl__
donk__

❷ Have your partner add y or ey to complete each word.

❸ Together, read the words aloud.

❹ Think of more words that end in y or ey. Add them to your list.

Grade 2 Lesson 12

What to Do at Recess

It's important to have fun at recess. There are many things you can do.

Find a friend to play hopscotch with.

Join other kids in a kickball game.

Sit on a swing and enjoy the sunshine

I like to imagine that I can fly.

I help my mom cook dinner each night.

furry
monkey
silly
quickly
donkey

DAILY ROUTINES

Day at a Glance

Day 1

 phonics and Spelling
- Introduce: Long Vowel /ē/ey, y
- Pretest

Reading/ Comprehension

 Review: Author's Purpose, *Student Edition,* pp. 360–361
- *Read-Aloud Anthology:* "Cardboard Box Joins Toy Hall of Fame"

Fluency
- Model Oral Fluency

Robust Vocabulary

Words from the Read-Aloud
- Introduce: *recently, housed, official, nominate*

Grammar
- Introduce: Singular Possessive Nouns

Writing
- Paragraph That Gives Information

Warm-Up Routines

Oral Language

Objective *To listen attentively and respond appropriately to oral communication*

Question of the Day

How do you play with your friends?

Ask children to brainstorm ways in which they play with friends. Group their ideas in a web. Use the following prompts.

- **Where do you play with your friends?**

- **What games do you play?**

- **When do you play?**

- **What do you play in the summer? In the winter?**

Have children complete the following sentence to describe how they play.

I play with my friends _____.

Read Aloud

Objective *To listen for information*

TRANSPARENCY Read aloud the passage "Native American Toys and Games" on **Transparency R57**. Use the following steps:

- **Set a purpose for listening.** Help children set a purpose for listening, such as to listen for information.

- **Model using punctuation to read accurately.** Read the passage aloud. Remind children that good readers pay attention to punctuation marks to help them read in a way that sounds like natural speech.

- **Discuss the passage.** Ask: **Why do you think the author wrote the passage?** (to give information about Native American toys and games)

Author's Purpose

Native American Toys and Games

Long ago, Native American children had just as much fun playing as children do today. They didn't buy toys at stores. Instead, they made toys from things found in nature.

Children who lived near forests formed dolls out of materials from trees. Some used pine needles to make dolls with pine "skirts." They made their dolls dance on a thin piece of wood.

Hopi children who lived in what is now Arizona played a board game on a flat stone. They tried to capture each other's animals by jumping over the pieces. It sounds a lot like checkers!

Grade 2, Lesson 12   R57   Comprehension

Transparency R57

Word Wall

Objective *To read high-frequency words*

REVIEW HIGH-FREQUENCY WORDS Review the following words: *draw, picture, question, minute* and any other high-frequency words from the previous lesson. Point to a card on the Word Wall, and have children take turns reading the word aloud. Continue until all children have had a chance to participate at least once.

draw   picture   question   minute

Long Vowel /ē/ ey, y

 phonics *and Spelling*

Objectives

- *To recognize and generate the /ē/ sound*
- *To read words with /ē/ey, y and other known letter-sounds*
- *To use /ē/ey, y and other known letter-sounds to spell words*

Skill Trace

Tested Long Vowel /ē/ *ey, y*

Introduce	Grade 1
Reintroduce	**T126–T129**
Reteach	S12
Review	T138–T139, T158–T159, T392
Test	Theme 3
Maintain	Theme 4, T168

Connect Letters to Sounds

WARM UP WITH PHONEMIC AWARENESS Say the words *money* and *candy*. Have children say the words. Say: **The words *money* and *candy* end with the /ē/ sound.** Repeat with the words *honey* and *silly*. Say: **The words *honey* and *silly* also end with the /ē/ sound.** Then have children say /ē/ several times.

Routine Card 1 **CONNECT LETTERS AND SOUNDS** Display the *Sound/Spelling Card* for long e. Point to the letters *ey* and review their letter/sound correspondence. Say: **The letters *ey* can stand for the /ē/ sound, the sound at the end of *money*.** Touch the letters several times, and have children say /ē/ each time. Repeat with /ē/y, using the word *candy*.

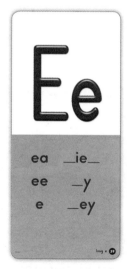

▲ **Sound/Spelling Card**

5-DAY PHONICS

DAY 1	Reintroduce /ē/ey, y
DAY 2	Word Building with /ē/ey, y
DAY 3	Word Building with /ē/ey, y
DAY 4	Inflections -ed, -es (y to i); Review /ē/ey, y
DAY 5	Inflections -ed, -es (y to i); Review /ē/ey, y

Work with Patterns

REINFORCE /ē/ey Write the following words on the board. Point out that each word ends with the letters *ey*. Read each word, and then have children read it with you.

hockey	alley	money
journey	honey	chimney
valley	monkey	trolley

REINFORCE /ē/y Repeat the procedure with the following words that end with the letter *y*.

candy	silly	lazy
lucky	study	foggy
funny	baby	tiny
rocky	ugly	penny

BELOW-LEVEL

Blend Words If children have difficulty reading a word, stop and blend the sounds. Slide your hand under each letter as you say the corresponding sound. Then read the word naturally.

valley
→

E L L

Support Word Meaning Use *Picture Cards* and other photos to support word meaning. For example, as children read *baby*, display the card for *baby*.

baby

▲ Picture Card 7

Long Vowel /ē/ey, y
phonics *and Spelling*

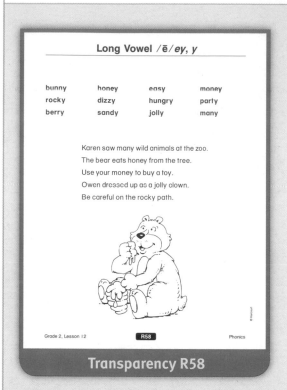

Long Vowel /ē/ ey, y

bunny	honey	easy	money
rocky	dizzy	hungry	party
berry	sandy	jolly	many

Karen saw many wild animals at the zoo.
The bear eats honey from the tree.
Use your money to buy a toy.
Owen dressed up as a jolly clown.
Be careful on the rocky path.

Grade 2, Lesson 12   R58   Phonics

Transparency R58

Reading Words

GUIDED PRACTICE Display **Transparency R58** or write the words and sentences on the board. Point to the word *bunny*. Read the word, and then have children read it with you.

INDEPENDENT PRACTICE Point to the remaining words in the top portion and have children read them. Then have children read aloud the sentences and identify words with /ē/*ey, y*.

Decodable Books

Additional Decoding Practice

- **Phonics**
  Long Vowel /ē/*ey, y*
- **Decodable Words**
- **High-Frequency Words**
  See the lists in *Decodable Book 10*.
  See also *Decodable Books*, online (Take-Home Version).

▲ Decodable Book 10 "Silly Donkey and His Missing Key"

BELOW-LEVEL | ON-LEVEL | ADVANCED

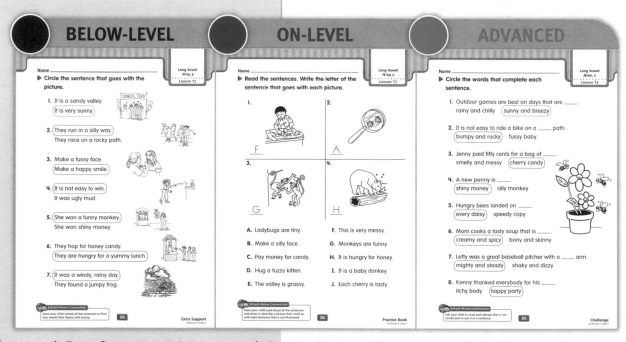

▲ Extra Support, p. 86   ▲ Practice Book, p. 86   ▲ Challenge, p. 86

ELL

- Group children according to academic levels, and assign one of the pages on the left.
- Clarify any unfamiliar concepts as necessary. See *ELL Teacher Guide* Lesson 12 for support in scaffolding instruction.

5-DAY SPELLING
DAY 1 Pretest
DAY 2 Word Building
DAY 3 State the Generalization
DAY 4 Review
DAY 5 Posttest

Introduce Spelling Words

PRETEST   Say the first word and read the dictation sentence. Repeat the word as children write it. Write the word on the board and tell children to check their spelling. Have them circle the word if they spelled it correctly or write it correctly if they did not. Repeat for words 2–10.

Words with /ē/*ey, y*

1. very	The rainstorm got us **very** wet.
2. messy	The **messy** girl spilled her food.
3. lady	The **lady** danced with the prince at the ball.
4. happy	The **happy** puppy ran around the room.
5. key	Use the **key** to open the lock.
6. baby	The **baby** likes to play with blocks.
7. money	Do you save your **money** in a piggy bank?
8. funny	Julian giggled at the **funny** joke.
9. candy	Frank made fudge and other **candy**.
10. sunny	Do you play outside on **sunny** days?

ADVANCED

Challenge Words   Use the challenge words in these dictation sentences.

11. chimney	The smoke rose out of the **chimney**.
12. nobody	**Nobody** makes mushroom ice cream.
13. breezy	The flags waved in the **breezy** weather.
14. twenty	We counted **twenty** grapes on the plate.
15. keyhole	The castle door has a large **keyhole**.

Spelling Words

1.	**very***	6.	**baby**
2.	**messy**	7.	**money**
3.	**lady**	8.	**funny**
4.	**happy**	9.	**candy**
5.	**key**	10.	**sunny**

Challenge Words

11.	**chimney**	14.	**twenty**
12.	**nobody**	15.	**keyhole**
13.	**breezy**		

* Word from "At Play: Long Ago and Today"

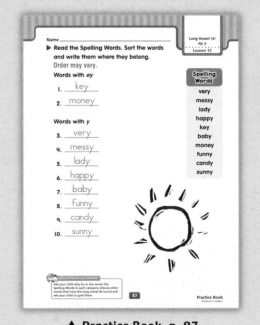

▲ Practice Book, p. 87

Lesson 12   **T129**

Author's Purpose
Comprehension

Objective

- *To identify an author's purpose for writing*

Daily Comprehension
 Author's Purpose

DAY 1:	Introduce Author's Purpose *Student Edition*
DAY 2:	Review Author's Purpose *Student Edition*
DAY 3:	Review Author's Purpose *Student Edition*
DAY 4:	Review Author's Purpose *Transparency*
DAY 5:	Review Author's Purpose *Read-Aloud Anthology*

✓ MONITOR PROGRESS

Author's Purpose

IF children have difficulty identifying the author's purpose,	**THEN** have them look at a how-to article or an informational book and help them figure out the author's purpose.

Small-Group Instruction, pp. S16–S17:

- ● **BELOW-LEVEL:** Reteach
- ● **ON-LEVEL:** Reinforce
- ● **ADVANCED:** Extend

Teach/Model

REVIEW AUTHOR'S PURPOSE Have children read *Student Edition* page 360. Model how to determine an author's purpose for writing.

Think Aloud As I read "Bicycles," I see that the author is telling me about the parts of a bicycle. That helps me know that the author's purpose is to give information. Understanding the author's purpose helps me read more carefully. As I continue to read, I will think about what I already know about bicycles and what I may learn from this passage.

Practice/Apply

GUIDED PRACTICE Display several nonfiction books that children have read. Guide them to identify the author's purpose for writing each one. Then read "Car Games" on page 361 with children. Discuss what the passage is about. Ask: **What kind of writing is this?** (how-to paragraph)

Try This! **INDEPENDENT PRACTICE** Ask children to determine the author's purpose for writing the paragraph. (Possible responses: to give information; to tell how to play a game) Ask volunteers to explain how they determined the author's purpose.

ADVANCED

Categorize Books Provide children with nonfiction books that give information or tell how to do something. Have them work with partners to stack the books in one of the two categories, according to the author's purpose. Invite children to explain their decisions.

Focus Skill

 Author's Purpose

Remember that authors write for different purposes. Authors write to entertain, to send messages, to give opinions, and to tell about their feelings. Sometimes an author writes to give facts about the world. An author may also write to tell how to do something.

Kind of Writing	Author's Purpose
research report	to give information
how-to paragraph	to tell how to do something

Bicycles

by Sonya K.

Bicycles have two wheels with

rubber tires. They have a handlebar for

steering, a seat, and two pedals.

360

Read the paragraph. What kind of writing is it?

Car Games

Games can help pass the time on a long car ride. "Car ABC" is easy and fun to play. Start with the letter *a*. The first person to see something that starts with *a* gets a point. Repeat until you have named an object for each letter of the alphabet. Some letters might be hard to find things for. Be creative!

Kind of Writing	Author's Purpose

GO online www.harcourtschool.com/storytown

Try This!

Look back at the paragraph. What is the author's purpose for writing it?

361

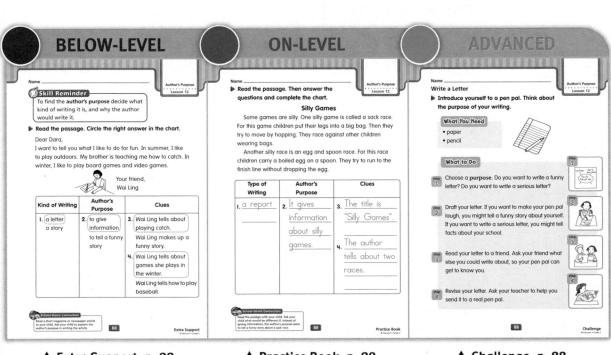

BELOW-LEVEL

Author's Purpose
Lesson 12

Skill Reminder
To find the **author's purpose** decide what kind of writing it is, and why the author would write it.

▶ Read the passage. Circle the right answer in the chart.

Dear Dara,
I want to tell you what I like to do for fun. In summer, I like to play outdoors. My brother is teaching me how to catch. In winter, I like to play board games and video games.

Your friend,
Wai Ling

Kind of Writing	Author's Purpose	Clues
1. a letter a story	**2.** to give information to tell a funny story	**3.** Wai Ling tells about playing catch. Wai Ling makes up a funny story. **4.** Wai Ling tells about games she plays in the winter. Wai Ling tells how to play baseball.

School-Home Connection
Read a short magazine or newspaper article to your child. Ask your child to explain the author's purpose in writing the article.

88

Extra Support

▲ **Extra Support, p. 88**

ON-LEVEL

Author's Purpose
Lesson 12

▶ Read the passage. Then answer the questions and complete the chart.

Silly Games

Some games are silly. One silly game is called a sack race. For this game children put their legs into a big bag. Then they try to move by hopping. They race against other children wearing bags.

Another silly race is an egg and spoon race. For this race children carry a boiled egg on a spoon. They try to run to the finish line without dropping the egg.

Type of Writing	Author's Purpose	Clues
1. a report	2. It gives information about silly games.	3. The title is "Silly Games". 4. The author tells about two races.

School-Home Connection
Read the passage with your child. Ask your child what would be different if, instead of giving information, the author's purpose were to tell a funny story about a sack race.

88

Practice Book

▲ **Practice Book, p. 88**

ADVANCED

Author's Purpose
Lesson 12

Write a Letter

▶ Introduce yourself to a pen pal. Think about the purpose of your writing.

What You Need
• paper
• pencil

What to Do

step 1 Choose a **purpose**. Do you want to write a funny letter? Do you want to write a serious letter?

step 2 Draft your letter. If you want to make your pen pal laugh, you might tell a funny story about yourself. If you want to write a serious letter, you might tell facts about your school.

step 3 Read your letter to a friend. Ask your friend what else you could write about, so your pen pal can get to know you.

step 4 Revise your letter. Ask your teacher to help you send it to a real pen pal.

88

Challenge

▲ **Challenge, p. 88**

ELL

• Group children according to academic levels, and assign one of the pages on the left.

• Clarify any unfamiliar concepts as necessary. See *ELL Teacher Guide* Lesson 12 for support in scaffolding instruction.

Listening Comprehension
Read Aloud

Objectives

- *To set a purpose for listening*
- *To identify the author's purpose for writing*

Build Fluency

Focus: Punctuation   Before you read, remind children that good readers pay attention to punctuation. They pause when they come to a comma, a period, a question mark, or an exclamation point.

▲ Read-Aloud Anthology, "Cardboard Box Joins Toy Hall of Fame," p. 46

Before Reading

CONNECT TO PRIOR KNOWLEDGE   Tell children that they will listen to a news story called "Cardboard Box Joins Toy Hall of Fame." Ask children to suggest some reasons that a cardboard box might be fun to play with.

Routine Card 2 **GENRE STUDY: NONFICTION**
Tell children that a news story is nonfiction. Remind them of the characteristics of this genre:

> **Think Aloud**   **A news story tells about events that really happened. It gives facts about the event, such as when and where the event happened and who was involved.**

After Reading

RESPOND   Have children summarize the selection by recalling what they learned from this news story. Ask: **Do you think the cardboard box should be in the Toy Hall of Fame? Tell why you think so.** (Responses will vary.)

REVIEW AUTHOR'S PURPOSE   Have children identify the author's purpose for writing "Cardboard Box Joins Toy Hall of Fame." (to give information)

E L L

Idioms   Explain that *natural fit* means that the cardboard box is similar to other toys in the museum that children use with their imagination.

Build Robust Vocabulary

Words from the Read-Aloud

Teach/Model

Routine Card 3

INTRODUCE ROBUST VOCABULARY   Use *Routine Card 3* to introduce the words.

> ❶ Put the word in **selection context**.
> ❷ Display Transparency R62 and read the word and the **Student-Friendly Explanation**.
> ❸ Have children **say the word** with you.
> ❹ Use the word in other contexts, and have children **interact with the word's meaning**.
> ❺ Remove the transparency. Say the Student-Friendly Explanation again, and ask children to **name the word** that goes with it.

❶ **Selection Context:** The cardboard box was **recently** added to a list of great toys.

❹ **Interact with Word Meaning:** I finished a book recently. Would you recently have learned to fly a plane or learned to ride a bike?

❶ **Selection Context:** The toy collection is **housed** at a museum.

❹ **Interact with Word Meaning:** Paintings are housed at an art museum. What is housed at a zoo, a tiger or a horse?

❶ **Selection Context:** The museum **official** thinks the cardboard box is a great toy.

❹ **Interact with Word Meaning:** Who do you think is a school official, a crossing guard or the principal?

❶ **Selection Context:** People can **nominate** their favorite toys online.

❹ **Interact with Word Meaning:** Who would you nominate for class president, your best friend or a teacher?

Practice/Apply

GUIDED PRACTICE   Ask children to use the vocabulary to tell what they think an *official* at a museum or a hospital might do.

Objective

- *To develop robust vocabulary through discussing a literature selection*

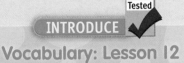

INTRODUCE ✓ | Tested

Vocabulary: Lesson 12

recently	**official**
housed	**nominate**

▼ **Student-Friendly Explanations**

Student-Friendly Explanations

recently	If something happened not long ago, it happened recently.
housed	If something is placed or lives somewhere, it is housed there.
official	If someone holds a position of authority in an organization, the person is called an official.
nominate	When you suggest that someone should get an office, job, or honor, you nominate the person.
recreation	When you do something fun and relaxing, it is recreation for you.
leisurely	If you do something in a leisurely way, you are not in a hurry.
ramble	When you ramble, you wander around.
archaic	If something is archaic, it is old and not used anymore.

Grade 2, Theme 3   R62   Vocabulary

Transparency R62

Grammar
Singular Possessive Nouns

5-DAY GRAMMAR	
DAY 1	Possessive Nouns
DAY 2	Identifying Singular Possessive Nouns
DAY 3	Sentence Formation with Possessive Nouns
DAY 4	Apply to Writing
DAY 5	Weekly Review

Objectives

- *To recognize that possessive nouns show ownership*
- *To speak in complete, coherent sentences*

Daily Proofreading

Mr Lynch threw the ball to home plate

(Mr., plate.)

TECHNOLOGY

 www.harcourtschool.com/ storytown

Grammar Glossary

Singular Possessive Nouns

The basketball _____ hoop is new. (court)

_____ soccer shoes got wet. (Vanessa)

The _____ plan is to play four-square. (girl)

At the _____ party, the children played tag. (boy)

_____ bike got a flat tire. (Liang)

The _____ slide has a tall ladder. (park)

The skateboard _____ sides are curved. (ramp)

_____ roller-skates have new wheels. (Min)

Grade 2, Lesson 12   LA25   Grammar

Transparency LA25

Teach/Model

INTRODUCE POSSESSIVE NOUNS   Explain that a **possessive noun** shows ownership. It tells *who or what something belongs to*. An apostrophe plus *s* (*'s*) is used to form a possessive noun. Tell children that they use possessive nouns all the time when they talk with others.

Write on the board this phrase based on "Cardboard Box Joins Toy Hall of Fame":

Toy Hall of Fame's star-studded lineup

Read aloud the phrase. Then explain how the phrase *Toy Hall of Fame's* shows what the star-studded lineup belongs to. Point out that the apostrophe plus *s* (*'s*) shows ownership by one person or thing. Write these single possessive nouns as examples:

Maggie's basketball   the bike's handlebars

Guided Practice

FORM POSSESSIVES   Display **Transparency LA25**. Explain to children that they will help you form the possessive of each word in parentheses. Read the first sentence and work with children to identify the possessive as *court's*. Complete the next three items together, eliciting responses from volunteers.

Practice/Apply

WRITE SENTENCES   Have children rewrite the last four items on **Transparency LA25** so that the words in parentheses are possessives. Have them read aloud their sentences to a partner.

5-DAY WRITING	
DAY 1	Introduce
DAY 2	Prewrite
DAY 3	Draft
DAY 4	Revise
DAY 5	Revise

Writing
Paragraph That Gives Information

Teach/Model

INTRODUCE "PARAGRAPH THAT GIVES INFORMATION"
Display **Transparency LA26** or write the paragraph on the
board. Explain that this paragraph was written by a child
to give information about a game. Read aloud the paragraph, and
discuss how it is organized. Work together to develop a list of characteristics. Display it for children to refer to on Days 3–5.

Paragraph That Gives Information

- The paragraph gives information about a real topic.

- The first sentence tells the main idea.

- The other sentences give more information about the main idea.

- Some of the sentences may tell what to do in the correct order, or sequence.

 VOICE Discuss with children how they can tell that the
WRITING TRAIT writer is interested in kickball. Explain that when writers
show they like their topic, readers are more interested, too.

Guided Practice

MODEL WRITING Model writing a main-idea sentence, such as,
"Jacks is a fun game to play." Have children use this sentence frame
to share their own main-idea sentences: _____ *is fun to play.*

Practice/Apply

MAKE WORD WEBS Have children make word webs with
"Games" in the center. In the outer circles, they can write
words about games. Tell them to share their word webs with a
partner and save them for use on Days 2–5.

Objectives

- *To read and respond to a paragraph that gives information and
to use the paragraph as a model
for writing*

- *To develop ideas and topics for
writing*

Writing Prompt

Illustrate and Write Have
children draw and write about a
game they played recently, using this
sentence starter: My neighborhood's
favorite game to play is_____.
Point out how the 's is used in
neighborhood's.

**Student Model: Paragraph That
Gives Information**

Kickball

Kickball is easy and fun to play. The teams take
turns being at bat. The pitcher rolls the ball and the
person at bat kicks it. Then the kicker tries to run to first
base without getting hit out. A run is scored when a
kicker goes around the bases to home plate.

Grade 2, Lesson 12 | **LA26** | Writing

Transparency LA26

Day at a Glance

Day 2

phonics and Spelling
- Review: Long Vowel /ē/*ey, y*
- Build Words

High-Frequency Words
- Introduce: *imagine*, *favorite*, *year*, *enjoy*, *cook*, *board*, *popular*, *expensive*

Comprehension

Focus Strategy Ask Questions

Focus Skill Author's Purpose

Reading
- "At Play: Long Ago and Today," *Student Edition*, pp. 364–381

Read!

Fluency
- Punctuation

Robust Vocabulary
Words About the Selection
- Introduce: *recreation*, *leisurely*, *ramble*, *archaic*

Grammar
- Review: Singular Possessive Nouns

Writing 🖉
- Paragraph That Gives Information

Warm-Up Routines

 Oral Language

Objectives *To listen attentively and respond appropriately to oral communication*

> ## Question of the Day
> How would you play a game with the sun, the Earth, or the sky?

Ask children to imagine they are friends with the sun, the Earth, and the sky. Have them plan ways to have fun playing with each one. Use the following prompts.

- **What do you think the sun would like to do?**
- **Do you think the sky would like to play with the sun?**
- **What could the Earth do for fun? What couldn't it do?**

Then have children complete the following sentence frame to describe their playtime.

If I played with _____, we would _____.

Read Aloud

Objective *To listen for a purpose*

BIG BOOK OF RHYMES AND POEMS
Display the poem "Play" on page 23 and
read aloud the title. Ask children to listen
for ways the sun, the Earth, and the sky like
to play. Then track the print as you read the
poem aloud, asking children to chime in on
the repeated phrase "Come play with me."
Invite children to tell what they imagined as
they listened to the poem.

▲ Big Book of Rhymes
and Poems, p. 23

Word Wall

Objective *To read high-frequency words*

REVIEW HIGH-FREQUENCY WORDS   Review the words *bought*, *worry*,
especially, and *sure*, as well as other previously learned high-frequency
words. Point to each word on the Word Wall, and have children read it, spell
it, and then read it again. Then point to words at random and have children
read them.

bought

worry

especially

sure

Long Vowel /ē/ ey, y

 phonics *and Spelling*

Objectives

- *To blend sounds into words*
- *To spell words that include long vowel /ē/ey, y*

Skill Trace

 Tested **Long Vowel /ē/ ey, y**

Introduce	Grade 1
Reintroduce	T126–T129
Reteach	S12
Review	**T138–T139, T158–T159, T392**
Test	Theme 3
Maintain	Theme 4, T168

Spelling Words

1.	**very***	6.	**baby**
2.	**messy**	7.	**money**
3.	**lady**	8.	**funny**
4.	**happy**	9.	**candy**
5.	**key**	10.	**sunny**

Challenge Words

11.	**chimney**	14.	**twenty**
12.	**nobody**	15.	**keyhole**
13.	**breezy**		

* Word from "At Play: Long Ago and Today"

Word Building

READ A SPELLING WORD   Write the word *funny* on the board. Ask children to identify the letter that stands for the /ē/ sound. (*y*) Then read the word, and have children repeat.

BUILD SPELLING WORDS   Ask children which letter you should change to make *funny* become *sunny*. (Change *f* to *s*.) Write the word *sunny* on the board, and have children read it. Continue building spelling words in this manner. Say:

- **Which letters do I have to change to make the word *money*?** (Change *su* to *mo* and the second *n* to *e*.)

- **Which letters do I have to change to make the word *key*?** (Change *mon* to *k*.)

- **Which letters do I have to change to make the word *very*?** (Change *k* to *v* and add *r* before *y*.)

- **Which letters do I have to change to make the word *messy*?** (Change *v* to *m* and *r* to *ss*.)

Continue building the remaining spelling words in this manner.

> funny
> sunny
> money
> key
> very
> messy

BELOW-LEVEL

Build Spelling Words   Write *-ey* and *-y* as headings on the board. Under *-ey*, write ___*ey*. Ask children to help you write the word *key*. Guide them to add the letter *k*. Repeat for other spelling words, providing the correct number of spaces for the letters of each word.

ADVANCED

Word Grids   Provide children with grid paper. Model writing *money* across and *funny* down so that the two words share the letter *n*. Challenge children to see how many spelling words they can link.

5-DAY PHONICS/SPELLING

DAY 1	Pretest
DAY 2	Word Building
DAY 3	State the Generalization
DAY 4	Review
DAY 5	Posttest

Read Words in Context

APPLY PHONICS Write the following sentences on the board or on chart paper. Have children read each sentence silently. Then track the print as children read the sentence aloud.

> Jaime counted the <u>money</u> in his piggy bank.
> Tomato plants grow in <u>sunny</u> weather.
> The <u>baby</u> crawls across the floor.
> Use the <u>key</u> to unlock the bike.
> The <u>lady</u> rode to the castle.

WRITE Dictate several spelling words. Have children write the words in their notebook or on a dry-erase board.

phonics Resources

Phonics Practice Book, pp. 73–78

✓ MONITOR PROGRESS

Long Vowel /ē/ey, y

| **IF** children have difficulty building and reading words with /ē/ey, y, | **THEN** help them blend and read the words *money*, *sunny*, *baby*, and *key*. |

Small-Group Instruction, p. S12:

● **BELOW-LEVEL:** Reteach
● **ON-LEVEL:** Reinforce
● **ADVANCED:** Extend

BELOW-LEVEL ON-LEVEL ADVANCED

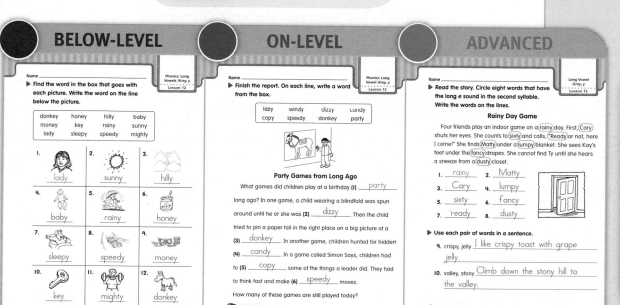

▲ Extra Support, p. 89   ▲ Practice Book, p. 89   ▲ Challenge, p. 89

ELL

- Group children according to academic levels, and assign one of the pages on the left.

- Clarify any unfamiliar concepts as necessary. See *ELL Teacher Guide* Lesson 12 for support in scaffolding instruction.

High-Frequency Words
Words to Know

Objective
- *To read high-frequency words*

High-Frequency Words

board	favorite
cook	imagine
enjoy	popular
expensive	year

Review High-Frequency Words
Hold up *Picture Card* 89 and say, **I enjoy the park.** Have children practice using the word *enjoy* in this sentence frame with other *Picture Cards*.

See *ELL Teacher Guide* Lesson 12 for support in scaffolding instruction.

park

▲ **Picture Card 89**

Teach/Model

Routine Card 5 **INTRODUCE WORDS**   Write the words *imagine*, *favorite*, *year*, *enjoy*, *cook*, *board*, *popular*, and *expensive* on the board.

- Point to and read *imagine*. Repeat it, having children say it with you.
- Say: **Can you *imagine* living in a world without cars?**
- Point to each letter as you spell the word. Have children spell the word with you.
- Have children reread the word.

Repeat for the remaining words. Use the following sentences:

- **Apple pie is Sonja's *favorite* dessert.**
- **In what *year* were you born?**
- **The children *enjoy* playing hopscotch.**
- **Can you *cook* rice for dinner?**
- **The checkers *board* has red and black squares.**
- **Kickball is the most *popular* game at recess.**
- **A football is more *expensive* than a marble.**

Guided Practice

STUDENT EDITION PAGES 362–363   Have children turn to *Student Edition* pages 362 and 363. Ask them to point to and read aloud each of the highlighted words. Talk about the games and toys that are pictured. Then ask children to read aloud the passage.

Words to Know

High-Frequency Words

Special Memories

imagine
favorite
board
enjoy
year
cook
popular
expensive

My grandparents like to tell me stories about when they were my age. Grandma asks me to **imagine** watching TV in black and white. Her **favorite** shows were funny stories about families.

Grandpa laughs when he tells me about the **board** games he played as a boy. He and Grandma still **enjoy** games with pieces that players move around the board.

Grandma says that her favorite toy was a little wooden stove. Her father made it the **year** she turned five. She and her brother would pretend to **cook** tasty meals on it.

Grandpa remembers that a lot of toys used to be handmade. That meant that many **popular** toys weren't very **expensive**. I tell him that some things have really changed!

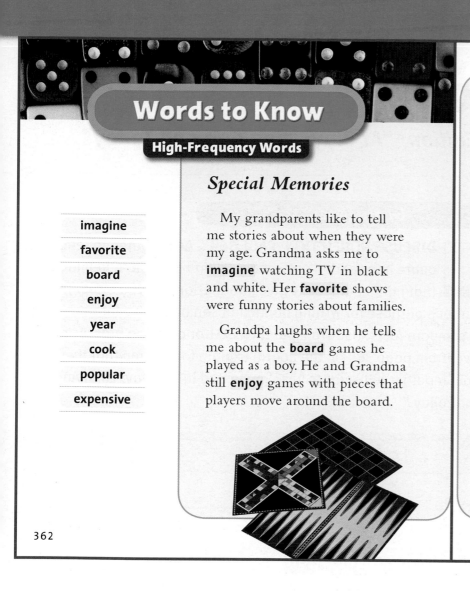

Go online www.harcourtschool.com/storytown

362

363

BELOW-LEVEL

Extra Support, p. 90

Name _____

▶ Write the word from the box that completes the sentence.

| imagine | favorite | year | enjoy |
| cook | board | popular | expensive |

1. We play in the snow at this time of __year__
2. We __enjoy__ singing.
3. This is a __board__ game.
4. Save money for an __expensive__ game.
5. Jumping rope is our __favorite__ game.
6. I like to __imagine__ a new game to play.
7. That singer is __popular__
8. Our school has a picnic every __year__
9. They __cook__ food on the grill.

ON-LEVEL

Practice Book, p. 90

Name _____

▶ Write the word from the box that completes the sentence.

| imagine | favorite | year | enjoy |
| cook | board | popular | expensive |

1. Chess is a game played on a __board__
2. Games of tag have been __popular__ with children for a long time.
3. Indoor games can be played all __year__
4. Some games are low cost, but others are __expensive__
5. Try to __imagine__ a time when there were no computer games.
6. Children often __enjoy__ a day at the park.
7. People __cook__ food for picnics at the park.
8. What is your __favorite__ game to play?

▶ Write sentences to tell about games you like. Use at least three words from the box in your sentences.

9. My _favorite_ games are _popular_ video games. I _enjoy_ playing them all _year_.

ADVANCED

Challenge, p. 90

Name _____

▶ Write the word from the box that belongs in each set.

| imagine | favorite | year |
| enjoy | cook | expensive |

1. best, first-choice, __favorite__
2. fancy, high-priced, __expensive__
3. dream, think, __imagine__
4. fry, boil, __cook__
5. day, week, __year__
6. laugh, feel happy, __enjoy__

▶ Use what you know to answer each question. Accept reasonable responses.

7. What is a **board** game that you and your friends **enjoy**?
We like playing checkers.

8. Do you think that the most **popular** games are **expensive**?
Yes. Video games are fun, but they can cost a lot of money.

ELL

• Group children according to academic levels, and assign one of the pages on the left.

• Clarify any unfamiliar concepts as necessary. See *ELL Teacher Guide* Lesson 12 for support in scaffolding instruction.

 Reading

Student Edition: "At Play: Long Ago and Today"

Objectives

- *To understand characteristics of nonfiction*
- *To ask questions as a strategy for comprehension*
- *To apply word knowledge to the reading of a text*

Options for Reading

 BELOW-LEVEL

Echo-Reading Read aloud the headings as children look at the photographs. Guide them to predict what each page will tell about the topic. Read each page to children, and have them read it after you.

 ON-LEVEL

Monitor Comprehension Have children read the story aloud, page by page. Ask the Monitor Comprehension questions as you go. Ask the children to compare play from long ago to play today.

 ADVANCED

Independent Reading Have children read each page silently, looking up when they finish a page. Ask the Monitor Comprehension questions as you go. Then lead them in a discussion about how play has changed over the years.

Genre Study

DISCUSS NONFICTION: PAGE 364 Ask children to read the genre information on *Student Edition* page 364. Remind them that nonfiction books give information about a topic. The author's purpose for writing nonfiction can be to give information or to compare facts. Use **Transparency GO 1** or copy the graphic organizer from page 364 on the board. Explain to children that they will work together to compare facts presented in "At Play: Long Ago and Today."

Long Ago	Today

Comprehension Strategies

ASK QUESTIONS: PAGE 364 Remind children that good readers ask themselves questions as they read to help them understand nonfiction writing. Have children read aloud the Comprehension Strategy information on page 364. Point out that they can look for the answers in the text, think about what they already know, or read on to see if their questions are answered.

Nonfiction

Genre Study

Nonfiction gives facts about a topic. Look for

- headings that help you find information.

- facts that you can compare.

Long Ago	Today

Comprehension Strategy

Ask questions that help you focus on the important ideas in a selection.

364

At Play
Long Ago and Today

by Lynnette R. Brent

365

Build Background

DISCUSS PLAYING   Tell children that they are going to read a nonfiction selection that tells how people play. Ask them to share how children play today. Write a list on the board. Read each item and ask children to raise their hands if they think those activities were enjoyed by children in the past, too.

Routine Card 6   **SET A PURPOSE AND PREDICT**   Tell children that this is a nonfiction selection they will read to get information.

- Have children read the title.

- Discuss what is happening in the photographs. Elicit that the inset shows children from long ago and the larger photo shows children on a modern playground.

- Have children read the selection to discover information about ways people played long ago and ways they play today.

Long Ago

Imagine that it is long ago. You have just finished listening to your favorite radio show. Now you are making your own scooter with the wheels from your old roller skates and a piece of wood your dad gave you. ❶

Your friends are calling you from outside! It is time for you to try the scooter you have made. You run outside and meet your friends. They love the new scooter!

366

This is what you may have been doing if you lived many years ago. What else would you have been doing with your friends and family long ago? Let's see what Americans did to play long ago.

▼ Long ago, children made their own scooters or rented them with their friends.

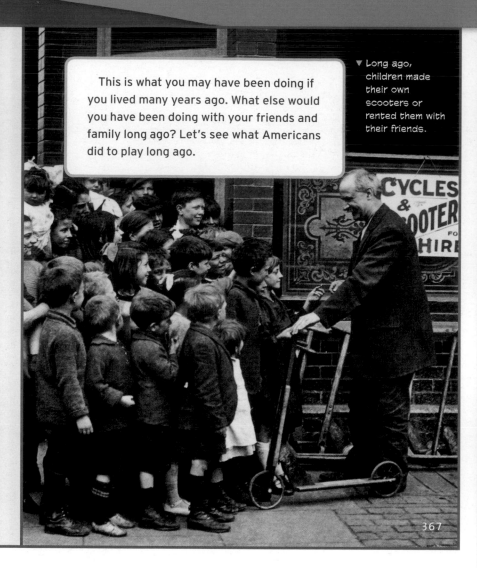

367

Monitor Comprehension

PAGES 366–367 Say: **The heading reads "Long Ago." I see pictures of roller skates and scooters. Read to find out how children played with these things long ago.**

❶ **NOTE DETAILS** How did children long ago make scooters? (They took wheels from old roller skates and put them on a piece of wood.)

❷ **DRAW CONCLUSIONS** How can you tell that these pages tell about children who lived long ago? (The heading says "Long Ago." The children are in old-fashioned clothing.)

Playing Sports

Long ago, children played many sports. Boys mostly played stickball, basketball, football, and field hockey. Girls mostly played tennis, golf, and croquet. **①**

Children usually played together in their own neighborhoods. They did not have special times of the year for each sport.

▼ Stickball was played with a broomstick and a small ball.

368

▲ Girls and boys play baseball during spring and summer.

Today, children still play sports that were played long ago. But now, both boys and girls play many of the same sports, like basketball or tennis.

Many children play sports in community programs or for their school teams. Children play different sports at different times of the year. **②** **③**

369

Monitor Comprehension

PAGES 368–369   Say: **The heading says, "Playing Sports." Read to find out about sports children played long ago and those they play today.**

① **COMPARE AND CONTRAST**   **Did boys and girls long ago play the same sports? Explain.** (No; boys mostly played stickball, basketball, football, and field hockey; girls mostly played tennis, golf, and croquet.)

② **AUTHOR'S PURPOSE**   **How can you tell that the author's purpose is to give information and not to tell a story?** (Possible responses: The author is telling us information about sports from long ago. There are no characters.)

③ **NOTE DETAILS**   **What sports do boys and girls play today?** (They play many of the same sports as long ago like baseball and basketball.)

Apply
Comprehension Strategies

Ask Questions   Explain to children that they can ask questions to make sure they understand the selection so far.

Think Aloud   What is stickball? I'm not sure, but I think it might be like baseball. I'll look at the picture and the caption to find the answer.

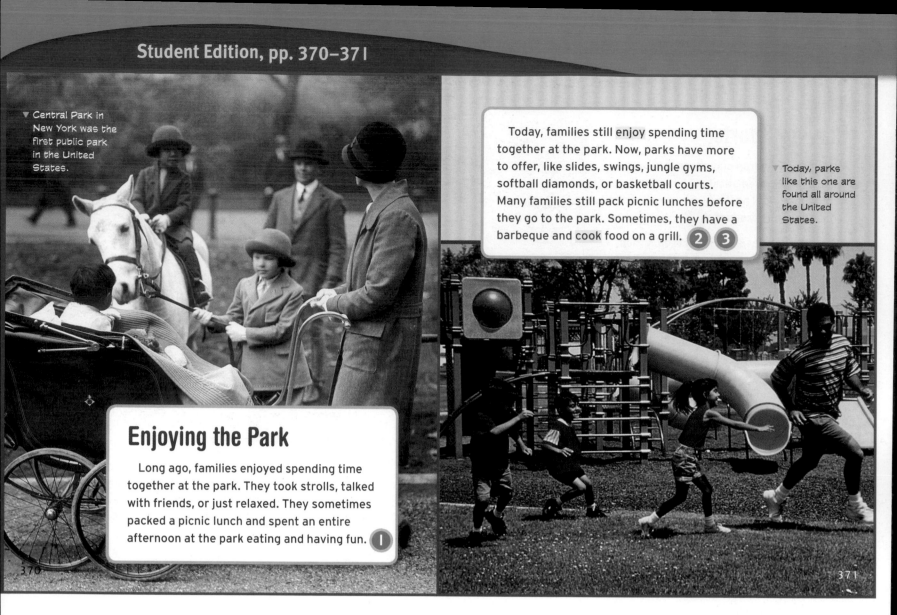

Central Park in New York was the first public park in the United States.

Today, families still enjoy spending time together at the park. Now, parks have more to offer, like slides, swings, jungle gyms, softball diamonds, or basketball courts. Many families still pack picnic lunches before they go to the park. Sometimes, they have a barbeque and cook food on a grill. **2 3**

Today, parks like this one are found all around the United States.

Enjoying the Park

Long ago, families enjoyed spending time together at the park. They took strolls, talked with friends, or just relaxed. They sometimes packed a picnic lunch and spent an entire afternoon at the park eating and having fun. **1**

370

371

Monitor Comprehension

PAGES 370–371 Have children read the heading. Say: **I see photos of people from the past and today at parks. Read to find out what people did at the park long ago.**

1 NOTE DETAILS What did people do at the park long ago? (took strolls, talked with friends, had a picnic)

2 AUTHOR'S VIEWPOINT Do you think the author thinks parks are better today? Why or why not? (Possible response: Yes; the author says that parks today have more to offer.)

3 EXPRESS PERSONAL OPINIONS What do you like to do at parks that is the same as what children on these pages like? (Possible response: I like to play on slides and swings with friends.)

E L L

Support Understanding Ask children to point to the pictures of the park, slide, and jungle gym in the photograph on page 371 as you say each word. Also use verbs such as *run*, *play*, and *reach*. Name other words and objects in the picture using the sentence frame "I see _____." Work with children to locate each word or object named.

Games

Long ago, people played different kinds of games. Board games, like checkers, were a popular family activity. Marbles was a game that children liked to play with their friends. To play this game, children bounced their marbles against other marbles in a circle. They won any marbles they could knock out of the circle. ❶

▼ Ringer and Rolley-hole were popular marble games.

Today, people still play many of the same games that were played long ago, such as checkers and marbles. But now, video games are also popular. Many children like to play video games on their televisions or on their computers. Some even have handheld video games that are so small they can be played anywhere! ❷ ❸

▲ Children can play sports, adventure, or puzzle video games.

372

373

Monitor Comprehension

PAGES 372–373   Say: **The photographs show children from long ago and today playing games. What games do you see in the pictures? Read to find out more.**

❶ **NOTE DETAILS**   How did children long ago win marbles? (They knocked the marbles out of a circle.) **Which sentence shows the answer?** (They won any marbles they could knock out of the circle.)

❷ **COMPARE AND CONTRAST**   Do children play the same games today as those children long ago played? (Possible response: They play some of the same games, but some games, such as video games, are new.)

❸ **SPECULATE**   Do you think children 100 years from now will play the same games? Explain. (Possible response: They might play some of the same games, but other games might be based on new inventions.)

Use Multiple Strategies

Use Prior Knowledge   Say: Thinking about what I already know about the topic can help me understand what the author is telling me. On page 372, I read about board games and marbles that were played long ago. I think about what I already know about those games to help me understand why people in the past enjoyed them, too.

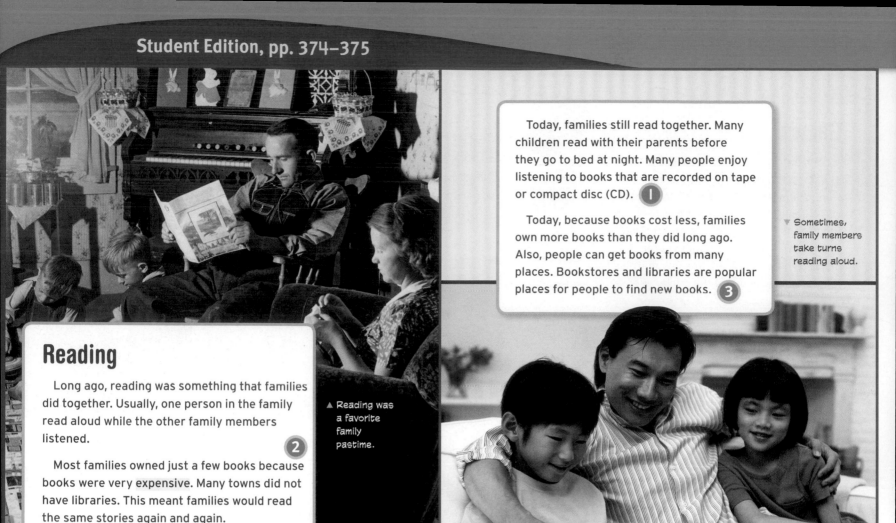

Reading

Long ago, reading was something that families did together. Usually, one person in the family read aloud while the other family members listened. **2**

Most families owned just a few books because books were very expensive. Many towns did not have libraries. This meant families would read the same stories again and again.

▲ Reading was a favorite family pastime.

Today, families still read together. Many children read with their parents before they go to bed at night. Many people enjoy listening to books that are recorded on tape or compact disc (CD). **1**

Today, because books cost less, families own more books than they did long ago. Also, people can get books from many places. Bookstores and libraries are popular places for people to find new books. **3**

▼ Sometimes, family members take turns reading aloud.

374

375

Monitor Comprehension

PAGES 374–375   Say: **Read aloud the heading. What do you see in the pictures? I wonder if reading could have changed over time. Read to find out.**

1 **NOTE DETAILS**   **What is the same about reading long ago and today?** (Possible response: families reading together)

2 **CAUSE/EFFECT**   **Why did families long ago own just a few books?** (Books were very expensive. Many people could not afford to buy them.) **Can you point to the clue word that helped you figure out the answer?** (Children should point to the word *because*.)

3 **SPECULATE**   **Why do you think libraries are popular places to find new books?** (Possible response: People can take books out for free.)

SOCIAL STUDIES

SUPPORTING STANDARDS

Libraries   Explain that local governments are in charge of community libraries. The local government collects taxes, or money, from its citizens, or people who live there. The taxes are used to help pay for the libraries. Have children explain who uses libraries and why they are important to their communities.

Family Vacations

Long ago, few families took vacations. If they did, they went camping in a nearby forest or visited beaches that were close to home. There were few roads, so people could not easily travel to the places they wanted to go. **1**

▼ Some families spent their vacations swimming or boating.

▲ Many families take vacations all over the world.

Today, more families go on vacation because traveling is easier. There are many more roads across the country. People can drive their cars to places that are far from home. Some families travel by train or by airplane. By taking cars, trains, and airplanes, families have many choices of vacation locations. **2**

376

377

Monitor Comprehension

PAGES 376–377   Say: **Read the heading together. What do you think we will learn about in this section? Read to find out.**

1 **CAUSE/EFFECT**   **Why didn't people travel far on their vacations long ago?** (There were few roads.)

2 **MAIN IDEA**   **How have cars, trains, and airplanes changed the ways people take vacations?** (Possible response: People can go to many different places far from home.)

ANALYZE AUTHOR'S PURPOSE

Author's Purpose   Remind children that authors have a purpose, or reason, for writing. After children have finished reading "At Play: Long Ago and Today," ask:

Why did the author write "At Play: Long Ago and Today"?

- to give information about how children played long ago and how they play today
- to compare facts and details

Lesson 12 (*Student Edition*, pages 376–377)   **T149**

▲ Circus parades let people know the circus was in town.

▼ Children of all ages enjoy carnival rides.

Special Events

Long ago, there were many special events children looked forward to. One was the circus coming to town! Children would line the streets with their parents to see the animals and clowns walk through the town. Some towns even had carnivals. Carnivals were a place for people to ride the Ferris wheel, eat food, and play games. **1**

Today, children enjoy some of the same events as long ago. Some children go to the circus when it comes to town. The carnival is still a place for families to have fun. Now, many children go to theme parks where fast roller coasters and merry-go-rounds are very popular. **2**

378

379

Monitor Comprehension

PAGES 378–379 Ask children to describe what they see. Say: **Read to find out what special events children enjoyed long ago.**

1 NOTE DETAILS What special events did children enjoy long ago? (circuses, parades, and carnivals)

2 COMPARE AND CONTRAST What do children enjoy today that children in the past were not able to enjoy? (Possible response: theme parks, roller coasters)

Apply Comprehension Strategies

Ask Questions Remind children that they can ask themselves questions to make sure they understand the information the author wants them to know.

Think Aloud What sorts of special events were there long ago? I wonder if the events are like those that we enjoy today. I see that people enjoyed circuses and carnivals, just as we do today. These details show that the author wants us to know that many special events were the same long ago as they are today.

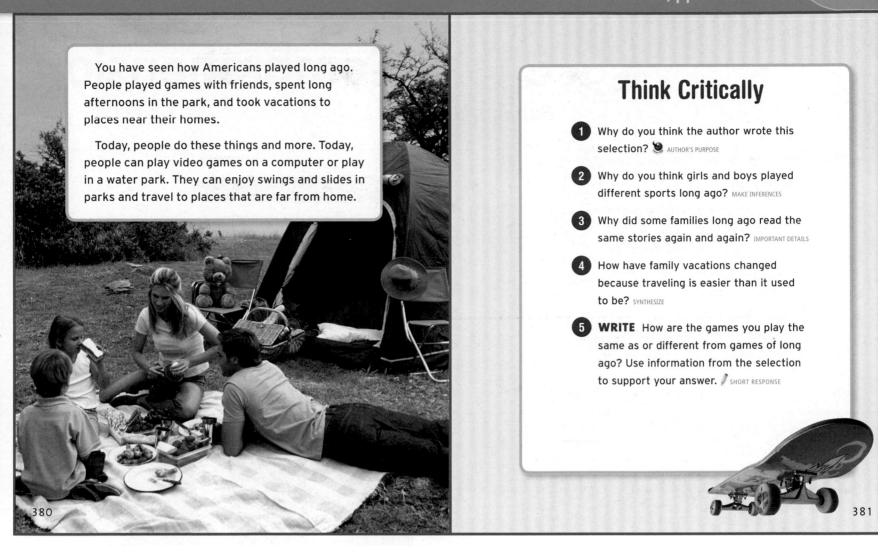

You have seen how Americans played long ago. People played games with friends, spent long afternoons in the park, and took vacations to places near their homes.

Today, people do these things and more. Today, people can play video games on a computer or play in a water park. They can enjoy swings and slides in parks and travel to places that are far from home.

380

Think Critically

1. Why do you think the author wrote this selection? 🌀 AUTHOR'S PURPOSE

2. Why do you think girls and boys played different sports long ago? MAKE INFERENCES

3. Why did some families long ago read the same stories again and again? IMPORTANT DETAILS

4. How have family vacations changed because traveling is easier than it used to be? SYNTHESIZE

5. **WRITE** How are the games you play the same as or different from games of long ago? Use information from the selection to support your answer. ✏ SHORT RESPONSE

381

Think Critically

Respond to the Literature

1. Possible response: to give information to readers about different ways people play. **AUTHOR'S PURPOSE**

2. Possible response: There may have been different rules about what boys and girls could play. **MAKE INFERENCES**

3. Possible response: Books were expensive. Most families had few books and many towns did not have libraries, so people read the same stories many times. **IMPORTANT DETAILS**

4. Possible response: People travel farther and go to different kinds of places. **SYNTHESIZE**

5. **WRITE** Possible response: I play baseball and basketball just as children long ago did. I like to play checkers too. **SHORT RESPONSE**

Check Comprehension
Summarizing

Objectives

- *To practice summarizing a non-fiction selection*
- *To use punctuation to read in a manner that sounds like natural speech*

RETELLING RUBRIC

4	Uses details to clearly summarize the selection
3	Uses some details to summarize the selection
2	Summarizes the selection with some inaccuracies
1	Is unable to summarize the selection

Professional Development

 Podcasting: Auditory Modeling

BELOW-LEVEL

Fluency Practice For fluency practice, have children read *Decodable Book 10*, the appropriate *Leveled Reader* (pp. T190–T193), or Story 12 in the *Intervention Reader*.

Summarize

 DIBELS Oral Reading Fluency ORF **AUTHOR'S PURPOSE** Have children identify the author's purpose for writing "At Play: Long Ago and Today." (to give information about how people played in the past and today)

REVISIT THE GRAPHIC ORGANIZER Display completed **Transparency GO1**. Guide children to use the graphic organizer to summarize the selection.

STORY RETELLING CARDS The cards for the selection can be used for summarizing or to help complete the graphic organizer.

▲ Story Retelling Cards 1–6, "At Play: Long Ago and Today"

 # Fluency
Punctuation

Teach/Model

 DIBELS Oral Reading Fluency ORF **USING PUNCTUATION** Have children track the print as you read *Student Edition* pages 368–369. Have them listen for the way you pause at commas and end marks.

Practice/Apply

 Routine Card 8 **ECHO-READ** Read aloud the rest of the selection, one page at a time. Have children echo-read each page after you.

Build Robust Vocabulary

Words About the Selection

Teach/Model

Routine Card 3

INTRODUCE ROBUST VOCABULARY Use *Routine Card 3* to introduce the words.

❶ Put the word in **selection context**.
❷ Display Transparency R62 and read the word and the **Student-Friendly Explanation**.
❸ Have children **say the word** with you.
❹ Use the word in other contexts, and have children **interact with the word's meaning**.
❺ Remove the transparency. Say the Student-Friendly Explanation again, and ask children to **name the word** that goes with it.

❶ **Selection Context:** Long ago, children played stickball and croquet for **recreation**.
❹ **Interact with Word Meaning:** If you play soccer for recreation, you do it for fun. Would you take a test or play outside for recreation?

❶ **Selection Context:** Families strolled **leisurely** through the park.
❹ **Interact with Word Meaning:** What might you do leisurely, come in from recess or clean your room? Why?

❶ **Selection Context:** Families could **ramble** when they went camping.
❹ **Interact with Word Meaning:** Would you ramble in a playground or in a parking lot? Why?

❶ **Selection Context:** In the future, video games might become **archaic**.
❹ **Interact with Word Meaning:** An archaic tool is not used anymore. Which is archaic, a typewriter or a computer?

Practice/Apply

GUIDED PRACTICE Ask children to use the vocabulary to tell about something that might be *archaic* one day.

Objective

- *To develop robust vocabulary through discussing a literature selection*

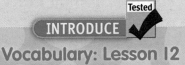
INTRODUCE ✔ Tested

Vocabulary: Lesson 12

| recreation | ramble |
| leisurely | archaic |

▼ **Student-Friendly Explanations**

Student-Friendly Explanations

recently	If something happened not long ago, it happened recently.
housed	If something is placed or lives somewhere, it is housed there.
official	If someone holds a position of authority in an organization, the person is called an official.
nominate	When you suggest that someone should get an office, job, or honor, you nominate the person.
recreation	When you do something fun and relaxing, it is recreation for you.
leisurely	If you do something in a leisurely way, you are not in a hurry.
ramble	When you ramble, you wander around.
archaic	If something is archaic, it is old and not used anymore.

Grade 2, Theme 3 — R62 — Vocabulary

Transparency R62

Grammar
Singular Possessive Nouns

5-DAY GRAMMAR

DAY 1	Possessive Nouns
DAY 2	Identifying Singular Possessive Nouns
DAY 3	Sentence Formation with Possessive Nouns
DAY 4	Apply to Writing
DAY 5	Weekly Review

Objective
- *To identify and form singular possessive nouns*

Daily Proofreading

Vicky soccer ball is white and black

(Vicky's, black.)

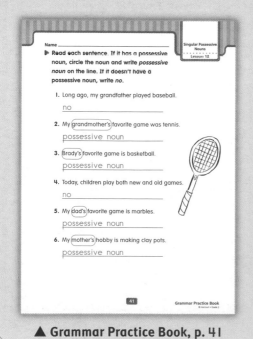

▲ Grammar Practice Book, p. 41

Review

IDENTIFY SINGULAR POSSESSIVE NOUNS   Write these sentences on the board.

Marissa borrowed her sister's books.
(sister's)

Do you like the story's characters?
(story's)

Ben played his friend's video games.
(friend's)

They sat in their mother's living room.
(mother's)

Have children read aloud the sentences. Explain that each sentence has a noun that shows ownership. Ask children to identify the noun that shows ownership in each sentence.

Practice/Apply

GUIDED PRACTICE   Write the following phrases on the board. Tell the children that these phrases are one way to show ownership. Then model how to rewrite the first phrase to include a possessive noun. Work with children to rewrite the remaining phrases.

the hat that belongs to the clown (the clown's hat)

the swing set that belongs to the playground
(the playground's swing set)

the roller coaster that belongs to the theme park
(the theme park's roller coaster)

INDEPENDENT PRACTICE   Write the following phrases on the board. Ask children to rewrite them, using possessive nouns.

the chairs that belong to the library (the library's chairs)

the picnic tables that belong to the campground
(the campground's picnic tables)

the ramp that belongs to the skateboard park
(the skateboard park's ramp)

5-DAY WRITING	
DAY 1	Introduce
DAY 2	Prewrite
DAY 3	Draft
DAY 4	Revise
DAY 5	Revise

Writing
Paragraph That Gives Information

Prewrite

GENERATE IDEAS Have children look again at the word webs they made on Day 1 (page T135). Ask them to think of more information about the games they listed. Then tell them to put a star beside the game they want to write about.

WRITING TRAIT **VOICE** Have children brainstorm words that show they are interested in the game.

MODEL PREWRITING Copy on the board the chart below. Tell children that they can use a graphic organizer to organize their ideas for a paragraph that gives information. Model writing ideas in sequence to give information about playing a game of hide-and-seek.

> **First**
> One child covers his or her eyes.
>
> ↓
>
> **Next**
> That same child counts to ten.
>
> ↓
>
> **Then**
> The other kids run and hide!
>
> ↓
>
> **Last**
> The child finds someone's hiding place and calls out "You're it!"

Practice/Apply

GUIDED PRACTICE Choose a game with which children are familiar. Work with them to complete a sequence chart that shows how to play the game. Discuss how you decide the order of actions or events.

INDEPENDENT PRACTICE Have children use their word webs and the group's sequence chart to develop a sequence chart for the game they want to write about. Tell children to save their sequence charts to use on Days 3–5.

Objectives

- *To develop ideas and topics for writing*
- *To use a graphic organizer for prewriting*

Writing Prompt

Record Reflections Have children record their reflections about a popular game.

BELOW-LEVEL

Explain Sequence Charts
If children have difficulty understanding the sequence chart, number each box and have children trace the path from first to last.

Day at a Glance

Day 3

phonics and Spelling
- Review: Long Vowel /ē/*ey, y*
- State the Generalization

High-Frequency Words
- Review: *imagine, favorite, year, enjoy, cook, board, popular, expensive*

Fluency
- Punctuation
- "At Play: Long Ago and Today," *Student Edition*, pp. 364–381

Comprehension

 Review: Author's Purpose

- "A History of Games and Toys in the United States," *Student Edition*, pp. 382–383

Read!

Robust Vocabulary
- Review: *recently, housed, official, nominate, recreation, leisurely, ramble, archaic*

Grammar
- Review: Singular Possessive Nouns

Writing
- Paragraph That Gives Information

Warm-Up Routines

 Oral Language

Objective *To listen attentively and respond appropriately to oral communication*

Question of the Day
What would you like about being a kite?

Use the following prompts to help children imagine what it would feel like to be a kite.

- **Where would you fly?**
- **What would you feel?**
- **What would you smell?**
- **What would you see?**
- **What would you hear?**

Have children complete the following sentence frame to share their feelings.

I would like to be a kite because _____.

Read Aloud

Objective *To identify rhymes and repetition in poetry*

BIG BOOK OF RHYMES AND POEMS Display "Play" on page 23 and ask children to tell what they remember about the poem. As you read the poem, emphasize the repeated rhyming words at the ends of lines 3 and 4 and lines 7 and 8 *(sky, I)*. Then reread the poem, encouraging children to join in.

▲ **Big Book of Rhymes and Poems, p. 23**

Word Wall

Objective *To read high-frequency words*

REVIEW HIGH-FREQUENCY WORDS Have children begin clapping their hands to keep time. Point to and read one of the high-frequency words below. Have children spell and read the word to the beat of the claps. Repeat the process until the class reviews each word several times.

favorite	popular	imagine	enjoy
expensive	year	cook	board

Long Vowel /ē/ey, y
 phonics *and Spelling*

5-DAY PHONICS	
DAY 1	Introduce /ē/ey, y
DAY 2	Word Building with /ē/ey, y
DAY 3	Word Building with /ē/ey, y
DAY 4	Inflections -ed, -es (y to i); Review /ē/ey, y
DAY 5	Inflections -ed, -es (y to i); Review /ē/ey, y

Objectives

- To read and write common word families
- To recognize spelling patterns

Skill Trace

Tested **Long Vowel /ē/ey, y**

Introduce	Grade 1
Reintroduce	T126–T129
Reteach	S12
Review	**T138–T139, T158–T159, T392**
Test	Theme 3
Maintain	Theme 4, T168

Long Vowel /ē/ey, y

Betty pets the friendly donkey.
The buggy bumped down the rocky path.
Gary gets dizzy when he spins around.
Billy went to a party at his friend's house.
A monkey and a pony are in the circus act.
Can you find the key to the heavy chest?

Grade 2, Lesson 12   R59   Phonics

Transparency R59

Work with Patterns

BUILD AND READ WORDS Write the word endings *-nny* and *-ney* at the top of two columns.

Tell children that these are the endings of some words. Point out that both endings sound the same, /nē/.

Then have children name words that end with *-nny*, such as *funny*, *runny*, *penny*, *skinny*, and *granny*, and words that end with *-ney*, such as *money*, *honey*, *chimney*, *journey*, and *kidney*. Have them tell which letter or letters to add to build each word, and write the word in the appropriate column. Have children read each column of words. Then point to words at random and have children read them.

Read Words in Context

READ SENTENCES Display **Transparency R59** or write the sentences on the board or on chart paper. Have children choral-read the sentences as you track the print. Then ask volunteers to read each sentence aloud and to underline words in which the letters *ey* or *y* stand for the /ē/ sound.

5-DAY SPELLING

DAY 1	Pretest
DAY 2	Word Building
DAY 3	State the Generalization
DAY 4	Review
DAY 5	Posttest

Review Spelling Words

STATE THE GENERALIZATION FOR /ē/ey, y List spelling words 1–10 on chart paper or on the board. Circle the words in which the letters *ey* stand for the /ē/ sound, and have children read them. Ask: **What is the same in each word?** (In each word, the letters *ey* stand for the /ē/ sound.) Then, using a different color pen, circle the words in which the letter *y* stands for the /ē/ sound, and repeat the procedure.

WRITE Have children write the spelling words in their note-books. Remind them to use their best handwriting and to use the chart to check their spelling.

Handwriting

Letter Spacing Remind children to make sure their letters are not too close together or too far apart.

Spelling Words

1. **very***	6. **baby**
2. **messy**	7. **money**
3. **lady**	8. **funny**
4. **happy**	9. **candy**
5. **key**	10. **sunny**

Challenge Words

11. **chimney**	14. **twenty**
12. **nobody**	15. **keyhole**
13. **breezy**	

* Word from "At Play: Long Ago and Today"

Decodable Books

Additional Decoding Practice

- **Phonics**
  Long Vowel /ē/ey, y
- **Decodable Words**
- **High-Frequency Words**
  See the lists in *Decodable Book 10.*

  See also *Decodable Books,* online (Take-Home Version).

▲ Decodable Book 10 "Monkeys"

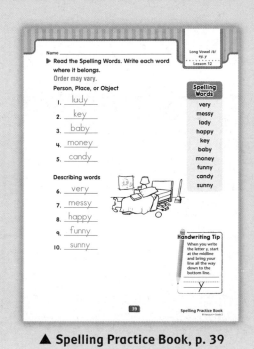

▲ Spelling Practice Book, p. 39

 High-Frequency Words

Objective

• *To read high-frequency words*

REVIEW ✓ Tested

High-Frequency Words

board	favorite
cook	imagine
enjoy	popular
expensive	year

Clarify Usage Tell children that in the selection they read yesterday, the word *board* means a flat piece of cardboard or wood. Show a game board. Ask: **Is this a board?** Have them answer using the word *board*. You may wish to explain that *board* can also mean an action, such as to board a bus.

Review

DISPLAY THE WORDS Write the words *imagine*, *favorite*, *year*, *enjoy*, *cook*, *board*, *popular*, and *expensive* on the board. Point to each word, and ask a volunteer to read it.

Practice/Apply

GUIDED PRACTICE Give each child a set of word cards (*Teacher Resource Book,* p. 77), and have children spread the cards out. Randomly call out each word, and have children hold up the matching card. Point to the word on the board so they can check their response. Repeat until children respond quickly and accurately.

INDEPENDENT PRACTICE Have children work with a partner and use only one set of word cards. Tell partners to take turns calling out a word while the other holds up the matching card.

 MONITOR PROGRESS

High-Frequency Words

IF children have difficulty reading the high-frequency words,	**THEN** have them set aside their word cards except for *imagine* and *favorite*. Call out each word. Have children hold up the matching card. Repeat, and then add another word each time.

Small-Group Instruction, p. S13:

● **BELOW-LEVEL:** Reteach   ● **ON-LEVEL:** Reinforce   ● **ADVANCED:** Extend

Fluency
Punctuation

Review

MODEL USING PUNCTUATION
Remind children that good readers use punctuation marks to read smoothly. Tell children to

▲ Student Edition, pp. 364–381

- pause briefly when they come to commas and periods.

- add strength to their voices when they come to a sentence with an exclamation point.

Think Aloud I'm going to read aloud part of "At Play: Long Ago and Today." I'll skim ahead to see what punctuation is at the end of a group of words or at the end of the sentence. Then I'll know when to pause and how to make my voice sound.

Practice/Apply

Routine Card 9

GUIDED PRACTICE Read pages 366–367 aloud. Then have children practice reading the same pages several times with a partner. Monitor children as they read, making sure they are paying attention to the punctuation marks.

INDEPENDENT PRACTICE Have partners reread sections of "At Play: Long Ago and Today" aloud two or three times. Have the partner who is listening follow along in the *Student Edition* and alert the reader when he or she misses punctuation.

Objective

- *To use punctuation to read fluently in a manner that sounds like natural speech*

BELOW-LEVEL

Fluency Practice Have children reread *Decodable Book 10*, Story 12 in the *Strategic Intervention Interactive Reader*, or the appropriate *Leveled Reader* (pp. T190–T193). Have them practice reading the text several times.

Additional Related Reading

- *Let's Play Soccer!* by Heather Adamson. Capstone, 2006. **EASY**

- *The Story of Figure Skating* by Anastasia Suen. Rigby, 2001. **AVERAGE**

- *Hoops* by Robert Burleigh. Harcourt, 2001. **CHALLENGE**

Author's Purpose
Comprehension

Objective

• *To identify an author's purpose for writing*

Skill Trace

 Tested **Author's Purpose**

Introduce	T34–T35
Reteach	S16–S17
Review	**T68, T82, T92, T130–T131, T162, T176, T186, T379, T394**
Test	Theme 3
Maintain	Theme 5, T278

Review

REVIEW AUTHOR'S PURPOSE Remind children that identifying an author's purpose for writing can help them make sense of what they read. Ask them to recall some purposes for writing. (Possible responses: to entertain readers; to give information; to tell how to do something)

Practice/Apply

GUIDED PRACTICE Have children turn to "Life as a Frog" on *Student Edition* page 80. Ask: **What is the author's purpose for writing this selection?** (Possible response: to tell what happens to a frog during its life) Guide children to think about how this knowledge can help them understand informational text. Ask: **Since I know the author's purpose, what should I expect to learn as I read "Life as a Frog"?** (Possible responses: how a frog changes during its life; what a frog eats)

INDEPENDENT PRACTICE Have children turn to other nonfiction selections in the *Student Edition*. Ask them to identify the author's purpose for writing each one and to explain how that knowledge can help them understand the selection.

Reading
Student Edition: Paired Selection

Read and Respond

USE PRIOR KNOWLEDGE/SET A PURPOSE   Have children use prior knowledge about games and toys to set a purpose for reading. Then have them read the time line. Point out that they should pause after reading the name of each game or toy in red.

MONITOR COMPREHENSION   Ask:

- **PERSONAL RESPONSE**   **What toys or games in this selection do you play with?** (Responses will vary.)

- **COMPARE AND CONTRAST**   **How are video games today different from the video game made by Ralph Baer?** (Possible responses: Video games are now in color. Some of them are played on small screens that you can hold.)

 Connections

Objectives

- *To compare texts*
- *To connect texts to personal experiences*

Comparing Texts

1 Possible response: They are alike because they both describe ways that children in the past and today like to play. They are different because "At Play: Long Ago and Today" has information about more than just games and toys.   **TEXT TO TEXT**

2 Responses will vary, but may include jump-rope, kickball, hopscotch, and tag.   **TEXT TO SELF**

3 Possible response: Children today also play tag, hide-and-seek, and other games. They play games in the snow and in the water.   **TEXT TO WORLD**

Connections

Comparing Texts

❶ How are "At Play: Long Ago and Today" and "A History of Games and Toys in the United States" alike? How are they different?

❷ What do you like to play at recess?

❸ What other games do children play today?

Phonics

Rhyming Words

Read each word in the box. Match each word with a picture whose name rhymes with it. Then say each rhyming pair to a partner.

> very
> funny
> dirty
> honey
> donkey

384

Fluency Practice

Timed Reading

Read aloud a section of "At Play: Long Ago and Today." Remember to pay attention to the punctuation to know how to read the sentences. Then time yourself as you read the section aloud several times. Try to read it a little faster without mistakes each time.

Writing

 Write About a Change

Think about things that were different long ago. Use a chart to list your ideas. Then choose one idea, and write a paragraph about it. Tell what has changed from long ago to today.

Long Ago	Today

My Writing Checklist

Writing Trait ▸ Voice

✔ I use a chart to list topics I could write about.

✔ I write about what is interesting to me.

385

PHONICS

Rhyming Words If necessary, review the name of what is shown in each picture: *thirty, berry, monkey, sunny,* and *money.* Extend the activity by having partners write the pairs of words on a sheet of paper. Challenge them to think of more words that rhyme with each pair.

> funny
> sunny
> bunny

FLUENCY

Timed Reading Children may wish to work with partners and take turns timing each other with a stopwatch and recording the times. Remind children that they should make sure they are reading accurately and paying attention to the punctuation, even as they try to improve their times.

WRITING

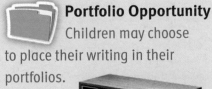 **Write About a Change** Help children brainstorm things that were different long ago. Prompt them to recall things their family members have said were different when they were growing up.

Portfolio Opportunity Children may choose to place their writing in their portfolios.

 # Build Robust Vocabulary

Objective

- *To review robust vocabulary*

Tested

REVIEW ✓

Vocabulary: Lesson 12

recently	recreation
housed	leisurely
official	ramble
nominate	archaic

▼ **Student-Friendly Explanations**

Student-Friendly Explanations

recently	If something happened not long ago, it happened recently.
housed	If something is placed or lives somewhere, it is housed there.
official	If someone holds a position of authority in an organization, the person is called an official.
nominate	When you suggest that someone should get an office, job, or honor, you nominate the person.
recreation	When you do something fun and relaxing, it is recreation for you.
leisurely	If you do something in a leisurely way, you are not in a hurry.
ramble	When you ramble, you wander around.
archaic	If something is archaic, it is old and not used anymore.

Grade 2, Theme 3   R62   Vocabulary

Transparency R62

Review Robust Vocabulary

USE VOCABULARY IN DIFFERENT CONTEXTS   Remind children of the Student-Friendly Explanations of the Vocabulary Words introduced on Days 1 and 2. Then discuss each word, using the following prompts:

recently

- **What books have you read recently?**
- **What did you do outside recently?**
- **What has the weather been like recently?**

housed

- **What can be housed in a museum?**
- **Why are some animals housed in a zoo?**
- **What might be housed in a garage?**

official

- **What might an official do at a parade?**
- **What would you say to a fire official?**
- **When might you see a police official?**

nominate

- **Which pet would you nominate as the best of all?**
- **Which toy would you nominate as the best of all?**

recreation

- What do you do for recreation in the winter?

- What do you do for recreation in the summer?

leisurely

- Do you play tag in a leisurely way? Explain.

- Is someone who walks in a leisurely way angry or relaxed?

- What are some activities that you can do in a leisurely way?

ramble

- Do you ramble if you are in a hurry? Explain.

- Name some things you might see and hear if you ramble at the beach.

- Do you ever ramble in your neighborhood? What do you see?

archaic

- Is a new invention archaic? Explain.

- Why do museums show archaic things?

- Would archaic things tell us about the past? Why?

Support Understanding Before you work through the exercises for *leisurely* with children, show them how you would walk in a leisurely way. For example, you might pause to look out the window or act out picking flowers. Have children demonstrate the actions. Do a similar demonstration for *ramble*.

Grammar
Singular Possessive Nouns

5-DAY GRAMMAR

DAY 1	Possessive Nouns
DAY 2	Identifying Singular Possessive Nouns
DAY 3	**Sentence Formation with Possessive Nouns**
DAY 4	Apply to Writing
DAY 5	Weekly Review

Objective

- *To form sentences with possessive nouns correctly*

Daily Proofreading

Leticias favorite game tag is.

(Leticia's, is tag.)

Review

FORMING SENTENCES WITH POSSESSIVE NOUNS Write and read aloud these sentences.

> **The tires of the bike were flat.**
>
> **The surface of the sidewalk was wet.**

Tell children that they can restate these sentences using possessive nouns. Underline the word *bike*. Ask: **What belongs to the bike?** (tires) Ask: **How do you write *bike* as a noun that shows ownership?** (*bike's*) Then rewrite the sentence using *bike's*. (The bike's tires were flat.) Repeat the steps with the second sentence. (The sidewalk's surface was wet.)

Practice/Apply

GUIDED PRACTICE Write these sentences on the board. Model how to make the underlined word a possessive noun in sentence one. Work with children to revise the remaining sentences.

> **Mike carried the stickball of <u>Jerome</u>.**
>
> **Leroy hit the marble that belonged to <u>Bill</u>.**
>
> **Mia bought lemonade that belonged to <u>Henry</u>.**

INDEPENDENT PRACTICE Have children revise the following sentences using singular possessive nouns.

> **Omar caught the ball that belonged to <u>Jerry</u>.**
>
> **Margo skipped down the path of the <u>park</u>.**
>
> **The families had a cookout at the house of a <u>neighbor</u>.**
>
> **The woman walked the dog of her <u>sister</u>.**
>
> **The worker fed the hippo that belonged to the <u>zoo</u>.**

Name _____

Singular Possessive Nouns
Lesson 12

▶ Complete each sentence. Change the noun in ( ) to show ownership, and write it on the line.

1. We went for a walk in ___Pam's___ neighborhood. (Pam)

2. We went to see ___Mrs. Stout's___ new house. (Mrs. Stout)

3. She was looking for ___Mr. Stout's___ eyeglasses. (Mr. Stout)

4. Are they under ___Peggy's___ pillow? (Peggy)

5. Are they in ___Bobby's___ toy box? (Bobby)

6. Mrs. Stout found the eyeglasses on ___Mr. Stout's___ dresser. (Mr. Stout)

42   Grammar Practice Book

▲ **Grammar Practice Book, p. 42**

5-DAY WRITING	
DAY 1	Introduce
DAY 2	Prewrite
DAY 3	Draft
DAY 4	Revise
DAY 5	Revise

Writing
Paragraph That Gives Information

Draft Sentences

REVIEW A LITERATURE MODEL   Tell children that "At Play: Long Ago and Today" has many paragraphs that give information. Read aloud the heading and the paragraph on page 372. Discuss how the paragraph gives information about games. Point out the following:

> • The paragraph gives information about games.
>
> • The first sentence tells the main idea—that people long ago played different games.
>
> • The other sentences give more information, or details, about the main idea.
>
> • Some of the sentences tell how to play marbles in the correct order, or sequence.

DRAFT A PARAGRAPH THAT GIVES INFORMATION   Have children use their word webs, filled-in sequence charts, and what they now know to write a paragraph that gives information about their favorite game.

WRITING TRAIT **VOICE**   As children write their sentences, remind them that they can choose action words or exact words to show that they are excited to share information about their favorite game.

CONFER WITH CHILDREN   Meet with individual children, helping them as they draft their paragraphs. Offer encouragement for what they are doing well, and make constructive suggestions for improving an aspect of the writing, as needed.

Objectives

• *To draft a paragraph that gives information*
• *To write a main-idea sentence and supporting details*

 ## Writing Prompt

Reflect   Have children write whether they think the author of "At Play: Long Ago and Today" had fun writing the selection.

▲ Writer's Companion, Lesson 12

BELOW-LEVEL

Write Possessive Nouns
Encourage children to include words that show ownership. Remind them that they can add an apostrophe and the letter *s* to form singular possessive nouns.

Day at a Glance

Day 4

phonics and Spelling

- Introduce: Inflections *-ed, -es* (*y* to *i*)
- Review: Long Vowel /ē/*ey, y*

High-Frequency Words

- Review: *imagine, favorite, year, enjoy, cook, board, popular, expensive*

Fluency

- Punctuation
- "At Play: Long Ago and Today," *Student Edition*, pp. 364–381

Comprehension

Review: Author's Purpose

Robust Vocabulary

- Review: *recently, housed, official, nominate, recreation, leisurely, ramble, archaic*

Grammar

- Review: Singular Possessive Nouns

Writing

- Paragraph That Gives Information

Warm-Up Routines

Oral Language

Objective *To listen attentively and respond appropriately to oral communication*

Question of the Day

Do you like to play alone or with friends?

Use the following prompts to help children compare and contrast playing alone and with friends.

- **How do you use your imagination when you're alone? With friends?**

- **What games or activities are more fun to play alone? Which are more fun with friends?**

Have children complete the following sentence frames to summarize their discussion.

> **When I play by myself I like to _____.**
>
> **When I play with friends I like to _____.**

Read Aloud

Objective *To listen for enjoyment*

BIG BOOK OF RHYMES AND POEMS Display the poem "Sharing the Swing" on page 24 and read the title. Tell children to listen to the poem for enjoyment. Then track the print as you read the poem aloud. Explain that a pantry often has many shelves for keeping food, pots, and pans and that these shelves might seem high to a child. Then discuss what makes having a friend push the swing more fun than doing it yourself.

▲ **Big Book of Rhymes and Poems, p. 24**

Word Wall

Objective *To read high-frequency words*

REVIEW HIGH-FREQUENCY WORDS Arrange the words *imagine*, *favorite*, *year*, *enjoy*, *cook*, *board*, *popular*, and *expensive* in two rows. Have children read the words as a group, snapping their fingers to the syllables. Then have each child read one word aloud, continuing the rhythm. Continue until each child has had a chance to read aloud a word at least once.

imagine	cook	favorite	board
year	popular	enjoy	expensive

Inflections -ed, -es (y to i) phonics

5-DAY PHONICS	
DAY 1	Introduce /ē/ey, y
DAY 2	Word Building with /ē/ey, y
DAY 3	Word Building with /ē/ey, y
DAY 4	Inflections -ed, -es (y to i); Review /ē/ey, y
DAY 5	Inflections -ed, -es (y to i); Review /ē/ey, y

Objective

- *To read two-syllable words with the inflections -ed and -es*

Skill Trace

 Tested **Inflections -ed, -es (y to i)**

Introduce	T172
Review	T182
Test	Theme 3

Inflections -ed, -es (y to i)

The squirrel buried a walnut in the ground.

We keep four ponies in the barn.

Which kind of berries do you like best?

That couple got married on Saturday.

Grade 2, Lesson 12   R60   Phonics

Transparency R60

Teach/Model

INTRODUCE y TO i Write the word *carry* on the board and have children read it. Say: **When a word ends in a consonant and the letter y, change the y to an i before adding -ed or -es.** Write the words *carried* and *carries*, demonstrating how the *y* changes to *i* before the inflection is added. Have children read the words.

carry
carried   carries

Point out that the letters *ied* stand for /ēd/ in words like *carried*, and the letters *ies* stand for /ēz/ in words like *carries*.

Guided Practice

READ WORDS Write the following words on the board. Read each word, and have children read it after you.

ponies	hurried	bunnies
studied	pennies	worried

Practice/Apply

READ SENTENCES Display **Transparency R60** or write the sentences on the board or on chart paper. Have children read the sentences aloud. Remind them to use what they have learned about words with *-ied* or *-ies* to help them read accurately.

Long Vowel /ē/ ey, y

phonics and Spelling

5-DAY SPELLING

DAY 1	Pretest
DAY 2	Word Building
DAY 3	State the Generalization
DAY 4	**Review**
DAY 5	Posttest

Build Words

REVIEW THE WORDS   Have children open their notebooks to the spelling words that they wrote on Day 3. Have them read the words several times and then close their notebooks.

MAP LETTERS TO SOUNDS   Have children follow your directions to change one or more letters in each of the following words to spell a spelling word. Have them write the spelling word on a sheet of paper. Then have a volunteer change the spelling of the word on the board so that children can self-check their spelling.

- Write *lad* on the board. Ask: **Which spelling word can you make by adding a letter?** *(lady)*

- Write *puppy* on the board. Ask: **Which spelling word can you make by changing the first two letters?** *(happy)*

- Write *keep* on the board. Ask: **Which spelling word can you make by changing the last two letters?** *(key)*

Follow a similar procedure with the following words: *berry (very), dressy (messy), batty (baby), monkcy (money), bunny (funny, sunny), sandy (candy).*

CHALLENGE WORDS   Write the consonants of each challenge word on the board. Ask volunteers to spell each word in its entirety and write the missing letters.

ch __ mn __ __

Objective

- *To use /ē/ ey, y, and other known letter-sounds to spell and write words*

Spelling Words

1. **very***
2. **messy**
3. **lady**
4. **happy**
5. **key**
6. **baby**
7. **money**
8. **funny**
9. **candy**
10. **sunny**

Challenge Words

11. **chimney**
12. **nobody**
13. **breezy**
14. **twenty**
15. **keyhole**

* Word from "At Play: Long Ago and Today"

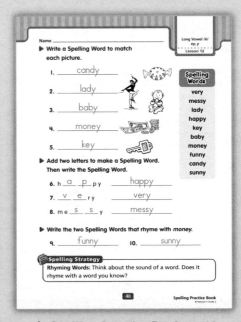

▲ Spelling Practice Book, p. 40

BELOW-LEVEL

Focus on *ey* and *y*   Write the spelling words on the board, with a blank where the letters *y* or *ey* should be. Help children complete each word by asking questions such as, "What letter can you add to *happ_* to make *happy*?" Have children spell aloud each completed word.

High-Frequency Words

Objective

* *To read high-frequency words*

High-Frequency Words

board	favorite
cook	imagine
enjoy	popular
expensive	year

Review

READ WORDS   Display **Transparency R61**. Have children read the words at the top. Then point to the words at random and have children read them.

Practice/Apply

GUIDED PRACTICE   Talk about the illustration. Then track the print as you read aloud the sentences. Have children echo-read after you.

Then have children create their own sentences using the high-frequency words. Write each sentence on the board, and read it with children.

INDEPENDENT PRACTICE   Have children write sentences using the high-frequency words. Then have them share their sentences with a partner.

High-Frequency Words

board	expensive	popular
cook	favorite	year
enjoy	imagine	

Alesha went to her <u>favorite</u> park.
The park is free, so it is not <u>expensive</u> to go there.
Ducks swim in the lake during part of the <u>year</u>.
The park is <u>popular</u> with people of all ages.
Alesha couldn't <u>imagine</u> a prettier place.
Her little brothers <u>enjoy</u> the playground.
Her dad plays chess on a game <u>board</u>.
They <u>cook</u> food on the grill.

Grade 2, Lesson 12   R61   High-Frequency Words

Transparency R61

Fluency
Punctuation

Review

DIBELS
Oral Reading Fluency
ORF

MODEL USING PUNCTUATION Read aloud page 372 of "At Play: Long Ago and Today." Point out the commas in the sentence *Board games,* like checkers, *were a popular family activity.*

▲ Student Edition, pp. 364–381

Think Aloud When I read sentences with commas, I pause slightly after each comma. This makes reading the sentence sound more like I'm speaking naturally.

Practice/Apply

Routine Card 8

GUIDED PRACTICE Have children echo-read pages 372–373 with you, matching your expression and pacing. Point out the pauses and changes in tone that result from the punctuation of the passage.

INDEPENDENT PRACTICE Have children read along with "At Play: Long Ago and Today" on *Audiotext 2*. Have them practice reading the selection several times until they can read it in "one voice." You may wish to divide the class into groups and assign a section to each group.

BELOW-LEVEL

Echo-Read Some children may pause awkwardly at the ends of lines of text, rather than at punctuation marks. Write some of the sentences from the selection on the board, with no line breaks. Read each sentence aloud and have children repeat, matching your speed, phrasing, and expression. Repeat until children can read each sentence with no difficulty.

Objective

• *To use punctuation to read fluently in a manner that sounds like natural speech*

 MONITOR PROGRESS

Fluency

IF children have difficulty using punctuation to read accurately and in a manner that sounds like natural speech,	**THEN** model reading a section of the selection and have children echo-read after you.

Small-Group Instruction, pp. S14–S15:

 BELOW-LEVEL: Reteach
● **ON-LEVEL:** Reinforce
● **ADVANCED:** Extend

Author's Purpose
Comprehension

Objective

- *To identify an author's purpose for writing*

Skill Trace

 Tested **Author's Purpose**

Introduce	T34–T35
Reteach	S16–S17
Review	**T68, T82, T92, T130–T131, T162, T176, T186, T379, T394**
Test	Theme 3
Maintain	Theme 5, T278

Author's Purpose

Native American Toys and Games

Long ago, Native American children had just as much fun playing as children do today. They didn't buy toys at stores. Instead, they made toys from things found in nature.

Children who lived near forests formed dolls out of materials from trees. Some used pine needles to make dolls with pine "skirts." They made their dolls dance on a thin piece of wood.

Hopi children who lived in what is now Arizona played a board game on a flat stone. They tried to capture each other's animals by jumping over the pieces. It sounds a lot like checkers!

Grade 2, Lesson 12   R57   Comprehension

Transparency R57

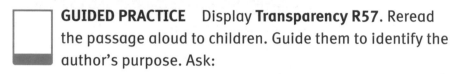

Review

EXPLAIN AUTHOR'S PURPOSE   Ask children to tell how they figure out an author's purpose for writing. (Possible response: I think about what kind of writing it is, and then I figure out why the author wrote it.) Remind children that good readers figure out an author's purpose for writing so they can understand what they are reading.

Practice/Apply

GUIDED PRACTICE   Display **Transparency R57**. Reread the passage aloud to children. Guide them to identify the author's purpose. Ask:

- **Is "Native American Toys and Games" fiction or nonfiction?** (nonfiction; the passage gives information)

- **Why did the author write this passage?** (to tell about Native American toys and games that are like toys and games we play today)

- **Does knowing the author's purpose help you understand the passage? Tell why or why not.** (Possible response: Yes; it helps me know to read for facts and information.)

INDEPENDENT PRACTICE   Ask children to identify the author's purpose for writing "A History of Games and Toys in the United States." (Possible responses: to inform; to tell when some games and toys were made and who created them)

Build Robust Vocabulary

Review Robust Vocabulary

USE VOCABULARY IN DIFFERENT CONTEXTS   Remind children of the Student-Friendly Explanations of the Vocabulary Words. Then discuss the words, using the following activities:

leisurely, ramble   Tell children that you will name some places. If they think these are places where they could leisurely ramble, they should say, "Yes." If they disagree, they should say, "No."

a busy airport	**a pretty garden**
a path in the woods	**a crowded shopping mall**

archaic   Tell children that you will name some activities. If they think the activity is archaic, they should say, "That's archaic!" If not, they should say nothing.

driving a horse-drawn wagon

building a castle wall

riding in a car

going to school

nominate, housed   Tell children that you will nominate some animals to be housed in a zoo. If they agree, they should raise their hand. If they disagree, they should do nothing.

a worm	**a monkey**
a lion	**a zebra**
an ant	**a crow**

Objective

• *To review robust vocabulary*

REVIEW   Tested ✔

Vocabulary: Lesson 12

recently	recreation
housed	leisurely
official	ramble
nominate	archaic

▼ **Student-Friendly Explanations**

Student-Friendly Explanations

recently	If something happened not long ago, it happened recently.
housed	If something is placed or lives somewhere, it is housed there.
official	If someone holds a position of authority in an organization, the person is called an official.
nominate	When you suggest that someone should get an office, job, or honor, you nominate the person.
recreation	When you do something fun and relaxing, it is recreation for you.
leisurely	If you do something in a leisurely way, you are not in a hurry.
ramble	When you ramble, you wander around.
archaic	If something is archaic, it is old and not used anymore.

Grade 2, Theme 3   R62   Vocabulary

Transparency R62

Grammar
Singular Possessive Nouns

5-DAY GRAMMAR

DAY 1	Possessive Nouns
DAY 2	Identifying Singular Possessive Nouns
DAY 3	Sentence Formation with Possessive Nouns
DAY 4	**Apply to Writing**
DAY 5	Weekly Review

Objective
• *To write singular possessive nouns correctly in sentences*

Daily Proofreading

ted ran laps at the schools track.

(Ted, school's)

Review

DISCUSS SINGULAR POSSESSIVE NOUNS   Review with children that a singular possessive noun tells who or what something belongs to. Write the following phrases on the board.

the shoes of the <u>soccer player</u>

the gloves of the <u>goalie</u>

the mitt of the <u>baseball player</u>

Tell children that these phrases can be rewritten so that the underlined words show ownership. Point to and read aloud "the shoes of the soccer player." Underneath, write *the soccer player's shoes*. Discuss how the apostrophe plus *s* (*'s*) shows that the shoes belong to the soccer player.

USE EDITOR'S MARKS   Work through each of the remaining phrases to make them show ownership with singular possessive nouns. Model using basic editor's marks to revise them.

Editor's Marks	
∧	Add
ℐ	Take out
⌐	Change
⊙	Add a period
≡	Capitalize

Practice/Apply

GUIDED PRACTICE   Model writing a sentence about outdoor activities, using singular possessive nouns. Call on volunteers to suggest additional sentences. After you write each sentence, model orally how to check that each is complete, uses singular possessive nouns correctly, begins with a capital letter, and ends with punctuation.

INDEPENDENT PRACTICE   Ask children to write three complete sentences that tell about outdoor activities they do after school or at recess. Make sure they include singular possessive nouns. Have partners exchange sentences and check that their sentences are complete thoughts, use singular possessive nouns correctly, begin with a capital letter, and have end punctuation. Have them use editor's marks as necessary.

Name _____
Singular Possessive Nouns
Lesson 12

▶ Read each group of words. Then write it with a possessive noun.

1. the house of Tony   Tony's house
2. the skateboard that belongs to Tim   Tim's skateboard
3. the bone that belongs to Fido   Fido's bone
4. the backpack that belongs to Marcia   Marcia's backpack

▶ Write each sentence so that the noun in ( ) shows ownership.

5. (Mr. Franklin) dog was lost.
   Mr. Franklin's dog was lost.
6. We checked (Mrs. Brown) yard.
   We checked Mrs. Brown's yard.
7. We looked in (the mailman) yard, too.
   We looked in the mailman's yard, too.
8. The dog was under (Mr. Franklin) car the whole time!
   The dog was under Mr. Franklin's car the whole time!

43   Grammar Practice Book

▲ **Grammar Practice Book, p. 43**

Day 4

5-DAY WRITING	
DAY 1	Introduce
DAY 2	Prewrite
DAY 3	Draft
DAY 4	**Revise**
DAY 5	Revise

Writing
Paragraph That Gives Information

Write and Revise

WRITE Have children continue writing their paragraphs. Remind them that the sentences in their paragraph should give more information about their main idea.

 VOICE Have children look for words that they can replace with action words or exact words so the reader knows they care about what they are writing about.

REVISE Have children read their paragraphs to a partner. They should check that the paragraph begins with a main idea and that all the other sentences tell more about the main idea. Suggest that children use the list of criteria for a Paragraph That Gives Information to improve their writing.

> ### Paragraph That Gives Information
>
> - The paragraph gives information about a real topic.
> - The first sentence tells the main idea.
> - The other sentences give more information about the main idea.
> - Some of the sentences tell what to do in the correct order, or sequence.

Have children revise their paragraphs. Let them work together to make sure any singular possessive nouns are used correctly. Encourage children to use editor's marks to revise their writing. Save children's paragraphs to continue revising on Day 5.

Editor's Marks

∧	Add
✐	Take out
⌐	Change
⊙	Add a period
≡	Capitalize
◯	Check Spelling

Objectives

- *To revise a paragraph that gives information*
- *To use singular possessive nouns correctly*

 ### Writing Prompt

Evaluate Have children write what they liked about their partners' paragraphs.

BELOW-LEVEL

Use Tape Recorders Allow children to record their ideas on audiotape; then work with them to listen to the tape and organize their ideas into a written paragraph.

DAILY ROUTINES

Day at a Glance

Day 5

 phonics and Spelling
- Review: Inflections *-ed, -es* (*y* to *i*)
- Posttest: Long Vowel /ē/*ey, y*

High-Frequency Words
- Cumulative Review

Fluency
- Punctuation
- "At Play: Long Ago and Today," *Student Edition*, pp. 364–381

Comprehension

 Review: Author's Purpose
- *Read-Aloud Anthology:* "Cardboard Box Joins Toy Hall of Fame"

Robust Vocabulary
- Cumulative Review

Grammar
- Review: Singular Possessive Nouns

Writing
- Paragraph That Gives Information

Warm-Up Routines

 Oral Language

Objective *To listen attentively and respond appropriately to oral communication*

Question of the Day

What are some ways to have fun with friends and family members?

Invite children to share ways that they have fun with friends and family members. Use the following prompts.

- **Do you share your toys? Which ones?**
- **What games and sports do you play?**
- **What do you do to make your friends or family members laugh?**

On the board, keep a list of ways children have fun with others.

Read Aloud

Objective *To identify rhymes in poetry*

BIG BOOK OF RHYMES AND POEMS
Display the poem "Sharing the Swing" on page 24. Ask children to listen for words that rhyme. Then read aloud the poem. Guide children to identify the rhyming words *myself/shelf*, *brother/other*, and *high/sky*. Lead children to notice that each set of two lines ends with rhyming words. Then read the poem again, inviting children to join in.

▲ **Big Book of Rhymes and Poems, p. 24**

Word Wall

Objective *To read high-frequency words*

REVIEW HIGH-FREQUENCY WORDS   Review the words *imagine*, *favorite*, *year*, *enjoy*, *cook*, *board*, *popular*, and *expensive*. Point to a card at random and ask children to read the word. Have children read the words several times.

favorite	imagine	year	enjoy
cook	popular	board	expensive

Inflections -ed, -es (y to i) phonics

5-DAY PHONICS	
DAY 1	Introduce /ē/ey, y
DAY 2	Word Building with /ē/ey, y
DAY 3	Word Building with /ē/ey, y
DAY 4	Inflections -ed, -es (y to i); Review /ē/ey, y
DAY 5	Inflections -ed, -es (y to i); Review /ē/ey, y

Objective

• To read two-syllable words with the inflections -ed and -es

Skill Trace

Tested **Inflections -ed, -es (y to i)**

Introduce	T172
Review	**T182**
Test	Theme 3

Review

READ y TO i WORDS Write the word *babies* on the board. Underline the letters *ies* and remind children that the *y* in the word *baby* was changed to *i* before adding -es. Have children read the word. Repeat the procedure with *scurried*.

Practice/Apply

GUIDED PRACTICE Write the following words on the board and have children read them: *blueberries*, *buried*, *cherries*, and *candies*. Then make a chart as shown. Guide children in sorting the words by consonants and adding them to the chart.

double consonants	no double consonants
blueberries	candies
cherries	buried

INDEPENDENT PRACTICE Ask children to add more words to the chart. Then point to the words at random and have children read them.

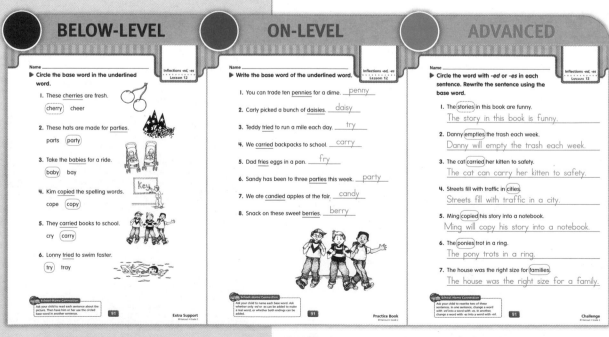

▲ **Extra Support, p. 91**   ▲ **Practice Book, p. 91**   ▲ **Challenge, p. 91**

BELOW-LEVEL · **ON-LEVEL** · **ADVANCED**

E L L

• Group children according to academic levels, and assign one of the pages on the left.

• Clarify any unfamiliar concepts as necessary. See *ELL Teacher Guide* Lesson 12 for support in scaffolding instruction.

Day **5**

5-DAY SPELLING
DAY 1 Pretest
DAY 2 Word Building
DAY 3 State the Generalization
DAY 4 Review
DAY 5 Posttest

Long Vowel /ē/ey, y
phonics and Spelling

Assess

POSTTEST   Assess children's progress. Use the dictation sentences from Day 1.

Words with /ē/ey, y

1.	very	The rainstorm got us **very** wet.
2.	messy	The **messy** girl spilled her food.
3.	lady	The **lady** danced with the prince at the ball.
4.	happy	The **happy** puppy ran around the room.
5.	key	Use the **key** to open the lock.
6.	baby	The **baby** likes to play with blocks.
7.	money	Do you save your **money** in a piggy bank?
8.	funny	Julian giggled at the **funny** joke.
9.	candy	Frank made fudge and other **candy**.
10.	sunny	Do you play outside on **sunny** days?

ADVANCED

Challenge Words   Use the challenge words in these dictation sentences.

11.	chimney	The smoke rose out of the **chimney**.
12.	nobody	**Nobody** makes mushroom ice cream.
13.	breezy	The flags waved in the **breezy** weather.
14.	twenty	We counted **twenty** grapes on the plate.
15.	keyhole	The castle door has a large **keyhole**.

WRITING APPLICATION

Have children write and illustrate a sentence using two of the spelling words.

We eat candy on a sunny day.

Objective

- *To use /ē/ey, y and other known letter-sounds to spell and write words*

Spelling Words

1.	**very***	6.	**baby**
2.	**messy**	7.	**money**
3.	**lady**	8.	**funny**
4.	**happy**	9.	**candy**
5.	**key**	10.	**sunny**

Challenge Words

11.	**chimney**	14.	**twenty**
12.	**nobody**	15.	**keyhole**
13.	**breezy**		

* Word from "At Play: Long Ago and Today"

High-Frequency Words

Objectives
- *To read high-frequency words*
- *To explore word relationships*

REVIEW **Tested**

High-Frequency Words

bought	board
draw	cook
especially	enjoy
minute	expensive
picture	favorite
question	imagine
sure	popular
worry	year

Cumulative Review

REINFORCE WORD RECOGNITION   Write the high-frequency words for Lessons 11 and 12 on the board. Point to words at random, and ask children to read them.

SORT WORDS   Guide children in sorting the words into columns according to the number of letters. Then have them read the words in each column again.

1–5 letters	6 or more letters
draw	picture
worry	question
sure	minute
year	especially
cook	bought
enjoy	imagine
board	popular
	favorite
	expensive

- Ask: **Which words begin with the /b/ sound?** (bought, board)
- Ask: **Which word has the word *pop* in it?** (popular)
- Ask: **Which word begins and ends with the /k/ sound?** (cook)
- Ask: **Which word has the word *joy* in it?** (enjoy)
- Ask: **Which word rhymes with *dear*?** (year)
- Ask: **Which words have more than two syllables?** (especially, imagine, popular, favorite, expensive)

Fluency
Punctuation

Readers' Theater

▲ Student Edition, pp. 364–381

DIBELS
Oral Reading Fluency
ORF

PERFORM "AT PLAY: LONG AGO AND TODAY" To help children improve their fluency, have them perform "At Play: Long Ago and Today" as Readers' Theater. Use the following procedures:

- Discuss with children how they can use punctuation to help them know when to pause to make their reading sound like natural speech.

- Have groups of three children read the selection together. Children should alternate sections or pages.

- Monitor the groups as they read. Provide feedback and support.

- Invite the groups to read the selection to classmates. Remind them to focus on using the punctuation to help them read accurately and with expression.

E L L

Questions and Exclamations Remind children who read Spanish that English does not have upside-down question marks and exclamation points at the beginning of sentences. Model how to let your eyes jump quickly to the end of a sentence to determine if it is a question or an exclamation.

Objective

- *To use punctuation to read fluently in a manner that sounds like natural speech*

 ASSESSMENT

Monitoring Progress Periodically, take a timed sample of children's oral reading and record the number of words read correctly per minute. Children should accurately read approximately 72 words per minute in the middle of Grade 2.

Fluency Support Materials

 Fluency Builders, Grade 2, Lesson 12

 Audiotext *Student Edition* selections are available on *Audiotext 2.*

 Strategic Intervention Teacher Guide, Lesson 12

Author's Purpose
Comprehension

Objective

- *To identify an author's purpose for writing*

Skill Trace

 Tested **Author's Purpose**

Introduce	T34–T35
Reteach	S16–S17
Review	**T68, T82, T92, T130–T131, T162, T176, T186, T379, T394**
Test	Theme 3
Maintain	Theme 5, T278

E L L

Build Background If children have difficulty understanding the concept of a hall of fame, name some hall of fame athletes with whom they are familiar. As an alternative, name well-known people in your school or community who could be part of a local hall of fame.

Review

REVIEW THE SKILL Remind children that good readers identify an author's purpose for writing. Point out that understanding the author's purpose can help them read more carefully.

SET A PURPOSE FOR LISTENING Guide children to set a purpose for listening that includes

- listening for information about the Toy Hall of Fame.
- listening to find out why the author wrote the selection.

▲ Read-Aloud Anthology, "Cardboard Box Joins Toy Hall of Fame," p. 46

Practice/Apply

GUIDED PRACTICE As you read aloud "Cardboard Box Joins Toy Hall of Fame," record information about the author's purpose in a chart.

Kind of Writing	Author's Purpose
nonfiction or news story	to give information about the National Toy Hall of Fame

INDEPENDENT PRACTICE Have children review what they know about the author's purpose by looking at the chart. Then have them tell how knowing the author's purpose helps them understand the selection. (Possible response: When I know that the author's purpose is to give information, I think about what I already know about the topic. I listen or read to find out new information about the topic.)

Build Robust Vocabulary

Cumulative Review

REINFORCE MEANINGS Ask children the following questions:

- **Would you be likely to ramble in a park that people are beautifying? Tell why or why not.**

- **Would an executive also be considered an official? Why or why not?**

- **What kind of recreation do you do with your kin? What kind of recreation do you do with your fellow students?**

MAKE WORD WEBS Using **Transparency GO9,** guide children to complete word webs to enrich their understanding of *recreation* and *ramble*. Write *recreation* in the center of a word web and have children name examples of *recreation*. Write their responses.

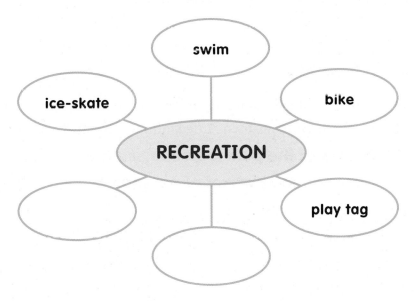

Then have children create their own web for *ramble*. Have them fill in the webs with places to ramble.

Objective
- *To review robust vocabulary*

REVIEW Vocabulary

Lesson 11	Lesson 12
filthy	recently
fellow	housed
executive	offical
beautifying	nominate
renowned	recreation
kin	leisurely
original	ramble
adorn	archaic

✔ MONITOR PROGRESS

Build Robust Vocabulary

IF children do not demonstrate understanding of the words and have difficulty using them,	THEN model using each word in several sentences, and have children repeat each sentence.

Small-Group Instruction, pp. S18–S19:

- ● **BELOW-LEVEL:** Reteach
- ● **ON-LEVEL:** Reinforce
- ○ **ADVANCED:** Extend

Grammar
Singular Possessive Nouns

5-DAY GRAMMAR

DAY 1	Possessive Nouns
DAY 2	Identifying Singular Possessive Nouns
DAY 3	Sentence Formation with Possessive Nouns
DAY 4	Apply to Writing
DAY 5	Weekly Review

Objectives

- *To write singular possessive nouns correctly in sentences*
- *To write in complete, coherent sentences*

Daily Proofreading

We picked the bushs berryes.

(bush's, berries)

 Language Arts Checkpoint

If children have difficulty with the concepts, see pages S20–S21 to reteach.

Review

REVIEW SINGULAR POSSESSIVE NOUNS   Review the rules for forming singular possessive nouns. Write these rules on the board.

> - **A singular possessive noun shows ownership.**
> - **It tells who or what something belongs to.**
> - **Add an apostrophe plus *s* ('s) to show ownership by one person, animal, or thing.**

Practice/Apply

GUIDED PRACTICE   Model revising the following phrase to use a singular possessive noun.

> **the carnival of the town** (the town's carnival)

Write the following sentences on the board. Ask volunteers to help you revise the phrases to include singular possessive nouns.

> **The hill of the park is steep.** (park's hill)
>
> **We sit on the blanket of our mother.** (our mother's blanket)

INDEPENDENT PRACTICE   Write the following sentences on the board. Explain that each needs a noun that shows ownership. Have children form the possessive of each word in parentheses and rewrite the sentence. Have volunteers read aloud their corrected sentences.

> **She washed her _____ car. (dad)** (dad's)
>
> **She sold lemonade in front of her _____ house. (aunt)** (aunt's)
>
> **The _____ piggybank was full. (girl)** (girl's)

Name _____

▶ Follow the directions to write the possessive form of each noun.

Singular Possessive Nouns
Lesson 12

1. American + apostrophe + s
   American's
2. country + apostrophe + s
   country's
3. eagle + apostrophe + s
   eagle's
4. flag + apostrophe + s
   flag's
5. George Washington + apostrophe + s
   George Washington's

▶ Write sentences for three of the possessive nouns you wrote above. Possible responses are shown.

6. Our country's name is the United States.
7. The eagle's wings are large.
8. The American flag's colors are red, white, and blue.

Point to three objects in your home. Ask your child to use a possessive noun to tell who owns each object.

92

Practice Book

▲ **Practice Book, p. 92**

Writing

Paragraph That Gives Information

5-DAY WRITING

DAY 1	Introduce
DAY 2	Prewrite
DAY 3	Draft
DAY 4	Revise
DAY 5	Revise

Revise

REVIEW PARAGRAPH CONTENT   Remind children to check that their paragraphs have a main-idea sentence and that the other sentences tell more about the main idea. Have them check again that any steps they describe are in an order that makes sense.

REVIEW CONVENTIONS   Remind children that any words that show ownership should be written with an apostrophe plus *s* (*'s*). Children should also make sure that their handwriting is neat.

WRITING TRAIT   **VOICE**   Have children share examples from their writing to show that they are excited about their topic. Discuss how showing an interest in the topic helps readers find the writing interesting, too.

Objective

- *To revise paragraphs to improve focus*

Writing Prompt

Record Reflections   Have children write about a game they learned from a classmate.

WEEKLY LESSON TEST

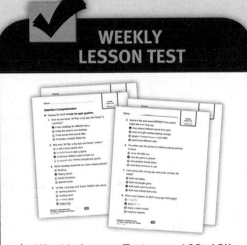

▲ **Weekly Lesson Tests, pp. 123–134**

- Selection Comprehension with Short Response
- Phonics and Spelling
- High-Frequency Words
- Focus Skill
- Robust Vocabulary
- Grammar
- Fluency Passage

 GO online   For prescriptions, see pp. A2–A6. Also available electronically on StoryTown Online Assessment and ExamView.

Podcasting: Assessing Fluency

NOTE: A 4-point rubric appears on page R8.

SCORING RUBRIC

	6	5	4	3	2	1
FOCUS	Completely focused, purposeful.	Focused on topic and purpose.	Generally focused on topic and purpose.	Somewhat focused on topic and purpose.	Related to topic but does not maintain focus.	Lacks focus and purpose.
ORGANIZATION	Ideas progress logically; paper conveys sense of completeness.	Organization mostly clear; paper gives sense of completeness.	Organization mostly clear, but some lapses occur; may seem unfinished.	Some sense of organization; seems unfinished.	Little sense of organization.	Little or no sense of organization.
SUPPORT	Strong, specific details; clear, exact language; freshness of expression.	Strong, specific details; clear, exact language.	Adequate support and word choice.	Limited supporting details; limited word choice.	Few supporting details; limited word choice.	Little development; limited or unclear word choice.
CONVENTIONS	Varied sentences; few, if any, errors.	Varied sentences; few errors.	Some sentence variety; few errors.	Simple sentence structures; some errors.	Simple sentence structures; many errors.	Unclear sentence structures; many errors.

REPRODUCIBLE RUBRICS for specific writing purposes and presentations are available on pages R3–R8.

Leveled Readers

Reinforcing Skills and Strategies

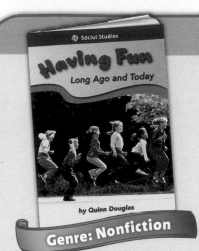

Genre: Nonfiction

by Quinn Douglas

BELOW-LEVEL

Having Fun: Long Ago and Today

SUMMARY Children's games, sports, and other activities from past and present are compared.

-  **phonics** Long Vowel /ē/ ey, y
- **High-Frequency Words**

  Author's Purpose

  Focus Skill

Before Reading

BUILD BACKGROUND/SET PURPOSE Have children name activities they do just to have fun. Then guide children to preview the story and set a purpose for reading it.

Reading the Book

PAGES 4–7 MAIN IDEA AND DETAILS What can you learn about board games and music from these pages? (Board games were played long ago, and they're still played today. Children of long ago liked listening to music on the radio, but children of today can listen on music players.)

PAGE 14 AUTHOR'S PURPOSE Why do you think the author decided to write about this topic? (The author wants to show that children of today like some of the same activities as children of long ago.)

REREAD FOR FLUENCY Have partners take turns pointing to a picture and reading the sentences that go with it as if talking naturally to each other. Remind them to make their voice go up at the end of a question.

Think Critically *(See inside back cover for questions.)*

1. **MAKE COMPARISONS** play games and sports, listen to music, read
2. **CAUSE AND EFFECT** Books were very expensive and hard to find.
3. **NOTE DETAILS** They played in their neighborhoods.
4. **AUTHOR'S PURPOSE** Responses will vary.
5. **PERSONAL RESPONSE** Responses will vary.

LEVELED READERS TEACHER GUIDE

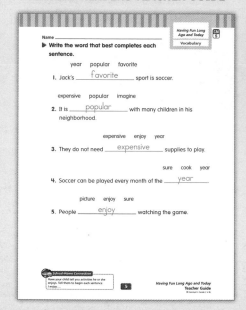

▲ High-Frequency Words, p. 5

▲ Comprehension, p. 6

ON-LEVEL

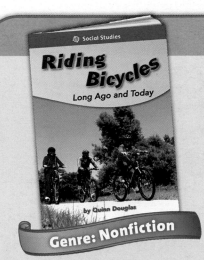

Genre: Nonfiction

Riding Bicycles: Long Ago and Today

SUMMARY   Bicycles and bicycle riding have changed from the 1860s until today.

• **phonics**   Long Vowel /ē/ *ey, y*

• **High-Frequency Words**

Focus Skill   Author's Purpose

LEVELED READERS TEACHER GUIDE

▲ **High-Frequency Words, p. 5**

▲ **Comprehension, p. 6**

Before Reading

BUILD BACKGROUND/SET PURPOSE   Ask children to describe a bicycle to someone who has never seen one. List several features they suggest, such as front and back wheels, hand brakes, and a padded seat. Ask children whether they think bicycles of long ago had the same features. Then guide children to preview the story and set a purpose for reading it.

Reading the Book

PAGES 3–9   **AUTHOR'S PURPOSE**   What is the author's purpose for writing "Riding Bicycles: Long Ago and Today?" (The author wants to give information about old-fashioned and new bicycles.)

PAGES 12–13   **MAIN IDEA AND DETAILS**   What do bicycle riders do today to stay safe? (They wear special protection for their heads, arms, and legs. They wear helmets. They learn rules. Children sometimes go to bicycle safety classes.)

REREAD FOR FLUENCY   Have each partner choose a page that is especially interesting and read it aloud so that it would sound interesting to a listener.

Think Critically   *(See inside back cover for questions.)*

1 **CONTEXT CLUES**   It had steel wheels that would shake the rider.

2 **SPECULATE**   Responses will vary.

3 **NOTE DETAILS**   Bicycle riders must wear helmets.

4 **AUTHOR'S PURPOSE**   Responses will vary.

5 **PERSONAL OPINION**   Responses will vary.

Leveled Readers
Reinforcing Skills and Strategies

ADVANCED

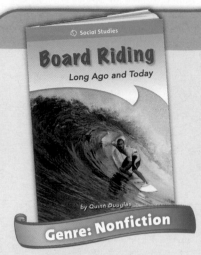

Genre: Nonfiction

Board Riding: Long Ago and Today

SUMMARY Surfboarding, skateboarding, snowboarding, and wakeboarding are four boarding sports that have developed from the past to the present.

- **phonics** Long Vowel /ē/ ey, y
- **High-Frequency Words**
  Author's Purpose

Before Reading

BUILD BACKGROUND/SET PURPOSE Ask children to think about riding a board on water or on snow. In what ways might the boards and the rides be different? Then guide children to preview the story and set a purpose for reading it.

Reading the Book

PAGES 9–11   MAIN IDEA AND DETAILS   How has snowboarding changed over the years? (The first snowboard was a small board with a rope handle. Today's snowboards have straps for the feet, and snowboarders wear special boots and other gear.)

PAGE 14   AUTHOR'S PURPOSE   What is the author's purpose for writing "Board Riding: Long Ago and Today?" (To give information about the four board sports and how they all came from surfing in Hawaii.)

REREAD FOR FLUENCY Have partners take turns reading the book a page at a time. Remind children to take a short pause for commas and a longer pause for periods.

Think Critically   *(See inside back cover for questions.)*

1. **NOTE DETAILS** Surfing began in Hawaii hundreds of years ago.

2. **COMPARE AND CONTRAST** Responses will vary.

3. **SPECULATE** Responses will vary.

4. **AUTHOR'S PURPOSE** Responses will vary.

5. **PERSONAL RESPONSE** Responses will vary.

LEVELED READERS TEACHER GUIDE

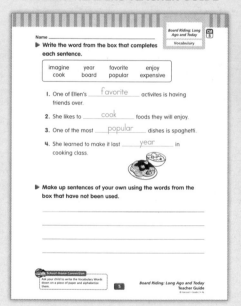

▲ High-Frequency Words, p. 5

▲ Comprehension, p. 6

Genre: **Realistic Fiction**

Toys: Long Ago and Today

SUMMARY As a boy plays with his grandfather, he tells how his toys are like and unlike the ones his grandfather had as a child.

- **Build Background**
- **Concept Vocabulary**
- **Scaffolded Language Development**

Before Reading

BUILD BACKGROUND/SET PURPOSE Ask children to give examples of battery-operated toys. Choose one example, and talk about whether there is a toy like it that does not need a battery to work. Then guide children to preview the story and set a purpose for reading it.

Reading the Book

PAGES 8–9 MAKE INFERENCES Why are the boy and the grandfather each good at different games? (Possible response: Grandfather has had a lot of practice with board games, and the boy has had a lot of practice with video games.)

PAGE 14 🌀 **AUTHOR'S PURPOSE** What was the author's purpose for writing "Toys: Long Ago and Today"? (The author wants to teach and entertain with a story.)

REREAD FOR FLUENCY Have partners take turns reading the story a page at a time. Remind children to be aware of punctuation.

Scaffolded Language Development

(See inside back cover for teacher-led activity.)

Provide additional examples and explanation as needed.

LEVELED READERS TEACHER GUIDE

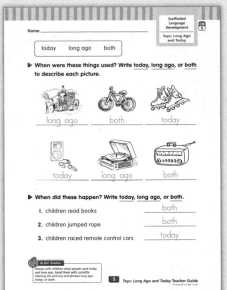

▲ **Scaffolded Language Development, p. 5**

▲ **Build Background and Vocabulary, p. 6**

Lesson 13

WEEK AT A GLANCE

✔ Phonics
Consonants /s/c; /j/g, dge
Inflections -ed, -ing (double final consonant)

✔ Spelling
slice, dodge, city, huge, nice, space, gem, price, cage, fudge

✔ High-Frequency Words
above, shoes, tough, wash, wear, woman, young

Reading
"Big Bushy Mustache" by Gary Soto
REALISTIC FICTION

"Changing" by Mary Ann Hoberman   POETRY

✔ Fluency
Phrasing

✔ Comprehension
 Fiction and Nonfiction

 Monitor Comprehension: Reread

✔ Robust Vocabulary
wilting, flitted, swirling, trance, route, semblance, distraught, improvise

✔ Grammar
Plural Possessive Nouns

Writing
Form: Story: Dialogue
Trait: Conventions

✔ Weekly Lesson Test

 = Focus Skill   = Focus Strategy   = Tested Skill

One stop *for all* your **Digital** needs

Digital
CLASSROOM

 www.harcourtschool.com/storytown
To go along with your print program

FOR THE TEACHER

Prepare Professional Development

 Videos for Podcasting

Plan & Organize Online TE & Planning Resources*

Teach Transparencies

for electronic projection

Assess Online Assessment*

with Student Tracking System and Prescriptions

FOR THE STUDENT

Read  Student eBook*

 Strategic Intervention Interactive Reader

 Decodable Books

 Leveled Readers

Practice & Apply Splash into Phonics CD-ROM

 Comprehension Expedition CD-ROM

 Also available on CD-ROM

Lesson 13 **T195**

Literature Resources

eBook
STUDENT EDITION

Big Bushy Mustache
by Gary Soto
illustrated by Joe Cepeda

Genre: Realistic Fiction

Changing
by Mary Ann Hoberman

Genre: Poetry

 ◀ **Audiotext** *Student Edition selections are available on Audiotext 2.*

Accelerated Reader ◀ *Practice Quizzes for the Selection*

THEME CONNECTION: CHANGING TIMES
Comparing Realistic Fiction and Poetry

Paired Selections

 SOCIAL STUDIES **Big Bushy Mustache, pp. 392–417**

SUMMARY In order to look more like his father, Ricky borrows a mustache from a school costume to wear home.

 LANGUAGE ARTS **Changing, pp. 418–419**

SUMMARY This poem describes what it might be like to change places with someone else.

Support for Differentiated Instruction

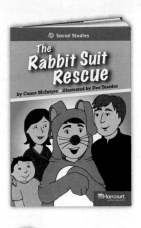

● **BELOW-LEVEL** ● **ON-LEVEL** ○ **ADVANCED**

E L L

LEVELED PRACTICE

◄ **Strategic Intervention Resource Kit, Lesson 13**

◄ **Strategic Intervention Interactive Reader, Lesson 13**

Strategic Intervention Interactive Reader Online

◄ **ELL Extra Support Kit, Lesson 13**

◄ **Challenge Resource Kit, Lesson 13**

● **BELOW-LEVEL**
Extra Support Copying Masters, pp. 93, 95–98

● **ON-LEVEL**
Practice Book, pp. 93–99

○ **ADVANCED**
Challenge Copying Masters, pp. 93, 95–98

E L L

ELL Copying Masters Lesson 13

ADDITIONAL RESOURCES

butterfly

firefighter

Read with a Recording

- Decodable Book 11
- Spelling Practice Book, pp. 41–43
- Grammar Practice Book, pp. 45–48
- Reading Transparencies R63–R68
- Language Arts Transparencies LA26–LA27
- Test Prep System
◄ Literacy Center Kit, Cards 61–65
- Sound/Spelling Cards
◄ Fluency Builders
◄ Picture Card Collection
- Read-Aloud Anthology, pp. 48–51

ASSESSMENT

✓ **Monitor Progress**

✓ **Weekly Lesson Tests, Lesson 13**

- Comprehension
- Phonics and Spelling
- Focus Skill
- Robust Vocabulary
- High-Frequency Words
- Grammar

 GO online
www.harcourtschool.com/storytown
Online Assessment
Also available on CD-ROM—Exam View

Suggested Lesson Planner

 GO online Online TE & Planning Resources

	Day 1	Day 2

Step 1 Whole Group

Daily Routines
- Oral Language
- Read Aloud
- High-Frequency Words

Day 1

QUESTION OF THE DAY, p. T206
Who is someone that you look up to? Why do you look up to this person?

READ ALOUD, p. T207
Transparency R63: Ana and Her Sister

WORD WALL, p. T207

Day 2

QUESTION OF THE DAY, p. T218
Are two people ever the same? Tell why.

READ ALOUD, p. T219
Big Book of Rhymes and Poems, "Did You Ever Think?"

WORD WALL, p. T219

Word Work

 • phonics
- Spelling
- High-Frequency Words

Day 1

 phonics, p. T208
Introduce: Consonants /s/c; /j/g, dge

SPELLING, p. T211
Pretest: *slice, dodge, city, huge, nice, space, hem, price, cage, fudge*

Day 2

 phonics, p. T220
Review: Consonants /s/c; /j/g, dge

SPELLING, p. T221
Word Building

HIGH-FREQUENCY WORDS
Words to Know, p. T222
Introduce: *above, shoes, tough, wash, wear, woman, young*

Skills and Strategies
- Reading
- Fluency
- Comprehension
- Build Robust Vocabulary

Day 1

READING Words with Soft *c* and Soft *g*, p. T209

COMPREHENSION, p. T212
Introduce: Fiction and Nonfiction

LISTENING COMPREHENSION, p. T214
Read-Aloud: "Butterfly Boy"

FLUENCY, p. T214
Focus: Phrasing

BUILD ROBUST VOCABULARY, p. T215
Words from the Read-Aloud

Day 2

READING, p. T224
"Big Bushy Mustache"
Options for Reading

COMPREHENSION, p. T224
Introduce: Monitor
Comprehension: Reread

▲ Student Edition

RETELLING/FLUENCY, p. T238
Phrasing

BUILD ROBUST VOCABULARY, p. T239
Words About the Selection

Step 2 Small Groups

Suggestions for Differentiated Instruction (See pp. T200–T201.)

Step 3 Whole Group

Language Arts
- Grammar
- Writing

Day 1

GRAMMAR, p. T216
Introduce: Plural Possessive Nouns

Daily Proofreading
tanyas dogs ran across the yard?
(Tanya's, yard.)

 WRITING, p. T217
Introduce: Story: Dialogue
Writing Trait: Conventions

Writing Prompt *Write out a short conversation that you had today with a friend at school.*

Day 2

GRAMMAR, p. T240
Introduce: Plural Possessive Nouns

Daily Proofreading
the three cats bed (the three cats' beds)
the mices cheese (the mice's cheese)

 WRITING, p. T241
Review: Story: Dialogue
Writing Trait: Conventions

Writing Prompt *Write your feelings about your story ideas.*

 = Focus Skill    = Focus Strategy    = Tested Skill

phonics
- Consonants /s/c; /j/g, dge
- Inflections -ed, -ing

Comprehension

 **Focus Skill**
Fiction and Nonfiction

 **Focus Strategy** Monitor
Comprehension: Reread

Fluency
Phrasing

Vocabulary
HIGH-FREQUENCY: *above, shoes, tough, wash, wear, woman, young*

ROBUST: *wilting, flitted, swirling, trance, route, semblance, distraught, improvise*

Day 3

QUESTION OF THE DAY, p. T242
In what ways can people be alike? In what ways is everyone special?

READ ALOUD, p. T243
Big Book of Rhymes and Poems, "Did You Ever Think?"

WORD WALL, p. T243

  phonics, p. T244
Review: Consonants /s/c; /j/g, dge

 SPELLING, p. T245
State the Generalization

 HIGH-FREQUENCY WORDS, p. T246
Review: *above, shoes, tough, wash, wear, woman, young*

FLUENCY, p. T247
Phrasing: "Big Bushy Mustache"

 COMPREHENSION, p. T248
 Review: Fiction and Nonfiction
Paired Selection: "Changing"

▲ Student Edition

CONNECTIONS, p. T250

 **BUILD ROBUST VOCABULARY,** p. T252
Review

Day 4

QUESTION OF THE DAY, p. T256
What are some things you do at home before you leave for school each morning?

READ ALOUD, p. T257
Big Book of Rhymes and Poems, "Aliona Says"

WORD WALL, p. T257

  phonics, p. T258
Introduce: Inflections -ed, -ing

SPELLING, p. T259
Review Spelling Words

HIGH-FREQUENCY WORDS, p. T260
Review: *above, shoes, tough, wash, wear, woman, young*

FLUENCY, p. T261
Phrasing: "Big Bushy Mustache"

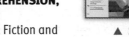 **COMPREHENSION,** p. T262
Review: Fiction and Nonfiction

▲ Student Edition

 BUILD ROBUST VOCABULARY, p. T263
Review

Day 5

QUESTION OF THE DAY, p. T266
What is good advice to give someone leaving for school in the morning? Why?

READ ALOUD, p. T267
Big Book of Rhymes and Poems, "Aliona Says"

WORD WALL, p. T267

 phonics, p. T268
Introduce: Inflections -ed, -ing

SPELLING, p. T269
Posttest

HIGH-FREQUENCY WORDS, p. T270
Cumulative Review: *imagine, favorite, year, enjoy, cook, board, popular, expensive, wear, tough, woman, young, shoes, wash, above*

FLUENCY, p. T271
Phrasing: "Big Bushy Mustache"

 **COMPREHENSION,** p. T272
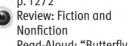 Review: Fiction and Nonfiction
Read-Aloud: "Butterfly Boy"

▲ Student Edition

 BUILD ROBUST VOCABULARY, p. T273
Cumulative Review

● **BELOW-LEVEL**   ● **ON-LEVEL**   ● **ADVANCED**   **E L L**

 **GRAMMAR,** p. T254
Review: Plural Possessive Nouns

Daily Proofreading
the childrens' bikes were all red.
(The, children's)

 WRITING, p. T255
Review: Story: Dialogue
Writing Trait: Conventions

Writing Prompt *Write more dialogue between Ricky and his mother.*

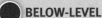 **GRAMMAR,** p. T264
Review: Plural Possessive Nouns

Daily Proofreading
Most peoples best Friends are nice to them.
(people's, friends)

  WRITING, p. T265
Review: Story: Dialogue
Writing Trait: Conventions

Writing Prompt *Use quotation marks to write a conversation that you heard today at school.*

  GRAMMAR, p. T274
Review: Plural Possessive Nouns

Daily Proofreading
my parents home is in ohio
(My, parents', Ohio.)

  WRITING, p. T275
Review: Story: Dialogue
Writing Trait: Conventions

Writing Prompt *Write your thoughts about writing with dialogue.*

Suggested Small-Group Planner

45–60 Minutes

 BELOW-LEVEL 15–20 Minutes

 ON-LEVEL 15–20 Minutes

 ADVANCED 15–20 Minutes

Day 1

Day 2

BELOW-LEVEL

Day 1

Teacher-Directed
Leveled Reader:
"The Hamster Escape"
p. T276
Before Reading

Independent
⭐ Listening/Speaking Center,
p. T204
Extra Support Copying Masters, pp. 93, 95

▲ Leveled Reader

Day 2

Teacher-Directed
Student Edition:
"Big Bushy Mustache"
p. T224

Independent
⭐ Reading Center, p. T205
Extra Support Copying Masters,
pp. 96–97

▲ Student Edition

ON-LEVEL

Day 1

Teacher-Directed
Leveled Reader:
"The Rabbit Suit Rescue"
p. T277
Before Reading

Independent
⭐ Reading Center, p. T204
Practice Book, pp. 93, 95

▲ Leveled Reader

Day 2

Teacher-Directed
Student Edition:
"Big Bushy Mustache"
p. T224

Independent
⭐ Letters and Sounds
Center, p. T205
Practice Book, pp. 96–97

▲ Student Edition

ADVANCED

Day 1

Teacher-Directed
Leveled Reader:
"The Dinosaur Drawing Delivery"
p. T277
Before Reading

Independent
⭐ Letters and Sounds Center, p. T205
Challenge Copying Masters, pp. 93, 95

▲ Leveled Reader

Day 2

Teacher-Directed
Leveled Reader: "The Dinosaur
Drawing Delivery" p. T277
Read the Book

Independent
⭐ Word Work Center, p. T205
Challenge Copying Masters,
pp. 96–97

▲ Leveled Reader

ELL

English-Language Learners

In addition to the small-group instruction above, use the ELL Extra Support Kit to promote language development.

LANGUAGE DEVELOPMENT SUPPORT
Teacher-Directed
ELL TG, Day 1
Independent
ELL Copying Masters, Lesson 13

▲ ELL Student Handbook

LANGUAGE DEVELOPMENT SUPPORT
Teacher-Directed
ELL TG, Day 2
Independent
ELL Copying Masters, Lesson 13

▲ ELL Student Handbook

Intervention

▲ Strategic Intervention
Resource Kit

▲ Strategic Intervention
Interactive Reader

Strategic Intervention TG, Day 1
Strategic Intervention Practice Book, Lesson 13

Strategic Intervention TG, Day 2
Strategic Intervention Interactive
Reader, Lesson 13

▲ Strategic Intervention
Interactive Reader

MONITOR PROGRESS

Small-Group Instruction

Comprehension	Phonics	High-Frequency Words	Fluency	Robust Vocabulary	Language Arts Checkpoint
Focus Skill Author's Purpose pp.S26–S27	Consonants /s/c; /j/g, dge p. S22	above, shoes, tough, wash, wear, woman, young p. S23	Phrasing pp. S24–S25	wilting, flitted, swirling, trance, route, semblance, distraught, improvise pp. S28–S29	**Grammar:** Plural Possessive Nouns **Writing:** Story: Dialogue pp. S30–S31

Day 3

Teacher-Directed
Leveled Reader: "The Hamster Escape" p. T276
Read the Book

Independent
⭐ Word Work Center, p. T205

▲ Leveled Reader

Teacher-Directed
Leveled Reader: "The Rabbit Suit Rescue" p. T277
Read the Book

Independent
⭐ Writing Center, p. T205

▲ Leveled Reader

Teacher-Directed
Leveled Reader: "The Dinosaur Drawing Delivery" p. T278
Think Critically

Independent
⭐ Listening/Speaking Center, p. T204

▲ Leveled Reader

LANGUAGE DEVELOPMENT SUPPORT

Teacher-Directed
Leveled Reader: "Just Like Olivia," p. T279
Before Reading; Read the Book
ELL TG, Day 3

Independent
ELL Copying Masters, Lesson 13

▲ Leveled Reader

Strategic Intervention TG, Day 3
Strategic Intervention Interactive Reader, Lesson 13
Intervention Practice Book, Lesson 13

▲ Strategic Intervention Interactive Reader

Day 4

Teacher-Directed
Leveled Reader: "The Hamster Escape" p. T276
Reread for Fluency

Independent
⭐ Letters and Sounds Center, p. T205

▲ Leveled Reader

Teacher-Directed
Leveled Reader: "The Rabbit Suit Rescue" p. T277
Reread for Fluency

Independent
⭐ Word Work Center, p. T205

▲ Leveled Reader

Teacher-Directed
Leveled Reader: "The Dinosaur Drawing Delivery" p. T278
Reread for Fluency

Independent
⭐ Writing Center, p. T205
Self-Selected Reading: Classroom Library Collection

▲ Leveled Reader

LANGUAGE DEVELOPMENT SUPPORT

Teacher-Directed
Leveled Reader: "Just Like Olivia" p. T279
Reread for Fluency
ELL TG, Day 4

Independent
ELL Copying Masters, Lesson 13

▲ Leveled Reader

Strategic Intervention TG, Day 4
Strategic Intervention Interactive Reader, Lesson 13

▲ Strategic Intervention Interactive Reader

Day 5

Teacher-Directed
Leveled Reader: "The Hamster Escape" p. T276
Think Critically

Independent
⭐ Writing Center, p. T205
Leveled Reader: Reread for Fluency
Extra Support Copying Masters, p. 98

▲ Leveled Reader

Teacher-Directed
Leveled Reader: "The Rabbit Suit Rescue" p. T277
Think Critically

Independent
⭐ Listening/Speaking Center, p. T204
Leveled Reader: Reread for Fluency
Practice Book, p. 98

▲ Leveled Reader

Teacher-Directed
Leveled Reader: "The Dinosaur Drawing Delivery" p. T278
Reread for Fluency

Independent
⭐ Reading Center, p. T204
Leveled Reader: Reread for Fluency
Self-Selected Reading: Classroom Library Collection
Challenge Copying Masters, p. 98

▲ Leveled Reader

LANGUAGE DEVELOPMENT SUPPORT

Teacher-Directed
Leveled Reader: "Just Like Olivia," p. T279
Think Critically
ELL TG, Day 5

Independent
Leveled Reader: Reread for Fluency
ELL Copying Masters, Lesson 13

▲ Leveled Reader

Strategic Intervention TG, Day 5
Strategic Intervention Interactive Reader, Lesson 13

▲ Strategic Intervention Interactive Reader

Leveled Readers & Leveled Practice

Reinforcing Skills and Strategies

LEVELED READERS SYSTEM

- **Leveled Readers**
- **Leveled Readers, CD**
- **Leveled Readers Teacher Guides**
  - *Comprehension*
  - *High-Frequency Words*
  - *Oral Reading Fluency Assessement*
- **Response Activities**
- **Leveled Readers Assessment**

See pages T276–T279 for lesson plans.

BELOW-LEVEL

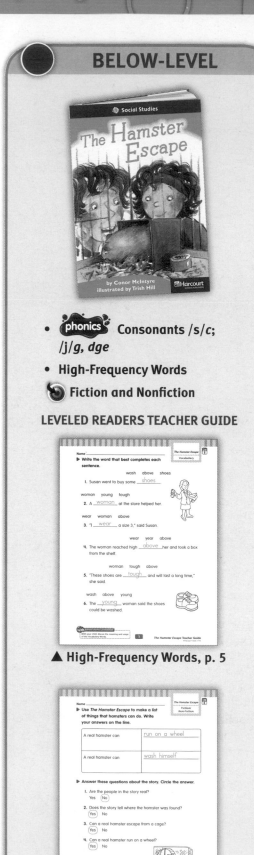

-  **phonics** Consonants /s/c; /j/g, dge
- **High-Frequency Words**
- **Fiction and Nonfiction**

LEVELED READERS TEACHER GUIDE

▲ High-Frequency Words, p. 5

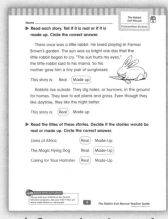

▲ Comprehension, p. 6

ON-LEVEL

- **phonics** Consonants /s/c; /j/g, dge
- **High-Frequency Words**
- **Fiction and Nonfiction**

LEVELED READERS TEACHER GUIDE

▲ High-Frequency Words, p. 5

▲ Comprehension, p. 6

ADVANCED

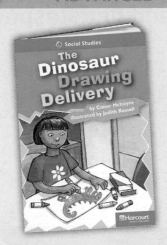

Social Studies

The Dinosaur Drawing Delivery
by Conor McIntyre
illustrated by Judith Rossell

- **phonics** Consonants /s/c;
/j/g, *dge*
- **High-Frequency Words**
- **Fiction and Nonfiction**

LEVELED READERS TEACHER GUIDE

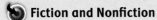

▲ **High-Frequency Words, p. 5**

▲ **Comprehension, p. 6**

ELL

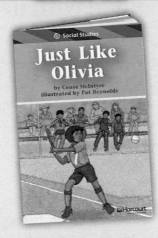

Social Studies

Just Like Olivia
by Conor McIntyre
illustrated by Pat Reynolds

- **Build Background**
- **Concept Vocabulary**
- **Scaffolded Language Development**

LEVELED READERS TEACHER GUIDE

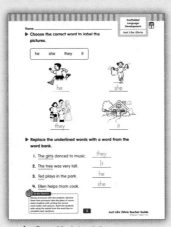

▲ **Scaffolded Language Development, p. 5**

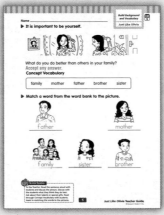

▲ **Build Background p. 6**

CLASSROOM LIBRARY
for Self-Selected Reading

EASY

▲ *Clown Fish* by Carol K. Lindeen, Capstone Press, 2005. NONFICTION

AVERAGE

▲ *Buster* by Denise Fleming, Henry Holt and Company, 2003. FICTION

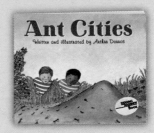

CHALLENGE

▲ *Ant Cities* by Arthur Dorros, HarperCollins, 1987. NONFICTION

▲ **Classroom Library Books Teacher Guide, Lesson 13**

15 Min. each Literacy Centers

Management Support

While you provide direct instruction to individuals or small groups, other children can work on literacy center activities.

▲ **Literacy Center Pocket Chart**

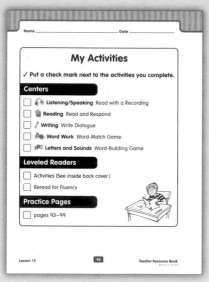

My Activities

✓ Put a check mark next to the activities you complete.

Centers

- ☐ Listening/Speaking Read with a Recording
- ☐ Reading Read and Respond
- ☐ Writing Write Dialogue
- ☐ Word Work Word-Match Game
- ☐ Letters and Sounds Word-Building Game

Leveled Readers

- ☐ Activities (See inside back cover.)
- ☐ Reread for Fluency

Practice Pages

- ☐ pages 93–99

Lesson 13 · 46 · Teacher Resource Book

▲ **Teacher Resource Book, p. 46**

Homework for the Week

TEACHER RESOURCE BOOK, PAGE 46

The Homework Copying Master provides activities to complete for each day of the week.

LISTENING/SPEAKING

Read with a Recording

Objective
To develop fluency by reading poems aloud and listening to them

LISTENING/SPEAKING — Card 61

Read with a Recording

MATERIALS
- CD/cassette player
- Audiotext
- Student Edition
- Reading Log or paper
- pencil

With a partner, listen to "Big Bushy Mustache" on the *Audiotext.*

❶ Follow along in your book while you listen.

❷ Listen to it again, and read aloud with the recording.

❸ Use your Reading Log to record what you read.

Grade 2 Lesson 13

⭐ **Literacy Center Kit • Card 61**

READING

Read and Respond

Objective
To read, retell and respond to self-selected stories

READING — Card 62

Read and Respond

MATERIALS
- Student Edition
- Leveled Readers
- library books
- paper
- pencil

❶ Work with a partner. Read a story silently while your partner reads a different story.

❷ Retell your story to your partner.

❸ Write a few sentences about the story your partner retold. Tell why you do or do not want to read the story yourself.

Grade 2 Lesson 13

⭐ **Literacy Center Kit • Card 62**

WRITING
Write Dialogue

Objective
To write story dialogue to show an understanding of characters

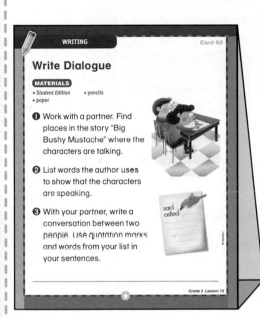

⭐ **Literacy Center Kit • Card 63**

 ## WORD WORK
Word-Match Game

Objective
To read high-frequency regular words

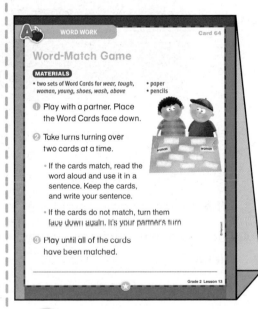

⭐ **Literacy Center Kit • Card 64**

ABC LETTERS AND SOUNDS
Word-Building Game

Objective
To build words using letters and sounds

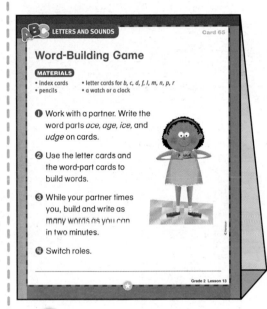

⭐ **Literacy Center Kit • Card 65**

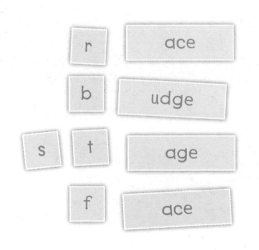

Day at a Glance

Day 1

phonics and Spelling

- Introduce: Consonants /s/*c*; /j/*g*, *dge*
- Pretest

Reading

- Words with Soft *c* and Soft *g*, *Student Edition*, pp. 388–389

Comprehension

- Introduce: Fiction and Nonfiction
- *Read-Aloud Anthology*: "Butterfly Boy"

Fluency

- Model Oral Fluency

Robust Vocabulary

Words from the Read-Aloud
- Introduce: *wilting, flitted, swirling, trance*

Grammar

- Introduce: Plural Possessive Nouns

Writing

- Story: Dialogue

Warm-Up Routines

Oral Language

Objective *To listen attentively and respond appropriately to oral communication*

> ### Question of the Day
>
> **Who is someone that you look up to?**
>
> **Why do you look up to this person?**

If necessary, explain that when you look up to or admire someone, you like something about that person. Have children discuss people they admire. Use the following prompts:

- **What kind of actions might make you look up to, or admire, someone?**
- **Can you admire someone you've never met, or only family members and friends? Why do you think so?**
- **Why might you admire an older brother or sister or an older friend?**

Then have children complete the following sentence frame to explain why they admire a certain person.

I admire _____ because _____.

Read Aloud

Objective *To listen for a purpose*

TRANSPARENCY Read aloud the story "Ana and Her Sister" on **Transparency R63**. Use the following steps:

- **Set a purpose for listening.** Tell children to listen to find out who Ana and her sister are and how Ana feels about her sister.

- **Model fluent reading.** Read the story aloud. Point out that good readers read long sentences by breaking them up into shorter groups of words that go together.

- **Discuss the story.** Ask: **How do you think Ana feels when she learns that Sarah needs help learning to throw a baseball?** (She feels happy; she feels good about herself.)

Fiction and Nonfiction

Ana and Her Sister

Ana loved her big sister Sarah and wanted to be a soccer player just like her. Every day Ana practiced kicking the soccer ball. It never went very far or very straight.

"I can't play soccer like Sarah," she said to her friend Timmy.

"Maybe we can play something else," said Timmy.

Timmy had a baseball and two gloves. Timmy and Ana put on the gloves. When Timmy tossed the ball to Ana, she caught it like a pro!

"I was just lucky," said Ana, but it wasn't luck. For the next hour they played catch. Ana caught every ball thrown to her.

"Hey," said Ana with a big grin. "I like baseball!"

Then Ana heard a voice behind her.

"Hey, Ana!" said Sarah. "Let me try. Throw the ball to me."

Ana tossed the ball to her sister very lightly. Sarah reached for it, but she missed it completely.

"Come on," Ana said to Sarah. "I'll teach you how to throw if you'll teach me how to kick."

"Deal!" said Sarah, and she ran to get her soccer ball.

Grade 2, Lesson 13   R63   Comprehension

Transparency R63

Word Wall

Objective *To read high-frequency words*

REVIEW HIGH-FREQUENCY WORDS Have children read the Word Wall to find answers to the following riddles.

- Which word means the same as 12 months and rhymes with *near*? (*year*)

- Which word's opposite is *cheap* and begins like *example*? (*expensive*)

- Which word means to think of something creative and ends like *engine*? (*imagine*)

- Which word means to fix a meal and rhymes with *book*? (*cook*)

| imagine | cook | year | expensive |

Consonants /s/ c; /j/ g, dge

 phonics *and Spelling*

Objectives

- *To recognize and generate the /s/ and /j/ sounds*
- *To read words with /s/ c; /j/ g, dge; and other known letter-sounds*
- *To use /s/ c; /j/ g, dge; and other known letter-sounds to spell words*

Skill Trace

Tested ✓ **Consonants /s/ c; /j/ g, dge**

Introduce	Grade 1
Reintroduce	**T208—T211**
Reteach	S22
Review	T220–T221, T244–T245, T402
Test	Theme 3
Maintain	Theme 4, T250

Connect Letters to Sounds

WARM UP WITH PHONEMIC AWARENESS   Say the words *city* and *circle*. Have children repeat the words. Say: **The words *city* and *circle* begin with the /s/ sound.** Repeat with the words *mice* and *place*. Say: **The words *mice* and *place* end with the /s/ sound.** Have children say /s/ several times. Repeat the procedure for /j/ using the words *giant*, *gentle*, *bridge*, and *page*.

Routine Card 1 **CONNECT LETTERS AND SOUNDS**   Display the *Sound/Spelling Cards* for the /s/ sound and the /j/ sound. Point to the letter *c* in *ci_* and *ce*. Review its letter/sound correspondence. Say: **The letter *c* sometimes stands for the /s/ sound, the sound at the beginning of *city* and at the end of *mice*.** Touch the letter several times, and have children say /s/ each time. Repeat with /j/ g, dge, using the words *giant* and *bridge*.

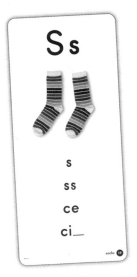

▲ **Sound/Spelling Cards**

Phonics Skill

Words with Soft *c* and Soft *g*

The letter **c** can stand for the *s* sound. The letter **g** can stand for the *j* sound. Read these words.

| city | fence | gem | page |

Now read these longer words.

center   advice   giraffe   village

Point to the letter in each word that stands for the *s* sound or the *j* sound.

388

Read each sentence. Tell which word has the same sound as the *c* in *city* or the *g* in *gem*.

> The mice are not afraid of the cat.

> Greg gave me a giant gift.

> Grandma and Grandpa grow cabbage in their garden.

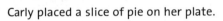

Try This!

Read the sentence. Which words have the same sound as the *c* in *city*?

Carly placed a slice of pie on her plate.

GO online www.harcourtschool.com/storytown

389

Reading Words

GUIDED PRACTICE   Have children read *Student Edition* page 388. Ask volunteers to read aloud the words below the pictures and the longer words, and have children repeat. Then work with children to read the sentences on page 389 and to identify the words with the /s/ and /j/ sounds. (*mice, giant, cabbage*)

Try This!   Have children use what they have learned to read the sentence and identify the words with /s/c. (*placed, slice*)

Consonants /s/c; /j/g, dge
phonics *and Spelling*

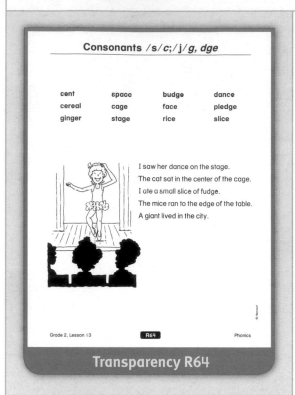

Consonants /s/c;/j/g, dge

cent	space	budge	dance
cereal	cage	face	pledge
ginger	stage	rice	slice

I saw her dance on the stage.
The cat sat in the center of the cage.
I ate a small slice of fudge.
The mice ran to the edge of the table.
A giant lived in the city.

Grade 2, Lesson 13   R64   Phonics

Transparency R64

Reading Words

INDEPENDENT PRACTICE Display **Transparency R64** or write the words and sentences on the board. Point to the words in the top portion and have children read them. Then have children read aloud the sentences and identify words with /s/c or /j/g, dge.

Decodable Books

Additional Decoding Practice

- **Phonics**
  Consonants /s/c; /j/g, dge
- **Decodable Words**
- **High-Frequency Words**
  See lists in *Decodable Book 11*.
  See also *Decodable Books*, online (Take-Home Version).

▲ **Decodable Book 11:** "City Bake Shop" and "Sarge Sits"

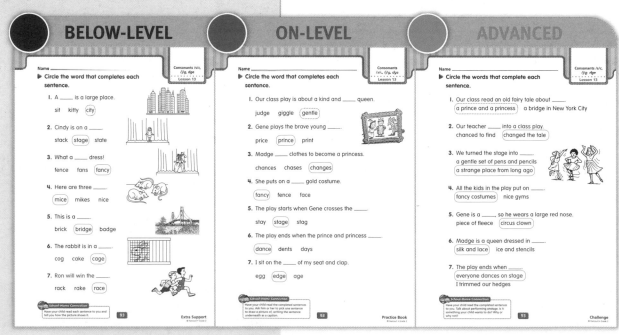

BELOW-LEVEL

Name ____
▶ Circle the word that completes each sentence.

1. A ____ is a large place.
   sit   kitty   (city)
2. Cindy is on a ____.
   stack   (stage)   state
3. What a ____ dress!
   fence   fans   (fancy)
4. Here are three ____.
   (mice)   mikes   nice
5. This is a ____.
   brick   (bridge)   badge
6. The rabbit is in a ____.
   cog   cake   (cage)
7. Ron will win the ____.
   rack   rake   (race)

▲ **Extra Support, p. 93**

ON-LEVEL

Name ____
▶ Circle the word that completes each sentence.

1. Our class play is about a kind and ____ queen.
   judge   giggle   (gentle)
2. Gene plays the brave young ____.
   price   (prince)   print
3. Madge ____ clothes to become a princess.
   chances   chases   (changes)
4. She puts on a ____ gold costume.
   (fancy)   fence   face
5. The play starts when Gene crosses the ____.
   stay   (stage)   stag
6. The play ends when the prince and princess ____.
   (dance)   dents   days
7. I sit on the ____ of my seat and clap.
   egg   (edge)   age

▲ **Practice Book, p. 93**

ADVANCED

Name ____
▶ Circle the words that complete each sentence.

1. Our class read an old fairy tale about ____
   (a prince and a princess)   a bridge in New York City
2. Our teacher ____ into a class play.
   chanced to find   (changed the tale)
3. We turned the stage into ____
   a gentle set of pens and pencils
   (a strange place from long ago)
4. All the kids in the play put on ____
   (fancy costumes)   nice gyms
5. Gene is a ____ so he wears a large red nose.
   piece of fleece   (circus clown)
6. Madge is a queen dressed in ____
   (silk and lace)   ice and stencils
7. The play ends when ____
   (everyone dances on stage)
   I trimmed our hedges

▲ **Challenge, p. 93**

ELL

- Group children according to academic levels, and assign one of the pages on the left.
- Clarify any unfamiliar concepts as necessary. See *ELL Teacher Guide* Lesson 13 for support in scaffolding instruction.

5-DAY SPELLING

DAY 1	Pretest
DAY 2	Word Building
DAY 3	State the Generalization
DAY 4	Review
DAY 5	Posttest

Introduce Spelling Words

PRETEST Say the first word and read the dictation sentence. Repeat the word as children write it. Write the word on the board and have children check their spelling. Tell them to circle the word if they spelled it correctly or write it correctly if they did not. Repeat for words 2–10.

Words with /s/c or /j/g, dge

1.	slice	I asked for a big **slice** of cake.
2.	dodge	Su jumped to **dodge** the ball.
3.	city	Juanita rode the subway in the **city**.
4.	huge	Deb's new dog is **huge**.
5.	nice	The doctor was **nice** when I was sick.
6.	space	Papi drove into the parking **space**.
7.	gem	There was a big, shiny **gem** in her ring.
8.	price	The **price** of the pen was one dollar.
9.	cage	The bird sang softly in its **cage**.
10.	fudge	The **fudge** melted in my mouth.

ADVANCED

Challenge Words Use the challenge words in these dictation sentences.

11.	central	My house is in the **central** part of town.
12.	fireplace	Mom put a big log in the **fireplace**.
13.	gentle	I had to be **gentle** with the little bird.
14.	gymnast	The **gymnast** performed on a mat.
15.	celebrate	I will **celebrate** with a big party!

Spelling Words

1.	**slice***	6.	**space**
2.	**dodge**	7.	**gem**
3.	**city**	8.	**price**
4.	**huge**	9.	**cage**
5.	**nice**	10.	**fudge**

Challenge Words

11.	**central**	14.	**gymnast**
12.	**fireplace**	15.	**celebrate**
13.	**gentle**		

* Word from "Big Bushy Mustache"

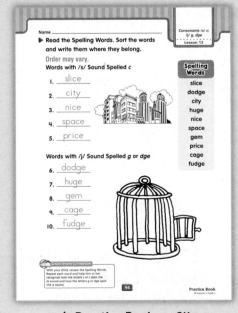

▲ Practice Book, p. 94

Fiction and Nonfiction
Comprehension

Objectives

- *To identify the elements of a fiction story*
- *To distinguish fiction from nonfiction elements*

Daily Comprehension

Fiction and Nonfiction

DAY 1:	Introduce Fiction and Nonfiction, *Student Edition*
DAY 2:	Review Fiction and Nonfiction, *Student Edition*
DAY 3:	Review Fiction and Nonfiction, *Student Edition*
DAY 4:	Review Fiction and Nonfiction, *Transparency*
DAY 5:	Review Fiction and Nonfiction, *Read-Aloud Anthology*

✔ MONITOR PROGRESS

Fiction and Nonfiction

IF children have difficulty identifying elements of fiction stories,	**THEN** have them look at a piece of fiction they are familiar with and help them identify the elements of fiction in that selection.

Small-Group Instruction, pp. S26–S27:

- ● **BELOW-LEVEL:** Reteach
- ● **ON-LEVEL:** Reinforce
- ● **ADVANCED:** Extend

Teach/Model

INTRODUCE FICTION AND NONFICTION Tell children that there are two main kinds of writing, fiction and nonfiction. Explain that fiction is written for readers to enjoy, while writers of nonfiction want readers to learn facts and information. On the board, draw a chart like the one below, or use **Transparency GO1**. Fill in the chart as you discuss the characteristics of fiction and nonfiction.

Fiction	Nonfiction
characters who are made up events that are made up	real people or animals real events

Refer to the chart as you model how to identify the *Student Edition* selection "Jamaica Louise James" as fiction.

 **As I read a story like "Jamaica Louise James," I look for clues that tell me whether it is fiction or nonfiction. Jamaica seems like a real girl I could know, but she is actually made up by the writer, Amy Hest. The illustrations are a clue, because if Jamaica were a real girl, there would probably be photographs of her instead of illustrations. The events that happen to Jamaica are also made-up.**

E L L

Clarify Terminology   Use photographs and illustrations from magazines or other parts of the *Student Edition* to clarify the meaning of *made-up*. Point to an image and ask: **Is this real or made-up?** Guide children in understanding that someone like a writer or an artist creates something that is made-up.

Guided Practice

IDENTIFY FICTION AND NONFICTION   Create a blank chart like the one below. Fill in the first column as you guide children in identifying the fiction characteristics of "Jamaica Louise James." Repeat the procedure with the nonfiction selection "At Play: Long Ago and Today."

Fiction—"Jamaica Louise James"	Nonfiction—"At Play: Long Ago and Today"
• characters are made up • events are made up • illustrations might be a clue that the story is made up	• photographs of real people and places • headings • gives facts about real toys, games, and pastimes

Practice/Apply

INDEPENDENT PRACTICE   Have partners take turns choosing other *Student Edition* selections and saying whether they are fiction or nonfiction. Have children discuss the clues that confirm their choices.

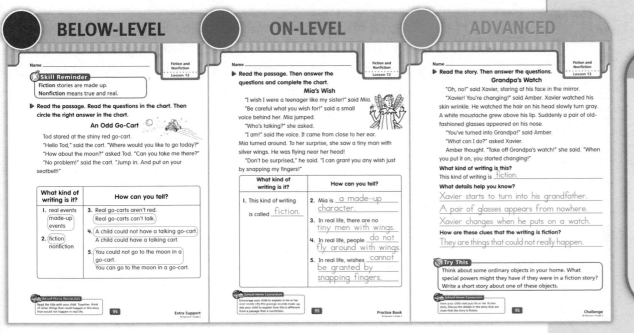

BELOW-LEVEL

▲ Extra Support, p. 95

ON-LEVEL

▲ Practice Book, p. 95

ADVANCED

▲ Challenge, p. 95

ELL

• Group children according to academic levels, and assign one of the pages on the left.

• Clarify any unfamiliar concepts as necessary. See *ELL Teacher Guide* Lesson 13 for support in scaffolding instruction.

Listening Comprehension
Read Aloud

Objectives
- *To set a purpose for listening*
- *To distinguish fiction elements from nonfiction elements*

Build Fluency

Focus: Phrasing   Tell children that good readers read long sentences by breaking them up into shorter groups of words that go together. Explain that reading groups of words without pausing helps you make sense of what you are reading, and it sounds more like natural speech.

E L L

Support Meaning   Display *Picture Card* 19 and other photos to support the meaning of the text. Ask several yes-no questions, such as *Do butterflies fly? Can butterflies sting?* and *Is the butterfly blue?*

Picture Card 19 ▶

butterfly

▲ Read-Aloud Anthology, "Butterfly Boy," p. 48

Before Reading

CONNECT TO PRIOR KNOWLEDGE   Tell children that they will listen to a story about a boy who shares a special love for butterflies with his grandfather. Ask children to share what they know about butterflies.

 **GENRE STUDY: SHORT STORY**
Tell children that "Butterfly Boy" is a short story. Explain the characteristics of this genre.

Think Aloud   **A short story usually tells about one event in the life of a character. A short story is fiction. It has characters, a setting, and a plot.**

After Reading

RESPOND   Have children discuss why the butterflies are so special to Emilio and his grandfather. Ask them to explain how Emilio knew that his grandfather liked the butterflies so much. Ask volunteers to tell about any experiences they may have had sharing something special with someone much older.

REVIEW FICTION AND NONFICTION   Reinforce that "Butterfly Boy" is fiction by asking: **Is "Butterfly Boy" a made-up story or does it give facts about real people and events?** (It's a made-up story.)

Build Robust Vocabulary
Words from the Read-Aloud

Teach/Model

 Routine Card 3 **INTRODUCE ROBUST VOCABULARY** Use *Routine Card 3* to introduce the words.

❶ Put the word in **selection context**.
❷ Display Transparency R68 and read the word and the **Student-Friendly Explanation**.
❸ Have children **say the word** with you.
❹ Use the word in other contexts, and have children **interact with the word's meaning**.
❺ Remove the transparency. Say the Student-Friendly Explanation again, and ask children to **name the word** that goes with it.

❶ **Selection Context:** The red admirals reminded Emilio of **wilting** leaves.
❹ **Interact with Word Meaning:** If you had a garden, would you rather have wilting weeds or wilting flowers? Why?

❶ **Selection Context:** The butterflies **flitted** about in the air.
❹ **Interact with Word Meaning:** Which would be more likely to flit about—a bird in a cage or a bird in a tree?

❶ **Selection Context:** Emilio watched the **swirling** snowflakes.
❹ **Interact with Word Meaning:** When would you most likely see swirling leaves—on a rainy day or on a windy day?

❶ **Selection Context:** Emilio watched the laundry as if in a **trance**.
❹ **Interact with Word Meaning:** Would you be more likely to feel like you were in a trance while riding a rollercoaster or while listening to a long speech? Why?

Practice/Apply

GUIDED PRACTICE Ask children to use the vocabulary to describe something they have seen that *flitted* about.

Objective

• *To develop robust vocabulary through discussing a literature selection*

 **Tested** **INTRODUCE** ✓

Vocabulary: Lesson 13

| wilting | swirling |
| flitted | trance |

▼ **Student-Friendly Explanations**

Student-Friendly Explanations

wilting	When a plant doesn't get enough water, its leaves start to droop because they are wilting.
flitted	If something moved quickly from place to place without stopping for long, it flitted.
swirling	If something is swirling, it is moving round and round quickly.
trance	When someone is in a trance, he or she seems to be asleep, but his or her eyes are open.
route	When you follow the same route to school or to the store every day, you are going the same way each time.
semblance	When you make a drawing that looks a lot like someone, it is a good semblance of that person.
distraught	When someone is distraught, that person is very, very unhappy.
improvise	If you improvise a song or a story, then you make it up as you sing the song or tell the story.

Grade 2, Lesson 13   R68   Vocabulary

Transparency R68

Grammar
Plural Possessive Nouns

5-DAY GRAMMAR

DAY 1	Introduce Plural Possessives
DAY 2	Plural Possessives in Sentences
DAY 3	Identify Singular and Plural Possessives
DAY 4	Apply to Writing
DAY 5	Weekly Review

Objectives

- *To recognize that plural possessive nouns show ownership by more than one person or thing*
- *To write phrases with plural possessive nouns*

Daily Proofreading

tanyas dogs ran across the yard?

(Tanya's, yard.)

TECHNOLOGY

 www.harcourtschool.com/storytown
Grammar Glossary

Plural Possessive Nouns

the boys library books
the ants nest
the teachers classrooms
the animals claws
the truck drivers trucks
the foxes pups
the peoples houses
the children parents

Grade 2, Lesson 13   LA27   Grammar

Transparency LA27

Teach/Model

INTRODUCE PLURAL POSSESSIVES   Remind children that a plural noun means more than one person or thing and usually ends in *s* or *es*. Explain that a plural possessive noun shows that something belongs to more than one person or thing. Like singular possessive nouns, plural possessives also have an apostrophe in them.

Write this sentence, based on "Butterfly Boy," on the board:

> The butterflies landed on his parents' garage.

Read aloud the sentence. Explain that the word *parents'* is a plural possessive noun because it shows that the garage belongs to both of Emilio's parents. Next, write these phrases on the board:

the girls' lunch boxes   **the women's clothes**

Point out that plural possessives usually end with the apostrophe placed after the plural ending, *s'*. Explain that some plural forms of words such as *women* and *mice* do not end with an *s*, so their possessive form is made by adding *'s*.

Guided Practice

REWRITE PHRASES   Display **Transparency LA27**. Read the first phrase and explain that it is supposed to show that the books belong to more than one boy. Rewrite the phrase with the apostrophe correctly in place (*boys'*). Continue with the same procedure for the remaining phrases, asking for responses from volunteers.

Practice/Apply

SHOW PLURAL POSSESSIVES   Write these phrases on the board. Have children rewrite them to show plural possession.

- **the cats toys**
- **the computers screens**
- **the mices cheese**

Writing
Story: Dialogue

5-DAY WRITING	
DAY 1	Introduce
DAY 2	Prewrite
DAY 3	Draft
DAY 4	Revise
DAY 5	Revise

Teach/Model

INTRODUCE DIALOGUE   Display **Transparency LA28** and explain that the story was written by a child. Read aloud the story. Explain that storywriters often include dialogue, or the exact words that characters say. Then develop a list of characteristics for story dialogue.

Dialogue
- Dialogue tells the words characters say.
- Dialogue is inside quotation marks.
- Words like <u>said</u> and <u>asked</u> tell how the character says the dialogue.

WRITING TRAIT **CONVENTIONS**   Discuss how quotation marks are used to show what Elena and Tim say. Use examples from the story to discuss the use of plural possessives.

Guided Practice

DRAFT MORE DIALOGUE   Model writing one more exchange between Elena and Tim, such as *"Do you think you can catch me?" asked Tim. "Yes! So you better watch out!" said Elena.* Invite children to suggest placement of quotation marks and other punctuation.

Practice/Apply

FRIENDS TALKING   Have children draw a picture of two friends speaking to each other. Have them draw a speech bubble over each person in their pictures and then write words that each person is saying. Ask children to share their pictures, reading aloud the dialogue. Have children save their pictures for use on Days 2–5.

Objectives
- *To read and respond to character dialogue in a fiction story*
- *To develop ideas and topics for writing*
- *To write dialogue in a story*

Writing Prompt

Record   Have children write out a short conversation that they had today with a friend at school.

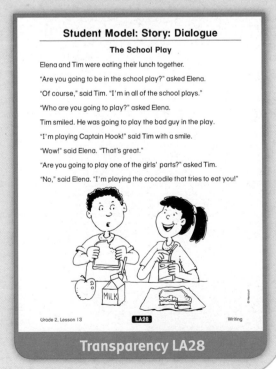

Student Model: Story: Dialogue

The School Play

Elena and Tim were eating their lunch together.

"Are you going to be in the school play?" asked Elena.

"Of course," said Tim. "I'm in all of the school plays."

"Who are you going to play?" asked Elena.

Tim smiled. He was going to play the bad guy in the play.

"I'm playing Captain Hook!" said Tim with a smile.

"Wow!" said Elena. "That's great."

"Are you going to play one of the girls' parts?" asked Tim.

"No," said Elena. "I'm playing the crocodile that tries to eat you!"

Grade 2, Lesson 13   LA28   Writing

Transparency LA28

DAILY ROUTINES

Day at a Glance

Day 2

 phonics and Spelling

- Review: Consonants /s/c; /j/g, dge
- Build Words

High-Frequency Words

- Introduce: *wear, tough, woman, young, shoes, wash, above*

Comprehension

 Focus Strategy Monitor Comprehension: Reread

Focus Skill Fiction and Nonfiction

Reading

- "Big Bushy Mustache," *Student Edition,* pp. 392–417

Read!

Fluency

- Phrasing

Robust Vocabulary

Words About the Selection

- Introduce: *route, semblance, distraught, improvise*

Grammar

- Review: Plural Possessive Nouns

Writing ✏️

- Story: Dialogue

Warm-Up Routines

Oral Language

Objective *To listen attentively and respond appropriately to oral communication*

Question of the Day

**Are two people ever exactly the same?
Tell why.**

Discuss with children what makes each person unique. Use the following prompts:

- **What makes the people we admire special?**
- **Are there children you know who are alike in some way? Tell how.**
- **People in the same family often look alike, but each family member is different in some way. Why do you think that is?**

Have children complete the following sentence to explain their thinking.

Two people ____ can/cannot ____ be alike because _____.

Read Aloud

Objective *To listen for a purpose*

BIG BOOK OF RHYMES AND POEMS   Display the poem "Did You Ever Think?" on page 25 and read aloud the title. Ask children to listen to ways that people are different as you read the poem aloud. Invite children to name other ways in which no two people are alike.

▲ Big Book of Rhymes and Poems, p. 25

Word Wall

Objective *To read high-frequency words*

REVIEW HIGH-FREQUENCY WORDS   Point to the following words on the Word Wall, and read them aloud: *favorite*, *enjoy*, *board*, and *popular*. Point to each word again and ask children to read the word aloud, spell it, and read it again.

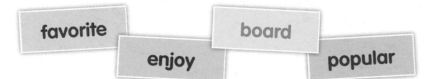

Consonants /s/c; /j/g, dge
 phonics *and Spelling*

Objectives

- *To blend sounds into words*
- *To spell words with /s/c and /j/g, dge*

Skill Trace

 Consonants /s/c; /j/g, dge

Introduce	Grade 1
Reintroduce	T208–T211
Reteach	S22
Review	**T220–T221, T244–T245, T402**
Test	Theme 3
Maintain	Theme 4, T250

Spelling Words

1.	slice*	6.	space
2.	dodge	7.	gem
3.	city	8.	price
4.	huge	9.	cage
5.	nice	10.	fudge

Challenge Words

11.	central	14.	gymnast
12.	fireplace	15.	celebrate
13.	gentle		

* Word from "Big Bushy Mustache"

Word Building

READ A SPELLING WORD Write the word *nice* on the board, and read it aloud. Ask children to name the letter that stands for the /s/ sound. (*c*) Then have children read the word aloud.

BUILD SPELLING WORDS Ask children which letter they should change in the word *nice* to make the word *slice*. (Change *n* to *sl*.) Write the word *slice* on the board below *nice*. Point to the word, and have children read it. Continue building spelling words in this manner. Say:

- **Which letters do I have to change to make the word *space*?** (Change *li* to *pa*.)
- **Which letters do I have to change to make the word *cage*?** (Change *sp* to *c* and *c* to *g*.)
- **Which letters do I have to change to make the word *huge*?** (Change *ca* to *hu*.)
- **Which letters do I have to change to make the word *fudge*?** (Change *h* to *f* and add *d* before *g*.)

Continue building the remaining spelling words in this manner.

> nice
> slice
> space
> cage
> huge
> fudge

BELOW-LEVEL	**ADVANCED**
Phonograms Have children build words with the same phonogram. Write the word *nice* on the board. Guide children to build *mice, rice, price,* and *slice*. Have children read each new word and point to and trace the letter or letters that have changed.	**Build Rhyming Pairs** Write the pairs *nice rice* and *budge fudge* on the board. Have children use the phonograms -ace, -ice, -age, -udge, and -odge to write similar rhyming pairs.

5-DAY PHONICS/SPELLING

DAY 1	Pretest
DAY 2	Word Building
DAY 3	State the Generalization
DAY 4	Review
DAY 5	Posttest

Read Words in Context

APPLY PHONICS Write the following sentences on the board or on chart paper. Have children read each sentence silently. Then track the print as children read the sentence aloud.

> The sign said the <u>price</u> for the <u>gem</u> is $500!
>
> You have to <u>dodge</u> many people when you walk in a busy <u>city</u>.
>
> Amanda poured hot <u>fudge</u> on a <u>huge</u> scoop of ice cream.

 WRITE Dictate several spelling words. Have children write the words in their notebook or on a dry-erase board.

phonics Resources

Phonics Practice Book, pp. 79–84

✓ **MONITOR PROGRESS**

Phonics: Consonants /s/c; /j/g, dge

| IF children have difficulty building and reading words with /s/c and /j/g, dge, | THEN help them blend and read the words cent, rice, gem, page, and budge. |

Small-Group Instruction, p. S22:

● **BELOW-LEVEL:** Reteach
● **ON-LEVEL:** Reinforce
● **ADVANCED:** Extend

BELOW-LEVEL

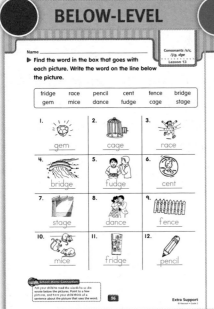

▲ Extra Support, p. 96

ON-LEVEL

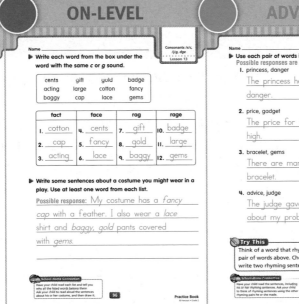

▲ Practice Book, p. 96

ADVANCED

Name ____
▶ Use each pair of words in a sentence. Possible responses are shown.
1. princess, danger
   The princess helped a prince who was in danger.
2. price, gadget
   The price for this strange gadget is too high.
3. bracelet, gems
   There are many bright gems on this bracelet.
4. advice, judge
   The judge gave me some advice about my problem.

Try This
Think of a word that rhymes with the shorter word in each pair of words above. Choose one set of rhyming words, and write two rhyming sentences.

▲ Challenge, p. 96

E L L

- Group children according to academic levels, and assign one of the pages on the left.

- Clarify any unfamiliar concepts as necessary. See *ELL Teacher Guide* Lesson 13 for support in scaffolding instruction.

High-Frequency Words

Words to Know

High-Frequency Words

Objective

• *To read high-frequency words*

 Tested

INTRODUCE ✓

High-Frequency Words

above	wear
shoes	woman
tough	young
wash	

E L L

Reinforce Meaning   Hold up *Picture Card 52* and say *The firefighter has to wear a helmet.* Have children practice using the word *wear* by completing the sentence frame *He has to wear _____* with other items in the picture, such as *a coat, boots,* and *gloves.*

See *ELL Teacher Guide* Lesson 13 for support in scaffolding instruction.

firefighter

▲ **Picture Card 52**

Teach/Model

Routine Card 5   **INTRODUCE WORDS**   Write the words *wear, tough, woman, young, shoes, wash,* and *above* on the board.

• Point to and read *wear*. Repeat it, having children read it with you.

• Say: **I am going to *wear* my new sneakers tonight.**

• Point to each letter as you spell the word. Have children spell the word with you.

• Have children reread the word.

Repeat for the remaining words. Use the following sentences:

• **Pat felt *tough* in her new jacket.**

• **A *woman* and a man walked by the store.**

• **The kittens were too *young* to eat adult cat food.**

• **Maria's *shoes* were so tight that they hurt her feet.**

• **I used a wet cloth to *wash* the board.**

• **Sasha keeps her books on a shelf *above* her desk.**

Guided Practice

STUDENT EDITION PAGES 390–391   Ask children to turn to *Student Edition* pages 390 and 391. Have children point to and read aloud each of the highlighted words on page 390. Talk about the photographs. Then ask volunteers to read aloud the passage.

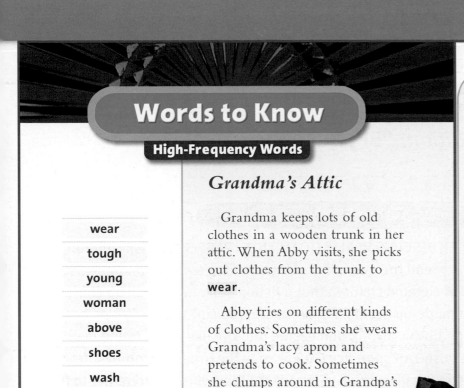

Words to Know

High-Frequency Words

wear

tough

young

woman

above

shoes

wash

Grandma's Attic

Grandma keeps lots of old clothes in a wooden trunk in her attic. When Abby visits, she picks out clothes from the trunk to **wear**.

Abby tries on different kinds of clothes. Sometimes she wears Grandma's lacy apron and pretends to cook. Sometimes she clumps around in Grandpa's **tough** old farm boots. Sometimes she wears a silky, white scarf and dances.

Abby likes to wear clothes Grandma wore when she was a **young woman**. Abby raises her hands **above** her head and slips on a long, white gown. Then she finds a pair of white **shoes** and puts them on.

Grandma climbs the stairs to check on Abby. "My wedding dress!" says Grandma.

"It makes me feel fancy," says Abby.

"It's dusty up in this attic," says Grandma. "Let's go down and **wash** off the dust of long ago!"

online www.harcourtschool.com/storytown

390

391

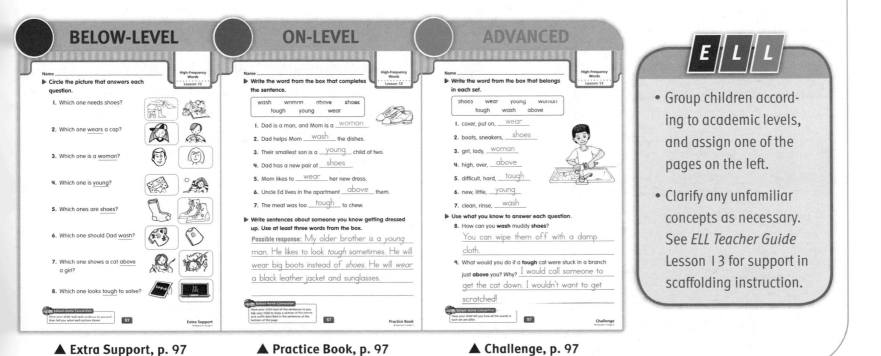

▲ Extra Support, p. 97　　▲ Practice Book, p. 97　　▲ Challenge, p. 97

Lesson 13 (*Student Edition*, pages 390–391)　**T223**

Reading

Student Edition: "Big Bushy Mustache"

Objectives

- *To understand characteristics of fiction*
- *To monitor comprehension by rereading*

Options for Reading

 BELOW-LEVEL

Preview   Have children preview the story by looking at the illustrations. Guide them to predict who the characters are. Read each page to children, and have them read it after you.

 ON-LEVEL

Monitor Comprehension
Have children read the story aloud, page by page. Ask the Monitor Comprehension questions as you go. Then lead them in a discussion about following rules.

 ADVANCED

Independent Reading   Have children read the story in pairs. When they have finished, ask the Monitor Comprehension questions. Then lead them in a discussion about the consequences of not following rules.

Genre Study

DISCUSS REALISTIC FICTION: PAGE 392   Ask children to read the genre information on *Student Edition* page 392. Remind children that a fiction story has made-up characters and made-up events. Point out that *realistic* fiction stories have made-up characters and events that are like those found in real life. Then use **Transparency GO4** or copy the graphic organizer from page 392 on the board. Tell children that they will work together to fill in the story map with examples of realistic fiction elements as they read "Big Bushy Mustache."

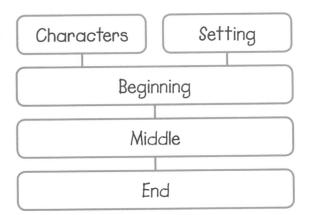

Comprehension Strategy

MONITOR COMPREHENSION—REREAD: PAGE 392   Remind children that good readers use strategies to make sense of what they read. Explain that one strategy readers can use is to reread parts that do not make sense to them. Have children read aloud the Comprehension Strategy information on page 392.

Realistic Fiction

Genre Study

Realistic fiction is a story that could really happen. Look for

- characters who do things that real people do.
- a realistic plot.

Characters → Setting
↓
Beginning
↓
Middle
↓
End

Comprehension Strategy

Monitor comprehension— Reread if you do not understand something.

392

BIG BUSHY MUSTACHE

by Gary Soto
illustrated by
Joe Cepeda

393

Build Background

DISCUSS WANTING TO BE LIKE SOMEONE YOU ADMIRE   Tell children that they are going to read about a character who admires his father and wants to look like him. Ask children if they have ever been told they look like someone they admire and how that made them feel.

Routine Card 6

SET A PURPOSE AND PREDICT   Remind children that this story is fiction. Ask them whether they will read it for enjoyment or to get information.

- Have children read the title.

- Identify Ricky and his father. Ask children what is unusual about a little boy with a mustache. Ask them how they think Ricky got a mustache.

- List their predictions on the board.

- Have children read to see how Ricky gets a big bushy mustache.

TECHNOLOGY

 GO online   **eBook**   "Big Bushy Mustache" is available in an eBook.

 Audiotext   "Big Bushy Mustache" is available on *Audiotext 2* for subsequent readings.

People always said Ricky looked just like his mother.

"He has beautiful eyes, exactly like yours, Rosa!" said Mrs. Sanchez, the crossing guard, as his mother took him to school one morning.

"Thanks!" Ricky's mother shouted, and turned a big smile on him. "Have a good day, *mi'jo*." Then she gave him a kiss.

Ricky went into school frowning. He was a boy. Why didn't people say he looked like his father? **1**

394

That morning his teacher, Mrs. Cortez, brought out a large box from the closet and set it on her desk. She took out a hat and a *sarape*. She took out a sword and raised it toward the ceiling.

"Class, for our next unit we're going to do a play about **2** *Cinco de Mayo*. That's a holiday that celebrates the Mexican victory over the French army."

395

Monitor Comprehension

PAGES 394–395 Say: **It looks as if the main character, Ricky, is on his way to school. He doesn't look happy. Read to find out more.**

1 **MAKE INFERENCES** **How does Ricky feel about being told he looks like his mother? How do you know?** (Ricky doesn't like it. I know because he frowns and wonders why people don't tell him he looks like his father.)

2 **DRAW CONCLUSIONS** **What will the class do with the things Mrs. Cortez is holding up? How do you know?** (Possible response: The class will probably use the things in a play. I know because Mrs. Cortez tells the class they will do a play, and people use costumes and props in plays.)

Apply
Comprehension Strategies

Monitor Comprehension— Reread Demonstrate how to reread to make sense of a part of the story that you didn't understand when you read it the first time.

Think Aloud I didn't understand why Mrs. Cortez was taking out a hat, a *sarape*, and a sword. When I reread page 395, I see that she wants the class to put on a play. That helps me understand that the things she is holding up are probably going to be used in the play.

Mrs. Cortez looked around the room. Her eyes settled on Ricky. "Ricky, do you want to carry the sword?"

Ricky shook his head no.

"Do you want to wear this white shirt?" she asked.

Again Ricky shook his head no. And he shook his head to the sombrero, the captain's hat, the purple cape, the tiny Mexican flag. **1**

396

But when Mrs. Cortez took out a big, bushy mustache, something clicked. This time Ricky nodded yes. **3**

2

397

Monitor Comprehension

PAGES 396–397 Say: **Ricky doesn't look happy on page 396. Read to find out why.**

1 **NOTE DETAILS** **Why does Ricky look sad?** (He doesn't like any of the costumes.)

2 **FICTION AND NONFICTION** **What clues tell you that this selection is fiction?** (Possible response: The illustrations are funny. The characters don't look like real people.)

3 **SPECULATE** **Why do you think Ricky nods yes to wearing the mustache? What makes you think this?** (Possible response: Maybe Ricky wants to look grown up. I remember that Ricky would like people to say he looks like his father.)

E L L

Idiomatic Expressions Point out that "something clicked" does not mean that there was a clicking sound. It means that suddenly Ricky had a good idea for the mustache.

For the rest of the day, the class practiced their parts. Some of the children played Mexican soldiers. Some of the children played French soldiers. ❶

All the while, Ricky played with his mustache. It tickled his lip. It made him feel tough. ❷

When school was over, Mrs. Cortez told the class to leave the costumes in their desks.

398

Ricky took off his mustache. But instead of leaving it behind, he put it in his pocket. He wanted to take it home. He wanted to surprise his father when he got home from work. ❸

Maybe Mami will take a picture of us, he thought. *We could stand next to each other in front of our new car.*

399

Monitor Comprehension

PAGES 398–399 Say: **Now it looks as if Ricky is wearing the mustache and the class is practicing for the play. Read to find out what happens.**

❶ **NOTE DETAILS** **What are the two groups of people in the play?** (Mexican soldiers and French soldiers)

❷ **MAKE INFERENCES** **Why do you think that the mustache makes Ricky feel tough?** (Possible response: The mustache is probably for a soldier in the play. I know soldiers are tough because they have to fight.)

❸ **MAKE JUDGMENTS** **Do you think it is a good idea for Ricky to take the mustache home? Why do you think this?** (Possible response: No, I don't think it is a good idea. Mrs. Cortez told everyone to leave their costumes in their desks. Ricky is not following her directions, so he might get into trouble.)

 **SOCIAL STUDIES**

SUPPORTING STANDARDS

Cinco de Mayo Locate Mexico and France on a world map. Explain that Cinco de Mayo is a holiday celebrated in Mexico every year on May 5 to remember a time when the Mexican army won a big victory over the French army. Ask children to discuss why armies from different countries sometimes fight. Ask children whether they think that fighting is a good way to solve problems between people and countries.

He passed a kindergartner, who said, "Mister, would you help me tie my shoes?" ❶ ❷

After Ricky left the school, he pressed the mustache back onto his lip. He felt grown-up.
A man on the street called out, "Hello, soldier."
Ricky passed a woman carrying groceries. She said, "What a handsome young man."

400

401

Monitor Comprehension

PAGES 400–401   Say: **Now it looks like Ricky is wearing the mustache by a barber shop. Read to see what is happening.**

❶ **DRAW CONCLUSIONS   Which of the people on the street think Ricky is really an adult? Why do you think this?** (Possible response: The kindergartner thinks he is an adult because she calls him mister and asks him to tie her shoes. The other people are older and are smiling. That makes me think they realize Ricky is pretending to be grown up.)

❷ **MAKE PREDICTIONS   What do you think Ricky's parents will say when he gets home with the mustache? Why do you think this?** (Possible response: I think they will smile, too, because a little boy with a mustache looks cute.)

Use Multiple Strategies

Ask Questions   Demonstrate how to ask questions to comprehend the story.

Think Aloud   Asking questions as I read helps me think about the events and characters. I can ask myself: "Why does Ricky feel grown up?" When I read, I see that other people on the street talk to him as if he is a grown-up when they see his mustache. That answers my question.

Ricky laughed and ran home. He climbed the wooden steps, pushed open the door, and rushed into the kitchen, where his mother was peeling apples.

"¡Hola, Mami!" he said. "I'm hungry."

He looked up and waited for her to say something about his big, bushy mustache. **2**

402

But she only smiled and handed him a slice of apple.

"Mi'jo, wash your hands and help me with the apples," she said.

Ricky's smile disappeared. Didn't she notice?

"Look, Mami. Isn't my bigote great?" he said, tugging at her apron.

His mother looked at him.

"¿Bigote? What are you talking about?"

"This one," he said. He touched his lip, but the mustache was gone! He felt around his face. It was not on his cheek. It was not on his chin. He looked down to the floor, but it wasn't there, either. **1** **3**

403

Monitor Comprehension

PAGES 402–403 Say: **It looks like Ricky is at home with his mother, but I don't see the mustache. Read to find out what happened to it.**

1 **NOTE DETAILS** What happened to Ricky's mustache? (Possible response: He lost it.)

2 **MAKE INFERENCES** What does Ricky hope his mother will think about his mustache? Why do you think this? (Possible response: He hopes she will think he looks grown-up, too. I know because he likes people to think he is grown up, and he runs home.)

3 **MAKE PREDICTIONS** What do you think Ricky will do now that he knows the mustache is gone? (Possible response: He will ask his mother to help him find it.)

ON-LEVEL

Spanish Phrases Point out that Ricky and his family speak both English and Spanish and that they use both English and Spanish words when they talk to each other. Discuss with children how the context of the story helps them infer what the Spanish words mean. You might ask any children in your class who speak Spanish to translate the Spanish words that Ricky and his family speak.

I must have lost it on the way home, Ricky thought. Without saying anything, he ran out the front door.

He retraced his steps, eyes wide open. He dug through a pile of raked leaves. He parted the tall grass that grew along a fence. He looked in the street, between parked cars, and in flower beds.

He jumped with hope when he saw a black thing. But when he bent over to pick it up, he discovered that it was a squashed crayon.

Ricky sat on the curb and cried. The mustache was gone.

404

405

Monitor Comprehension

PAGES 404–405 Say: **Read to find out why Ricky is sitting on the curb.**

1 CHARACTER'S EMOTIONS How do you think Ricky feels when he can't find the mustache? Why do you think this? (Possible response: He feels sad and scared because it doesn't belong to him. I think this because he's crying.)

2 CONFIRM PREDICTIONS Was your prediction about what Ricky would do correct? Why or why not? (Possible response: It was partly correct. Ricky does look for the mustache, but he does not ask his mother to help him.)

Demonstrate a Concept Explain that when Ricky retraced his steps, he walked back over the path he took when he walked home from school. Draw a diagram of your classroom on the board. Trace and retrace over a route that you can follow to walk from one point in the classroom to another. Then invite volunteers to walk a route through the classroom and to show how they would retrace that route.

When he got home, Ricky told his mother what had happened. She wiped her hands on a dish towel and hugged him.

406

At dinner, he wanted to tell Papi too, but the words would not come out. They were stuck in his throat.

He watched his father's big, bushy mustache move up and down when he chewed.

Under his breath, Ricky whispered, "Mustache," but his father didn't hear. He talked about his work.

407

Monitor Comprehension

PAGES 406–407   Say: **On one page Ricky is getting a hug from his mother. Read to find out what his mother thinks.**

1 CHARACTERS   **What is Ricky's mother like? How do you know?** (Possible response: She is kind and understanding. She doesn't get mad at Ricky when he tells her his problem. She tries to make him feel better. I know this because she hugs him.)

2 MAKE INFERENCES   **Why does Ricky whisper "Mustache" under his breath at dinner?** (Possible response: Ricky wants to tell his father about the mustache but he is afraid, so he only whispers.)

After dinner, Ricky went to his bedroom. With a black crayon, he colored a sheet of paper and then cut it into the shape of a mustache. He taped it to his mouth and stood before the mirror. But it didn't look real. He tore it off, crumpled it, and tossed it on the floor.

In the closet, Ricky found a can of black shoe polish. He looked in the mirror and smeared a line above his lip, but it was too flat, not thick and bushy at all.

408

Finally, he dug out a pair of old shoes. The strings were black. He cut them in short strips and bound them together with a rubber band. He held the creation above his lip. It looked like a black mop. And smelled like old socks. **①**

That night, after he put on his pajamas, Ricky went into the living room, where his father was listening to the radio.

"Papi, I lost my mustache . . . *mi bigote*."

His father laughed. "What mustache?"

Ricky climbed into his father's lap and told him everything. His father smiled and told him a story about a hen that tried to become a swan. It was a good story, but it **②** still didn't solve his problem.

Tomorrow he would have to face Mrs. Cortez. **③**

409

Monitor Comprehension

PAGES 408–409 Say: **Read to find out how Ricky tries to solve his problem.**

① **NOTE DETAILS** **What three things does Ricky do to try to replace the mustache? Do they work?** (He tapes a paper mustache to his face. He puts black shoe polish on his lip. He makes a mustache out of old shoelaces. None of them work.)

② **MAKE INFERENCES** **Why do you think Ricky's father tells him the story about a hen that wanted to be a swan?** (Possible response: He wants Ricky to know that it is okay to be just the way he is.)

③ **MAKE PREDICTIONS** **Do you think Ricky will solve his problem? If so, how will he do it?** (Possible response: Yes. His parents will help him make or buy another mustache.)

Apply
Comprehension Strategies

Focus Strategy

Monitor Comprehension— Reread Demonstrate how to reread to make sense of a part of the story that you didn't understand when you first read it.

Think Aloud I wasn't sure how the story Ricky's father tells helps him. I reread the page and saw that the story Ricky's father told doesn't solve the problem. Ricky will still have to tell his teacher about the mustache.

Mami held out a closed fist and let it open like a flower. Sitting in her palm was a mustache. It was big and bushy. **2**

"You found it!" Ricky shouted happily. "Well, yes and no," Mami said as she poured herself a cup of coffee.

The next morning, Ricky got out of bed slowly. He dressed slowly. He combed his hair slowly. At breakfast, he chewed his cereal slowly. He raised his eyes slowly when his father came into the kitchen. *"Buenos días,"* he greeted Ricky. **1**

Then Ricky's mother came into the kitchen. *"Mi'jo,* I have a surprise for you," she said.

410

411

Monitor Comprehension

PAGES 410–411 Say: **It looks like Ricky has his mustache again. Read to see how he got it.**

1 **MAKE INFERENCES** **Why does Ricky do everything slowly? Why do you think this?** (Possible response: Ricky doesn't want to go to school because he thinks Mrs. Cortez will be angry with him when he tells her about the mustache. I know I wouldn't be in a hurry to get to school if I was going to be in trouble with my teacher.)

2 **AUTHOR'S PURPOSE** **Why does the author write that Ricky's mother opens her hand like a flower?** (Possible response: A flower opening is very special and beautiful. The author wants to show that the new mustache is special and beautiful to Ricky.)

ANALYZE AUTHOR'S PURPOSE

Author's Purpose Remind children that authors have a purpose, or reason, for writing. After children have finished reading the story, ask:

Why did the author write "Big Bushy Mustache"?

- to explain why it's important to follow rules
- to tell facts about Cinco de Mayo
- to entertain readers with a story about a boy and his family

Ricky pressed the new mustache to his lip. He ate his cereal, and the mustache moved up and down, just like his father's.

But something was different about his father's smile. His lip looked funny. Ricky jumped up and threw his arms around Papi's neck.
"*Gracias*, Papi! Thank you!" he cried.

"That's okay," Papi told him. "But next time listen to your teacher."
Then Papi touched his son's hair softly. "And, hey, now I look just like you!"
Ricky grinned a mile wide.

412

413

Monitor Comprehension

PAGES 412–414   Say: **Read to find out how Ricky's parents got the new mustache.**

1 **DRAW CONCLUSIONS**   **Where does the new mustache come from? How do you know?** (Ricky's father shaved his mustache to make the new mustache. I know because Ricky's father doesn't have his mustache in the illustration.)

2 **CONFIRM PREDICTIONS**   **Was your prediction about how Ricky would solve his problem correct? Why or why not?** (Responses will vary.)

3 **MAKE INFERENCES**   **On page 414, why does Ricky put his father's mustache in his pocket instead of wearing it?** (Possible response: He doesn't want to lose the mustache because his father gave it to him.)

Apply
Comprehension Strategies

Monitor Comprehension— Reread   Demonstrate how to reread to make sense of a part of the story that you didn't understand when you first read it.

Think Aloud   I wasn't sure why Ricky's father said "Now I look just like you" to Ricky. I reread the last three pages of the story. I see that Ricky's father doesn't have a mustache now. That's why he looks like Ricky.

When Ricky walked to school, he carried the mustache not on his lip, but safely in his pocket. **3**
  It wasn't just a bushy disguise anymore, but a gift from his papi.

414

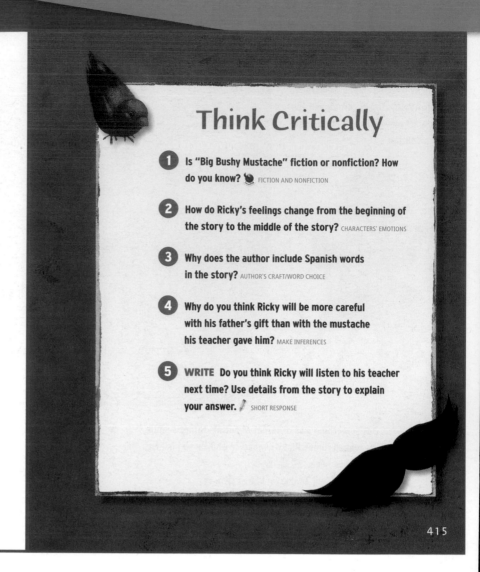

Think Critically

1 Is "Big Bushy Mustache" fiction or nonfiction? How do you know? FICTION AND NONFICTION

2 How do Ricky's feelings change from the beginning of the story to the middle of the story? CHARACTERS' EMOTIONS

3 Why does the author include Spanish words in the story? AUTHOR'S CRAFT/WORD CHOICE

4 Why do you think Ricky will be more careful with his father's gift than with the mustache his teacher gave him? MAKE INFERENCES

5 WRITE Do you think Ricky will listen to his teacher next time? Use details from the story to explain your answer. SHORT RESPONSE

415

Think Critically

Respond to the Literature

1 FocusSkill The selection is fiction because it is a made-up story with characters, a setting, and a plot. **FICTION AND NONFICTION**

2 Possible response: At first, the mustache makes Ricky feel tough, grown up, and happy. When he loses it, Ricky feels very sad and worried. **CHARACTER'S EMOTIONS**

3 Possible response: Gary Soto includes Spanish words to show that Ricky's family and some people in his neighborhood speak Spanish. **AUTHOR'S CRAFT/WORD CHOICE**

4 Possible response: Ricky will be more careful because this mustache was a gift from his father. **MAKE INFERENCES**

5 WRITE Possible response: I think Ricky will listen to his teacher next time. Ricky found out that bad things can happen when he doesn't listen to the teacher. He lost the mustache and worried about what he would tell his teacher. Also, his father told him to listen to his teacher next time. **SHORT RESPONSE**

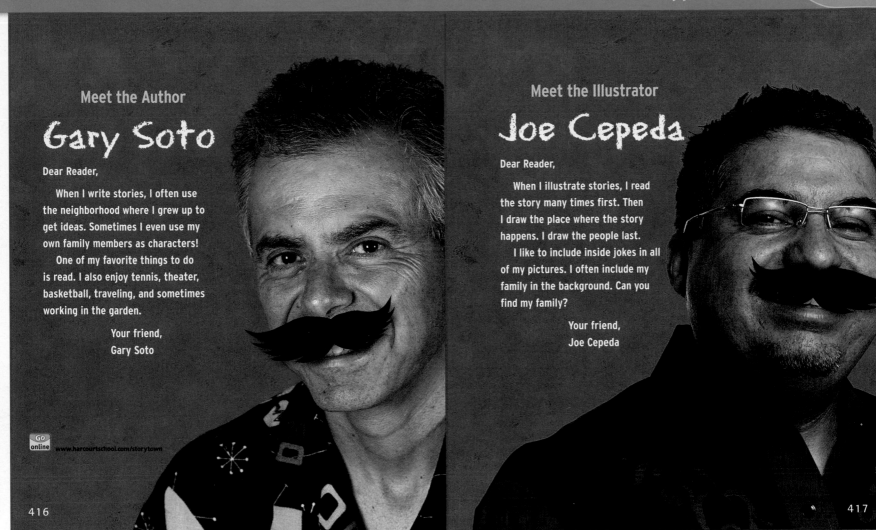

Meet the Author
Gary Soto

Dear Reader,

When I write stories, I often use the neighborhood where I grew up to get ideas. Sometimes I even use my own family members as characters!

One of my favorite things to do is read. I also enjoy tennis, theater, basketball, traveling, and sometimes working in the garden.

Your friend,
Gary Soto

www.harcourtschool.com/storytown

416

Meet the Illustrator
Joe Cepeda

Dear Reader,

When I illustrate stories, I read the story many times first. Then I draw the place where the story happens. I draw the people last.

I like to include inside jokes in all of my pictures. I often include my family in the background. Can you find my family?

Your friend,
Joe Cepeda

417

Meet the Author and Illustrator

PAGES 416–417 Explain that these pages tell about the writer and the illustrator of "Big Bushy Mustache." Point to the photograph of Gary Soto on page 416. Explain that often people become writers because they love to read good stories. Ask children why a love for reading might make someone want to become a writer. Then have children read Gary Soto's letter.

Then point out the photograph of Joe Cepeda, on page 417. Ask children what they thought of Joe Cepeda's illustrations for this story. Then have children read Joe Cepeda's letter. Encourage children to look back through the selection to find Joe Cepeda's family in the background of one of the pictures. They are standing behind Ricky when he is sitting on the curb (*Student Edition*, page 405).

Check Comprehension
Retelling

Objectives

- *To practice retelling a story*
- *To use phrasing to read in a manner that sounds like natural speech*

RETELLING RUBRIC

4	Uses details to clearly retell the story.
3	Uses some details to retell the story.
2	Retells the story with some inaccuracies.
1	Is unable to retell the story.

Professional Development

 Podcasting: Auditory Modeling

BELOW-LEVEL

Fluency Practice   For fluency practice, have children read *Decodable Book 11*, the appropriate *Leveled Reader* (pp. T276–T279), or Story 13 in the *Intervention Reader*.

Retell

  FICTION AND NONFICTION   Ask children to explain how they know that "Big Bushy Mustache" is fiction. (The characters and plot are made up.)

REVISIT THE GRAPHIC ORGANIZER   Display completed **Transparency GO4**. Guide children to use the story map to discuss the characters, setting, and plot.

STORY RETELLING CARDS   The cards for "Big Bushy Mustache" can be used for retelling or as an aid to completing the story map.

▲ **Story Retelling Cards 1–6, "Big Bushy Mustache"**

Fluency
Phrasing

Teach/Model

READING PHRASES   Explain that good readers break up sentences into groups of words that go together. Have children turn to *Student Edition* pages 402–403 and track the print as you read aloud. Demonstrate reading chunks of words.

Practice/Apply

Routine Card 9

PARTNER-READ   Have partners take turns reading aloud the rest of the story, one page at a time, paying close attention to phrasing.

Build Robust Vocabulary

Words About the Selection

Teach/Model

Routine Card 3

INTRODUCE ROBUST VOCABULARY Use *Routine Card 3* to introduce the words.

❶ Put the word in **selection context**.
❷ Display Transparency R68 and read the word and the **Student-Friendly Explanation**.
❸ Have children **say the word** with you.
❹ Use the word in other contexts, and have children **interact with the word's meaning**.
❺ Remove the transparency. Say the Student-Friendly Explanation again, and ask children to **name the word** that goes with it.

❶ **Selection Context:** Ricky retraced the **route** that he took home.
❹ **Interact with Word Meaning:** Who might use the same route every day, a mail carrier or a police officer?

❶ **Selection Context:** Ricky used shoe polish to make a **semblance** of a mustache.
❹ **Interact with Word Meaning:** Which would be a better semblance of something, a photograph or a clay sculpture?

❶ **Selection Context:** Ricky was **distraught** when he couldn't find the mustache.
❹ **Interact with Word Meaning:** Would you be distraught if you got good grades or poor grades on your report card? Why?

❶ **Selection Context:** Ricky tried to **improvise** to make a mustache.
❹ **Interact with Word Meaning:** Would you improvise if you forgot your lines in a play or if you missed your bus? Explain.

Practice Apply

GUIDED PRACTICE Ask children to describe the *route* you take to go from the classroom to the playground.

Objective

• *To develop robust vocabulary through discussing a literature selection*

Tested ✔

INTRODUCE

Vocabulary: Lesson 13

route	semblance
distraught	improvise

▼ **Student-Friendly Explanations**

Student-Friendly Explanations

wilting	When a plant doesn't get enough water, its leaves start to droop because they are wilting.
flitted	If something moved quickly from place to place without stopping for long, it flitted.
swirling	If something is swirling, it is moving round and round quickly.
trance	When someone is in a trance, he or she seems to be asleep, but his or her eyes are open.
route	When you follow the same route to school or to the store every day, you are going the same way each time.
semblance	When you make a drawing that looks a lot like someone, it is a good semblance of that person.
distraught	When someone is distraught, that person is very, very unhappy.
improvise	If you improvise a song or a story, then you make it up as you sing the song or tell the story.

Grade 2, Lesson 13   **R68**   Vocabulary

Transparency R68

Grammar
Plural Possessive Nouns

5-DAY GRAMMAR	
DAY 1	Introduce Plural Possessives
DAY 2	Plural Possessives in Sentences
DAY 3	Identify Singular and Plural Possessives
DAY 4	Apply to Writing
DAY 5	Weekly Review

Objective

- *To recognize and write plural possessive nouns in sentences*

Daily Proofreading

the three cats beds
(the three cats' beds)

the mices cheese
(the mice's cheese)

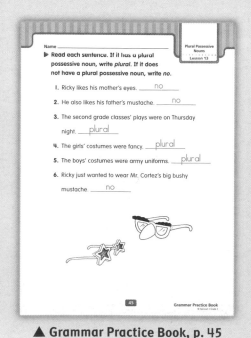

Name _____
▶ Read each sentence. If it has a plural possessive noun, write *plural*. If it does not have a plural possessive noun, write *no*.

Plural Possessive Nouns
Lesson 13

1. Ricky likes his mother's eyes. ___no___
2. He also likes his father's mustache. ___no___
3. The second grade classes' plays were on Thursday night. ___plural___
4. The girls' costumes were fancy. ___plural___
5. The boys' costumes were army uniforms. ___plural___
6. Ricky just wanted to wear Mr. Cortez's big bushy mustache. ___no___

45   Grammar Practice Book

▲ **Grammar Practice Book, p. 45**

Review

WRITE PLURAL POSSESSIVES   Write the following sentences on the board.

The teachers students put on a play.
(The teachers' students put on a play.)

The girls costumes were green.
(The girls' costumes were green.)

Have children read aloud the sentences. Point out that each sentence includes something that belongs to more than one person. Explain that you could also use an apostrophe to make the plural noun show ownership. Rewrite the sentences using plural possessive nouns. Then have children read the sentences with you.

Practice/Apply

GUIDED PRACTICE   Write the following sentences on the board. Model how to rewrite the first sentence to show that something belongs to more than one person or thing. Then ask volunteers to tell how to rewrite the remaining sentences.

Marco used the boys bats. (Marco used the boys' bats.)

Kitty watched the mices tails. (Kitty watched the mice's tails.)

My parents car is red. (My parents' car is red.)

INDEPENDENT PRACTICE   Write the following sentences on the board. Ask children to rewrite them to show that something belongs to more than one person or thing.

The dogs tails are wagging.
(The dogs' tails are wagging.)

Two girl's dresses are blue.
(Two girls' dresses are blue.)

The singers voices are strong.
(The singers' voices are strong.)

Writing

Story: Dialogue

5-DAY WRITING	
DAY 1	Introduce
DAY 2	**Prewrite**
DAY 3	Draft
DAY 4	Revise
DAY 5	Revise

Prewrite

GENERATE IDEAS Have children look again at the picture they drew on Day 1 (page T217). Ask children to think of other things the two children in the picture might say to each other.

CONVENTIONS Use an example from a volunteer's picture to write out the dialogue using quotation marks. Remind children that quotation marks show where the words a character says begin and end. Also, point out that the names of the characters are proper nouns and must begin with capital letters.

MODEL PREWRITING Copy the story map below. Remind children that using a story map can help them plan a story. Model filling in the story map. Explain that children can plan what the characters will say to each other in their story maps.

> **Characters**
> Sarah, Jorge

> **Setting**
> lunchtime, at school

> **Plot**
> Beginning: Sarah asks Jorge to eat with her.
> Middle: Jorge tells Sarah he got a new bike.
> End: Sarah tells Jorge she wants to see the bike.

Practice/Apply

GUIDED PRACTICE Have volunteers dictate dialogue that the characters might say to each other. Write their suggestions on the board, pointing out the correct use of quotation marks and dialogue words such as *asked* and *said*.

INDEPENDENT PRACTICE Have children use their pictures and the story map to brainstorm writing ideas for their own stories. Remind them to think about what the two characters will say to each other in their story and to include that in their story map. Have children save their pictures and story ideas to use on Days 3–5.

Objectives

- *To develop ideas and topics for writing*
- *To use a graphic organizer for prewriting*

Writing Prompt

Record Have children record their feelings about their story ideas.

Use Total Physical Response
Children may wish to act out the characters' actions and dialogue in their stories and then dictate ideas for their story maps.

DAILY ROUTINES

Day at a Glance

Day 3

phonics and Spelling

- Review: Consonants /s/c; /j/g, dge
- State the Generalization

High-Frequency Words

- Review: *wear, tough, woman, young, shoes, wash, above*

Fluency

- Phrasing
- "Big Bushy Mustache," *Student Edition*, pp. 392–417

Comprehension

Review: Fiction and Nonfiction

- "Changing," *Student Edition*, pp. 418–419

Robust Vocabulary

- Review: *wilting, flitted, swirling, trance, route, semblance, distraught, improvise*

Grammar

- Review: Plural Possessive Nouns

Writing

- Story: Dialogue

Warm-Up Routines

Oral Language

Objective *To listen attentively and respond appropriately to oral communication*

Question of the Day

In what ways can people be alike?

In what ways is everyone special?

Use the following prompts to help children think about ways in which people are similar and ways in which they may be unique.

- **How are you and your friends alike?**

- **How is each person unlike anyone else?**

Have children complete the following sentence frame to explain how each child is unique.

I am unlike anyone else because _____.

Objective *To identify rhythm and rhymes in poetry*

BIG BOOK OF RHYMES AND POEMS Display "Did You Ever Think?" on page 25 and have children read aloud the first four lines. Ask a volunteer to point to and read the words that repeat (*No one*) and the words that rhyme (*you* and *do*). Point out that the repeating words give the poem a rhythm that makes the poem fun to read and listen to. Repeat the procedure for the last four lines of the poem. Then reread the poem, encouraging children to join in.

▲ **Big Book of Rhymes and Poems, p. 25**

Objective *To read high-frequency words*

REVIEW HIGH-FREQUENCY WORDS Point to and read aloud the following words on the Word Wall: *wear, tough, woman, young, shoes, wash,* and *above*. Ask volunteers to read each word and spell it. Once you have gone through all the words, repeat the process.

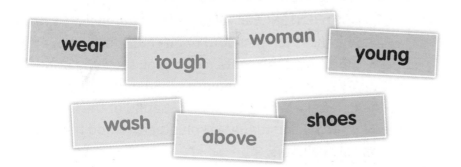

wear · tough · woman · young · wash · above · shoes

Consonants /s/c; /j/g, dge *phonics* and Spelling

5-DAY PHONICS

DAY 1	Reintroduce /s/c and /j/g, dge
DAY 2	Word Building with /s/c and /j/g, dge
DAY 3	**Word Building with /s/c and /j/g, dge**
DAY 4	Inflections -ed, -ing; Review /s/c; /j/g, dge
DAY 5	Inflections -ed, -ing; Review /s/c; /j/g, dge

Objectives

- *To read phonetically regular words*
- *To read and write common word families*
- *To recognize spelling patterns*

Skill Trace

Tested **Consonants /s/c; /j/g, dge**

Introduce	Grade 1
Reintroduce	T208–T211
Reteach	S22
Review	**T220–T221, T244–T245, T402**
Test	Theme 3
Maintain	Theme 4, T250

Consonants /s/c;/j/g, dge

Two mice were asleep in their cage.
One mouse woke up.
"Look!" she said to the other mouse with a nudge.
She had a huge grin on her face.
"There's a nice slice of cheese on the table!" she said.
"It would taste so good with rice!" said the mice.
"Let's get out of this place," they said.
They tried to get out, but the door would not budge.
Just then a cat raced to the cage and leapt for the mice!
The mice had to dodge the cat's huge paw.
"There won't be a slice for you mice!" said the cat.

Grade 2, Lesson 13   R65   Phonics

Transparency R65

Work with Patterns

INTRODUCE PHONOGRAMS   Write the following phonograms at the top of five columns.

-ice   -ace   -age   -uge   -udge

Tell children that these are the endings of some words. Slide your hand under the letters as you read each phonogram. Repeat, having children read the phonograms with you.

BUILD AND READ WORDS   Write the words *rice*, *race* and *rage* under the first three phonograms. Guide children to read each word: /r/-ice, rice; /r/-ace, race; /r/-age, rage. Continue the process using the letter *h* to build *huge* and the letter *f* to build *fudge*.

Then have children name other words that end with these phonograms. Have them tell which letter or letters to add to build each word, and write the word in the appropriate column. Have children read each column of words. Then point to words at random and have children read them.

Read Words in Context

READ SENTENCES   Display **Transparency R65** or write the sentences on the board or on chart paper. Have children choral-read the sentences as you track the print. Then ask volunteers to read each sentence aloud and to underline words in which the letter *c* stands for the /s/ sound or the letters *g* or *dge* stand for the /j/ sound. Invite volunteers to add the words to the appropriate columns.

5-DAY SPELLING

DAY 1	Pretest
DAY 2	Word Building
DAY 3	**State the Generalization**
DAY 4	Review
DAY 5	Posttest

Review Spelling Words

STATE THE GENERALIZATION FOR /s/c AND /j/g, dge List spelling words 1–10 on chart paper or on the board. Circle the words in which the letter *c* stands for the /s/ sound, and have children read them. Ask: **What is the same in each word?** (In each word, the letter *c* stands for the /s/ sound.) Then, using a different color pen, circle the words in which the letters *g* or *dge* stand for the /j/ sound, and repeat the procedure.

 WRITE Have children write the spelling words in their note-books. Remind them to use their best handwriting.

Handwriting

OPEN AND CLOSED LETTERS Remind children to close the top part of the letter *g* all the way and to curve the lower stem to the left so that it does not look like the letter *q*.

Spelling Words

1.	**slice***	6.	**space**
2.	**dodge**	7.	**gem**
3.	**city**	8.	**price**
4.	**huge**	9.	**cage**
5.	**nice**	10.	**fudge**

Challenge Words

11.	**central**	14.	**gymnast**
12.	**fireplace**	15.	**celebrate**
13.	**gentle**		

* Word from "Big Bushy Mustache"

Decodable Books

Additional Decoding Practice

• **Phonics**
 Consonants /s/c; /j/g, dge
• **Decodable Words**
• **High-Frequency Words**
 See lists in *Decodable Book 11*.
 See also *Decodable Books*, online (Take-Home Version).

▲ Decodable Book 11: "A Nice Place for Mice" and "Strange Gadgets"

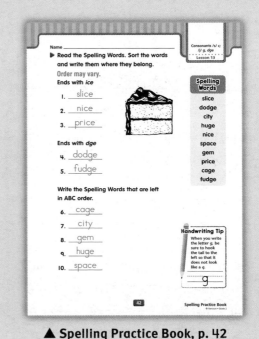

▲ Spelling Practice Book, p. 42

 # High-Frequency Words

Objective

- *To read high-frequency words*

REVIEW ✓ Tested

High-Frequency Words

above	wear
shoes	woman
tough	young
wash	

ELL

Clarify Usage Explain to children that *tough* describes someone who is strong and not afraid, like a firefighter running into a dangerous fire. Say: **A firefighter is tough.** Then say other sentences about people who are strong and courageous, and have children repeat them, using the word *tough*.

Review

DISPLAY THE WORDS Write the words *wear*, *tough*, *woman*, *young*, *shoes*, *wash*, and *above* on the board. Point to each word, and ask a volunteer to read it.

Practice/Apply

GUIDED PRACTICE Give each child a set of word cards (*Teacher Resource Book*, p. 78), and have children spread the cards out in front of them. Randomly call out each of the words, and have children hold up the matching card. Point to the word on the board so that children can check their response.

INDEPENDENT PRACTICE Have partners take turns picking a word card and reading the word aloud. The other child should hold up the matching card and use the word in a sentence. Have partners go through all seven word cards a few times.

✓ MONITOR PROGRESS

High-Frequency Words

IF children have difficulty reading the high-frequency words,	**THEN** display two sets of word cards, and have children read and match the words.

Small-Group Instruction, p. S23:

● **BELOW-LEVEL:** Reteach ● **ON-LEVEL:** Reinforce ● **ADVANCED:** Extend

Fluency

Phrasing

Review

DIBELS
Oral
Reading
Fluency
ORF

MODEL READING WITH NATURAL PHRASING
Remind children that good readers break up sentences into smaller groups of words, or chunks, that go together. Tell children to

▲ **Student Edition, pp. 392–417**

- break a long sentence into chunks that are complete thoughts and make sense.

- read the chunks without pausing.

- read in a way that sounds as if they are speaking to a friend.

Think Aloud   I'm going to read the first few paragraphs of "Big Bushy Mustache." I will break up the longer sentences into smaller chunks. I'll make sure each chunk makes sense. Sometimes a comma can help me break a sentence into chunks.

Practice/Apply

Routine Card 9   **GUIDED PRACTICE**   Read pages 394–395 aloud. Then have children practice reading the same pages several times with a partner. Monitor children as they read, guiding them in breaking the sentences into meaningful chunks.

Routine Card 10   **INDEPENDENT PRACTICE**   Have partners take turns rereading "Big Bushy Mustache" aloud, a page at a time. Remind the partner who is listening to offer feedback on whether or not the reader is making sense and is reading in a natural way.

Objective

- *To use phrasing to read fluently in a manner that sounds like natural speech*

BELOW-LEVEL

Fluency Practice   Have children reread *Decodable Book 11*, Story 13 in the *Strategic Intervention Interactive Reader*, or the appropriate *Leveled Reader* (pp. T276–T279). Have them practice reading the text several times.

Additional Related Reading

- *I Love My Mama* by Peter Kavanagh. Simon & Schuster, 2003. **EASY**

- *Grandfather and I* by Helen E. Buckley. HarperTrophy, 2000. **AVERAGE**

- *Just My Dad & Me* by Leah Komaiko. HarperTrophy, 1999. **CHALLENGE**

Fiction and Nonfiction
Comprehension

Objective

- *To distinguish fiction from nonfiction elements*

Skill Trace

 Fiction and Nonfiction

Introduce	T212–T213
Reteach	S16–S17
Review	**T248, T262, T272, T298–T299, T330, T344, T354, T404, T425**
Test	Theme 3
Maintain	Theme 4, T271

Review

REVIEW FICTION AND NONFICTION Remind children that there are two main kinds of writing, fiction and nonfiction. Ask them to recall some characteristics of fiction. (made-up characters; made-up events) Then ask them to recall some characteristics of nonfiction. (real people or animals; real events) Tell children that knowing whether a selection is fiction or nonfiction helps them set a purpose for reading.

Practice/Apply

GUIDED PRACTICE Have children turn to "Frog and Toad All Year" on *Student Edition* page 62. Flip through the selection together, and ask volunteers to recall what the story is about. Ask: **Is this selection fiction or nonfiction?** (fiction) Guide children to explain how they know, including a title that refers to made-up characters and illustrations that show made-up events. Repeat the procedure for "Life as a Frog" on *Student Edition* page 80. Guide children to notice the characteristics of the selection that show that it is nonfiction, including photographs that show real frogs, labels that give information about the photographs, and heads that tell the topic of each section.

INDEPENDENT PRACTICE Have children turn in the *Student Edition* to "Henry and Mudge" on page 94 and "Dogs" on page 118. Ask them to identify each selection as fiction or nonfiction and to explain how they know.

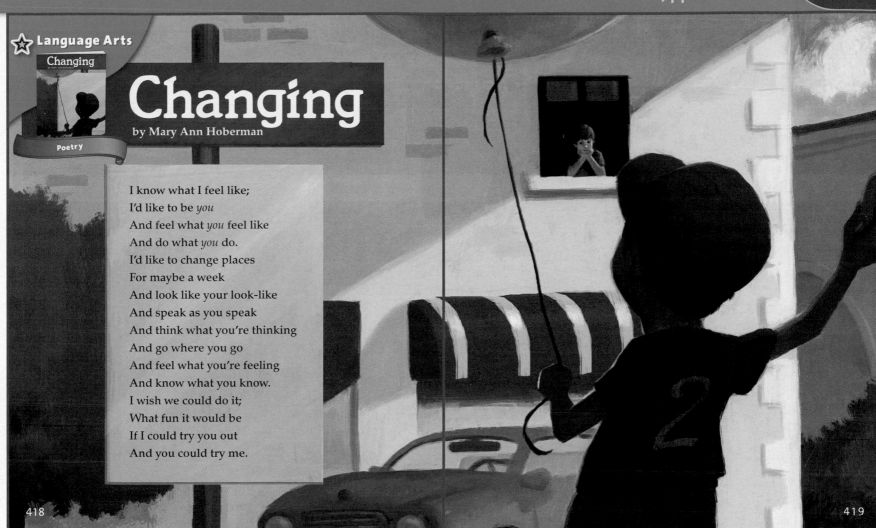

Changing
by Mary Ann Hoberman

I know what I feel like;
I'd like to be *you*
And feel what *you* feel like
And do what *you* do.
I'd like to change places
For maybe a week
And look like your look-like
And speak as you speak
And think what you're thinking
And go where you go
And feel what you're feeling
And know what you know.
I wish we could do it;
What fun it would be
If I could try you out
And you could try me.

418   419

Reading
Student Edition: Paired Selection

Read and Respond

USE PRIOR KNOWLEDGE/SET A PURPOSE   Guide children to use prior knowledge and set a purpose for reading. Then have them read the poem.

MONITOR COMPREHENSION   Ask children to reread the poem. Ask:

- **GENRE   What rhyming words do you hear in the poem?** (you/do; week/speak; go/know; be/me)

- **PERSONAL RESPONSE   Why might it be fun to change places with someone else for a week?** (Responses will vary.)

 SOCIAL STUDIES

SUPPORTING STANDARDS

If You Could Be the President   Ask children what they would do if they could change places with the President of the United States for one day. Have them name the current President. Point out that the President is the leader of the country.

 Connections

Comparing Texts

① Possible response: Both Ricky and the boy in the poem "Changing" want to be like someone else. Ricky wants to be like his father. The boy in the poem wants to change places with the boy he sees on the street. **TEXT TO TEXT**

② Responses will vary. **TEXT TO SELF**

③ Possible response: They can cut their hair or grow it longer. They can wear disguises like a fake mustache or a fake beard. Adult men can grow real mustaches or beards. People can also wear different clothes or costumes to look different. **TEXT TO WORLD**

Connections

Comparing Texts

❶ How are Ricky and the boy in the poem "Changing" alike?

❷ What costumes do you like to wear?

❸ What are some ways people can change the way they look?

Phonics

Make a Match

On one index card, write two words in which *c* has the soft sound. On another card, write two words in which *g* has the soft sound. Switch cards with a partner. Take turns naming rhyming words for the words on the cards.

trace
ice

edge
rage

420

Fluency Practice

Read with a Partner

Take turns reading the story again with a partner. As a reader, work on keeping groups of words together. If you make a mistake, go back and reread. As a listener, follow along and help the reader with hard words. Switch roles after every page.

Writing

Write About a Story

Write about the different mustaches Ricky makes. Look back at the story and your story map for details about each mustache. Use the details to help you write your sentences.

Characters — Setting
Beginning
Middle
End

My Writing Checklist
Writing Trait ▸ Conventions
✓ I use a story map to help me plan my writing.
✓ I use correct punctuation.

421

PHONICS

Make a Match Encourage children to think of different words than those shown in the *Student Edition*. After partners have switched cards, suggest that they list the new rhyming words on a sheet of paper. Have partners read aloud their lists of words.

trace
face
space
race
place

FLUENCY

Read with a Partner Remind children that the goal is for the reader to speak in a natural way, as if talking to a friend. As children read, encourage the listening partner to offer feedback to the reader: Can the listener follow what the reader is saying? Is the reader keeping groups of words together?

WRITING

Write About a Story Remind children that Ricky made mustaches in the middle of the story (*Student Edition* pages 408–409). You may wish to provide the following sentence frames: *Ricky's first mustache was _____. Ricky's second mustache was _____. and Ricky's last mustache was _____.*

Portfolio Opportunity Children may choose to illustrate their sentences and place them in their portfolios.

Build Robust Vocabulary

Objective

• *To review robust vocabulary*

REVIEW

Vocabulary: Lesson 13

wilting	flitted
swirling	trance
route	semblance
distraught	improvise

▼ Student-Friendly Explanations

Student-Friendly Explanations

wilting	When a plant doesn't get enough water, its leaves start to droop because they are wilting.
flitted	If something moved quickly from place to place without stopping for long, it flitted.
swirling	If something is swirling, it is moving round and round quickly.
trance	When someone is in a trance, he or she seems to be asleep, but his or her eyes are open.
route	When you follow the same route to school or to the store every day, you are going the same way each time.
semblance	When you make a drawing that looks a lot like someone, it is a good semblance of that person.
distraught	When someone is distraught, that person is very, very unhappy.
improvise	If you improvise a song or a story, then you make it up as you sing the song or tell the story.

Grade 2, Lesson 13   R68   Vocabulary

Transparency R68

Review Robust Vocabulary

USE VOCABULARY IN DIFFERENT CONTEXTS   Remind children of the Student-Friendly Explanations of the Vocabulary Words introduced on Days 1 and 2. Then discuss each word, using the following prompts:

wilting

• **Name some reasons why plants might be wilting.**

• **If someone wilts from being outside in the heat, how does that person feel?**

flitted

• **Would a class flit from room to room? Why or why not?**

• **Would you be more likely to flit about a toy store or a doctor's office? Why?**

swirling

• **Would it be a good idea to swirl hot soup in a bowl? Why or why not?**

• **When does water swirl in a bathtub—when it's being added or when it's being drained out?**

trance

• **Would you like for your friends to act like they are in a trance when you are telling them a story? Why or why not?**

• **If you were watching a movie as if you were in a trance, would you be enjoying the movie? Why or why not?**

route

- What route did you take to get to school today?

- What would you be doing if you retraced your route to the classroom?

- Could a river be part of a route? Why?

semblance

- Why could a doll be a semblance of a person?

- Would a baby's drawing of you be a good semblance of you? Why or why not?

- How could a twin be a good semblance of someone else?

distraught

- Would you be smiling if you were distraught? Why or why not?

- How might someone who is distraught act?

- What kinds of events might make a person distraught?

improvise

- If you improvise a song, what are you doing?

- How might a cook improvise a special dish?

- If you are following very closely the directions of how to play a game, are you improvising? Why?

ADVANCED

Tell Stories Challenge children to use four of the Vocabulary Words to tell a short story about a special day at school. Children can make up their oral stories with a partner. Then have them share their stories with classmates.

Grammar
Plural Possessive Nouns

5-DAY GRAMMAR	
DAY 1	Introduce Plural Possessives
DAY 2	Plural Possessives in Sentences
DAY 3	**Identify Singular and Plural Possessives**
DAY 4	Apply to Writing
DAY 5	Weekly Review

Objective
• *To identify and write singular and plural possessive nouns*

Daily Proofreading

the childrens' bikes were all red.

(The, children's)

Read each sentence. Circle each *singular* possessive noun. Underline each *plural* possessive noun.

Plural Possessive Nouns
Lesson 13

1. Mrs. Moseley's class went to the aquarium.
2. They watched the underwater creatures' movements.
3. The sharks' bodies were sleek, so they could swim fast.
4. Juan's favorite fish was the clownfish.

Write each sentence. Make the plural noun in ( ) show ownership.

5. The (teachers) lounge was filled with balloons.
   The teachers' lounge was filled with balloons.
6. The (girls) camp was at the lake.
   The girls' camp was at the lake.

46   Grammar Practice Book

▲ **Grammar Practice Book, p. 46**

Review

IDENTIFY SINGULAR AND PLURAL POSSESSIVES   Write the following sentences on the board.

The girl's mouse ate the cheese.
The girls' mice ate the cheese.

Read aloud the sentences. Explain that in each sentence, there is a word that shows ownership. Ask children to identify which sentence shows that just one person owns something. (the first sentence) Ask children how they are able to tell this. (The apostrophe in *girl's* comes before the *s*.) Then ask children how they know that the second sentence shows that more than one person owns something. (The apostrophe in *girls'* comes after the *s*.)

Practice/Apply

GUIDED PRACTICE   Write these sentences on the board. Model how to identify the singular possessive noun in the first sentence by looking at the placement of the apostrophes. Work with children to identify the singular or plural possessive nouns in the remaining sentences.

Mr. Patrick's mustache is brown.
The hamsters' cage was messy.
This mouse's baby looks like all the mice's babies.

INDEPENDENT PRACTICE   Have children rewrite the following sentences with singular or plural possessive nouns.

The boys lunch boxes were lost.
The cat kittens all looked alike.
The people homes lined the street.
I could see into the house windows.

Writing

Story: Dialogue

5-DAY WRITING	
DAY 1	Introduce
DAY 2	Prewrite
DAY 3	Draft
DAY 4	Revise
DAY 5	Revise

Draft Dialogue

REVIEW A LITERATURE MODEL Have children open their *Student Edition* to "Big Bushy Mustache," page 403. Read aloud the page, focusing on the dialogue between Ricky and his mother. Point out the following:

> • The writer uses quotation marks to show the exact words that Ricky and his mother say to each other.
>
> • The word *said* shows who is speaking and how the person speaks.
>
> • The dialogue is written the way real people speak, including Spanish words because these characters speak Spanish.

DRAFT DIALOGUE Have children use their pictures and filled-in story maps to write a short story that includes dialogue between the two people in their pictures.

WRITING TRAIT **CONVENTIONS** As children write, remind them of the correct usage of quotation marks in dialogue. Also remind them that proper nouns such as character names should be capitalized and that plural possessives usually have an apostrophe after the plural ending. Tell children they will be able to correct their sentences later when they revise them.

CONFER WITH CHILDREN Meet with individual children, helping them as they write their short stories. Offer encouragement for what they are doing well, and make constructive suggestions for improving an aspect of the writing, as needed.

Objectives

- *To draft a story with dialogue*
- *To use quotation marks and other punctuation correctly in story dialogue*

 Writing Prompt

Dialogue Have children write another exchange of dialogue between Ricky and his mother.

▲ Writer's Companion, Lesson 13

E L L

Support Writing Have children work with English-proficient partners to write their stories. Children can dictate their characters' dialogue to their partners. Then have children copy the dialogue that they dictated.

Day at a Glance

Day 4

 phonics and Spelling
- Introduce: Inflections *-ed, -ing*
- Review: Consonants /s/c; /j/g, *dge*

High-Frequency Words
- Review: *wear, tough, woman, young, shoes, wash, above*

Fluency
- Phrasing
- "Big Bushy Mustache," *Student Edition*, pp. 392–417

Comprehension
 Review: Fiction and Nonfiction

Robust Vocabulary
- Review: *wilting, flitted, swirling, trance, route, semblance, distraught, improvise*

Grammar
- Review: Plural Possessive Nouns

Writing ✏
- Story: Dialogue

Warm-Up Routines

 Oral Language

Objective *To listen attentively and respond appropriately to oral communication*

Question of the Day

What are some things you do at home before you leave for school each morning?

Encourage children to describe the routine they follow just before they leave for school each day. Use the following prompts.

- **What are some things you do to get ready for school each day?**
- **Who might you say goodbye to before leaving home each morning? How do you say goodbye to this person?**
- **What is the last thing you do before you leave for school?**

Read Aloud

Objective *To listen for enjoyment*

BIG BOOK OF RHYMES AND POEMS Display "Aliona Says" on page 26 and read the title aloud. Point out that the Aliona in the title is probably a child and the poem is written as if Aliona were talking. Tell children to listen to the poem for enjoyment. Then read the poem aloud, encouraging children to join in. Ask children what kind of advice a child might receive before leaving for school.

Aliona Says

An off-to-school hug
Is quick but nice.
Mine always comes
with some words
Of advice.

Emily George

▲ Big Book of Rhymes and Poems, p. 26

Word Wall

Objective *To read high-frequency words*

REVIEW HIGH-FREQUENCY WORDS Arrange the words *wear*, *tough*, *woman*, *young*, *shoes*, *wash*, and *above* in two columns. Divide the class into two groups. Have children in the first group take turns reading aloud the words in the first column and using each word in a sentence. Have the second group do the same with the second column of words. Then have the groups switch columns and repeat.

wear tough woman young

shoes wash above

Inflections -ed, -ing  phonics

5-DAY PHONICS	
DAY 1	Reintroduce /s/c and /j/g, dge
DAY 2	Word Building with /s/c and /j/g, dge
DAY 3	Word Building with /s/c and /j/g, dge
DAY 4	Inflections -ed, -ing; Review /s/c; /j/g, dge
DAY 5	Inflections -ed, -ing; Review /s/c; /j/g, dge

Objective

• To read words with doubled consonants and inflections -ed and -ing

Skill Trace

 Inflections -ed, -ing (double final consonant)

Introduce	Grade 1
Reintroduce	**T258**
Review	T268
Test	Theme 3

Teach/Model

INTRODUCE DOUBLING CONSONANTS   Write the word *hop* on the board, and have children read it. Ask volunteers to identify the vowel and consonants. Point out that *hop* has the CVC pattern. Say: **When -ed or -ing is added to the end of a CVC word, the final consonant is doubled.** Write the words *hopped* and *hopping*, demonstrating how the *p* is doubled before the inflection is added. Read the words, pointing out that the vowel sound does not change when -ed and -ing are added. Then have children read the words with you.

hop
hopped
hopping

Guided Practice

READ WORDS   Write the following words on the board. Read each word, and have children read it after you.

stopped	chatted	grabbed
hugging	skidding	popping

Practice/Apply

READ SENTENCES   Display **Transparency R66** or write the sentences on the board or on chart paper. Have children read the sentences aloud. Remind them to use what they have learned about doubling consonants in words with the endings -ed and -ing.

Inflections -ed, -ing

Maria was so happy she hopped and skipped all the way home.

The race horse trotted across the field.

Marco was shopping for a new baseball glove all day at the mall.

Freddie and Ana were running for the bus when I saw them after school.

Grade 2, Lesson 13   R66   Phonics

Transparency R66

Consonants /s/ c; /j/ g, dge and Spelling

5-DAY SPELLING

DAY 1	Pretest
DAY 2	Word Building
DAY 3	State the Generalization
DAY 4	**Review**
DAY 5	Posttest

Build Words

REVIEW THE WORDS Have children open their notebooks to the spelling words that they wrote on Day 3. Have them read the words several times and then close their notebooks.

MAP LETTERS TO SOUNDS Have children follow your directions to change one letter in each of the following words to make a spelling word. Have them write the spelling word on a sheet of paper. Then have a volunteer change the spelling of the word on the board so that children can self-check their spelling.

- Write *lodge* on the board. Ask: **Which spelling word can you make by changing the first letter?** (dodge)

- Write *twice* on the board. Ask: **Which spelling words can you make by changing the first two letters?** (slice, nice, price)

- Write *them* on the board. Ask: **Which spelling word can you make by changing the first two letters?** (gem)

Follow a similar procedure with the following words: *pity (city), hug (huge), face (space), page (cage), judge (fudge)*.

CHALLENGE WORDS Write the first syllable of each challenge word on the board. Say each word, and ask volunteers to spell the second syllable. Then have children write each word in its entirety two or three times.

BELOW-LEVEL

Silent *e* Words Some children may have difficulty discriminating between the long-vowel sound in the CVC*e* pattern and the short-vowel sound in words ending in *dge*. Write *c_ge* and *d_dge* on the board. Work with children to complete each word, pointing out that when they see the *dge* pattern, the vowel before it has a short sound.

Objective

- *To use /s/ c; /j/ g, dge; and other known letter-sounds to spell and write words*

Spelling Words

1.	**slice***	6.	**space**
2.	**dodge**	7.	**gem**
3.	**city**	8.	**price**
4.	**huge**	9.	**cage**
5.	**nice**	10.	**fudge**

Challenge Words

11.	**central**	14.	**gymnast**
12.	**fireplace**	15.	**celebrate**
13.	**gentle**		

* Word from "Big Bushy Mustache"

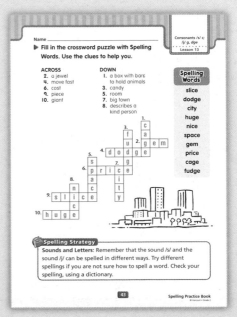

▲ Spelling Practice Book, p. 43

High-Frequency Words

Objective

• *To read high-frequency words*

REVIEW ✓

High-Frequency Words

above	wear
shoes	woman
tough	young
wash	

Review

READ SENTENCES Display **Transparency R67**. Have children read the words at the top in order. Then point to the words at random and have children read them.

Practice/Apply

GUIDED PRACTICE Talk about the illustration. Then track the print as you read aloud the sentences. Have children choral-read with you.

Ask children to create their own sentences with high-frequency words. Write each sentence on the board as children dictate it. Then have children read the sentences aloud.

INDEPENDENT PRACTICE Have children write three sentences using one or more high-frequency words in each one. Then have them share their sentences with a partner.

High-Frequency Words

above	shoes	tough	wash
wear	woman	young	

Angel watched the man <u>wash</u> the store window.

He could see the shelf <u>above</u> the counter inside.

"Those are the <u>shoes</u> I want," he said to his friend Ruben.

"You're too <u>young</u> to <u>wear</u> them," said Ruben. "They're for adults to wear at work."

"That's okay," said Angel. "I want to look <u>tough</u> like my Uncle Juan."

Angel went inside to ask the <u>woman</u> if he could try them on.

Grade 2, Lesson 13   R67   High-Frequency Words

Transparency R67

Fluency
Phrasing

Review

MODEL READING WITH NATURAL PHRASING Read aloud the first paragraph on page 412 of "Big Bushy Mustache," breaking the text into natural, meaningful phrases. Point out that the natural breaks in the text are often marked by punctuation.

▲ Student Edition, pp. 392–417

Think Aloud In the first sentence, there is no punctuation mark in the middle, but I know I can take a tiny pause before *to his lip* because that is a chunk of words that go together. In the next sentence, there are commas that help me know where to pause.

Practice/Apply

 Routine Card 8

GUIDED PRACTICE Have children echo-read pages 412–414 with you, matching your phrasing. Remind them to pay attention to the punctuation in the sentences as clues to how to chunk text.

 Routine Card 9

INDEPENDENT PRACTICE Ask partners to reread "Big Bushy Mustache" aloud two or three times. Remind them to read in chunks that make sense.

✓ MONITOR PROGRESS

Fluency

IF children have difficulty reading with appropriate phrasing and in a manner that sounds like natural speech,	**THEN** write several sentences on the board, dividing the text into meaningful chunks using slash marks.

Small-Group Instruction, pp. S24–S25:

● **BELOW-LEVEL:** Reteach   ● **ON-LEVEL:** Reinforce   ● **ADVANCED:** Extend

Objective

- *To use phrasing to read fluently in a manner that sounds like natural speech*

BELOW-LEVEL

Choral-Read Model reading the story dialogue in natural-sounding phrases that sound like real speech. Have children choral-read the dialogue with you until they can read it with natural phrasing.

"Research Says"

Repeated Reading "The major conclusion of this study was that repeated reading worked."
—Dowhower 1987, p. 402

Fiction and Nonfiction
Comprehension

Objectives

- *To identify the elements of a fiction story*
- *To distinguish fiction from nonfiction elements*

Skill Trace

 Tested Fiction and Nonfiction

Introduce	T212–T213
Reteach	S16–S17
Review	**T248, T262, T272, T298–T299, T330, T344, T354, T404, T425**
Text	Theme 3
Maintain	Theme 4, T271

Fiction and Nonfiction

Ana and Her Sister

Ana loved her big sister Sarah and wanted to be a soccer player just like her. Every day Ana practiced kicking the soccer ball. It never went very far or very straight.

"I can't play soccer like Sarah," she said to her friend Timmy.

"Maybe we can play something else," said Timmy.

Timmy had a baseball and two gloves. Timmy and Ana put on the gloves. When Timmy tossed the ball to Ana, she caught it like a pro!

"I was just lucky," said Ana, but it wasn't luck. For the next hour they played catch. Ana caught every ball thrown to her.

"Hey," said Ana with a big grin. "I like baseball!"

Then Ana heard a voice behind her.

"Hey, Ana!" said Sarah. "Let me try. Throw the ball to me."

Ana tossed the ball to her sister very lightly. Sarah reached for it, but she missed it completely.

"Come on," Ana said to Sarah. "I'll teach you how to throw if you'll teach me how to kick."

"Deal!" said Sarah, and she ran to get her soccer ball.

Grade 2, Lesson 13   R63   Comprehension

Transparency R63

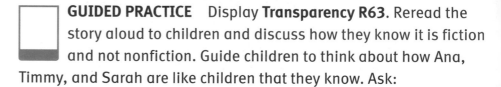

EXPLAIN FICTION AND NONFICTION   Ask children to explain how they can tell a fiction selection from a nonfiction selection. (Fiction selections are made-up stories. Nonfiction selections are about real-life people, places, or things.) Remind children that some fiction stories, like "Arthur's Reading Race," are easy to identify because the characters are not like real people. Some fiction stories have made-up characters that look, act, and speak like real people, so these stories can be harder to identify as fiction.

Practice/Apply

GUIDED PRACTICE   Display **Transparency R63**. Reread the story aloud to children and discuss how they know it is fiction and not nonfiction. Guide children to think about how Ana, Timmy, and Sarah are like children that they know. Ask:

- **What is Ana doing that is like something that you or a friend might do?** (She is playing sports.)

- **Are Ana's feelings like feelings a real person might have, or are her feelings different? Why or why not?** (They are like a real person's feelings. Real children sometimes wish they could be like someone else.)

- **If this were a nonfiction selection, how might you be able to tell?** (There might be a photograph of a real person named Ana. It would give more facts about Ana.)

INDEPENDENT PRACTICE   Ask children to tell how Ricky behaves like a real child in "Big Bushy Mustache." (Possible response: He goes to school. He wants to be like his father. He feels bad when he does something he should not have done.)

Build Robust Vocabulary

Review Robust Vocabulary

USE VOCABULARY IN DIFFERENT CONTEXTS Remind children of the Student-Friendly Explanations of the Vocabulary Words. Then discuss the words, using the following activities.

improvise, route Tell children to think about travelers riding in a car across the country. Say that some of the time, they will follow a route that they have planned, but some of the time, they will improvise their route. Tell children you will say different types of travel routes. Ask children to make the sound of a car horn, "Beep! Beep!" if the plans are improvised.

The travelers follow a route on a map.

The travelers just drive wherever they feel like going.

The travelers follow directions from a website.

The travelers take a new route to avoid a traffic jam.

semblance, distraught Tell children that a painter is going to paint pictures of a family. You will describe each picture. Have children say, "Cheer up!" when you describe a semblance of a distraught family member.

A six-year-old is laughing.

A ten-year-old is crying.

A father is smiling.

A mother is jumping up and down.

trance Tell children that you will name some activities. Ask them to raise a hand if they might seem to be in a trance while doing the activity.

watching a favorite TV program

playing on a playground

listening to a good story

swimming in a pool

Objective

• *To review robust vocabulary*

Tested

REVIEW ✓

Vocabulary: Lesson 13

wilting	flitted
swirling	trance
route	semblance
distraught	improvise

▼ **Student-Friendly Explanations**

Student-Friendly Explanations

wilting	When a plant doesn't get enough water, its leaves start to droop because they are wilting.
flitted	If something moved quickly from place to place without stopping for long, it flitted.
swirling	If something is swirling, it is moving round and round quickly.
trance	When someone is in a trance, he or she seems to be asleep, but his or her eyes are open.
route	When you follow the same route to school or to the store every day, you are going the same way each time.
semblance	When you make a drawing that looks a lot like someone, it is a good semblance of that person.
distraught	When someone is distraught, that person is very, very unhappy.
improvise	If you improvise a song or a story, then you make it up as you sing the song or tell the story.

Grade 2, Lesson 13   R68   Vocabulary

Transparency R68

Lesson 13   **T263**

Grammar
Plural Possessive Nouns

5-DAY GRAMMAR

DAY 1 Introduce Plural Possessives
DAY 2 Plural Possessives in Sentences
DAY 3 Identify Singular and Plural Possessives
DAY 4 Apply to Writing
DAY 5 Weekly Review

Objective
- *To identify and write singular and plural possessive nouns*

Daily Proofreading

Most peoples best Friends are nice to them.

(people's, friends)

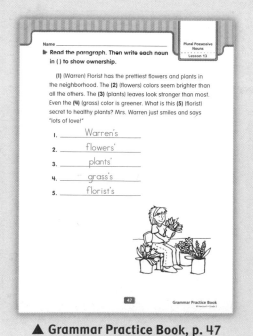

▲ Grammar Practice Book, p. 47

Review

DISCUSS PLURAL POSSESSIVES Review with children that plural possessive nouns show that something belongs to more than one person or thing. Elicit that the apostrophe is usually placed after the *s* in a plural noun. Point out that some plural words, such as *children* and *mice* add an apostrophe plus *s* to show ownership. Write the following sentences on the board:

Jorge likes to watch the mices' whiskers move. (mice's)

The three cat's kittens are cute. (cats')

All of that girl's dresses are red.

Tell children that each sentence has a plural possessive, but only one sentence is written correctly. Point to and read aloud the first sentence. Ask children if the word *mices'* is written correctly and to explain why or why not. Continue with the next two sentences, leading children to understand that the third sentence is correct.

USE EDITOR'S MARKS Model using basic Editor's Marks to revise each of the three sentences.

Editor's Marks

∧	Add
℘	Take out
⌃	Change
⊙	Add a period

Practice/Apply

GUIDED PRACTICE Have children help you write three sentences that each have at least one plural possessive. After you have written each sentence, model how to check it to make sure the plural possessive is written correctly and that the sentence uses correct punctuation. Use Editor's Marks as necessary.

INDEPENDENT PRACTICE Ask children to write three complete sentences about your school that each include at least one plural possessive noun. Have partners exchange sentences and check that the sentences are correctly punctuated.

5-DAY WRITING	
DAY 1	Introduce
DAY 2	Prewrite
DAY 3	Draft
DAY 4	**Revise**
DAY 5	Revise

Writing
Story: Dialogue

Write Dialogue

 WRITE Have children continue writing their short stories with dialogue. Remind them that the dialogue should be the exact words the characters say.

CONVENTIONS Remind children that sentences with dialogue begin and end with quotation marks and also include speaking words such as *said* or *asked*. Have them check their writing for the correct use of quotation marks.

REVISE Have children read their short stories to partners and check that they have included dialogue that makes the stories more interesting to listen to. Children can use the list of criteria for Dialogue to improve their writing.

Dialogue

- Dialogue tells the words characters say.
- Dialogue is inside quotation marks.
- Words like <u>said</u> and <u>asked</u> tell how the character says the dialogue.

Have children revise their short stories. Encourage them to work with a partner to make sure that they have used dialogue and quotation marks correctly. Encourage children to use Editor's Marks to revise their writing. Save children's writing for use on Day 5.

Editor's Marks	
∧	Add
℘	Take out
⌃	Change
⊙	Add a period
≡	Capitalize
◠	Check Spelling

Objectives

- *To revise dialogue in a story*
- *To use quotation marks correctly*

 ## Writing Prompt

Dialogue Have children use quotation marks to write a short conversation that they overheard today at school.

BELOW-LEVEL

Story Conferencing Have children work with an On-Level partner to review their drafts. Encourage children to offer constructive feedback on each other's stories and to check each other's drafts for the correct use of quotation marks and other punctuation.

Day at a Glance
Day 5

 and Spelling
- Review: Inflections *-ed, -ing*
- Posttest: Consonants /s/*c*; /j/*g, dge*

High-Frequency Words
- Cumulative Review

Fluency
- Phrasing
- "Big Bushy Mustache," *Student Edition*, pp. 392–417

Read!

Comprehension

Focus Skill
Review: Fiction and Nonfiction
- *Read-Aloud Anthology*: "Butterfly Boy"

Robust Vocabulary
- Cumulative Review

Grammar
- Review: Plural Possessive Nouns

Writing
- Story: Dialogue

Warm-Up Routines

Oral Language

Objective *To listen attentively and respond appropriately to oral communication*

> ### Question of the Day
>
> What is good advice to give to someone leaving for school in the morning? Why?

Invite children to discuss what they think is good advice for a child heading to school in the morning. Use the following prompts:

- **Has anyone ever given you good advice about school or something else? How did it help you?**

- **What kind of advice would you give to a child who is going to school if you were an adult?**

On the board, list children's advice.

Read Aloud

Objective *To identify rhymes in poetry*

BIG BOOK OF RHYMES AND POEMS Display "Aliona Says" on page 26. Tell children to listen for two words that rhyme in the poem. Then read the poem aloud. Guide children to identify the two rhyming words, *nice* and *advice*. Ask children to name other words that rhyme with *nice* and *advice*. Then read the poem again, encouraging children to join in.

▲ **Big Book of Rhymes and Poems, p. 26**

Word Wall

Objective *To read high-frequency words*

REVIEW HIGH-FREQUENCY WORDS Review the words *wear, tough, woman, young, shoes, wash,* and *above*. Point to the words on the Word Wall in random order and call on individual children to read the words quickly. Repeat a number of times so that each child gets to read at least one word. Then repeat, this time calling on children to use each word in a sentence.

Inflections -ed, -ing phonics

5-DAY PHONICS

DAY 1	Reintroduce /s/c and /j/g, dge
DAY 2	Word Building with /s/c and /j/g, dge
DAY 3	Word Building with /s/c and /j/g, dge
DAY 4	Inflections -ed, -ing; Review /s/c; /j/g, dge
DAY 5	Inflections -ed, -ing; Review /s/c; /j/g, dge

Objective

- *To read words with doubled consonants and inflections -ed and -ing*

Skill Trace

Tested ✓ **Inflections -ed, -ing (double final consonant)**

Introduce	Grade 1
Reintroduce	T258
Review	**T268**
Test	Theme 3

Review

READ WORDS WITH -ed, -ing   Write the words *pat*, *patted*, and *patting* on the board. Ask a volunteer to explain how the base word changed when the endings -ed and -ing were added. (The final consonant was doubled.) Then have children read the words.

Practice/Apply

GUIDED PRACTICE   Write the following words on the board and have children read them: *grab*, *pop*, *clean*, and *park*. Then make a chart as shown. Guide children in sorting the words and adding the endings -ed and -ing. Have children read the words with you.

Double the Final Consonant	Do Not Double the Final Consonant
grab, grabbed, grabbing pop, popped, popping	clean, cleaned, cleaning park, parked, parking

INDEPENDENT PRACTICE   Have children add other words to the chart. Point to the words at random and have children read them.

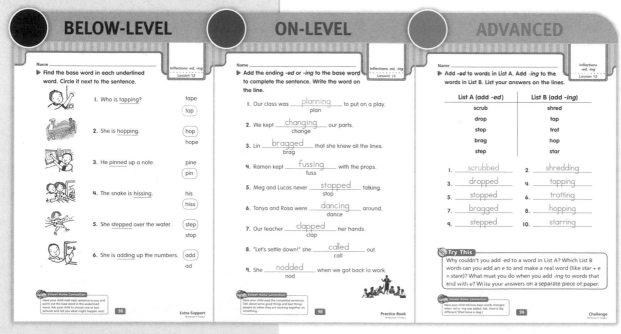

▲ **Extra Support, p. 98**   ▲ **Practice Book, p. 98**   ▲ **Challenge, p. 98**

ELL

- Group children according to academic levels, and assign one of the pages on the left.

- Clarify any unfamiliar concepts as necessary. See *ELL Teacher Guide* Lesson 13 for support in scaffolding instruction.

Consonants /s/ c; /j/ g, dge phonics and Spelling

5-DAY SPELLING
DAY 1 Pretest
DAY 2 Word Building
DAY 3 State the Generalization
DAY 4 Review
DAY 5 Posttest

Assess

POSTTEST Assess children's progress. Use the dictation sentences from Day 1.

Words with /s/ c or /j/ g, dge

1.	slice	I asked for a big **slice** of cake.
2.	dodge	Su jumped to **dodge** the ball.
3.	city	Juanita rode the subway in the **city**.
4.	huge	Deb's new dog is **huge**.
5.	nice	The doctor was **nice** when I was sick.
6.	space	Papi drove into the parking **space**.
7.	gem	There was a big, shiny **gem** in her ring.
8.	price	The **price** of the pen was one dollar.
9.	cage	The bird sang softly in its **cage**.
10.	fudge	The **fudge** melted in my mouth.

ADVANCED

Challenge Words Use the challenge words in these dictation sentences.

11.	central	My house is in the **central** part of town.
12.	fireplace	Mom put a big log in the **fireplace**.
13.	gentle	I had to be **gentle** with the little bird.
14.	gymnast	The **gymnast** performed on a mat.
15.	celebrate	I will **celebrate** with a big party!

WRITING APPLICATION
Have children write and illustrate a sentence using one of the spelling words.

Mom and I like to make fudge.

Objective

• To use /s/ c; /j/ g, dge; and other known letter-sounds to spell and write words

Spelling Words

1.	slice*	6.	space
2.	dodge	7.	gem
3.	city	8.	price
4.	huge	9.	cage
5.	nice	10.	fudge

Challenge Words

11.	central	14.	gymnast
12.	fireplace	15.	celebrate
13.	gentle		

* Word from "Big Bushy Mustache"

High-Frequency Words

Objectives

- *To read high-frequency words*
- *To explore word relationships*

REVIEW Tested ✓

High-Frequency Words

board	above
cook	shoes
enjoy	tough
expensive	wash
favorite	wear
imagine	woman
popular	young
year	

Cumulative Review

REINFORCE WORD RECOGNITION   Write the high-frequency words for Lessons 12 and 13 on the board. Point to words at random, and ask volunteers to read them.

SORT WORDS   Guide children in sorting the words into columns according to the number of syllables. Then have them read the words in each column again.

I Syllable	2 Syllables	3 Syllables
year	enjoy	imagine
cook	woman	favorite
board	above	popular
wear		expensive
tough		
young		
shoes		
wash		

- Ask: **Which word rhymes with *cheer*?** (year)
- Ask: **Which words begin with the letter *w*?** (wear, wash, woman)
- Ask: **Which word has two *p*'s?** (popular)
- Ask: **Which words end with the letter *e*?** (above, imagine, favorite, expensive)
- Ask: **Which words begin and end with a vowel?** (above, imagine, expensive)

Fluency
Phrasing

Readers' Theater

DIBELS
Oral Reading Fluency
ORF

PERFORM "BIG BUSHY MUSTACHE"   To help children improve their fluency, have them perform "Big Bushy Mustache" as Readers' Theater. Use the following procedures:

▲ **Student Edition, pp. 392–417**

- Ask children to describe how Ricky feels at different times in the story and how they would show this with their voices as they read aloud.

- Have groups of six children read the story together. Assign the roles of the narrator, Ricky, Mrs. Cortez, Ricky's mother, and Ricky's father. Another child can read all the additional parts of the people in Ricky's town, such as Mrs. Sanchez, the man on the street, and the woman carrying groceries.

- Monitor the groups as they read. Provide feedback and support.

- Invite groups to read the story or sections of it to classmates. Remind them to break up long sentences in natural-sounding chunks that sound like real people talking.

E L L

Develop Vocabulary   As you discuss how Ricky feels, call children's attention to words and phrases such as *frowning*, *shook his head no*, *nodded yes*, *laughed*, and *cried*. Model the actions that these words describe. Have children imitate your actions as they say the words and tell how Ricky feels at each point.

Objective

- *To read fluently with phrasing in a manner that sounds like natural speech*

ASSESSMENT

Monitoring Progress   Periodically, take a timed sample of children's oral reading and record the number of words read correctly per minute. Children should accurately read approximately 72 words per minute in the middle of Grade 2.

Fluency Support Materials

Fluency Builders, Grade 2, Lesson 13

Audiotext   *Student Edition* selections are available on *Audiotext 2*.

Strategic Intervention Teacher Guide, Lesson 13

Fiction and Nonfiction
Comprehension

Objectives

- *To identify the elements of a fiction story*
- *To distinguish fiction from non-fiction elements*

Skill Trace

 Fiction and Nonfiction

Introduce	T212–T213
Reintroduce	S16–S17
Review	**T248, T262, T272, T298– T299, T330, T344, T354, T404, T425**
Test	Theme 3
Maintain	Theme 4, T271

E L L

Build Background If children have difficulty understanding the concept of how the butterflies are drawn to bright white surfaces only, use visual aids such as colored paper to demonstrate it.

Review

REVIEW THE SKILL Remind children that fiction stories are different from nonfiction selections because they are made-up. Point out that in fiction, the characters, settings, and events are created by the author.

SET A PURPOSE FOR LISTENING Guide children in setting a purpose for listening that includes

- listening for clues that this is realistic fiction, such as characters who act and speak like real people.
- listening to recall who the Butterfly Boy is and why he has that name.

▲ **Read-Aloud Anthology, "Butterfly Boy," p. 48**

Practice/Apply

GUIDED PRACTICE As you read aloud "Butterfly Boy," use a chart to record information about the characters, setting, and dialogue that are similar to those in real life.

Characters	Setting	Dialogue
Emilio acts like a real boy. Emilio loves his grandfather. Abuelo seems like a real person who is sick.	The story is set in a home that seems like a real home. Real homes have windows, garages, and laundry lines.	Emilio talks to his grandfather and to his parents like a real boy would.

INDEPENDENT PRACTICE Have children use the chart to tell how they know the story is realistic fiction.

Build Robust Vocabulary

Cumulative Review

REINFORCE MEANINGS   Ask children the following questions:

- If you ramble through your neighborhood, are you going to stick to a planned route? Explain.

- If someone went to a shopping mall and leisurely flitted from store to store, what did that person do?

- How might you act around a distraught person? Why?

MEANINGS AND EXAMPLES   Using **Transparency GO10**, guide children to tell what *flitted* means. Write the meaning on the chart, and then ask volunteers to name examples of things that might flit about.

Word	Meaning	Examples
flitted	moved quickly from place to place without stopping for long	• birds in the trees • butterflies • flies at a picnic

Repeat the procedure for *archaic* and *swirling*.

Objective
- *To review robust vocabulary*

REVIEW Tested

Vocabulary

Lesson 12	Lesson 13
recently	wilting
housed	flitted
official	swirling
nominate	trance
recreation	route
leisurely	semblance
ramble	distraught
archaic	improvise

✓ MONITOR PROGRESS

Build Robust Vocabulary

IF children do not demonstrate understanding of the words and have difficulty using them,	**THEN** use each word in several sentences, and have children repeat each sentence.

Small-Group Instruction, pp. S28–S29:

⬤ **BELOW-LEVEL:** Reteach
⬤ **ON-LEVEL:** Reinforce
⬤ **ADVANCED:** Extend

Grammar
Plural Possessive Nouns

5-DAY GRAMMAR

DAY 1 Introduce Plural Possessives
DAY 2 Plural Possessives in Sentences
DAY 3 Identify Singular and Plural Possessives
DAY 4 Apply to Writing
DAY 5 Weekly Review

Objectives

• *To recognize that plural possessive nouns show ownership by more than one person or thing*
• *To write phrases with plural possessive nouns*

Daily Proofreading

my parents home is in ohio

(My; parents'; Ohio.)

 Language Arts Checkpoint

If children have difficulty with the concepts, see pages S30–S31 to reteach.

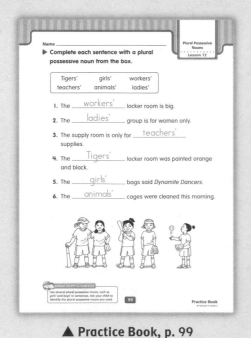

▲ Practice Book, p. 99

Review

REVIEW PLURAL POSSESSIVES Review the rules for forming plural possessive nouns. Write these points on the board.

> • **Plural possessive nouns show that something belongs to more than one person or thing.**
>
> • **An apostrophe usually comes after the <u>s</u> or <u>es</u>.**
>
> • **Some plural words, such as <u>children</u> and <u>mice</u>, have the apostrophe before the <u>s</u>.**

Practice/Apply

GUIDED PRACTICE Model revising the following phrases to show the correct form of plural possessive nouns.

the three sister's coats (the three sisters' coats)
the soccer players's coach (the soccer players' coach)
the childrens' lunchboxes (the children's lunchboxes)

INDEPENDENT PRACTICE Write the following sentences on the board. Explain that the plural possessive is not correct in each sentence. Have partners work together to rewrite the sentences with the correct form for the plural possessives. Have each pair of partners review the work of another pair of partners.

The students's teacher was nice.
(The students' teacher was nice.)

Jack washed all the actors costumes.
(Jack washed all the actors' costumes.)

The childrenss books were on the shelf.
(The children's books were on the shelf.)

Writing
Story: Dialogue

5-DAY WRITING	
DAY 1	Introduce
DAY 2	Prewrite
DAY 3	Draft
DAY 4	Revise
DAY 5	Revise

Revise

REVISE SHORT STORIES WITH DIALOGUE   Have children exchange short stories with a partner. Tell partners to review the stories, looking for a clear sequence of events as well as for interesting dialogue. Allow partners time to discuss each other's comments and questions. Then tell children to think about ways to improve and clarify their short stories.

WRITING TRAIT **CONVENTIONS**   After children revise their short stories, discuss as a class how to include dialogue in a story to show what characters say. Review how to use quotation marks at the beginning and end of the speakers' exact words, as well as the correct style for proper nouns and plural possessives.

NOTE: A 4-point rubric appears on page R8.

SCORING RUBRIC					
6	**5**	**4**	**3**	**2**	**1**
FOCUS Completely focused, purposeful.	Focused on topic and purpose.	Generally focused on topic and purpose.	Somewhat focused on topic and purpose.	Related to topic but does not maintain focus.	Lacks focus and purpose.
ORGANIZATION Ideas progress logically; paper conveys sense of completeness.	Organization mostly clear; paper gives sense of completeness.	Organization mostly clear, but some lapses occur; may seem unfinished.	Some sense of organization; seems unfinished.	Little sense of organization.	Little or no sense of organization.
SUPPORT Strong, specific details; clear, exact language; freshness of expression.	Strong, specific details; clear, exact language.	Adequate support and word choice.	Limited supporting details; limited word choice.	Few supporting details; limited word choice.	Little development; limited or unclear word choice.
CONVENTIONS Varied sentences; few, if any, errors.	Varied sentences; few errors.	Some sentence variety; few errors.	Simple sentence structures; some errors.	Simple sentence structures; many errors.	Unclear sentence structures; many errors.

REPRODUCIBLE RUBRICS for specific writing purposes and presentations are available on pages R2–R8.

Objective
- *To revise dialogue in stories*

Writing Prompt

Record   Have children record dialogue that they had with a classmate.

WEEKLY LESSON TEST

▲ **Weekly Lesson Tests, pp. 135–146**

- Selection Comprehension with Short Response
- Phonics and Spelling
- High-Frequency Words
- Focus Skill
- Robust Vocabulary
- Grammar
- Fluency Passage

 For prescriptions, see pp. A2–A6. Also available electronically on StoryTown Online Assessment and ExamView.

 Podcasting: Assessing Fluency

Leveled Readers

Reinforcing Skills and Strategies

Social Studies

The Hamster Escape

by Conor McIntyre

Genre: Realistic Fiction

BELOW-LEVEL

The Hamster Escape

SUMMARY   Jenna takes Henry the hamster home from school for the holidays. When Henry escapes, Jenna and her mother look everywhere and finally discover him in Mom's purse.

- **phonics**   Consonants /s/c; /j/g, dge
- **High-Frequency Words**

  Focus Skill   Fiction and Nonfiction

Before Reading

BUILD BACKGROUND/SET PURPOSE   Have children name animals that are often kept in classrooms. Then guide children to preview the story and set a purpose for reading it.

Reading the Book

PAGE 3   MAKE PREDICTIONS   What is a detail on page 3 that helps you predict what will happen in the story? (The teacher warns Jenna not to let Henry out of his cage because he might escape.)

PAGES 1—14   FICTION AND NONFICTION   Is this story about something that really happened? How do you know? (This is a made-up story with characters, so it didn't happen in real life, even though it seems real.)

REREAD FOR FLUENCY   Have partners take turns pointing to a picture and reading the sentences that go with it as if talking naturally to each other. Remind them to read groups of words that go together rather than word by word.

Think Critically   *(See inside back cover for questions.)*

① **NOTE DETAILS**   They looked in the plants, behind the curtains, inside the blue shoes.

② **INTERPRET CHARACTER'S EMOTIONS**   Responses will vary.

③ **PERSONAL RESPONSE**   Responses will vary.

④ **CAUSE AND EFFECT**   Henry got lost because Jenna opened the cage door.

⑤ **FICTION AND NONFICTION**   Responses will vary.

LEVELED READERS TEACHER GUIDE

Name _____

▶ Write the word that best completes each sentence.

wash   above   shoes

1. Susan went to buy some ___shoes___

woman   young   tough

2. A ___woman___ at the store helped her.

wear   woman   above

3. "I ___wear___ a size 3," said Susan.

wear   year   above

4. The woman reached high ___above___ her and took a box from the shelf.

woman   tough   above

5. "These shoes are ___tough___ and will last a long time," she said.

wash   above   young

6. The ___young___ woman said the shoes could be washed.

▲ **High-Frequency Words, p. 5**

Name _____

▶ Use *The Hamster Escape* to make a list of things that hamsters can do. Write your answers on the line.

A real hamster can	run on a wheel
A real hamster can	wash himself

▶ Answer these questions about the story. Circle the answer.

1. Are the people in the story real?
   Yes   (No)

2. Does the story tell where the hamster was found?
   (Yes)   No

3. Can a real hamster escape from a cage?
   (Yes)   No

4. Can a real hamster run on a wheel?
   (Yes)   No

▲ **Comprehension, p. 6**

www.harcourtschool.com/storytown

★ Leveled Readers Online Database
Searchable by Genre, Skill, Vocabulary, Level, or Title
★ Student Activities and Teacher Resources, online

ON-LEVEL

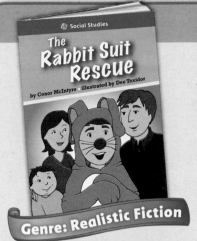

Genre: Realistic Fiction

The Rabbit Suit Rescue

SUMMARY Joseph can't resist taking home the rabbit suit he will wear in the class play. When it rips, Dad is able to mend it. After the performance, Joseph promises not to take home any more costumes.

• **phonics** Consonants /s/*c*; /j/*g, dge*

• **High-Frequency Words**

Fiction and Nonfiction

Before Reading

BUILD BACKGROUND/SET PURPOSE Have children share their experiences wearing costumes. Then guide children to preview the story and set a purpose for reading it.

Reading the Book

PAGES 3–4 MAKE PREDICTIONS What details on pages 3 and 4 help you predict that something may go wrong with Joseph's costume? (He disobeys his teacher, who tells the children to leave their costumes at school.)

PAGES 1–14 FICTION AND NONFICTION How can you tell that this story is fiction? (It has characters who are not real people. The story includes the words they say to each other.)

REREAD FOR FLUENCY Have partners take turns reading aloud pages of the story. Remind them to pay attention to the words in quotation marks and to say those words in the same way the character who is speaking says them.

Think Critically *(See inside back cover for questions.)*

1 **CAUSE AND EFFECT** The ear came off the rabbit suit.

2 **INTERPRET CHARACTER'S EMOTIONS** Responses will vary.

3 **PROBLEM/SOLUTION** Dad mended the ear and washed the suit.

4 **PERSONAL RESPONSE** Responses will vary.

5 **FICTION AND NONFICTION** Responses will vary.

LEVELED READERS TEACHER GUIDE

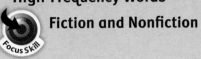

▲ **High-Frequency Words, p. 5**

▲ **Comprehension, p. 6**

Leveled Readers

Reinforcing Skills and Strategies

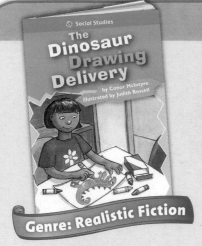

Genre: Realistic Fiction

ADVANCED

The Dinosaur Drawing Delivery

SUMMARY Lily takes her drawing home to show her mother instead of storing it in the classroom as she is told. She forgets to take it back, but her mother delivers it in time for the school art exhibit.

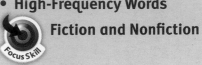

- **phonics** Consonants /s/c; /j/g, dge
- **High-Frequency Words**

  Fiction and Nonfiction

Focus Skill

Before Reading

BUILD BACKGROUND/SET PURPOSE Talk with children about a school art exhibit. Then guide children to preview the story and set a purpose for reading it.

Reading the Book

PAGES 5–6 MAKE PREDICTIONS At what point in the story can you predict that something will probably go wrong? (Lily slips the picture into her backpack even though she was told to put it on the shelf. Usually in stories, if a character breaks a rule, something goes wrong.)

PAGE 14 FICTION AND NONFICTION How is the ending of this story like the endings of many fiction stories? (It ends with a problem that is solved, and happy characters.)

REREAD FOR FLUENCY Groups may read the story as Readers' Theater, taking the parts of the four characters and the narrator. Remind children to say the words inside quotation marks in the voice of the character.

Think Critically *(See inside back cover for questions.)*

1. **NOTE DETAILS** He told them to leave their drawings on the shelf above the crayons.

2. **STORY EVENTS** when Lily's mom came to school with the drawing

3. **INTERPRET CHARACTER'S EMOTIONS** Responses will vary.

4. **FICTION AND NONFICTION** Responses will vary.

5. **PERSONAL RESPONSE** Responses will vary.

LEVELED READERS TEACHER GUIDE

▲ **High-Frequency Words, p. 5**

▲ **Comprehension, p. 6**

E L L

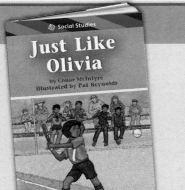

Genre: Realistic Fiction

Just Like Olivia

SUMMARY When Olivia hits a home run in a softball game, she is pleased to be a better runner and hitter than anyone else in her family.

- **Build Background**
- **Concept Vocabulary**
- **Scaffolded Language Development**

Before Reading

BUILD BACKGROUND/SET PURPOSE Ask children why someone might say, "I don't want to be like everybody else." Talk about why a child likes being different from other family members. Then guide children to preview the story and set a purpose for reading it.

Reading the Book

PAGES 3–6 MAKE INFERENCES Why does Olivia say, "I just want to be me"? (Her mother, father, and brother say she is just like other people in the family.)

PAGE 14 FICTION AND NONFICTION How can you tell that this story is fiction? (It has made-up characters. The main character has a problem that is solved at the end.)

REREAD FOR FLUENCY Have partners take turns reading the story a page at a time. Remind children to read groups of words rather than word by word.

Scaffolded Language Development

(See inside back cover for teacher-led activity.)

Provide additional examples and explanation as needed.

LEVELED READERS TEACHER GUIDE

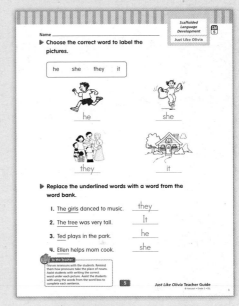

▲ **Scaffolded Language Development**

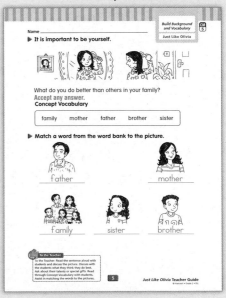

▲ **Build Background and Vocabulary**

Lesson 14

WEEK AT A GLANCE

✔ **Phonics**
r–Controlled Vowel /ûr/ir, ur, er, ear
Syllable Pattern VCCV

✔ **Spelling**
fur, shirt, burn, stir, bird, turn, herd, third, learn, search

✔ **High-Frequency Words**
care, father, interesting, sweat, thumb, touch

Reading
"Rain Forest Babies" by Kathy Darling
NONFICTION
"Baby Tapir Is Born!" WEBSITE

✔ **Fluency**
Phrasing

✔ **Comprehension**
 Fiction and Nonfiction
 Monitor Comprehension: Reread

✔ **Robust Vocabulary**
dappled, entranced, trooped, circling, adorable assortment, habitat, immense

✔ **Grammar**
Pronouns

Writing
Form: Paragraph That Explains
Trait: Conventions

✔ **Weekly Lesson Test**

 = Focus Skill   = Focus Strategy   ✔ = Tested Skill

One stop
for all
your Digital *needs*

Digital
CLASSROOM

 www.harcourtschool.com/storytown
To go along with your print program

FOR THE TEACHER

Prepare   Professional Development

 Videos for Podcasting

Plan & Organize   Online TE & Planning Resources*

Teach   Transparencies

for electronic projection

Assess   Online Assessment*

with Student Tracking System and Prescriptions

FOR THE STUDENT

Read   Student eBook*

 Strategic Intervention Interactive Reader

 Decodable Books

 Leveled Readers

Practice & Apply   Splash into Phonics CD-ROM

 Comprehension Expedition CD-ROM

 Also available on CD-ROM

Lesson 14 **T281**

Literature Resources

STUDENT EDITION

 **eBook** STUDENT EDITION

Rain Forest Babies

Genre: Nonfiction

Tapir

Baby Tapir is Born!

Genre: Website

 ◀ **Audiotext** *Student Edition selections are available on Audiotext 2.*

 Accelerated Reader ◀ *Practice Quizzes for the Selection*

THEME CONNECTION: CHANGING TIMES
Comparing Nonfiction and Website

Paired Selections

 SCIENCE **Rain Forest Babies, pp. 428–445**

SUMMARY Facts and photos combine to give descriptions of some of the interesting animal babies found in rain forests around the world.

SCIENCE **Baby Tapir is Born!, pp. 446–447**

SUMMARY This website announces the birth of a baby tapir at a zoo in Texas and also gives basic facts about the animal.

Support for Differentiated Instruction

Go online LEVELED READERS

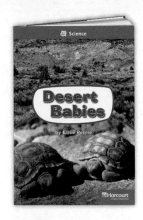

 ● **BELOW-LEVEL**

 ● **ON-LEVEL**

● **ADVANCED**

E L L

LEVELED PRACTICE

◀ **Strategic Intervention Resource Kit, Lesson 14**

◀ **Strategic Intervention Interactive Reader, Lesson 14**

Strategic Intervention Interactive Reader eBook

◀ **ELL Extra Support Kit, Lesson 14**

◀ **Challenge Resource Kit, Lesson 14**

● **BELOW-LEVEL**

Extra Support Copying Masters, pp. 100, 102–105

● **ON-LEVEL**

Practice Book, pp. 100–106

● **ADVANCED**

Challenge Copying Masters, pp. 100, 102–105

E L L

ELL Copying Masters Lesson 14

ADDITIONAL RESOURCES

- Decodable Book 12
- Spelling Practice Book, pp. 44–46
- Grammar Practice Book, pp. 49–52
- Reading Transparencies R69–R74
- Language Arts Transparencies LA28–LA29
- Test Prep System
- ◀ Literacy Center Kit, Cards 66–70
- Sound/Spelling Cards
- ◀ Fluency Builders
- ◀ Picture Card Collection
- Read-Aloud Anthology, p. 52–55

ASSESSMENT

✔ **Monitor Progress**

✔ **Weekly Lesson Tests, Lesson 14**

- Comprehension
- Robust Vocabulary
- Phonics and Spelling
- High-Frequency Words
- Focus Skill
- Grammar

Go online www.harcourtschool.com/storytown
Online Assessment
Also available on CD-ROM—Exam View

Suggested Lesson Planner

Go online Online TE & Planning Resources

	Day 1	**Day 2**
Step 1 **Whole Group** **Daily Routines** • *Oral Language* • *Read Aloud* • *High-Frequency Words*	**QUESTION OF THE DAY,** p. T292 *What do you think a rainforest looks like?* **READ ALOUD,** p. T293 *Transparency R00: Rain Forests* **WORD WALL,** p. T293	**QUESTION OF THE DAY,** p. T304 *What do you think is most interesting about birds?* **READ ALOUD,** p. T305 *Big Book of Rhymes and Poems,* "Macaw" **WORD WALL,** p. T305
Word Work • **phonics** • *Spelling* • *High-Frequency Words*	☑ **phonics**, p. T294 Introduce: *r*–Controlled Vowel /ûr/*ir, ur, er, ear* ☑ **SPELLING,** p. T297 Pretest: *fur, shirt, burn, stir, bird, turn, herd, third, learn, search*	☑ **phonics**, p. T306 Review: *r*–Controlled Vowel /ûr/*ir, ur, er, ear* ☑ **SPELLING,** p. T307 Word Building ☑ **HIGH-FREQUENCY WORDS** Words to Know, p. T308 Introduce: *care, father, interesting, sweat, thumb, touch*
Skills and Strategies • *Reading* • *Fluency* • *Comprehension* • *Build Robust Vocabulary*	☑ **READING/COMPREHENSION,** p. T298 Introduce: Fiction and Nonfiction **LISTENING COMPREHENSION,** p. T300 Read-Aloud: "Laurel's Rainforest" **FLUENCY,** p. T300 Focus: Phrasing ☑ **BUILD ROBUST VOCABULARY,** p. T301 *Words from the Read-Aloud*	☑ **READING,** p. T310 "Rain Forest Babies" *Options for Reading* ☑ **COMPREHENSION,** p. T310 Introduce: Monitor Comprehension: Reread ▲ Student Edition 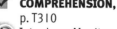 **RETELLING/FLUENCY,** p. T320 Reading with Phrasing ☑ **BUILD ROBUST VOCABULARY,** p. T321 *Words About the Selection*

 Step 2 **Small Groups**

Suggestions for Differentiated Instruction (See pp. T286–T287.)

 Step 3 **Whole Group**

Language Arts • *Grammar* • *Writing*

☑ **GRAMMAR,** p. T302 Introduce: Pronouns *Daily Proofreading* Did kim see a frog cling to a vine (Kim, vine?) **WRITING,** p. T303 Introduce: Paragraph That Explains Writing Trait: Conventions **Writing Prompt** *Write about something that changes during the school year.*	☑ **GRAMMAR,** p. T322 Introduce: Pronouns *Daily Proofreading* Cadies brother likes to read to her (Cadie's, her.) **WRITING,** p. T323 Review: Paragraph That Explains Writing Trait: Conventions **Writing Prompt** *Write your reflections about how you have changed since you were younger.*

 = **Focus Skill**   = **Focus Strategy**   ☑ = **Tested Skill**

Skills at a Glance

phonics
- r–Controlled Vowel /ûr/ir, ur, er, ear
- Syllable Pattern VCCV

Comprehension

Focus Skill
Fiction and Nonfiction

Focus Strategy Monitor
Comprehension: Reread

Fluency
Phrasing

Vocabulary

HIGH-FREQUENCY: *care, father, interesting, sweat, thumb, touch*

ROBUST: *dappled, entranced, trooped, circling, adorable, assortment, habitat, immense*

Day 3

QUESTION OF THE DAY, p. T324
What words would you use to tell how a macaw looks, sounds, and moves?

READ ALOUD, p. T325
Big Book of Rhymes and Poems, "Macaw"

WORD WALL, p. T325

, p. T326
Review: *r*–Controlled Vowel /ûr/*ir, ur, er, ear*

SPELLING, p. T327
State the Generalization

HIGH-FREQUENCY WORDS, p. T328
Review: *care, father, interesting, sweat, thumb, touch*

FLUENCY, p. T329
Phrasing:
"Rain Forest Babies"

COMPREHENSION,
p. T330
Review: Fiction and Nonfiction
Paired Selection:
"Pygmy Marmoset is Born!"

▲ Student Edition

CONNECTIONS, p. T332

BUILD ROBUST VOCABULARY, p. T333
Review

GRAMMAR, p. T334
Review: Pronouns

Daily Proofreading
some frogses live in the rain forest.
(Some, frogs)

WRITING, p. T335
Review: Paragraph That Explains
Writing Trait: Conventions

Writing Prompt Write a sentence to explain why people stay away from rain forest frogs.

Day 4

QUESTION OF THE DAY, p. T338
Why should you be kind to animals?

READ ALOUD, p. T339
Big Book of Rhymes and Poems, "Always Be Kind to Animals"

WORD WALL, p. T339

, p. T340
Introduce: Syllable Pattern VCCV

SPELLING, p. 341
Review Spelling Words

HIGH-FREQUENCY WORDS, p. T342
Review: *care, father, interesting, sweat, thumb, touch*

FLUENCY, p. T343
Phrasing:
"Rain Forest Babies"

COMPREHENSION,
p. T344
Review: Fiction and Nonfiction

▲ Student Edition

BUILD ROBUST VOCABULARY, p. T345
Review

GRAMMAR, p. T346
Review: Pronouns

Daily Proofreading
Zoe and zeke turned eight in october.
(Zeke, October)

WRITING, p. T347
Review: Paragraph That Explains
Writing Trait: Conventions

Writing Prompt Write to explain a favorite game or sport.

Day 5

QUESTION OF THE DAY, p. T341
Imagine that you get a new pet. What should you do to care for it?

READ ALOUD, p. T342
Big Book of Rhymes and Poems, "Always Be Kind to Animals"

WORD WALL, p. T343

, p. T350
Review: Syllable Pattern VCCV

SPELLING, p. T351
Posttest

HIGH-FREQUENCY WORDS, p. T352
Cumulative Review: *wear, tough, woman, young, shoes, wash, above, interesting, thumb, touch, care, sweat, father*

FLUENCY, p. T353
Phrasing:
"Rain Forest Babies"

COMPREHENSION,
p. T354
Review: Fiction and Nonfiction
Read-Aloud: "Laurel's Rainforest"

▲ Student Edition

BUILD ROBUST VOCABULARY, p. T355
Cumulative Review

● **BELOW-LEVEL**   ● **ON-LEVEL**   ○ ADVANCED   **E L L**

GRAMMAR, p. T356
Review: Pronouns

Daily Proofreading
We will go to the Beach on sunday.
(beach, Sunday)

WRITING, p. T357
Review: Paragraph That Explains
Writing Trait: Conventions

Writing Prompt Write another paragraph that explains.

Suggested Small-Group Planner

45-60 Minutes

	Day 1	Day 2
BELOW-LEVEL 15-20 Minutes	**Teacher-Directed** Leveled Reader: "Mountain Babies," p. T358 Before Reading **Independent** ⭐ Listening/Speaking Center, p. T290 Extra Support Copying Masters, pp. 100, 102 ▲ Leveled Reader	**Teacher-Directed** Student Edition: "Rain Forest Babies," p. T310 **Independent** ⭐ Reading Center, p. T290 Extra Support Copying Masters, pp. 103–104  ▲ Student Edition
ON-LEVEL 15-20 Minutes	**Teacher-Directed** Leveled Reader: "Desert Babies," p. T359 Before Reading **Independent** ⭐ Reading Center, p. T290 Practice Book, pp. 100,102 ▲ Leveled Reader	**Teacher-Directed** Student Edition: "Rain Forest Babies," p. T310 **Independent** ⭐ Letters and Sounds Center, p. T291 Practice Book, pp. 103–104  ▲ Student Edition

ADVANCED
 15-20 Minutes
	Teacher-Directed
	 Leveled Reader: "Prairie Babies," p. T360
	 Before Reading
	
	 Independent
	 ⭐ Letters and Sounds Center, p. T291
	 Challenge Copying Masters, pp. 100, 102
	
	  ▲ Leveled Reader
		Teacher-Directed
		 Leveled Reader: "Prairie Babies," p. T360
		 Read the Book
		
		 Independent
		 ⭐ Word Work Center, p. T291
		 Challenge Copying Masters, pp. 103–104
		
		  ▲ Leveled Reader

E L L

English-Language Learners

In addition to the small-group instruction above, use the ELL Extra Support Kit to promote language development.

LANGUAGE DEVELOPMENT SUPPORT

Teacher-Directed
ELL TG, Day 1

Independent
ELL Copying Masters, Lesson 14

 ▲ ELL Student Handbook

LANGUAGE DEVELOPMENT SUPPORT

Teacher-Directed
ELL TG, Day 2

Independent
ELL Copying Masters, Lesson 14

 ▲ ELL Student Handbook

Intervention

▲ Strategic Intervention Resource Kit

▲ Strategic Intervention Interactive Reader

Strategic Intervention TG, Day 1
Strategic Intervention Practice Book, Lesson 14

Strategic Intervention TG, Day 2
Strategic Intervention Interactive Reader, Lesson 14

 ▲ Strategic Intervention Interactive Reader

MONITOR PROGRESS

Small-Group Instruction

Comprehension	Phonics	High-Frequency Words	Fluency	Robust Vocabulary	Language Arts Checkpoint
Focus Skill Author's Purpose pp.S36–S37	*r*-Controlled Vowel /ûr/*ir, ur, er, ear* p. S32	*care, father, interesting, sweat, thumb, touch* p. S33	Phrasing pp. S34–S35	*dappled, entranced, trooped, circling, adorable, assortment, habitat, immense* pp. S38–S39	**Grammar:** Pronouns **Writing:** Paragraph That Explains pp. S40–S41

Day 3

Teacher-Directed
Leveled Reader: "Mountain Babies," p. T358
Read the Book

Independent
 Word Work Center, p. T291

▲ Leveled Reader

Teacher-Directed
Leveled Reader: "Desert Babies," p. T359
Read the Book

Independent
 Writing Center, p. T291

▲ Leveled Reader

Teacher-Directed
Leveled Reader: "Prairie Babies," p. T360
Think Critically

Independent
 Listening/Speaking Center, p. T290

▲ Leveled Reader

LANGUAGE DEVELOPMENT SUPPORT

Teacher-Directed
Leveled Reader: "Rain Forest Homes," p. T361
Before Reading; Read the Book
ELL TG, Day 3

Independent
ELL Copying Masters, Lesson 14

▲ Leveled Reader

Strategic Intervention TG, Day 3
Strategic Intervention Interactive Reader, Lesson 14
Strategic Intervention Practice Book, Lesson 14

▲ Strategic Intervention Interactive Reader

Day 4

Teacher-Directed
Leveled Reader: "Mountain Babies," p. T358
Reread for Fluency

Independent
 Letters and Sounds Center, p. T291

▲ Leveled Reader

Teacher-Directed
Leveled Reader: "Desert Babies," p. T359
Reread for Fluency

Independent
 Word Work Center, p. T291

▲ Leveled Reader

Teacher-Directed
Leveled Reader: "Prairie Babies," p. T360
Reread for Fluency

Independent
 Writing Center, p. T291
Self-Selected Reading: Classroom Library Collection

▲ Leveled Reader

LANGUAGE DEVELOPMENT SUPPORT

Teacher-Directed
Leveled Reader: "Rain Forest Homes," p. T361
Reread for Fluency
ELL TG, Day 4

Independent
ELL Copying Masters, Lesson 14

▲ Leveled Reader

Strategic Intervention TG, Day 4
Strategic Intervention Interactive Reader, Lesson 14

▲ Strategic Intervention Interactive Reader

Day 5

Teacher-Directed
Leveled Reader: "Mountain Babies," p. T358
Think Critically

Independent
 Writing Center, p. T291
Leveled Reader: Reread for Fluency
Extra Support Copying Masters, p. 105

▲ Leveled Reader

Teacher-Directed
Leveled Reader: "Desert Babies," p. T359
Think Critically

Independent
 Listening/Speaking Center, p. T290
Leveled Reader: Reread for Fluency
Practice Book, p. 105

▲ Leveled Reader

Teacher-Directed
Leveled Reader: "Prairie Babies," p. T360
Reread for Fluency

Independent
 Reading Center, p. T290
Leveled Reader: Reread for Fluency
Self-Selected Reading: Classroom Library Collection
Challenge Copying Masters, p. 105

▲ Leveled Reader

LANGUAGE DEVELOPMENT SUPPORT

Teacher-Directed
Leveled Reader: "Rain Forest Homes," p. T361
Think Critically
ELL TG, Day 5

Independent
Leveled Reader: Reread for Fluency
ELL Copying Masters, Lesson 14

▲ Leveled Reader

Strategic Intervention TG, Day 5
Strategic Intervention Interactive Reader, Lesson 14

▲ Strategic Intervention Interactive Reader

Leveled Readers & Leveled Practice
Reinforcing Skills and Strategies

LEVELED READERS SYSTEM

- ■ **Leveled Readers**
- ■ **Leveled Readers, CD**
- ■ **Leveled Readers Teacher Guides**
  - *Comprehension*
  - *High-Frequency Words*
  - *Oral Reading Fluency Assessement*
- ■ **Response Activities**
- ■ **Leveled Readers Assessment**

See pages T358–T361 for lesson plans.

BELOW-LEVEL

- • **phonics** *r*-Controlled Vowel /ûr/ *ir, ur, er, ear*
- • **High-Frequency Words**
- 🔁 **Fiction and Nonfiction**

LEVELED READERS TEACHER GUIDE

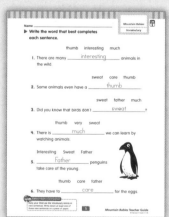

▲ High-Frequency Words, p. 5

▲ Comprehension, p. 6

ON-LEVEL

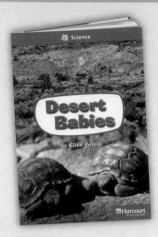

- • **phonics** *r*-Controlled Vowel /ûr/ *ir, ur, er, ear*
- • **High-Frequency Words**
- 🔁 **Fiction and Nonfiction**

LEVELED READERS TEACHER GUIDE

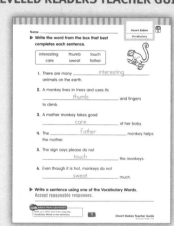

▲ High-Frequency Words, p. 5

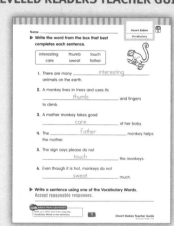

▲ Comprehension, p. 6

www.harcourtschool.com/storytown

Go online

★ Leveled Readers, Online Database
Searchable by Genre, Skill, Vocabulary, Level, or Title
★ Student Activities and Teacher Resources, online

ADVANCED

- **phonics** *r*-Controlled Vowel /ûr/ *ir, ur, er, ear*
- High-Frequency Words
- Fiction and Nonfiction

LEVELED READERS TEACHER GUIDE

▲ High-Frequency Words, p. 5

▲ Comprehension, p. 6

E L L

- Build Background
- Concept Vocabulary
- Scaffolded Language Development

LEVELED READERS TEACHER GUIDE

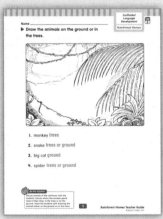

▲ Scaffolded Language Development, p. 5

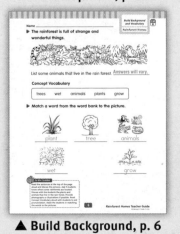

▲ Build Background, p. 6

CLASSROOM LIBRARY

for Self-Selected Reading

EASY

▲ *Clown Fish* by Carol K. Lindeen, Capstone Press, 2005. NONFICTION

AVERAGE

▲ *Buster* by Denise Fleming, Henry Holt and Company, 2003. FICTION

CHALLENGE

▲ *Ant Cities* by Arthur Dorros, HarperCollins, 1987. NONFICTION

▲ Classroom Library Books Teacher Guide, Lesson 14

Literacy Centers

15 Min. each

Management Support

While you provide direct instruction to individuals or small groups, other children can work on literacy center activities.

▲ Literacy Center Pocket Chart

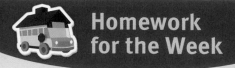

My Activities

✓ Put a check mark next to the activities you complete.

Centers

☐ 👟 Listening/Speaking Read with a Recording
☐ 📖 Reading Read and Respond
☐ ✏️ Writing Paragraph of Information
☐ 🔤 Word Work Word Game
☐ 🔠 Letters and Sounds Sort Words

Leveled Readers

☐ Activities (See inside back cover.)
☐ Reread for Fluency

Practice Pages

☐ pages 100–106

Lesson 14   47   Teacher Resource Book

▲ Teacher Resource Book, p. 47

🏠 Homework for the Week

TEACHER RESOURCE BOOK, PAGE 47
The Homework Copying Master provides activities to complete for each day of the week.

🎧 LISTENING/SPEAKING

Read with a Recording

Objective
To develop fluency by listening to familiar stories and reading them aloud

LISTENING/SPEAKING   Card 66

Read with a Recording

MATERIALS
• CD/cassette player   • Student Edition   • pencil
• Audiotext   • Reading Log or paper

❶ With a partner, listen to "Rain Forest Babies" on the *Audiotext*.

❷ Follow along in your book while you listen.

❸ Listen to it again, and read aloud with the recording.

❹ Use your Reading Log to record what you read.

Grade 2 Lesson 14

⭐ **Literacy Center Kit • Card 66**

Rain Forest Babies

Tara Darling

📖 READING

Read and Respond

Objective
To develop comprehension by rereading familiar stories and responding to them

READING   Card 67

Read and Respond

MATERIALS
• Student Edition   • library books   • pencil
• Leveled Readers   • paper

❶ Choose a favorite story that you have read in class.

❷ Read the story aloud to your partner.

❸ Then write the title and a few sentences telling why you like the story.

Grade 2 Lesson 14

⭐ **Literacy Center Kit • Card 67**

I like Click, Clack, Moo: Cows That Type because it is funny. Cows and ducks type messages to Farmer Brown.

Go online

www.harcourtschool.com/storytown

★ Additional Literacy Center Activities
★ Resources for Parents and Teachers

Differentiated
for Your Needs

WRITING

Paragraph That Explains

Objective
To practice writing a paragraph that explains

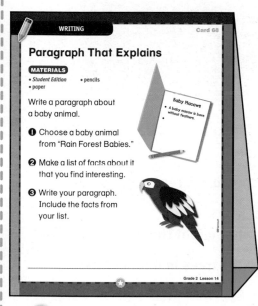

⭐ **Literacy Center Kit • Card 68**

WORD WORK

Word Game

Objective
To read common sight words

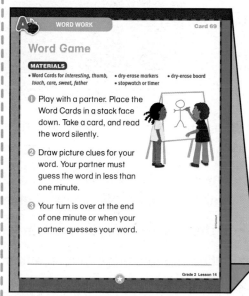

⭐ **Literacy Center Kit • Card 69**

ABC LETTERS AND SOUNDS

Sort Words

Objective
To read words with /ûr/ir, ur, er, ear, and other known letter sounds

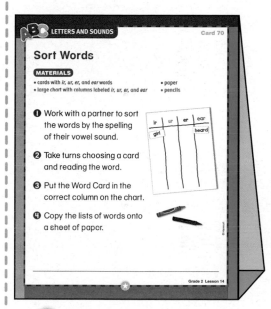

⭐ **Literacy Center Kit • Card 70**

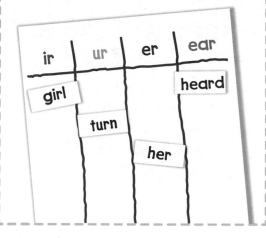

Day at a Glance

Day 1

 phonics and Spelling

- Introduce: *r*-Controlled Vowel /ûr/ *ir, ur, er, ear*
- Pretest

Reading/ Comprehension

 Review: Fiction and Nonfiction, *Student Edition*, pp. 424–425
- *Read-Aloud Anthology*: "Laurel's Rainforest"

Fluency
- Model Oral Fluency

Robust Vocabulary
Words from the Read-Aloud
- Introduce: *dappled, entranced, trooped, circling*

Grammar
- Introduce: Pronouns

Writing
- Paragraph That Explains

Warm-Up Routines

 Oral Language

Objective *To listen attentively and respond appropriately to oral communication*

Question of the Day

What do you think a rain forest looks like?

Help children talk about what a rain forest might look like. Record their ideas in a web. Use the following prompts:

- **The words *rain* and *forest* are in the name *rain forest*. What do those words make you think you might see?**
- **If there is a lot of rain in a rain forest, what might the plants look like?**
- **What animals might live in and around the trees in a rain forest?**

Read Aloud

Objective *To listen for a purpose*

TRANSPARENCY Read aloud the story "Rain Forests" on **Transparency R69**. Use the following steps:

- **Set a purpose for listening.** Tell children to listen to find out what a rain forest is.

- **Model fluent reading.** Read the story aloud. Point out that good readers read groups of words rather than one word at a time.

- **Discuss the selection.** Ask: **What does a rain forest look like?** (tall trees, wet and rainy)

Fiction and Nonfiction

Rain Forests

Have you ever wondered what a rain forest would be like? Picture trees that stretch so high you cannot see their tops. Raindrops fall onto the leaves of lush, green plants. Water drips from long vines. Birds squawk, monkeys chatter, insects hum, and frogs croak. These are some things you might find in a rain forest.

A rain forest is a woodland where more than 70 inches of rain falls each year. Rain forests are in many parts of the world. They are in cool places and in hot places.

Rain forests are a major source for fresh water. Rain forest plants make lots of oxygen. People need to breathe oxygen to stay alive. Rain forests also provide people with resources for food, medicine, and building. Half of Earth's plants and animals live in rain forests. So rain forests are important to both people and animals.

Grade 2, Lesson 14   R69   Comprehension

Transparency R69

Word Wall

Objective *To read high-frequency words*

REVIEW HIGH-FREQUENCY WORDS Remove from the Word Wall the cards for *wear*, *tough*, *woman*, and *young*, as well as other previously learned high-frequency words. Hold up a card at random, and ask children to read the word. Flip through the word cards several times.

wear	woman
tough	young

r-Controlled Vowel /ûr/ir, ur, er, ear and Spelling

Objectives

- *To recognize and blend the r-controlled vowel sound /ûr/ir, ur, er, ear*
- *To read words with /ûr/ir, ur, er, ear, and other known letter-sounds*
- *To use /ûr/ir, ur, er, ear, and other known letter-sounds to spell words*

Skill Trace

 Tested **r-Controlled Vowel /ûr/ir, ur, er, ear**

Introduce	Grade I
Reintroduce	**T294–T297**
Reteach	S32
Review	T306–T307, T326–T327, T412
Test	Theme 3
Maintain	Theme 5, T286

Connect Letters to Sound

WARM UP WITH PHONEMIC AWARENESS Say the words *earth* and *urge*. Have children say the words. Say: **The words *earth* and *urge* begin with the /ûr/ sound.** Then say *shirt* and *nurse*. Have children say the words. Say: **The /ûr/ sound comes in the middle of the words *shirt* and *nurse*.** Have children say /ûr/ several times.

Routine Card I **CONNECT LETTERS AND SOUNDS** Display the *Sound/Spelling Card* for *ir, er, ur, ear*. Point to the letters *ir* and review their letter/sound correspondence. Say: **The letters *ir* can stand for the /ûr/ sound, the sound you hear at the end of the word *sir*.** Touch the letters *ir* several times, and have children say /ûr/ each time. Repeat the process for *er, ur,* and *ear*.

▲ Sound/Spelling Card

5-DAY PHONICS

DAY 1	Reintroduce /ûr/*ir*, *ur*, *er*, *ear*
DAY 2	Word Building with /ûr/*ir*, *ur*, *er*, *ear*
DAY 3	Word Building with /ûr/*ir*, *ur*, *er*, *ear*
DAY 4	VCCV; Review /ûr/*ir*, *ur*, *er*, *ear*
DAY 5	VCCV; Review /ûr/*ir*, *ur*, *er*, *ear*

Work with Patterns

REINFORCE /ûr/*ir* Write the following words on the board. Point out that each word has the letters *ir* in the middle of the word. Read each word, and then have children read it with you.

girl	first
dirt	third
skirt	circle

REINFORCE /ûr/*er*, *ur* Repeat the procedure with the following words that have the letters *er* or *ur* in the middle.

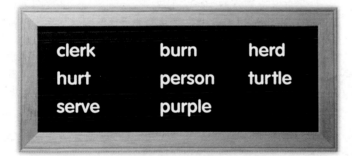

clerk	burn	herd
hurt	person	turtle
serve	purple	

REINFORCE /ûr/*ear* Repeat the procedure with the following words that have the letters *ear* at the beginning or in the middle.

earnings	heard
earl	search

BELOW-LEVEL

Identify Rhyming Words Help children identify words with the /ûr/ sound. Point out that some rhyming words with the /ûr/ sound may have very different spellings, such as *hurt*, *dirt*, *learn*, *turn*, and *bird*, *herd*.

r-Controlled Vowel /ûr/ir, ur, er, ear phonics and Spelling

r-Controlled Vowel /ûr/ir, ur, er, ear

hurt	girl	hers	earth
pearl	perch	dirt	stir
third	curb	learn	birth
lurk	blurb	thirsty	earthquake

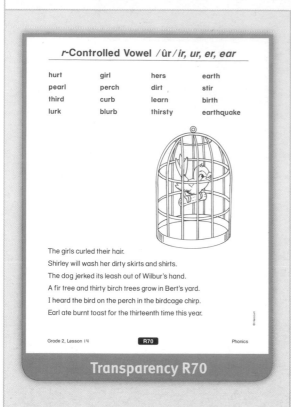

The girls curled their hair.
Shirley will wash her dirty skirts and shirts.
The dog jerked its leash out of Wilbur's hand.
A fir tree and thirty birch trees grow in Bert's yard.
I heard the bird on the perch in the birdcage chirp.
Earl ate burnt toast for the thirteenth time this year.

Grade 2, Lesson 14   **R70**   Phonics

Transparency R70

Reading Words

GUIDED PRACTICE   Display **Transparency R70** or write the words and sentences on the board. Point to the word *hurt*. Read the word, and then have children read it with you.

INDEPENDENT PRACTICE   Point to the remaining words in the top portion and have children read them. Then have children read aloud the sentences and identify words with /ûr/*ir*, *ur*, *er*, or *ear*.

Decodable Books

Additional Decoding Practice

- **Phonics**
  r-Controlled Vowel /ûr/*ir, ur, er, ear*
- **Decodable Words**
- **High-Frequency Words**
  See lists in *Decodable Book 12*.
  See also *Decodable Books*, online (Take-Home Version).

▲ **Decodable Book 12: "A Birthday Surprise for Bird" and "Bertha the Sales Clerk"**

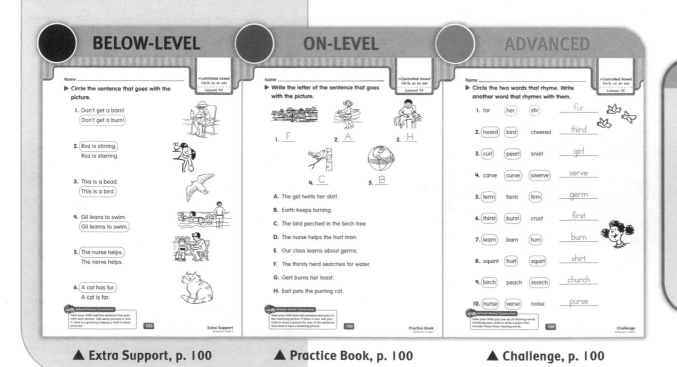

▲ **Extra Support, p. 100**   ▲ **Practice Book, p. 100**   ▲ **Challenge, p. 100**

ELL

- Group children according to academic levels, and assign one of the pages on the left.

- Clarify any unfamiliar concepts as necessary. See *ELL Teacher Guide* Lesson 14 for support in scaffolding instruction.

5-DAY SPELLING	
DAY 1	Pretest
DAY 2	Word Building
DAY 3	State the Generalization
DAY 4	Review
DAY 5	Posttest

Introduce Spelling Words

PRETEST Say the first word and read the dictation sentence. Repeat the word as children write it. Write the word on the board and have children check their spelling. Tell them to circle the word if they spelled it correctly or write it correctly if they did not. Repeat for words 2–10.

Words with *r*-Controlled Vowel /ûr/*ir, ur, er, ear*

1.	fur	My cat's **fur** is soft and silky.
2.	shirt	Rajiv bought a **shirt** at the mall.
3.	burn	Dad heated the soup slowly so it would not **burn**.
4.	stir	Dara helped Grandma **stir** the pancake batter.
5.	bird	The ostrich is the largest **bird** in the world.
6.	turn	Today it is Omar's **turn** to erase the board.
7.	herd	Devon saw a **herd** of cattle at her uncle's ranch.
8.	third	My family's apartment is on the **third** floor.
9.	learn	I want to **learn** how to surf.
10.	search	Everyone helped Ricardo **search** for his lost dog.

ADVANCED

Challenge Words Use the challenge words in these dictation sentences.

11.	perfect	A warm, sunny day is **perfect** for a picnic.
12.	birthday	Sonia's **birthday** is in October.
13.	purple	My favorite color is **purple**.
14.	circus	Mia saw elephants and clowns at the **circus**.
15.	surprise	Rafi's parents gave him a puppy as a **surprise**.

Spelling Words

1.	**fur***	6.	**turn**
2.	**shirt**	7.	**herd***
3.	**burn**	8.	**third**
4.	**stir**	9.	**learn***
5.	**bird**	10.	**search**

Challenge Words

11.	**perfect**	14.	**circus**
12.	**birthday**	15.	**surprise***
13.	**purple**		

* Words from "Rain Forest Babies"

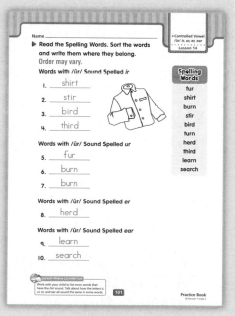

▲ Practice Book, p. 101

Fiction and Nonfiction
Comprehension

Objectives

- *To distinguish fiction from nonfiction*
- *To know the basic characteristics of fiction and nonfiction*

Daily Comprehension
 ### Fiction and Nonfiction

DAY 1:	Introduce Fiction and Nonfiction, *Student Edition*
DAY 2:	Review Fiction and Nonfiction, *Student Edition*
DAY 3:	Review Fiction and Nonfiction, *Student Edition*
DAY 4:	Review Fiction and Nonfiction, *Transparency*
DAY 5:	Review Fiction and Nonfiction, *Read-Aloud Anthology*

✔ MONITOR PROGRESS

Fiction and Nonfiction

IF children have difficulty distinguishing fiction from nonfiction,	**THEN** provide examples of more fiction and nonfiction books and help them determine whether a book is fiction or nonfiction.

Small-Group Instruction, pp. S36–S37:

- ● **BELOW-LEVEL:** Reteach
- ● **ON-LEVEL:** Reinforce
- ● **ADVANCED:** Extend

Before Reading

INTRODUCE FICTION AND NONFICTION Have children read *Student Edition* page 424. Model how to distinguish fiction from nonfiction.

> **Think Aloud** When I read a selection, I pay attention to the characters and events to help me figure out whether the story is fiction or nonfiction. Does the selection have information about real people and events? If so, it is nonfiction. If the characters and events are made up, then it is fiction.

Practice/Apply

GUIDED PRACTICE Have children read the passage on *Student Edition* page 425. Explain that Theodore Roosevelt was the twenty-sixth President of the United States. Ask children to identify the kind of writing the passage is. (nonfiction) Discuss how knowing that Theodore Roosevelt was a real person helped them distinguish fiction from nonfiction.

Try This! **INDEPENDENT PRACTICE** Have children identify other details that show that the writing is nonfiction. Discuss their responses.

 ### BELOW-LEVEL

Build Background After reading "Tropical Trip" with children, ask questions such as "Is South America a real place?" "Are there really jungles in Brazil?" Confirm that these places are real, and point to them on a map.

Focus Skill

Fiction and Nonfiction

There are two main kinds of writing—fiction and nonfiction. **Fiction** is about made-up events and characters. A fiction writer wants to tell a story for you to enjoy. **Nonfiction** is about real events and real people or animals. A nonfiction writer wants to give you information.

Fiction	Nonfiction
made-up events	real events
made-up characters	real people or animals

Read the paragraph. What kind of writing is it? How can you tell?

Tropical Trip

President Theodore Roosevelt set sail for South America on October 4, 1913. He was on a trip to learn about jungles in Brazil. For two months, he explored a river that flowed through the rain forest. President Roosevelt traveled in canoes with his son, Kermit, and about twenty other people.

Fiction	Nonfiction

Try This!

Look back at the paragraph. What other details show what kind of writing this is?

GO online www.harcourtschool.com/storytown

424

425

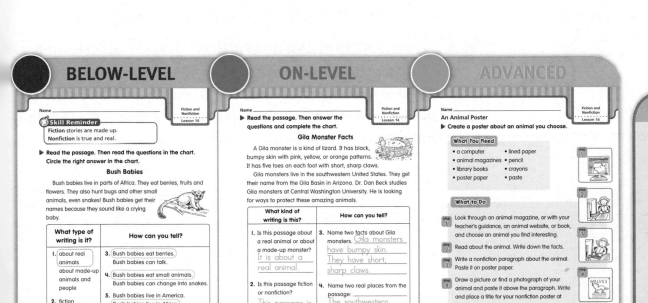

▲ Extra Support, p. 102   ▲ Practice Book, p. 102   ▲ Challenge, p. 102

ELL

- Group children according to academic levels, and assign one of the pages on the left.

- Clarify any unfamiliar concepts as necessary. See *ELL Teacher Guide* Lesson 14 for support in scaffolding instruction.

Listening Comprehension
Read Aloud

Objectives

- *To set a purpose for listening*
- *To distinguish fiction from nonfiction*

Build Fluency

Focus: Phrasing Tell children that good readers try to read groups of words that go together without pausing. They pay attention to punctuation marks to help them identify phrases.

Clarify Vocabulary Show children drawings and photographs to clarify unknown vocabulary. For example, if children do not know what a frog is, show *Picture Card 56* and say **This is a frog.**

frog

▲ Picture Card 56

Before Reading

CONNECT TO PRIOR KNOWLEDGE Tell children that they will listen to a story about a girl's first morning in a rain forest. Ask children to share what they know about rain forests.

▲ Read-Aloud Anthology, "Laurel's Rainforest," p. 52

Routine Card 2 **GENRE STUDY: REALISTIC FICTION** Tell children that the story, "Laurel's Rainforest," is realistic fiction. Remind them that realistic fiction stories are make-believe but may have parts that are like real life.

Think Aloud **I know that Laurel is a made-up character, but she acts like a real person. She's taken airplanes, buses, and vans to reach the rain forest, which is a real place.**

After Reading

RESPOND Have children identify the things Laurel saw, heard, and did in the rain forest. List them on the board. Then ask children to identify events in the story that are similar to things in real life.

REVIEW FICTION AND NONFICTION Have children identify the characters and events in "Laurel's Rainforest" that are like people and events in real life. Discuss why this is a fiction selection. Then remind children that nonfiction is about real people and events.

Build Robust Vocabulary

Words from the Read-Aloud

Teach/Model

 INTRODUCE ROBUST VOCABULARY   Use *Routine Card 3* to introduce the words.

> ❶ Put the word in **selection context**.
> ❷ Display Transparency R74 and read the word and the **Student-Friendly Explanation**.
> ❸ Have children **say the word** with you.
> ❹ Use the word in other contexts, and have children **interact with the word's meaning**.
> ❺ Remove the transparency. Say the Student-Friendly Explanation again, and ask children to **name the word** that goes with it.

❶ **Selection Context:** Monkeys swing in and out of the **dappled** light.

❹ **Interact with Word Meaning:** Which would be called dappled, the light at the beach or the light coming through the trees in a park?

❶ **Selection Context:** Laurel was **entranced** by the animals she saw.

❹ **Interact with Word Meaning:** Would you be entranced by a magazine or by cute puppies playing?

❶ **Selection Context:** The leafcutter ants **trooped** forward, carrying pieces of leaves.

❹ **Interact with Word Meaning:** Would people troop into a water park when it opened or into a store that was open all the time?

❶ **Selection Context:** Three butterflies were **circling** Laurel's head.

❹ **Interact with Word Meaning:** What might you see circling, a plane waiting to land or a person taking a walk?

Practice/Apply

GUIDED PRACTICE   Ask children to use the vocabulary to describe a sight that *entranced* them.

Objective

• *To develop robust vocabulary through discussing a literature selection*

INTRODUCE ✓ Tested

Vocabulary: Lesson 14

dappled	trooped
entranced	circling

▼ **Student-Friendly Explanations**

Student-Friendly Explanations

dappled	If something is dappled, it has spots, streaks, or patches of different colors or shades.
entranced	If you are entranced by something, it has delighted or amazed you.
trooped	If you trooped someplace, you moved along with a group of people.
circling	If something is circling you, it is moving around you.
adorable	If something is very cute, it is adorable.
assortment	If you see a variety or mixture of things, you see an assortment.
habitat	If a plant or an animal lives in a particular place in nature, that is its habitat.
immense	If something is really big or huge, it is immense.

Grade 2, Theme 3   R74   Vocabulary

Transparency R74

Grammar
Pronouns

5-DAY GRAMMAR

DAY 1 Pronouns
DAY 2 He, She, It, We, They
DAY 3 Using I and Me
DAY 4 Apply to Writing
DAY 5 Weekly Review

Objectives

• *To recognize and use pronouns*
• *To identify the noun that a pronoun takes the place of*

Daily Proofreading

**Did kim see a frog cling
to a vine**
(Kim, vine?)

TECHNOLOGY

 www.harcourtschool.com/
storytown
Grammar Glossary

▼ **Student-Friendly Explanations**

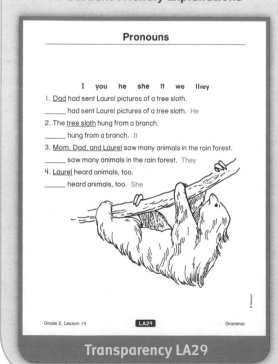

Transparency LA29

Teach/Model

INTRODUCE PRONOUNS   Explain that a **pronoun** is a word that takes the place of a noun. Review that nouns are words that name people, places, things, and animals. Write the pronouns *I*, *he*, *she*, *it*, *we*, and *they* on the board. Read them aloud. Tell children the following about pronouns:

• Use *I* and *me* to tell about yourself. Capitalize *I*.

• Use *he* to tell about a man or boy and *she* to tell about a woman or girl.

• Use *it* to tell about an animal or a thing.

• Use *they* to tell about more than one.

• Use *we* to tell about yourself and someone or something else.

Then write on the board these sentences from "Laurel's Rainforest" (*Read-Aloud Anthology*, p. 16):

**Laurel yawned and stretched.
She thought she knew how Dasher felt.**

Read aloud the first sentence, and identify the noun (Laurel). Then read aloud the second sentence, and identify the pronouns (She, she). Explain that each *she* takes the place of *Laurel*.

Guided Practice

READ PRONOUNS   Display **Transparency LA29**. Have children read the pronouns. Then read aloud item one. Point out the underlined noun *Dad*. Then complete the sentence with the pronoun *He* to take the place of *Dad*. Complete item two together, eliciting responses from volunteers.

Practice/Apply

WRITE PRONOUNS   Have children replace the underlined nouns with pronouns for items three and four on **Transparency LA29**. Ask volunteers to read the sentences aloud.

5-DAY WRITING	
DAY 1	Introduce
DAY 2	Prewrite
DAY 3	Draft
DAY 4	Revise
DAY 5	Revise

Writing
Paragraph That Explains

Teach/Model

INTRODUCE PARAGRAPH THAT EXPLAINS   Display **Transparency LA30,** and explain that this paragraph was written by a child to explain what a tadpole is. Read it aloud. Together, develop a list of characteristics for a paragraph that explains. Keep it on display for children to refer to on Days 3–5.

> ## Paragraph That Explains
>
> • The topic sentence tells about the main idea.
>
> • The other sentences give more details about the main idea.
>
> • The writer may do research to find facts.

WRITING TRAIT **CONVENTIONS**   Point out that the writer uses correct grammar, punctuation, and spelling. Discuss how the writer often used *it* to replace *tadpole.*

Guided Practice

DRAFT A SENTENCE THAT EXPLAINS   Model writing a main idea sentence that explains an object, such as "An elephant's trunk is useful in many ways." Talk about how the sentence explains the object. Then have children share sentences that explain an object or an event.

Practice/Apply

WRITE SENTENCES THAT EXPLAIN   Have children write sentences that explain one way that they have changed from when they were younger. They should save their sentences for use on Days 2–5.

Objectives

• *To read and respond to a paragraph that explains*

• *To develop ideas and topics for writing*

• *To write sentences that explain*

Writing Prompt

Reflect   Have children write about something that changes during the school year.

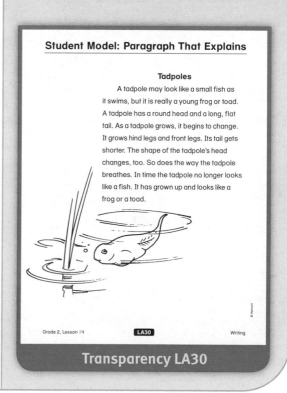

Student Model: Paragraph That Explains

Tadpoles

A tadpole may look like a small fish as it swims, but it is really a young frog or toad. A tadpole has a round head and a long, flat tail. As a tadpole grows, it begins to change. It grows hind legs and front legs. Its tail gets shorter. The shape of the tadpole's head changes, too. So does the way the tadpole breathes. In time the tadpole no longer looks like a fish. It has grown up and looks like a frog or a toad.

Grade 2, Lesson 14   LA30   Writing

Transparency LA30

Warm-Up Routines

 phonics **and Spelling**

- Review: *r*-Controlled Vowel /ûr/*ir*, *ur*, *er*, *ear*
- Build Words

High-Frequency Words

- Introduce: *interesting, thumb, touch, care, sweat, father*

Comprehension

 Monitor Comprehension: Reread

Fiction and Nonfiction

Reading

- "Rain Forest Babies," *Student Edition*, pp. 428–445

Read!

Fluency

- Phrasing

Robust Vocabulary

Words About the Selection

- Introduce: *adorable, assortment, habitat, immense*

Grammar

- Review: Pronouns

Writing ✏️

- Paragraph That Explains

 Oral Language

Objective *To listen attentively and respond appropriately to oral communication*

Question of the Day

What do you think is most interesting about birds? Why?

Guide children to describe things they find interesting about birds. Use the following prompts:

- **What color birds have you seen?**
- **What sounds have you heard birds make?**
- **What are some things that birds like to eat?**
- **What do you think birds can see when they fly?**

Then have children complete the following sentence to tell more about birds:

I think the most interesting thing about birds is _____ because _____.

Read Aloud

Objective *To listen for a purpose*

BIG BOOK OF RHYMES AND POEMS Display the poem "Macaw" on page 27 and read aloud the title. Ask children to listen for the color words in the poem and what they describe. Then read the poem aloud. Ask: **What colors did the author mention and what did they describe?** (blue feathers; yellow squawking) Invite children to use color words to describe objects and sounds at school.

▲ Big Book of Rhymes and Poems, p. 27

Word Wall

Objective *To read high-frequency words*

REVIEW HIGH-FREQUENCY WORDS Review the words *woman*, *young*, *shoes*, *wash*, and *above*, as well as previously learned high-frequency words. Point to each word on the Word Wall, and have children read it, spell it, and then read it again.

woman	young	shoes

wash	above

r-Controlled Vowel /ûr/ *ir, ur, er, ear* phonics *and Spelling*

Objectives

- *To blend sounds into words*
- *To spell three-, four-, five-, and six-letter words with r-controlled vowel /ûr/ir, ur, er, ear*

Skill Trace

 Tested **r-Controlled Vowel /ûr/ ir, ur, er, ear**

Introduce	Grade 1
Reintroduce	T294–T297
Reteach	S32
Review	T306–T307, T326–T327, T412
Test	Theme 3
Maintain	Theme 5, T286

Spelling Words

1. **fur***	6. **turn**
2. **shirt**	7. **herd***
3. **burn**	8. **third**
4. **stir**	9. **learn***
5. **bird**	10. **search**

Challenge Words

11. **perfect**	14. **circus**
12. **birthday**	15. **surprise***
13. **purple**	

Words from "Rain Forest Babies"

Word Building

READ A SPELLING WORD Write the word *turn* on the board. Ask children to identify the letters that stand for the /ûr/ sound. Then read the word, and have children do the same.

BUILD SPELLING WORDS Ask children which letter you should change to make *turn* become *burn*. (Change *t* to *b*.) Write the word *burn* on the board. Point to the word, and have children read it. Continue building spelling words in this manner. Say:

- **Which letters do I have to change to make the word *bird*?** (Change *u* to *i* and *n* to *d*.)
- **Which letter do I have to change to make the word *third*?** (Change *b* to *th*.)
- **Which letters do I have to change to make the word *herd*, as in the sentence *I see a herd of elephants*?** (Take away *t* and change *i* to *e*.)
- **Which letters do I have to change to make the word *learn*?** (Change *h* to *l*, add *a* after *e*, and change *d* to *n*.)

Continue building the remaining spelling words in this manner.

BELOW-LEVEL

Kinesthetic Reinforcement
List the spelling words on the board. Read each word aloud. Have children repeat it and trace it in the air with their index finger.

ADVANCED

Silly Sentences List the spelling words on the board. Challenge children to write silly sentences using the spelling words. Have partners share their sentences.

5-DAY PHONICS/SPELLING

DAY 1	Pretest
DAY 2	**Word Building**
DAY 3	State the Generalization
DAY 4	Review
DAY 5	Posttest

Read Words in Context

APPLY PHONICS Write the following sentences on the board or on chart paper. Have children read each sentence silently. Then track the print as children read the sentence aloud.

Earl's dog has brown <u>fur</u>.

Mom helped me <u>search</u> for my red <u>shirt</u>.

It is Curt's <u>turn</u> to pick a book to read.

My pet <u>bird</u> is green and yellow.

The dog kept the <u>herd</u> of sheep together.

WRITE Dictate several spelling words. Have children write the words in their notebook or on a dry-erase board.

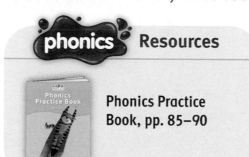

phonics Resources

Phonics Practice Book, pp. 85–90

✓ **MONITOR PROGRESS**

r-Controlled Vowel /ûr/ir, ur, er, ear

IF children have difficulty building and reading words with *r*-controlled vowel /ûr/ir, ur, er, and ear,	**THEN** help them blend and read the words *sir, girl, hurt, curl, her, perch, earth,* and *pearl.*

Small-Group Instruction, p. S32:

● **BELOW-LEVEL:** Reteach

● **ON-LEVEL:** Reinforce

● **ADVANCED:** Extend

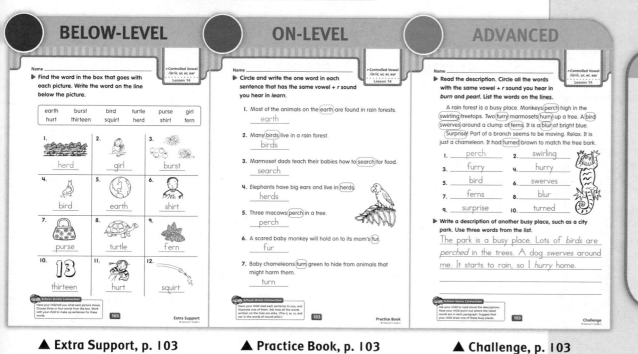

▲ Extra Support, p. 103   ▲ Practice Book, p. 103   ▲ Challenge, p. 103

ELL

• Group children according to academic levels, and assign one of the pages on the left.

• Clarify any unfamiliar concepts as necessary. See *ELL Teacher Guide* Lesson 14 for support in scaffolding instruction.

High-Frequency Words

Words to Know

Objectives

• *To read high-frequency words*

INTRODUCE ✔

High-Frequency Words

care	sweat
father	thumb
interesting	touch

Review High-Frequency Words   Hold up *Picture Card* 47 (family) and say *This is the father.* Have children practice using the word *father* by telling about their father or other fathers they know as they point to the picture of the father.

See *ELL Teacher Guide* Lesson 14 for support in scaffolding instruction.

Picture Card 47 ▶   family

Teach/Model

Routine Card 5   **INTRODUCE WORDS**   Write the words *interesting*, *thumb*, *touch*, *care*, *sweat*, and *father* on the board.

• Point to and read *interesting*. Repeat it, having children say it with you.

• Say: **I watched an *interesting* television program last night.**

• Point to each letter as you spell the word. Have children spell the word with you.

• Have children reread the word.

Repeat for the remaining words. Use the following sentences:

• **I hurt my *thumb* playing baseball.**

• **Be careful not to *touch* poison ivy.**

• **Sharon helped Dad take *care* of the baby.**

• **We were so hot from running that we were dripping with *sweat*.**

• **Miguel's *father* is a police officer.**

Guided Practice

STUDENT EDITION PAGES 426–427   Ask children to turn to *Student Edition* pages 426 and 427. Have children point to and read aloud each of the highlighted words on page 426. Talk about the photograph and map. Then ask volunteers to read aloud the passage.

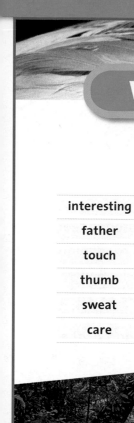

Words to Know

High-Frequency Words

interesting

father

touch

thumb

sweat

care

November 15

Dear Kayla,

I took an **interesting** trip last month. My **father** took me with him on a research trip to a rain forest. He said I would see, hear, smell, taste, and **touch** some amazing things in the rain forest. He was right!

My dad studies the plants that grow in rain forests. He's good with plants. My mom says he has a green **thumb**.

We flew to the Amazon rain forest in South America. This is the largest rain forest in the world! I was covered with **sweat** the whole time I was there. That's because the rain forest is warm and wet all year.

I learned on this trip that we need to take **care** of the rain forests. Did you know that more than half of the world's plants and animals live in rain forests?

Your friend,

David

GO online www.harcourtschool.com/storytown

426

427

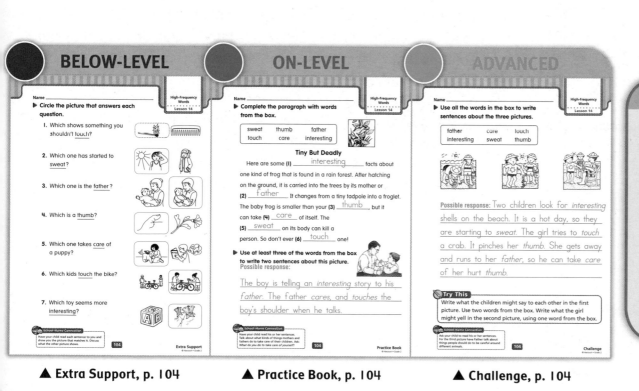

▲ Extra Support, p. 104   ▲ Practice Book, p. 104   ▲ Challenge, p. 104

ELL

- Group children according to academic levels, and assign one of the pages on the left.

- Clarify any unfamiliar concepts as necessary. See *ELL Teacher Guide* Lesson 14 for support in scaffolding instruction.

Reading

Student Edition: **"Rain Forest Babies"**

Objectives

- *To understand characteristics of nonfiction*
- *To reread as a strategy for comprehension*
- *To apply word knowledge to the reading of a text*

Options for Reading

 BELOW-LEVEL

Preview   Have children preview the selection by looking at the photos and the headings. Guide them in filling in the K and W columns of their K-W-L charts. Read each page to children, and have them read it after you.

 ON-LEVEL

Monitor Comprehension
Have children complete the K and W columns of their K-W-L charts before they read the selection aloud. Ask the Monitor Comprehension questions as you go. Then lead them in retelling the selection.

 ADVANCED

Independent Reading   Have children fill in the K and W columns of their K-W-L charts before they read. Ask the Monitor Comprehension questions as you go. Then discuss rain forest animals.

Genre Study

DISCUSS NONFICTION: PAGE 428   Ask children to read the genre information on *Student Edition* page 428. Remind them that nonfiction gives information about a topic. It has ideas that are supported by facts. Then use **Transparency GO5** or copy the graphic organizer from page 428 onto the board. Tell children that they will work together to complete the K-W-L chart as they read "Rain Forest Babies."

K What I Know	**W** What I Want to Know	**L** What I Learned

Comprehension Strategies

REREAD: PAGE 428   Remind children that good readers use strategies to make sure they understand what they are reading. Explain that if they do not understand a sentence or a paragraph they are reading, they should reread it. Have children read the Comprehension Strategies information on page 428. Tell children that they should reread any part of the selection that confuses them or doesn't make sense.

Think Aloud   When I read a nonfiction selection such as "Rain Forest Babies," I know there will be a lot of information to remember and understand. Sometimes, I might miss a fact or not be certain what it means. When that happens, I need to go back and reread.

RAIN FOREST BABIES

BY KATHY DARLING

Genre Study

Nonfiction gives facts about a topic. Look for

- main ideas in paragraphs.
- facts about subjects you want to learn more about.

K	W	L
What I Know	What I Want to Know	What I Learned

Comprehension Strategy

Monitor Comprehension— Reread a section if something does not make sense to you.

Build Background

DISCUSS RAIN FOREST ANIMALS   Tell children that they are going to read a story about animal babies that live in rain forests. Invite volunteers to name and share facts that they know about rain forest animals.

[Routine Card 6] **SET A PURPOSE AND PREDICT**   Tell children that they will read this selection to get information about baby animals that live in rain forests.

- Have children read the title.

- Identify the animals. Ask: **What do you think these animal babies eat and do?**

- List their predictions on the board.

- Have children read the selection to learn what the animal babies eat and do.

TECHNOLOGY

 eBook   "Rain Forest Babies" is available in an eBook.

 Audiotext   "Rain Forest Babies" is available on *Audiotext 2* for subsequent readings.

Tropical Rain Forests of the World

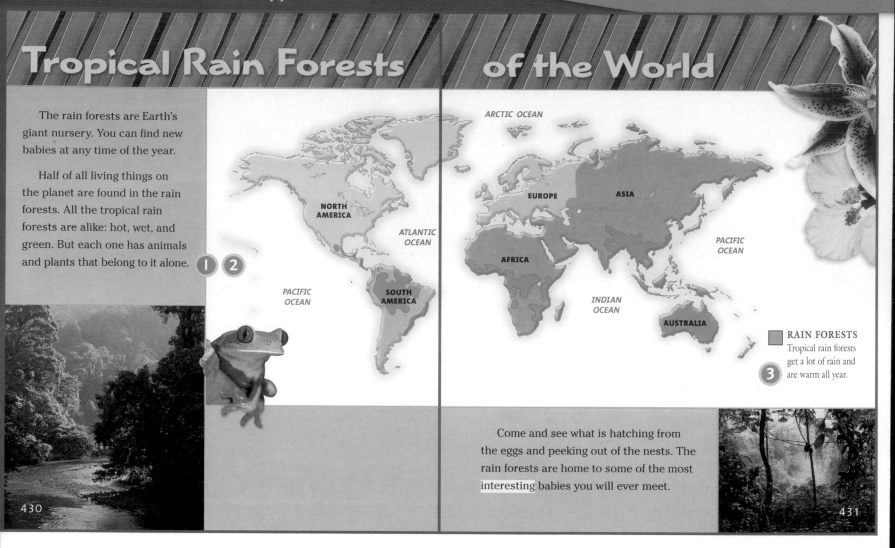

The rain forests are Earth's giant nursery. You can find new babies at any time of the year.

Half of all living things on the planet are found in the rain forests. All the tropical rain forests are alike: hot, wet, and green. But each one has animals and plants that belong to it alone. **1** **2**

ARCTIC OCEAN

EUROPE   ASIA

NORTH AMERICA

ATLANTIC OCEAN

AFRICA

PACIFIC OCEAN

PACIFIC OCEAN

SOUTH AMERICA

INDIAN OCEAN

AUSTRALIA

RAIN FORESTS
Tropical rain forests get a lot of rain and are warm all year. **3**

Come and see what is hatching from the eggs and peeking out of the nests. The rain forests are home to some of the most interesting babies you will ever meet.

430   431

Monitor Comprehension

PAGES 430–431   Say: **The heading at the top of these pages is "Tropical Rain Forests of the World." Read to find out what tropical rain forests are like.**

1 **NOTE DETAILS**   **What are tropical rain forests like?** (All tropical rain forests are hot, wet, and green. They get a lot of rain and are warm all year. Half of all living things on the planet are found in the rain forests.)

2 **MAKE COMPARISONS**   **How are tropical rain forests different from one another?** (Each one has animals and plants that belong to it alone.)

3 **MAKE INFERENCES**   **How might you feel in a rain forest? Explain.** (Possible response: Damp and sticky, as rain forests get a lot of rain and are warm.)

SUPPORTING STANDARDS

Map Skills   Tell children that tropical rain forests are found mainly in South America, Central America, west and central Africa, Indonesia, parts of Southeast Asia, and parts of Australia. Help children find these places on a world map. Have them use this sentence frame to describe where the rain forests are:

The rain forest in _____ is near _____.

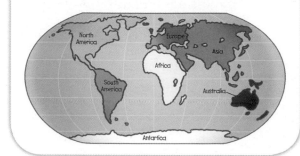

Elephant

The biggest animal in the rain forest is the elephant. The biggest baby is the elephant calf. Three hundred pounds at birth, it will become a thousand-pound baby in less than two years. That elephant milk is powerful stuff! **2**

Elephant
(Sumatran Elephant)

- **Baby name:** Calf
- **Birth weight:** 300 pounds **1**
- **Favorite food:** Babies drink milk; adults eat leaves and grass.
- **Parent care:** Baby stays with mother for 10 or more years in a herd of related females.

The elephant baby sucks on its trunk just as a human baby sucks on its thumb. Trunks are good for other things too: sniffing, putting food and water into the mouth, and playing with sticks and leaves. This calf is part of a big family called a *herd*. There are lots of other elephant babies in the herd, but this calf is only two weeks old and still too little to play with the other babies. **3**

432

433

Monitor Comprehension

PAGES 432–433   Say: **I see a lot of elephants in the photo. Read to find out about the size of baby elephants.**

1 **NOTE DETAILS**   How heavy is an elephant at birth? (three hundred pounds)

2 **AUTHOR'S CRAFT**   Why does the author say that elephant milk is "powerful stuff"? (Possible response: The author is explaining how nutritious elephant milk is. Baby elephants grow quickly while drinking it.)

3 **MAKE COMPARISONS**   Elephants use their trunks to do things that people do. What can elephants do with their trunks that people do with some body parts? (Elephants use their trunks like noses to sniff, like thumbs to suck on, and like hands to lift food to their mouths and to play.)

Apply Comprehension Strategies

Reread   Demonstrate how to reread to comprehend the selection to this point.

Think Aloud   Before reading, I wanted to know how big elephant babies are at birth. I thought that page 432 said 1,000 pounds. That didn't make sense, so I reread the page. Actually, they weigh 300 pounds at birth and will be 1,000 pounds by age 2.

Tiger

This cute little tiger cub will grow up to be a hundred times bigger than the kitty in your house. It will do a lot of the same things a house cat does, but it will not be able to purr.

Tiger
(Bengal Tiger)

• **Baby name:** Cub

• **Birth weight:** 2 pounds

• **Favorite food:** Babies drink milk; adults eat meat.

• **Parent care:** Cubs stay with mother for 2 years. Father does not help.

The tiger is one of the "four who can roar." Three of the roaring cats—the tigers, the leopards, and the jaguars—live in rain forests. Lions, the fourth roarer, sometimes live in forests, but never in rain forests.

434

435

Monitor Comprehension

PAGES 434–435 Say: **Tigers are a kind of cat. Read to find out how tigers are different from house cats.**

1 **NOTE DETAILS** **How are tigers different from house cats?** (They grow up to be a hundred times bigger than house cats. They cannot purr. They can roar.)

2 **MAKE COMPARISONS** **In what way is a tiger cub like an elephant calf?** (Possible responses: They both drink milk. Both tiger and elephant babies stay with their mother.)

3 **FICTION AND NONFICTION** **How do you know that the section called "Tiger" is nonfiction?** (Possible response: It gives facts about tigers.)

ELL

Nouns Point out the nouns *cat*, *tiger*, *leopard*, and *lion*. Discuss how each noun names an animal. Then display photos of a tiger, lion, leopard, and cat. Have children point to the corresponding photo(s) as you ask questions, such as *Which animals can roar? Which animal cannot roar? Which animals live in a rain forest? Which do not?*

Macaw

Mother and father macaw have the most beautiful feathers in the forest. But their chicks have none at all. Only for a few days, though. Then fluffy "baby feathers" called *down* cover their wrinkly skin. This two-week-old Hahn's macaw (right) is warm in its down coat, but it can't fly with this kind of feather. Down is not waterproof, either, so the baby macaw won't go far from the nest hole.

Macaw
(Hahn's Macaw,
Blue and Gold Macaw)

- **Baby name:** Chick, called a fledgling when it can fly
- **Birth weight:** 1 ounce
- **Favorite food:** Partly digested fruit and seeds brought by parents
- **Parent care:** Both mother and father feed, protect, and teach the babies for 2 or 3 years. **2**

3

At nine weeks, a blue and gold macaw baby already has most of the bright, strong feathers it will need to fly away. But the fledgling is in no hurry to leave its loving parents. Young macaws stay with their family for two or three years.

436

437

Monitor Comprehension

PAGES 436–437   Ask children to describe what they see in the photos. Say: **Read to find out how baby macaws change as they grow.**

1 NOTE DETAILS   How do macaw chicks change as they grow? (They have no feathers for a few days. Then fluffy down covers their wrinkly skin. At nine weeks, a macaw baby has most of the feathers it will need to fly.)

2 MAKE COMPARISONS   What is different about the way macaw parents and tiger parents care for their young? (Macaw mothers and fathers feed, protect, and teach the babies for two or three years. Tiger cubs stay with their mothers for two years, but tiger fathers do not help care for the young.)

3 TEXT STRUCTURE   Why does the author include, in the side column, the bulleted items about each animal? (The author wants to provide the same facts for each animal, and placing them on the side column makes them easy to find.)

Apply
Comprehension Strategies

Reread   Demonstrate how to reread to comprehend the selection to this point.

Think Aloud   I wanted to know why newborn macaws can't fly and why they stay near the nest. The text on page 436 must have the answer, but I was confused by what I read. I didn't see the reason. When I reread, I see that it's the down feathers that keep them from flying and from leaving the area.

Lesson 14 (*Student Edition*, pages 436–437)   **T315**

Frog

Look, but don't touch! People who live in the rain forest know to keep away from these beautiful baby frogs. The golden froglets are small, but they are able to take care of themselves. If danger comes, a poison oozes out of their skin. This "sweat" is very deadly.

Frog
(Poison Arrow Frog)

- **Baby name:** Tadpole when young, froglet when older
- **Birth size:** No bigger than a raisin
- **Favorite food:** Insects, ants, tiny water animals
- **Parent care:** Tadpoles are fed by both parents.

Bright gold is one of the warning colors that ❶ poison frogs use. Here are some of the bright patterns they use to say, *Danger! Keep away.* ❷ ❸

438

439

Monitor Comprehension

PAGES 438–439 Say: **Look at the colorful frogs on these pages. Read to find out what kind of frogs they are.**

❶ **NOTE DETAILS** **What kind of frogs do these pages show?** (poisonous frogs)

❷ **MAKE INFERENCES** **What do you think might happen to a person who touched one of these frogs? Why do you think so?** (Possible response: The person would die. A very deadly poison oozes out of the frog's skin.)

❸ **EXPRESS PERSONAL OPINIONS** **Do you think it is good or bad that poison frogs are brightly colored? Explain.** (Possible response: Good, because people can see them easily and stay away from them.)

Use Multiple Strategies

Use Graphic Organizers Demonstrate how to use the K-W-L chart to comprehend the selection.

Think Aloud Before reading, I filled in the K and W part. As I read, I fill in what I have learned.

K What I Know	W What I Want to Know	L What I Learned
• There are a lot of animals in rain forests.	• What animals are found in rain forests?	• Elephants, tigers, macaws, and frogs are in the rain forests.

Kangaroo

Kangaroo
(Red-legged Pademelon)

- **Baby name:** Joey
- **Birth weight:** About the same as a grain of rice
- **Favorite food:** Babies drink milk; adults eat leaves and grass. ③
- **Parent care:** Mother carries baby in pouch. Father does not help.

Surprise! There are kangaroos in rain forests. These red-legged pademelons live on the ground. Other kinds hop around in the treetops.
   All baby kangaroos have the same name. When they are carried in Mother's pouch, both boy and girl babies are called *joey*.

This little one is too big for the pouch, but it will keep close to its mother's side for protection. Don't let Mom's sweet face fool you. She can deliver a kick that would make a karate champion proud. ②

440

441

Monitor Comprehension

PAGES 440–441   Say: **I didn't know that kangaroos lived in the rain forest. Read to find out about the rain forest kangaroos.**

① **NOTE DETAILS**   Where in the rain forest do kangaroos live? (Red-legged pademelons live on the ground. Other kinds of kangaroos live in the treetops.)

② **MAKE INFERENCES**   How might a mother kangaroo protect its baby from enemies? Explain. (Possible response: She kicks enemies. The author writes that her kick "would make a karate champion proud.")

③ **DRAW CONCLUSIONS**   Why do you think a joey is carried in its mother's pouch? (Possible response: Joeys are as small as a grain of rice at birth. Being in the pouch keeps them safe as they grow.)

BELOW-LEVEL

Descriptive Words   Point out descriptive words used to tell about kangaroos, such as *red-legged* and *sweet face*. Elicit that these words help readers visualize kangaroos and that they appeal to the senses. Work with children to identify words used to describe other rain forest animals.

Sugar Glider

② The sugar glider jumps out of trees. Without a parachute . . . and at night. Its target is not the ground but a nearby tree. It leaps from tree to tree to get the sweet sap.

Sugar Glider
(Lesser Sugar Glider)

- **Birth weight:** Less than a grain of rice
- **Favorite food:** Babies drink only milk for the first 100 days; adults prefer tree sap and insects.
- **Parent care:** Mother keeps babies in pouch for 70 days and then feeds them in nest for another month. Although gliders live in a colony and share a nest, the mother does all the child-raising chores.

Although it looks like a flying squirrel, the sugar glider is not even a close relative. It is a ① marsupial—an animal with a pouch. Only as big as a mouse, this baby, four weeks out of the pouch, is already a fearless leaper.

442

443

Monitor Comprehension

PAGES 442–443 Say: **The sugar glider looks like a squirrel to me. Read to find out if it's a kind of squirrel.**

① **NOTE DETAILS** **Is a sugar glider a kind of squirrel?** (No.) **What kind of animal is a sugar glider?** (It is a marsupial.)

② **AUTHOR'S CRAFT** **Which sentence helps you know that a sugar glider is a "fearless leaper"?** ("Without a parachute . . . and at night")

ANALYZE AUTHOR'S PURPOSE

Author's Purpose Remind children that authors have a purpose, or reason, for writing. After children have finished reading the selection, ask:

Why did the author write "Rain Forest Babies"?

- to entertain readers with a story about baby animals
- to tell facts about baby animals living in a rain forest
- to inform readers about people who visit rain forests

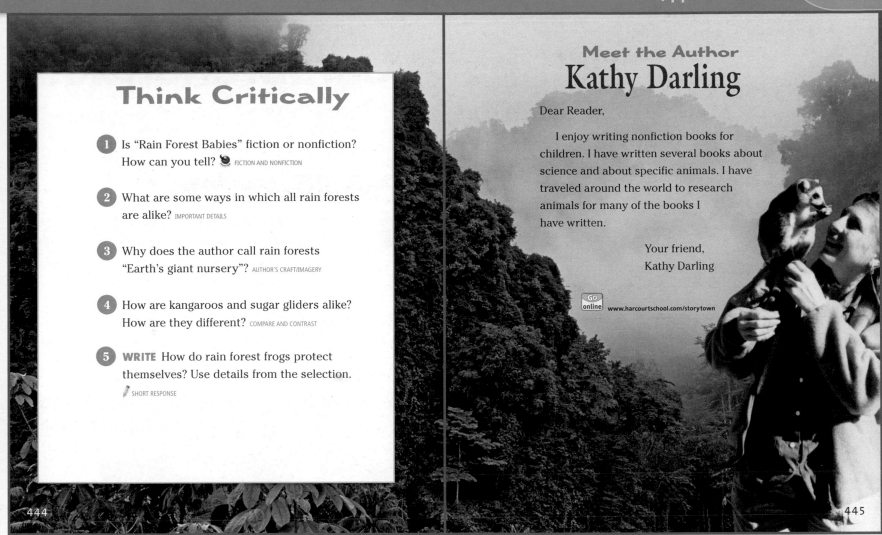

Think Critically

1. Is "Rain Forest Babies" fiction or nonfiction? How can you tell? FICTION AND NONFICTION

2. What are some ways in which all rain forests are alike? IMPORTANT DETAILS

3. Why does the author call rain forests "Earth's giant nursery"? AUTHOR'S CRAFT/IMAGERY

4. How are kangaroos and sugar gliders alike? How are they different? COMPARE AND CONTRAST

5. WRITE How do rain forest frogs protect themselves? Use details from the selection. SHORT RESPONSE

Meet the Author
Kathy Darling

Dear Reader,

I enjoy writing nonfiction books for children. I have written several books about science and about specific animals. I have traveled around the world to research animals for many of the books I have written.

Your friend,
Kathy Darling

GO online www.harcourtschool.com/storytown

444   445

Think Critically

Respond to the Literature

1. Focus Skill Possible response: Nonfiction; it gives factual information about real animals in a real place.   **FICTION AND NONFICTION**

2. Possible response: All rain forests are hot, wet, and green.   **IMPORTANT DETAILS**

3. Possible response: The author wants readers to know that lots of baby animals live there.   **AUTHOR'S CRAFT/IMAGERY**

4. Possible response: Both keep their babies in pouches. Kangaroos hop to get around. Sugar gliders leap from tree to tree.   **COMPARE AND CONTRAST**

5. **WRITE** Possible response: They sweat a poison that is very dangerous to anything it touches.   **SHORT RESPONSE**

Meet the Author

PAGE 445 Explain that this page tells about Kathy Darling, the author of this story. Read aloud Kathy Darling's letter on page 445. Discuss where she might have traveled to learn about the animals in "Rain Forest Babies." (Possible responses: to rain forests, to zoos, to libraries)

Check Comprehension
Summarizing

Objectives

- *To practice summarizing a non-fiction selection*
- *To use proper phrasing to read fluently in a manner that sounds like natural speech*

RETELLING RUBRIC

4	Uses details to clearly summarize the selection
3	Uses some details to summarize the selection
2	Summarizes the selection with some inaccuracies
1	Is unable to summarize the selection

Professional Development

 Podcasting: Auditory Modeling

BELOW-LEVEL

Fluency Practice   For fluency practice, have children read *Decodable Book 12*, the appropriate *Leveled Reader* (pp. T358–T361), or Story 14 in the *Intervention Reader*.

Summarize

 DIBELS Oral Reading Fluency **ORF**

 FICTION AND NONFICTION   Ask children to tell what kind of story "Rain Forest Babies" Is and to explain how they know. (Nonfiction; it gives facts about real animals in a real place.)

 REVISIT THE GRAPHIC ORGANIZER   Display completed **Transparency GO5**. Guide children to use the K-W-L chart to help them recall important details.

STORY RETELLING CARDS   The cards for "Rain Forest Babies" can be used for summarizing or as an aid to completing the K-W-L chart.

▲ Story Retelling Cards 1–6, "Rain Forest Babies"

 # Fluency
Phrasing

Teach/Model

 DIBELS Oral Reading Fluency **ORF**

PHRASING   Explain that good readers read without pausing when they read words that belong together. Have children open to pages 432–433 of "Rain Forest Babies" and track the print as you model reading phrases.

Practice/Apply

Routine Card 8

 ECHO-READ   Read aloud the rest of the selection, modeling reading with phrasing. Have children echo-read each page.

Build Robust Vocabulary

Words About the Selection

Teach/Model

 Routine Card 3

INTRODUCE ROBUST VOCABULARY Use *Routine Card 3* to introduce the words.

❶ Put the word in **selection context**.
❷ Display Transparency R74 and read the word and the **Student-Friendly Explanation**.
❸ Have children **say the word** with you.
❹ Use the word in other contexts, and have children **interact with the word's meaning**.
❺ Remove the transparency. Say the Student-Friendly Explanation again, and ask children to **name the word** that goes with it.

❶ **Selection Context:** Many baby animals are **adorable**.
❹ **Interact with Word Meaning:** Is a puppy or a snake adorable?

❶ **Selection Context:** An **assortment** of animals live in rain forests.
❹ **Interact with Word Meaning:** Would you prefer to have an assortment of toys or an assortment of homework assignments? Why?

❶ **Selection Context:** Rain forests are the **habitat** for many living things on Earth.
❹ **Interact with Word Meaning:** Is your habitat a rain forest or a house?

❶ **Selection Context:** Elephant calves are **immense** compared to other animal babies.
❹ **Interact with Word Meaning:** Which do you think is immense, an ocean or a pond? Explain.

Practice/Apply

GUIDED PRACTICE Ask children to use the vocabulary to tell about a place where they might see an *assortment* of animals.

Objectives

• *To develop robust vocabulary through discussing a literature selection*

 **Tested**

INTRODUCE

Vocabulary: Lesson 14

| adorable | habitat |
| assortment | immense |

▼ **Student-Friendly Explanations**

Student-Friendly Explanations

dappled	If something is dappled, it has spots, streaks, or patches of different colors or shades.
entranced	If you are entranced by something, it has delighted or amazed you.
trooped	If you trooped someplace, you moved along with a group of people.
circling	If something is circling you, it is moving around you.
adorable	If something is very cute, it is adorable.
assortment	If you see a variety or mixture of things, you see an assortment.
habitat	If a plant or an animal lives in a particular place in nature, that is its habitat.
immense	If something is really big or huge, it is immense.

Grade 2, Theme 3   R74   Vocabulary

Transparency R74

Grammar
Pronouns

5-DAY GRAMMAR

DAY 1	Define Pronouns
DAY 2	*He, She, It, We, They*
DAY 3	Using *I* and *Me*
DAY 4	Apply to Writing
DAY 5	Weekly Review

Objectives

- *To identify pronouns*
- *To use pronouns correctly*

Daily Proofreading

Cadies brother likes to read to her

(Cadie's, her.)

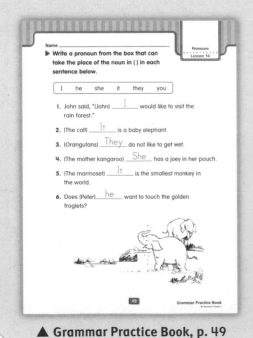

▲ Grammar Practice Book, p. 49

Review

PRONOUNS Remind children that a pronoun is a word that takes the place of a noun. Write the following sentences on the board.

My sister and I like animals. (We)

So does May Ling. (she)

Hanna, Lee, and Mike like animals, too. (They)

The dog likes us! (It)

Have children read aloud the sentences. Explain that the underlined nouns can be replaced by pronouns. Rewrite each sentence, replacing the underlined word with the correct pronoun. Then have children read the sentences with you. Ask them to identify the pronoun in each sentence and tell which noun(s) it replaced.

Practice/Apply

GUIDED PRACTICE Explain that people use pronouns to avoid repeating words. Say: **An egg started to hatch. It had a baby chick in it**. Explain that *it* was used to replace *An egg*. Write the following sentences on the board. Invite children to tell which pronouns should replace the nouns.

Mike and I looked. (We)

Liz came to look. (She)

Liz and Mike saw a beak. (They)

Mike said, "This is fun!" (He)

INDEPENDENT PRACTICE Write the following sentences on the board. Have children replace the underlined word(s) with a pronoun.

<u>Hal</u> went swimming. (He)

<u>Jill and I</u> went with him. (We)

<u>Some ducks</u> joined us. (They)

<u>Jill</u> said, "What funny ducks!" (She)

Writing
Paragraph That Explains

5-DAY WRITING	
DAY 1	Introduce
DAY 2	Prewrite
DAY 3	Draft
DAY 4	Revise
DAY 5	Revise

Prewrite

GENERATE IDEAS   Have children reread the sentences they wrote on Day 1 (page T303). Ask them to think of details that give more information about the sentences.

 CONVENTIONS   Tell children to use pronouns in place of nouns if it is clear what noun the pronoun is replacing. Demonstrate as you complete the chart below.

MODEL PREWRITING   Copy on the board the chart below. Tell children that they can use a chart or other graphic organizer to record ideas for writing a paragraph that explains. Model adding a main idea sentence and details that tell more about the main idea.

> **Main Idea**
> Elephants use their trunks in many ways.
>
> **Detail**
> Elephants use their trunks to get food.
>
> **Detail**
> They use their trunks to sniff.
>
> **Detail**
> They use their trunks to play.

Practice/Apply

GUIDED PRACTICE   Ask children to brainstorm a main idea and details for their paragraphs. Invite volunteers to share the sentences they wrote on Day 1 about how they have changed since they were younger. Record their sentences as the main idea in a new chart. Elicit details that tell more about the main idea, and add them to the chart.

INDEPENDENT PRACTICE   Have children use the chart to brainstorm a main idea and details to use in their paragraph that explains. Have children save their charts for use on Days 3–5.

Objectives

- *To develop ideas and topics for writing*
- *To use a graphic organizer for prewriting*
- *To use pronouns in place of nouns*

 Writing Prompt

Reflect and Record   Have children record their reflections about how they know they have changed since they were younger.

Demonstrate Meaning   If children have difficulty completing the chart, allow them to use oral language, point to pictures, and role-play to communicate main ideas and details. Repeat their responses, and then write them in the chart. Read aloud the completed chart for children, and then invite them to read it aloud with you.

Day at a Glance

Day 3

 phonics and Spelling
- Review: *r*-Controlled Vowel /ûr/*ir*, *ur*, *er*, *ear*
- State the Generalization

High-Frequency Words
- Review: *interesting*, *thumb*, *touch*, *care*, *sweat*, *father*

Fluency
- Phrasing
- **"Rain Forest Babies,"** *Student Edition*, pp. 428–445

Comprehension

 Review: Fiction and Nonfiction

- **"Baby Tapir Is Born!",** *Student Edition*, pp. 446–447

 **Read!**

Robust Vocabulary
- Review: *dappled, entranced, trooped, circling, adorable, assortment, habitat, immense*

Grammar
- Review: Pronouns

Writing
- Paragraph That Explains

Warm-Up Routines

Oral Language

Objective *To listen attentively and respond appropriately to oral communication*

Question of the Day

What words would you use to tell how a macaw looks, sounds, and moves?

Use prompts such as the following to help children think about how a macaw looks, sounds, and moves.

- **What colors are macaws?**
- **What do their feathers look like?**
- **How does a macaw sound? Is it loud or soft?**
- **What does a macaw use to move? How does it move?**

Record children's responses on the board.

Read Aloud

Objective *To appreciate poetic language*

BIG BOOK OF RHYMES AND POEMS Display "Macaw" on page 27, and ask children to tell what they remember about the poem. Remind them that the poet describes the parrot's yellow squawking as brash. Say: **When someone does something in a brash way, he or she does it in a lively or harsh way, without holding back.** Then reread the poem, encouraging children to join in. Invite children to read "quiet blue feathers" quietly and "brash yellow squawking" as though they are squawking.

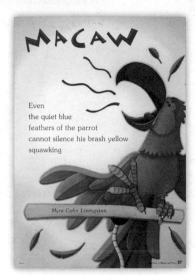

▲ Big Book of Rhymes and Poems, p. 27

Word Wall

Objective *To read high-frequency words*

REVIEW HIGH-FREQUENCY WORDS Have children begin tapping a finger on their desk to keep time. Point to a card and have children spell and read the word to the beat of their taps. Repeat the process several times.

thumb	touch	care
sweat	father	interesting

r-Controlled Vowel /ûr/
ir, ur, er, ear

 phonics and Spelling

5-DAY PHONICS	
DAY 1	Reintroduce /ûr/ir, ur, er, ear
DAY 2	Word Building with /ûr/ir, ur, er, ear
DAY 3	**Word Building with /ûr/ir, ur, er, ear**
DAY 4	VCCV; Review /ûr/ir, ur, er, ear
DAY 5	VCCV; Review /ûr/ir, ur, er, ear

Objectives

- *To use common spelling patterns to build and read words*
- *To read and write common word families*
- *To recognize spelling patterns*

Skill Trace

Tested ✔ **r-Controlled Vowel /ûr/ir, ur, er, ear**

Introduce	Grade 1
Reintroduce	T294–T297
Reteach	S32
Review	**T306–T307, T326–T327, T412**
Test	Theme 3
Maintain	Theme 5, T286

r-Controlled Vowel /ûr/ir, ur, er, ear

The bird hurt its wing.
Let Curt take a turn.
He can stir the mix a third time.
A speck of dirt fell on my shirt.
Did the sun burn your nose?
I did not mean to squirt water on your skirt!

Grade 2, Lesson 14   R71   Phonics

Transparency R71

Work with Patterns

INTRODUCE PHONOGRAMS Write the following phonograms at the top of five columns.

-ir   -ird   -irt   -urn   -urt

Tell children that these are the endings of some words. Slide your hand under the letters as you read each phonogram. Repeat, having children read the phonograms with you.

BUILD AND READ WORDS Write the letter *s* in front of the phonogram *-ir*. Guide children to read the word: /s/ *-ir*, *sir*. Have children identify the letters that stand for the /ûr/ sound. (ir) Continue the process, writing *b* in front of *-ird* and *-urn*; *d* in front of *-irt*; and *h* in front of *-urt* to make the words *bird*, *burn*, *dirt*, and *hurt*.

Then have children name other words that end with *-ir*, *-ird*, *-irt*, *-urn*, or *-urt*. Have them tell which letter or letters to add to build each word, and write the word in the appropriate column. Have children read each column of words. Then point to words at random and have children read them.

Read Words in Context

READ SENTENCES Display **Transparency R71** or write the sentences on the board. Have children choral-read the sentences as you track the print. Then ask volunteers to read each sentence aloud and underline words with /ûr/. Invite volunteers to add the words *Curt*, *turn*, *stir*, *third*, *shirt*, *squirt*, and *skirt* to the appropriate columns.

5-DAY SPELLING	
DAY 1	Pretest
DAY 2	Word Building
DAY 3	**State the Generalization**
DAY 4	Review
DAY 5	Posttest

Review Spelling Words

STATE THE GENERALIZATION FOR /ûr/ir, ur, er, ear List spelling words 1–10 on chart paper or on the board. Circle the words with /ûr/ spelled *ir*, and have children read them aloud. Ask: **What is the same in each word?** (The letters ir stand for the /ûr/ sound.) Ask volunteers to circle the other spelling words with /ûr/ spelled *ur*, /ûr/ spelled *er*, and /ûr/ spelled *ear*. Have them use a different color for each group of words.

 WRITE Have children write the spelling words in their notebooks. Remind children to use their best handwriting.

Handwriting

POSTURE Remind children to hold their pens and pencils correctly before they begin writing.

Spelling Words

1. **fur***   6. **turn**
2. **shirt**   7. **herd***
3. **burn**   8. **third**
4. **stir**   9. **learn***
5. **bird**   10. **search**

Challenge Words

11. **perfect**   14. **circus**
12. **birthday** 15. **surprise***
13. **purple**

* Words from "Rain Forest Babies"

Decodable Books

Additional Decoding Practice

- **Phonics**
  r-Controlled Vowel /ûr/*ir*, *ur*, *er*, *ear*

- **Decodable Words**

- **High-Frequency Words**
  See lists in *Decodable Book 12*.

  See also *Decodable Books*, online (Take-Home Version).

▲ Decodable Book 12: "A Pet That Purrs" and "Earth Day"

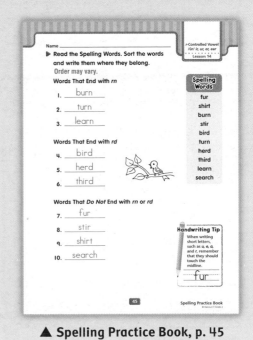

▲ Spelling Practice Book, p. 45

High-Frequency Words

Objective

• *To read high-frequency words*

REVIEW ✓ High-Frequency Words

care	sweat
father	thumb
interesting	touch

Model Usage Tell children that the word *touch* can mean "to cause part of your body to come into contact with something or someone." Touch your toes, and say: **I can touch my toes**. Have children touch their toes and repeat the sentence after you. Repeat the process, using other sentences.

Review

DISPLAY THE WORDS Write the words *interesting*, *thumb*, *touch*, *care*, *sweat*, and *father* on the board. Point to each word, and ask a volunteer to read it.

Practice/Apply

GUIDED PRACTICE Give each child a set of word cards (*Teacher Resource Book*, p. 79), and have children spread the cards out in front of them. Randomly call out each of the words, and have children hold up the matching card. Point to the word on the board. Repeat until children respond quickly and accurately.

INDEPENDENT PRACTICE Have children work with a partner. One partner should read a word while the other holds up the matching card. Have them repeat the process for all the words. Then have them take turns using the words in sentences.

MONITOR PROGRESS

High-Frequency Words

IF children have difficulty reading the high-frequency words,	**THEN** display two sets of word cards, and have them read and match the words.

Small-Group Instruction, p. S33:

● **BELOW-LEVEL:** Reteach   ● **ON-LEVEL:** Reinforce   ● **ADVANCED:** Extend

Fluency

Phrasing

Review

MODEL USING PROPER PHRASING Remind children that good readers group words into phrases so their reading sounds like they are speaking. Tell children to

▲ Student Edition, pp. 428–445

- look ahead as they read to see which groups of words should be connected.

- use punctuation clues, such as commas, to group words.

Think Aloud **I'm going to read part of "Rain Forest Babies" aloud. I'll read without pausing when I come to groups of words that go together. That way, my reading aloud will be easier to understand.**

Practice/Apply

Routine Card 9

GUIDED PRACTICE Read pages 432–433 aloud. Then have children practice reading the same two pages several times with a partner. Circulate, correcting any children who are reading word-by-word rather than reading groups of words that belong together.

INDEPENDENT PRACTICE Have partners take turns reading, "Rain Forest Babies" aloud, two pages at a time. Remind them to look ahead as they read to identify groups of words that belong together.

Objective

- *To use proper phrasing to read fluently in a manner that sounds like natural speech*

Additional Related Reading

- ***Life in a Rain Forest*** by Carol K. Lindeen. Capstone, 2004. **EASY**

- ***Here Is the Tropical Rain Forest*** by Madeleine Dunphy. Web of Life, 2006. **AVERAGE**

- ***The Great Kapok Tree: A Tale of the Amazon Rain Forest*** by Lynne Cherry. Harcourt, 2000. **CHALLENGE**

BELOW-LEVEL

Fluency Practice Have children reread *Decodable Book 12*, Story 14 in the *Intervention Reader*, or the appropriate *Leveled Reader* (pp. T358–T361). Have them practice reading the text several times.

"Research Says"

Repeated Reading "Repeated reading provides students with the necessary practice to build fluency, acquire new information, and maintain established information."
—O'Shea, Sindelar, & O'Shea (1985), p. 140

Fiction and Nonfiction
Comprehension

Objective

• *To distinguish fiction from nonfiction*

Skill Trace

 Fiction and Nonfiction

Introduce	T212–T213
Reteach	S36–S37
Review	**T248, T262, T272, T298–T299, T330, T344, T354, T404, T425**
Test	Theme 3
Maintain	Theme 4, T271

Review

REVIEW FICTION AND NONFICTION Remind children that a nonfiction book is about real people and events and a fiction book is about made-up characters and events. Guide them to identify topics that might be found in nonfiction and fiction. (Possible responses: Nonfiction—Animal Homes, Famous People; Fiction—Flying Dogs, Susie and Lee)

Tell children that distinguishing fiction from nonfiction can help them understand what they read.

Practice/Apply

GUIDED PRACTICE Have children turn to "Dogs" on *Student Edition* page 118. Look through the selection together, and ask volunteers to recall whether the story is fiction or nonfiction. Ask: **Is the selection fiction or nonfiction? How do you know?**

INDEPENDENT PRACTICE Have children turn to other selections in the *Student Edition* that they have read. Ask them to identify whether each selection is fiction or nonfiction and why.

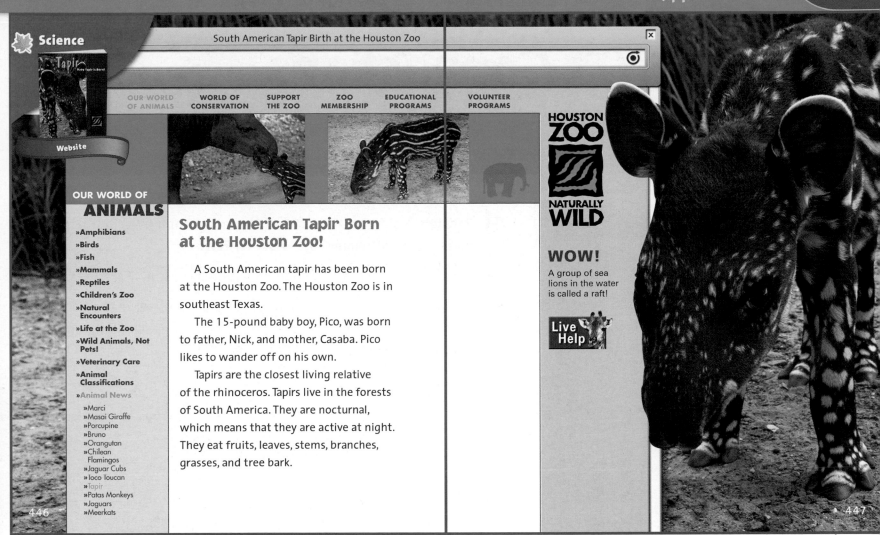

Science

Website

South American Tapir Birth at the Houston Zoo

OUR WORLD OF ANIMALS

WORLD OF CONSERVATION | SUPPORT THE ZOO | ZOO MEMBERSHIP | EDUCATIONAL PROGRAMS | VOLUNTEER PROGRAMS

OUR WORLD OF ANIMALS

»Amphibians
»Birds
»Fish
»Mammals
»Reptiles
»Children's Zoo
»Natural Encounters
»Life at the Zoo
»Wild Animals, Not Pets!
»Veterinary Care
»Animal Classifications
»Animal News
  »Marci
  »Masai Giraffe
  »Porcupine
  »Bruno
  »Orangutan
  »Chilean Flamingos
  »Jaguar Cubs
  »Ioco Toucan
  »Tapir
  »Patas Monkeys
  »Jaguars
  »Meerkats

South American Tapir Born at the Houston Zoo!

A South American tapir has been born at the Houston Zoo. The Houston Zoo is in southeast Texas.

The 15-pound baby boy, Pico, was born to father, Nick, and mother, Casaba. Pico likes to wander off on his own.

Tapirs are the closest living relative of the rhinoceros. Tapirs live in the forests of South America. They are nocturnal, which means that they are active at night. They eat fruits, leaves, stems, branches, grasses, and tree bark.

HOUSTON ZOO NATURALLY WILD

WOW!
A group of sea lions in the water is called a raft!

Live Help

446

447

Reading

Student Edition: Paired Selection

Read and Respond

USE PRIOR KNOWLEDGE/SET A PURPOSE Guide children to use prior knowledge and set a purpose for reading. Then have them read the article.

MONITOR COMPREHENSION Ask children to reread the article. Ask:

- **FICTION AND NONFICTION Is "Baby Tapir Is Born!" about real or make-believe things?** (real) **How can you tell?** (It tells facts about a real animal at a real place.)

- **PERSONAL RESPONSE Would you like to see a South American tapir? Explain.** (Responses will vary.)

SCIENCE

SUPPORTING STANDARDS

Understand Adaptations Tell children that the South American tapir has three hooved toes on its rear feet. This makes it possible for the tapir to form trails through the rain forest's undergrowth. The tapir also has a short proboscis, or flexible trunk. It is similar to an elephant's trunk. This helps the tapir pick up grasses and other foods.

 Connections

Objectives

- *To compare texts*
- *To connect texts to personal experiences*

Comparing Texts

1. Possible response: Yes; a South American tapir lives in the rain forests of South America. **TEXT TO TEXT**

2. Responses will vary and should include a reason. **TEXT TO SELF**

3. Possible response: They go to rain forests to observe the baby animals. They read books and learn what other scientists already know about the babies. **TEXT TO WORLD**

Connections

Comparing Texts

❶ Could a tapir have been in "Rain Forest Babies"? Why or why not?

❷ What rain forest baby do you want to learn more about? Why?

❸ How do you think scientists learn about rain forest babies?

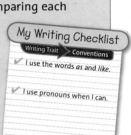

Phonics

Make Word Cards

On index cards, write words in which the letters *ir, ur, er,* or *ear* stand for the vowel sound in *turn.* Draw a picture on each card to show the word. Then share your word cards with a partner. Ask your partner to read each word.

stir

448

Fluency Practice

Read with a Partner

Read "Rain Forest Babies" aloud with a partner. Take turns reading one page at a time. Be sure to read the headings, too. Without pausing, read groups of words that go together.

Writing

Write a Poem

With a partner, write sentences comparing each rain forest baby to something else using *as* or *like.* Use your sentences to write a poem about rain forest babies.

The macaw's feathers are <u>as</u> colorful <u>as</u> a rainbow.

The kangaroo kicks <u>like</u> a karate champ.

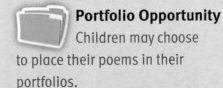
My Writing Checklist
Writing Trait → Conventions
✔ I use the words *as* and *like.*
✔ I use pronouns when I can.

449

⏱ PHONICS

Make Word Cards Have children first write *ir, ur, er,* and *ear* words. Then have them illustrate the words. Once children have completed their word cards, have partners read each other's word cards and use the words in sentences.

Herd

⏱ FLUENCY

Read with a Partner Before they begin reading, have partners decide how they will take turns reading the selection aloud. Model how to read phrases. Read *Student Edition* page 430 aloud. Point out the punctuation that has to do with phrasing in the sentence that begins, "All the tropical . . ."

⏱ WRITING

Write a Poem Help partners brainstorm things they could compare animals to. Then suggest they brainstorm rhyming words for their comparison.

Portfolio Opportunity Children may choose to place their poems in their portfolios.

 Build Robust Vocabulary

Objective

- *To review robust vocabulary*

Tested

REVIEW ✓

Vocabulary: Lesson 14

dappled	adorable
entranced	assortment
trooped	habitat
circling	immense

▼ **Student-Friendly Explanations**

Student-Friendly Explanations

dappled	If something is dappled, it has spots, streaks, or patches of different colors or shades.
entranced	If you are entranced by something, it has delighted or amazed you.
trooped	If you trooped someplace, you moved along with a group of people.
circling	If something is circling you, it is moving around you.
adorable	If something is very cute, it is adorable.
assortment	If you see a variety or mixture of things, you see an assortment.
habitat	If a plant or an animal lives in a particular place in nature, that is its habitat.
immense	If something is really big or huge, it is immense.

Grade 2, Theme 3   R74   Vocabulary

Transparency R74

Review Robust Vocabulary

USE VOCABULARY IN DIFFERENT CONTEXTS   Remind children of the Student-Friendly Explanations of the Vocabulary Words introduced on Days 1 and 2. Then discuss each word, using the following prompts:

dappled

- **Look for a dappled shirt or dress. What colors are dappled on it?**

- **What are some kinds of animals that can be dappled?**

entranced

- **Would you feel bored if something entranced you? Explain.**

- **What is something that you have been entranced by? Why?**

trooped

- **If you went someplace by yourself, would you have trooped there? Why or why not?**

- **Describe a time when you saw people who trooped.**

circling

- **Tell about a time you saw an animal circling something or someone.**

- **If you were circling a park, would you be walking through the park or around the park? Explain.**

- **If you see a shark swimming around its food, would it be correct to say *The shark is circling its food*? Explain.**

adorable

- Tell about something that is adorable.

- What other words could you use to describe an adorable baby?

assortment

- If you see a lot of green beans, do you see an assortment of green beans? Explain.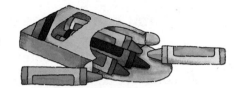

- If you have ten different colors, do you have an assortment of colors? Explain.

- Describe what an assortment of toys might include.

habitat

- What kind of habitat do fish live in?

- Describe the habitat you live in.

- Would a rain forest be a good place for an animal that likes dry weather and a lot of sand? Explain.

immense

- Would you use the word *immense* to describe a castle? Why or why not?

- Would you use the word *immense* to describe an ant? Why or why not?

- What word is the opposite of *immense*?

Reinforce Understanding
Help children understand the meanings of *entranced* and *circled*. For *entranced*, look closely at a small object with an expression of interest and fascination. Have children demonstrate the action. For *circling*, move around the group. Then have volunteers do the same.

Grammar
Pronouns

5-DAY GRAMMAR

DAY 1 Define Pronouns
DAY 2 *He, She, It, We, They*
DAY 3 Using *I* and *Me*
DAY 4 Apply to Writing
DAY 5 Weekly Review

Objective

• *To use the pronouns* I *and* me *correctly*

Daily Proofreading

some frogses live in the rain forest.

(Some, frogs)

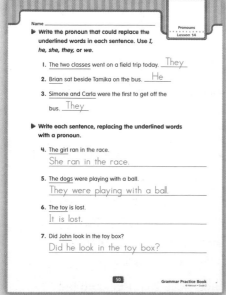

▲ **Grammar Practice Book, p. 50**

Review

USING *I* AND *ME*   Write and read aloud these sentences.

> **Vong said, "I want to go to the park."**
> **Mom replied, "I will take you to the park."**
> **"You can help me make a picnic," said Mom.**

Read aloud the first sentence. Explain that Vong uses the pronoun *I* because he is talking about himself. Read aloud the next sentence. Identify the speaker (Mom). Explain that Mom uses *I* to talk about herself. Read aloud the last sentence. Identify *me* as a pronoun. Explain that *me* refers back to the speaker, Mom. Tell children that a person who is speaking uses the pronoun *me* instead of *I* when the pronoun follows a verb or words such as *for*, *to*, *by*, *on*, and *under*.

Practice/Apply

GUIDED PRACTICE   Write these sentences on the board. Read the first sentence aloud. Model how to add *I* or *me* to the sentence. Work with children to complete the remaining sentences.

> Dad said, "_____ went for a jog at lunchtime." (I)
>
> Vong said, "Mom and _____ went to the park." (I)
>
> "Vong helped _____ make a picnic," said Mom. (me)
>
> "Did you save a snack for _____?" asked Dad. (me)

INDEPENDENT PRACTICE   Have children add *I* or *me* to complete each sentence. Remind children that *I* is always capitalized.

> **"Jim gave ___ a game for my birthday," said Lee.** (me)
> **"___ think that is very nice," said Mom.** (I)
> **"Here is another gift for ___," said Lee.** (me)
> **Lee asked Mom, "Did you give it to ____?"** (me)

Writing
Paragraph That Explains

5-DAY WRITING

DAY 1	Introduce
DAY 2	Prewrite
DAY 3	**Draft**
DAY 4	Revise
DAY 5	Revise

Draft a Paragraph That Explains

REVIEW A LITERATURE MODEL   Tell children that "Rain Forest Babies" is made up of many paragraphs that explain. Have children turn to page 443 in their *Student Edition* and read the paragraph. Invite them to tell what the writer included in the paragraph. Point out the following:

> - The first two sentences explain what a sugar glider is.
>
> - The pronoun *it* is used to refer to the sugar glider.
>
> - A dash is used to emphasize what a marsupial is.
>
> - The writer most likely did research to find this information.

 DRAFT A PARAGRAPH THAT EXPLAINS   Have children use their sentences, filled-in charts, and what they now know to write a paragraph that explains how they have changed since they were younger.

WRITING TRAIT **CONVENTIONS**   As children write their drafts, encourage them to use correct pronouns and correct grammar, punctuation, and spelling. Tell them that they will also be able to correct any mistakes when they revise and edit later.

CONFER WITH CHILDREN   Meet with children, helping them as they write their paragraph that explains. Offer encouragement for what they are doing well and make constructive suggestions for improving an aspect of writing, as needed.

Objectives
- *To draft a paragraph that explains*
- *To group related ideas and maintain a consistent focus*
- *To include details that tell more about the main idea*

 ### Writing Prompt

Explain   Have children write a sentence that explains why people stay away from rain forest frogs.

▲ Writer's Companion, Lesson 14

Day at a Glance

Day
4

 phonics and Spelling

- Introduce: Syllable Pattern VCCV
- Review: *r*-Controlled Vowel /ûr/*ir*, *ur*, *er*, *ear*

High-Frequency Words

- Review: interesting, thumb, touch, care, sweat, father

Fluency

- Phrasing
- "Rain Forest Babies," *Student Edition*, pp. 428–445

Comprehension

Review: Fiction and Nonfiction

Robust Vocabulary

- Review: *dappled, entranced, trooped, circling, adorable, assortment, habitat, immense*

Grammar

- Review: Pronouns

Writing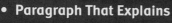

- Paragraph That Explains

Warm-Up Routines

 Oral Language

Objective *To listen attentively and respond appropriately to oral communication*

Question of the Day

Why should you be kind to animals?

Encourage children to share their ideas about why it is important to be kind to animals. Use the following prompts:

- **How do you treat animals that you know, such as pets? Tell why.**

- **When you see an animal that you don't know, what do you do? Why?**

- **Would you want to be treated the way you treat animals? Why or why not?**

Then have children complete the following sentence frame to explain their reasons.

I am kind to animals because _____.

Read Aloud

Objective *To listen for a purpose*

BIG BOOK OF RHYMES AND POEMS   Display "Always Be Kind to Animals" on page 28 and read the title. Tell children to listen for the poet's reasons for being kind. Then read the poem aloud. Explain that *furthermore* means "also" or "in addition." Invite children to tell the poet's reasons for being kind to animals. (Animals have feelings; animals bite.) Then read the poem again, and invite children to join in.

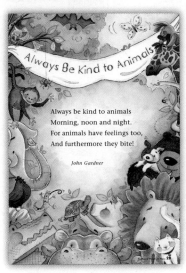

▲ **Big Book of Rhymes and Poems, p. 28**

Word Wall

Objective *To read high-frequency words*

REVIEW HIGH-FREQUENCY WORDS   Arrange the words *interesting*, *thumb*, *touch*, *care*, *sweat*, and *father* in two columns. Divide the class into two groups. Have children in the first group choral-read the first column of words, snapping their fingers to keep time. Have the second group do the same with the second column of words. Then have the groups switch columns and repeat.

Syllable Pattern VCCV phonics

5-DAY PHONICS	
DAY 1	Reintroduce /ûr/ir, ur, er, ear
DAY 2	Word Building with /ûr/ir, ur, er, ear
DAY 3	Word Building with /ûr/ir, ur, er, ear
DAY 4	**VCCV; Review /ûr/ir, ur, er, ear**
DAY 5	VCCV; Review /ûr/ir, ur, er, ear

Objectives

- *To identify the VCCV pattern in two-syllable words*
- *To read longer words with the VCCV pattern*

Skill Trace

 Tested **Syllable Pattern VCCV**

Introduce	T78
Review	T88, T340, T350

Syllable Pattern VCCV

Anna patted a furry puppy.

Shirley saw thirteen birds on a tree.

The children saw a hermit crab scurry to the sea.

Vincent spent thirty cents on popcorn.

Grade 2, Lesson 14   R72   Phonics

Transparency R72

Teach/Model

Routine Card 11 **REVIEW VCCV** Remind children that good readers look for familiar syllable patterns in words they do not know. Write the word *perturb* on the board. Ask: **How many syllables does this word have?** (two) Ask children to identify the vowels and the consonants between them. Label the vowels with **V** and the middle consonants with **C**.

per|turb
VC CV

Then model how to blend the syllables together to read *perturb*.

- Cover the second syllable and have children read /pûr/.
- Cover the first syllable and have children read /tûrb/.
- Then have children read the word, *perturb*.

Refer to Syllabication Card 8 (*Teacher Resource Book*, page 91) for more VCCV words.

Guided Practice

NONSENSE WORDS Write the words *turken, firley,* and *burfon* on the board. Note that the words are made-up. Have children identify the VCCV pattern and blend the syllables to read each word.

Practice/Apply

INDEPENDENT PRACTICE Display **Transparency R72** or write the sentences on the board or chart paper. Have children read the sentences aloud.

r-Controlled Vowel
/ûr/ ir, ur, er, ear phonics and Spelling

5-DAY SPELLING
DAY 1 Pretest
DAY 2 Word Building
DAY 3 State the Generalization
DAY 4 Review
DAY 5 Posttest

Build Words

REVIEW THE WORDS   Have children open their notebooks to the spelling words that they wrote on Day 3. Have them read the words several times and then close their notebooks.

MAP LETTERS TO SOUNDS   Have children follow your directions to change one element in each of the following words to make a spelling word. Have them write the spelling word on a sheet of paper. Then have a volunteer change the spelling of the word on the board so that children can self-check their spelling.

- Write *thud* on the board. Ask: **Which spelling word can you make by changing the third letter?** *(third)*

- Write *earn* on the board. Ask: **Which spelling word can you make by adding a letter at the beginning?** *(learn)*

- Write *such* on the board. Ask: **Which spelling word can you make by changing the second letter to letters that stand for the /ûr/ sound?** *(search)*

- Write *far* on the board. Ask: **Which spelling word can you make by changing the middle letter?** *(fur)*

Follow a similar procedure with the following words: *star (stir), turf (turn), barn (burn), skirt (shirt), hard (herd), bind (bird)*.

CHALLENGE WORDS   Write the first or second syllable of each challenge word on the board. Ask volunteers to spell each word in its entirety and write the missing letters.

BELOW-LEVEL

Focus on *r*-Controlled Vowels   Write the spelling words on the board, with blanks where the letters that stand for the /ûr/ sound should be. Then prompt children to complete each word, asking questions such as, "What letters can you add to *l _ _ _ n* to make *learn*?" Have children spell each completed word.

Objective

- *To use /ûr/ir, ur, er, ear, and other known letter-sounds to spell and write words*

Spelling Words

1. **fur***	6. **turn**
2. **shirt**	7. **herd***
3. **burn**	8. **third**
4. **stir**	9. **learn***
5. **bird**	10. **search**

Challenge Words

11. **perfect**	14. **circus**
12. **birthday**	15. **surprise***
13. **purple**	

* Words from "Rain Forest Babies"

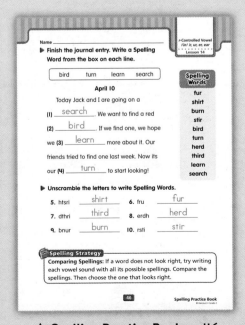

▲ Spelling Practice Book, p. 46

High-Frequency Words

Objective

- *To read high-frequency words*

REVIEW ✓ **Tested**

High-Frequency Words

care	sweat
father	thumb
interesting	touch

Review

READ WORDS   Display **Transparency R73.** Have children read the words at the top in order. Then point to the words at random and have children read them.

Practice/Apply

GUIDED PRACTICE   Talk about the illustration. Then track the print as you read aloud the sentences. Have children echo-read after you.

Then have children create their own sentences using the high-frequency words. Write each sentence on the board. Have children choral-read the sentences.

INDEPENDENT PRACTICE   Have children write three sentences, using one or more high-frequency words in each one. Ask them to share their sentences with a partner.

High-Frequency Words

interesting
thumb
touch
care
sweat
father

Martin went to the rain forest with his <u>father</u>.
It was hot, and soon they were covered with <u>sweat</u>.
Martin saw many <u>interesting</u> animals and plants.
He did not <u>touch</u> any of them, but one touched him.
A butterfly landed on his <u>thumb</u>!
Dad took <u>care</u> to leave the woods clean.

Grade 2, Lesson 14   R73   High-Frequency Words

Transparency R73

Fluency
Phrasing

Review

MODEL USING PHRASING Read aloud page 435 of "Rain Forest Babies." Point out the quotation marks, periods, dashes, and commas.

▲ Student Edition, pp. 428–445

Think Aloud The quotation marks, commas, and end marks on this page help me know which words should be grouped together. The quotation marks show that "four who can roar" should be read without pausing. Words between dashes should be grouped together, too. I paused for a moment when I reached the dashes—just as I was supposed to do—but I read the words between the dashes as a group, pausing only slightly at each comma. I paused slightly at the end of each sentence, too.

Practice/Apply

Routine Card 8

GUIDED PRACTICE Have children echo-read pages 434–435 with you, matching your expression and phrasing.

INDEPENDENT PRACTICE Have children read along with "Rain Forest Babies" on *Audiotext 2*. Have children practice reading the selection several times until they are able to read it with appropriate phrasing.

✓ MONITOR PROGRESS

Fluency

IF children have difficulty using proper phrasing,	**THEN** model how you identify phrases, and have children echo-read the phrases after you.

Small-Group Instruction, pp. S34–S35:

● **BELOW-LEVEL:** Reteach ● **ON-LEVEL:** Reinforce ● **ADVANCED:** Extend

Objective

• *To use proper phrasing to read fluently in a manner that sounds like natural speech*

BELOW-LEVEL

Echo-Read On the board, write sentences from the story that children have trouble reading fluently. Read each sentence aloud. Have children repeat it, matching your speed, phrasing, and expression. Repeat until children can read each sentence effortlessly.

Fiction and Nonfiction
Comprehension

Objectives

- *To distinguish fiction from nonfiction*
- *To know the basic characteristics of fiction and nonfiction*

Skill Trace

 Tested **Fiction and Nonfiction**

Introduce	T212–T213
Reteach	S36–S37
Review	T248, T262, T272, T298–T299, T330, T344, T354, T404, T425
Test	Theme 3
Maintain	Theme 4, T271

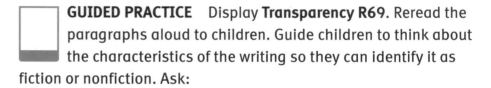

Review

EXPLAIN FICTION AND NONFICTION Remind children that there are two main kinds of writing—fiction and nonfiction. Ask: **How is fiction different from nonfiction?** (Fiction is about made-up characters and events. Nonfiction is about real people, real places, and real events. It gives information about a topic and has ideas that are supported by facts.) Ask children why authors write fiction and nonfiction. (They write fiction to tell a story for readers to enjoy and nonfiction to give readers information.)

Practice/Apply

GUIDED PRACTICE Display **Transparency R69**. Reread the paragraphs aloud to children. Guide children to think about the characteristics of the writing so they can identify it as fiction or nonfiction. Ask:

- **Is a rain forest a real place or a make-believe place?** (real)

- **Why do you think the author wrote this story?** (to give readers information about rain forests)

- **Is this story fiction or nonfiction?** (nonfiction) **How do you know?** (It gives information about a real place—rain forests—and has ideas that are supported by facts.)

INDEPENDENT PRACTICE Ask children to tell whether "Rain Forest Babies" is fiction or nonfiction and to tell how they know. Ask children to give an example from the selection to support each of their reasons. (Possible response: Nonfiction. The author writes about real animals, such as elephants, macaws, and sugar gliders, that live in a real place, the rain forest. The author gives information and facts about rain-forest animals. For example, she writes that the biggest baby in the rain forest is the elephant calf, which weighs three hundred pounds at birth.)

Fiction and Nonfiction

Rain Forests

Have you ever wondered what a rain forest would be like? Picture trees that stretch so high you cannot see their tops. Raindrops fall onto the leaves of lush, green plants. Water drips from long vines. Birds squawk, monkeys chatter, insects hum, and frogs croak. These are some things you might find in a rain forest.

A rain forest is a woodland where more than 70 inches of rain falls each year. Rain forests are in many parts of the world. They are in cool places and in hot places.

Rain forests are a major source for fresh water. Rain forest plants make lots of oxygen. People need to breathe oxygen to stay alive. Rain forests also provide people with resources for food, medicine, and building. Half of Earth's plants and animals live in rain forests. So rain forests are important to both people and animals.

Grade 2, Lesson 14 | R69 | Comprehension

Transparency R69

Build Robust Vocabulary

Review Robust Vocabulary

USE VOCABULARY IN DIFFERENT CONTEXTS Remind children of the Student-Friendly Explanations of the Vocabulary Words. Then discuss the words, using the following activities:

adorable, immense Tell children that you will name some things. If something is adorable, children should say, "Adorable." If something is immense, children should say, "Immense."

a whale   a puppy   a giant   a mountain

entranced Tell children that you will describe some things. If children think that they would be entranced by the thing, they should say, "I would be entranced!" If not, they should remain silent.

a bird building a nest   **a new video game**

a boy doing dishes   **a talking cow**

trooped Tell children that you will say some sentences. If the people in the sentences trooped, children should say, "They trooped." If not, children should remain silent.

The people waited in line.   **All the children got onto the bus.**

A couple of people danced.   **Groups of shoppers walked from store to store.**

circling Tell children that you will name some actions. If the actions describe circling, children should say, "Circling." If not, they should remain silent.

walking around a pond   diving into a pool

flying around a town   driving around the block

Objective

• *To review robust vocabulary*

REVIEW ✔ [Tested]

Vocabulary: Lesson 14

dappled	adorable
entranced	assortment
trooped	habitat
circling	immense

▼ **Student-Friendly Explanations**

Student-Friendly Explanations

dappled	If something is dappled, it has spots, streaks, or patches of different colors or shades.
entranced	If you are entranced by something, it has delighted or amazed you.
trooped	If you trooped someplace, you moved along with a group of people.
circling	If something is circling you, it is moving around you.
adorable	If something is very cute, it is adorable.
assortment	If you see a variety or mixture of things, you see an assortment.
habitat	If a plant or an animal lives in a particular place in nature, that is its habitat.
immense	If something is really big or huge, it is immense.

Grade 2, Theme 3   R74   Vocabulary

Transparency R74

Grammar
Pronouns

5-DAY GRAMMAR

DAY 1	Define Pronouns
DAY 2	*He, She, It, We, They*
DAY 3	Using *I* and *Me*
DAY 4	**Apply to Writing**
DAY 5	Weekly Review

Objectives

- *To identify pronouns*
- *To use pronouns correctly in writing*

Daily Proofreading

Zoe and zeke turned eight in october.

(Zeke, October)

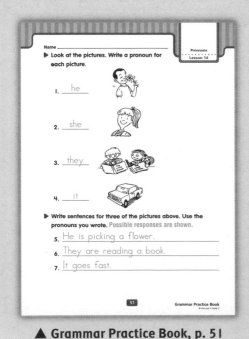

▲ **Grammar Practice Book, p. 51**

Review

DISCUSS PRONOUNS   Review what children have learned about the pronouns *I, he, she, it, we, they,* and *me,* using the following points:

- Use *he* to tell about a man or boy and *she* to tell about a woman or girl.

- Use *it* to tell about an animal or a thing.

- Use *they* to tell about more than one.

- Use *we* to tell about yourself and someone or something else.

- Use *I* and *me* to tell about yourself.

Write the following sentences on the board:

> **Beth said, "Dad and I are going to the woods."**
>
> **Ray also wanted to go. So he went with Beth and Dad.**
>
> **They saw a chipmunk in the woods. It was so cute!**

Have children point at and read aloud each pronoun.

Practice/Apply

GUIDED PRACTICE   Tell children that you are going to write three sentences about animals and people you see at a park, and you will include a pronoun in each sentence. Model writing the first sentence. Elicit additional ideas from children. After you write each sentence, model orally how to check that the correct pronoun is used.

INDEPENDENT PRACTICE   Ask children to write three sentences about the kinds of things they might see in a park. Tell children to use a pronoun in each sentence. Have partners exchange sentences and check that pronouns are used correctly.

5-DAY WRITING

DAY 1	Introduce
DAY 2	Prewrite
DAY 3	Draft
DAY 4	**Revise**
DAY 5	Revise

Writing
Paragraph That Explains

Write a Paragraph That Explains

WRITE Have children continue writing their paragraph that explains. Remind them to include facts in their writing so the reader gains information.

WRITING TRAIT → **CONVENTIONS** Remind children to use correct grammar, spelling, and punctuation in their paragraphs. Have them check that they use pronouns correctly.

REVISE Have children read their paragraph that explains to a partner. They can use the list of criteria for a paragraph that explains to improve their writing.

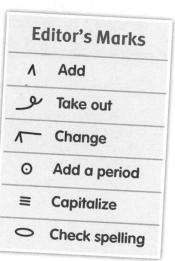

Paragraph That Explains

- The topic sentence tells about the main idea.
- The other sentences give more details about the main idea.
- The writer may do research to find facts.

Tell children to make notes on their drafts of the changes they will make. Encourage them to use Editor's Marks. Remind them to check that they have used pronouns correctly. Save children's paragraphs so they can continue revising on Day 5.

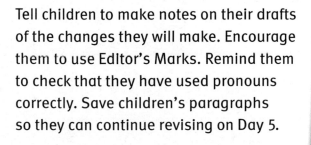

Editor's Marks

∧	Add
⤲	Take out
⌃—	Change
⊙	Add a period
≡	Capitalize
⬯	Check spelling

Objectives

- *To revise a draft of a paragraph that explains*
- *To use pronouns correctly*
- *To edit a draft for appropriate grammar, spelling, and punctuation*

Writing Prompt

Explain Have children write to explain a favorite game or sport.

E L L

Editor's Marks If children are hesitant to revise their work, model using Editor's Marks to revise. Speak slowly as you show and explain what you are doing. Explain why you are making changes. Then have children demonstrate how to use the Editor's Marks to revise their writing.

Day at a Glance

Day 5

phonics and Spelling

- Review: Syllable Pattern VCCV
- Posttest: *r*-Controlled Vowel /ûr/*ir, ur, er, ear*

High-Frequency Words

- Cumulative Review

Fluency

- Phrasing
- "Rain Forest Babies," *Student Edition*, pp. 428–445

Read!

Comprehension

Focus Skill

Review: Fiction and Nonfiction
- *Read-Aloud Anthology:* "Laurel's Rainforest"

Robust Vocabulary

- Cumulative Review

Grammar

- Review: Pronouns

Writing

- Paragraph That Explains

Warm-Up Routines

Oral Language

Objective *To listen attentively and respond appropriately to oral communication*

Question of the Day

Imagine that you get a new pet. What should you do to care for it?

Use the following prompts to help children tell about ways to care for pets. List their ideas on the board.

- **What are some things that a new pet needs?**
- **Why is it important to take care of a pet?**

Read Aloud

Objective *To identify rhymes in poetry*

BIG BOOK OF RHYMES AND POEMS Display "Always Be Kind to Animals" on page 28. Ask children to listen for words that rhyme. Then read aloud the poem. Guide children to identify the rhyming words *night* and *bite*. Then read the poem again, encouraging children to join in.

▲ **Big Book of Rhymes and Poems, p. 28**

Word Wall

Objective *To read high-frequency words*

REVIEW HIGH-FREQUENCY WORDS Review the words *interesting*, *thumb*, *touch*, *care*, *sweat*, and *father*. Point to a card at random, and have children read the word. Have them read the words several times.

interesting	touch	sweat
thumb	care	father

Syllable Pattern VCCV

phonics *and Spelling*

5-DAY PHONICS	
DAY 1	Reintroduce /ûr/ir, ur, er, ear
DAY 2	Word Building with /ûr/ir, ur, er, ear
DAY 3	Word Building with /ûr/ir, ur, er, ear
DAY 4	VCCV; Review /ûr/ir, ur, er, ear
DAY 5	VCCV; Review /ûr/ir, ur, er, ear

Objectives

- *To identify the VCCV pattern in two-syllable words*
- *To read two-syllable words with the VCCV pattern*

Skill Trace

 Tested **Syllable Pattern VCCV**

Introduce	T78
Review	T88, T340, T350

Review

READ VCCV WORDS Write the words *perfect* and *compare* on the board. Guide children to label the VCCV pattern in each word and read it aloud.

Practice/Apply

GUIDED PRACTICE Write the following words on the board: *circus, letter, pearl, church, tiger,* and *parrot.* Then make a chart as shown. Guide children to sort the words and add them to the chart.

VCCV Words	Not VCCV Words
circus	pearl
letter	church
parrot	tiger

INDEPENDENT PRACTICE Have children read aloud the words in the chart.

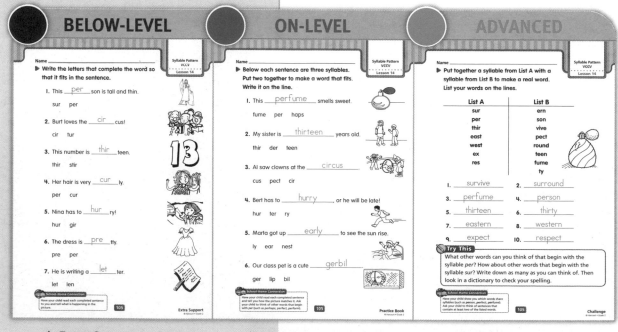

BELOW-LEVEL

▲ Extra Support, p. 105

ON-LEVEL

▲ Practice Book, p. 105

ADVANCED

▲ Challenge, p. 105

E L L

- Group children according to academic levels, and assign one of the pages on the left.

- Clarify any unfamiliar concepts as necessary. See *ELL Teacher Guide* Lesson 14 for support in scaffolding instruction.

Day 5

5-DAY SPELLING
DAY 1 Pretest
DAY 2 Word Building
DAY 3 State the Generalization
DAY 4 Review
DAY 5 Posttest

r-Controlled Vowel
/ûr/ ir, ur, er, ear phonics and Spelling

Assess

POSTTEST Assess children's progress. Use the dictation sentences from Day 1.

Words with r-Controlled Vowel /ûr/ir, ur, er, ear

1.	fur	My cat's **fur** is soft and silky.
2.	shirt	Rajiv bought a **shirt** at the mall.
3.	burn	Dad heated the soup slowly so it would not **burn**.
4.	stir	Dara helped Grandma **stir** the pancake batter.
5.	bird	The ostrich is the largest **bird** in the world.
6.	turn	Today it is Omar's **turn** to erase the board.
7.	herd	Devon saw a **herd** of cattle at her uncle's ranch.
8.	third	My family's apartment is on the **third** floor.
9.	learn	I want to **learn** how to surf.
10.	search	Everyone helped Ricardo **search** for his lost dog.

ADVANCED

Challenge Words Use the challenge words in these dictation sentences.

11.	perfect	A warm, sunny day is **perfect** for a picnic.
12.	birthday	Sonia's **birthday** is in October.
13.	purple	My favorite color is **purple**.
14.	circus	Mia saw elephants and clowns at the **circus**.
15.	surprise	Rafi's parents gave him a puppy as a **surprise**.

WRITING APPLICATION
Have children write and illustrate a silly sentence using one or more of the spelling words.

Would a bird like a fur shirt?

Objective

- *To use /ûr/ir, ur, er, ear, and other known letter-sounds to spell and write words*

Spelling Words

1.	fur*	6.	turn
2.	shirt	7.	herd*
3.	burn	8.	third
4.	stir	9.	learn*
5.	bird	10.	search

Challenge Words

11.	perfect	14.	circus
12.	birthday	15.	surprise*
13.	purple		

* Words from "Rain Forest Babies"

 High-Frequency Words

Objectives

- *To read high-frequency words*
- *To explore word relationships*

REVIEW ✓ Tested

High-Frequency Words

above	care
shoes	father
tough	interesting
wash	sweat
wear	thumb
woman	touch
young	

Cumulative Review

REINFORCE WORD RECOGNITION   Write on the board the high-frequency words for Lessons 13 and 14. Point to words at random, and ask volunteers to read them.

SORT WORDS   Guide children in sorting the words into columns according to the number of syllables. Then have them read the words in each column.

1 Syllable		2 Syllables	4 Syllables
touch	care	woman	interesting
sweat	tough	above	
wear	young	father	
shoes	wash		
thumb			

- Ask: **Which two words begin with vowels?** (above, interesting)
- Ask: **Which three words begin with two consonants?** (shoes, thumb, sweat)
- Ask: **Which word has the word *rest* in it?** (interesting)
- Ask: **Which three words begin with the /w/ sound?** (wear, wash, woman)
- Ask: **Which word has the word *car* in it?** (care)
- Ask: **Which two words begin with the /t/ sound?** (touch, tough)
- Ask: **Which word begins with the /sh/ sound?** (shoes)

Fluency

Phrasing

Readers' Theater

PERFORM "RAIN FOREST BABIES" To help children improve their fluency using phrasing, have them perform "Rain Forest Babies" as Readers' Theater. Use the following procedures:

▲ **Student Edition, pp. 428–445**

- Discuss with children how you use proper phrasing to guide the listener to understand important ideas.

- Have groups of three children read the story together. One child should read the sections "Tropical Rain Forests of the World," "Macaw," and "Sugar Glider." Have a second child read the sections "Elephant" and "Frog," and a third child read the sections "Tiger" and "Kangaroo."

- Monitor the groups as they read. Provide feedback and support, paying particular attention to how readers group ideas, or phrases, together.

Develop Vocabulary Remind children to keep number and time words and descriptive phrases together so listeners will understand important ideas. Demonstrate with the phrase "fluffy 'baby feathers' called *down*" from page 436.

Objective

- *To use proper phrasing to read fluently in a manner that sounds like natural speech*

✓ ASSESSMENT

Monitoring Progress

Periodically, take a timed sample of children's oral reading and record the number of words read correctly per minute. Children should accurately read approximately 72 words per minute in the middle of Grade 2.

Fluency Support Materials

Fluency Builders, Grade 2, Lesson 14

 Audiotext *Student Edition* selections are available on *Audiotext 2.*

 **Strategic Intervention Teacher Guide,** Lesson 14

Fiction and Nonfiction
Comprehension

Objectives

- *To distinguish fiction from nonfiction*
- *To know the basic characteristics of fiction and nonfiction*

Skill Trace

Tested **Fiction and Nonfiction**

Introduce	T212–T213
Reintroduce	S36–S37
Review	**T248, T262, T272, T298–T299, T330, T344, T354, T404, T425**
Test	Theme 3
Maintain	Theme 4, T271

E L L

Build Background If children have difficulty understanding the concepts of made-up and real, show children familiar books. For each book, point to and name the characters, and identify them as made-up or real. Do the same for the setting and story events. Explain that if one or more parts of a story are made-up, then the whole story is fiction.

Review

REVIEW THE SKILL Remind children that fiction is about made-up characters and events, and that authors write fiction to tell a story for readers to enjoy. Lead children to define nonfiction as writing about real events and real people or animals. Point out that authors write nonfiction to give readers information.

▲ **Read-Aloud Anthology, "Laurel's Rainforest," p. 52**

SET A PURPOSE FOR LISTENING Guide children to set a purpose for listening that includes

- listening to find out whether the people, places, and events in "Laurel's Rainforest" are real or made-up.

- listening to decide whether "Laurel's Rainforest" is fiction or nonfiction.

Practice/Apply

GUIDED PRACTICE As you read aloud "Laurel's Rainforest," record details about the people, places, and events in a chart.

Fiction	Nonfiction
Made-up characters: Laurel; her mother; her father Made-up events that seem real	Real place: Costa Rican rain forest

INDEPENDENT PRACTICE Have children use the chart to tell whether the people, places, and events in "Laurel's Rainforest" are real or made-up. Ask whether "Laurel's Rainforest" is fiction or nonfiction and why. (Possible response: "Laurel's Rainforest" takes place in a real place. The events seem real: Laurel sees animals and plants that live in a rain forest. But the characters are made-up, so I know this must be fiction.)

Build Robust Vocabulary

Cumulative Review

REINFORCE MEANINGS   Ask children to respond to the following:

- Would an animal be distraught if it was taken out of its habitat?
- Why might you take a route circling a park or a trail?
- What might you do if you had a garden with a wilting assortment of flowers?

MAKE WORD WEBS   Using **Transparency GO9**, guide children to complete word webs for *immense* and *semblance*. Write *immense* in the center of a word web, and have children name things that are immense. Write their responses in the web.

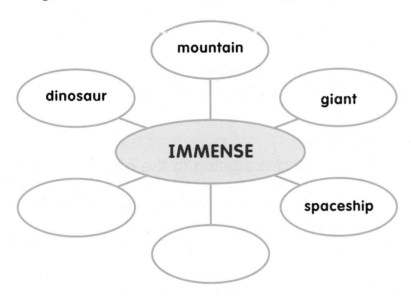

Then have children create their own web for *semblance*. Have them fill in the web with things that are like each other.

Objective
- *To review robust vocabulary*

REVIEW Tested
Vocabulary

Lesson 13	Lesson 14
wilting	dappled
flitted	entranced
swirling	trooped
trance	circling
route	adorable
semblance	assortment
distraught	habitat
improvise	immense

 MONITOR PROGRESS

Build Robust Vocabulary

IF children do not demonstrate understanding of the words and have difficulty using them, | **THEN** model using each word in several sentences, and have children repeat each sentence.

Small-Group Instruction, pp. S38–S39:

- **BELOW-LEVEL:** Reteach
- **ON-LEVEL:** Reinforce
- **ADVANCED:** Extend

Grammar
Pronouns

5-DAY GRAMMAR	
DAY 1	Define Pronouns
DAY 2	*He, She, It, We, They*
DAY 3	Using *I* and *Me*
DAY 4	Apply to Writing
DAY 5	**Weekly Review**

Objectives

- *To identify pronouns*
- *To use pronouns correctly*

Daily Proofreading

We will go to the Beach on sunday.

(beach, Sunday)

 Language Arts Checkpoint

If children have difficulty with the concepts, see pages S40–S41 to reteach.

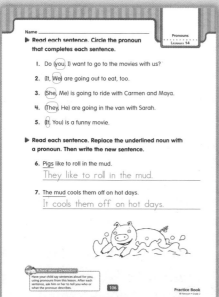

▲ Practice Book, p. 106

Review

REVIEW PRONOUNS   Write these pronouns on the board: *he, she, it, we, they, I,* and *me.* Use the following questions to review pronouns. Have volunteers write answers on the board. Ask:

- **What takes the place of a noun?** (pronoun)
- **Which pronoun tells about a man or boy?** (*he*) **a woman or girl?** (*she*)
- **What does *it* tell about?** (an animal or thing)
- **What word tells about more than one?** (*they*)
- **What does *we* tell about?** (yourself and someone else)
- **What pronouns tell about you?** (*I, me*)

Practice/Apply

GUIDED PRACTICE   Model correcting the pronoun in the following sentence.

> **Rosa said, "I are going to the beach."** (*We* or *They*)

Write the following sentences on the board. Ask volunteers to help you correct the pronouns in each sentence.

> Me saw a baby bird. (*I*)
>
> He was a seagull. (*It*)
>
> They is a nice brother! (*He*)

INDEPENDENT PRACTICE   Have partners take turns saying sentences with nouns. Have one partner say the sentence and the other rewrite the sentence using the correct pronoun. Then have partners switch and repeat the process.

 # Writing
Paragraph That Explains

5-DAY WRITING

DAY 1	Introduce
DAY 2	Prewrite
DAY 3	Draft
DAY 4	Revise
DAY 5	Revise

Revise

REVISE A PARAGRAPH THAT EXPLAINS Explain that good writers look back at their writing to be sure it is clear and meets its purpose. Tell children to reread their paragraph that explains and ask themselves these questions:

- Does the topic sentence tell about the main idea?

- Have I included sentences that give more details about the main idea?

- Have I included facts from research?

WRITING TRAIT **CONVENTIONS** Encourage children to read aloud their paragraphs to be sure that pronouns are used correctly. Encourage children to revise their paragraph that explains to correct convention errors and add any missing information.

NOTE: A 4-point rubric appears on page R8.

SCORING RUBRIC

	6	5	4	3	2	1
FOCUS	Completely focused, purposeful.	Focused on topic and purpose.	Generally focused on topic and purpose.	Somewhat focused on topic and purpose.	Related to topic but does not maintain focus.	Lacks focus and purpose.
ORGANIZATION	Ideas progress logically; paper conveys sense of completeness.	Organization mostly clear; paper gives sense of completeness.	Organization mostly clear, but some lapses occur; may seem unfinished.	Some sense of organization; seems unfinished.	Little sense of organization.	Little or no sense of organization.
SUPPORT	Strong, specific details; clear, exact language; freshness of expression.	Strong, specific details; clear, exact language.	Adequate support and word choice.	Limited supporting details; limited word choice.	Few supporting details; limited word choice.	Little development; limited or unclear word choice.
CONVENTIONS	Varied sentences; few, if any, errors.	Varied sentences; few errors.	Some sentence variety; few errors.	Simple sentence structures; some errors.	Simple sentence structures; many errors.	Unclear sentence structures; many errors.

REPRODUCIBLE RUBRICS for specific writing purposes and presentations are available on pages R2–R8.

Objectives
- *To revise a paragraph that explains*
- *To use pronouns correctly*

 ## Writing Prompt

Write a Paragraph Have children write another paragraph that explains.

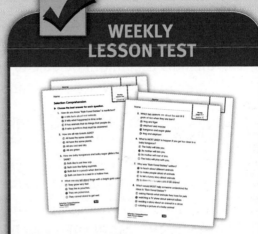 ## WEEKLY LESSON TEST

▲ Weekly Lesson Tests, pp. 147–158
- Selection Comprehension
- Phonics and Spelling
- High-Frequency Words
- Focus Skill
- Robust Vocabulary
- Grammar
- Fluency Passage

 GO online For prescriptions, see pp. A2–A6. Also available electronically on StoryTown Online Assessment and ExamView.

 Podcasting: Assessing Fluency

Leveled Readers

Reinforcing Skills and Strategies

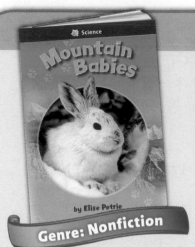
by Elise Petrie

Genre: Nonfiction

BELOW-LEVEL

Mountain Babies

SUMMARY Mountains are home to baby brown bears, lynx, snowshoe hares, mountain goats, and porcupines.

 phonics *r*-Controlled Vowel /ûr/*ir, ur, er, ear*

• High-Frequency Words

Focus Skill Fiction and Nonfiction

Before Reading

BUILD BACKGROUND/SET PURPOSE Ask children to describe mountains. Make sure that snowy peaks are mentioned. Ask for ideas about the kinds of animals that might be able to live in snowy mountains. Then guide children to preview the story and set a purpose for reading it.

Reading the Book

PAGE 3 **FICTION AND NONFICTION** **How can you tell from the very first page that this book is nonfiction?** (There is a photograph of a real place, and the sentence gives facts.)

PAGES 1–14 **MAIN IDEA AND DETAILS** **What do all the pictures and words in this book tell about?** (different baby animals that live in the mountains)

REREAD FOR FLUENCY Have partners take turns reading the sentences about each kind of animal. While one partner reads, the other should point to details in the photograph. Remind children to read phrases rather than word by word.

Think Critically *(See inside back cover for questions.)*

1 **NOTE DETAILS** baby brown bears, and baby mountain goats

2 **GENERALIZE** Responses will vary.

3 **TEXT STRUCTURE** Responses will vary.

4 **EXPRESS PERSONAL OPINION** Responses will vary.

5 **FICTION AND NONFICTION** Responses will vary.

LEVELED READERS TEACHER GUIDE

Name _____
▶ Write the word that best completes each sentence.

thumb interesting much

1. There are many ___interesting___ animals in the wild.

sweat care thumb

2. Some animals even have a ___thumb___

sweat father much

3. Did you know that birds don't ___sweat___ ?

thumb very sweat

4. There is ___much___ we can learn by watching animals.

Interesting Sweat Father

5. ___Father___ penguins take care of the young.

thumb care father

6. They have to ___care___ for the eggs.

▲ High-Frequency Words, p. 5

Name _____
▶ Write facts from *Mountain Babies* on the lines below.

Facts About Bears

1. Accept all reasonable answers.

2. _____

Facts About Lynx

1. Accept all reasonable answers.

2. _____

Facts About Porcupines

1. Accept all reasonable answers.

2. _____

▲ Comprehension, p. 6

www.harcourtschool.com/storytown

★ **Leveled Readers Online Database**
Searchable by Genre, Skill, Vocabulary, Level, or Title
★ **Student Activities and Teacher Resources, online**

ON-LEVEL

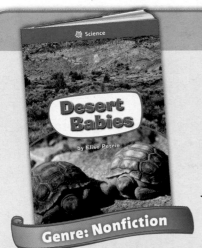

Desert Babies

SUMMARY   This book describes adaptations of desert animals and their babies: desert tortoise, bighorn sheep, roadrunner, spadefoot toad, and jackrabbit.

Genre: Nonfiction

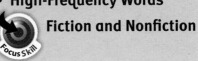

- **phonics**   *r*-Controlled Vowel /ûr/*ir, ur, er, ear*
- **High-Frequency Words**

  Fiction and Nonfiction

Before Reading

BUILD BACKGROUND/SET PURPOSE   Write the word *desert*, and have children name any desert characteristics they know. Explain that the one thing all deserts have in common is very little rainfall. Ask what would be most important to animals that live in dry lands like deserts. Then guide children to preview the story and set a purpose for reading it.

Reading the Book

PAGES 3–5   **FICTION AND NONFICTION**   **How can you tell that this book is nonfiction?** (It has photographs of real places and animals. The heading "Desert Tortoise Babies" tells you about the information on the pages.)

PAGES 8–9   **MAIN IDEA AND DETAILS**   **How do roadrunner parents help their babies?** (The parents keep the eggs in a safe place. When the eggs hatch, the parents give their babies water and food.)

REREAD FOR FLUENCY   Have partners take turns choosing a favorite picture and reading the accompanying text aloud. Remind them that they should read groups of words that go together as phrases.

Think Critically
(See inside back cover for questions.)

1. **NOTE DETAILS**   Females hatch in warm sand, males in cool.
2. **SEQUENCE**   Parents make the baby drink water from their stomachs.
3. **COMPARE AND CONTRAST**   They go under the sand to stay cool.
4. **FICTION AND NONFICTION**   Responses will vary.
5. **EXPRESS PERSONAL OPINION**   Responses will vary.

LEVELED READERS TEACHER GUIDE

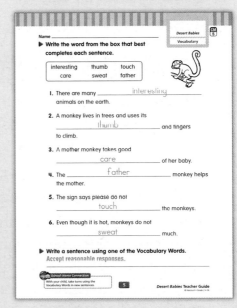

▲ **High-Frequency Words, p. 5**

▲ **Comprehension, p. 6**

Leveled Readers
Reinforcing Skills and Strategies

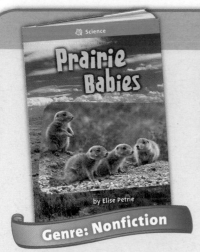

 **ADVANCED**

Prairie Babies

SUMMARY   This book describes adaptations of prairie animals and their babies: bison, prong-horns, coyotes, prairie dogs, and burrowing animals.

Genre: Nonfiction

by Elise Petrie

- **phonics** *r*-Controlled Vowel /ûr/*ir, ur, er, ear*
- **High-Frequency Words**

  Fiction and Nonfiction

Focus Skill

Before Reading

BUILD BACKGROUND/SET PURPOSE   Tell children that a prairie is a large area of grassland. Then guide children to preview the story and set a purpose for reading it.

Reading the Book

PAGES 4–5 **FICTION AND NONFICTION**   **If this were a fiction book about bison babies, how might it be different from this nonfiction book?** (In fiction, the bison babies might talk to each other and act like people. In nonfiction, the author gives facts about bison babies.)

PAGES 1–14   **MAIN IDEA AND DETAILS**   **What is true about all the animal babies shown in this book?** (They need to stay safe and get food from their parents.)

REREAD FOR FLUENCY   Groups of two or three children may take turns playing the role of story-hour librarian, reading portions of this book aloud and displaying the accompanying photos. Remind children to try to make the information sound clear and interesting.

Think Critically   *(See inside back cover for questions.)*

1. **NOTE DETAILS**   The largest animal on the prairie is the bison.
2. **CAUSE/EFFECT**   The chicks make sounds like rattlesnakes.
3. **AUTHOR'S PURPOSE**   Responses will vary.
4. **FICTION AND NONFICTION**   Responses will vary.
5. **EXPRESS PERSONAL OPINION**   Responses will vary.

LEVELED READERS TEACHER GUIDE

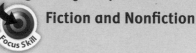

Name _____

▶ Write the word from the box that completes each sentence.

| interesting | thumb | much |
| care | sweat | father |

1. The baby panda is one of the most ___interesting___ animals in the world.
2. There is still ___much___ to learn about them.
3. When they are born they not much bigger than a ___thumb___
4. They need a lot of special ___care___ when they are babies.
5. When they get bigger, ___much___ of their food is bamboo.

▶ Write two sentences using the words *sweat* and *father*.

1. _____
2. _____

▲ **High-Frequency Words, p. 5**

Name _____
Make a Diorama

▶ A diorama is a mini world in a box. Here is how to build your own prairie diorama

What You Need
- Shoebox,
- cardboard, paper
- Scissors
- Markers or Paint
- Magazines
- Glue

What to Do

step 1 Use paper or magazines to find pictures of grass and sky.

step 2 Glue the scene of grass and sky to the inside back and sides of the shoe box.

step 3 Draw two prairie babies on cardboard. Draw tabs on their feet. Color and cut them out.

step 4 Bend tabs backwards and tape or glue to the floor of the shoebox.

step 5 Display your diorama at home or at school.

step 6 Tell your friends about baby prairie animals.

▲ **Comprehension, p. 6**

E L L

Genre: Nonfiction

Rainforest Homes

SUMMARY Rainforests are home to tall trees and animals that depend on the trees for food and shelter. Plants, frogs, monkeys, birds, bats, snakes, cats, insects, spiders, and people live in the rainforest.

- **Build Background**
- **Concept Vocabulary**
- **Scaffolded Language Development**

Before Reading

BUILD BACKGROUND/SET PURPOSE Write the word *rainforest*. Point to each part of the compound word as you ask children what a *forest* that gets a lot of *rain* might be like. Then guide children to preview the story and set a purpose for reading it.

Reading the Book

PAGE 7 MAKE INFERENCES Why do monkeys live high up in the trees? (They are safe from animals on the ground that might eat them. They find fruit and flowers to eat in the high branches.)

PAGES 1–14 FICTION AND NONFICTION How can you tell that this book is nonfiction? (It has photographs of real rainforests. It has facts about plants and animals.)

REREAD FOR FLUENCY Have partners take turns reading a page at a time and pointing to elements in the pictures that are described. Remind children to read groups of words rather than word by word.

Scaffolded Language Development

(See inside back cover for teacher-led activity.)

Provide additional examples and explanation as needed.

LEVELED READERS TEACHER GUIDE

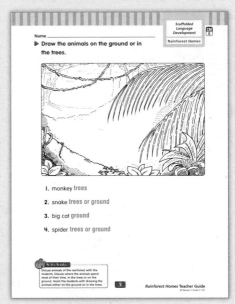

▲ **Scaffolded Language Development, p. 5**

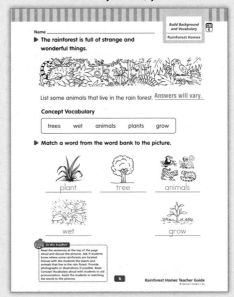

▲ **Build Background and Vocabulary, p. 6**

Lesson 15
Theme Review and Vocabulary Builder

WEEK AT A GLANCE

 **Phonics**
REVIEW
- Digraphs /ch/*ch, tch*; /sh/*sh*; /th/*th*
- Long Vowel /ē/*ey, y*
- Consonants /s/*c*; /j/*g, dge*
- *r*–Controlled Vowel /ûr/*ir, ur, er, ear*

 **Spelling**
REVIEW
- Words with *ch, tch, sh*, and *th*
- Words with *ey* and *y*
- Words with Soft *c* and Soft *g*
- Words with *ir, ur, er*, and *ear*

High-Frequency Words
REVIEW   *draw, picture, question, minute, bought, worry, especially, sure, imagine, favorite, year, enjoy, cook, board, popular, expensive, wear, tough, woman, young, shoes, wash, above, interesting, thumb, touch, care, sweat, father*

Reading
READERS' THEATER
"A Birthday Mystery"   MYSTERY
COMPREHENSION STRATEGIES
Reading Your Science Book:
"The Life Cycle of a Frog"   SCIENCE TEXTBOOK

Fluency
REVIEW
- Punctuation
- Phrasing

Comprehension
REVIEW
-  Author's Purpose
- Ask Questions
- Fiction and Nonfiction
- Monitor Comprehension: Reread

Robust Vocabulary
INTRODUCE *distrust, witness, lock, beneath, bewildered, evasive, mull, startle*

Grammar
REVIEW
- Abbreviations
- Singular Possessive Nouns
- Plural Possessive Nouns
- Pronouns

Writing: Revise and Publish
REVIEW Writing Trait: Voice
REVIEW Writing Trait: Conventions

 = Focus Skill   = Focus Strategy   = Tested Skill

Digital
CLASSROOM

 www.harcourtschool.com/storytown
To go along with your print program

FOR THE TEACHER

Prepare Professional Development

 Videos for Podcasting

Plan & Organize Online TE & Planning Resources*

Teach Transparencies

for electronic projection

Assess Online Assessment*

with Student Tracking System and Prescriptions

FOR THE STUDENT

Read  Student eBook*

 Strategic Intervention Interactive Reader

 Leveled Readers

Practice & Apply Splash into Phonics CD-ROM

 Comprehension Expedition CD-ROM

 Also available on CD-ROM

Literature Resources

STUDENT EDITION

 eBook STUDENT EDITION

Readers' Theater
MYSTERY

Reading Your Science Textbook

 ◀ **Audiotext** *Student Edition Readers' Theater selections are available on Audiotext 2.*

REVIEW THEME CONCEPTS
Using Readers' Theater and a Science Textbook

 READERS' THEATER

🍁 **SCIENCE** **A Birthday Mystery, pp. 452–459**

SUMMARY A boy tries to guess what gift he will receive for his birthday by asking his siblings to give him clues.

 COMPREHENSION STRATEGIES

🍁 **SCIENCE** **Reading Your Science Textbook: The Life Cycle of a Frog, pp. 460–463**

SUMMARY Children will learn about the stages of a frog's life cycle.

Support for Differentiated Instruction

GO online **LEVELED READERS**

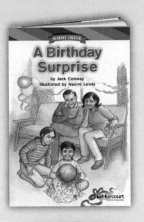

● **BELOW-LEVEL**   ● **ON-LEVEL**   ● **ADVANCED**   **E L L**

LEVELED PRACTICE

◀ **Strategic Intervention Resource Kit, Lesson 15**

◀ **Strategic Intervention Interactive Reader, Lesson 15**

Strategic Intervention Interactive Reader Online

◀ **ELL Extra Support Kit, Lesson 15**

◀ **Challenge Resource Kit, Lesson 15**

● **BELOW-LEVEL**
Extra Support Copying Masters, pp. 107, 109–112, 114–115, 117

● **ON-LEVEL**
Practice Book, pp. 107–117

● **ADVANCED**
Challenge Copying Masters, pp. 107, 109–112, 114–115, 117

E L L

ELL Copying Masters, Lesson 15

ADDITIONAL RESOURCES

- Teacher Resource Book, pp. 48, 114, 130–133
- Spelling Practice Book, pp. 47–50
- Grammar Practice Book, pp. 53–54
- Reading Transparencies R75
- Test Prep System
◀ **Literacy Center Kit, Cards 71–75**
- Sound/Spelling Card
◀ **Fluency Builders**
◀ **Picture Card Collection**

ASSESSMENT

✓ **Weekly Lesson Tests, Lesson 15**
- Comprehension   • Robust Vocabulary

✓ **Rubrics, pp. R3–R8**

GO online www.harcourtschool.com/ **storytown**
Online Assessment
Also available on CD-ROM—Exam View

Suggested Lesson Planner

90+ Minutes

GO online Online TE & Planning Resources

	Day 1	**Day 2**
Step 1 Whole Group **Daily Routines** • Oral Language • Read Aloud • High-Frequency Words	**QUESTION OF THE DAY,** p. T374 *What is the best thing about birthdays?* **READ ALOUD,** p. T375 *Big Book of Rhymes and Poems,* "My Name" **WORD WALL,** p. T375	**QUESTION OF THE DAY,** p. T390 *How do you feel when you are playing with your friends?* **READ ALOUD,** p. T391 *Big Book of Rhymes and Poems,* "Play" **WORD WALL,** p. T391
Word Work • phonics • Spelling • High-Frequency Words	✔ **phonics**, p. T376 Review: Digraphs /ch/*ch, tch*; /sh/*sh*; /th/*th* ✔ **SPELLING,** p. T378 Pretest: *wish, catch, bath, very, money, huge, price, stir, turn, learn* ✔ **HIGH-FREQUENCY WORDS,** p. T380 Review: *enjoy, especially, father, imagine, interesting, minute, question, wash, wear, year*	✔ **phonics**, p. T392 Review: Long Vowel /ē/*ey, y* ✔ **SPELLING,** p. T393 Word Building ✔ **HIGH-FREQUENCY WORDS,** p. T395 Review: *enjoy, especially, father, imagine, interesting, minute, question, wash, wear, year*
Skills and Strategies • Reading • Fluency • Comprehension • Build Robust Vocabulary	🕹 **COMPREHENSION,** p. T379 Review: Author's Purpose ✔ **READING** **READERS' THEATER** Read Aloud/Read Along: "A Birthday Mystery," p. T382 **FLUENCY:** p. T382 Model Oral Fluency ✔ **BUILD ROBUST VOCABULARY,** p. T387 *Words About the Readers' Theater* ▲ Student Edition	🕹 **COMPREHENSION,** p. T394 Review: Author's Purpose ✔ **READING** **READERS' THEATER** Read Together: "A Birthday Mystery," p. T396 **FLUENCY,** p. T396 Punctuation and Phrasing ✔ **BUILD ROBUST VOCABULARY,** p. T397 *Words from the Read-Aloud* ▲ Student Edition 
Step 2 Small Groups	**Suggestions for Differentiated Instruction (See pp. T368–T369.)**	
Step 3 Whole Group **Language Arts** • Grammar • Writing	✔ **GRAMMAR,** p. T388 Review: Abbreviations ***Daily Proofreading*** Do you know where mr Grady lives (Mr., lives?) ✏ **WRITING,** p. T389 Revise Writing Trait: Ideas **Writing Prompt** *Add new ideas to your notebook.*	✔ **GRAMMAR,** p. T398 Review: Singular Possessive Nouns ***Daily Proofreading*** Dr Smiths bag was on the flor. (Dr., Smith's, floor) ✏ **WRITING,** p. T399 Revise Writing Trait: Ideas **Writing Prompt** *Write a paragraph telling why a selection was interesting to you.*

🕹 = **Focus Skill**   🕹 = **Focus Strategy**   ✔ = **Tested Skill**

phonics REVIEW

Skills at a Glance

• Lessons 11–14

Comprehension REVIEW

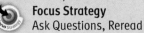

Focus Skills
Author's Purpose, Fiction/Nonfiction

Focus Strategy
Ask Questions, Reread

Fluency REVIEW

• Punctuation

• Phrasing

Vocabulary INTRODUCE

bewildered, evasive, mull, startle, distrust, witness, lock, beneath

Day 3

QUESTION OF THE DAY, p. T400
In what ways are you like other second graders? In what ways are you different?

READ ALOUD, p. T401
Big Book of Rhymes and Poems, "Did You Ever Think?"

WORD WALL, p. T401

 **phonics**, p. T402
Review: Consonants /s/c; /j/g, dge

 SPELLING, p. T403
State the Generalization

HIGH-FREQUENCY WORDS, p. T405
Review: *enjoy, especially, father, imagine, interesting, minute, question, wash, wear, year*

COMPREHENSION, p. T404
Review: Fiction and Nonfiction

FLUENCY

READERS' THEATER
Choose Roles/Rehearse: "A Birthday Mystery," a p. T406

▲ Student Edition

BUILD ROBUST VOCABULARY, p. T407
Review

Day 4

QUESTION OF THE DAY, p. T410
If you were an animal, what are some reasons that you might bite a person?

READ ALOUD, p. T411
Big Book of Rhymes and Poems, "Always Be Kind to Animals"

WORD WALL, p. T411

phonics, p. T412
Review r-Controlled Vowel /ûr/ir, ur, er, ear

SPELLING, p. T413
Review Spelling Words

HIGH-FREQUENCY WORDS, p. T417
Review: *enjoy, especially, father, imagine, interesting, minute, question, wash, wear, year*

READING **COMPREHENSION STRATEGIES**

Review: Ask Questions and Reread, p. T414

FLUENCY

READERS' THEATER
Rehearse Roles: "A Birthday Mystery," p. T418

▲ Student Edition

BUILD ROBUST VOCABULARY, p. T419
Review

Day 5

QUESTION OF THE DAY, p. T422
What advice would you give a child going to school for the first time?

READ ALOUD, p. T423
Big Book of Rhymes and Poems, "Aliona Says"

WORD WALL, p. T423

phonics, SPELLING, p. T424
Posttest

HIGH-FREQUENCY WORDS, p. T426
Review: *enjoy, especially, father, imagine, interesting, minute, question, wash, wear, year*

COMPREHENSION, p. T425
Review: Fiction and Nonfiction

FLUENCY

READERS' THEATER
Perform: "A Birthday Mystery," p. T427

▲ Student Edition

● **BELOW-LEVEL** ● ON-LEVEL ● ADVANCED **E L L**

GRAMMAR, p. T408
Review: Plural Possessive Nouns

Daily Proofreading
That is Stacys Bike. (Stacy's, bike)

WRITING, p. T409
Publish
Writing Trait: Presentation

Writing Prompt *Write a paragraph about a character.*

GRAMMAR, p. T420
Review: Pronouns

Daily Proofreading
Can Joseph come to the movies with I. (me?)

WRITING, p. T421
Publish
Writing Trait: Conventions

Writing Prompt *Write about your publishing idea.*

GRAMMAR, p. T428
Review: Lessons 11–14

Daily Proofreading
Shondras shoes got wet in yesterdays rain storm. (Shondra's, yesterday's)

WRITING, p. T429
Present
Writing Trait: Conventions

Writing Prompt *Write about a piece of writing shared by a classmate.*

Suggested Small-Group Planner

45–60 Minutes

	Day 1	Day 2
BELOW-LEVEL 15–20 Minutes	**Teacher-Directed** Leveled Reader: "A Going Away Present," p. T430 Before Reading **Independent** ⭐ Listening/Speaking Center, p. T372 Extra Support Copying Masters, pp. 107, 109 ▲ Leveled Reader	**Teacher-Directed** Student Edition: "A Birthday Mystery," p. T382 **Independent** ⭐ Reading Center, p. T372 Extra Support Copying Masters, pp. 110–112  ▲ Student Edition
ON-LEVEL 15–20 Minutes	**Teacher-Directed** Leveled Reader: "A Surprise for Mom," p. T431 Before Reading **Independent** ⭐ Reading Center, p. T372 Practice Book, pp. 107, 109 ▲ Leveled Reader	**Teacher-Directed** Student Edition: "A Birthday Mystery," p. T382 **Independent** ⭐ Letters and Sounds Center, p. T373 Practice Book, pp. 110–112  ▲ Student Edition
ADVANCED 15–20 Minutes	**Teacher-Directed** Leveled Reader: "Clues for Grandma," p. T432 Before Reading **Independent** ⭐ Letters and Sounds Center, p. T373 Challenge Copying Masters, pp. 107, 109 ▲ Leveled Reader	**Teacher-Directed** Leveled Reader: "Clues for Grandma," p. T432 Read the Book **Independent** ⭐ Word Work Center, p. T373 Challenge Copying Masters, pp. 110–112 ▲ Leveled Reader

ELL

English-Language Learners

In addition to the small-group instruction above, use the ELL Extra Support Kit to promote language development.

LANGUAGE DEVELOPMENT SUPPORT	**LANGUAGE DEVELOPMENT SUPPORT**
Teacher-Directed ELL TG, Day 1 **Independent** ELL Copying Masters, Lesson 15 ▲ ELL Student Handbook	**Teacher-Directed** ELL TG, Day 2 **Independent** ELL Copying Masters, Lesson 15 ▲ ELL Student Handbook

Intervention

▲ Strategic Intervention Resource Kit   ▲ Strategic Intervention Interactive Reader

| Strategic Intervention TG, Day 1 Strategic Intervention Practice Book, Lesson 15 | Strategic Intervention TG, Day 2 Strategic Intervention Interactive Reader, Lesson 15 ▲ Strategic Intervention Interactive Reader |

Day 3

Teacher-Directed
Leveled Reader:
"A Going Away Present," p. T430
Read the Book

Independent
 Word Work Center, p. T373
Extra Support Copying Masters, p. 114

▲ Leveled Reader

Teacher-Directed
Leveled Reader:
"A Surprise for Mom,"
p. T431
Read the Book

Independent
 Writing Center, p. T373
Practice Book, p. 114

▲ Leveled Reader

Teacher-Directed
Leveled Reader:
"Clues for Grandma," p. T432
Think Critically

Independent
 Listening/Speaking Center,
p. T372
Challenge Copying Masters, p. 114

▲ Leveled Reader

LANGUAGE DEVELOPMENT SUPPORT

Teacher-Directed
Leveled Reader: "A Birthday Surprise,"
p. T433
Before Reading; Read the Book
ELL TG, Day 3

Independent
ELL Copying Masters, Lesson 15

▲ Leveled Reader

Strategic Intervention TG, Day 3
Strategic Intervention Interactive
Reader, Lesson 15
Strategic Intervention Practice Book,
Lesson 15

▲ Strategic Intervention
Interactive Reader

Day 4

Teacher-Directed
Leveled Reader:
"A Going Away Present," p. T430
Reread for Fluency

Independent
 Letters and Sounds Center,
p. T373
Extra Support Copying Masters, p. 115

▲ Leveled Reader

Teacher-Directed
Leveled Reader:
"A Surprise for Mom,"
p. T431
Reread for Fluency

Independent
 Word Work Center, p. T373
Practice Book, p. 115

▲ Leveled Reader

Teacher-Directed
Leveled Reader:
"Clues for Grandma," p. T432
Reread for Fluency

Independent
 Writing Center, p. T373
Challenge Copying Masters, p. 115
Self-Selected Reading: Classroom
Library Collection

▲ Leveled Reader

LANGUAGE DEVELOPMENT SUPPORT

Teacher-Directed
Leveled Reader: "A Birthday Surprise,"
p. T433
Reread for Fluency
ELL TG, Day 4

Independent
ELL Copying Masters, Lesson 15

▲ Leveled Reader

Strategic Intervention TG, Day 4
Strategic Intervention Interactive
Reader, Lesson 15

▲ Strategic Intervention
Interactive Reader

Day 5

Teacher-Directed
Leveled Reader:
"A Going Away Present," p. T430
Think Critically

Independent
 Writing Center, p. T373
Leveled Reader: Reread for Fluency
Extra Support Copying Masters, p. 117

▲ Leveled Reader

Teacher-Directed
Leveled Reader:
"A Surprise for Mom,"
p. T431
Think Critically

Independent
 Listening/Speaking Center,
p. T372
Leveled Reader: Reread for Fluency
Practice Book, p. 117

▲ Leveled Reader

Teacher-Directed
Leveled Reader:
"Clues for Grandma," p. T432
Reread for Fluency
Self-Selected Reading: Classroom
Library Collection

Independent
 Reading Center, p. T372
Leveled Reader: Reread for Fluency
Challenge Copying Masters, p. 117

▲ Leveled Reader

LANGUAGE DEVELOPMENT SUPPORT

Teacher-Directed
Leveled Reader: "A Birthday Surprise,"
p. T433
Think Critically
ELL TG, Day 5

Independent
Leveled Reader: Reread for Fluency
ELL Copying Masters, Lesson 15

▲ Leveled Reader

Strategic Intervention TG, Day 5
Strategic Intervention Interactive
Reader, Lesson 15

▲ Strategic Intervention
Interactive Reader

Leveled Readers & Leveled Practice
Reinforcing Skills and Strategies

LEVELED READERS SYSTEM

- Leveled Readers
- Leveled Readers, CD
- Leveled Readers Teacher Guides
  - *Comprehension*
  - *High-Frequency Words*
  - *Oral Reading Fluency Assessement*
- Response Activities
- Leveled Readers Assessment

See pages T430–T433 for lesson plans.

BELOW-LEVEL

- **phonics**
- **High-Frequency Words**
- **Author's Purpose; Fiction and Nonfiction**

LEVELED READERS TEACHER GUIDE

▲ **High-Frequency Words, p. 5**

▲ **Comprehension, p. 6**

ON-LEVEL

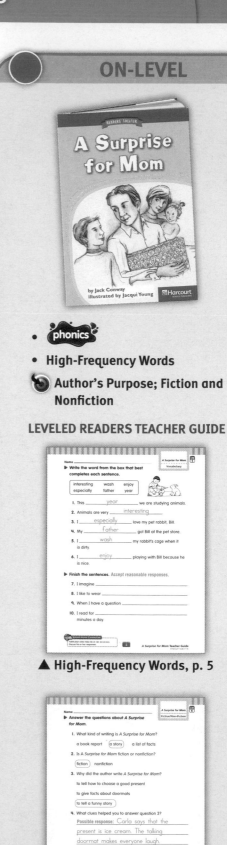

- **phonics**
- **High-Frequency Words**
- **Author's Purpose; Fiction and Nonfiction**

LEVELED READERS TEACHER GUIDE

▲ **High-Frequency Words, p. 5**

▲ **Comprehension, p. 6**

ADVANCED

-  **phonics**
- **High-Frequency Words**
- **Author's Purpose, Fiction and Nonfiction**

LEVELED READERS TEACHER GUIDE

▲ **High-Frequency Words, p. 5**

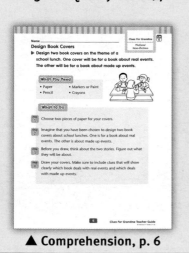

▲ **Comprehension, p. 6**

ELL

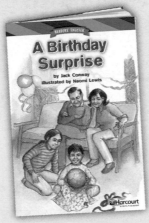

- **Build Background**
- **Concept Vocabulary**
- **Scaffolded Language Development**

LEVELED READERS TEACHER GUIDE

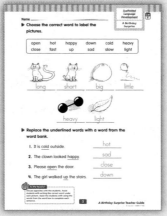

▲ **Scaffolded Language Development, p. 5**

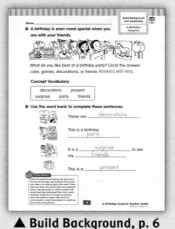

▲ **Build Background, p. 6**

CLASSROOM LIBRARY

for Self-Selected Reading

EASY

▲ *Clown Fish* by Carol K. Lindeen, Capstone Press, 2005. NONFICTION

AVERAGE

▲ *Buster* by Denise Fleming, Henry Holt and Company, 2003. FICTION

CHALLENGE

▲ *Ant Cities* by Arthur Dorros, HarperCollins, 1987. NONFICTION

▲ **Classroom Library Books Teacher Guide, Lesson 15**

Literacy Centers

15 Min. each

Management Support

While you provide direct instruction to individuals or small groups, other children can work on literacy center activities.

▲ **Literacy Center Pocket Chart**

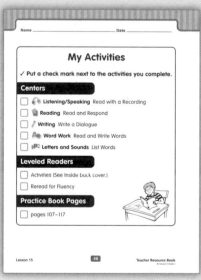

▲ **Teacher Resource Book, p. 48**

Homework for the Week

TEACHER RESOURCE BOOK, PAGE 48
The *Homework Copying Master* provides activities to complete for each day of the week.

 LISTENING/SPEAKING

Read with a Recording

Objective
To develop fluency by listening to familiar selections and reading them aloud

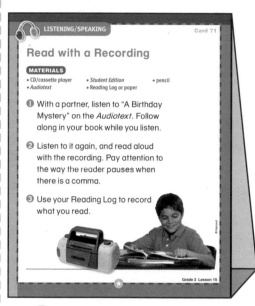

⭐ **Literacy Center Kit • Card 71**

 READING

Read and Respond

Objective
To develop comprehension by reading fiction selections and responding to them

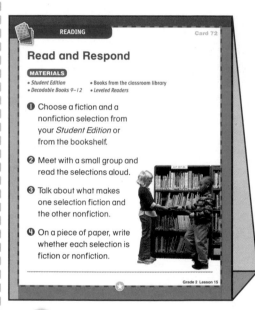

⭐ **Literacy Center Kit • Card 72**

www.harcourtschool.com/storytown

GO online

★ Additional Literacy Center Activities

★ Resources for Parents and Teachers

Differentiated *for Your Needs*

 WRITING

Write a Dialogue

Objective
To practice writing dialogue

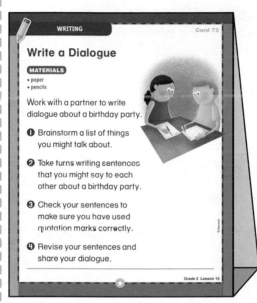

WRITING — Card 73

Write a Dialogue

MATERIALS
• paper
• pencils

Work with a partner to write dialogue about a birthday party.

❶ Brainstorm a list of things you might talk about.

❷ Take turns writing sentences that you might say to each other about a birthday party.

❸ Check your sentences to make sure you have used quotation marks correctly.

❹ Revise your sentences and share your dialogue.

Grade 2 Lesson 15

⭐ **Literacy Center Kit** • Card 73

"Can you come to my birthday party on Saturday?"

 WORD WORK

Read and Write Words

Objective
To practice spelling and writing High-Frequency Words

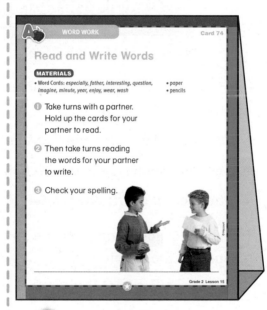

WORD WORK — Card 74

Read and Write Words

MATERIALS
• Word Cards: *especially, father, interesting, question, imagine, minute, year, enjoy, wear, wash*
• paper
• pencils

❶ Take turns with a partner. Hold up the cards for your partner to read.

❷ Then take turns reading the words for your partner to write.

❸ Check your spelling.

Grade 2 Lesson 15

⭐ **Literacy Center Kit** • Card 74

especially
father
interesting
question
imagine
minute
year
enjoy
wear
wash

ABC LETTERS AND SOUNDS

Sounds in Words

Objective
To use spelling patterns to read and write words

LETTERS AND SOUNDS — Card 75

List Words

MATERIALS
• dry-erase board
• dry-erase markers

❶ Make a chart like this one.

chill	money	city	stir

❷ Read the words. Listen for the sounds the underlined letters stand for.

❸ Add words to each column on the chart. List words that use the underlined letters to stand for the same sound.

Grade 2 Lesson 15

⭐ **Literacy Center Kit** • Card 75

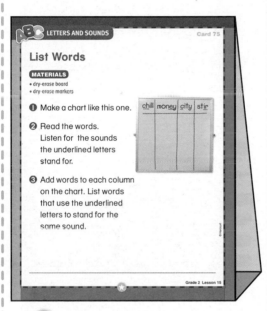

chill	money	city	stir
chin		nice	
watch			

Day at a Glance

Day 1

phonics and Spelling

- Digraphs /ch/*ch, tch*; /sh/*sh*; /th/*th*
- Pretest

Reading/ Comprehension

Focus Skill
Review: Author's Purpose
Monitor Comprehension

High-Frequency Words

- Review: *especially, interesting, question, imagine, minute, year, enjoy, wear, wash, father*

Fluency

READERS' THEATER

- Read Aloud/ Read Along
- Model Fluent Reading
- "A Birthday Mystery," *Student Edition,* pp. 452–459

Read!

Robust Vocabulary

Words About the Readers' Theater

- Introduce: *bewildered, evasive, mull, startle*

Grammar

- Review: Abbreviations

Writing

- Select and Revise

Warm-Up Routines

Oral Language

Objective *To listen attentively and respond appropriately to oral communication*

Question of the Day

What is the best thing about birthdays?

Have children brainstorm a list of fun things associated with birthdays. Use the following prompts.

- **What happens at birthday parties?**
- **What do families do to celebrate birthdays?**
- **What part of a birthday celebration makes you smile?**

Then have children complete the following sentence frame to explain the reasons for their choice.

The best thing about birthdays is _____.

Read Aloud

Objective *To listen for a purpose*

BIG BOOK OF RHYMES AND POEMS   Display "My Name" on page 21 and read the title aloud. Ask children to recall what happens each time the poet writes his name. Then have the children read the poem aloud. Discuss what is special about birthday cards, and why the poet's name stays on the card he gives his mother.

▲ Big Book of Rhymes and Poems, p. 21

Word Wall

Objective *To read high-frequency words*

REVIEW HIGH-FREQUENCY WORDS   Point to and read aloud the following words from the Word Wall: *especially, interesting, question, imagine, minute, year, enjoy, wear, wash,* and *father.* Point to words at random and have children read the words as a group several times. Then ask each child to read three words that you point to in quick succession. Continue until all children have had a chance to participate at least once.

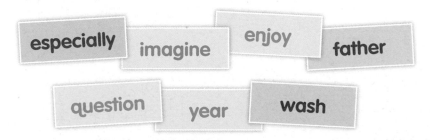

Digraphs /ch/ *ch, tch*; /sh/ *sh*; /th/ *th*

 phonics *and Spelling*

Objectives

- *To recognize and blend the digraphs /ch/ch, tch; /sh/sh; /th/th*
- *To read words with the digraphs /ch/ch, tch; /sh/sh; /th/th and other known letter-sounds*
- *To use the digraphs /ch/ch, tch; /sh/sh; /th/th and other known letter-sounds to spell words*

Skill Trace

Tested ✔ **/ch/*ch, tch*; /sh/*sh*; /th/*th***

Introduce	Grade 1
Reintroduce	T30–T33
Reteach	S2
Review	**T42–T43, T64–T65, T376–T377**
Test	Theme 3
Maintain	Theme 5, T168–T169

Review

REVIEW PHONICS ELEMENTS   Explain to children that during this week, they will review the phonics elements they learned during Theme 3.

WARM UP WITH PHONEMIC AWARENESS   Say the words *chill* and *chin*. Have children repeat the words. Say: **The words *chill* and *chin* begin with the /ch/ sound.** Repeat with the words *beach* and *match*. Say: **The words *beach* and *match* end with the /ch/ sound.** Have children say /ch/ several times.

Follow a similar procedure for /sh/, using the words *ship* and *dish*, and for /th/, using the words *think* and *path*.

Routine Card 1 **CONNECT LETTERS AND SOUNDS**   Review the letter/sound correspondences for digraphs /ch/*ch, tch*; /sh/*sh*; and /th/*th*. Display the *Sound/Spelling Cards* for *ch/tch, sh,* and *th*. Begin with /ch/ by pointing to *ch* and *tch*. Ask children to say the sound that the letters stand for. Ask volunteers to name some words that include the /ch/ sound, and on the board begin a list of the words they suggest. Ask children to identify in each word the letters that stand for the /ch/ sound. Follow a similar procedure for the digraphs /sh/*sh* and /th/*th*.

▲ **Sound/Spelling Cards**

5-DAY PHONICS

DAY 1	Review /ch/*ch*, *tch*; /sh/*sh*; /th/*th*
DAY 2	Review /ē/*ey*, *y*
DAY 3	Review Consonants /s/*c*; /j/*g*, *dge*
DAY 4	Review /û/*ir*, *ur*, *er*, *ear*
DAY 5	Cumulative Review

Practice/Apply

GUIDED PRACTICE   Using the lists you have created, ask volunteers to read four words by choosing one word from each column. Then have the group choral-read four words that you point to in rapid succession. Finally, ask volunteers to suggest sentences using the words. Write their ideas on the board, underlining any words with the digraphs /ch/*ch*, *tch*; /sh/*sh*; and /th/*th*.

> There was a <u>chill</u> in the air.
>
> We followed a <u>path</u> to <u>reach</u> the <u>shore</u>.
>
> Did you <u>catch</u> any <u>fish</u> today?

INDEPENDENT PRACTICE   Have children work with a partner to write sentences using words with the digraphs /ch/*ch, tch*; /sh/*sh*; and /th/*th*. Tell partners to exchange papers with another pair to read aloud each other's sentences.

ADVANCED

Multisyllabic Words   Challenge children to add two- and three-syllable words with digraphs /ch/*ch, tch*; /sh/*sh*; and /th/*th* to the chart begun on page T376.

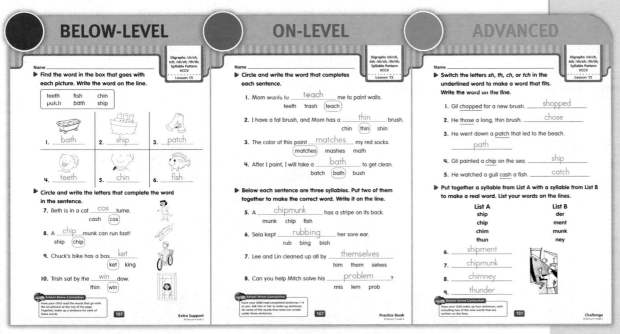

▲ **Extra Support, p. 107**   ▲ **Practice Book, p. 107**   ▲ **Challenge, p. 107**

E L L

• Group children according to academic levels, and assign one of the pages on the left.

• Clarify any unfamiliar concepts as necessary. See *ELL Teacher Guide*, Lesson 15, for support in scaffolding instruction.

Spelling
Review

5-DAY SPELLING

DAY 1	Pretest
DAY 2	Word Building
DAY 3	State the Generalization
DAY 4	Review
DAY 5	Posttest

Objective

• *To review spelling words from previous lessons*

Spelling Words

1.	**wish**	6.	**huge**
2.	**catch***	7.	**price**
3.	**bath**	8.	**stir**
4.	**very***	9.	**turn**
5.	**money**	10.	**learn**

* Words from "A Birthday Mystery"

Reinforce the Skill

PRETEST Say the first word and read the dictation sentence. Repeat the word as children write it. Write the word on the board and have children check their spelling. Tell them to circle the word if they spelled it correctly or write it correctly if they did not. Repeat for words 2–10.

Words with /ch/*ch, tch*; /sh/*sh*; or /th/*th*; /ē/*ey, y*; /s/*c*; /j/*g, dge*; /ûr/*ir, ur, er, ear*

1.	wish	Sam made a **wish** as he blew out his birthday candles.
2.	catch	Lulu tried to **catch** me in a game of tag.
3.	bath	We gave our puppy a **bath** after she played in the mud.
4.	very	Jamal studied **very** hard for his math test.
5.	money	Our class had a bake sale to raise **money** for our field trip.
6.	huge	Dad made a **huge** pizza to share with everyone at lunch.
7.	price	Do you know the **price** of that red jacket?
8.	stir	The recipe says to **stir** the soup as you heat it.
9.	turn	Mom asked me to **turn** around before I saw my surprise.
10.	learn	We **learn** how to spell ten new words each week.

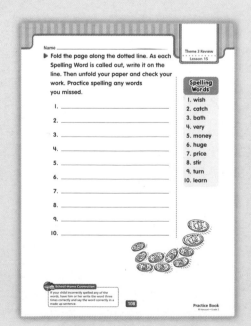

▲ Practice Book, p. 108

Author's Purpose

Comprehension: Review

Reinforce the Skill

DISCUSS AUTHOR'S PURPOSE   Have children turn to and reread *Student Edition* page 325 to determine author's purpose. Model how to identify an author's purpose.

Think Aloud   Before I think about why an author wrote something, I check whether what I'm reading is fiction or nonfiction. I know that most fiction stories are written to entertain the reader. Most nonfiction selections are written to give information.

Tell children that this selection is fiction and was written to entertain.

Practice/Apply

GUIDED PRACTICE   Draw a chart like the one below. Point to and read aloud the entries. Then ask children to identify other kinds of writing they know about, such as poems, folktales, and magazine articles, and add them to the chart. Work together to identify the author's purpose for each kind of writing.

INDEPENDENT PRACTICE   Have children look back at the selections they read in Theme 3 and think about the author's purpose for writing each one. Have children draw and complete a chart like the one below. Discuss children's responses, and ask volunteers to explain how they determined the author's purpose.

Selection	Kind of Writing	Author's Purpose
Jamaica Louise James	fiction	to entertain
At Play: Long Ago and Today	nonfiction	to give information

Objective

• *To identify an author's purpose for writing*

Skill Trace

 Author's Purpose

Introduce	T34–T35
Reteach	S6–S7, S16–S17
Review	**T68, T82, T92, T130–T131, T162, T176, T186, T379, T394**
Test	Theme 3
Maintain	Theme 5, T278

High-Frequency Words
Review

Objective

- *To read high-frequency words*

REVIEW **Tested** ✓

High-Frequency Words

These words are reviewed from Lessons 11–14.

especially	year
interesting	enjoy
question	wear
imagine	wash
minute	father

Reinforce

REVIEW WORDS Play a "Mystery Word" game with children. Write the high-frequency words on the board and read them with children several times. Call on volunteers to say and point to the word when they have figured out the clue. Provide the following clues:

- This mystery word names a short amount of time. (minute)

- This mystery word has the word *rest* in it. (interesting)

- This mystery word ends with the same sound as *toy*. (enjoy)

- These two mystery words have the /sh/ sound in them. (especially, wash)

- This mystery word begins with the same sound as *fast*. (father)

- This mystery word rhymes with *deer*. (year)

- This mystery word is something you can do with your mind. (imagine)

- This mystery word asks for an answer. (question)

- This mystery word rhymes with *bear*. (wear)

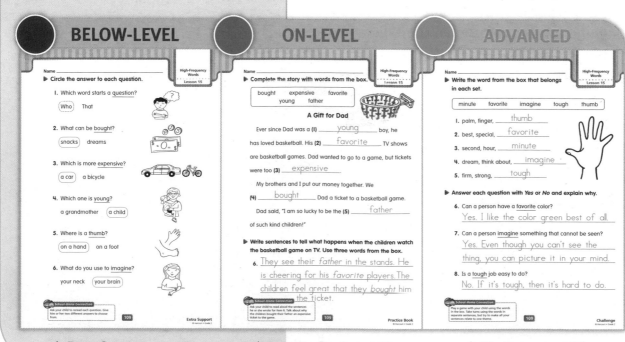

▲ Extra Support, p. 109   ▲ Practice Book, p. 109   ▲ Challenge, p. 109

- Group children according to academic levels, and assign one of the pages on the left.

- Clarify any unfamiliar concepts as necessary. See *ELL Teacher Guide*, Lesson 15, for support in scaffolding instructions.

Managing Readers' Theater

"A Birthday Mystery"

Set the Stage

OVERVIEW Use the following suggestions to help children prepare a Readers' Theater presentation of "A Birthday Mystery." See page T427 for additional performance ideas.

MODEL FLUENT READING Model fluent, expressive reading by reading aloud the script on *Student Edition* pages 452–459 (pp. T383–T386) as children follow along. Then read the script again, using the Monitor Comprehension questions to assess children's comprehension of the selection. Consider performance options for the end of the week. You may want to invite parents or other guests and allow children to create invitations.

READ TOGETHER Have children read the script on their own for the first time. Guide children to read with appropriate accuracy, reading rate, and expression. Encourage them to use the fluency tips to help them read more fluently.

CHOOSE ROLES AND REHEARSE Distribute copies of the script (*Teacher Resource Book*, pp. 130–133). Assign children to groups and have them practice reading different roles aloud. After children read, assign roles or have children choose their own. Encourage children to highlight their part and to practice reading their script at home.

REHEARSE Have children work in their assigned groups to read the script as many times as possible. Informally observe the groups and give feedback on children's accuracy and expression. You may want to have children rehearse while using the backdrop for "A Birthday Mystery" (*Teacher Resource Book*, p. 114).

PERFORM Assign each group a scene to perform. Have children stand in a row at the front of the classroom and read the script aloud. Groups who aren't performing become part of the audience. Encourage the audience to give feedback after the performances about each group's accuracy, reading rate, and expression.

Professional Development

 Podcasting: Readers' Theater

READERS' THEATER SCRIPTS

STORYTOWN

Teacher Resource Book

Grade 2

Harcourt School Publishers

▲ Teacher Resource Book, pp. 130–133

▲ Teacher Resource Book, p. 114

READERS' THEATER

Read Aloud/Read Along: "A Birthday Mystery"

5-DAY READERS' THEATER

DAY 1	Read Aloud/Read Along
DAY 2	Read Together
DAY 3	Choose Roles/Rehearse
DAY 4	Rehearse Roles
DAY 5	Perform

Objective

• *To develop fluency by listening to a model read aloud*

TECHNOLOGY

 eBook "A Birthday Mystery" is available in an eBook.

Audiotext "A Birthday Mystery" is available on *Audiotext 2* for subsequent readings.

 E L L

Phrasing Point out that grouping phrases together helps the listener understand what is being read aloud. Write *Group words together to read smoothly* on the board. Use your hands to frame *Group words together* as you read this sentence part aloud. Then use your hands to frame and read *to read smoothly*. Reread the entire sentence again, using phrasing to read the sentence smoothly.

Build Background

DISCUSS GENRE Remind children that Readers' Theater is like a play that is read aloud rather than acted out. Tell them that the genre of "A Birthday Mystery" is a mystery play. Explain that in mysteries, characters must use clues to figure out something or to solve a special problem.

REVIEW HIGH-FREQUENCY WORDS Review the following words taught in Lessons 11–14 from *Student Edition* page 452: *year, especially, enjoy, wear, interesting, question, wash, imagine, minute,* and *father.* Have children read them aloud with you.

PREDICT Have students predict what will happen in the play.

Reading for Fluency

DISCUSS FLUENCY TIPS Have children read the Reading for Fluency text on *Student Edition* page 452. Remind them that these are the two fluency strategies they learned to use in Lessons 11–14. Explain that throughout the Readers' Theater, they will find fluency tips that will help them use punctuation and phrasing to read smoothly and with expression.

SET A PURPOSE Tell children to listen to hear how you read with expression and ease.

READ ALOUD/READ ALONG Have children follow along as you read aloud the script. Remind them to pay close attention to how you use end punctuation to speak expressively, and how you group phrases together to make the words sound as though you are talking rather than reading.

> **Think Aloud** I am going to read "A Birthday Mystery" aloud. I know you will be listening carefully to hear how I make my voice sound when I notice punctuation. As I read, I will also try to sound as if I am speaking naturally rather than reading.

Read the script aloud a second time. This time, tell children to listen to what happens in the story, because you will ask them questions.

Monitor Comprehension

PAGES 452–453   Have children look at the illustrations. Ask them what is happening. Have them read along to find out.

1 **NOTE DETAILS   What is happening so far?** (It is Alex's birthday and his family is giving him a special gift.)

2 **AUTHOR'S PURPOSE   What do you think was the author's purpose in writing a mystery?** (Possible response: to entertain)

Focus Skill

3 **MAKE INFERENCES   Do you think that Alex likes puzzles? Why or why not?** (Yes; if he likes guessing games, then he probably likes puzzles.)

Reading for Fluency

Fluency Tip   **Punctuation**   Tell children that good readers look for punctuation in the sentences they are reading to help them read with expression or know when to pause when reading.

Think Aloud   I know that if I see a comma in a sentence, I should pause or slow down briefly after it. So this is what I do.

Narrator: First, Alex asks Nicky.

Alex: Hi, Nicky. Why don't you give me a hint about my present?

Nicky: If I do, it won't be a surprise.

Alex: I'm not going to figure it out from one little hint.

Nicky: Okay, I'll give you one little hint. It's something that's very soft.

Alex: It's something that's soft? Maybe it's something that I can wear. Will you give me another hint?

Nicky: Alex, you said just one hint, and that's what you got. If you can't figure it out, you'll just have to wait.

Fluency Tip

Remember to pause briefly when you come to a comma.

454

Narrator: Next, Alex asks Pat.

Alex: Pat, why don't you give me a hint about what I'm getting for my birthday?

Pat: Gifts are supposed to be surprises. It wouldn't be much fun if I told you.

Alex: Please, just give me one little hint to make it interesting. I won't be able to figure out what it is from one hint.

Pat: Okay, I'll give you one little hint. It's something you can play with. ❶

Alex: It's something I can play with? That could be anything. Can't you give me a better hint than that?

Pat: I gave you one hint, and that's all I'm going to tell you. ❷ ❸

455

Monitor Comprehension

PAGES 454–455 Ask children what questions they have about what is happening. Have them read along carefully to find out.

❶ **COMPARE/CONTRAST How are Nicky's and Pat's answers different?** (Nicky hints that Alex's gift is very soft; Pat says it's something he can play with.)

❷  **FICTION/NONFICTION Do you think "A Birthday Mystery" is fiction or nonfiction? How can you tell?** (It is fiction. We are not given any information, like exact dates, that make it true and real.)

❸ **EXPRESS PERSONAL OPINIONS Do you think it is a good idea for Alex to question each of this brothers and sisters about his gift? Why or why not?** (Possible response: No. He could guess what the gift is, and then he wouldn't have a surprise for his birthday.)

SOCIAL STUDIES

SUPPORTING STANDARDS

CULTURAL TRADITIONS Birthday celebrations are cultural traditions. Not all cultures celebrate birthdays, but many do, and in many different ways. Have children share why families and friends get together to celebrate, and in what ways. Have them describe the best kind of family celebration they know of.

Theme Review

Narrator: Then Alex asks Sam.

Alex: Hey, Sam, why don't you give me a hint about my birthday present?

Sam: That would ruin the surprise. A present that isn't a surprise is not much fun.

Alex: It will still be a surprise. I'm not going to figure it out from one little hint.

Sam: Okay, here's one little hint. It's something that's hard to catch. ❶

Alex: It's something that's hard to catch? Let me ask you one question. Is it a ball?

Sam: If I tell you, it won't be a surprise. Sorry, Alex. You're just going to have to wait.

Narrator: Last, Alex asks Lee.

Alex: Lee, how about giving me a hint about my present?

Lee: Presents should be surprises. You don't want to ruin your surprise, do you?

Alex: A hint won't ruin the surprise. I won't be able to figure out what the present is.

Lee: Okay, I'll give you one little hint. You sometimes have to wash it. ❶

Alex: Now I'm really confused. I can't imagine what it could be if you have to wash it. Give me another hint, okay?

Lee: Sorry, Alex. You said one little hint. That's the only one you are going to get.

Fluency Tip
Let your voice rise at the end of questions that have a yes or no answer.

456   457   ❷ ❸

Monitor Comprehension

PAGES 456–457   Ask children to read carefully to find out what clues are given next.

❶ **NOTE DETAILS**   What clue does Sam give about the present? What clue does Lee give about the present? (Sam says that it is difficult to catch. Lee says that sometimes you have to wash it.)

❷ **AUTHOR'S PURPOSE**   Why do you think the author wrote the conversations between Alex and each brother or sister so that they are alike? (Possible response: to entertain; to show that Alex is determined to find out what his present is.)

❸ **MAKE PREDICTIONS**   What do you think Alex's gift is? Why do you think that? (Responses will vary but should include hints from the story to support the answer.)

Reading for Fluency

Fluency Tip   **Punctuation**
Remind children to raise their voice slightly when they read a question.

Think Aloud   I see from all the question marks that Alex continues to ask a lot of questions. When I read Lee's line, "I don't think you want to ruin your surprise, do you?" I know that I need to change my voice when I say "do you?" That way, anyone who is listening will know that it is a question.

Narrator: Now it's time for the party.

Nicky: Alex, are you ready to find out what your present is? It's really special!

Alex: I sure am! I don't want to wait another minute.

Nicky: Remember, it's something very soft.

Pat: It's something you can play with.

Sam: It's hard to catch.

Lee: It also needs to be washed sometimes.

Alex: I give up. I know it's all of those things, but I can't guess what it is. May I have the present now?

Everyone: Okay, Alex, here it is!

Narrator: Alex's mother and father walk in with the present. His father puts it down, and it runs right over to Alex.

458

Fluency Tip

How would you group the words in these sentences? Read the lines that way.

Nicky: I told you that it was very soft!

Pat: I told you that it was something you could play with!

Sam: I told you that it was hard to catch!

Lee: I told you that you had to wash it sometimes!

Alex: You were all right. Those were all good clues, but there's just one hint you didn't give me.

Everyone: What's that?

Alex: That it would lick my face! ① ②

459

Monitor Comprehension

PAGES 458–459   Ask children if they can tell if their prediction was correct. Have them read along carefully to find out from the text if their guess is correct.

① **MAKE PREDICTIONS**   **Was your prediction correct? How do you know?** (Possible response: Yes, I guessed it was a dog. I know because it ran over to Alex and licked his face.)

② **DRAW CONCLUSIONS**   **Were all the clues true statements about the puppy? Why couldn't Alex figure out what his present was from the clues?** (Possible response: All the clues were true, but Alex thought about each separate clue instead of putting them together.)

Reading for Fluency

Fluency Tip   **Phrasing**   Point out that the lines spoken by Nicky, Pat, Sam, and Lee on page 459 all begin with the words "I told you." Demonstrate how to read each line by saying those words together as a phrase, followed by the phrase that repeats the clue each child gives.

Build Robust Vocabulary

Words About the Readers' Theater

Teach/Model

Routine Card 3

INTRODUCE ROBUST VOCABULARY Use *Routine Card 3* to introduce the words.

❶ Put the word in **selection context**.

❷ Display Transparency R75, and read the word and the **Student-Friendly Explanation**.

❸ Have children **say the word** with you.

❹ Use the word in other contexts, and have children **interact with the word's meaning**.

❺ Remove the transparency. Say the Student-Friendly Explanation again, and ask children to **name the word** that goes with it.

❶ **Selection Context:** Alex is **bewildered** by the hints about his gift.

❹ **Interact with Word Meaning:** When school started in the fall, I was bewildered by all the new things to learn. What bewildered you?

❶ **Selection Context:** Alex receives **evasive** answers about his gift.

❹ **Interact with Word Meaning:** Should you be evasive when you answer questions on a test? Why or why not?

❶ **Selection Context:** Alex has to **mull** over the clues he hears.

❹ **Interact with Word Meaning:** Do you have to mull it over when you are asked what kind of birthday cake you want? Why or why not?

❶ **Selection Context:** The puppy will **startle** Alex by licking his face.

❹ **Interact with Word Meaning:** Would a scary movie startle you or relax you? Why?

Practice/Apply

GUIDED PRACTICE Ask children to use facial expressions and movements to demonstrate the vocabulary words.

Objective

• *To develop robust vocabulary through discussing a literature selection.*

INTRODUCE **Tested** ✓
Vocabulary

bewildered	mull
evasive	startle

▼ **Student-Friendly Explanations**

Student-Friendly Explanations

bewildered When you are bewildered, you are confused and unable to understand something.

evasive When someone tries to avoid answering a question, that person is being evasive.

mull When you think through possible solutions to a problem, or the answer to a question, you mull over the information.

startle If someone comes up quietly behind you and surprises you, the person may startle you.

distrust When someone is not honest with you, you might distrust that person.

witness If someone sees an event and can tell about it, that person is a witness.

lock A group of hairs that hang together is a lock of hair.

beneath If you stand under a tree, you are standing beneath the tree.

Grade 2, Lesson 15   R75   Vocabulary

Transparency R75

Grammar
Review: Abbreviations

5-DAY GRAMMAR

DAY 1	Review Abbreviations
DAY 2	Review Singular Possessive Nouns
DAY 3	Review Plural Possessive Nouns
DAY 4	Review Pronouns
DAY 5	Cumulative Review

Objective

- *To use correct capitalization and punctuation in abbreviations*

Daily Proofreading

Do you know where mr Grady lives

(Mr., lives?)

Reinforce the Skill

REVIEW ABBREVIATIONS   Review what children have learned about abbreviations by using the following points:

- An abbreviation is a short way to write a word.

- Most abbreviations end with a period.

- Abbreviations for proper nouns begin with capital letters.

- Abbreviations are sometimes used for days of the week and months of the year. There is no abbreviation for the month of May.

Write the following names and dates on the board:

Mr. Simmons	Tues.	Oct. 6
Dr. Gray	Fri.	Jan. 30

Have children point out and read aloud each abbreviation. Remind children that abbreviations are pronounced as if they were written out.

Practice/Apply

GUIDED PRACTICE   Read aloud the following names and dates one at a time, and have children write the abbreviation for each: *Mister Rose, August 31, Monday, February 4, Missus Wilder, Doctor Green, Saturday, July 2, Tuesday*. Invite volunteers to take turns writing a response on the board and reading it aloud.

INDEPENDENT PRACTICE   Provide a current calendar so that children can find next Saturday. Have children create an invitation for an imaginary party on that day. Tell them to write the complete day and date, as well as the abbreviated day and date, on the invitation. Have children include their names, using their appropriate title.

Writing
Revise

5-DAY WRITING

DAY 1	Select a Piece and Revise
DAY 2	Revise
DAY 3	Proofread and Publish
DAY 4	Publish
DAY 5	Present

Revise

SELECT WRITING   Tell children to choose one of the writing pieces they started earlier in this theme, such as the personal narrative, that they would like to publish. Tell them to reread it and think about what they could do to make it better. Explain that they will revise the piece of writing that they select and will decide on a way to publish their writing to share it with others.

Point out that when children reread their writing from earlier in the theme, they may notice parts that are unclear or descriptions that could be more vivid. Explain that as they revise their writing, they will have an opportunity to address any problems they notice and to generally improve their writing.

ADD DESCRIPTIVE WORDS   Tell children that one way to improve their writing is to use colorful descriptive words. Help children to brainstorm words that tell the size, shape, and color of things they describe.

IDEAS   Tell children that they may have new ideas about the topic of their piece of writing. Suggest that they think about where any new ideas best fit in their writing and that they use editing marks to indicate where they will add these ideas.

GRAMMAR-WRITING CONNECTION   Remind children to check that they use the correct abbreviations for any titles used in their writing, and that any abbreviations end with a period.

Mister
Mr.

Street
St.

Objectives

- *To select a piece of writing for revision*
- *To revise by adding descriptive words*
- *To revise for abbreviations*

Writing Prompt

Review   Suggest that children review what they have written in their notebooks during Theme 3. Tell them to add new ideas and to indicate places where they have changed their mind about a subject.

Create Synonym Lists   Work with children to identify some familiar descriptive words, such as *big, little, tall, short, hot,* and *cold.* Guide them to begin synonym lists for these words in their notebook. Help children to read and pronounce the new words.

Warm-Up Routines

Day at a Glance

Day 2

phonics and Spelling
- Review: Long Vowel /ē/*ey, y*

Comprehension

Focus Skill

Review: Author's Purpose

High-Frequency Words
- Review: *especially, year, interesting, enjoy, question, wear, imagine, wash, minute, father*

Fluency

READERS' THEATER

- Read Together: "A Birthday Mystery," *Student Edition* pp. 452–459

Read!

Robust Vocabulary
- *Read-Aloud Anthology:* "The Missing Baseball Mystery"
- *Words from the Read-Aloud* Introduce: *distrust, witness, lock, beneath*

Grammar
- Review: Singular Possessive Nouns

Writing ✏
- Revise

Oral Language

Objective *To listen attentively and respond appropriately to oral communication*

Question of the Day

How do you feel when you're playing with friends?

Discuss with children the games that they like to play outdoors and how they feel when they are playing with friends. Use prompts like the following:

- **What are some games you like to play outdoors?**

- **What are some ways that children can play together so that everyone has fun?**

Then have children complete the following sentence frame to describe their playtime:

I like to play _____ with _____ because _____.

Read Aloud

Objective *To listen for a purpose*

BIG BOOK OF RHYMES AND POEMS   Display "Play" on page 23 and read aloud the title. Remind children that they read this poem earlier in the theme. Have children read the poem aloud and listen to how repeated phrases such as "Come play with me" add a feeling of fun and playfulness to the poem. Reread the poem, having children read with you. Then ask children to share how the poem makes them feel.

▲ **Big Book of Rhymes and Poems, p. 23**

Word Wall

Objective *To read high-frequency words*

REVIEW HIGH-FREQUENCY WORDS   Point to the following words from the Word Wall: *especially, year, interesting, enjoy, question, wear, imagine, wash, minute,* and *father*. For each word, have children read it, spell it, and finally read it again.

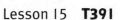

Long Vowel /ē/ey, y
phonics and Spelling

Objectives

- *To recognize and blend the long-vowel /ē/ sound of ey, y*
- *To read words with /ē/ey, y and other known letter-sounds*
- *To use /ē/ey, y and other known letter-sounds to spell words*

Spelling Words

1. wish	6. huge
2. catch*	7. price
3. bath	8. stir
4. very*	9. turn
5. money	10. learn

* Words from "A Birthday Mystery"

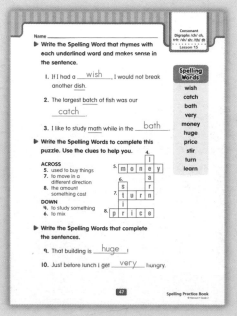

▲ Spelling Practice Book, p. 47

Review

READ A SPELLING WORD   Write the words *very* and *money* on the board. Ask children to identify the letter or letters that stand for the /ē/ vowel sound in each word. Remind children that they have learned that the letters *y* and *ey* at the end of words can stand for the /ē/ sound. Have them read the words aloud.

BUILD SPELLING WORDS   Have children follow your directions to change one or more letters in each of the words *bury* or *honey* to make a spelling word. Have them write the word on a sheet of paper or in their notebook. Then have a volunteer change the spelling of the word on the board so that children can self-check their spelling.

- Write *bury* on the board. Ask: **Which spelling word can you make by changing the first two letters?** *(very)*

- Write *honey* on the board. Ask: **Which spelling word can you make by changing the first letter?** *(money)*

Follow a similar procedure with the words *dish (wish), match (catch), path (bath), cage (huge), spice (price), star (stir), burn (turn),* and *earn (learn).*

BELOW-LEVEL	ADVANCED
Build Spelling Words List the spelling words on the board. Point to the words one at a time. Read each word possible, pantomime a related action, and then spell the word out loud. Have children imitate what you do. Repeat with each spelling word.	**Rhyming Words in Poems** Have children think of words that rhyme with four of the spelling words. Then have children write an eight-line poem, using the rhyming pairs to create lines that rhyme. Have children share their poems with the class.

5-DAY PHONICS

DAY 1	Review /ch/*ch, tch*; /sh/*sh*, /th/*th*
DAY 2	Review /ē/*y, ey*
DAY 3	Review /s/*c*; /j/*g, dge*
DAY 4	Review /ûr/*ir, ur, er, ear*
DAY 5	Cumulative Review

Read Words in Context

APPLY PHONICS   Write the following sentences on the board or on chart paper. Have children read each sentence silently. Then track the print as children read the sentence aloud.

Yuri made a <u>wish</u> and blew out the candles on the cake.

Su tried to <u>catch</u> the ball with one hand.

Mom gives the baby a <u>bath</u> every day.

The sale <u>price</u> for the bike was just what I had saved.

Now you have to <u>stir</u> the pot for five minutes.

WRITE   Dictate a number of the spelling words to children. Have them write the words in their notebook or on a separate sheet of paper.

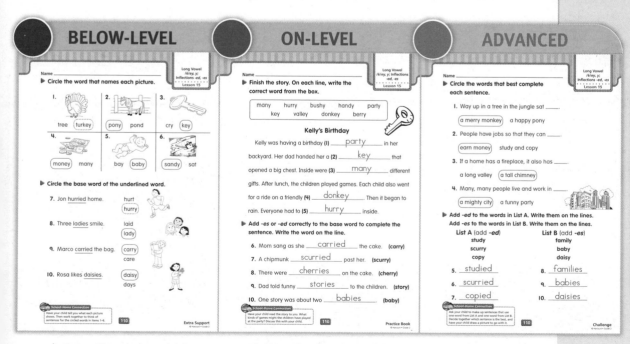

BELOW-LEVEL

▲ Extra Support, p. 110

ON-LEVEL

▲ Practice Book, p. 110

ADVANCED

▲ Challenge, p. 110

E L L

- Group children according to academic levels, and assign one of the pages on the left.

- Clarify any unfamiliar concepts as necessary. See *ELL Teacher Guide* Lesson 15 for support in scaffolding instruction.

Focus Skill

Author's Purpose
Comprehension: Review

Objectives
- *To identify the characteristics of a genre*
- *To use genre to identify the author's purpose in writing*

Skill Trace
 Tested **Author's Purpose**

Introduce	T34–T35
Reteach	S6–S7, S16–S17
Review	**T68, T82, T92, T130–T131, T162, T176, T186, T379, T394**
Test	Theme 3
Maintain	Theme 5, T278

Review

DISCUSS AUTHOR'S PURPOSE Remind children that authors write for different purposes. Have children turn to *Student Edition* page 361 and read the text with you to determine the purpose.

> **Think Aloud** I know that an author of a how-to paragraph wants to explain how to do something. I see that this selection was written to tell the reader how to do something.

Practice/Apply

GUIDED PRACTICE Draw a two-column chart like the one below. Review selections from an earlier theme children have read, guiding children in identifying the author's purpose.

Selection/Kind of Writing	Author's Purpose

INDEPENDENT PRACTICE Have children complete the chart for other literature selections they have read in an earlier theme.

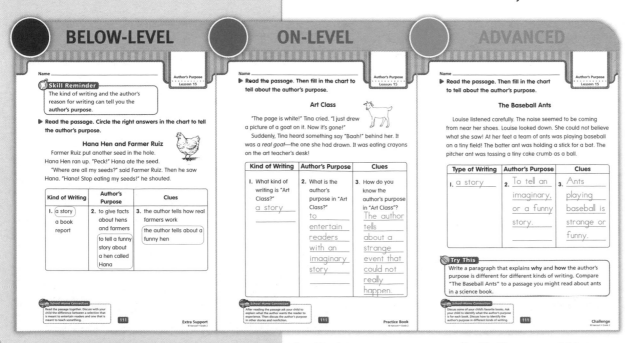

BELOW-LEVEL ▲ Extra Support, p. 111

ON-LEVEL ▲ Practice Book, p. 111

ADVANCED ▲ Challenge, p. 111

ELL
- Group children according to academic levels, and assign one of the pages on the left.
- Clarify any unfamiliar concepts as necessary. See *ELL Teacher Guide* Lesson 15 for support in scaffolding instruction.

High-Frequency Words
Review

Reinforce

REVIEW WITH STUDENT EDITION   Have children turn to *Student Edition* page 452. Point out the list of words on the left side of the page, and remind children that they studied these words in Lessons 11–14, as well as on Day 1 of Lesson 15. Explain that they will see these words again as they read "A Birthday Mystery."

Practice/Apply

GUIDED PRACTICE   Read through the list of high-frequency words on page 452 with children. Then have them read the list aloud on their own.

INDEPENDENT PRACTICE   Have children read through the list of words with partners. Tell children to read the list twice and then listen as their partner does the same. Then have one child point to words at random for his or her partner to read. Partners may then reverse roles.

Objective
• *To read high-frequency words*

REVIEW   **Tested**

High-Frequency Words

These words are reviewed from Lessons 11–14.

enjoy	minute
especially	question
father	wash
imagine	wear
interesting	year

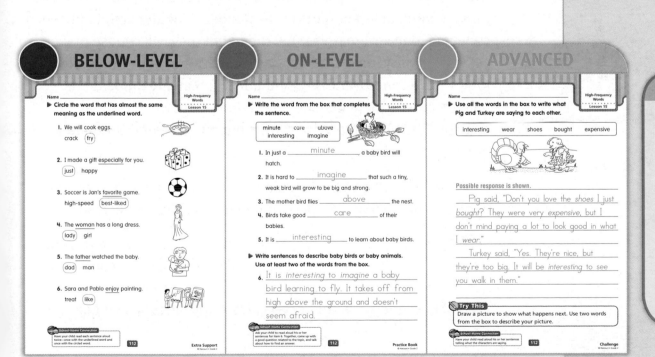

▲ Extra Support, p. 112   ▲ Practice Book, p. 112   ▲ Challenge, p. 112

E L L

• Group children according to academic levels, and assign one of the pages on the left.

• Clarify any unfamiliar concepts as necessary. See *ELL Teacher Guide* Lesson 15 for support in scaffolding instruction.

READERS' THEATER

Read Together: "A Birthday Mystery"

5-DAY READERS' THEATER	
DAY 1	Read Aloud/Read Along
DAY 2	**Read Together**
DAY 3	Choose Roles/Rehearse
DAY 4	Rehearse Roles
DAY 5	Perform

Objectives

- *To practice reading fluently with correct punctuation and phrasing*

Fluency Support Materials

Fluency Builders, Grade 2, Lesson 15

Audiotext "A Birthday Mystery" is available on *Audiotext 2.*

A Birthday Mystery

Characters

Narrator	Nicky	Sam
Alex	Pat	Lee

Narrator: Today is Alex's birthday.

Alex: My birthday is one of my favorite days of the year to celebrate. This year I'm especially excited, because my family told me I'm going to get a special present.

Narrator: Alex can't wait to find out what the present is.

Alex: I know what I'll do! I'll ask my brothers and sisters for hints. I enjoy guessing games. If someone gives me hints, there's nothing I can't figure out.

Narrator: First, Alex asks Nicky.

Alex: Hi, Nicky. Why don't you give me a hint about my present?

Nicky: If I do, it won't be a surprise.

Alex: I'm not going to figure it out from one little hint.

Nicky: Okay, I'll give you one little hint. It's something that's very soft.

Lesson 15: A Birthday Mystery 130 Teacher Resource Book

▲ **Teacher Resource Book, pp. 130–133**

Preview

GENRE Have children open their books to page 452, or distribute photocopies of the script from *Teacher Resource Book* pages 130–133. Help children recall that this Readers' Theater is a mystery. Remind them that a mystery is a story in which characters use clues to figure out something unknown.

Focus on Fluency

DISCUSS PUNCTUATION AND PHRASING Remind children that in this theme they learned that good readers use punctuation and phrasing to help them read more fluently. Remind them also that a period signals a stop, but a question mark or an exclamation point means that the sentence should be read with special expression. Likewise, phrasing, or grouping text into "chunks" of words that go together, can make their reading sound more fluent.

Read Together

ORAL READING Place children in small groups. Have children take turns reading different parts in the Readers' Theater script until each child has read several roles. Tell them that they will choose or you will assign parts on a different day. Explain that in this first reading, they should concentrate on using punctuation and phrasing to help them read more fluently. Tell children that when they make a mistake, they should stop, correct the mistake, and continue practicing reading.

Visit the different groups, listening to children read. Offer encouragement, and modify reading for fluency as children need it.

Think Aloud I see how some sentences that begin with *What* or *How* give me a clue that the sentences should be read as questions. I will try reading them that way, as I am practicing right now and know that I can correct any mistakes I make.

Build Robust Vocabulary

Words from the Read-Aloud

Teach/Model

Routine Card 3

INTRODUCE ROBUST VOCABULARY Use *Routine Card 3* to introduce the words.

▶ Read-Aloud Anthology, "The Missing Baseball Mystery," p. 452

❶ Put the word in **selection context**.
❷ Display Transparency R75 and say the word and the **Student-Friendly Explanation**.
❸ Have children **say the word** with you.
❹ Use the word in other contexts, and have children **interact with the word's meaning**.
❺ Remove the transparency. Say the Student-Friendly Explanation again, and ask children to **name the word** that goes with it.

❶ **Selection Context:** Will said that friends never **distrust** friends.
❹ **Interact with Word Meaning:** If you distrust someone, would you leave your bicycle alone with the person, or would you lock it up?

❶ **Selection Context:** Charlie was the only **witness** to the crime.
❹ **Interact with Word Meaning:** Can you be a witness to an event that happened at school while you were at home? Why?

❶ **Selection Context:** Will brushed back a **lock** of his hair.
❹ **Interact with Word Meaning:** A lock of hair can fall in front of your eyes when your head is down. What can you do?

❶ **Selection Context:** The children found the ball **beneath** a tree.
❹ **Interact with Word Meaning:** Name something that is beneath your table right now.

Practice/Apply

GUIDED PRACTICE Ask children to do the following:
• Show what you do when a *lock* of hair blocks your eyes.
• Name something that is *beneath* your feet when you walk.

Objective

• *To develop robust vocabulary through discussing a literature selection*

INTRODUCE Tested ✓

Vocabulary: Lesson 15

distrust	lock
witness	beneath

▼ **Student-Friendly Explanations**

Student-Friendly Explanations

bewildered When you are bewildered, you are confused and unable to understand something.

evasive When someone tries to avoid answering a question, that person is being evasive.

mull When you think through possible solutions to a problem, or the answer to a question, you mull over the information.

startle If someone comes up quietly behind you and surprises you, the person may startle you.

distrust When someone is not honest with you, you might distrust that person.

witness If someone sees an event and can tell about it, that person is a witness.

lock A group of hairs that hang together is a lock of hair.

beneath If you stand under a tree, you are standing beneath the tree.

Grade 2, Lesson 15 R75 Vocabulary

Transparency R75

Grammar
Review: Singular Possessive Nouns

5-DAY GRAMMAR	
DAY 1	Review Abbreviations
DAY 2	Review Singular Possessive Nouns
DAY 3	Review Plural Possessive Nouns
DAY 4	Review Pronouns
DAY 5	Cumulative Review

Objective
- *To identify and form singular possessive nouns*

Daily Proofreading

Dr smiths bag was on the flor.

(Dr.; Smith's; floor)

Reinforce the Skill

REVIEW SINGULAR POSSESSIVE NOUNS   Remind children that a singular possessive noun shows who or what something belongs to. Point out that there is always an apostrophe plus *s* ('*s*) in a singular possessive noun. Tell children that they use possessive nouns all the time when they talk with others.

Write the following phrase on the board: *the cat's claws*. Have a volunteer read the phrase and tell who or what the claws belong to. Review how the singular possessive word *cat's* is formed by adding an apostrophe in front of the *s*.

Practice/Apply

GUIDED PRACTICE   Write the following sentences on the board.

> **Maria shook the dog's paw.** (dog's)
>
> **Trina liked the cover of the book a lot.** (book's)

Have a volunteer read the first sentence aloud. Guide children in identifying the singular possessive noun in the sentence, explaining how the apostrophe and *s* have been added to show that something belongs to something else or to someone. Then have a volunteer read aloud the last sentence. Guide children in rewriting the possessive noun in the sentence.

INDEPENDENT PRACTICE   Write the following sentences on the board. Have children rewrite them, using possessive nouns.

> **The tractor that belongs to the farmer is broken.** (The farmer's tractor is broken.)
> **The player shook the hand of the fan.** (The player shook the fan's hand.)
> **The kittens of the mother cat were sleeping.** (The mother cat's kittens were sleeping.)

Name _____

Abbreviations;
Singular Possessive
Nouns
Lesson 15

▶ Write an abbreviation to answer each question. **Answers will vary.**

1. What month is it now? _____
2. What day is today? _____
3. In which month is your birthday? _____
4. What day was yesterday? _____

▶ Follow the directions to write the possessive form of each noun.

5. Mexico + apostrophe + s   Mexico's
6. flower + apostrophe + s   flower's
7. rabbit + apostrophe + s   rabbit's
8. Anne + apostrophe + s   Anne's
9. house + apostrophe + s   house's

Practice Book

113

▲ **Practice Book, p. 113**

5-DAY WRITING	
DAY 1	Select a Piece and Revise
DAY 2	Revise
DAY 3	Proofread and Publish
DAY 4	Publish
DAY 5	Present

Writing
Revise

Revise

REVISE Remind children that good writers often revise their writing many times before they are satisfied with their work. Point out that having a friend or an adult read through a draft and offer suggestions for making it better can be very helpful.

Think Aloud **When I revise a draft, I read through it to make sure that the ideas are clear and that the writing is interesting. Sometimes I'll ask someone to read through my draft and offer suggestions for ways to make the writing clearer and more interesting.**

Have children work with a partner to continue to revise the piece of writing that they have chosen to publish. Encourage partners to offer each other positive feedback and helpful suggestions.

GRAMMAR-WRITING CONNECTION Remind children to check that they have correctly used singular possessive nouns to show that something belongs to something or someone else. Have them use Editor's Marks to mark corrections.

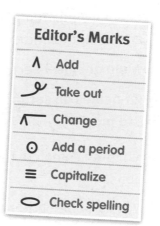

Editor's Marks	
∧	Add
✐	Take out
⌐	Change
⊙	Add a period
≡	Capitalize
⟠	Check spelling

WRITING TRAIT **IDEAS** Remind children that good writers often write about topics that interest them. As children revise their writing, have them check it to make sure that they are including only details that they find interesting.

CONFER WITH CHILDREN Meet with individual children, helping them as they revise their writing. Offer encouragement for what they are doing well, and make constructive suggestions for improving an aspect of the writing, as needed. If necessary, review the use of Editor's Marks to indicate changes and corrections on their drafts.

Objectives

- *To progress through the stages of the writing process*
- *To revise a self-selected piece of assigned writing*
- *To use singular possessive nouns correctly in a piece of writing*

Writing Prompt

Write About a Selection from the Theme Have children write a short paragraph telling why one of the selections they read in this theme was interesting to them. Encourage them to tell about the words the author used.

▲ **Writer's Companion**

Day at a Glance

Day 3

 phonics and Spelling

- Review: Consonants /s/*c*; /j/*g*, *dge*
- State the Generalization

Comprehension

Review: Fiction and Nonfiction

High-Frequency Words

- Review: *especially, interesting, question, imagine, minute, year, enjoy, wear, wash, father*

Fluency

READERS' THEATER

- Choose Roles/ Rehearse: "A Birthday Mystery," *Student Edition* pp. 452–459

Robust Vocabulary

- Review: *bewildered, evasive, mull, startle, distrust, witness, lock, beneath*

Grammar

- Review: Plural Possessive Nouns

Writing

- Proofread and Publish

Warm-Up Routines

 Oral Language

Objective *To listen attentively and respond appropriately to oral communication*

> ## Question of the Day
>
> **In what ways are you like other second graders? In what ways are you different?**

Use the following prompts to help children think about ways in which they are similar to and different from other second graders.

- **How old are most second graders? How old are you?**

- **What games do second graders like to play? What games do you like to play?**

Have children complete the following sentence frames to answer the questions.

One way I am like other second graders is _____.

One way I am different from other second graders is _____.

Read Aloud

Objective *To listen for rhyming words*

BIG BOOK OF RHYMES AND POEMS
Display "Did You Ever Think?" on page 25, and read aloud the title. Remind children of previous discussions about each person's unique qualities. Then ask children to listen for rhyming words as they read the poem aloud with you. Call on volunteers to name any rhyming words they heard in the poem. (you, do; name, same)

▲ **Big Book of Rhymes and Poems, p. 25**

Word Wall

Objective *To read high-frequency words*

REVIEW HIGH-FREQUENCY WORDS Point to the following words on the Word Wall: *especially, year, interesting, enjoy, question, wear, imagine, wash, minute,* and *father.* Choral-read the words with children, clapping out the number of syllables as you read each one. Then point to the words again. For each word, have a volunteer clap out the number of syllables as he or she reads. Then have the whole group read the word and clap out its syllables. Continue until all of the words have been read.

Consonants /s/c; /j/g, dge

 phonics and Spelling

5-DAY PHONICS	
DAY 1	Review /ch/ch, tch; /sh/sh; /th/th
DAY 2	Review /ē/y, ey
DAY 3	Review /s/c; /j/g, dge
DAY 4	Review /ûr/ir, ur, er, ear
DAY 5	Cumulative Review

Objectives

- *To recognize and blend the soft sounds of* c *and* g
- *To read words with* /s/c *and* /j/g, dge, *and other known letter-sounds*
- *To use* /s/c *and* /j/g, dge, *and other known letter-sounds to spell words*

Skill Trace

 Tested **Consonants /s/c; /j/g, dge**

Introduce	Grade 1
Reintroduce	T208–T211
Reteach	S22
Review	**T220–T221, T244–T245, T402**
Test	Theme 3
Maintain	Theme 4, T250

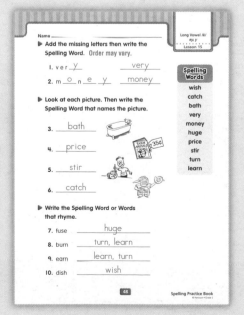

▲ Spelling Practice Book, p. 48

Review

CONNECT LETTERS AND SOUNDS Remind children that they have learned that the letter *c* can stand for the /s/ sound, and that *g* and *dge* can stand for the /j/ sound. Display the *Sound/Spelling Cards* for the /s/ sound and the /j/ sound. Review the letter/sound correspondences for *c* and *g/dge*.

Routine Card 1

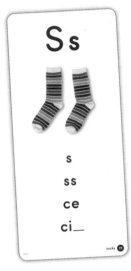 

▲ Sound/Spelling Cards

Read Words in Context

APPLY PHONICS Write the following sentences on the board or on chart paper. Have children read each sentence silently. Then track the print as children read the sentences aloud.

The singer stood at the <u>edge</u> of the <u>stage</u>.

Her <u>voice</u> filled the <u>huge</u> <u>concert</u> hall.

Her <u>fancy</u> dress had a <u>gem</u> at the neck.

5-DAY SPELLING

DAY 1	Pretest
DAY 2	Word Building
DAY 3	State the Generalization
DAY 4	Review
DAY 5	Posttest

Review Spelling Words

STATE THE GENERALIZATION FOR /s/c AND /j/g, dge   List spelling words 1–10 on chart paper or on the board. Circle the word *price* and ask children to read it. Ask a volunteer to identify the letter that stands for the /s/ sound and underline it. Then, repeat the process with the word *huge*, leading children to identify the letter that stands for the /j/ sound. Follow a similar procedure to identify the letters that stand for the following phonic elements:

- digraphs /ch/*ch, tch*; /sh/*sh*; /th/*th*

- long vowel /ē/*ey, y*

- *r*-controlled vowel /ûr/*ir, ur, er, ear*

 WRITE   Have children write the spelling words in their notebooks. Remind them to use their best handwriting.

Handwriting

OPEN AND CLOSED LETTERS   Remind children to leave an opening on the side of the letter *c* so that it does not look like the letter *o*.

Spelling Words

1.	**wish**	6.	**huge**
2.	**catch***	7.	**price**
3.	**bath**	8.	**stir**
4.	**very***	9.	**turn**
5.	**money**	10.	**learn**

* Words from "A Birthday Mystery"

BELOW-LEVEL

Sound Spelling   Write the spelling words on the board, leaving blanks for the target phonics elements. Work with children to complete each word by connecting the sound to the appropriate missing letter.

ELL

- Group children according to academic levels and assign one of the pages on the left.

- Clarify any unfamiliar concepts as necessary. See *ELL Teacher Guide* Lesson 15 for support in scaffolding instruction.

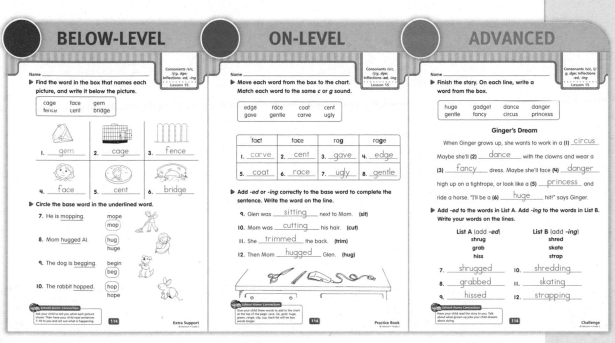

▲ Extra Support, p. 114   ▲ Practice Book, p. 114   ▲ Challenge, p. 114

Fiction and Nonfiction
Comprehension: Review

Objectives

- *To identify the elements of a fiction story*
- *To distinguish fiction from nonfiction elements*

Skill Trace

Tested **Fiction and Nonfiction**

Introduce	Grade 1
Reintroduce	T212–T213
Reteach	S26–S27, S36–S37
Review	**T248, T262, T272, T298–T299, T330, T344, T354, T404, T425**
Test	Theme 3
Maintain	Theme 4, T271

Reinforce the Skill

DISCUSS FICTION AND NONFICTION   Remind children that fiction is written for readers to enjoy, while writers of nonfiction want readers to learn facts and information. Remind children that they have read fiction stories such as "Big Bushy Mustache" and nonfiction selections such as "Rain Forest Babies." Review and list the characteristics of fiction and nonfiction on the board.

Fiction	Nonfiction
made-up characters	real people or animals
made-up events	real events

Practice/Apply

GUIDED PRACTICE   Draw on the board a blank chart like the one below. Discuss "Big Bushy Mustache" with children, filling in the left-hand column with clues that show the story is fiction. Guide children in identifying the nonfiction characteristics of "Rain Forest Babies," and list them in the right-hand column.

Fiction—"Big Bushy Mustache"	Nonfiction—"Rain Forest Babies"
Ricky is a made-up character. The events are made up, too. The illustrations might be a clue that the story is about made-up people.	There are photographs of real animals. There are headings. The selection gives facts about baby animals.

INDEPENDENT PRACTICE   Have partners take turns choosing other selections from the *Student Edition* and saying whether they are fiction or nonfiction. Have children complete charts of their own like the one above.

High-Frequency Words
Review

Reinforce

SEE THE WORDS Display word cards, or write the high-frequency words on the board. Read through the list several times, inviting children to join in after your first reading.

READ THE WORDS Call on volunteers to read the words as you point to them at random. Continue until all of the words have been read several times. Then, write the following sentences on the board and read each one aloud. Ask a volunteer to identify and underline the high-frequency word in each sentence.

- I thought "Rain Forest Babies" was <u>interesting</u> to read.
- Sal raised his hand to ask a <u>question</u>.
- Can you <u>imagine</u> what the world's biggest birthday cake looks like?
- It will take exactly one <u>minute</u> to walk to the bus stop.
- Michael and Kim <u>enjoy</u> playing soccer after school.
- Be sure to <u>wear</u> your jacket on a cold day.
- Rose went to the market with her mother and <u>father</u>.

Objective
- *To read common sight words*

REVIEW | Tested

High-Frequency Words

These words are reviewed from Lessons 11–14.

especially	year
interesting	enjoy
question	wear
imagine	wash
minute	father

READERS' THEATER

Choose Roles: "A Birthday Mystery"

5-DAY READERS' THEATER

DAY 1 Read Aloud/Read Along
DAY 2 Read Together
DAY 3 Choose Roles/Rehearse
DAY 4 Rehearse Roles
DAY 5 Perform

Objective

- *To read fluently using punctuation and phrasing as aids to expression*

Fluency Support Materials

Fluency Builders, Grade 2, Lesson 15

 Audiotext "A Birthday Mystery" is available on *Audiotext 2*.

E L L

Special Roles The role of the narrator in "A Birthday Mystery" is designed for ELL students needing language development support. Assign this role to those children who need the extra support. However, you may want to allow ELL students who need less support to choose their own roles.

Focus on Fluency

READ USING PUNCTUATION AND PHRASING Remind children that when they read aloud, they want to read with accuracy and at an appropriate rate, as well as with expression. Tell them that paying attention to punctuation and phrasing can help them do just that. Remind them to divide sentences into meaningful parts that make sense together.

Practice Reading

CHOOSE/ASSIGN ROLES You may want to distribute copies of the script to the children if you have not already done so. Assign or have children choose roles. More challenging roles, such as Alex, should be assigned to advanced readers, and shorter, less challenging roles, such as Pat, to below level readers. After you assign roles, encourage children to highlight the parts they will read aloud. Encourage them also to mark their scripts for phrasing or punctuation.

PRACTICE AND REHEARSE Remind children how to follow along as others read. Some children may still need to place a card or ruler under the lines to follow along, but others may be comfortable holding the pages farther from their bodies.

As children read aloud the script, circulate, providing feedback to individuals and groups by modeling, encouraging, and praising children for their efforts and enthusiasm. If children make a mistake, encourage them to try again. Also encourage children to give positive feedback to each other as they read their parts.

Tell children to notice how well they time their starting point, how smoothly they end, and how well they mimic natural speech.

Build Robust Vocabulary

Review

Reinforce Word Meanings

USE VOCABULARY IN DIFFERENT CONTEXTS Remind children of the Student-Friendly Explanations of the Vocabulary Words introduced on Days I and 2. Then discuss each word, using the following examples.

bewildered

- Would you be bewildered about finding your way in a new city? Why?

evasive

- Is it good to be evasive when someone asks for directions? Why?

mull

- When you are asked a difficult question, do you answer right away or do you mull it over? Explain.

startle

- What might happen if you startled a sleeping baby?

distrust

- Would friends distrust you if you followed the rules of a game? Why?

witness

- Are you a witness to what astronauts do on the space shuttle? Explain.

lock

- Why might you brush a lock of hair off your face?

beneath

- If you wanted to show a drawing, would you put it beneath a book? Why?

Objectives

- *To review robust vocabulary*
- *To demonstrate knowledge of word meaning*

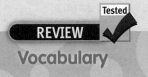

REVIEW Tested

Vocabulary

bewildered	distrust
evasive	witness
mull	lock
startle	beneath

▼ **Student-Friendly Explanations**

Student-Friendly Explanations

bewildered When you are bewildered, you are confused and unable to understand something.

evasive When someone tries to avoid answering a question, that person is being evasive.

mull When you think through possible solutions to a problem, or the answer to a question, you mull over the information.

startle If someone comes up quietly behind you and surprises you, the person may startle you.

distrust When someone is not honest with you, you might distrust that person.

witness If someone sees an event and can tell about it, that person is a witness.

lock A group of hairs that hang together is a lock of hair.

beneath If you stand under a tree, you are standing beneath the tree.

Grade 2, Lesson 15   R75   Vocabulary

Transparency R75

Grammar

Review: Plural Possessive Nouns

5-DAY GRAMMAR	
DAY 1	Review Abbreviations
DAY 2	Review Singular Possessive Nouns
DAY 3	**Review Plural Possessive Nouns**
DAY 4	Review Pronouns
DAY 5	Cumulative Review

Objectives

- *To recognize that plural possessive nouns show ownership by more than one person or thing*
- *To write phrases with plural possessive nouns*

Daily Proofreading

That is Stacys Bike.

(Stacy's, bike.)

Reinforce the Skill

REVIEW PLURAL POSSESSIVES Remind children that a plural possessive noun shows that something belongs to more than one person or thing.

Write the following sentence on the board:

The three boys' books are on the table.

Read aloud the sentence. Explain that the word *boys'* is a plural possessive noun because it shows that the books belong to all three of the boys. Underline the *s'*. Point out that plural possessives usually end with the apostrophe placed after the plural ending, *s'*. Explain that some plural forms of words, such as *children* and *mice*, do not end with an *s*, so their possessive form is made by adding *'s*. Write these phrases to illustrate these points:

the two dogs' tails   **the children's pets**

Practice/Apply

GUIDED PRACTICE Write the following phrases on the board.

the girls dresses

three mens hats

two childrens noses

Point to the first phrase and explain that it is supposed to show that the dresses belong to more than one girl. Rewrite the phrase with the apostrophe correctly in place *(girls')*. Ask volunteers to correct the remaining phrases.

INDEPENDENT PRACTICE Write these phrases on the board. Have children rewrite them to show plural possession.

- the hamsters cage
- the boys birthday presents
- the pens ink
- the mices paws

Writing
Publish

5-DAY WRITING
DAY 1	Select a Piece and Revise
DAY 2	Revise
DAY 3	**Proofread and Publish**
DAY 4	Publish
DAY 5	Present

Publish

CHOOSE A PUBLISHING IDEA   Have children choose a publishing idea that "fits" the kind of writing they have chosen to revise and publish. You may wish to suggest the following options.

- **Create a Tri-Fold:**   To highlight the sequence of events in a story or narrative, or in an informational paragraph, have children fold a large sheet of construction paper into three sections. Tell them that each section can hold a portion of the writing, such as the beginning, middle, and ending of a story. Tell children that they can illustrate each section.

My Birthday Party

- **Make a Shape Book:**   Tell children they can focus on an important character from a story or the topic of an informational paragraph by writing on a shape cutout. For example, children might cut out the shape of an animal from their story or cut out the shape of a ball for a paragraph about a sport or game.

Rain Forest Kangaroos

> **WRITING TRAIT** ▶ **PRESENTATION**   Remind children that in order for other people to read and enjoy the writing that the children have chosen to publish, it is important to use good handwriting. Point out that children should proofread their final drafts carefully to be sure that there are no new errors.

PREPARE FINAL WRITING   Tell children that they can begin to work on the final version of their piece of writing. Depending on the publishing idea they have chosen, children may either write on paper in their best handwriting or use available technology to type and print their writing.

Objectives

- *To progress through the stages of the writing process*
- *To publish a self-selected piece of assigned writing*

Warm-Up Routines

Day at a Glance

Day 4

phonics and Spelling
- Review: *r*-Controlled Vowel /ûr/*ir*, *ur*, *er*, *ear*
- Build Words

COMPREHENSION STRATEGIES
Review: Ask Questions, Monitor Comprehension—Reread

Reading
- Reading a Science Textbook: "The Life Cycle of a Frog," *Student Edition*, pp. 460–463

High-Frequency Words
- Review: *especially*, *interesting*, *question*, *imagine*, *minute*, *year*, *enjoy*, *wear*, *wash*, *father*

Fluency
READERS' THEATER
- Rehearse Roles: "A Birthday Mystery," *Student Edition*, pp. 452–459

Robust Vocabulary
- Review: *bewildered*, *evasive*, *mull*, *startle*, *distrust*, *witness*, *lock*, *beneath*

Grammar
- Review: Pronouns

Writing
- Publish

Oral Language

Objective *To listen attentively and respond appropriately to oral communication*

Question of the Day
If you were an animal, what are some reasons that you might bite a person?

Brainstorm a list of situations in which an animal might bite a person. As needed, explain that an animal may bite to protect itself, its territory, or its babies, and remind children to always be cautious around unfamiliar animals.

- **Why might a dog or cat bite someone?**
- **Why might a wild animal such as a bear or a tiger bite someone?**
- **What can you do to avoid being bitten by an animal?**

List children's ideas on the board.

Read Aloud

Objective *To listen for a purpose*

BIG BOOK OF RHYMES AND POEMS Display "Always Be Kind to Animals" on page 28 and read aloud the title. Remind children of their ideas about why animals bite, and ask them to listen for the poet's idea about how to avoid animal bites. Then have children read the poem aloud with you. Invite children to tell the poet's suggestion. (Always be kind to animals.) Ask children whether they think that advice is always good.

▲ **Big Book of Rhymes and Poems, p. 28**

Word Wall

Objective *To read high-frequency words*

REVIEW HIGH-FREQUENCY WORDS Point to the following words from the Word Wall: *especially, year, interesting, enjoy, question, wear, imagine, wash, minute,* and *father*. Ask volunteers to read each word and use it in a sentence. Repeat until all children have had a turn.

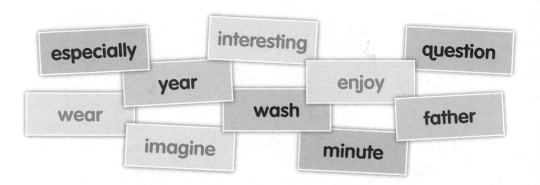

r-Controlled Vowel /ûr/ir, ur, er, ear

phonics *and Spelling*

Objectives

- *To recognize and blend the sound /ûr/ir, ur, er, and ear*
- *To read words with /ûr/ir, ur, er, ear, and other known letter-sounds*
- *To use /ûr/ir, ur, er, ear, and other known letter-sounds to spell words*

Spelling Words

1.	wish	6.	huge
2.	catch*	7.	price
3.	bath	8.	stir
4.	very*	9.	turn
5.	money	10.	learn

* Words from "A Birthday Mystery"

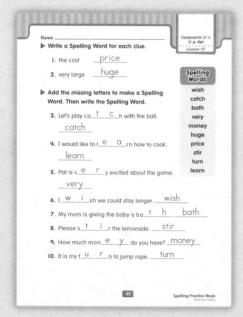

▲ Spelling Practice Book, p. 49

Review

READ A SPELLING WORD Write the word *stir* on the board. Ask children to identify the letters that stand for the /ûr/ sound and to read the word. Remind them that the letters *ir, ur, er,* and *ear* can all stand for the /ûr/ sound.

BUILD SPELLING WORDS Have children follow your directions to change one or more letters in each of the following words to make a spelling word. Have them write the word on a sheet of paper or in their notebook. Then have a volunteer change the spelling of the word on the board so that children can self-check their spelling.

- Write *still* on the board. Ask: **Which spelling word can you make by replacing the last two letters with one letter?** (stir)

- Write *torn* on the board. Ask: **Which spelling word can you make by changing the second letter?** (turn)

- Write *lean* on the board. Ask: **Which spelling word can you make by adding one letter?** (learn)

Use a similar procedure with the following words: *fish* (wish), *watch* (catch), *both* (bath), *vent* (very), *monkey* (money), *hug* (huge), *pride* (price).

BELOW-LEVEL

Build Spelling Words List the spelling words on the board. Point to the words one at a time and read each word aloud. Have children repeat each word, spell it, and then say it again.

ADVANCED

Write Clues List the spelling words on the board. Ask children to write clues for each word, without identifying the word. Have them change papers with a partner and identify the word that goes with each of their partner's clues.

Day 4

5-DAY PHONICS

DAY 1	Review /ch/ch, tch; /sh/sh; /th/th
DAY 2	Review /ē/y, ey
DAY 3	Review /s/c; /j/g, dge
DAY 4	**Review /ûr/ir, ur, er, ear**
DAY 5	Cumulative Review

Read Words in Context

APPLY PHONICS Write the following sentences on the board or on chart paper. Have children read each sentence silently. Then track the print as children read the sentence aloud.

Close your eyes and <u>turn</u> around.

Ernie wants to <u>learn</u> to play chess.

Today was a <u>very</u> rainy day.

Zoe has just enough <u>money</u> left to buy an ice cream cone.

There was a <u>huge</u> rainbow after the storm passed.

WRITE Have children use each spelling word in a new sentence.

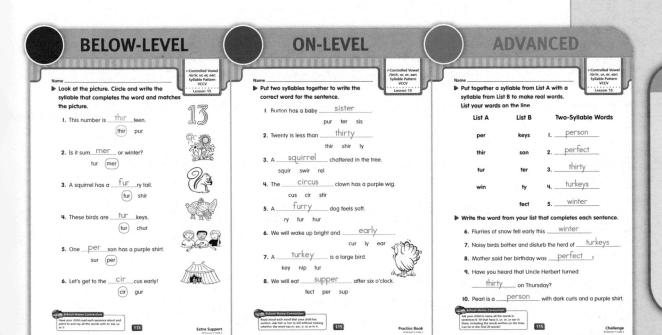

▲ Extra Support, p. 115   ▲ Practice Book, p. 115   ▲ Challenge, p. 115

E L L

- Group children according to academic levels, and assign one of the pages on the left.

- Clarify any unfamiliar concepts as necessary. See *ELL Teacher Guide* Lesson 15 for support in scaffolding instruction.

Comprehension Strategies
Review

Objectives

- *To analyze genre features*
- *To apply reading strategies to content-area reading*

Reading Your Science Book

PREVIEW PAGES 460–463   Have children scan the pages. Point out the smaller pages with callouts on pages 460–461. Also point out to children that pages 462–463 show the same pages, only at full size.

SET A PURPOSE   Tell children that their purpose for reading the text on these pages is to learn more about the features of science textbooks and how to use these features and comprehension strategies to help them read and understand.

DISCUSS TEXT FEATURES   Have children read the first two paragraphs under Reading Your Science Book. Then guide them in reading about the text features pointed out in the callouts on page 461. Explain to children that each time they read their science books, they will likely see the following text features:

- **VOCABULARY**   Important science words are highlighted.

- **LABELS**   Labels on photographs and drawings tell the names of things or parts of things.

- **QUESTIONS**   One or more questions are often found at the end of a section to help children summarize.

Review the Focus Strategies

DISCUSS COMPREHENSION STRATEGIES   Have children read and discuss the information about asking questions and rereading.

APPLY TO CONTENT-AREA READING   Explain to children that as soon as they begin reading a science lesson, they can use comprehension strategies to help them.

SET A PURPOSE AND READ THE SELECTION   Have children turn to pages 462–463. Tell children that "The Life Cycle of a Frog" is from a science textbook. Tell them that their purpose for reading these two pages is to use comprehension strategies and what they now know about science textbooks to read and understand the pages.

BELOW-LEVEL

Use Visuals   Point out the labels in the life cycle of the frog to explain how they name what is shown in the photographs. Explain that these labels appear in a flowchart that "flows" in order across the pages from left to right.

COMPREHENSION STRATEGIES
Review

Reading Your Science Book

Bridge to Content-Area Reading Science books have special features that help you read for information. Some of these features are labels, questions, and special vocabulary.

Read the notes on page 461. How can the features help you read a science lesson?

Review the Focus Strategies

The strategies you learned in this theme can help you read your science book.

👁 **Ask Questions**

Ask yourself questions before, while, and after you read. What is this science lesson mostly about? What parts will give you answers to your questions?

👁 **Monitor Comprehension—Reread**

Reread parts of a lesson you do not understand.

Use comprehension strategies as you read "The Life Cycle of a Frog" on pages 462–463.

VOCABULARY
New vocabulary words are in dark print. The meaning of the word is explained in the sentence. Vocabulary words are also in the glossary of your science book.

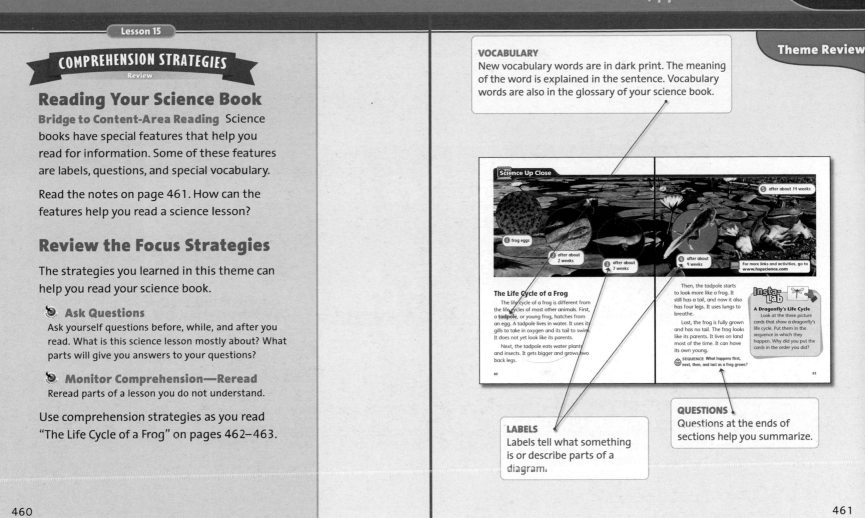

LABELS
Labels tell what something is or describe parts of a diagram.

QUESTIONS
Questions at the ends of sections help you summarize.

460

461

Science Textbook Features

Point out the special features of science textbooks noted in the callouts on page 461.

Vocabulary In science and social studies textbooks, highlighted vocabulary words are usually defined in the sentences in which they first appear.

Labels Labels name things to help readers understand what they are reading or seeing.

Questions Questions at the end of sections are there for readers to think about and check their understanding of what they have just read.

Apply the Strategies Read these pages from a science book. As you read, stop and think about how you are using comprehension strategies.

Stop and Think

How did rereading help if you didn't understand part of the lesson? What questions do you still have?

Science Up Close

 1 frog eggs

2 after about 2 weeks

3 after about 7 weeks

4 after about 9 weeks

 5 after about 14 weeks

For more links and activities, go to www.hspscience.com

The Life Cycle of a Frog 1 2

The life cycle of a frog is different from the life cycles of most other animals. First, a **tadpole**, or young frog, hatches from an egg. A tadpole lives in water. It uses its gills to take in oxygen and its tail to swim. It does not yet look like its parents.

Next, the tadpole eats water plants and insects. It gets bigger and grows two back legs.

60

Then, the tadpole starts to look more like a frog. It still has a tail, and now it also has four legs. It uses lungs to breathe.

Last, the frog is fully grown and has no tail. The frog looks like its parents. It lives on land most of the time. It can have its own young.

 Insta-Lab

A Dragonfly's Life Cycle
Look at the three picture cards that show a dragonfly's life cycle. Put them in the sequence in which they happen. Why did you put the cards in the order you did?

SEQUENCE What happens first, next, then, and last as a frog grows?

61

462

463

Monitor Comprehension

PAGES 462–463 Have children scan both pages. Point out that the main text begins with the heading "The Life Cycle of a Frog." Then have them read the pages, using comprehension strategies.

1 **AUTHOR'S PURPOSE** **What do you think was the author's purpose in writing this science lesson?** (to explain science information about the life cycle of a frog)

2 **FICTION AND NONFICTION** **Is this information fiction or nonfiction? How do you know?** (nonfiction; because it gives facts about frogs)

Stop and Think

Apply Comprehension Strategies

Asking Questions and Rereading Review with children how to use comprehension strategies such as asking questions and rereading.

Think Aloud After I read the sentence with the Vocabulary Word *tadpole* in it, I decided to reread it. I didn't understand it the first time I read it, and I wanted to remember that a tadpole is a young frog. After I read the last sentence on the first page, I asked myself, "What happens next?"

Encourage children to use the comprehension strategies as they continue reading.

High-Frequency Words

Review

Reinforce Words

RECOGNIZE HIGH-FREQUENCY WORDS   Give each child a set of word cards (*Teacher Resource Book* p. 80) and have children spread the cards out in front of them. Randomly call out each of the words, and have children hold up the matching card. Repeat until children respond quickly and accurately.

Tell children you will give a clue for each word. Explain that they should hold up the word card that matches your clue. Use the following clues.

- This word names an amount of time that is less than an hour. (minute)

- This word names a long amount of time. (year)

- This word names something you find on a test. (question)

- This word tells what you do when your hands are dirty. (wash)

- You could use this word instead of "very" in the sentence "It is very hot today." (especially)

- This word names a person in a family. (father)

- This word names what you do when you picture something in your mind. (imagine)

- You could use this word to tell about something you really like. (enjoy)

- This word is used to tell about something that holds your attention because it is exciting or challenging. (interesting)

- This word tells what you do when you put on a sweater or jacket. (wear)

Objective

- *To read high-frequency words*

REVIEW

High-Frequency Words

These words are reviewed from Lessons 11–14.

enjoy	minute
especially	question
father	wash
imagine	wear
interesting	year

 BELOW-LEVEL

Choral-Read   Have children read the high-frequency words with you as you flip through a set of the word cards several times. Then have children read the words.

 ADVANCED

Complete Sentences   Have children write a sentence for each high-frequency word, leaving a blank space for the target word. Tell them to exchange papers with a partner and fill in the blanks.

READERS' THEATER

5-DAY READERS' THEATER	
DAY 1	Read Aloud/Read Along
DAY 2	Read Together
DAY 3	Choose Roles/Rehearse
DAY 4	**Rehearse Roles**
DAY 5	Perform

Rehearse Roles: "A Birthday Mystery"

Objective

- *To read for fluency and expression*

Fluency Support Materials

Fluency Builders, Grade 2, Lesson 15

Audiotext *"A Birthday Mystery"* is available on *Audiotext 2.*

"Research Says"

Repeated Reading "Reading rate increased significantly from one to three readings, an occurence that brought instructional-level readers to near mastery-level performance."

–Rasinki, et al. (1994), p. 224

▲ **Teacher Resource Book, pp. 130–133**

Focus on Fluency

USE PUNCTUATION AND PHRASING   Have children continue to rehearse reading aloud fluently in their groups. They should each read aloud their part. Explain to children that since they are going to perform the Readers' Theater tomorrow, they need to pretend that they are in front of their audience when they rehearse. Remind children to read aloud expressively, loudly, and clearly so that the audience will be able to understand them. Call their attention again to punctuation and phrasing clues.

Think Aloud   **I read the role of Alex several times. I was paying close attention to ending punctuation so I knew how to speak. I also looked for phrases that went well together so I'd know when to pause to make my part sound like I was really talking instead of reading.**

Practice Reading

REHEARSE ROLES   Have children who are reading the same roles assemble in groups so they can help one another with how the character speaks. Have one group member read the role while other group members listen and offer positive comments.

Circulate and model reading particular lines if children are struggling. If you copied pages 130–133 in the *Teacher Resource Book* so children have individual scripts, they may want to double-underline or highlight in a different color words or sections that give them particular difficulty.

After children have read through the script in their character groups, have them reassemble with their whole group. Have them practice reading together, as if their audience is listening to them read. Tell them to stand or sit in the positions they will take on Day 5. Prepare the backdrop on page 114 of the *Teacher Resource Book*.

Build Robust Vocabulary

Review

Reinforce Word Meanings

USE VOCABULARY IN DIFFERENT CONTEXTS   Remind children of the Student-Friendly Explanations of the words. Then discuss each word in a new context.

bewildered, startle   Tell children to cover their eyes if the event would startle them, and to put their heads down if the event would leave them bewildered.

> **hearing a sudden boom of thunder**
>
> **missing a cookie from their lunch bag**

distrust, witness   Tell children to say nothing if they think it is possible that a witness saw an event, and to say, "I distrust this witness!" if they think it is unlikely that the witness saw the event.

> **space creatures playing in the school yard**
>
> **children getting off a school bus**

beneath   Tell children that if the thing you name can be beneath them, they should raise their hands. If not, they should do nothing.

> **a chair   stars   a ceiling   the floor   a sidewalk**

lock   Remind children that *lock* can mean a group of hairs, or it can describe the act of turning a key to close something. Ask them to raise their hands if you describe a lock of hair. Tell them to do nothing if you describe turning a key.

> **I brush away a lock from my eyes.**
>
> **I lock the classroom door.**

Objectives

- *To review robust vocabulary*
- *To figure out a word's meaning based on its context*

REVIEW Vocabulary

bewildered	distrust
evasive	witness
mull	lock
startle	beneath

▼ **Student-Friendly Explanations**

Student-Friendly Explanations

bewildered When you are bewildered, you are confused and unable to understand something.

evasive When someone tries to avoid answering a question, that person is being evasive.

mull When you think through possible solutions to a problem, or the answer to a question, you mull over the information.

startle If someone comes up quietly behind you and surprises you, the person may startle you.

distrust When someone is not honest with you, you might distrust that person.

witness If someone sees an event and can tell about it, that person is a witness.

lock A group of hairs that hang together is a lock of hair.

beneath If you stand under a tree, you are standing beneath the tree.

Grade 2, Lesson 15   R75   Vocabulary

Transparency R75

Grammar
Review: Pronouns

5-DAY GRAMMAR

DAY 1	Review Abbreviations
DAY 2	Review Singular Possessive Nouns
DAY 3	Review Plural Possessive Nouns
DAY 4	**Review Pronouns**
DAY 5	Cumulative Review

Objectives

- *To identify pronouns*
- *To use pronouns correctly in writing*

Daily Proofreading

Can Joseph come to the movies with I.

(me?)

▲ Practice Book, p. 116

Reinforce the Skill

REVIEW PRONOUNS   Review the pronouns *I, he, she, it, we, they,* and *me* with children and elicit that pronouns take the place of nouns. Ask children to respond to the following questions.

- What pronoun replaces a man or boy? (he)
- What pronoun replaces a woman or girl? (she)
- What pronoun replaces an animal or a thing? (it)
- What pronouns replace more than one person? (we, they)
- What pronoun replaces you and someone else? (we)
- What two pronouns replace you? (I, me)

Practice/Apply

GUIDED PRACTICE   Write the following sentences on the board. Work with children to replace each underlined word with an appropriate pronoun.

> **<u>Shannon and Lucy</u> sat together on the bus.** (They)
>
> **Lucy said, "<u>Shannon and Lucy</u> talked all the way to school!"** (We)
>
> **Shannon said, "Oh, no. You talked. <u>Shannon</u> listened!"** (I)

INDEPENDENT PRACTICE   Write the following sentences on the board. Have children work with a partner to rewrite the sentences, using appropriate pronouns to replace the underlined nouns.

> **<u>Davis</u> plans to go to the library today.** (He)
>
> **Davis asked his friend Matt, "Will you go to the library with <u>Davis</u>?"** (me)
>
> **<u>Davis and Matt</u> chose three books each.** (They)

Writing
Publish

5-DAY WRITING

DAY 1 Select a Piece and Revise
DAY 2 Revise
DAY 3 Proofread and Publish
DAY 4 Publish
DAY 5 Present

Publish

MODEL WRITING TITLES   Point out that the title of a piece of writing is the first thing a reader sees, and that an interesting or unusual title can make it more likely that someone will decide to read the piece. As you mention the titles below, write them on the board.

Think Aloud   **I like to think of fun titles for whatever I write because it makes people interested in reading what I write. If I wrote a paragraph about rain forest kangaroos, I might call it "What Kangaroos Carry" or "Keeping Up with Kangaroos." I could decorate the letter *K* in the title, or I could use a special font on the computer when I type it.**

Have volunteers share the title of the piece of writing they are publishing. Discuss how they might enhance its appearance or work together to brainstorm alternatives that are more creative.

Handwriting

NEATNESS COUNTS   Remind children to use their best printing for any information that they add to their writing. Point out that in addition to making their writing easier to read, neat printing will draw attention to their published piece when it is displayed.

 CONVENTIONS   Suggest that children review their writing to be sure that each sentence begins with a capital letter and ends with the appropriate end mark. Tell them to check their spelling and to be sure that they have correctly used any pronouns in their writing.

What Kangaroos Carry

Objectives

- *To progress through the stages of the writing process*
- *To publish a self-selected piece of assigned writing*

 ### Writing Prompt

Reflect   Ask children to write about why they decided to use the publishing idea they have chosen.

TECHNOLOGY

GO online   Children can use a word-processing program to design creative formats for the titles of their writing.

Day at a Glance

Day 5

 phonics and Spelling

- Lessons 11–14 Review
- Posttest

Comprehension

Focus Skill Review: Fiction and Nonfiction

High-Frequency Words

- Review: *especially, interesting, question, imagine, minute, year, enjoy, wear, wash, father*

Fluency

READERS' THEATER

- Reading Using Punctuation and Phrasing
- Perform: "A Birthday Mystery," *Student Edition,* pp. 452–459

Robust Vocabulary

- Review: *bewildered, evasive, mull, startle, distrust, witness, lock, beneath*

Grammar

- Review: Lessons 11–14

Writing ✏

- Present

Warm-Up Routines

 ## Oral Language

Objective *To listen attentively and respond appropriately to oral communication*

Question of the Day

What advice would you give to a child going to school for the first time?

Discuss children's ideas about how to make a school experience successful and fun. Use the following prompts.

- **What are some things about school that a young child might not know?**

- **What hints did you get, or do you wish you had been given, when you started school?**

- **Which is more difficult in school— doing your assignments, or learning how to behave? Why do you think so?**

Have children use the following sentence frame to share the advice they would give.

The most important thing to tell a child about school is _____.

Read Aloud

Objective *To listen for enjoyment*

BIG BOOK OF RHYMES AND POEMS Display "Aliona Says" on page 26 and read the title. Then reread the poem several times, inviting children to join in. Remind children of their ideas about advice for a child going to school, and ask them to speculate about the advice that the poet receives.

Aliona Says

An off-to-school hug
Is quick but nice.
Mine always comes
with some words
Of advice.

Emily George

**Big Book of Rhymes ▶
and Poems, p. 26**

Word Wall

Objective *To read high-frequency words*

REVIEW HIGH-FREQUENCY WORDS Show the following words from the Word Wall: *especially, year, interesting, enjoy, question, wear, imagine, wash, minute,* and *father*. Give the following clues for the words. Have children guess the word being described:

- **I spy a word that rhymes with *bear*. It has the same beginning sound as *wash*.** (wear)

- **I spy a word that means the same as *sixty seconds*.** (minute)

- **I spy a word that means the opposite of *answer*.** (question)

Continue asking clues until all words have been used.

> especially   enjoy   imagine
> interesting   wear   minute   father

Lessons 11–14 Review
phonics *and Spelling*

5-DAY SPELLING	
DAY 1	Pretest
DAY 2	Review
DAY 3	Review/Handwriting
DAY 4	Review
DAY 5	Posttest

Objective

- *To review spelling words*

Spelling Words

1.	wish	6.	huge
2.	catch*	7.	price
3.	bath	8.	stir
4.	very*	9.	turn
5.	money	10.	learn

* Words from "A Birthday Mystery"

Review

SPELLING TEST Assess children's progress using the dictation sentences.

Words with /ch/*ch, tch*; /sh/*sh*; /th/*th*; /ē/*ey, y*; /s/*c*; /j/*g, dge*; or /ûr/*ir, ur, er, ear*

1.	wish	Sam made a **wish** as he blew out his birthday candles.
2.	catch	Lulu tried to **catch** me in a game of tag.
3.	bath	We gave our puppy a **bath** after she played in the mud.
4.	very	Jamal studied **very** hard for his math test.
5.	money	Our class held a bake sale to raise **money** for our field trip.
6.	huge	Dad made a **huge** pizza to share with everyone at lunch.
7.	price	Do you know the **price** of that red jacket?
8.	stir	The recipe says to **stir** the soup as you heat it.
9.	turn	Mom asked me to **turn** around before I saw my surprise.
10.	learn	We **learn** how to spell ten new words each week.

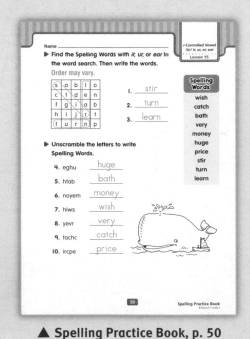

▲ Spelling Practice Book, p. 50

Fiction and Nonfiction
Comprehension: Review

Reinforce the Skill

REVIEW FICTION AND NONFICTION Remind children that fiction has made-up characters and events, and nonfiction is about real people, animals, or events. Review the selections in Theme 3, and identify each one as fiction or nonfiction in a chart on the board.

Fiction	Nonfiction
"Jamaica Louise James"	"At Play: Long Ago and Today"
"Big Bushy Mustache"	"Rain Forest Babies"

Practice/Apply

GUIDED PRACTICE Review the *Read-Aloud Anthology* selections for Theme 3, and work with children to identify each one as fiction or nonfiction. Add the titles to the chart above.

INDEPENDENT PRACTICE Have partners take turns choosing other selections they have read from the *Student Edition* and say whether they are fiction or nonfiction.

Objectives
- To identify the elements of fiction and nonfiction
- To distinguish fiction from nonfiction elements

Skill Trace
 Fiction and Nonfiction

Introduce	Grade 1
Reintroduce	T212–T213
Reteach	S26–S27, S36–S37
Review	**T248, T262, T272, T298–T299, T330, T344, T354, T404, T425**
Test	Theme 3
Maintain	Theme 4, T271

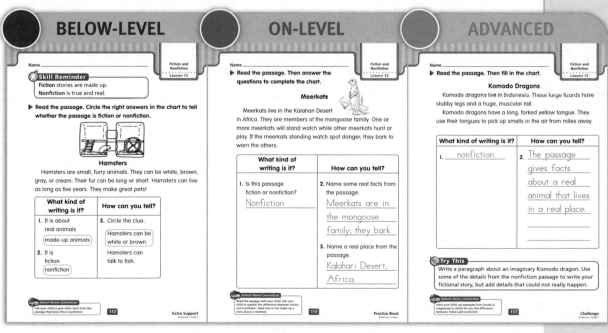

▲ Extra Support, p. 117   ▲ Practice Book, p. 117   ▲ Challenge, p. 117

E L L
- Group children according to academic levels, and assign one of the pages on the left.
- Clarify any unfamiliar concepts as necessary. See *ELL Teacher Guide* Lesson 15 for support in scaffolding instruction.

 High-Frequency Words

Review

Objective

• *To read high-frequency words*

REVIEW

High-Frequency Words

These words are reviewed from Lessons 11–14.

enjoy	minute
especially	question
father	wash
imagine	wear
interesting	year

Reinforce

REINFORCE WORD RECOGNITION Write the following words on the board: *especially, year, interesting, enjoy, question, wear, imagine, wash, minute,* and *father*. Have children choral-read the words several times. Then point to words at random and have the group read them aloud.

SORT WORDS Guide children in sorting the words into columns according to the number of syllables. Then have them read the words in each column again.

1 Syllable	2 Syllables	3 Syllables	4 Syllables
year	question	imagine	especially
wear	minute		interesting
wash	enjoy		
	father		

READERS' THEATER

Perform: "A Birthday Mystery"

5-DAY READERS' THEATER
DAY 1	Read Aloud/Read Along
DAY 2	Read Together
DAY 3	Choose Roles/Rehearse
DAY 4	Rehearse Roles
DAY 5	Perform

Performance Ideas

PRESENTATION STRATEGIES   Tell children that it is okay to be nervous but to keep going once they begin reading. Remind them that after they finish reading aloud, the cast should take a bow. Also emphasize the importance of being polite and listening attentively if groups are taking turns reading aloud for each other. You may want to project the backdrop for "A Birthday Mystery" against a board or screen.

Focus on Fluency

USING PUNCTUATION AND PHRASING   Remind children to use the following fluency tips they've been practicing all this week:

- Use punctuation as clues to reading smoothly and with feeling.

- Use phrasing to make the reading sound more natural.

Perform

SPEAKING AND LISTENING   Before children perform, review rules for reading before an audience and for being a listener.

Performance Checklist

- I look up occasionally at the audience as I read.

- I read clearly and with feeling.

- I listen quietly and politely as others read.

RUBRIC   See rubric for Speaking and Listening on page R5.

EVALUATE   Invite children or others in the audience to comment in a positive way about how the readers read. Encourage children to speak in complete sentences.

Objectives

- *To self-evaluate oral reading for fluency*
- *To speak in complete sentences*

▲ Teacher Resource Book, p. 114

▲ Teacher Resource Book, pp. 130–133

Grammar

Review: Lessons 11–14

5-DAY GRAMMAR

DAY 1	Review: Abbreviations
DAY 2	Review: Singular Possessive Nouns
DAY 3	Review: Plural Possessive Nouns
DAY 4	Review: Pronouns
DAY 5	Cumulative Review

Objectives

- *To use correct capitalization and punctuation in abbreviations*
- *To identify and form singular possessive nouns*
- *To identify and form plural possessive nouns*
- *To identify pronouns*

Daily Proofreading

Shondras shoes got wet in yesterdays rain storm.

(Shondra's, yesterday's)

Reinforce the Skills

MIXED REVIEW   Discuss with children the following points:

- An abbreviation is a short way to write a word. Most abbreviations end with a period.

- A singular possessive noun shows that something belongs to one person, animal, or thing. Singular possessives are often formed by adding an apostrophe plus *s*.

- A plural possessive noun shows that something belongs to more than one person, animal, or thing. Plural possessives are often formed by adding an apostrophe after a final *s*.

- Pronouns take the place of nouns. Commonly used pronouns include *I, he, she, it, we, they,* and *me*.

Practice/Apply

GUIDED PRACTICE   Write the following sentences on the board. Work with children to identify any abbreviations, singular possessive nouns, plural possessive nouns, and pronouns.

Dr. Foster's office is on the second floor.
She is my two sisters' dentist.
The building's elevator was broken last week.
A sign on it said, "Tues., Apr. 3: Use the stairs."
Many children's feet climbed the stairs that day!

INDEPENDENT PRACTICE   Have partners work together to write one sentence for each of the following: an abbreviation, a singular possessive noun, a plural possessive noun, and a pronoun. Tell partners to exchange their sentences with another pair and to identify any abbreviations, singular possessive nouns, plural possessive nouns, and pronouns in the other pair's sentences.

Writing
Present

5-DAY WRITING

DAY 1	Select a Piece and Revise
DAY 2	Revise
DAY 3	Proofread and Publish
DAY 4	Publish
DAY 5	Present

Share

CELEBRATE WRITING Provide an opportunity for children to share their published pieces of writing. Some children may enjoy a chance to read aloud to the group, while others may prefer to display their writing for others to read silently.

 **CONVENTIONS** Take time to highlight accurate use of conventions in finished writing, especially for those children who find it a challenge.

LISTENING AND SPEAKING SKILLS Remind children that when they are reading aloud, they should

- speak clearly and at an appropriate pace.
- use proper phrasing.

Remind listeners that they should

- listen critically and responsively.
- ask for clarification as needed.

NOTE: A 4-point rubric appears on page R8.

SCORING RUBRIC

	6	5	4	3	2	1
FOCUS	Completely focused, purposeful.	Focused on topic and purpose.	Generally focused on topic and purpose.	Somewhat focused on topic and purpose.	Related to topic but does not maintain focus.	Lacks focus and purpose.
ORGANIZATION	Ideas progress logically; paper conveys sense of completeness.	Organization mostly clear; paper gives sense of completeness.	Organization mostly clear, but some lapses occur; may seem unfinished.	Some sense of organization; seems unfinished.	Little sense of organization.	Little or no sense of organization.
SUPPORT	Strong, specific details; clear, exact language; freshness of expression.	Strong, specific details; clear, exact language.	Adequate support and word choice.	Limited supporting details; limited word choice.	Few supporting details; limited word choice.	Little development; limited or unclear word choice.
CONVENTIONS	Varied sentences; few, if any, errors.	Varied sentences; few errors.	Some sentence variety; few errors.	Simple sentence structures; some errors.	Simple sentence structures; many errors.	Unclear sentence structures; many errors.

REPRODUCIBLE STUDENT RUBRICS for specific writing purposes and presentations are available on pages R2–R8.

Objectives

- *To publish and share writing*
- *To listen attentively to oral presentations*
- *To speak clearly using an appropriate pace and phrasing*

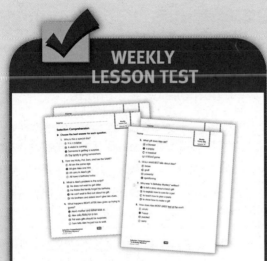

WEEKLY LESSON TEST

▲ **Weekly Lesson Tests, pp. 159–163**

- Selection Comprehension
- Phonics and Spelling
- High-Frequency Words
- Focus Skill
- Robust Vocabulary
- Grammar
- Fluency Passage **FRESH READS**

 For prescriptions, see pp. A2–A6. Also available electronically on StoryTown Online Assessment and ExamView.

 Podcasting: Assessing Fluency

Leveled Readers

Reinforcing Skills and Strategies

Genre: Fiction

BELOW-LEVEL

A Going Away Present

SUMMARY   With the help of the school principal, the children in Mr. Fletcher's class prepare a surprise going-away party for him.

 **phonics**   Lessons 11–14 Review

• **High-Frequency Words**

 Focus Skill **Author's Purpose; Fiction and Nonfiction**

Before Reading

BUILD BACKGROUND/SET A PURPOSE   Ask children if they have ever been to a going-away party. Guide children to preview the story and set a purpose for reading it.

Reading the Book

PAGES 3–14 **FICTION AND NONFICTION**   **Is this story fiction or nonfiction? How do you know?** (Fiction; It has illustrations. The characters and the story are made up.)

PAGES 3–14 **AUTHOR'S PURPOSE**   **Why do you think the author wrote this story?** (to entertain; to share a story about a nice teacher)

READING FOR FLUENCY   Have children reread pages 4–8. Remind them to pause briefly at commas, and to use the commas to help them read phrases rather than word-by-word.

Think Critically   *(See inside back cover for questions.)*

1 **NOTE DETAILS**   They planned a surprise party for Mr. Fletcher.

2 **INTERPRET CHARACTER TRAITS**   Responses will vary.

3 **AUTHOR'S PURPOSE**   Responses will vary.

4 **FICTION AND NONFICTION**   Responses will vary.

5 **PERSONAL RESPONSE**   Responses will vary.

LEVELED READERS TEACHER GUIDE

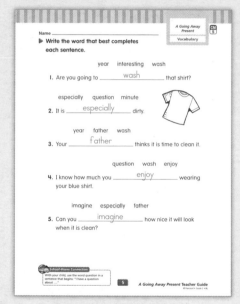

▲ High-Frequency Words, p. 5

▲ Comprehension, p. 6

www.harcourtschool.com/storytown

★ Leveled Readers Online Database
Searchable by Genre, Skill, Vocabulary, Level, or Title
★ Student Activities and Teacher Resources, online

ON-LEVEL

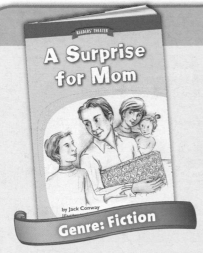

A Surprise for Mom
by Jack Conway
illustrated by
Genre: Fiction

A Surprise for Mom

SUMMARY   Dad returns home from a business trip with gifts for everyone in the family, including a special surprise for Mom. No one is able to guess what her gift might be, but when Mom opens the package, everyone agrees it's the perfect present.

- **phonics** **Lessons 11–14 Review**
- **High-Frequency Words**

Author's Purpose; Fiction and Nonfiction

Focus Skill

Before Reading

BUILD BACKGROUND/SET A PURPOSE   Ask children how they choose gifts for family and friends. Guide children to preview the story and set a purpose for reading it.

Reading the Book

PAGES 3–14 🌀 **FICTION AND NONFICTION**   **Is this story fiction or nonfiction? How do you know?** (Fiction; It has illustrations. The characters and the story are made up.)

PAGES 3–14 🌀 **AUTHOR'S PURPOSE**   **Why do you think the author wrote about the children trying to guess what Mom's gift was?** (to entertain; to make the story funny)

READING FOR FLUENCY   Have children reread pages 4–8. Remind them to change their voices when they see exclamation points and question marks, and to read phrases rather than word-by-word.

Think Critically   *(See inside back cover for questions.)*

① **NOTE DETAILS**   Mom was always telling someone to shut the door.

② 🌀 **FICTION AND NONFICTION**   Responses will vary.

③ **CHARACTER TRAITS**   Responses will vary.

④ 🌀 **AUTHOR'S PURPOSE**   Responses will vary.

⑤ **PERSONAL RESPONSE**   Responses will vary.

LEVELED READERS TEACHER GUIDE

Name _____
▶ Write the word from the box that best completes each sentence.

interesting	wash	enjoy
especially	father	year

1. This ___year___ we are studying animals.
2. Animals are very ___interesting___.
3. I ___especially___ love my pet rabbit, Bill.
4. My ___father___ got Bill at the pet store.
5. I ___wash___ my rabbit's cage when it is dirty.
6. I ___enjoy___ playing with Bill because he is nice.

▶ Finish the sentences. Accept reasonable responses.

7. I imagine _____
8. I like to wear _____
9. When I have a question _____
10. I read for _____ minutes a day.

A Surprise for Mom Teacher Guide

▲ **High-Frequency Words, p. 5**

Name _____
▶ Answer the questions about *A Surprise for Mom*.

1. What kind of writing is *A Surprise for Mom*?
   a book report   (a story)   a list of facts
2. Is *A Surprise for Mom* fiction or nonfiction?
   (fiction)   nonfiction
3. Why did the author write *A Surprise for Mom*?
   to tell how to choose a good present
   to give facts about doormats
   (to tell a funny story)
4. What clues helped you to answer question 3?
   Possible response: Carla says that the present is ice cream. The talking doormat makes everyone laugh.

A Surprise for Mom Teacher Guide

▲ **Comprehension, p. 6**

Leveled Readers

Reinforcing Skills and Strategies

Genre: Fiction

ADVANCED

Clues for Grandma

SUMMARY Grandma cleverly gets clues from her grandchildren about the gift she will get for her seventieth birthday. Though the children give away some bits of information, they are still able to keep the surprise a secret until Grandma opens her present—a necklace made of seventy pearls.

Before Reading

BUILD BACKGROUND/SET A PURPOSE Ask volunteers how many candles were on their last birthday cake. Guide children to preview the story and set a purpose for reading it.

Reading the Book

PAGES 3–14 **FICTION AND NONFICTION** **Is this story fiction or nonfiction? How do you know?** (Fiction; It has illustrations. The characters and the story are made up.)

PAGES 13–14 **AUTHOR'S PURPOSE** **Why do you think the author wrote "Clues for Grandma"?** (to entertain)

READING FOR FLUENCY Have children reread pages 13–14. Remind them to show the characters' excitement when they see exclamation points, and to use the commas to read phrases rather than word-by-word.

Think Critically *(See inside back cover for questions.)*

1. **NOTE DETAILS** Because it was Grandma's seventieth birthday.

2. **FICTION AND NONFICTION** Responses will vary.

3. **AUTHOR'S PURPOSE** Responses will vary.

4. **TEXT STRUCTURE AND FORMAT** Responses will vary.

5. **PERSONAL RESPONSE** Responses will vary.

- **phonics** **Lessons 11–14 Review**
- **High-Frequency Words**

  Focus Skill Author's Purpose; Fiction and Nonfiction

LEVELED READERS TEACHER GUIDE

▲ High-Frequency Words, p. 5

▲ Comprehension, p. 6

www.harcourtschool.com/storytown

★ **Leveled Readers Online Database**
Searchable by Genre, Skill, Vocabulary, Level, or Title
★ **Student Activities and Teacher Resources, online**

A Birthday Surprise

Genre: Fiction

SUMMARY Juan is celebrating his first birthday since he and his family moved to a new neighborhood. He is excited about his birthday present and his party, but the real surprise comes when his friends from his old neighborhood arrive to join in the fun.

- Build Background
- Concept Vocabulary
- Scaffolded Language Development

Before Reading

BUILD BACKGROUND/SET A PURPOSE Ask children to brainstorm some ideas about what makes a party fun. Guide children to preview the story and set a purpose for reading it.

Reading the Book

PAGES 3–14 🔘 **FICTION AND NONFICTION** **Is this story fiction or nonfiction? How do you know?** (Fiction; It has illustrations. The characters and the story are made up.)

PAGES 13–14 🔘 **AUTHOR'S PURPOSE** **Why do you think the author wrote "A Birthday Surprise"?** (to entertain)

READING FOR FLUENCY Have children reread pages 6–8. Remind them to show the characters' excitement when they see exclamation points, and to use the commas to read phrases rather than word-by-word.

Scaffolded Language Development

(See inside back cover for teacher-led activity.)

Provide additional examples and explanation as needed.

LEVELED READERS TEACHER GUIDE

▲ Scaffolded Language Development, p. 5

▲ Build Background and Vocabulary, p. 6

Theme Wrap-up and Review

Discuss the Literature

Use the questions below to guide children in making connections across the texts in this theme.

- **In what ways do the selections in this theme tell about growth and change?** (Possible response: The selections show ways that things can change or grow, and that sometimes we need the help of family or friends to make that happen.)

- **Why do your think "Rain Forest Babies" was included in this theme?** (Possible response: "Rain Forest Babies" was included in this theme to show that animals are different when they are young and change as they grow.)

- **Which character from the theme do you think showed the most growth or change?** (Responses will vary but should include examples of how specific characters showed growth or change.)

Return to the Theme Connections

Complete a graphic organizer to show information compiled from all the selections children have read and listened to in this theme.

Response Option

✎ **REFLECT** Have children reflect on and write about what they have learned about growing and changing.

SELF-ASSESSMENT Children can reflect on their own progress using the My Reading Log copying master on *Teacher Resource Book* p. 64.

LITERATURE CRITIQUE CIRCLES Have children meet in small groups to discuss and reflect on the literature in this theme. Encourage children to share their likes and dislikes about the following:

- genres
- subjects/topics
- illustrations or photographs

Remind children to support their opinions with examples found in the selections.

Children may also like to use this time to recommend to classmates any books they read and enjoyed during independent reading. Have them list titles for future reading.

My Reading Log

Date _____
Title: _____ Author: _____
Pages read _____
Write at least one sentence about what you read: _____
_____

Date _____
Title: _____ Author: _____
Pages read _____
Write at least one sentence about what you read: _____
_____

Date _____
Title: _____ Author: _____
Pages read _____
Write at least one sentence about what you read: _____
_____

Date _____
Title: _____ Author: _____
Pages read _____
Write at least one sentence about what you read: _____
_____

64   Teacher Resource Book

▲ Teacher Resource Book, p. 64

Then and Now

PRESENT TABLETOP DISPLAYS Group members may present and explain their displays to an audience. Encourage them to demonstrate what they have learned in a creative way.

PRESENTATION IDEA Suggest that children show the contrasts in their Then-and-Now Displays by putting on short performances in which they take the roles of a child of fifty years ago and a child of today.

- **Tell group members to decide** what each pair of children will discuss. Have each group make two signs to hold while performing: *Then* and *Now*.

- **Have pairs of children role-play a conversation** about how times have changed. Suggest that they focus on one topic or object shown in their group's display.

To evaluate children's work, you may wish to use the Rubric for Presentations on page R5.

School-Home Connection

Theme Project Presentations
You may want to invite family members and other interviewees to see the completed tabletop displays and children's presentations. Guide children in writing an invitation for the event that includes the appropriate date, time, and location.

Monitor Progress
at the End of Theme 3

THEME 3 TEST After instruction for Book 1–2, assess student progress in the following areas:

- Decoding/Phonics
- Comprehension of grade-level text
- Vocabulary
- Spelling
- Writing to a prompt
- Grammar
- Fluency*

(*Note on Fluency: Assessment can be staggered to make sure all students can be individually assessed.)

 PODCASTING: ASSESSING FLUENCY

GO online ONLINE ASSESSMENT

✓ Theme 3 Benchmark Test
✓ Weekly Lesson Tests
✓ Student Profile System to track student growth
✓ Prescriptions for Reteaching

GO online www.harcourtschool.com/storytown

MONITOR PROGRESS

Use Data to Inform Instruction for Theme 3

IF performance was	THEN, in addition to core instruction, use these resources:
● **BELOW-LEVEL: Reteach**	• Below-Level Leveled Readers • Leveled Readers System • Strategic Intervention Resource Kit • Extra Support Copying Masters • Intensive Intervention Program
● **ON-LEVEL: Reinforce**	• On-Level Leveled Readers • Leveled Readers System • Practice Book
● **ADVANCED: Extend**	• Advanced Leveled Readers • Leveled Readers System • Challenge Copying Masters • Challenge Resource Kit

BENCHMARK ASSESSMENT

Mid-Year Test

- Phonics/Spelling
- Comprehension
- Fluency
- Grammar
- Writing
- Vocabulary

▲ **Benchmark Assessment**

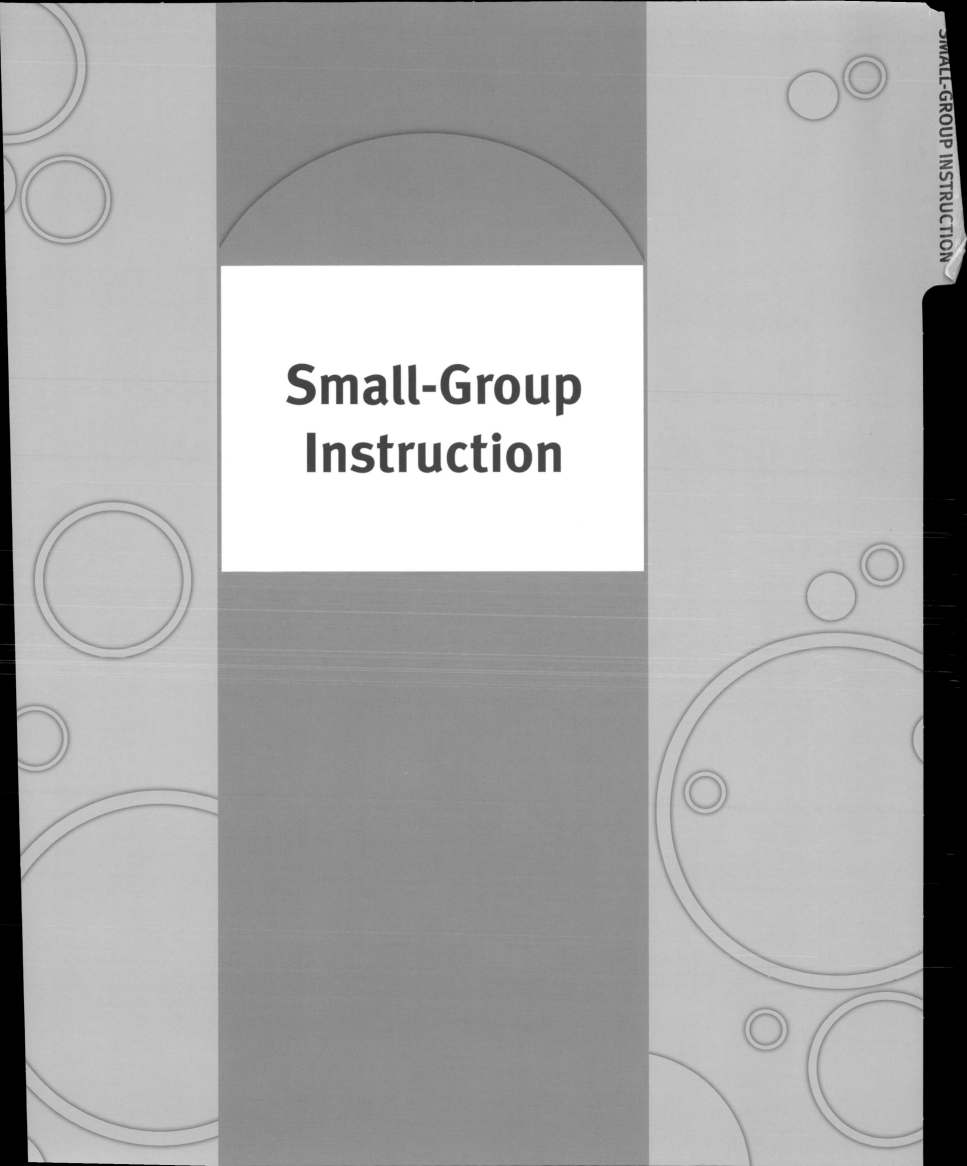

Small-Group Instruction

SMALL-GROUP INSTRUCTION

Phonics

Objective
To practice and apply knowledge of the digraphs /ch/ch, tch, /sh/sh, /th/th

Decodable Book 9

"The Bad Itch," "Flash Gets a Shave," and "Ruth, Thad, and the Pie Contest" ▶

MONITOR PROGRESS

Phonics After small-group instruction, are children able to blend and read words with *ch, tch, sh,* and *th*?

If not, provide additional small-group practice with the sound-spellings. See the *Strategic Intervention Resource Kit* for additional support.

Strategic ▶ Intervention Resource Kit

 **BELOW-LEVEL RETEACH**

Discriminate Letters

Routine Card 1 Use *Routine Card 1* and the *Sound/Spelling Card* to review the letter/sound correspondences /ch/*ch*, *tch*, /sh/*sh* and /th/*th*. Write the digraphs *ch, tch, sh,* and *th* on the board. Remind children *ch* and *tch* stand for the /ch/ sound as in the beginning of *chop* and the end of *catch*, *sh* stands for the /sh/ sound as in *shoe*, and *th* stands for the /th/ sound as in *think*. Hold up each digraph at random, having children name the sound each one stands for. Then have children read aloud Decodable Book 9. Pause at the end of each page to review any words children struggled to read.

 **ON-LEVEL REINFORCE**

Word Building

Write the letters *ch, tch, sh,* and *th* on the board. Add letters to build the following words: *beach, batch, bash, bath, thin, shin* and *chin*. Have children read each new word as it is built. Then have children read Decodable Book 9 aloud. Ask questions about each story to make sure children understood what they read.

 **ADVANCED EXTEND**

Write Silly Sentences with Digraphs

Have children brainstorm a list of words with the digraphs *ch, tch, sh,* and *th,* and have a volunteer write the words on the board or on chart paper. Ask children to use the words in silly sentences, such as *I watched Chip chip his teeth when he chomped on the shoe.* Challenge them to create a number of silly sentences that use all of the digraphs, as well as sentences that use words with the same digraph, such as *Sharks shy away from ships.*

High-Frequency Words

• BELOW-LEVEL RETEACH •

Match Words

Reintroduce the words using *Routine Card 5*. List the words on the board. Then, flip through a set of word cards (*Teacher Resource Book*, page 76), asking children to say the word, point to its match on the board and read the word aloud. Run through the cards until children are able to recognize each word quickly.

 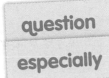

draw
bought
picture
worry
question
especially
minute
sure

• ON-LEVEL REINFORCE •

Rapid Word Naming

Hold up the word card (*Teacher Resource Book*, page 76) for each of the lesson's words, one at a time, and guide children to read the word. Then randomly display the words, having children name the word each time. Finally, ask children to write each word on the board, on chart paper, or in their notebooks.

ADVANCED EXTEND

Play "I Spy"

Display the eight word cards along with several cards from previous lessons. Hold up the cards at random, and have children name each word. Invite children to think of sentences that include one or more of the words. Then play "I Spy" with the words, having children suggest clues such as the following:

I spy two words with four letters. *(draw, sure)*

I spy a word with four syllables. *(especially)*

E L L

Model usage of each word with sentences such as the following:

*I can **draw** with a crayon.*

*I made a **picture** of a cat.*

*I want to ask a **question**.*

*The clock shows the hour and the **minute**.*

*I **bought** milk at the store.*

*Do not **worry** about the test.*

*I **especially** like cats.*

*I am **sure** you will like school.*

Have children repeat each sentence.

✓ MONITOR PROGRESS

High-Frequency Words After small-group instruction, are children able to recognize and read the words *draw, picture, question, minute, bought, worry, especially,* and *sure?*

If not, provide additional small-group practice with the words. See the *Intensive Intervention Program* for additional support.

Fluency

Objective

To use punctuation to read fluently in a manner that sounds like natural speech

Use Punctuation Point to question marks and exclamation points from the appropriate *Leveled Reader*. Model how to change your vocal level and expression for each type of punctuation. Write two short sentences on the board, one ending with an exclamation point, the other with a question? Model reading each, having children echo-read with you. Then have children read each sentence on their own.

Fluency After small-group instruction, are children able to read their *Leveled Reader* with punctuation?

If not, provide additional small-group practice with the words. See the *Strategic Intervention Resource Kit* for additional support.

Strategic ▶ Intervention Resource Kit

 BELOW-LEVEL **RETEACH**

Model Fluent Reading

Routine Card 8 Remind children that fluent readers pay attention to punctuation marks in the text they read to help them understand feelings, story events, and ideas. Explain that different punctuation marks—such as commas, periods, exclamation points, and question marks—are clues to how a word, phrase, or sentence should be read.

Distribute copies of *Lucia's Gift* to children. Read the book aloud to them, modeling fluency by reading in a natural-sounding way. Point out how the punctuation marks in the text give you clues about how to read. After reading, review a few sentences, pointing out the punctuation marks and explaining how they help you with your reading. Have children echo-read the sentences, imitating your attention to the punctuation. Then have them read the story with a partner, practicing paying attention to punctuation.

Echo-Reading

Routine Card 8

Distribute *Measuring Max* to children, and explain that they will practice reading the story in a natural-sounding voice by paying attention to the punctuation. Read each page aloud to children, modeling how you pause, adjust tone, and change expression with each punctuation mark. Have children read aloud after you, adjusting their reading to the punctuation. After reading the story through this way, have children practice reading the story with partners. Listen to them read, and give them feedback about how well they use the punctuation to read fluently.

Independent Reading

Routine Card 10

Ask a volunteer to explain how different types of punctuation are clues to help them read more fluently. Distribute *On Stage!* to children, and tell them that they will read the book, practicing using the punctuation to help them read more fluently. Have children work in pairs, having one child read the story aloud while the other listens. After the first child is done, have the listener offer constructive feedback about reading with punctuation. Then have children swap roles and repeat the reading aloud.

LEVELED READERS

● **BELOW-LEVEL**

▲ Lucia's Gift

● **ON-LEVEL**

▲ Measuring Max

● **ADVANCED**

▲ On Stage!

Comprehension
Author's Purpose

Objective

To identify an author's purpose for writing

ELL

Clarify Meaning The phrase *author's purpose* may be unfamiliar to children. Explain that *author* is the same as *writer*—the person who writes a book. Explain that *purpose* is the same as *reason:* It tells why. Explain that an author's purpose is the reason why the author writes a book, a report, or another type of writing.

MONITOR PROGRESS

After small-group instruction, are children able to identify and describe the author's purpose for writing different kinds of writing?

If not, provide additional small-group practice with the skill. See the *Strategic Intervention Resource Kit* for additional support.

Strategic ▶ Intervention Resource Kit

BELOW-LEVEL **RETEACH**

Review Author's Purpose

Have children turn to pages 324–325 in their *Student Edition*, and review with them the concept of author's purpose. Discuss the different kinds of writing in the chart on page 324, using examples of different types of literature from your classroom library. Hold up books or reports and preview the text of each example. Guide children to understand why the author wrote it and what the author wants the reader to think or feel when reading it. Use prompts such as the following:

Would you read a fiction story to get facts or would you read for enjoyment? Why?

Would you read a book report to get facts about a subject or would you read it to find out what the writer thought about a book?

ON-LEVEL REINFORCE

Identifying Author's Purpose

Remind children of the definition of *author's purpose,* and ask a volunteer to identify the author's purpose for writing "Serious Farm." Ask children to look through several of the *Student Edition* longer and shorter selections that they have already read. Have children identify each type of writing and tell what the author wants the reader to feel, learn, or understand in each. Have children fill in a two-column chart such as the one on *Student Edition* page 325 for each different type of writing.

ADVANCED EXTEND

Explore Author's Purpose

Explain to children that throughout the year they have been and will continue to be authors of different types of writing. Point out that each time they write something, they have a purpose for writing that the readers of their writing should be able to identify. Have each child select a sample of writing that she or he has written this year. Have children work in pairs and exchange their writing samples. Each partner should read the other partner's sample aloud and tell what the author's purpose is. Have the author of the piece explain what he or she wanted readers to learn or experience from reading the sample.

Robust Vocabulary

Objective
To review robust vocabulary

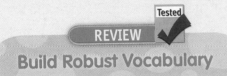

REVIEW Tested ✓

Build Robust Vocabulary

filthy	renowned
fellow	kin
executive	original
beautifying	adorn

MONITOR PROGRESS

After small-group instruction, are children able to use and understand the robust vocabulary words?

If not, provide additional small-group practice with the words. See the *Strategic Intervention Resource Kit* for additional support.

Strategic ▶ Intervention Resource Kit

⬤ BELOW-LEVEL RETEACH

Reintroduce the Words

Routine Card 3 Use *Routine Card 3* and **Transparency R56** to reintroduce all eight words to children. Review the Student-Friendly Explanations until they are familiar with the words. Then ask questions such as the following to check for understanding. Be sure children explain their answer each time.

filthy If your clothes were filthy, would you need to clean them or put them in the closet?

fellow Who would be more likely to be fellow classmates, you and your friends or you and your parents?

executive Would an executive work in an office or on a farm?

beautifying If you were beautifying the school, would you clean it up or would you put trash all around it?

renowned Might a renowned person be famous or not well known?

kin Who would be kin, a brother and sister or two people from two different families?

original If an idea is original, is it the first time someone thought of it or has someone already thought of it?

adorn Would you adorn a gift box with ribbon or with mud?

ON-LEVEL   REINFORCE

Apply Word Knowledge

Review for children the Student-Friendly Explanations on **Transparency R56**. Then give illustrative examples of the words. For example, name a way you might try beautifying the classroom or what you might adorn the walls of your home with. Then have children suggest other illustrative examples. Repeat the activity using non-examples for as many words as possible. For instance, tell something that would not be filthy such as a brand new car or a shirt from the cleaners. Have children explain why each of their choices is a good example of the word.

ADVANCED   EXTEND

Word Round Robin

Write the eight Vocabulary Words on index cards and use them as you review the Student-Friendly Explanations. Then place the cards in a stack face down. Have children take turns drawing a card, turning it over, reading the word, and using it in a sentence that begins with *I*, such as *I like to swim with my fellow swimmers*. Once the child has said his or her sentence, the child should pass the card to the next child, who should read the word and use it in a different sentence that starts with *I*. Children should pass around the card until each child has used the word in a new sentence. Then, the last child with the card places it face down and draws a new card, repeating the procedure in the opposite direction. Once all the cards have been passed around, children can begin again, using each word in a sentence that begins with *He*, *She*, or *They*.

Grammar and Writing
Language Arts Checkpoint

Objectives
- *To recognize and write abbreviations*
- *To compose a personal narrative*

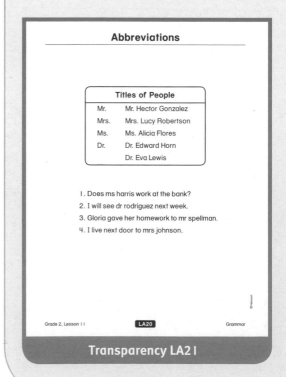

Abbreviations

Titles of People

Mr.	Mr. Hector Gonzalez
Mrs.	Mrs. Lucy Robertson
Ms.	Ms. Alicia Flores
Dr.	Dr. Edward Horn
	Dr. Eva Lewis

1. Does ms harris work at the bank?
2. I will see dr rodriguez next week.
3. Gloria gave her homework to mr spellman.
4. I live next door to mrs johnson.

Grade 2, Lesson 11   LA20   Grammar

Transparency LA21

BELOW-LEVEL   RETEACH

Review Abbreviations

Display **Transparency LA21**, reminding children that they have seen it before. Read each abbreviation and its example to children. Then do the following:

- Explain that abbreviations, such as these titles, are short forms of longer words.

- Point out the capital letter at the beginning and the period at the end.

Read the first sentence aloud, underlining the person's name and title. Rewrite the sentence with the correct form of the abbreviated title and proper name. Then, have a volunteer reread the sentence, pointing out what changed. Guide children in repeating these steps for the remaining sentences.

REVIEW WRITING A PERSONAL NARRATIVE   Remind children that a personal narrative is a story that contains sentences that tell about something that happened to the writer. Invite a volunteer to say a sentence about himself or herself that would be a good beginning for a personal narrative, such as *I was walking to school one morning.* Write the sentence on the board. Point out that some sentences in a personal narrative may contain abbreviations. Invite the remaining children to suggest sentences that they might write to begin a personal narrative. Write the sentences on the board. Encourage pairs of children to work together to brainstorm and write two more sentences to add to their personal narratives.

ON-LEVEL REINFORCE

Connect Grammar and Writing

Explain that many personal narratives contain people, such as teachers and adult friends, whose names begin with a title. Write the following sentences from a personal narrative on the board or on chart paper:

> **At the theater, I ran into Mr. and Dr. Garland. Mr. Garland had been my first grade teacher. Dr. Garland was his wife.**
> **"Hi, there, Mr. Garland," I said to him.**

Guide children in identifying and reading the abbreviations in the passage. Explain that if children include in their personal narratives names of people who have titles, such as *Mr.* and *Dr.*, they should make sure each abbreviation begins with a capital letter and ends with a period.

ADVANCED EXTEND

Apply the Skills

Remind children that in a personal narrative they should carefully choose words to describe people, places, and events. Point out that including titles such as *Dr.* or *Mrs.* are good choices, because the titles help identify more exactly the people the writers are describing. Remind children to use abbreviations when writing titles. Explain that exact, descriptive words can also help writers add energy and excitement to their writing. Ask a volunteer to read aloud a short paragraph or a number of sentences from his or her personal narrative. Discuss the descriptive word choices. Brainstorm words and phrases that the writer might add to the passage to give it more energy and to show enthusiasm.

ELL

First Person Subject *I* The subject in sentences in some children's home languages may often be dropped. Model and reinforce that, in English, the subject in sentences about the person writing or speaking is *I* and that it is not dropped. Write examples such as *I went to the store. I am in school. I like books.* Read the examples to children and then have them read them with you.

Phonics

Objective

To practice and apply knowledge of the long vowel /ē/y, ey

Decodable Book 10

"Silly Donkey and His Missing Key" and "Monkeys" ▶

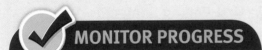

MONITOR PROGRESS

Phonics   After small-group instruction, are children able to blend and read words with /ē/ *y* and *ey*?

If not, provide additional small-group practice with the sound-spellings. See the *Strategic Intervention Resource Kit* for additional support.

Strategic ▶ **Intervention Resource Kit**

BELOW-LEVEL RETEACH

Blend Words

Routine Card 1 Use *Routine Card 1* and the *Sound/Spelling Card* to review the letter/sound correspondence /ē/y, ey. Write the words *very* and *money* on the board, underlining the *y* and the *ey*. Read the words aloud, emphasizing the /ē/ sound at the end. Remind children that the letter *y* and the letters *ey* can stand for the /ē/ sound at the end of words. Write the words *honey, baby, happy,* and *donkey* on the board. Guide children in reading the words and identifying the letters that stand for /ē/. Then have children read aloud Decodable Book 10. Pause at the end of each page to review any words children struggled to read.

ON-LEVEL REINFORCE

Word Building

Write the letters *y* and *ey* on the board. Add letters to build the following words: *key, donkey, honey, funny,* and *candy.* Have children read each new word as it is built. Then have children read Decodable Book 10 aloud. Ask questions about each story to make sure children understood what they read.

ADVANCED EXTEND

Write Fun Phrases

Have children make a list of words with /ē/y and *ey* by looking through literature in the classroom. Have a volunteer write the words on the board or on chart paper. Then ask children to brainstorm and write fun two-word phrases that use both a word with *y* and a word with *ey*, such as *funny money*.

High-Frequency Words

Objective
To read high-frequency words

BELOW-LEVEL RETEACH

Match Words

ELL

Model usage of each word with sentences such as the following:

> I like to **imagine** I am a bird.
>
> Pizza is my **favorite** food.
>
> I will be in third grade next **year**.
>
> I **enjoy** playing in the rain.
>
> I can **cook** eggs.
>
> I got a **board** game to play.
>
> I am **popular** with lots of friends.
>
> I can't buy **expensive** shoes.

Have children repeat each sentence.

Routine Card 5

Reintroduce the words using *Routine Card 5*. Display two sets of word cards (*Teacher Resource Book*, page 77), and ask children to match the words from each set. As you match each word, have children say the word. Randomly display the cards, and ask children to call out each word. Run through the cards until children are able to recognize each word quickly.

imagine favorite year enjoy

cook board popular expensive

ON-LEVEL REINFORCE

Rapid Word Naming

Hold up the word cards (*Teacher Resource Book*, page 77) for each of the lesson's words, one at a time, and guide children to read the word. Then randomly display the words, having children name the word each time. Finally, ask children to write each word on the board, on chart paper, or in their notebooks.

MONITOR PROGRESS

High-Frequency Words After small-group instruction, are children able to recognize and read the words *imagine, favorite, year, enjoy, cook, board, popular,* and *expensive*?

If not, provide additional small-group practice with the words. See the *Intensive Intervention Program* for additional support.

ADVANCED EXTEND

Fill in the Blanks

Ask children to write sentences using the lesson's high-frequency words. Have them write one sentence for each word, leaving a blank in place of the high-frequency word. Then have children trade sentences with a partner and fill in the blanks. Have them read the completed sentences aloud.

Fluency

Objective

To use punctuation to read fluently in a manner that sounds like natural speech

Use Punctuation Point to periods and commas in one paragraph from the appropriate *Leveled Reader*. Point to each mark and say: **A period lets me know to take a longer pause at the end of a sentence. A comma lets me know to take just a little pause between words.** Model the difference in reading the two types of punctuation by reading aloud a section of the selection. Have children follow along and echo-read with you.

 **MONITOR PROGRESS**

After small-group instruction, are children able to use punctuation to read their *Leveled Reader* fluently?

If not, provide additional modeling of fluent reading with small groups. See the *Strategic Intervention Resource Kit* for additional support

Strategic ▶ Intervention Resource Kit

 **BELOW-LEVEL RETEACH**

Model Fluent Reading

Routine Card 10 Remind children that fluent readers pay attention to punctuation marks in nonfiction texts to help them better understand the ideas and information. On the board, write examples of simple sentences and questions containing commas and exclamation points. Model reading each sentence, pointing to the punctuation marks and noting how you pause or change tone. Then distribute copies of *Having Fun: Long Ago and Today* to children. Read the book aloud to them, modeling fluency by reading in a naturally sounding way. Point out how the punctuation marks in the text give you clues about how to read. After reading, reread a few sentences with commas in a series, pointing out the commas as you read. Have children echo-read the sentences, imitating your attention to the punctuation. Then have them read the book with a partner, reminding them to monitor each other's reading and to offer corrections as they listen.

ON-LEVEL REINFORCE

Echo-Reading

Routine Card 8

Distribute *Riding Bicycles: Long Ago and Today* to children, and explain that they will practice reading aloud in a natural sounding voice. Read each page aloud to children, modeling how you pause, adjust tone, and change expression with each punctuation mark. Have children read aloud after you, adjusting their reading to the punctuation. After reading the book through this way, have children practice reading it with partners. Listen to them read, giving them feedback about how well they use the punctuation to read fluently.

ADVANCED EXTEND

Independent Reading

Routine Card 10

Ask a volunteer to explain how different types of punctuation are clues to good readers to help them read more fluently. Distribute *Board Riding: Long Ago and Today* to children, and tell them that they will be practicing using punctuation to help them read more fluently. Group children in pairs, having one child read the book aloud while the other listens. After the first child is done, have the listener offer constructive feedback about reading with punctuation. Then have children swap roles and repeat the reading aloud.

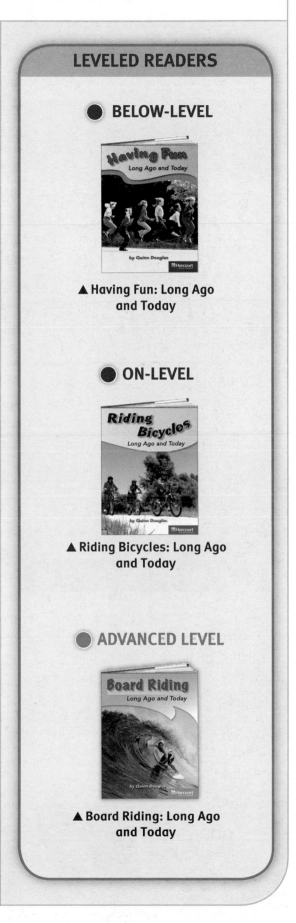

LEVELED READERS

● **BELOW-LEVEL**

▲ Having Fun: Long Ago and Today

● **ON-LEVEL**

▲ Riding Bicycles: Long Ago and Today

● **ADVANCED LEVEL**

▲ Board Riding: Long Ago and Today

Comprehension
Author's Purpose

Objective
To identify an author's purpose for writing

Clarify Meaning
Remind children that the author's purpose is the reason that he or she wrote a book or a selection. Review the meanings of the following phrases to help children better understand author's purpose:

To have fun

To learn

To feel something (emotional as opposed to tactile)

After small-group instruction, are children able to identify and describe the author's purpose for writing different kinds of writing?

If not, provide additional small-group practice with the skill. See the *Strategic Intervention Resource Kit* for additional support.

Strategic ▶
Intervention
Resource Kit

Guided Reveiw

Have children turn in their *Student Edition* to pages 360–361. Read aloud the paragraph on page 360 and discuss the chart to review author's purpose for different kinds of nonfiction writing. Then read aloud and discuss the passage on page 361. Guide children to understand that the writer of a how-to selection wants the reader to learn how to do something. Use prompts such as the following:

What does this paragraph tell you about?

What do you think the writer wants you to learn from reading this?

Go through the *Student Edition* with children to find a few previously-read examples of nonfiction writing. Preview the title, headings, and images and read aloud the first paragraph of each selection. Use prompts such as the ones above to guide children in identifying what the author wants the reader to learn from each selection.

Identify Author's Purpose

Remind children that an author might write a selection to entertain readers, to present information, to tell how she or he feels about something, or to make the reader feel a certain way. Look through copies of children's magazines from the classroom or school library with children. Stop and discuss different kinds of nonfiction writing such as how-to articles, reports, biographies, and letters to the editor. Have volunteers read aloud the beginning of each example, and then discuss what the writer of each nonfiction work wants the readers to know or learn. Guide children in understanding how the author's purpose is different depending on the type of nonfiction writing.

ADVANCED EXTEND

Play An Author's Purpose Game

Have children brainstorm a list of author's purposes, such as *to entertain, to give information, to tell how to do something, to given an opinion,* and *to make the reader feel something.* Have children write each example on a different index card. Then have children play an Author's Purpose Game. Stack the index cards face down. Have one child select a card and read the author's purpose aloud. Then, when that child says "Go," the other children should each look through their *Student Edition* or other books to find an example of a selection that matches the author's purpose. Each child should find a different example, if possible. Each child should present his or her example to the group and explain how the author's purpose for writing the selection matches that on the card. Then, a different child should draw and read a new Author's Purpose card to begin the next round.

Robust Vocabulary

Objective
To review robust vocabulary

REVIEW Tested ✓

Vocabulary: Lesson 12

recently	recreation
housed	leisurely
official	ramble
nominate	archaic

 **MONITOR PROGRESS**

After small-group instruction, are children able to use and understand the Vocabulary Words?

If not, provide additional small-group practice with the words. See the *Strategic Intervention Resource Kit* for additional support.

 **Strategic ▶ Intervention Resource Kit**

 **BELOW-LEVEL RETEACH**

Reintroduce the Words

Routine Card 3 Use *Routine Card 3* and **Transparency R62** to reintroduce all eight words to children. Review the Student-Friendly Explanations until they are familiar with the words. Then ask questions such as the following to check for understanding. Be sure children explain their answer each time.

recently — If you went to the dentist recently, might you have gone last week or last year?

housed — Might a lion in the zoo be housed in a cage or in a pool?

official — Who would be an official for the government, the President or a house painter?

nominate — If you nominate someone for a club, do you want that person to be in the club or to be kicked out of the club?

recreation — What is an example of recreation, water skiing on a lake or writing a report in an office?

leisurely — What would be an example of doing something leisurely, walking very slowly or racing down the street?

ramble — If you were to ramble through the woods, would you go straight on one path, or walk around a number of paths?

archaic — Which would be archaic, a cell phone you bought today or a telephone from a hundred years ago?

ON-LEVEL REINFORCE

Apply Word Knowledge

Review for children the Student-Friendly Explanations on **Transparency R62**. Then, for each word, have children name two examples. For example, for the word *leisurely,* children might say *walking slowly on the beach* and *riding a bike slowly through the park.* List children's examples on the board. Then have them use each example in a sentence, such as *The boy rode his bike leisurely through the park.*

ADVANCED EXTEND

Quick Sentences

Write the eight Vocabulary Words on the board. Point to each word, asking a child to read it and quickly use it in a sentence about the Read-Aloud, "Cardboard Box Joins Toy Hall of Fame," or the selection "At Play: Long Ago and Today." Once you have gone through the list a few times, quickly go around the group at random, asking each child to choose a word and use it in another sentence about the literature.

Clarify Meaning Use pantomime to help children understand the words *leisurely* and *ramble.* Say: **I am walking in a leisurely way.** Act out the meaning by walking slowly. Say: **I will ramble through the classroom.** Act out this sentence as well. Then have children act out the meaning for each word, repeating each of the sentences above as they go.

Student-Friendly Explanations

recently	If something happened not long ago, it happened recently.
housed	If something is placed or lives somewhere, it is housed there.
official	If someone holds a position of authority in an organization, the person is called an official.
nominate	When you suggest that someone should get an office, job, or honor, you nominate the person.
recreation	When you do something fun and relaxing, it is recreation for you.
leisurely	If you do something in a leisurely way, you are not in a hurry.
ramble	When you ramble, you wander around.
archaic	If something is archaic, it is old and not used anymore.

Grade 2, Theme 3   R62   Vocabulary

Transparency R62

Grammar and Writing
Language Arts Checkpoint

Objectives

- *To recognize and write abbreviations*
- *To write a personal narrative*

Student Model: Paragraph That Gives Information

Kickball

Kickball is easy and fun to play. The teams take turns being at bat. The pitcher rolls the ball and the person at bat kicks it. Then the kicker tries to run to first base without getting hit out. A run is scored when a kicker goes around the bases to home plate.

Grade 2, Lesson 12   LA25   Writing

Transparency LA25

BELOW-LEVEL   **RETEACH**

Review Singular Possessive Nouns

Write the following phrases on the board and read them aloud: *Miguel's coat, the coat's sleeves*. Underline *Miguel's* in the first phrase and explain that this shows that the coat belongs to Miguel. Explain it is a shorter way of saying "The coat that belongs to Miguel." Repeat the procedure for the other example. Then review the following:

- A singular possessive noun shows that something belongs to someone or something.

- There is always an apostrophe and *s* at the end of a singular possessive noun.

Display **Transparency LA25,** reminding children that they have seen it before. Guide children in completing each sentence with the correct singular possessive noun. Write each singular possessive on the board, demonstrating how to add the apostrophe *s*.

REVIEW PARAGRAPH THAT GIVES INFORMATION   Remind children that a paragraph that gives information tells about a real topic. Write the following paragraph on the board or on chart paper:

> **This is how to take care of your cat. First, make sure it has clean water to drink every day. Next, feed your cat each day. Once a week you should brush your cat. Finally, you need to take your cat to the vet for a check-up at least once a year.**

Read the paragraph to children. Guide them in identifying the main idea and the sequence words. Discuss the different information it tells about caring for cats. Then, work with children to write another paragraph about caring for another kind of pet.

Connect Grammar and Writing

Explain that paragraphs that give information often contain singular possessive nouns. Write the following main idea sentence on the board:

Sometimes you need to change a fishtank's water.

Guide children in identifying the singular possessive in the sentence. Then, have children brainstorm the steps to changing the water in a fishtank. List their ideas on the board. Work with children to complete the paragraph on the board, using the children's ideas. Stop to have volunteers explain how to write any singular possessives that might appear in the paragraph. When the paragraph is complete, review it with the group to make sure the steps are in order and that all the information tells about the main idea.

ADVANCED EXTEND

Apply the Skills

Have children work together to write a paragraph that gives information about one of the daily routines in your classroom. Have children brainstorm a topic and write a main idea sentence. Then have the group work together to complete the paragraph. Once the first draft is complete, have them edit and revise it using editor's marks. Remind children to check that they have correctly used any singular possessive nouns. Have one student write a finished draft on nice paper. Then post the paragraph as a reminder of this daily routine for the rest of the class.

Sequence Help children understand and use sequence words such as *first, next, then,* and *finally* by demonstrating a task such as erasing the board or sharpening a pencil. Talk through the steps of the task as you do it, carefully emphasizing the order of the steps using sequence words. Then have children repeat the task. Say each step, having children repeat it as they complete the action.

Phonics

Objective

To practice and apply knowledge of the consonants /s/c and /j/g, dge

Decodable Book 11

"A Nice Place for Mice" and "Strange Gadgets" ▶

✓ MONITOR PROGRESS

Phonics After small-group instruction, are children able to blend and read words with /s/c; /j/g, dge?

If not, provide additional small-group practice with the sound-spellings. See the *Strategic Intervention Resource Kit* for additional support.

Strategic ▶
Intervention
Resource Kit

BELOW-LEVEL RETEACH

Blend Words

Routine Card 1 Use *Routine Card 1* and the Sound/Spelling Card to review the letter/sound correspondences /s/c and /j/g, dge. Write the words *city, slice, huge,* and *judge* on the board, underlining the *c* in *city* and *slice*, the *g* in *huge*, and the *dge* in *judge*. Read the words aloud, emphasizing the /s/ and /j/ sounds. Explain that the letter *c* can sometimes stand for the /s/ sound. Repeat the procedure for /j/g and dge. Write the words *center, place, gem,* and *fudge* on the board. Guide children in reading the words and identifying the letters that stand for /s/ and /j/. Then have children read aloud Decodable Book 11. Pause at the end of each page to review any words children struggled to read.

ON-LEVEL REINFORCE

Word Building

Write the letters *c, g,* and *dge* on the board. Add letters to build the following words: *nice, city, cage, huge, fudge,* and *gem.* Have children read each new word as it is built. Then have children read Decodable Book 11 aloud. Ask questions about each story to make sure children understood what they read.

ADVANCED EXTEND

Write Rhyming Couplets

Have children make a list of words with *c, g,* and *dge* by looking through literature in the classroom. Then ask children to work together to write rhyming couplets such as the following:

All day long I did not budge

Until mother made her delicious fudge.

Have children pick three or four couplets to share with the class.

High-Frequency Words

- - - BELOW-LEVEL **RETEACH** - - - -

Match Words

 Reintroduce the words using *Routine Card 5*. Display two sets of word cards (*Teacher Resource Book*, page 78), and ask children to match the words from each set. As you match each word, have children say the word. Randomly display the cards, and ask children to call out each word. Run through the cards until children are able to recognize each word quickly.

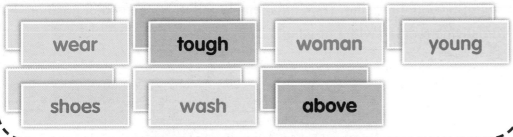

wear   tough   woman   young

shoes   wash   above

- - - ON-LEVEL **REINFORCE** - - - -

Rapid Word Naming

Hold up the word cards for each of the lesson's words, one at a time, and guide children to read the words. Then randomly display the cards, having children name each word. Finally, ask children to write each word on the board, on chart paper, or in their notebooks.

- - - ADVANCED **EXTEND** - - - -

Write Analogies

Write on the board the Lesson 13 words as well as a few additional words from Lesson 12. Then write the following analogies on the board:

Under is to ***over*** as ***below*** is to _____. (***above***)

Boy is to ***girl*** as ***man*** is to _____. (***woman***)

Model how to complete each analogy with a high-frequency word listed on the board. Discuss the relationships the words have to each other. Then have pairs of children work together to write two other analogies.

Objectives
To read high-frequency words

Model usage of each word with sentences such as the following:

> I ***wear*** colorful shirts.
>
> I want to be as ***tough*** as a hockey player.
>
> I watched a ***woman*** and a man walk down the street.
>
> I knew the boy was too ***young*** to ride.
>
> I like ***shoes*** that make my feet look big!
>
> I will ***wash*** the window.
>
> I watched the bird fly ***above*** the building.

Have children repeat each sentence.

✓ MONITOR PROGRESS

High-Frequency Words   After small-group instruction, are children able to recognize and read the words *wear, tough, woman, young, shoes, wash,* and *above*?

If not, provide additional small-group practice with the words. See the *Intensive Intervention Program* for additional support.

Fluency

Objective
To use phrasing to read fluently in a manner that sounds like natural speech

Phrases   Have children look at a sentence in an appropriate *Leveled Reader*. Point to individual words and say: **This is one word.** Have children read with you as you read one word at a time. Then point to a phrase and say: **This is several words together. It is called a *phrase*.** Model reading in phrases as children track the print with their fingers and read with you.

✓ MONITOR PROGRESS

After small-group instruction, are children able to use phrasing to read their *Leveled Readers* fluently?

If not, provide additional modeling of fluent reading with small groups. See the *Strategic Intervention Resource Kit* for additional support.

Strategic ▶ **Intervention Resource Kit**

BELOW-LEVEL   RETEACH

Model Fluent Reading

Routine Card **9**

Remind children that fluent readers do not read just one word at a time, but that they read in chunks of words, or phrases, that make sense together. Distribute copies of *The Hamster Escape*. Read the book aloud, modeling the use of natural phrasing. After reading, reread a few sentences, pointing out how you chunk the words together in phrases as you read. Have children echo-read the sentences, imitating your phrasing. Then have them read the book with a partner, practicing reading with phrasing.

⬤ ON-LEVEL **REINFORCE**

Echo-Reading

Routine Card 8

Distribute *The Rabbit Suit Rescue* to children, and explain that they will practice reading aloud with phrasing. Read each page aloud to children, modeling how to read in phrases. Have children read aloud after you, encouraging them to read in phrases, too. After reading the book through this way, have children practice reading it with partners. Listen to them read, giving them feedback about how fluently they read in phrases.

● **BELOW-LEVEL**

▲ **The Hamster Escape**

● **ON-LEVEL**

▲ **The Rabbit Suit Rescue**

⬤ ADVANCED **EXTEND**

Independent Reading

Routine Card 10

Ask a volunteer to explain why reading in phrases helps a reader sound natural, as if speaking to a friend. Distribute *The Dinosaur Drawing Delivery* to children, and tell them that they will be practicing reading with phrasing. Group children in pairs, having one child read the book aloud while the other listens. After the first child is done, have the listener offer constructive feedback about reading with phrasing. Then have children swap roles and repeat the reading aloud.

◍ **ADVANCED LEVEL**

▲ **The Dinosaur Drawing Delivery**

Comprehension
Fiction and Nonfiction

Focus Skill

Objective
To identify the elements of a fiction story

Clarify Meaning
Clarify the meanings of *real* and *made-up* for children, using images from books or magazines. Point to photographs of real people and things and say: **These are real.** Point to images of fictional characters and situations in a piece of fiction, such as animals speaking. Say: **These are made-up. They are not real.** Then hold up various images and ask children to say whether they are real or made-up.

 MONITOR PROGRESS

After small-group instruction, are children able to identify and describe the elements of fiction and nonfiction?

If not, provide additional small-group practice with the skill. See the *Strategic Intervention Resource Kit* for additional support.

Strategic ▶ Intervention Resource Kit

 BELOW-LEVEL RETEACH

Guided Review

Remind children that fiction stories are about made-up people and made-up events. Ask children to raise their hands when they hear you name some things that are not real. Then name the following:

a boy who runs   a girl who talks   a girl who floats in the air

Review what is real and not real about each item. Then have children turn to the selection *Click, Clack, Moo: Cows That Type* on page 270 of the *Student Edition*. Guide them in understanding that this is a made-up story, or fiction. Point out that while a farmer could have cows, cows cannot really type. Then have children turn to *Henry and Mudge* on page 94. Explain that this is also a made-up story, but it is harder to tell why. Point out that Henry acts like a real boy, and Mudge acts like a real dog. Explain that the illustrations and the information that they read before and after the story, such as the author's biography, sometimes give clues that this is a made-up story.

 ON-LEVEL REINFORCE

Identify the Elements of Fiction

Provide copies of two or three fiction books children have read in the classroom or school library. Remind children that fiction stories are about made-up characters and made-up events. Further explain that if the characters act and talk like real people and live in places that seem real, the story is realistic fiction. Have children work together to review each of the books. Then have them list each title on the board. Under each title, they should write whether the book is fiction or realistic fiction. Then, for each book, they should list at least two story elements that are clues to why the story is fiction or realistic fiction.

ADVANCED EXTEND

Explore the Elements of Fiction

Have children pick an article from a children's magazine. Explain that fiction writers often base their made-up stories on real-life people and events. Have a volunteer read aloud the article. Discuss how children know that this story is a real-life story. Have children suggest ways they might change this story to make it fiction. List the fiction elements that children might add to turn the story into fiction. Then have children work together to rewrite the story as fiction.

Robust Vocabulary

Objective
To review robust vocabulary

REVIEW Tested ✓

Vocabulary: Lesson 13

wilting	route
flitted	semblance
swirling	distraught
trance	improvise

 **MONITOR PROGRESS**

After small-group instruction, are children able to use and understand the Vocabulary Words?

If not, provide additional small-group practice with the words. See the *Strategic Intervention Resource Kit* for additional support.

Strategic ▶
Intervention
Resource Kit

BELOW-LEVEL RETEACH

Reintroduce the Words

Routine Card 3 Use *Routine Card 3* and **Transparency R68** to reintroduce all eight words to children. Review the Student-Friendly Explanations until they are familiar with the words. Then ask questions such as the following to check for understanding. Be sure children explain their answer each time.

wilting What would be an example of something wilting, a plant whose leaves have died or a plant with green leaves?

flitted If a dragonfly flitted by you, did it fly straight or did it fly all over, here and there?

swirling If water is swirling down the drain, is it going straight down or spinning first?

trance If someone is in a trance, does that person look all around or does that person look straight ahead?

route If you go to the store using the same route every day, would you see the same things or different things?

semblance What would be an example of a good semblance of someone, a photograph or a drawing done by a two-year-old?

distraught If you were distraught, might you laugh or might you cry?

improvise If you improvise a song, do you make it up as you sing or do you read it from a music book?

Apply Word Associations

Review for children the Student-Friendly Explanations on **Transparency R68**. Then ask children word-association questions for the words, such as *Which word goes with dying leaves on a plant? (wilting)* and *Which word goes with sad? (distraught)* Continue with this format for the rest of the words. Then have children work in pairs to think of other word-association questions. Have children take turns asking a new question until each child has covered all of the words.

Clarify Meaning You can use pantomime to help children understand the meanings of most of the words on the list. For example, say: **I gobble my food.** Act out gobbling an imaginary plate of food. Have children repeat the sentence as they mimic your actions.

ADVANCED **EXTEND**

Is/Is Not Examples

Write the eight Vocabulary Words on the board, and have children read each one with you. Repeat a few times with the words in random order. Then review the Student-Friendly Explanations on **Transparency R68**. Ask children to give *is/is not* examples for each word, such as the following: *A trance is someone looking off into space. A trance is not someone talking to a friend. Someone who is distraught is sad. Someone who is distraught is not happy.* After giving children the examples, have them take turns selecting words and giving other *is/is not* examples.

Student-Friendly Explanations

wilting	When a plant doesn't get enough water, its leaves start to droop because they are wilting.
flitted	If something moved quickly from place to place without stopping for long, it flitted.
swirling	If something is swirling, it is moving round and round quickly.
trance	When someone is in a trance, he or she seems to be asleep, but his or her eyes are open.
route	When you follow the same route to school or to the store every day, you are going the same way each time.
semblance	When you make a drawing that looks a lot like someone, it is a good semblance of that person.
distraught	When someone is distraught, that person is very, very unhappy.
improvise	If you improvise a song or a story, then you make it up as you sing the song or tell the story.

Grade 2, Lesson 13 　　　　R68 　　　　Vocabulary

Transparency R68

Grammar and Writing

Language Arts Checkpoint

Objectives

- *To recognize and write plural possessive nouns*
- *To write story dialogue*

BELOW-LEVEL RETEACH

Review Singular Possessive Nouns

Give the boys in the group a single sheet of paper, and give the girls in the group a single pencil. Point out that the single sheet of paper belongs to all of the boys and that the pencil belongs to all of the girls. Write the following phrases on the board: *the boys' paper, the girls' pencil, the children's supplies.* Read the phrases, guiding children to understand how the apostrophe is added at the end of most plurals without adding another *s.* Point out that some words that name more than one, such as *children* and *people,* do not end with an *s.* Explain that in those words, the apostrophe *s* is added. Display **Transparency LA27,** reminding children that they have seen it before. Guide children in completing each plural possessive noun.

REVIEW STORY DIALOGUE   Remind children that stories often include the words characters say. Explain that this is called dialogue and is written in a special way. Write the following sentence on the board or on chart paper:

> **"Hello!" said Arthur to his new friend, Jorge.**
> **"Hello, Arthur," said Jorge. "How are you today?"**

Read the sentences to children. Guide them in identifying that these sentences show the exact words Arthur and Jorge say to each other. Discuss how the word *said* is used to show who is talking, and point out how the punctuation is different in this kind of sentence than in other kinds of sentences. Then point out the quotation marks and other punctuation, and explain how they are used to show what the characters are saying.

Transparency LA27

ON-LEVEL REINFORCE

Connect Grammar and Writing

Explain that sometimes, story characters use plural possessive nouns while speaking. Write the following dialogue on the board:

"What is my costume?" asked Alma.

"It is a big tiger suit," said Mr. Jenks. "It is hanging up with the rest of the girls' costumes."

Read the dialogue aloud. Guide children in identifying the plural possessive nouns and in using the words *asked* and *said* to show who is speaking. Then have children brainstorm other exchanges of dialogue that might happen between Alma and Mr. Jenks. Write the dialogue on the board as children dictate it. Encourage them to include at least one plural possessive noun in the dialogue. Stop to have volunteers explain how to write plural possessives and how to write the dialogue using quotation marks.

ADVANCED EXTEND

Act Out and Write Dialogue

Have children pick two characters, each from a different story they have recently read. Ask them to think about what these two characters might say to each other if they were to meet. Have children brainstorm and act out the possible dialogue between the two characters. Then have each child write a short exchange of dialogue between his or her characters. Before children begin writing, ask volunteers to explain how to use quotation marks in story dialogue. Once children have finished their writing, have partners exchange papers and read aloud each other's dialogues to the rest of the group.

ELL

Role-Play Simple Dialogue

Have children role-play simple dialogue such as an exchange of greetings. Work with a volunteer to model an exchange, then have pairs of children role-play similar exchanges. On the board, write one of the exchanges as story dialogue. Read the dialogue back to children, having them read along with you. Point out how quotation marks, commas, and the word *said* are used to show what each character says.

Phonics

Objective

To practice and apply knowledge of the r-controlled vowel /ûr/ir, ur, er, and ear

Decodable Book 12

"A Birthday Surprise for Bird,"
"A Pet That Purrs,"
"Bertha the Sales Clerk,"
and "Earth Day" ▶

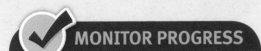

MONITOR PROGRESS

Phonics After small-group instruction, are children able to blend and read words with /ûr/ir, ur, er, and ear?

If not, provide additional small-group practice with the sound-spellings. See the *Strategic Intervention Resource Kit* for additional support.

Strategic ▶
Intervention
Resource Kit

BELOW-LEVEL RETEACH

Blend Words

Routine Card 1

Use *Routine Card 1* and the *Sound/Spelling Card* to review the letter/sound correspondence /ûr/*ir, ur, er,* and *ear*. Write the words *sir, fur, her,* and *earn* on the board. Read the words aloud, emphasizing the /ûr/ sound in each. Explain that these letters followed by the letter *r* can stand for the /ûr/ sound. Write the words *stir, turn, herd,* and *learn* on the board. Guide children in reading the words and identifying the letters that stand for /ûr/. Then have children read aloud Decodable Book 12. Pause at the end of each page to review any word children struggled to read.

ON-LEVEL REINFORCE

Word Building

Write the letters *ir, ur, er,* and *ear* on the board. Add letters to build the following words: *fur, burn, bird, third, herd,* and *learn*. Have children read each new word as it is built. Then have children read Decodable Book 12 aloud. Ask questions about each story to make sure children understood what they read.

ADVANCED EXTEND

Use Clues

Have children flip through children's magazines or their *Student Edition* to find and list words with /ûr/*ir, ur, er,* and *ear*. Then ask children to take turns giving clues for a word on the list for a partner to guess. For example, a clue for *bird* might include: **The word begins with *b* and ends with *d*. It's something that can fly.** Challenge children to see which partner can guess the most words correctly in a set amount of time.

High-Frequency Words

BELOW-LEVEL RETEACH

Match Words

Reintroduce the words using *Routine Card 5*. Display two sets of word cards (*Teacher Resource Book,* page 79) and ask children to match the words from each set. As you match each word, have children say the word. Randomly display the cards, and ask children to call out each word. Run through the cards until children are able to recognize each word quickly.

ON-LEVEL REINFORCE

Rapid Word Naming

Hold up the word card for each of the lesson's words, one at a time, and guide children to read the word. Then randomly display the words, having children name the word each time. Finally, ask children to write each word on the board, on chart paper, or in their notebooks.

ADVANCED EXTEND

Write Word Clues

Write on the board the Lesson 14 words as well as a few additional words from Lesson 13. Then write the following word clues on the board.

This word has the letters <u>fat</u> in it. (father)

This word begins with the letters <u>sw</u>. (sweat)

Have volunteers read aloud the clues and name the answers from the list of words. Then have pairs of children work together to write similar clues for the other words on the board. Have each pair swap their completed clues with another pair of children and see if they can name the word that goes with each clue.

Model usage of each word with sentences such as the following:

*I think books are **interesting**.*

*My sister sucks her **thumb**.*

*I like to **touch** soft fur.*

*I take **care** of my pets.*

*I **sweat** a lot when I run.*

*I called my **father** on the phone.*

Have children repeat each sentence.

 MONITOR PROGRESS

High-Frequency Words After small-group instruction, are children able to recognize and read the words *interesting, thumb, touch, care, sweat,* and *father*?

If not, provide additional small-group practice with the words. See the *Intensive Intervention Program* for additional support.

Fluency

Objective
To read fluently with phrasing in a manner that sounds like natural speech

Practice Reading Phrases

Give children additional practice reading with phrasing, using a page from the appropriate *Leveled Reader*. First, read aloud the page, pointing with your finger to the phrases. Have children listen, following along in their books with their fingers. Then, reread the section, having children echo-read with you.

 MONITOR PROGRESS

After small-group instruction, are children able to use phrasing to read their *Leveled Reader* fluently?

If not, provide additional modeling of fluent reading with small groups. See the *Strategic Intervention Resource Kit* for additional support.

Strategic ▶
Intervention
Resource Kit

 BELOW-LEVEL **RETEACH**

Model Fluent Reading

 Routine Card 9

Demonstrate how difficult it is to understand someone when just one word at a time is spoken. Say: **How. Does. It. Sound. When. I. Speak. Just. One. Word. At. A. Time?** Then repeat the sentence in a natural-sounding way. Discuss the difference with children. Remind them that fluent readers read in chunks of words that make sense together, called phrases. Distribute copies of *Mountain Babies* to children. Read the book aloud, modeling the use of natural phrasing. After reading, reread a few sentences, pointing out phrases as you read. Have children echo-read the sentences, imitating your phrasing. Then have them read the book with a partner, practicing reading with phrasing.

● ON-LEVEL REINFORCE

Echo-Reading

Routine Card 8
Distribute *Desert Babies* to children, and explain that they will practice reading aloud with phrasing. Read each page aloud to children, modeling how to read in phrases. Have children read aloud after you, imitating your phrasing. After reading the book through this way, have children practice reading it with partners. Listen to them read, giving them feedback about how well they read in phrases.

● ADVANCED EXTEND ✏

Independent Reading

Routine Card 10
Distribute *Prairie Babies* to children. Ask a volunteer to read the first page to model how to read fluently in phrases. Discuss how reading in phrases makes the reader sound as if he or she is reading in a natural way. Then tell children they will all be practicing reading with phrasing to read more fluently. Group children in pairs, having one child read the book aloud while the other listens. After the first child is done, have the listener offer constructive feedback about reading with phrasing. Then have children swap roles and repeat the reading aloud.

LEVELED READERS

● BELOW-LEVEL

▲ Mountain Babies

● ON-LEVEL

▲ Desert Babies

● ADVANCED

▲ Prairie Babies

Comprehension
Fiction and Nonfiction

Objective
To identify the elements of nonfiction

Clarify Meaning Clarify the meanings of the elements of nonfiction selection by leafing through "Rain Forest Babies" with children. Point out the different elements. For example, point to a heading and say: **This is a heading.** Have children point to the element in their books and repeat the sentence. Continue through the selection, identifying a map, photographs, captions, and a sidebar.

MONITOR PROGRESS

After small-group instruction, are children able to identify and describe the elements of nonfiction?

If not, provide additional small-group practice with the skill. See the *Strategic Intervention Resource Kit* for additional support.

Strategic ▶ Intervention Resource Kit

BELOW-LEVEL **RETEACH**

Guided Review

Have children open their *Student Edition* to pages 424–425, and review with them the differences between fiction and nonfiction. Then have children turn to *Student Edition* page 428, and discuss the nonfiction elements in "Rain Forest Babies." Guide children in understanding that this selection presents facts about animals in the rain forest. Point out the examples of nonfiction elements in the selection, such as headings, a map, photographs of real animals and places with captions, and sidebars. Discuss how this kind of selection looks different from a fiction story, such as "Big Bushy Mustache" on *Student Edition* pages 392–417. Then have children look through the pages of "At Play: Long Ago and Today" on *Student Edition* pages 364–381. Ask them to tell whether this is fiction or nonfiction and then to identify the elements of nonfiction in the selection.

Kathy Darling • Photographs by Tara Darling

Identify the Elements of Nonfiction

Review the definition of nonfiction with children. Then have children select an example of a nonfiction magazine article or a nonfiction book from the classroom library. Have children identify the subject of the book or article. Then have children take turns identifying the elements of nonfiction in the selection, such as the following:

- **headings**
- **photographs with captions**
- **fact files and sidebars**
- **maps**

Have children explain how these elements let you know that the book or article is about a real topic with facts and not a made-up story.

Find Examples of Fiction and Nonfiction

Display six fiction books and six nonfiction books from the classroom or school library. Review with the group the differences between fiction and nonfiction selections. Then have each child write the titles of the fiction selections on one sheet of paper and the titles of the nonfiction selections on another sheet. Next to each title, children should write one reason the book is either fiction or nonfiction. Have children come together and compare their lists of titles and reasons.

Robust Vocabulary

Objective
To review robust vocabulary

REVIEW ✓ Tested

Vocabulary: Lesson 14

dappled	adorable
entranced	assortment
trooped	habitat
circling	immense

MONITOR PROGRESS

After small-group instruction, are children able to use and understand the Vocabulary Words?

If not, provide additional small-group practice with the words. See the *Strategic Intervention Resource Kit* for additional support.

Strategic ▸ Intervention Resource Kit

● **BELOW-LEVEL** **RETEACH**

Reintroduce the Words

Routine Card 3 Use *Routine Card 3* and **Transparency R74** to reintroduce all eight words to children. Review the Student-Friendly Explanations until children are familiar with the words. Then ask questions such as the following to check understanding. Be sure children explain their answers each time.

dappled	What would be an example of an animal with dappled fur or hair, a zebra with stripes or a jungle cat with spots?
entranced	If a person is entranced, would that person be standing still and staring or would that person be running around?
trooped	If a group of people trooped over a mountain, would they be flying or would they be walking?
circling	If a bird is circling over your head, is it flying around and around or is it diving straight down?
adorable	What would be adorable, a basket full of worms or a basket full of kittens?
assortment	Would an assortment of fruit have just apples, or would it have apples, oranges, pears, grapes, and berries?
habitat	If an animal has a jungle habitat, does the animal live in the jungle or in the ocean?
immense	What would be an example of an immense animal, an elephant or a mouse?

ON-LEVEL REINFORCE

Word Relationships

Review for children the Student-Friendly Explanation on **Transparency R74**. Then have children sit in a circle. For each word, go around the circle asking each child to name a word that is related to the vocabulary word and tell why or how it is related. For example, for the word *assortment*, children might say *candy, crayons, many, different,* and *variety*. Help children who get stuck by using prompts such as *What kinds of school supplies come in an assortment of colors?* or *What are some animals that you think are adorable?*

ADVANCED EXTEND

Sentence Stems

Review for children the Student-Friendly Explanation on **Transparency R74** for each word, and use each word in a sentence. Then have children complete sentence stems for each word that follow the following format:

I could tell the horse was dappled because _____. (it was covered with spots)

Many animals won't survive outside of their habitats because _____. (that is where they live)

Once children have completed the sentence stems for each of the words, have them work in pairs to create their own sentence stems for each word. Have partners take turns saying the beginning and completing the stem.

Clarify Meaning   Use the photographs in the selection "Rain Forest Babies" to clarify the meanings of the Vocabulary words. Point to examples such as the kangaroo baby on page 441 and say: **This baby kangaroo is adorable. It is cute.** Have children point to the photograph and repeat what you say.

Student-Friendly Explanations

dappled	If something is dappled, it has spots, streaks, or patches of different colors or shades.
entranced	If you are entranced by something, it has delighted or amazed you.
trooped	If you trooped someplace, you moved along with a group of people.
circling	If something is circling you, it is moving around you.
adorable	If something is very cute, it is adorable.
assortment	If you see a variety or mixture of things, you see an assortment.
habitat	If a plant or an animal lives in a particular place in nature, that is its habitat.
immense	If something is really big or huge, it is immense.

Grade 2, Theme 3   R74   Vocabulary

Transparency R74

Grammar and Writing
Language Arts Checkpoint

Objectives
- *To recognize and write pronouns*
- *To compose a paragraph that explains*

BELOW-LEVEL RETEACH

Review Pronouns

Remind children that pronouns are words that stand for other nouns. Write the following sentences on the board and read them aloud: *Mick gives Anna the pencil. He gives it to her.* Reread the sentences, underlining the pronouns in the second sentence. Ask a volunteer to name the noun from the first sentence that each pronoun stands for in the second sentence. Then create a simple chart such as the following on the board.

I	we	he	she	they	it
Tells about me	Tells about me and someone else	boy man father	girl woman mother	men women children animals	horse car book

Use the chart to help children understand what each pronoun can stand for. Display **Transparency LA29,** reminding children that they have seen it before. Guide children in completing the sentences.

REVIEW PARAGRAPH THAT EXPLAINS   Remind children that a paragraph can explain something about a person, place, or thing. Write the following paragraph on the board or on chart paper:

> **Some cats have thumbs. Most cats have five fingers on their front paws. Some cats grow another finger on each front paw. It looks like a thumb.**

Read the paragraph to children. Ask them what the paragraph explains. (how some cats have thumbs) Guide them in identifying the main idea sentence at the beginning and the details that support the main idea.

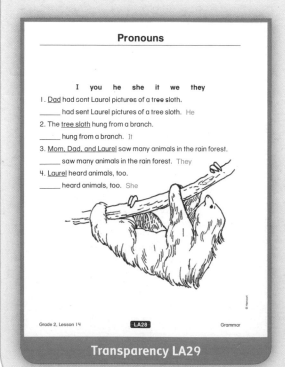

Pronouns

I   you   he   she   it   we   they

1. <u>Dad</u> had sent Laurel pictures of a tree sloth.

_____ had sent Laurel pictures of a tree sloth.   He

2. The <u>tree sloth</u> hung from a branch.

_____ hung from a branch.   It

3. <u>Mom, Dad, and Laurel</u> saw many animals in the rain forest.

_____ saw many animals in the rain forest.   They

4. <u>Laurel</u> heard animals, too.

_____ heard animals, too.   She

Grade 2, Lesson 14   LA28   Grammar

Transparency LA29

ON-LEVEL REINFORCE

Connect Grammar and Writing

Explain that writers often use pronouns in paragraphs that explain. Write the following paragraph on the board:

The Fourth of July is a big holiday. It is the day when Americans celebrate the nation's birthday. People have cookouts and go to parades. At night, many go to see fireworks. It is a special day in America.

Have a volunteer read the paragraph aloud. Guide children in identifying what is being explained as well as the main idea sentence and supporting details. Then underline the pronouns and ask children which noun each pronoun stands for. Work with children to write another short paragraph that explains another national holiday. Guide them in writing a main idea sentence and adding supporting details. Guide children to use pronouns to take the place of other nouns mentioned earlier in the paragraph.

ADVANCED EXTEND

Write About a Special Day at School

Have children write a paragraph that explains a special event or day that takes place in your school each year. Have the group brainstorm and list ideas for paragraphs. Then have each child choose one idea to write about. Remind children to include a main idea sentence that tells what is being explained as well as supporting details that further explain what happens during the special day or event. Once each child has completed the paragraph, have children swap paragraphs with partners. Ask them to read each other's paragraphs and offer helpful suggestions for fixing errors or for improving the paragraph. Remind children to check to make sure that pronouns have been used correctly.

E L L

Pronoun Support In some languages, nouns are assigned a gender, so some children may have difficulty using the non-gender-specific pronoun *it*. Provide children with additional practice with sentence pairs such as:

The dog barks. It is hungry.

The car is fast. It is painted red.

Write the sentences on the board. Read each pair aloud, pointing to *it*. Then have children practice saying the sentences.

Teacher's Notes

Assessment

# Assessment

Good assessments tell you what your students need to learn to meet grade-level standards.

It's not just about scoring the students—or the teacher, for that matter. It's about helping teachers **know what to teach and how much.**

Reading education is a **growing science.** We know more about how children learn to read than we did in the past. This **knowledge gives us the power** to use assessment to inform instruction. Assessment exposes the missing skills so that teachers can fill in the gaps.

Good assessment is part of instruction.

Think about it: if you are testing what you are teaching, then the test is another **practice and application** opportunity for children. In addition, when tests focus on the skills that are essential to better reading, testing informs teachers about which students need more instruction in those essential skills.

What is the best kind of assessment to use?

Using more than one kind of assessment will give you the clearest picture of your students' progress. **Multiple measures** are the key to a well-rounded view.

First, consider the assessments that are already **mandated** for you: your school, your district, and your state will, of course, tell you which tests you must use, and when. In addition to these, you should use **curriculum-based assessments** to monitor your students' progress in *StoryTown*.

The following curriculum-based assessments are built into *StoryTown*.

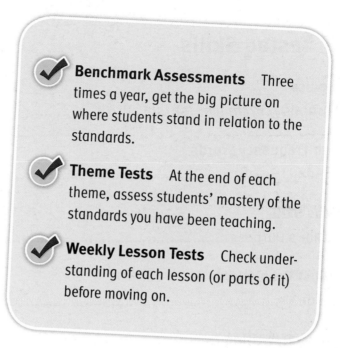

Benchmark Assessments Three times a year, get the big picture on where students stand in relation to the standards.

Theme Tests At the end of each theme, assess students' mastery of the standards you have been teaching.

Weekly Lesson Tests Check understanding of each lesson (or parts of it) before moving on.

On a daily basis, point-of-use **Monitor Progress** notes help you check understanding and reteach or extend instruction. Additional checklists and rubrics are provided to help you monitor students' comprehension, writing, listening, and speaking.

The *Benchmark Assessments,* the *Theme Tests,* and the *Weekly Lesson Tests* are all available online. Students can take the tests on the computer, or you can use pencil-and-paper and enter the scores into the database later. Either way, *StoryTown Online Assessment* will help you track students' progress and share their growth with administrators and families.

 StoryTown Online Assessment

Weekly Test

Using Assessment to Inform Instruction

Specific prescriptions based on Harcourt Reading Assessments.

✔ Tested Skills   Prescriptions

Phonics

Digraphs /ch/*ch*, *tch*; /sh/*sh*; /th/*th* .... Reteach, p. S2

High-Frequency Words

Lesson 11 .... Reteach, p. S3

Focus Skill

Author's Purpose.. Reteach, pp. S6–S7

Robust Vocabulary

Lesson 11 .... Reteach, pp. S8–S9

Grammar/Writing

Abbreviations .... Reteach, pp. S10–S11

Fluency

Punctuation .... Reteach, pp. S4–S5

Lesson 12   Weekly Test

✔ Tested Skills

Prescriptions

Phonics

Long Vowel /ē/*ey, y*.. Reteach, p. S12

High-Frequency Words

Lesson 12.. Reteach, p. S13

Focus Skill

Author's Purpose.. Reteach, pp. S16–S17

Robust Vocabulary

Lesson 12.. Reteach, pp. S18–S19

Grammar/Writing

Singular Possessive Nouns... Reteach, pp. S20–S21

Fluency

Punctuation .... Reteach, pp. S14–S15

Weekly Test

✔ Tested Skills

Prescriptions

Phonics

Consonants /s/c; /j/g, dge .... Reteach, p. S22

High-Frequency Words

Lesson 13...Reteach, p. S23

Focus Skill

Fiction and Nonfiction......................................Reteach, pp. S26–S27

Robust Vocabulary

Lesson 13...Reteach, pp. S28–S29

Grammar/Writing

Plural Possessive Nouns..................................Reteach, pp. S30–S31

Fluency

Phrasing ....Reteach, pp. S24–S25

Lessons 14–15 Weekly Tests

✔ Lesson 14 Tested Skills   Prescriptions

Phonics
r-Controlled Vowel /ûr/*ir, ur, er, ear*............................... Reteach, p. S32

High-Frequency Words
Lesson 14... Reteach, p. S33

Focus Skill
Fiction and Nonfiction.................................... Reteach, pp. S36–S37

Robust Vocabulary
Lesson 14.. Reteach, pp. S38–S39

Grammar/Writing
Pronouns .... Reteach, pp. S40–S41

Fluency
Phrasing .... Reteach, pp. S34–S35

✔ Lesson 15 Tested Skills

Selection Comprehension
"A Birthday Mystery" .... Monitor Comprehension,
         pp. T383–T386

Robust Vocabulary
Lesson 15.. Build Robust Vocabulary,
         pp. T387, T397, T407, T419

Theme 3 Test

☑ Tested Skills

Tested Skills	Prescriptions
Phonics	Reteach, pp. S2, S12, S22, S32,
High-Frequency Words	Reteach, pp. S3, S13, S23, S33
Focus Skill	Reteach, pp. S6–S7, S16–S17, S26–S27, S36–S37
Robust Vocabulary	Reteach, pp. S8–S9, S18–S19, S28–S29, S38–S39
Grammar/Writing	Reteach, pp. S10–S11, S20–S21, S30–S31, S40–S41
Spelling	*Spelling Practice Book,* pp. 35–37, 38–40, 41–43, 44–46, 47–50
Fluency	Reteach, pp. S4–S5, S14–S15, S24–S25, S34–S35

● BELOW-LEVEL RETEACH
- Below-Level Leveled Readers
- Leveled Reader System
- Extra Support Copying Masters
- Strategic Intervention Resource Kit
- Intensive Intervention Program

● ON-LEVEL REINFORCE
- On-Level Leveled Readers
- Leveled Reader System
- Practice Book

● ADVANCED EXTEND
- Advanced Leveled Readers
- Leveled Reader System
- Challenge Copying Masters
- Challenge Resource Kit

To determine whether students need even more support, use your district-approved diagnostic and screening assessments.

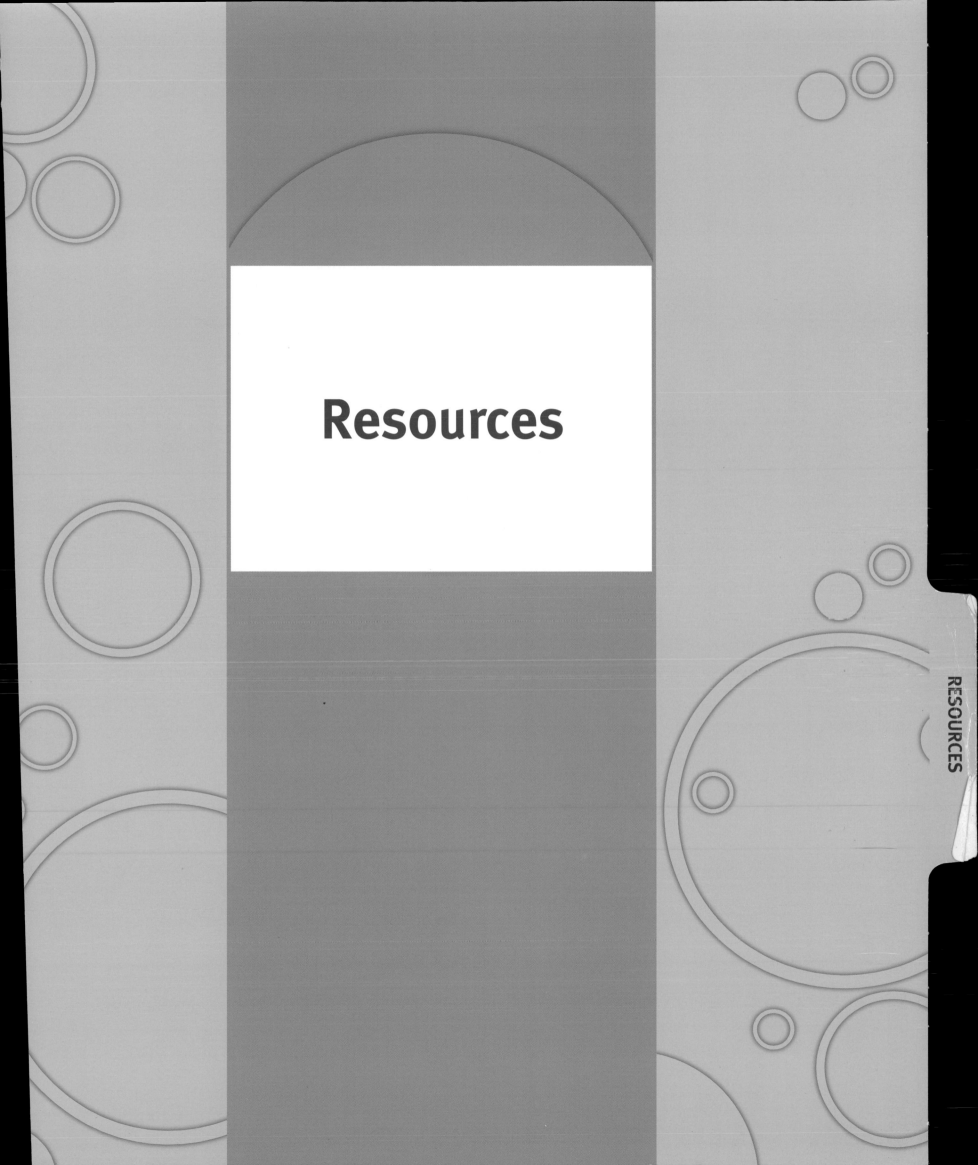

Resources

ADDITIONAL RESOURCES

Using Rubrics

A **rubric** *is a tool a teacher can use to score a student's work.*

A **rubric** *lists the criteria for evaluating the work, and it describes different levels of success in meeting those criteria.*

Rubrics *are useful assessment tools for teachers, but they can be just as useful for students. They explain expectations, and can be powerful teaching tools.*

RUBRIC Rubrics for Retelling and Summarizing

- There is a separate rubric for fiction and nonfiction. Before students begin their retellings or summaries, ask them which rubric should be used. Then point out the criteria and discuss each one.

- Have students focus on the criteria for excellence listed on the rubric so that they have specific goals to aim for.

RUBRIC Rubrics for Presentations: Speaking and Listening

- Before students give a presentation, discuss the criteria listed on the rubric. Help them focus on the criteria for excellence listed on the rubric so that they have specific goals to aim for.

- Discuss the criteria for listening with students who will be in the audience. Point out the criteria for excellence listed on the rubric so that they have specific goals to aim for.

RUBRIC Rubrics for Short- and Extended-Response

- Before students begin a short- and extended-response, discuss the criteria for excellence listed on the rubrics so that they have specific goals to aim for.

- Tell students that the short-response task should take about five to ten minutes to complete, and the extended-response should take much longer to complete.

RUBRIC Rubric for Writing

- When you introduce students to a new kind of writing through a writing model, discuss the criteria listed on the rubric, and ask students to decide how well the model meets each criterion.

- Before students attempt a new kind of writing, have them focus on the criteria for excellence listed on the rubric so that they have specific goals to aim for.

- During both the drafting and revising stages, remind students to check their writing against the rubric to keep their focus and to determine if there are any aspects of their writing they can improve.

- Students can use the rubrics to score their own writing. They can keep the marked rubric in their portfolios with the piece of writing it refers to. The marked rubrics will help students see their progress through the school year. In conferences with students and family members, you can refer to the rubrics to point out both strengths and weaknesses.

Score of 4

The student:

- names and describes the main and supporting characters and tells their actions
- tells about the setting, including both time and place
- retells the plot in detail
- describes the problems and solutions in the story
- accurately defines the theme or meaning of the story
- provides extensions of the story such as making connections to other texts, relating experiences, making inferences and/or making generalizations
- uses phrases, language, vocabulary, or sentence structure from the story
- discriminates between reality and fantasy, fact and fiction
- requires little or no prompting

Score of 3

The student:

- names and describes the main characters
- tells about the setting
- retells most of the plot accurately with some details
- describes some of the problems and solutions in the story
- relates some aspects of the theme or meaning of the story
- uses some phrases, language, or vocabulary from the story
- provides some extensions of the story such as making connections to other texts or relating relevant experiences
- discriminates between reality and fantasy, fact and fiction
- may require some prompting

Score of 2

The student:

- tells some details about the story elements, including characters, setting, and plot, with some omissions or errors
- cannot correctly identify problems or corresponding solutions in the story
- uses very little language and vocabulary from story
- shows minimal understanding of the theme or meaning
- provides minimal extensions of the story
- confuses reality and fantasy, and fact and fiction
- requires some prompting to retell the story

Score of 1

The student:

- tells few if any details about the story elements, possibly with errors
- has little or no awareness of the theme of the story
- provides no extensions of the story
- confuses reality and fantasy, and fact and fiction
- unable to retell the story without prompting

Scoring RUBRIC for Summarizing Nonfiction

Score of 4

The student:

- provides a summarizing statement
- relates the main idea and important supporting details
- creates a focused, coherent, logical, and organized structure; stays on topic; and relates important points to the text
- understands relationships in the text such as recognizing cause and effect relationships, chronological order, or comparing and contrasting information
- uses phrases, language, or vocabulary from the text
- clearly identifies the conclusion
- identifies the author's purpose for creating the text
- provides extensions of the text such as making connections to other texts, relating relevant experiences, making inferences and/or making generalizations
- requires little or no prompting

Score of 3

The student:

- tells the topic of the text
- relates the main idea and relevant details
- creates a coherent structure and stays on topic
- mostly understands relationships in the text such as recognizing cause and effect relationships, chronological order, or comparing and contrasting information
- uses some language, or vocabulary from the text
- tells the conclusion or point of the text
- identifies the author's purpose
- provides some extensions of the text such as making connections to other texts or relating relevant experiences
- may require some prompting

Score of 2

The student:

- minimally relates the topic of the text
- shows minimal understanding of main idea and omits many important details
- provides some structure; might stray from topic
- understands few, if any, relationships in the text or recognizes chronological order
- uses little or no language and vocabulary from the text
- does not fully understand conclusion or point of the text
- shows some awareness of author's purpose
- provides few, if any, extensions of the text
- requires some prompting to retell the story

Score of 1

The student:

- shows little or no understanding of main idea and omits important details
- provides a poorly organized or unclear structure
- does not understand relationships in or of the text
- does not understand conclusion of the text
- provides no extensions of the text
- unable to retell the story without prompting

Scoring RUBRIC for Presentations

	Score of 6	Score of 5	Score of 4	Score of 3	Score of 2	Score of 1
HANDWRITING	The slant of the letters is consistent throughout. The letters are clearly formed, spaced equally, and easy to read.	The slant of the letters is almost the same throughout. The letters are clearly formed. Spacing is nearly equal.	The slant and form of the letters is usually consistent. The spacing between words is usually equal.	The handwriting is readable. There are some inconsistencies in shape, form, slant, and spacing.	The handwriting is somewhat readable. There are many inconsistencies in shape, form, slant, and spacing.	The letters are not shaped, formed, slanted, or spaced correctly. The paper is very difficult to read.
WORD PROCESSING	Fonts and sizes are used very well, which helps the reader enjoy reading the text.	Fonts and sizes are used well.	Fonts and sizes are used fairly well, but could be improved upon.	Fonts and sizes are used well in some places, but make the paper look cluttered in others.	Fonts and sizes are not used well. The paper looks cluttered.	The writer has used too many different fonts and sizes. It is very distracting to the reader.
MARKERS	The title, side heads, page numbers, and bullets are used very well. They make it easy for the reader to find information in the text.	The title, side heads, page numbers, and bullets are used well. They help the reader find most information.	The title, side heads, page numbers, and bullets are used fairly well. They usually help the reader find information.	The writer uses a title, or page numbers, or bullets. Improvement is needed.	The writer uses few markers. This makes it hard for the reader to find and understand the information in the text.	There are no markers such as title, page numbers, bullets, or side heads.
VISUALS	The writer uses visuals such as illustrations and props. The text and visuals clearly relate.	The writer uses visuals well. The text and visuals relate to each other.	The writer uses visuals fairly well.	The writer uses visuals with the text, but the reader may not understand how they are related.	The writer tries to use visuals with the text, but the reader is confused by them.	The visuals do not make sense with the text.
SPEAKING	The speaker uses very effective pacing, volume, intonation, and expression.	The speaker uses effective pacing, volume, intonation, and expression.	The speaker uses effective pacing, volume, intonation, and expression.	The speaker uses effective pacing, volume, intonation, and expression.	The speaker needs to work on pacing, volume, intonation, and expression.	The speaker's techniques are unclear or distracting to the listener.

Scoring RUBRIC for Short- and Extended-Response

	Score of 4	Score of 3	Score of 2	Score of 1	Score of 0
EXTENDED-RESPONSE	The response indicates that the student has a thorough understanding of the reading concept embodied in the task. The student has provided a response that is accurate, complete, and fulfills all the requirements of the task. Necessary support and/or examples are included, and the information is clearly text-based.	The response indicates that the student has an understanding of the reading concept embodied in the task. The student has provided a response that is accurate and fulfills all the requirements of the task, but the required support and/or details are not complete or clearly text-based.	The response indicates that the student has a partial understanding of the reading concept embodied in the task. The student has provided a response that includes information that is essentially correct and text-based, but the information is too general or too simplistic. Some of the support and/or examples and requirements of the task may be incomplete or omitted.	The response indicates that the student has very limited understanding of the reading concept embodied in the task. The response is incomplete, may exhibit many flaws, and may not address all requirements of the task.	The response indicates that the student does not demonstrate an understanding of the reading concept embodied in the task. The student has provided a response that is inaccurate; the response has an insufficient amount of information to determine the student's understanding of the task; or the student has failed to respond to the task.
SHORT-RESPONSE			The response indicates that the student has a complete understanding of the reading concept embodied in the task. The student has provided a response that is accurate, complete, and fulfills all the requirements of the task. Necessary support and/or examples are included, and the information given is clearly text-based.	The response indicates that the student has a partial understanding of the reading concept embodied in the task. The student has provided a response that includes information that is essentially correct and text-based, but the information is too general or too simplistic. Some of the support and/or examples may be incomplete or omitted.	The response indicates that the student does not demonstrate an understanding of the reading concept embodied in the task. The student has provided a response that is inaccurate; the response has an insufficient amount of information to determine the student's understanding of the task; or the student has failed to respond to the task.

Scoring RUBRIC for Writing

	Score of 6	Score of 5	Score of 4	Score of 3	Score of 2	Score of 1
FOCUS	The writing is narrowly focused on the main topic and subtopics, and has a clearly defined purpose.	The writing is focused on the topic and purpose.	The writing is generally focused on the topic and purpose with occasional drifts.	The writing is somewhat focused on the topic and purpose with off-topic sentences common.	The writing is related to the topic but does not have a clear focus.	The writing is not focused on the topic and/or purpose.
ORGANIZATION	The ideas in the paper are well-organized and presented in logical order. The paper seems complete to the reader.	The organization of the paper is mostly clear. The paper seems complete.	The organization is mostly clear, but the paper may seem unfinished.	The paper is somewhat organized, but seems unfinished.	There is little organization to the paper.	There is no organization to the paper.
SUPPORT	The writing has strong, specific details. The word choices are clear and fresh.	The writing has strong, specific details and clear word choices.	The writing has supporting details and some variety in word choice.	The writing has few supporting details. It needs more variety in word choice.	The writing uses few supporting details and very little variety in word choice.	There are few or no supporting details. The word choices are unclear, misused, or confusing.
CONVENTIONS	The writer uses a variety of sentences. There are few or no errors in grammar, spelling, punctuation, and capitalization.	The writer uses a variety of sentences. There are a few errors in grammar, spelling, punctuation, and capitalization.	The writer uses some variety in sentences. There are quite a few errors in grammar, spelling, punctuation, and capitalization.	The writer uses simple sentences. There are often errors in grammar, spelling, punctuation, and capitalization.	The writer uses unclear sentences. There are many errors in grammar, spelling, punctuation, and capitalization.	The writer uses awkward sentences. There are numerous errors in grammar, spelling, punctuation, and capitalization.

Scoring RUBRIC for Presentations

	Score of 4	Score of 3	Score of 2	Score of 1
IDEAS	The paper is clear and focused. It is engaging and includes enriching details.	The paper is generally clear and includes supporting details, with minor focusing problems.	The paper is somewhat clear but the writer does not effectively use supporting details.	The paper has no clear central theme. The details are either missing or sketchy.
ORGANIZATION	The ideas are well organized and in a logical order.	The ideas are generally well organized and in a logical order.	The ideas are somewhat organized.	The ideas are not well organized and there is no logical order.
VOICE	The writer consistently uses creative ideas and expressions.	The writer's ideas and expressions are generally creative.	The writer's ideas and expressions are somewhat creative.	The writer lacks creativity in ideas and expressions.
WORD CHOICE	The writing uses vivid verbs, specific nouns, and colorful adjectives well. The writing is very detailed.	The writing may use some vivid verbs, specific nouns, and colorful adjectives. The writing is detailed.	The writing may use few interesting words. The writing is only somewhat detailed.	The writing lacks interesting word choice. The writing also lacks detail.
SENTENCE FLUENCY	The writing flows smoothly. The writer uses transitions, and a variety of sentences.	The writing flows generally well. The writer uses some variety in sentences.	The writing flows somewhat. The writer does not use much variety in his or her sentence structure.	The writing does not flow. The writer uses little or no variety in sentences, and some sentences are unclear.
CONVENTIONS	The writer uses standard writing conventions well, with few or no errors.	The writer uses most standard writing conventions well, but makes some errors.	The writer uses some writing conventions well, but makes distracting errors.	The writer makes continuous errors with most writing conventions, making text difficult to read.

Additional Reading

ROLLING ALONG This list is a compilation of the additional theme- and topic-related books cited in the lesson plans. You may wish to use this list to provide students with opportunities **to read at least thirty minutes a day** outside of class.

Theme 3 CHANGING TIMES

Adamson, Heather.
Let's Play Soccer! Capstone, 2006. Simple text and photographs present the skills, equipment, and safety concerns of playing soccer. **EASY**

Buckley, Helen E.
Grandfather and I. HarperTrophy, 2000. A child considers how Grandfather is the perfect person to spend time with because he is never in a hurry. **AVERAGE**

Burleigh, Robert.
Hoops. Harcourt, 2001. Illustrations and poetic text describe the movement and feel of the game of basketball. *ALA Notable Book; Children's Choice; SLJ Best Book.* **CHALLENGE**

Cherry, Lynne.
The Great Kapok Tree: A Tale of the Amazon Rain Forest. Harcourt, 2000. The many different animals that live in a great kapok tree in the Brazilian rain forest try to convince a man with an ax of the importance of not cutting down their home. *Teachers' Choice; Outstanding Science Trade Book.* **CHALLENGE**

Dunphy, Madeleine.
Here Is the Tropical Rain Forest. Web of Life, 2006. Cumulative text presents the animals and plants of the tropical rain forest and their relationship with one another and their environment. *Award-Winning Author.* **AVERAGE**

Gibbons, Gail.
The Art Box. Holiday House, 1998. What will you find in an art box? Large illustrations show the variety of tools that artists use to express themselves. *Award-Winning Author.* **AVERAGE**

Kavanagh, Peter.
I Love My Mama. Simon & Schuster, 2003. Readers spend the day with a mother elephant and her baby as they splash in the water, soak up the sun, and lie in the grass. *Award-Winning Author.* **EASY**

Komaiko, Leah.
Just My Dad & Me. HarperTrophy, 1999. When other family members infringe on what she had hoped would be a special day with her father, a young girl imagines herself alone with fish that take on familiar appearances. *Award-Winning Author.* **CHALLENGE**

Lindeen, Carol K.
Life in a Rain Forest. Capstone, 2004. Simple text and photographs introduce the rain forest biome, including the environment, plants, and animals. **EASY**

Lithgow, John.
Micawber. Simon & Schuster, 2002. Micawber, a squirrel fascinated by art, leaves a museum with an art student and secretly uses her supplies to makes his own paintings. *Award-Winning Author.* **CHALLENGE**

Mayer, Mercer.
Just Me and My Puppy. Golden, 1998. A child trades his baseball mitt for a puppy and learns the importance of responsibility and playtime in this comical story. *Award-Winning Author.* **EASY**

Miller, Heather.
Artist. Heinemann, 2003. Readers learn what it is like to be an artist—from materials to workspaces—and the different art professions that exist. Includes a quiz and a glossary. **EASY**

Mora, Pat.
A Birthday Basket for Tía. Aladdin, 1997. With the help and interference of her cat Chica, Cecilia prepares a surprise for her great-aunt's ninetieth birthday. *Award-Winning Author.* **CHALLENGE**

Suen, Anastasia.
The Story of Figure Skating. Rigby, 2001. Readers explore the history of figure skating in this fascinating book, which includes references to popular skaters from around the world. *Award-Winning Author.* **AVERAGE**

Wells, Rosemary.
Bunny Cakes. Puffin, 2000. Max makes an earthworm cake for Grandma's birthday and helps Ruby with her angel surprise cake. At the store, the grocer can't read the entire shopping list, until Max solves the problem by drawing pictures. *Children's Choice; SLJ Best Book; Booklist Editors' Choice.* **AVERAGE**

Lesson Vocabulary

Theme 3

The following listening-speaking vocabulary words are introduced in Lessons 11–15.

Lesson 11	Lesson 12	Lesson 13	Lesson 14	Lesson 15
adorn	archaic	distraught	adorable	beneath
beautifying	housed	flitted	assortment	bewildered
executive	leisurely	gobble	circling	distrust
fellow	nominate	improvise	dappled	evasive
filthy	official	route	entranced	lock
kin	ramble	semblance	habitat	mull
original	recently	trance	immense	startle
renowned	recreation	wilting	trooped	witness

High-Frequency Words

Theme 3

The following high-frequency words are introduced in Lessons 11–15.

Lesson 11	Lesson 12	Lesson 13	Lesson 14	Lesson 15
draw	board	above	care	Review:
bought	cook	shoes	father	enjoy
especially	enjoy	tough	interesting	father
minute	expensive	wash	sweat	especially
picture	favorite	wear	thumb	imagine
question	imagine	woman	touch	interesting
sure	popular	young		minute
worry	year			question
				wash
				wear
				year

Cumulative Vocabulary

The following words appear in the *Student Edition* selections in Grade 2.

absolutely*
absurd*
accent*
accolade*
accomplish
accurately
ached*
acquired*
admit
adorable*
adorn*
affinity*
agile*
allowance*
alternatives*
announcement*
anonymous*
area
archaic*
aspire*
assistance*
assortment*
assumed*
attached*
attack
attempt*
attend
attract*
audible*
award
barely
bargain
beautifying*
belongings*

beneath*
bewildered*
beyond
bizarre*
blended
blockades*
boost
brew*
brisk*
budge
bulk*
career*
carefree
carefully
celebrate
challenge*
chilly*
circling*
clambered*
clumsy*
clutched*
collection
comfortable
committee
common
competitive*
compromise*
concentrate
consider*
correspond*
cozy
cradled
crave*
create

creative
crop
crowd (v.)
crumpled
dangerous*
dappled*
defeated*
delay
delivered
deny*
depend*
described*
diligent*
disability*
disappear
discovery
distance
distraught*
distrust*
disturb*
diversion*
drench*
durable*
earn
edge*
edible*
efficient*
enchanting
encountered*
entertain
enthusiast*
entire
entranced*
evasive*

except
exchanged
excitable*
executive*
experiments
expression
extinct*
extinguish*
extravaganza*
extremely
fantastic
feasible
fellow*
feud*
filthy*
fleeing*
flitted*
flutters*
fragrant
frail*
frisky*
gently
gobbled*
grand
grunted
habitat*
halfheartedly*
hazard*
heed*
hesitate*
hilarious
historical
horrendous*
host

housed*
identify*
ignore*
immense*
impatiently*
impressive
improve*
improvise*
impulsive*
industrious*
inexplicable*
innovation*
instantly*
instead
insult (v.)*
itinerary*
journeyed*
jubilant*
juggling*
kin*
last (v.)
leisurely*
literature
location*
lock*
majestic
master (v.)*
melodious*
minor*
misplaced*
mull*
native*
negotiate*
neighborly*

nominate*
noticed
official*
opinionated*
opponent*
original*
originated*
paced*
passion*
patience*
pattern
peered
penalty*
performance
personalities
pleaded
pledge*
plentiful*
position*
positive*
preference*
previous*
principles*
priorities*
procrastinate*
proficient*
provide
prying*
race*
raggedy
ramble*
rare
rattling*
recently*

recreation*
refuse*
relieved
renowned*
replied
report
request*
responds
responsibility*
review
rickety*
risk
role*
romp*
rosy*
route*
satisfied*
scampering
screeching
sealed
selected*
semblance*
separated
serious
serve
settled
sipped
sleuths
smothered
snug*
soaked*
spare
specially*
spectator*

spoiled
squatted*
startle*
statue
stomped
struggle*
strutted*
style*
superior*
supplies
swirling*
technique*
tedious*
territory*
thickens*
thrifty*
thrilled
traction*
trance*
trooped (v.)*
underestimate*
underneath*
universal*
unselfish*
upbeat
ventured*
volume
wilting*
witness*
witty
worthwhile*
zoom*

High-Frequency Vocabulary

above
accept
ago
already
believe
bicycle
board
bought
brother
brought
care

caught
cheer
children
clear
coming
cook
covered
curve
different
draw
early

ears
eight
enjoy
enough
especially
everything
exercise
expensive
fair
father
favorite

finally
guess
half
hundred
idea
imagine
impossible
interesting
knee
laughed
learn

lose
million
minute
picture
police
popular
prove
question
quite
shoes
short

sign
sometimes
special
straight
sugar
sure
sweat
though
through
thumb
touch

tough
understand
wash
wear
woman
woods
world
worry
year
young

* Listening and Speaking Vocabulary

Handwriting

Individual students have various levels of handwriting skills, but they all have the desire to communicate effectively. To write correctly, they must be familiar with concepts of

- size (tall, short)
- open and closed
- capital and lowercase letters
- manuscript vs. cursive letters
- letter and word spacing
- punctuation

To assess students' handwriting skills, review samples of their written work. Note whether they use correct letter formation and appropriate size and spacing. Note whether students follow the conventions of print such as correct capitalization and punctuation. Encourage students to edit and proofread their work and to use editing marks. When writing messages, notes, and letters, or when publishing their writing, students should leave adequate margins and indent new paragraphs to help make their work more readable for their audience.

Stroke and Letter Formation

Most manuscript letters are formed with a continuous stroke, so students do not often pick up their pencils when writing a single letter. When students begin to use cursive handwriting, they will have to lift their pencils from the paper less frequently and will be able to write more fluently. Models for Harcourt and D'Nealian handwriting are provided on pages R25–R28.

Position for Writing

Establishing the correct posture, pen or pencil grip, and paper position for writing will help prevent handwriting problems.

Posture Students should sit with both feet on the floor and with hips to the back of the chair. They can lean forward slightly but should not slouch. The writing surface should be smooth and flat and at a height that allows the upper arms to be perpendicular to the surface and the elbows to be under the shoulders.

Writing Instrument An adult-sized number-two lead pencil is a satisfactory writing tool for most students. As students become proficient in the use of cursive handwriting, have them use pens for writing final drafts. Use your judgment in determining what type of instrument is most suitable.

Paper Position and Pencil Grip The paper is slanted along the line of the student's writing arm, and the student uses his or her nonwriting hand to hold the paper in place. The student holds the pencil or pen slightly above the paint line—about one inch from the lead tip.

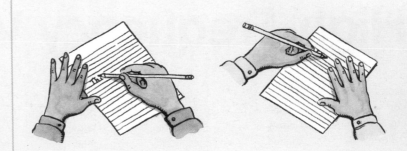

Meeting the Needs of All Learners

The best instruction builds on what students already now and can do. Given the wide range in students' handwriting abilities, a variety of approaches may be needed.

Extra Support For students who need more practice keeping their handwriting legible, one of the most important understandings is that legible writing is important for clear communication. Provide as many opportunities for classroom writing as possible. For example, students can

- **Make a class directory listing the names of their classmates.**
- **Draw and label graphic organizers, pictures, and maps.**
- **Contribute entries weekly to their vocabulary journals.**
- **Write and post messages about class assignments or group activities.**
- **Record observations during activities.**

ELL English-Language Learners can participate in meaningful print experiences. They can

- **Write signs, labels for centers, and other messages.**
- **Label graphic organizers and drawings.**
- **Contribute in group writing activities.**
- **Write independently in journals.**

You may also want to have student practice handwriting skills in their first language.

Challenge To ensure continued rapid advancement of students who come to second grade writing fluently, provide

- **A wide range of writing assignments.**
- **Opportunities for independent writing on self-selected and assigned topics.**

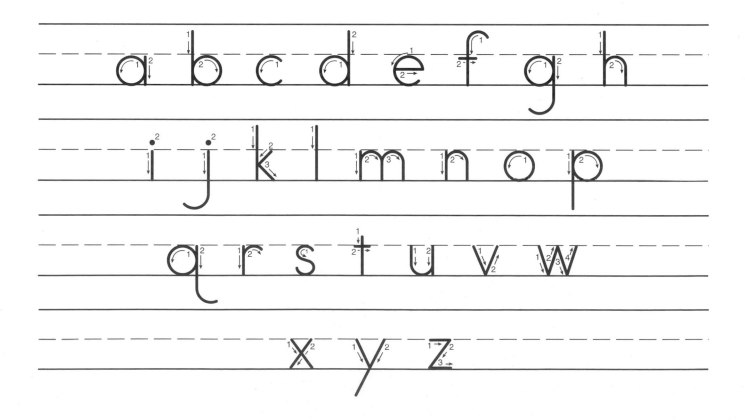

© Harcourt

A B C D E F G H

I J K L M N O P

Q R S T U V W

X Y Z

a b c d e f g h

i j k l m n o p

q r s t u v w

x y z

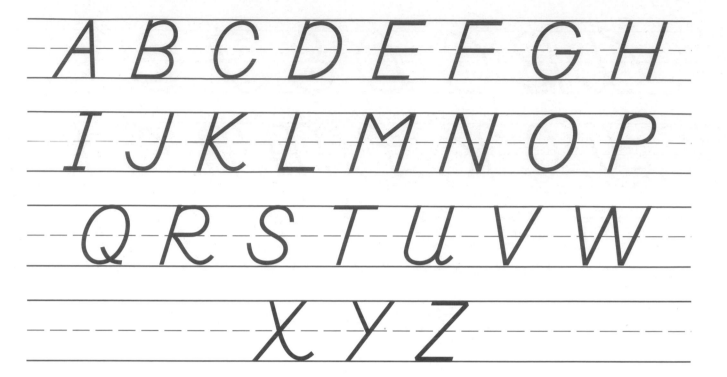

A B C D E F G H
I J K L M N O P
Q R S T U V W
X Y Z

a b c d e f g h
i j k l m n o p
q r s t u v w
x y z

© Harcourt

A B C D E F G H
I J K L M N O P
Q R S T U V W
X Y Z

a b c d e f g h
i j k l m n o p
q r s t u v w
x y z

Introducing the Glossary

MODEL USING THE GLOSSARY Explain to children that a glossary often is included in a book so that readers can find the meanings of words used in the book. Tell children that this glossary is different from most because it provides sample sentences rather than word meanings.

- Read aloud the introductory pages.

- Model looking up one or more words.

- Point out how you rely on **alphabetical order** and the **guide words** at the top of the Glossary pages to locate the **entry word**.

As children look over the Glossary, point out that illustrations accompany some of the example sentences.

Encourage children to look up several words in the Glossary, identifying the correct page and the guide words. Then have them explain how using alphabetical order and the guide words at the top of each page helped them locate the words.

Tell children to use the Glossary to help them better understand how to use some of the words that they often see in the *Student Edition*.

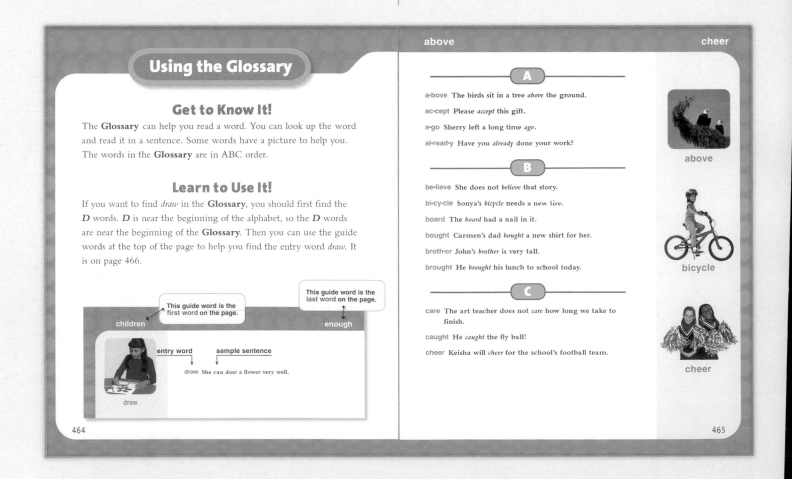

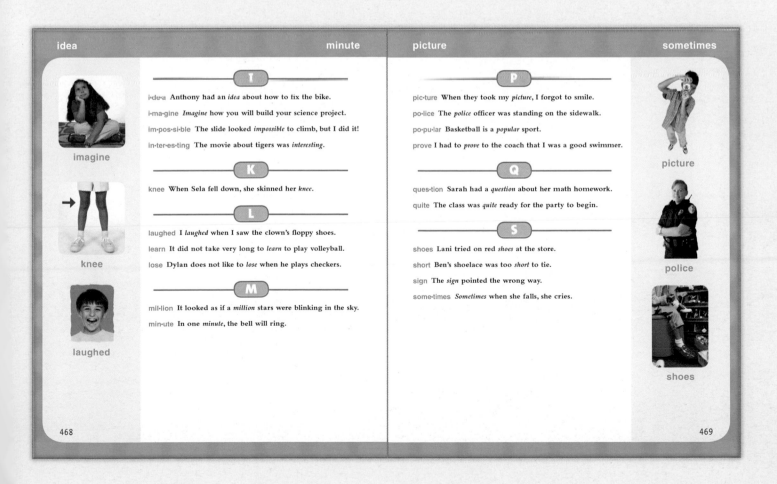

cook

draw

ears

chil·dren The *children* were noisy.

clear The rain made it *clear* that we would not have a picnic today.

com·ing The storm is *coming* this way.

cook Dad will *cook* hot dogs on the grill.

cov·ered Be sure the picnic food is *covered*.

curve We could not see past the *curve* in the road.

D

dif·fer·ent His painting was *different* from the others.

draw She can *draw* a flower very well.

E

ear·ly The bus came *early* this morning.

ears The elephant's *ears* are huge.

eight Jamal is *eight* years old.

en·joy I *enjoy* any kind of pizza.

e·nough We have *enough* people for a kickball game.

466

es·pe·cial·ly The room was *especially* quiet.

eve·ry·thing Why is *everything* the same color?

ex·er·cise I like to *exercise* with my mom.

ex·pen·sive The computer was *expensive*.

F

fair It was a *fair* race, even though we lost.

fa·ther His *father* is a teacher at this school.

fa·vo·rite My *favorite* pet is a snake.

fi·nal·ly He *finally* stopped to tie his shoe.

G

guess *Guess* what I got for my birthday.

H

half Ron finished only *half* of his math work.

hun·dred This giant oak tree is about one *hundred* years old.

exercise

father

467

imagine

knee

laughed

I

i·de·a Anthony had an *idea* about how to fix the bike.

i·ma·gine *Imagine* how you will build your science project.

im·pos·si·ble The slide looked *impossible* to climb, but I did it!

in·ter·es·ting The movie about tigers was *interesting*.

K

knee When Sela fell down, she skinned her *knee*.

L

laughed I *laughed* when I saw the clown's floppy shoes.

learn It did not take very long to *learn* to play volleyball.

lose Dylan does not like to *lose* when he plays checkers.

M

mil·lion It looked as if a *million* stars were blinking in the sky.

min·ute In one *minute*, the bell will ring.

468

P

pic·ture When they took my *picture*, I forgot to smile.

po·lice The *police* officer was standing on the sidewalk.

po·pu·lar Basketball is a *popular* sport.

prove I had to *prove* to the coach that I was a good swimmer.

Q

ques·tion Sarah had a *question* about her math homework.

quite The class was *quite* ready for the party to begin.

S

shoes Lani tried on red *shoes* at the store.

short Ben's shoelace was too *short* to tie.

sign The *sign* pointed the wrong way.

some·times *Sometimes* when she falls, she cries.

picture

police

shoes

469

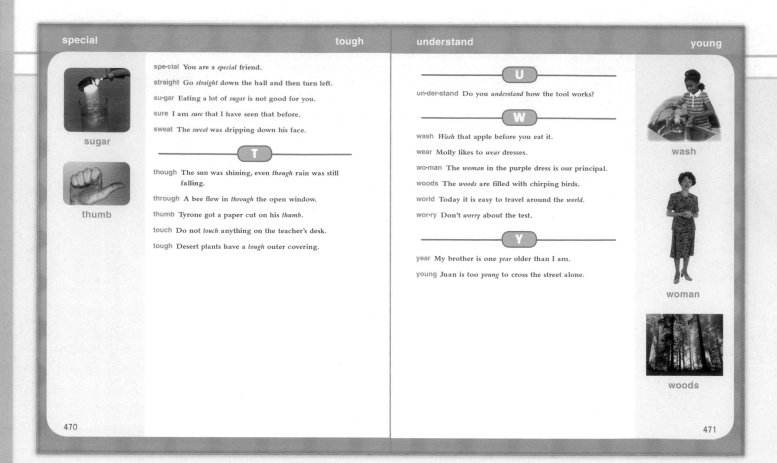

sugar

thumb

spe·cial You are a *special* friend.

straight Go *straight* down the hall and then turn left.

su·gar Eating a lot of *sugar* is not good for you.

sure I am *sure* that I have seen that before.

sweat The *sweat* was dripping down his face.

T

though The sun was shining, even *though* rain was still falling.

through A bee flew in *through* the open window.

thumb Tyrone got a paper cut on his *thumb*.

touch Do not *touch* anything on the teacher's desk.

tough Desert plants have a *tough* outer covering.

U

un·der·stand Do you *understand* how the tool works?

W

wash *Wash* that apple before you eat it.

wear Molly likes to *wear* dresses.

wo·man The *woman* in the purple dress is our principal.

woods The *woods* are filled with chirping birds.

world Today it is easy to travel around the *world*.

wor·ry Don't *worry* about the test.

Y

year My brother is one *year* older than I am.

young Juan is too *young* to cross the street alone.

wash

woman

woods

470

471

Index of Titles and Authors

Professional Bibliography

Armbruster, B.B., Anderson, T.H., & Ostertag, J.
(1987). Does text structure/summarization instruction facilitate learning from expository text? *Reading Research Quarterly,* 22 (3), 331–346.

Ball, E., & Blachman, B.
(1991). Does phoneme awareness training in kindergarten make a difference in early word recognition and developmental spelling? *Reading Research Quarterly,* 26 (1), 49–66.

Baumann, J.F. & Bergeron, B.S.
(1993). Story map instruction using children's literature: effects on first graders' comprehension of central narrative elements. *Journal of Reading Behavior,* 25 (4), 407–437.

Baumann, J.F., Seifert-Kessell, N., & Jones, L.A.
(1992). Effect of think-aloud instruction on elementary students' comprehension monitoring abilities. *Journal of Reading Behavior,* 24 (2), 143–172.

Beck, I.L., Perfetti, C.A., & McKeown, M.G.
(1982). Effects of long-term vocabulary instruction on lexical access and reading comprehension. *Journal of Educational Psychology,* 74 (4), 506–521.

Bereiter, C. & Bird, M.
(1985). Use of thinking aloud in identification and teaching of reading comprehension strategies. *Cognition and Instruction,* 2, 131–156.

Blachman, B.
(2000). Phonological awareness. In M. Kamil, P. Mosenthal, P.D. Pearson, & R. Barr (Eds.), *Handbook of reading research,* (Vol. 3). Mahwah, NJ: Erlbaum.

Blachman, B., Ball, E.W., Black, R.S., & Tangel, D.M.
(1994). Kindergarten teachers develop phoneme awareness in low-income, inner-city classrooms: Does it make a difference? *Reading and Writing: An Interdisciplinary Journal,* 6 (1), 1–18.

Brown, I.S. & Felton, R.H.
(1990). Effects of instruction on beginning reading skills in children at risk for reading disability. *Reading and Writing: An Interdisciplinary Journal,* 2 (3), 223–241.

Chall, J.
(1996). *Learning to read: The great debate (revised, with a new foreword).* New York: McGraw-Hill.

Dowhower, S.L.
(1987). Effects of repeated reading on second-grade transitional readers' fluency and comprehension. *Reading Research Quarterly,* 22 (4), 389–406.

Ehri, L., & Wilce, L.
(1987). Does learning to spell help beginners learn to read words? *Reading Research Quarterly,* 22 (1), 48–65.

Fletcher, J.M. & Lyon, G.R.
(1998) Reading: A research-based approach. In Evers, W.M. (Ed.) *What's gone wrong in America's classroom?,* Palo Alto, CA: Hoover Institution Press, Stanford University.

Foorman, B., Francis, D., Fletcher, J., Schatschneider, C., & Mehta, P.
(1998). The role of instruction in learning to read: Preventing reading failure in at-risk children. *Journal of Educational Psychology,* 90 (1), 37–55.

Fukkink, R.G. & de Glopper, K.
(1998). Effects of instruction in deriving word meaning from context: A meta-analysis. *Review of Educational Research,* 68 (4), 450–469.

Gipe, J.P. & Arnold, R.D.
(1979). Teaching vocabulary through familiar associations and contexts. *Journal of Reading Behavior,* 11 (3), 281–285.

Griffith, P.L., Klesius, J.P., & Kromrey, J.D.
(1992). The effect of phonemic awareness on the literacy development of first grade children in a traditional or a whole language classroom. *Journal of Research in Childhood Education,* 6 (2), 85–92.

Juel, C.
(1988). Learning to read and write: A longitudinal study of fifty-four children from first through fourth grades. *Journal of Educational Psychology,* 80, 437–447.

Lundberg, I., Frost, J., & Petersen O.
(1988). Effects of an extensive program for stimulating phonological awareness in preschool children. *Reading Research Quarterly,* 23 (3), 263–284.

McKeown, M.G., Beck, I.L., Omanson, R.C., & Pople, M.T.
(1985). Some effects of the nature and frequency of vocabulary instruction on the knowledge and use of words. *Reading Research Quarterly,* 20 (5), 522–535.

Nagy, W.E. & Scott, J.A.
(2000). Vocabulary processes. In M. Kamil, P. Mosenthal, P.D. Pearson, & R. Barr (Eds.), *Handbook of reading research,* (Vol. 3) Mahwah, NJ: Erlbaum.

National Reading Panel
(2000). *Teaching children to read.* National Institute of Child Health and Human Development, National Institutes of Health, Washington, D.C.

O'Connor, R., Jenkins, J.R., & Slocum, T.A.
(1995). Transfer among phonological tasks in kindergarten: Essential instructional content. *Journal of Educational Psychology,* 87 (2), 202–217.

O'Shea, L.J., Sindelar, P.T., & O'Shea, D.J.
(1985). The effects of repeated readings and attentional cues on reading fluency and comprehension. *Journal of Reading Behavior,* 17 (2), 129–142.

Paris, S.G., Cross, D.R., & Lipson, M.Y.
(1984). Informed strategies for learning: A program to improve children's reading awareness and comprehension. *Journal of Educational Psychology,* 76 (6), 1239–1252.

Payne, B.D., & Manning, B.H.
(1992). Basal reader instruction: Effects of comprehension monitoring training on reading comprehension, strategy use and attitude. *Reading Research and Instruction,* 32 (1), 29–38.

Rasinski, T.V., Padak, N., Linek, W., & Sturtevant, E.
(1994). Effects of fluency development on urban second-grade readers. *Journal of Educational Research,* 87 (3), 158–165.

Rinehart, S.D., Stahl, S.A., & Erickson, L.G.
(1986). Some effects of summarization training on reading and studying. *Reading Research Quarterly,* 21 (4), 422–438.

Robbins, C. & Ehri, L.C.
(1994). Reading storybooks to kindergartners helps them learn new vocabulary words. *Journal of Educational Psychology,* 86 (1), 54–64.

Rosenshine, B., & Meister, C.
(1994). Reciprocal teaching: A review of research. *Review of Educational Research,* 64 (4), 479–530.

Rosenshine, B., Meister, C., & Chapman, S.
(1996). Teaching students to generate questions: A review of the intervention studies. *Review of Educational Research,* 66 (2), 181–221.

Sénéchal, M.
(1997). The differential effect of storybook reading on preschoolers' acquisition of expressive and receptive vocabulary. *Journal of Child Language,* 24 (1), 123–138.

Shany, M.T. & Biemiller, A.
(1995) Assisted reading practice: Effects on performance for poor readers in grades 3 and 4. *Reading Research Quarterly,* 30 (3), 382–395.

Sindelar, P.T., Monda, L.E., & O'Shea, L.J.
(1990). Effects of repeated readings on instructional- and mastery-level readers. *Journal of Educational Research,* 83 (4), 220–226.

Snow, C.E., Burns, S.M., & Griffin, P.
(1998). *Preventing reading difficulties in young children.* Washington, D.C.: National Academy Press.

Stahl, S.A. & Fairbanks, M.M.
(1986). The effects of vocabulary instruction: A model-based meta-analysis. *Review of Educational Research,* 56 (1), 72–110.

Stanovich, K.E.
(1986) Matthew effects in reading: Some consequences of individual differences in the acquisition of literacy. *Reading Research Quarterly,* 21 (4), 360–406.

Torgesen, J., Morgan, S., & Davis, C.
(1992). Effects of two types of phonological awareness training on word learning in kindergarten children. *Journal of Educational Psychology,* 84 (3), 364–370.

Torgesen, J., Wagner, R., Rashotte, C., Rose, E., Lindamood, P., Conway, T., & Garvan, C.
(1999). Preventing reading failure in young children with phonological processing disabilities: Group and individual responses to instruction. *Journal of Educational Psychology,* 91(4), 579–593.

Vellutino, F.R., & Scanlon, D.M.
(1987). Phonological coding, phonological awareness, and reading ability: Evidence from a longitudinal and experimental study. *Merrill-Palmer Quarterly,* 33 (3), 321–363.

White, T.G., Graves, M.F., & Slater, W.H.
(1990). Growth of reading vocabulary in diverse elementary schools: Decoding and word meaning. *Journal of Educational Psychology,* 82 (2), 281–290.

Wixson, K.K.
(1986). Vocabulary instruction and children's comprehension of basal stories. *Reading Research Quarterly,* 21 (3), 317–329.

Program Reviewers

Elizabeth A. Adkins,
Teacher
Ford Middle School
Brook Park, Ohio

Jean Bell,
Principal
Littleton Elementary School
Avondale, Arizona

Emily Brown,
Teacher
Orange Center Elementary School
Orlando, Florida

Stephen Bundy,
Teacher
Ventura Elementary School
Kissimmee, Florida

Helen Comba,
Language Arts Supervisor K-5
Southern Boulevard School
Chatham, New Jersey

Marsha Creese,
Reading/Language Arts Consultant
Marlborough Elementary School
Marlborough, Connecticut

Wyndy M. Crozier,
Teacher
Mary Bryant Elementary School
Tampa, Florida

Shirley Eyler,
Principal
Martin Luther King School
Piscataway, New Jersey

Sandy Hoffman,
Teacher
Heights Elementary School
Fort Myers, Florida

Amy Martin,
Reading Coach
Kingswood Elementary School
Wickenburg, Arizona

Rachel A. Musser,
Reading Coach
Chumuckla Elementary School
Jay, Florida

Dr. Carol Newton,
Director of Elementary Curriculum
Millard Public Schools
Omaha, Nebraska

Alda P. Pill,
Teacher
Mandarin Oaks Elementary School
Jacksonville, Florida

Dr. Elizabeth V. Primas,
Director
Office of Curriculum and Instruction
Washington, District of Columbia

Candice Ross,
Staff Development Teacher
A. Mario Loiderman Middle School
Silver Spring, Maryland

Sharon Sailor,
Teacher
Conrad Fischer Elementary School
Elmhurst, Illinois

Lucia Schneck,
Supervisor/Language Arts, Literacy
Irvington Board of Education
Irvington, New Jersey

RuthAnn Shauf,
District Resource Teacher
Hillsborough County Public Schools
Tampa, Florida

Jolene Topping,
Teacher
Palmetto Ridge High School
Bonita Springs, Florida

Betty Tubon,
Bilingual Teacher
New Field Primary School
Chicago, Illinois

Janet White,
Assistant Principal
MacFarlane Park Elementary School
Tampa, Florida

KINDERGARTEN REVIEWERS

Denise Bir,
Teacher
Destin Elementary School
Destin, Florida

Linda H. Butler,
Reading First State Director
Office of Academic Services
Washington, District of Columbia

Julie Elvers,
Teacher
Aldrich Elementary School
Omaha, Nebraska

Rosalyn Glavin,
Principal
Walter White Elementary School
River Rouge, Michigan

Jo Anne M. Kershaw,
Language Arts Program Leader, K-5
Longhill Administration Building
Trumbull, Connecticut

Beverly Kibbe,
Teacher
Cherry Brook Elementary School
Canton, Connecticut

Bonnie B. Macintosh,
Teacher
Glenallan Elementary School
Silver Spring, Maryland

Laurin MacLeish,
Teacher
Orange Center Elementary School
Orlando, Florida

Mindy Steighner,
Teacher
Randall Elementary School
Waukesha, Wisconsin

Paula Stutzman,
Teacher
Seven Springs Elementary School
New Port Richey, Florida

Martha Tully,
Teacher
Fleming Island Elementary School
Orange Park, Florida

Scope and Sequence

	Gr K	Gr 1	Gr 2	Gr 3	Gr 4	Gr 5	Gr 6
Reading							
Concepts About Print							
Understand that print provides information	░						
Understand how print is organized and read	░						
Know left-to-right and top-to-bottom directionality	░						
Distinguish letters from words	░						
Recognize name	░						
Name and match all uppercase and lowercase letter forms	░						
Understand the concept of word and construct meaning from shared text, illustrations, graphics, and charts	░						
Identify letters, words, and sentences	░						
Recognize that sentences in print are made up of words	░						
Identify the front cover, back cover, title page, title, and author of a book	░	░					
Match oral words to printed words	░						
Phonemic Awareness							
Understand that spoken words and syllables are made up of sequence of sounds	░						
Count and track sounds in a syllable, syllables in words, and words in sentences	░						
Know the sounds of letters	░	░					
Track and represent the number, sameness, difference, and order of two or more isolated phonemes	░						
Match, identify, distinguish, and segment sounds in initial, final, and medial position in single-syllable spoken words	░						
Blend sounds (phonemes) to make words or syllables	░						
Track and represent changes in syllables and words as target sound is added, substituted, omitted, shifted, or repeated	░						
Distinguish long- and short-vowel sounds in orally stated words	░	░					
Identify and produce rhyming words	░	░					
Decoding: Phonic Analysis							
Understand and apply the alphabetic principle	░	░					
Consonants; single, blends, digraphs in initial, final, medial positions	•	•	•	•			
Vowels: short, long, digraphs, r-controlled, variant, schwa		•	•	•			
Match all consonant and short-vowel sounds to appropriate letters	•	•					
Understand that as letters in words change, so do the sounds	•	•					
Blend vowel-consonant sounds orally to make words or syllables	•	•					
Blend sounds from letters and letter patterns into recognizable words	░	░					
Decoding: Structural Analysis							
Inflectional endings, with and without spelling changes: plurals, verb tenses, possessives, comparatives-superlatives		•	•	•			
Contractions, abbreviations, and compound words		•	•	•			
Prefixes, suffixes, derivations, and root words				•	•	•	•
Greek and Latin roots					•	•	•
Letter, spelling, and syllable patterns							
Phonograms/word families/onset-rimes	░	░					
Syllable rules and patterns							
Decoding: Strategies							
Visual cues: sound/symbol relationships, letter patterns, and spelling patterns	░	•					
Structural cues: compound words, contractions, inflectional endings, prefixes, suffixes, Greek and Latin roots, root words, spelling patterns, and word families	░	•					
Cross check visual and structural cues to confirm meaning	░						

Key:

Shaded area - Explicit Instruction/Modeling/Practice and Application

- *Tested—Assessment Resources: Weekly Lesson Tests, Theme Tests, Benchmark Assessments*

	Gr K	Gr 1	Gr 2	Gr 3	Gr 4	Gr 5	Gr 6
Word Recognition							
One-syllable and high-frequency words	•	•	•				
Common, irregular sight words	•	•	•				
Common abbreviations			•				
Lesson vocabulary		•	•	•	•	•	•
Fluency							
Read aloud in a manner that sounds like natural speech							
Read aloud accurately and with appropriate intonation and expression		•	•	•	•	•	•
Read aloud narrative and expository text with appropriate pacing, intonation, and expression			•	•	•	•	•
Read aloud prose and poetry with rhythm and pace, appropriate intonation, and vocal patterns			•	•	•	•	•
Vocabulary and Concept Development							
Academic language							
Classify-categorize		•					
Antonyms			•	•	•	•	
Synonyms			•	•	•	•	
Homographs				•			
Homophones				•			
Multiple-meaning words			•		•	•	•
Figurative and idiomatic language					•		•
Context/context clues			•	•	•	•	•
Content-area words							
Dictionary, glossary, thesaurus			•	•	•		
Foreign words							•
Connotation-denotation							
Word origins (acronyms, clipped and coined words, regional variations, etymologies, jargon, slang)							
Analogies							
Word structure clues to determine meaning			•	•	•		•
Inflected nouns and verbs, comparatives-superlatives, possessives, compound words, prefixes, suffixes, root words			•	•	•	•	•
Greek and Latin roots, prefixes, suffixes, derivations, and root words					•	•	•
Develop vocabulary							
Listen to and discuss text read aloud							
Read independently							
Use reference books							
Comprehension and Analysis of Text							
Ask/answer questions							
Author's purpose		•	•	•	•	•	
Author's perspective					•	•	
Propaganda/bias							
Background knowledge: prior knowledge and experiences							
Cause-effect		•	•	•	•	•	
Compare-contrast		•	•	•	•	•	•
Details		•	•	•	•	•	•
Directions: one-, two-, multi-step			•	•	•		•
Draw conclusions		•			•	•	•
Fact-fiction					•	•	•

Key:

Shaded area - Explicit Instruction/Modeling/Practice and Application

• *Tested—Assessment Resources: Weekly Lesson Tests, Theme Tests, Benchmark Assessments*

	Gr K	Gr 1	Gr 2	Gr 3	Gr 4	Gr 5	Gr 6
Fact-opinion					•	•	
Higher order thinking							
Analyze, critique and evaluate, synthesize, and visualize text and information							
Interpret information from graphic aids			•	•		•	
Locate information			•		•		
Book parts				•	•		
Text features				•	•		
Alphabetical order		•		•			
Main idea: stated/unstated		•			•	•	•
Main idea and supporting details		•	•	•	•	•	•
Make generalizations						•	
Make inferences		•	•	•		•	
Make judgments						•	•
Make predictions/predict outcomes		•	•	•	•		
Monitor comprehension							
Adjust reading rate, create mental images, reread, read ahead, set/adjust purpose, self-question, summarize/paraphrase, use graphic aids, text features, and text adjuncts					•		
Paraphrase/restate facts and details					•	•	
Preview							
Purpose for reading							
Organize information							
Alphabetical order							
Numerical systems/outlines							
Graphic organizers							
Referents							
Retell stories and ideas			•	•			
Sequence		•		•	•	•	•
Summarize			•	•	•	•	•
Text structure							
Narrative text			•	•	•	•	
Informational text (compare and contrast, cause and effect, sequence/chronological order, proposition and support, problem and solution)			•	•	•	•	•
Study Skills							
Follow and give directions			•	•	•		•
Apply plans and strategies: KWL, question-answer-relationships, skim and scan, note taking, outline, questioning the author, reciprocal teaching							•
Practice test-taking strategies							
Research and Information							
Use resources and references			•		•	•	•
Understand the purpose, structure, and organization of various reference materials							
Title page, table of contents, chapter titles, chapter headings, index, glossary, guide words, citations, end notes, bibliography			•	•	•		
Picture dictionary, software, dictionary, thesaurus, atlas, globe, encyclopedia, telephone directory, on-line information, card catalog, electronic search engines and data bases, almanac, newspaper, journals, periodicals			•	•	•	•	
Charts, maps diagrams, timelines, schedules, calendar, graphs, photos			•		•	•	•
Choose reference materials appropriate to research purpose					•	•	•
Viewing/Media							
Interpret information from visuals (graphics, media, including illustrations, tables, maps, charts, graphs, diagrams, timelines)			•	•			•

Key:

Shaded area - Explicit Instruction/Modeling/Practice and Application

    • *Tested—Assessment Resources: Weekly Lesson Tests, Theme Tests, Benchmark Assessments*

	Gr K	Gr 1	Gr 2	Gr 3	Gr 4	Gr 5	Gr 6
Analyze the ways visuals, graphics, and media represent, contribute to, and support meaning of text							•
Select, organize, and produce visuals to complement and extend meaning							
Use technology or appropriate media to communicate information and ideas							
Use technology or appropriate media to compare ideas, information, and viewpoints							
Compare, contrast, and evaluate print and broadcast media							
Distinguish between fact and opinion							
Evaluate the role of media							
Analyze media as sources for information, entertainment, persuasion, interpretation of events, and transmission of culture							
Identify persuasive and propaganda techniques used in television and identify false and misleading information							
Summarize main concept and list supporting details and identify biases, stereotypes, and persuasive techniques in a nonprint message							
Support opinions with detailed evidence and with visual or media displays that use appropriate technology							

Literary Response and Analysis

Genre Characteristics

	Gr K	Gr 1	Gr 2	Gr 3	Gr 4	Gr 5	Gr 6
Know a variety of literary genres and their basic characteristics			•	•			
Distinguish between fantasy and realistic text							
Distinguish between informational and persuasive texts							
Understand the distinguishing features of literary and nonfiction texts: everyday print materials, poetry, drama, fantasies, fables, myths, legends, and fairy tales			•	•			
Explain the appropriateness of the literary forms chosen by an author for a specific purpose							

Literary Elements

Plot/Plot Development

	Gr K	Gr 1	Gr 2	Gr 3	Gr 4	Gr 5	Gr 6
Important events		•	•	•			
Beginning, middle, end of story		•	•	•			
Problem/solution		•	•	•			•
Conflict					•	•	•
Conflict and resolution/causes and effects					•	•	•
Compare and contrast			•	•	•	•	

Character

	Gr K	Gr 1	Gr 2	Gr 3	Gr 4	Gr 5	Gr 6
Identify		•	•				
Identify, describe, compare and contrast			•	•	•		
Relate characters and events							•
Traits, actions, motives				•	•	•	•
Cause for character's actions					•	•	
Character's qualities and effect on plot					•	•	•

Setting

	Gr K	Gr 1	Gr 2	Gr 3	Gr 4	Gr 5	Gr 6
Identify and describe		•	•	•			
Compare and contrast			•	•			•
Relate to problem/resolution							•

Theme

	Gr K	Gr 1	Gr 2	Gr 3	Gr 4	Gr 5	Gr 6
Theme/essential message				•	•	•	•
Universal themes							•

Mood/Tone

	Gr K	Gr 1	Gr 2	Gr 3	Gr 4	Gr 5	Gr 6
Identify							•
Compare and contrast							

Key:

Shaded area - Explicit Instruction/Modeling/Practice and Application

   • *Tested— Assessment Resources: Weekly Lesson Tests, Theme Tests, Benchmark Assessments*

	Gr K	Gr 1	Gr 2	Gr 3	Gr 4	Gr 5	Gr 6
Literary Devices/Author's Craft							
Rhythm, rhyme, pattern, and repetition							•
Alliteration, onomatopoeia, assonance, imagery						•	•
Figurative language (similes, metaphors, idioms, personification, hyperbole)				•	•	•	•
Characterization/character development				•	•	•	•
Dialogue							
Narrator/narration							
Point of view (first-person, third-person, omniscient)						•	•
Informal language (idioms, slang, jargon, dialect)							
Response to Text							
Relate characters and events to own life							
Read to perform a task or learn a new task							
Recollect, talk, and write about books read							
Describe the roles and contributions of authors and illustrators							
Generate alternative endings and identify the reason and impact of the alternatives							
Compare and contrast versions of the same stories that reflect different cultures							
Make connections between information in texts and stories and historical events							
Form ideas about what had been read and use specific information from the text to support these ideas							
Know that the attitudes and values that exist in a time period or culture affect stories and informational articles written during that time period							
Self-Selected Reading							
Select material to read for pleasure							
Read a variety of self-selected and assigned literary and informational texts							
Use knowledge of authors' styles, themes, and genres to choose own reading							
Read literature by authors from various cultural and historical backgrounds							
Cultural Awareness							
Connect information and events in texts to life and life to text experiences							
Compare language, oral traditions, and literature that reflect customs, regions, and cultures							
Identify how language reflects regions and cultures							
View concepts and issues from diverse perspectives							
Recognize the universality of literary themes across cultures and language							

Writing

	Gr K	Gr 1	Gr 2	Gr 3	Gr 4	Gr 5	Gr 6
Writing Strategies							
Writing process: prewriting, drafting, revising, proofreading, publishing							
Collaborative, shared, timed writing, writing to prompts		•	•	•	•	•	•
Evaluate own and other's writing							
Proofread writing to correct convention errors in mechanics, usage, punctuation, using handbooks and references as appropriate				•	•	•	•
Organization and Focus							
Use models and traditional structures for writing							
Select a focus, structure, and viewpoint							
Address purpose, audience, length, and format requirements							
Write single- and multiple-paragraph compositions			•	•	•	•	•
Revision Skills							
Correct sentence fragments and run-ons							
Vary sentence structure, word order, and sentence length							
Combine sentences							

Key:

Shaded area - Explicit Instruction/Modeling/Practice and Application

- *Tested Assessment Resources: Weekly Lesson Tests, Theme Tests, Benchmark Assessments*

	Gr K	Gr 1	Gr 2	Gr 3	Gr 4	Gr 5	Gr 6
Improve coherence, unity, consistency, and progression of ideas	▒		▒	▒	▒	▒	▒
Add, delete, consolidate, clarify, rearrange text	▒	▒	▒	▒	▒	▒	▒
Choose appropriate and effective words: exact/precise words, vivid words, trite/overused words	▒	▒	▒	▒	▒	▒	▒
Elaborate: details, examples, dialogue, quotations	▒	▒	▒	▒	▒	▒	▒
Revise using a rubric		▒	▒	▒	▒	▒	▒

Penmanship/Handwriting

	Gr K	Gr 1	Gr 2	Gr 3	Gr 4	Gr 5	Gr 6
Write uppercase and lowercase letters	▒	▒	▒	▒			
Write legibly, using appropriate word and letter spacing	▒	▒	▒	▒			
Write legibly, using spacing, margins, and indention		▒	▒	▒	▒	▒	▒

Writing Applications

	Gr K	Gr 1	Gr 2	Gr 3	Gr 4	Gr 5	Gr 6
Narrative writing (stories, paragraphs, personal narratives, journal, plays, poetry)	▒	•	•	•	•	•	•
Descriptive writing (titles, captions, ads, posters, paragraphs, stories, poems)	▒	•	•				
Expository writing (comparison-contrast, explanation, directions, speech, how-to article, friendly/business letter, news story, essay, report, invitation)		▒	▒	▒	•	•	•
Persuasive writing (paragraph, essay, letter, ad, poster)					•	•	•
Cross-curricular writing (paragraph, report, poster, list, chart)	▒	▒	▒	▒	▒	▒	▒
Everyday writing (journal, message, forms, notes, summary, label, caption)	▒	▒	▒	▒	▒	▒	▒

Written and Oral English Language Conventions

Sentence Structure

	Gr K	Gr 1	Gr 2	Gr 3	Gr 4	Gr 5	Gr 6
Types (declarative, interrogative, exclamatory, imperative, interjection)		•	•	•	•	•	•
Structure (simple, compound, complex, compound-complex)		•	•	•	•	•	•
Parts (subjects/predicates: complete, simple, compound; clauses; independent, dependent, subordinate; phrase)		•	•	•	•	•	•
Direct/indirect object						•	•
Word order		•	▒				

Grammar

	Gr K	Gr 1	Gr 2	Gr 3	Gr 4	Gr 5	Gr 6
Nouns (singular, plural, common, proper, possessive, collective, abstract, concrete, abbreviations, appositives)	▒	•	•	•	•	•	•
Verbs (action, helping, linking, transitive, intransitive, regular, irregular; subject-verb agreement)	▒	•	•	•	•	•	•
Verb tenses (present, past, future; present, past, and future perfect)		•	•	•	•	•	•
Participles; infinitives						•	•
Adjectives (common, proper; articles; comparative, superlative)		•	•	•	•	•	•
Adverbs (place, time, manner, degree)					•	•	•
Pronouns (subject, object, possessive, reflexive, demonstrative, antecedents)		•	•	•	•	•	•
Prepositions; prepositional phrases					•	•	•
Conjunctions					•	•	•
Abbreviations, contractions		▒	•	•	•	•	•

Punctuation

	Gr K	Gr 1	Gr 2	Gr 3	Gr 4	Gr 5	Gr 6
Period, exclamation point, or question mark at end of sentences	▒	•	•	•	•	•	•
Comma							
Greeting and closure of a letter		▒	▒	▒	▒	•	•
Dates, locations, and addresses			▒	▒	▒	•	•
For items in a series			▒	▒	•	•	•
Direct quotations					▒	•	•
Link two clauses with a conjunction in compound sentences					•	•	•
Quotation Marks							
Dialogue, exact words of a speaker					•	•	•
Titles of books, stories, poems, magazines					•	•	•

Key:

Shaded area - Explicit Instruction/Modeling/Practice and Application

- *Tested—Assessment Resources: Weekly Lesson Tests, Theme Tests, Benchmark Assessments*

	Gr K	Gr 1	Gr 2	Gr 3	Gr 4	Gr 5	Gr 6
Parentheses/dash/hyphen						•	•
Apostrophes in possessive case of nouns and in contractions		•	•	•	•	•	•
Underlining or italics to identify title of documents					•	•	•
Colon							
Separate hours and minutes						•	•
Introduce a list						•	•
After the salutation in business letters						•	•
Semicolons to connect dependent clauses							

Capitalization

	Gr K	Gr 1	Gr 2	Gr 3	Gr 4	Gr 5	Gr 6
First word of a sentence, names of people, and the pronoun *I*		•	•	•	•	•	•
Proper nouns, words at the beginning of sentences and greetings, months and days of the week, and titles and initials of people		•	•	•	•	•	•
Geographical names, holidays, historical periods, and special events			•	•			•
Names of magazines, newspapers, works of art, musical compositions, organizations, and the first word in quotations when appropriate						•	•
Use conventions of punctuation and capitalization			•	•	•	•	•

Spelling

	Gr K	Gr 1	Gr 2	Gr 3	Gr 4	Gr 5	Gr 6
Spell independently by using pre-phonetic knowledge, sounds of the alphabet, and knowledge of letter names							
Use spelling approximations and some conventional spelling							
Common, phonetically regular words		•	•	•	•	•	•
Frequently used, irregular words		•	•	•	•	•	•
One-syllable words with consonant blends			•	•	•	•	•
Contractions, compounds, orthographic patterns, and common homophones				•	•	•	•
Greek and Latin roots, inflections, suffixes, prefixes, and syllable constructions				•	•	•	•
Use a variety of strategies and resources to spell words							

Listening and Speaking

Listening Skills and Strategies

	Gr K	Gr 1	Gr 2	Gr 3	Gr 4	Gr 5	Gr 6
Listen to a variety of oral presentations such as stories,k poems, skits, songs, personal accounts, or informational speeches							
Listen attentively to the speaker (make eye contact and demonstrate appropriate body language)							
Listen for a purpose							
Follow oral directions (one-, two-, three-, and multi-step)							
For specific information							
For enjoyment							
To distinguish between the speaker's opinions and verifiable facts							
To actively participate in class discussions							
To expand and enhance personal interest and personal preferences							
To identify, analyze, and critique persuasive techniques							
To identify logical fallacies used in oral presentations and media messages							
To make inferences or draw conclusions							
To interpret a speaker's verbal and nonverbal messages, purposes, and perspectives							
To identify the tone, mood, and emotion							
To analyze the use of rhetorical devices for intent and effect							
To evaluate classroom presentations							
To respond to a variety of media and speakers							
To paraphrase/summarize directions and information							
For language reflecting regions and cultures							

Key:

Shaded area - Explicit Instruction/Modeling/Practice and Application

    • *Tested—Assessment Resources: Weekly Lesson Tests, Theme Tests, Benchmark Assessments*

	Gr K	Gr 1	Gr 2	Gr 3	Gr 4	Gr 5	Gr 6
To recognize emotional and logical arguments						�	
To identify the musical elements of language			▨	▨	▨		
Listen critically to relate the speaker's verbal communication to the nonverbal message					▨	▨	

Speaking Skills and Strategies

	Gr K	Gr 1	Gr 2	Gr 3	Gr 4	Gr 5	Gr 6
Speak clearly and audibly and use appropriate volume and pace in different settings	▨	▨	▨	▨	▨	▨	▨
Use formal and informal English appropriately	▨	▨	▨	▨	▨	▨	▨
Follow rules of conversation	▨	▨	▨	▨	▨	▨	▨
Stay on the topic when speaking		▨	▨	▨	▨	▨	▨
Use descriptive words		▨	▨	▨	▨	▨	▨
Recount experiences in a logical sequence			▨	▨	▨	▨	▨
Clarify and support spoken ideas with evidence and examples			▨	▨	▨	▨	▨
Use eye contact, appropriate gestures, and props to enhance oral presentations and engage the audience			▨	▨	▨	▨	▨
Give and follow two-, three-, and four-step directions		▨	▨	▨	▨	▨	▨
Recite poems, rhymes, songs, stories, soliloquies, or dramatic dialogues	▨	▨	▨	▨	▨	▨	▨
Plan and present dramatic interpretations with clear diction, pitch, tempo, and tone				▨	▨	▨	▨
Organize presentations to maintain a clear focus			▨	▨	▨	▨	▨
Use language appropriate to situation, purpose, and audience			▨	▨	▨	▨	▨
Make/deliver							
Oral narrative, descriptive, informational, and persuasive presentations			▨	▨	▨	▨	▨
Oral summaries of articles and books			▨	▨	▨	▨	▨
Oral responses to literature			▨	▨	▨	▨	▨
Presentations on problems and solutions			▨	▨	▨	▨	▨
Presentation or speech for specific occasions, audiences, and purposes			▨	▨		▨	▨
Vary language according to situation, audience, and purpose			▨	▨	▨	▨	▨
Select a focus, organizational structure, and point of view for an oral presentation					▨	▨	▨
Participate in classroom activities and discussions	▨	▨	▨	▨	▨	▨	▨

Key:

Shaded area - Explicit Instruction/Modeling/Practice and Application

- *Tested— Assessment Resources: Weekly Lesson Tests, Theme Tests, Benchmark Assessments*

Index

A

Abbreviations
See **Grammar,** abbreviations
Academic Language
See **Vocabulary**
Academic Vocabulary
See ***Student Edition,*** Glossary;
Vocabulary
Accelerated Reader, 2-3: T18
Accuracy
See **Fluency,** accuracy
Acknowledgments, 2-3: R74
Activity Cards
See **Literacy Centers**
Adjust Reading Rate
See **Focus Strategies,** adjust reading
rate
Advanced Readers
See **Leveled Readers,** Advanced
Readers
Advanced Learners, Activities for
See **Differentiated Instruction,** notes
for Advanced Learners
Art
See **Content-Area Reading,** art;
Cross-Curricular Connections,
art activities, fine art
Ask Questions
See **Focus Strategies,** ask questions
Assessment, 2-3: A1–A6
See also **Conferences; Monitor**
Progress; Rubrics
Benchmark Assessments, **2-3:** T436
decoding assessment, **2-3:** T43, T95,
T139, T221, T307
StoryTown Online Assessment, **2-3:**
T7, T436
Oral Reading Fluency Assessment,
2-3: T58, T67, T81, T91, T152,
T161, T175, T185, T238, T247,
T261, T271, T320, T329, T343,
T353

Portfolio Opportunity, **2-3:** T71, T109,
T165, T251, T333
prescriptions, **2-3:** T95, A2–A6
Self-Assessment, **2-3:** T108–T109,
T434
Spelling Posttest, **2-3:** T89, T183,
T269, T351
Spelling Pretest, **2-3:** T33, T129,
T211, T297
Theme Test, **2-3:** T436
Weekly Lesson Test, **2-3:** T95, T189,
T275, T357, T429
Assessment Prescriptions
See **Assessment,** assessment
prescriptions
Audience
See **Speaking and Listening,**
audience; **Writing,** audience
Audiotext
See **Technology,** technology resources,
Audiotext
Author Features
See ***Student Edition,*** author features
Authors, Program, 2-3: iii
Author's Purpose
See **Comprehension Skills,** author's
purpose; **Focus Skills,** author's
purpose
Authors, *Student Edition* Literature
See ***Student Edition,*** author features
Autobiography
See **Genre,** autobiography; **Writing**

Backdrops
See **Teachers' Resource Book,**
Readers' Theater, backdrops
Background, Build, 2-3: T14, T47, T96,
T97, T98, T99, T143, T190, T191,
T192, T193, T225, T276, T277, T278,
T279, T311, T358, T359, T360, T361,
T430, T431, T432, T433

Background Knowledge
See **Prior Knowledge**
Base Words
See **Decoding/Word Work,** base words
Below-Level Learners, activities for
See **Differentiated Instruction,** note
for Below-Level Learners
Below-Level Readers
See **Leveled Readers,** Below-Level
Readers
Benchmark Assessments
See **Assessment,** Benchmark
Assessments
Bibliography, Professional, 2-3: R22
Big Book of Rhymes and Poems
"Aliona Says," **2-3:** T257, T267, T423
"Always Be Kind to Animals," **2-3:**
T339, T349, T411
"Brush Dance," **2-3:** T77, T87
"Did You Ever Think?," **2-3:** T219,
T243, T401
"Macaw," **2-3:** T305, T325
"My Name," **2-3:** T41, T63, T375
"Play," **2-3:** T137, T157, T391
"Sharing the Swing," **2-3:** T171, T181
Books on Tape
See **Technology,** technology resources,
Audiotext
Brainstorming
See **Writing,** process writing, prewrite

Capitalization
See **Abbreviations**
Center Activity Kit Cards
See **Literacy Centers,** Center Activity
Kit Cards
Centers
See **Literacy Centers**
Challenge Copying Masters
See **Differentiated Instruction,**
Challenge Copying Masters

organizers; **Transparencies,** graphic organizers

charts, **2-3:** T36, T46, T61, T88, T90, T92, T142, T145, T155, T182, T184, T212, T213, T251, T259, T268, T270, T272, T273, T298, T310, T316, T320, T323, T327, T350, T352, T354, T373, T376, T379, T394, T404, T425, T426

story map, **2-3:** T50, T224, T241

word web, **2-3:** T93, T187, T355

Handwriting, 2-3: T65, T129, T245, T327, T403, T409, T421, R12–R17

High-Frequency Words, 2-3: T27, T29, T41, T44–T45, T63, T66, T77, T80, T87, T90, T96, T97, T98, T99, T123, T125, T137, T140–T141, T157, T160, T174, T181, T190, T191, T192, T193, T207, T219, T222–T223, T243, T257, T260, T267, T270, T276, T277, T278, T279, T293, T305, T308–309, T325, T339, T342, T349, T352, T358, T359, T360, T361, T373, T375, T380, T382, T391, T395, T401, T405, T411, T417, T423, T426, T430, T431, T432, T433, R10

See also **Leveled Reader Teacher Guide,** high-frequency words; **Literacy Center,** Word Work; **Monitor Progress,** high-frequency words; **Vocabulary,** vocabulary review, cumulative

History/Social Science
See **Cross-Curricular Connections,** social studies

Homework
See **Literacy Centers,** Homework Copying Master; **Teacher**

Resource Book, School-Home Connection

Ideas
See **Writing,** traits, ideas

Illustrators, *Student Edition* Literature
See *Student Edition,* illustrator features

Index of Titles and Authors
See *Student Edition,* Index of Titles and Authors

Inferences, Make
See **Comprehension Skills,** inferences, make

Inflected Forms
See **Decoding/Word Work,** inflections

Inflections
See **Decoding/Word Work,** inflections

Informal Assessment
See **Monitor Progress; Assessment**

Information Books
See **Genre,** nonfiction

Informational Text
See **Genre,** nonfiction

Inquiry
See **Theme Project**

Intensive Intervention Program
See **Intervention,** Intensive Intervention Program

Internet
See **Technology,** web site

Intervention
See also **Lesson Planner,** 5-Day Small-Group Planner
Intensive Intervention Program, **2-3:** T5
Strategic Intervention Interactive Reader, **2-3:** T58, T67, T152, T161, T238, T247, T329
Strategic Intervention Resource Kit, **2-3:** T5

Strategic Intervention Teacher Guide, **2-3:** T5, T91, T185, 271, T353

Intervention Reader
See **Intervention,** Intervention Reader

Intonation
See **Fluency,** intonation

Introduce the Theme, 2-3: T14–T15

Introducing the Book, 2-3: xvi

Judgments, Make
See **Comprehension Skills,** judgments, make

KWL Charts, 2-3: T316
See **Graphic Organizers,** charts

Labels, 2-3: T415–T416

Language Arts
See **Content-Area Reading,** language arts; **Grammar; Spelling; Transparencies,** language arts; **Writing**

Language Arts Checkpoint, 2-3: T94, T188, T274, T356

Language Development
See **ELL; Lesson Planner,** 5-Day Small-Group Planner; **Literacy Centers**

Language Structures
See **Grammar**

Learning Centers
See **Literacy Centers**

Learning Stations
See **Literacy Centers**

Universal Access

See **Differentiated Instruction**

Usage

See **Grammar**

Use Graphic Organizers

See **Focus Strategies,** use graphic
organizers

Use Multiple Strategies

See **Focus Strategies,** use multiple
strategies

Use Story Structure

See **Focus Strategies,** use story
structure

Vocabulary

See also **High-Frequency Words;**
Literacy Centers, Word Work
Center; **Monitor Progress,**
vocabulary; *Student Edition,*
Vocabulary; **Word Wall**

content-area vocabulary, **2-3:** T59,
T153, T321

context clues, **2-3:** T37, T59, T72,
T73, T83, T133, T153, T166–
T167, T177, T191, T215, T239,
T252–T253, T263, T301, T321,
T334–T335, T345, T397, T407,
T419

robust vocabulary, **2-3:** T11, T37, T59,
T72–T73, T83, T133, T153, T166–
T167, T177, T187, T251, T239,
T252–T253, T263, T273, T301,
T321, T334–T335, T345, T355,
T387, T397, T407, T419

Student-Friendly Explanations, **2-3:**
T37, T59, T72, T83, T133, T153,
T166, T177, T215, T239, T252,

T263, T301, T321, T334, T345,
T387, T397, T407, T419

vocabulary and concept development,
2-3: T11, T37, T59, T72–T73,
T83, T133, T153, T166–T167,
T177, T187, T251, T239, T252–
T253, T263, T273, T301, T321,
T334–T335, T345, T355, T387,
T397, T407, T419

vocabulary review, cumulative, **2-3:**
T90, T93, T184, T187, T270,
T273, T352, T355, R11

word wall, **2-3:** T29, T41, T63, T77,
T87, T125, T137, T157, T171, T181,
T207, T219, T243, T257, T267,
T293, T305, T325, T339, T349,
T375, T391, T401, T411, T423

word web, **2-3:** T93, T187, T355

Vocabulary and Concept Development

See **Vocabulary,** vocabulary and
concept development

Voice

See **Writing,** traits, voice

Website

See **Technology,** technology
resources

Weekly Lesson Tests

See **Assessment,** Weekly Lesson
Tests

Whole-Group Planner

See **Lesson Planners,** 5-Day Whole-
Group Planner

Word Analysis

See **Decoding/Word Work**

Word Attack

See **Decoding/Word Work**

Word Blending

See **Decoding/Word Work,** word
blending

Word Building

See **Decoding/Word Work,** word
building

Word Cards

See **Teacher Resource Book,** word
cards

Word Choice

See **Writing,** dialogue

Word Families, 2-3: T64–T65, T158–
T159, T244–T245, T326–T327

Word-Learning Strategies, 2-3: T11,
T37, T59, T72–T73, T83, T133,
T153, T166–T167, T177, T187,
T251, T239, T252–T253, T263,
T273, T301, T321, T334–T335,
T345, T355, T387, T397, T407,
T419

Word Lists, 2-3: T33, T44, T65, T66,
T79, T80, T140, T159, T160,
T222, T245, T246, T308, T327,
T328, T380, T403, T405

Word-Processing Skills

See **Technology,** technology skills,
word-processing skills

Word Recognition

See **Decoding/Word Work; High-
Frequency Words; Word Wall**

Word Sort, 2-3: T64, T65, T88, T90,
T184, T270, T326, T327, T350,
T352, T376, T426

Words to Know

See **High-Frequency Words**

Word Wall, 2-3: T29, T41, T63, T77,
T87, T125, T137, T157, T171,
T181, T207, T219, T243, T257,
T267, T293, T305, T325, T339,
T349, T375, T391, T401, T411,
T423

See also **High-Frequency Words**

Word Web

See **Vocabulary,** word web; **Graphic
Organizers,** word web

Word Work, 2-3: T27, T30–T33,
T42–T45, T64–T66, T78–T80,

Acknowledgments

For permission to reprint copyrighted material, grateful acknowledgment is made to the following sources:

Robin Bernard: "Brush Dance" by Robin Bernard. Text copyright © 2004 by Robin Bernard.

Georges Borchardt, Inc., on behalf of the Estate of John Gardner: "Always Be Kind to Animals" and "The Lizard" from *A Child's Bestiary* by John Gardner. Text copyright © 1977 by Boskydell Artists, Ltd.

Boyds Mills Press, Inc.: "Bumblebees" from *Lemonade Sun and Other Summer Poems* by Rebecca Kai Dotlich. Text copyright © 1998 by Rebecca Kai Dotlich. Published by Wordsong, an imprint of Boyds Mills Press.

Curtis Brown, Ltd.: "My Name" from *Kim's Place and Other Poems* by Lee Bennett Hopkins. Text copyright © 1974 by Lee Bennett Hopkins. Published by Henry Holt and Company. "Night Game" from *Sports! Sports! Sports!* by Lee Bennett Hopkins. Text copyright © 1999 by Lee Bennett Hopkins. Published by HarperCollins Publishers. "Quiet Morning" from *Climb Into My Lap* by Karen Winnick. Text copyright © 1998 by Karen Winnick. Published by Simon & Schuster, Inc.

Sandra Gilbert Brüg: "Soccer Feet" by Sandra Gilbert Brüg.

Estate of William Rossa Cole: "Here Comes the Band" by William Cole.

Trustees of Mrs. F. C. Cornford Will Trust: "Dogs" from *Collected Poems* by Frances Cornford. Published by Cresset Press, 1954.

The Cricket Magazine Group, a division of Carus Publishing Company: "Bat Habits" by Mary Ann Coleman and Oliver M. Coleman, Jr. from *Click Magazine*, April 2004. Text © 2004 by Mary Ann Coleman.

Farrar, Straus and Giroux, LLC: "the drum" from *Spin a Soft Black Song* by Nikki Giovanni. Text copyright © 1971, 1985 by Nikki Giovanni. "Sun" from *Small Poems* by Valerie Worth. Text copyright © 1972 by Valerie Worth.

Betsy Franco: "At the Bike Rack" by Betsy Franco. Text copyright © 2004 by Betsy Franco.

Emily George: "Aliona Says" by Emily George from *Pocket Poems*, selected by Bobbi Katz. Text copyright © 2004 by Emily George.

Harcourt, Inc.: "Nuts to You and Nuts to Me" from *The Llama Who Had No Pajama: 100 Favorite Poems* by Mary Ann Hoberman. Text copyright © 1974 by Mary Ann Hoberman.

HarperCollins Publishers: "Play" from *Country Pie* by Frank Asch. Text copyright © 1979 by Frank Asch. "Benita Beane" from *Something BIG Has Been Here* by Jack Prelutsky. Text copyright © 1990 by Jack Prelutsky.

Florence Parry Heide: "Rocks" by Florence Parry Heide. Text copyright © 1969 by Florence Parry Heide.

Henry Holt and Company, LLC: "Keepsakes" from *Is Somewhere Always Far Away?* by Leland B. Jacobs. Text © 1967 by Leland B. Jacobs; text © 1995 by Allen D. Jacobs.

Judith Infante: "The Poet Pencil" by Jesús Carlos Soto Morfín, translated by Judith Infante from *The Tree Is Older Than You Are*, selected by Naomi Shihab Nye. Text copyright © by Jesús Carlos Soto Morfín; English translation copyright © by Judith Infante.

Bobbi Katz: From "Did You Ever Think?" by Bobbi Katz. Text copyright © 1981, renewed 1996 by Bobbi Katz. "When You Can Read" from *Could We Be Friends? Poems for Pals* by Bobbi Katz. Text copyright © 1994 by Bobbi Katz. Published by Mondo Publishing, 1997.

Little, Brown and Co. Inc.: "Far Away" from *One at a Time* by David McCord. Text copyright © 1965, 1966 by David McCord.

Gina Maccoby Literary Agency: "Bookworm" by Mary Ann Hoberman. Text copyright © 1975 by Mary Ann Hoberman.

Marian Reiner: "Macaw" from *I Never Told and Other Poems* by Myra Cohn Livingston. Text copyright © 1992 by Myra Cohn Livingston. "Night Creature" from *Little Raccoon and Poems from the Woods* by Lilian Moore. Text copyright © 1975 by Lilian Moore.

Marian Reiner, on behalf of the Boulder Public Library Foundation, Inc.: "My Cat and I" from *Out in the Dark and Daylight* by Aileen Fisher. Text copyright © 1980 by Aileen Fisher.

Marian Reiner, on behalf of Constance Levy: "Cowscape" from *A Crack in the Clouds and Other Poems* by Constance Levy. Text copyright © 1998 by Constance Kling Levy. "Hide-and-Seek" from *A Tree Place and Other Poems* by Constance Levy. Text copyright © 1994 by Constance Kling Levy.

Marian Reiner, on behalf of Judith Thurman: "New Notebook" from *Flashlight and Other Poems* by Judith Thurman. Text copyright © 1976 by Judith Thurman.

Joanne M. Roberts: "My Snake" by Jo Roberts. Text copyright © 2004 by Jo Roberts.

Scholastic Inc.: "The Swarm of Bees" by Elsa Gorham Baker, "Sharing the Swing" by Alice Crowell Hoffman, "My Bike" by Bobbe Indgin, and "Tiny Seeds" by Vera L. Stafford from *Poetry Place Anthology*. Text copyright © 1983 by Edgell Communications, Inc. Published by Scholastic Teaching Resources.

Tiger Tales, an imprint of ME Media LLC, Wilton, CT: "Chimpanzee" from *Rumble in the Jungle* by Giles Andreae. Text © 1996 by Giles Andreae.

S©ott Treimel NY: "First Snow" and "Grown-ups" from *Seasons: A Book of Poems* by Charlotte Zolotow. Text copyright © 2002 by Charlotte Zolotow. "People" from *All That Sunlight* by Charlotte Zolotow. Text copyright © 1967, text copyright renewed © 1995 by Charlotte Zolotow. Published by HarperCollins Publishers.